THE CONTINENTAL LEGAL HISTORY SERIES

Published under the auspices of the

ASSOCIATION OF AMERICAN LAW SCHOOLS

A HISTORY OF CONTINENTAL CRIMINAL PROCEDURE

WITH SPECIAL REFERENCE TO FRANCE

BY

A. ESMEIN

PROFESSOR IN THE FACULTY OF LAW OF PARIS

TRANSLATED BY

JOHN SIMPSON

OF NEW YORK

WITH AN EDITORIAL PREFACE BY

WILLIAM E. MIKELL

PROFESSOR OF LAW IN THE UNIVERSITY OF PENNSYLVANIA

AND INTRODUCTIONS BY

NORMAN M. TRENHOLME

PROFESSOR OF HISTORY IN THE UNIVERSITY OF MISSOURI

AND

WILLIAM RENWICK RIDDELL

JUDGE OF THE HIGH COURT OF JUSTICE FOR ONTARIO

THE LAWBOOK EXCHANGE, LTD.

UNION, NEW JERSEY

2000

ISBN-13: 978-1-58477-042-8
ISBN-10: 1-58477-042-2

Fifth printing 2009

Printed in the United States of America on acid-free paper

THE LAWBOOK EXCHANGE, LTD.
33 Terminal Avenue
Clark, New Jersey 07066-1321

Please see our website for a selection of our other publications and fine facsimile reprints of classic works of legal history:
www.lawbookexchange.com

Library of Congress Cataloging-in-Publication Data

Esmein, A. (Adhemar), 1848-1913.
A history of continental criminal procedure with special reference to France / by A. Esmein; translated by John Simpson of New York; with an editorial preface by William E. Mikell and introductions by Norman M. Trenholme and William Renwick Riddell.
p. cm.
Originally published: Boston : Little, Brown, 1913. (the continental legal history series)
Includes bibliographical references and index.
ISBN 1-58477-042-2 (cloth : alk. paper)
1. Criminal procedure—Europe—History. 2. Criminal procedure—France—History. I. Title. II. Continental legal history series.

KJC9400 .E83 1999
345.4'05'09—dc21

99-045906
CIP

THE CONTINENTAL LEGAL HISTORY SERIES
Published under the auspices of the
ASSOCIATION OF AMERICAN LAW SCHOOLS

A HISTORY OF CONTINENTAL CRIMINAL PROCEDURE

WITH SPECIAL REFERENCE TO FRANCE

BY

A. ESMEIN

PROFESSOR IN THE FACULTY OF LAW OF PARIS

TRANSLATED BY

JOHN SIMPSON

OF NEW YORK

WITH AN EDITORIAL PREFACE BY

WILLIAM E. MIKELL

PROFESSOR OF LAW IN THE UNIVERSITY OF PENNSYLVANIA

AND INTRODUCTIONS BY

NORMAN M. TRENHOLME

PROFESSOR OF HISTORY IN THE UNIVERSITY OF MISSOURI

AND

WILLIAM RENWICK RIDDELL

JUDGE OF THE HIGH COURT OF JUSTICE FOR ONTARIO

BOSTON
LITTLE, BROWN, AND COMPANY
1913

Set up and electrotyped by J. S. Cushing Co., Norwood, Mass., U.S.A.
Presswork by S. J. Parkhill & Co., Boston, Mass., U.S.A.

THE CONTINENTAL
LEGAL HISTORY SERIES.

VOLUME FIVE

A HISTORY OF CONTINENTAL
CRIMINAL PROCEDURE

The Continental Legal History Series

Published under the auspices of the

Association of American Law Schools

I. A GENERAL SURVEY OF EVENTS, SOURCES, PERSONS, AND MOVEMENTS IN CONTINENTAL LEGAL HISTORY. By VARIOUS AUTHORS. Translated by RAPELJE HOWELL, F. S. PHILBRICK, JOHN WALGREN, and JOHN H. WIGMORE. $6.00 *net.*

II. GREAT JURISTS OF THE WORLD, FROM PAPINIAN TO VON IHERING. By VARIOUS AUTHORS. Illustrated. (Extra volume. By arrangement with John Murray, London.) $5.00 *net.*

III. HISTORY OF FRENCH PRIVATE LAW. By J. BRISSAUD, late of the University of Toulouse. Translated by RAPELJE HOWELL, of the New York Bar. $5.00 *net.*

IV. HISTORY OF GERMANIC PRIVATE LAW. By RUDOLPH HUEBNER, of the University of Rostock. Translated by DR. FRANCIS S. PHILBRICK, of New York, N. Y. $4.50 *net.*

V. HISTORY OF CONTINENTAL CRIMINAL PROCEDURE. By A. ESMEIN, Professor in the University of Paris, with chapters by FRANÇOIS GARRAUD, of the University of Lyon, and C. J. A. MITTERMAIER, late of the University of Heidelberg. Translated by JOHN SIMPSON, of the New York Bar. $4.50 *net.*

VI. HISTORY OF CONTINENTAL CRIMINAL LAW. By LUDWIG VON BAR, of the University of Göttingen. Translated by THOMAS S. BELL, of the Pasadena Cal. Bar. $4.00 *net.*

VII. HISTORY OF CONTINENTAL CIVIL PROCEDURE. By ARTHUR ENGELMANN, Chief Justice of the Court of Appeals at Breslau, with a chapter by E. GLASSON, late of the University of Paris. Translated by ROBERT W. MILLAR, of Northwestern University. $4.00 *net.*

VIII. HISTORY OF ITALIAN LAW. By CARLO CALISSE, of the Italian Council of State. Translated by JOHN LISLE, of the Philadelphia Bar. $5.00 *net.*

IX. HISTORY OF FRENCH PUBLIC LAW. By J. BRISSAUD, late of the University of Toulouse. Translated by JAMES W. GARNER, of the University of Illinois. $4.50 *net.*

X. HISTORY OF CONTINENTAL COMMERCIAL LAW. By PAUL HUVELIN, of the University of Lyon. Translated by ERNEST G. LORENZEN, of the University of Wisconsin. $5.50 *net.*

XI. THE EVOLUTION OF LAW IN EUROPE. By GABRIEL TARDE, RAOUL DE LA GRASSERIE, and others. $5.00 *net.*

EDITORIAL COMMITTEE

OF THE

ASSOCIATION OF AMERICAN LAW SCHOOLS

ERNST FREUND, Professor of Law in the University of Chicago.

CHARLES H. HUBERICH, of Berlin, former Professor of Law in Stanford University.

ERNEST G. LORENZEN, Professor of Law in the University of Wisconsin.

WM. E. MIKELL, Professor of Law in the University of Pennsylvania.

MUNROE SMITH, Professor of Jurisprudence in Columbia University.

JOHN H. WIGMORE, *Chairman*, Professor of Law in Northwestern University.

LIST OF TRANSLATORS

THOMAS S. BELL, of the Pasadena Bar.

JAMES W. GARNER, Professor in the State University of Illinois.

RAPELJE HOWELL, of the New York Bar.

JOHN LISLE, of the Philadelphia Bar.

ERNEST G. LORENZEN, of the Editorial Committee.

ROBERT W. MILLAR, of the Chicago Bar, Lecturer in Northwestern University.

FRANCIS S. PHILBRICK, of New York, N. Y.

JOHN SIMPSON, of the New York Bar.

JOHN WALGREN, of the Chicago Bar.

JOHN H. WIGMORE, of the Editorial Committee.

I might instance in other professions the obligation men lie under of applying themselves to certain parts of History; and I can hardly forbear doing it in that of the Law, — in its nature the noblest and most beneficial to mankind, in its abuse and debasement the most sordid and the most pernicious. A lawyer now is nothing more (I speak of ninety-nine in a hundred at least), to use some of Tully's words, "nisi leguleius quidem cautus, et acutus praeco actionum, cantor formularum, auceps syllabarum." But there have been lawyers that were orators, philosophers, historians: there have been Bacons and Clarendons. There will be none such any more, till in some better age true ambition, or the love of fame, prevails over avarice; and till men find leisure and encouragement to prepare themselves for the exercise of this profession, by climbing up to the vantage ground (so my Lord Bacon calls it) of Science, instead of grovelling all their lives below, in a mean but gainful application of all the little arts of chicane. Till this happen, the profession of the law will scarce deserve to be ranked among the learned professions. And whenever it happens, one of the vantage grounds to which men must climb, is Metaphysical, and the other, Historical Knowledge. HENRY ST. JOHN, Viscount BOLINGBROKE, *Letters on the Study of History* (1739).

Whoever brings a fruitful idea to any branch of knowledge, or rends the veil that seems to sever one portion from another, his name is written in the Book among the builders of the Temple. For an English lawyer it is hardly too much to say that the methods which Oxford invited Sir Henry Maine to demonstrate, in this chair of Historical and Comparative Jurisprudence, have revolutionised our legal history and largely transformed our current text-books. — Sir FREDERICK POLLOCK, Bart., *The History of Comparative Jurisprudence* (Farewell Lecture at the University of Oxford, 1903).

No piece of History is true when set apart to itself, divorced and isolated. It is part of an intricately pieced whole, and must needs be put in its place in the netted scheme of events, to receive its true color and estimation. We are all partners in a common undertaking, — the illumination of the thoughts and actions of men as associated in society, the life of the human spirit in this familiar theatre of coöperative effort in which we play, so changed from age to age, and yet so much the same throughout the hurrying centuries. The day for synthesis has come. No one of us can safely go forward without it. — WOODROW WILSON, *The Variety and Unity of History* (Address at the World's Congress of Arts and Science, St. Louis, 1904).

CONTINENTAL LEGAL HISTORY SERIES

GENERAL INTRODUCTION TO THE SERIES

"ALL history," said the lamented master Maitland, in a memorable epigram, "is but a seamless web; and he who endeavors to tell but a piece of it must feel that his first sentence tears the fabric."

This seamless web of our own legal history unites us inseparably to the history of Western and Southern Europe. Our main interest must naturally center on deciphering the pattern which lies directly before us, — that of the Anglo-American law. But in tracing the warp and woof of its structure we are brought inevitably into a larger field of vision. The story of Western Continental Law is made up, in the last analysis, of two great movements, racial and intellectual. One is the Germanic migrations, planting a solid growth of Germanic custom everywhere, from Danzig to Sicily, from London to Vienna. The other is the posthumous power of Roman law, forever resisting, struggling, and coalescing with the other. A thousand detailed combinations, of varied types, are developed, and a dozen distinct systems now survive in independence. But the result is that no one of them can be fully understood without surveying and tracing the whole.

Even insular England cannot escape from the web. For, in the first place, all its racial threads — Saxons, Danes, Normans — were but extensions of the same Germanic warp and woof that was making the law in France, Germany, Scandinavia, Netherlands, Austria, Switzerland, Northern Italy, and Spain. And, in the next place, its legal culture was never without some of the same intellectual influence of Roman law which was so thoroughly overspreading the Continental peoples. There is thus, on the one hand, scarcely a doctrine or rule in our own system which cannot be definitely and profitably traced back, in comparison, till we come to the point of divergence, where we once shared it in common with them. And, on the other hand, there is, during all the intervening centuries, a more or less constant juristic sociability (if it may be so called) between Anglo-American and Continental Law; and its reciprocal influences make the story one and inseparable. In short, there is a tangled common ancestry, racial or intellectual, for the law of all Western Europe and ourselves.

For the sake of legal science, this story should now become a familiar one to all who are studious to know the history of our own law. The time is ripe. During the last thirty years European scholars have placed the history of their law on the footing of modern critical and philosophical research. And to-day, among ourselves, we find a marked widening of view and a vigorous interest in the comparison of other peoples' legal institutions. To the satisfying of that interest in the present field, the only obstacle is the lack of adequate materials in the English language.

That the spirit of the times encourages and demands the study of Continental Legal History and all useful aids to it was pointed out in a memorial presented at the annual meeting of the Association of American Law Schools in August, 1909:

"The recent spread of interest in Comparative Law in general is notable. The Comparative Law Bureau of the American Bar Association; the Pan-American Scientific Congress; the American Institute of Criminal Law and Criminology; the Civic Federation Conference on Uniform Legislation; the International Congress of History; the libraries' accessions in foreign law, — the work of these and other movements touches at various points the bodies of Continental law. Such activities serve to remind us constantly that we have in English no histories of Continental law. To pay any attention at all to Continental law means that its history must be more or less considered. Each of these countries has its own legal system and its own legal history. Yet the law of the Continent was never so foreign to English as the English law was foreign to Continental jurisprudence. It is merely maintaining the best traditions of our own legal literature if we plead for a continued study of Continental legal history.

"We believe that a better acquaintance with the results of modern scholarship in that field will bring out new points of contact and throw new light upon the development of our own law. Moreover, the present-day movements for codification, and for the reconstruction of many departments of the law, make it highly desirable that our profession should be well informed as to the history of the nineteenth century on the Continent in its great measures of law reform and codification.

"For these reasons we believe that the thoughtful American lawyers and students should have at their disposal translations of some of the best works in Continental legal history."

And the following resolution was then adopted unanimously by the Association:

"That a committee of five be appointed, on Translations of Continental Legal History, with authority to arrange for the translation and publication of suitable works."

The Editorial Committee, then appointed, spent two years in studying the field, making selections, and arranging for translations. It resolved to treat the undertaking as a whole; and to co-ordinate the series as to (1) periods, (2) countries, and (3) topics, so as to give the most adequate survey within the space-limits available.

(1) As to *periods*, the Committee resolved to include modern times, as well as early and medieval periods; for in usefulness and importance they were not less imperative in their claim upon our attention. Each volume, then, was not to be merely a valuable torso, lacking important epochs of development; but was to exhibit the history from early to modern times.

(2) As to *countries*, the Committee fixed upon France, Germany, and Italy as the central fields, leaving the history in other countries to be touched so far as might be incidentally possible. Spain would have been included as a fourth; but no suitable book was in existence; the unanimous opinion of competent scholars is that a suitable history of Spanish law has not yet been written.

(3) As to *topics*, the Committee accepted the usual Continental divisions of Civil (or Private), Commercial, Criminal, Procedural, and Public Law, and endeavored to include all five. But to represent these five fields under each principal country would not only exceed the inevitable space-limits, but would also duplicate much common ground. Hence, the grouping of the individual volumes was arranged partly by topics and partly by countries, as follows:

Commercial Law, Criminal Law, Civil Procedure, and Criminal Procedure, were allotted each a volume; in this volume the basis was to be the general European history of early and medieval times, with special reference to one chief country (France or Germany) for the later periods, and with an excursus on another chief country. Then the Civil (or Private) Law of France and of Germany was given a volume each. To Italy was then given a volume covering all five parts of the field. For Public Law (the subject least related in history to our own), a volume was given to France, where the common starting point with England, and the later divergences, have unusual importance for the history of our courts and legal methods. Finally, two volumes were allotted to general surveys indispensable for viewing the connection of parts. Of these, an introductory volume deals with Sources, Literature, and General Movements, — in short, the external history of the law, as the Continentals call it (corresponding to the aspects covered by Book I of Sir F. Pollock and Professor F. W. Maitland's "History of the English Law before Edward I"); and a final volume analyzes the specific features, in the evolution of doctrine, common to all the modern systems.

Needless to say, a Series thus co-ordinated, and precisely suited for our own needs, was not easy to construct out of materials written by Continental scholars for Continental needs. The Committee hopes that due allowance will be made for the difficulties here encountered. But it is convinced that the ideal of a co-ordinated Series, which should collate and fairly cover the various fields as a connected whole, is a correct one; and the endeavor to achieve it will sufficiently explain the choice of the particular materials that have been used.

It remains to acknowledge the Committee's indebtedness to all those who have made this Series possible.

To numerous scholarly advisers in many European universities the Committee is indebted for valuable suggestions towards choice of the works to be translated. Fortified by this advice, the Committee is confident that the authors of these volumes represent the highest scholarship, the latest research, and the widest repute, among European legal historians. And here the Committee desires also to express its indebtedness to Elbert H. Gary, Esq., of New York City, for his ample provision of materials for legal science in the Gary Library of Continental Law (in Northwestern University). In the researches of preparation for this Series, those materials were found indispensable.

To the authors the Committee is grateful for their willing co-operation in allowing this use of their works. Without exception, their consent has been cheerfully accorded in the interest of legal science.

To the publishers the Committee expresses its appreciation for the cordial interest shown in a class of literature so important to the higher interests of the profession.

To the translators, the Committee acknowledges a particular gratitude. The accomplishments, legal and linguistic, needed for a task of this sort are indeed exacting; and suitable translators are here no less needful and no more numerous than suitable authors. The Committee, on behalf of our profession, acknowledges to them a special debt for their cordial services on behalf of legal science, and commends them to the readers of these volumes with the reminder that without their labors this Series would have been a fruitless dream.

So the Committee, satisfied with the privilege of having introduced these authors and their translators to the public, retires from the scene, bespeaking for the Series the interest of lawyers and historians alike.

THE EDITORIAL COMMITTEE.

A HISTORY OF CONTINENTAL CRIMINAL PROCEDURE

CONTENTS

PRELIMINARY TOPICS

CHAPTER I

THE DIFFERENT TYPES OF CRIMINAL PROCEDURE

CHAPTER II

ROMAN CRIMINAL PROCEDURE

CHAPTER III

PRIMITIVE GERMANIC CRIMINAL PROCEDURE

CONTENTS

PART I

HISTORY OF CRIMINAL PROCEDURE IN FRANCE FROM THE 1200s TO THE 1600s

INTRODUCTORY

GENERAL FEATURES OF THE EVOLUTION

TITLE I

THE CRIMINAL JURISDICTIONS IN ANCIENT FRANCE

TITLE II

THE PROCEDURE

CHAPTER I

THE ACCUSATORY PROCEDURE OF THE FEUDAL COURTS

CHAPTER II

THE ORIGIN OF THE INQUISITORIAL PROCEDURE AND ITS GROWTH DURING THE 1200s AND 1300s

CHAPTER III

FRENCH CRIMINAL PROCEDURE UNDER THE ORDINANCES OF THE 1400s AND 1500s

PART II

HISTORY OF CRIMINAL PROCEDURE IN THE LATE 1600s AND THE 1700s

TITLE I

THE FRENCH ORDINANCE OF 1670

CHAPTER I

THE DRAFTING OF THE ORDINANCE OF 1670

CHAPTER II

CHAPTER III

THEORY OF PROOF

CHAPTER IV

INFLUENCE OF THE ORDINANCE OF 1670 UPON THE ADMINISTRATION OF JUSTICE

TITLE II

CRIMINAL PROCEDURE IN EUROPE GENERALLY

CHAPTER I

CRIMINAL PROCEDURE IN OTHER COUNTRIES

CHAPTER II

CRIMINAL PROCEDURE AND PUBLIC OPINION IN THE 1600s AND 1700s

PART III

HISTORY OF CRIMINAL PROCEDURE SINCE THE FRENCH REVOLUTION

TITLE I

THE LAWS OF THE FRENCH REVOLUTION

CHAPTER I

THE AMENDMENTS TO THE ORDINANCE OF 1670

CHAPTER II

THE CODES OF THE INTERMEDIARY PERIOD

CHAPTER III

THE LAWS OF THE YEAR IX

TITLE II

THE FRENCH CODE OF CRIMINAL EXAMINATION, 1808

CHAPTER I

THE DRAFT OF THE CRIMINAL CODE

CHAPTER II

THE QUESTION OF THE JURY BEFORE THE STATE'S COUNCIL

CHAPTER III

THE ORDINANCE OF 1670 AND THE REVOLUTIONARY LAWS IN THE CODE OF CRIMINAL EXAMINATION

CHAPTER IV

CRIMINAL PROCEDURE IN FRANCE SINCE THE CODE OF 1808

TITLE III

CRIMINAL PROCEDURE SINCE 1800 IN OTHER COUNTRIES

APPENDICES

APPENDIX A

THE SCIENTIFIC LITERATURE OF CRIMINAL PROCEDURE

APPENDIX B

HISTORY OF THE CONTINENTAL SYSTEM OF EVIDENCE

EDITORIAL PREFACE

BY WILLIAM E. MIKELL[1]

NOTHING behooves us so much, in these days of reconsideration of the fundamentals in criminal procedure, as to consult experience, in the shape of the history of that subject. In no part of the law's framework are the scars of the past so deeply indented. No body of rules is so largely based on policies consciously adopted to safeguard against felt abuses. Nowhere in the law are the warnings of history more explicit and more valuable for our own generation. And the story of the process by which two systems of criminal procedure, starting as close together as the English and the Continental, diverged to become typical opposites, is fascinating in its interest.

The lack of material in English on the history of the Continental system has hitherto prevented any general familiarity with it. Indeed, in the Continental languages practically the only modern work of the kind is that of Professor Esmein, here presented.

ADHÉMAR ESMEIN, born February 1, 1848, at Touverac (in Charente), received his first appointment as Fellow ("agrégé") in 1875; became professor of law at Douai, and then at Paris in 1879. He has since been elected a member of the Institute of France. He has also been a member of the Superior Council of Public Instruction, and is Professor in the Free School of Political Science, and Section President in the Practical School of Higher Studies. His work in a variety of fields of legal history has placed his name in the front rank of French legal scholars.[2]

[1] Professor of Criminal Law and Procedure in the University of Pennsylvania, member of the Editorial Committee for this Series.

[2] Among his principal works may be named: "Etudes sur les contrats dans le très ancien droit français," 1883; "Mélanges d'histoire du droit et de critique; Droit romain," 1886; "Cours élémentaire d'histoire du droit français," 1892, 5th ed. 1903; "Précis Elémentaire de l'histoire du droit français de 1789 a 1814; Révolution, Consulat, et Empire," 1909; "Eléments de droit constitutionnel français et comparé," 5th ed. 1909. He has also written a monograph on "Gouverneur Morris," and contributed largely to the legal journals.

The work here translated was first published in 1882, under the title "Histoire de la procédure criminelle en France, et spécialement de la procédure inquisitoire depuis le XIII° siècle jusqu'à nos jours." M. Dareste, the veteran professor of comparative law,[1] said of M. Esmein's book, in announcing the report of the Academy awarding to it the prize in a competition for which it was presented, "This work, well constructed and well written, is notable for the keen judgment and the accuracy of treatment shown throughout." It is marked by all the sterling qualities of French scholarship at its best; and this important subject is fortunate in receiving so thoroughly satisfying a treatment. The author has thoroughly revised it for this edition, making copious additions to the notes and occasional substitutions in the text.

Though the breadth of view in Professor Esmein's work would make it an adequate guide to the development of Continental criminal procedure in general, yet it was not composed for that purpose. To render the present volume, therefore, more comprehensive and serviceable to Anglo-American readers, who need a larger perspective by reason of their peculiar standpoint, the Editorial Committee has added a few chapters from other works. These chapters trace the general lines of development for the Continent generally, and fill out more of the details for Germany; the special history in Italy, the home of criminal law movements, will be treated in the volume of this Series on the History of Italian law. These added chapters (three at the beginning, on types of Procedure, Roman Procedure, and Primitive Germanic Procedure; and three at the end, on Continental Legislation of the 1800s, the Literature of Criminal Procedure, and the History of Law of Evidence) are from the pens of Professor Garraud and Professor Mittermaier.

François Garraud, Professor in the Faculty of Law of Lyon, is the leading authority in France on modern criminal law and procedure. The chapters here used are from his "Traité théorique et pratique d'instruction criminelle et de procédure pénale," 1907, 1909; of which the concluding volumes have not yet been published.[2]

Carl Josef Anton Mittermaier (born in 1787, died 1867), Professor of Law at Heidelberg after 1821, became the most famous criminal scientist of his day in Europe. His life and

[1] We have to lament his decease since this Preface was penned.

[2] Reviewed in vol. II of the Journal of the American Institute of Criminal Law and Criminology. His other principal work in criminal law is, "Traité théorique et pratique du droit pénal," 6 vols., 1898–1902.

labors are fully told in vol. II of the present Series, "Great Jurists of the World." The chapters of his here used (on Roman Procedure, Primitive, Medieval, and Modern German Procedure) are taken from his "Das deutsche Strafverfahren, in der Fortbildung durch Gerichtsgebrauch und Landesgesetzgebung und in genauer Fergleichung mit dem englischen und französischen Strafverfahren." This work, first published in 1827, went into its fourth and last edition in 1846; and has since remained the best exposition of the history of German criminal procedure; nor has any later German scholar (singularly enough) offered anyth'ng so extensive in this field.

The translator of Professor Esmein's work and Professor Garraud's chapters is JOHN SIMPSON, of New York. Mr. Simpson is a contributor to the "American and English Encyclopedia of Law," a legal correspondent for numerous technical journals, and the translator of several masterpieces of French literature.

The translator of Professor Mittermaier's chapters is THOMAS S. BELL, formerly of the Tacoma Bar and Lecturer in the University of Washington, and now of Pasadena, California. Mr. Bell, after graduating from the University of Colorado, and going as Rhodes Scholar to Oxford, completed there a course in law and jurisprudence (B.C.L. 1908), and was afterwards Fellow in Jurisprudence at Columbia University.

Whatever the debt the student of English law owes to Sir William Blackstone, it must be said that to him in no small degree is due the lack of interest of the English and American lawyer of the past hundred years in the laws and legal institutions of other nations.

Blackstone never tired of giving thanks that the English law was not like other law. It has been a source of wonder to the youthful students of his pages how other nations preserved any semblance of civilization and freedom without the many great "palladia of liberty" possessed by the Anglo-Saxon. He never tired of drawing comparisons between the English law and the laws of other countries, always to the detriment of the latter. It may not be the result, but it is at least a coincidence, that with the cessation of the use of Blackstone's Commentaries as an entrance to the study of English law there is a growing demand for a knowledge of the legal systems of other countries.

From a practical point of view a knowledge of the criminal procedure of other countries is perhaps of less value than a knowledge of foreign law on any other branch of jurisprudence. Our own criminal procedure has been the avowed model for foreign countries. To the student of institutions, however; to him who joys in watching the never ceasing battle between the forces of repression and liberty — the nice adjustment of which spells true civilization; to him who would see how a great people have worked out a great problem,— the study of the history of French criminal procedure offers a fascinating subject. Our own procedure is the result of a slow evolution. In the French criminal procedure we see the rare phenomenon of a combination of evolution and adoption and then of an evolution of the adoption, yet with all a constant tendency to a reversion to type.

Nothing could be more interesting than Esmein's study of this evolution of French criminal procedure from Roman, through Germanic, to Canon law; the play and counter-play of various forces for two centuries, making for the permanence first of the accusatory and then of the inquisitorial system.

The reader will here find set forth the struggle between the *enquête du pays* and the "inquest" of the Canon law. He will learn how the former lost to the latter at the same time that the English equivalent of the *enquête du pays* — the *inquisitio patriæ* — the grand jury — was triumphant in England.

The Ordinance of 1670 definitely fixed the inquisitorial procedure in French law for a century. The Revolution, however, will bring to the battle new forces, and the accusatory procedure of England will be bodily transplanted into French soil. Later, the need of strengthening the authority of the State will cause a reversion. The Code of Offenses and Punishments of the year IV will show a tendency to return to the secret examination of the inquisitorial system, a tendency that the law of the year IX will accentuate. Then a compromise will be effected by the Code of 1808, which will reënact in part the inquisitorial, while retaining in part the accusatory system. The adoption of the Code of 1808, however, only marks a pause in the battle, a battle that begins again every time the government undergoes a notable change.

In studying French criminal procedure, considering it both in its broad sweep and in detail, one cannot fail to be struck with the unity of history. Different in many respects as has been the history of French and English procedure, so different indeed that the two have, at certain periods, offered opposing types, we see that both began as one type — the accusatory. English procedure remained true to type, with a few unimportant aberrations, such as the Star Chamber afforded. In France, though for many centuries this type was abandoned, we now see it restored in almost its pristine vigor. In details we see the same unity. Torture runs through both like a scarlet thread, though the thread is larger and the dye deeper in France. Shudder as we may at the institution of torture, it is something to know that the necessity for it was due, not to innate cruelty, but that it sprang from a regard for the innocent accused which demanded such perfect proof for conviction that nothing short of confession would satisfy it. The Frenchman's "house was his castle" even more than the Englishman's, for the former could not even be arrested in his home. In both countries the right of the accused to counsel, in serious crime, was first denied and then granted. The language of PUSSORT in the debate on the Ordinance of 1670 read like a modern political indictment of a "corporation lawyer." Pussort says: "We know how fertile these kinds of counsel are in finding openings to frame conflicts of jurisdiction, how they often scheme to discover nullities in the proceedings and to give birth to an infinitude of side issues. It is therefore peculiarly in the interests of the wealthy that counsel is granted." In both countries the right was granted by the judges before legal warrant by legislation.

In England the proof required to convict was always proof "beyond a reasonable doubt." In France the proof must be "clearer than the sun at noonday."

The doubts as to the necessity for a unanimous verdict; the right of the accused to be free from the necessity of incriminating himself,— these are a few of the many things the student of English law finds reproduced in France.

In law as in other sciences we have our recurring cycles of thought. The present-day alienist harks back to the ancient Greek where Homer ascribed guilt to Até. We are saying again the criminal is not so much a knave as a fool or a madman; his intellect is darkened. Simonides is quoted by Plato as saying, "A man cannot but be bad when the force of circumstances overpower him." The modern sociologist makes crime the product of environment. Humanism in the 1400s, on the Continent, inveighed against the theories and the technicalities of the Jurists. The social scientists of the 1900s are voicing the same cry — with this difference, that the Humanist cared nothing for the practical importance of the administration of the law; his interest, was in origins, and his effort, to take men's minds back to the purity of original sources. The present-day movement cares little for sources, its effort is directed to practical results.

In the French criminal procedure we may find many a precedent for provisions in our law which are anomalies with us.

Probably the most interesting feature of the building up of the French procedure is the struggle with the jury system. It is met at every turn in French legal history.

"The French inquest has in it the germ of all that becomes distinctly English in the English law of the later Middle Ages, the germ of trial by jury and of a hard and fast formulary system of actions which will be tough enough to resist the attacks of Romanism." Maitland has also told us how the fate of the inquest was still in the balance a century after the Conquest, and how Henry II, in the nick of time, by placing at the disposal of litigants in certain actions the "inquest of the country" which the Romans had brought from France, established trial by jury in England. Esmein shows us the steps by which this same "*enquête du pays*" lost in France in the struggle with the "inquest" of the Canon law. The jury early lost to France; imported as an alien institution in its entirety in 1791; its subsequent history, in which four times the fight for it was lost and won, won even against the opposition of Napoleon,—is treated with a masterly hand by our author.

Nothing could be more interesting to the American or English reader, to whom the jury is the "Palladium of Liberty," than to read the debates, set out at length by our author, on the value of, and the advisability of adopting, trial by jury in criminal cases. The recurrence of the argument that what has proved valuable among the English would not suit the "genius of the French people," reminds us of the phrase "un-American" which meets every effort at reform with us. Yet notwithstanding this "genius of the French people," the jury has won a permanent place in French law. As our author says: "A great civilized nation cannot renounce it without losing its rank. . . . It is indestructible . . . in spite of its defects."

Esmein's chapter on the function of the jury in criminal trials is well worth study. It has long been a mooted question with us whether the jury is legally bound to take the law from the court or is itself to be judge of the law as well as the facts in rendering a general verdict.

It is known to all who have eyes to see and ears to hear that there exists grave dissatisfaction with the administration of the criminal law in the United States. We used to be satisfied with the explanation that it was due to the fact that we were a new country, until we learned that the same phenomenon did not exist in newer countries than our own. The explanation that it was due to the immigrant is not weighty when we consider that our budget of crime is greater than that of the countries from which the immigrant comes. Opinion is crystallizing into the belief that it is due to our procedure in prosecuting criminals, and the public mind is open as never before in our history to the adoption of practicable means for the reform of the procedure where it is shown to be archaic or otherwise inadequate. No student of our criminal jurisprudence can fail to be impressed with the efforts of our criminal courts with the machinery at hand to render more effective the administration of the penal law. Decisions are daily rendered upholding indictments, ignoring errors in instructions, and validating verdicts that a few years ago would have been regarded as a denial of some fundamental constitutional right. But the judges — anxious as the vast majority of them are to render effective the administration of the criminal law — cannot do all that is needed. The more drastic power of the legislature and of the constitutional convention are necessary for the cure of some evils. To the legislator this book may be commended — not perhaps as a study in direct legislation — but for its broadening effect in showing how a great nation has tried to work out the problem that confronts us.

It is a curious fact that during the last century opposite tendencies have been working and continue to work in French procedure on one hand and English and American procedure on the other. In France the tendency has been to ameliorate the severities of the law, to surround the accused with greater safeguards at the expense of the prosecuting power. In England and the United States there is a strong tendency to strengthen the hand of the state at the expense of the accused, by a process of elimination of the technical rules that covered the accused as with a coat of mail. Recently the old inquisitorial procedure has shown its head in America in the so-called "Third Degree." Whether this is sporadic and will remain extra-legal or will find recognition remains to be seen. It has already reached sufficient magnitude to call forth legislation. So far this legislation has been against it, and in the extra-legal way in which it is practised it is, undoubtedly, vicious. But it may well be that, protected as the criminal is in Anglo-American jurisprudence from the time of arrest to final judgment, surrounded as he is not only with all the presumptions and technicalities of the old English procedure, but also by the added constitutional safeguard of State and Federal constitutions, we may yet find it necessary to adopt something corresponding to the examination of the French *juge d'instruction;* in some States we have already followed France and practically abolished the grand jury.

Another matter that may well engage those who would reform criminal procedure is that of the necessity, for conviction, of unanimity among the jury. With this, as with most other fundamentals of criminal procedure, the French have not scrupled to experiment, and their experience is well worth study.

Payment of damages by the State to one who has been wrongfully convicted and suffered punishment, is a feature of French law that we are likely soon to adopt. Agitation for a "public defender" has begun. He would be rash who would predict the future of penal legislation in the United States. Is it too much to hope that in making the changes that are coming we will study the history of criminal procedure in France — the country which for four hundred years has been the laboratory for legislation on this branch of law?

INTRODUCTION

By Norman Maclaren Trenholme[1]

In an age of growing internationalism, law should become more international as well as more rational and scientific. Lawyers as well as legal historians and teachers of law should become acquainted with the legal history and procedure of other countries, and develop a broad comparative knowledge of the principles, practices, and procedure of the past and present. In bringing this about, books such as the present volume are most effective and absolutely necessary. It is their absence heretofore that has made the legal profession of America and England somewhat narrow and national in its outlook.

Criminal procedure to-day is so much a matter of ordinary legal training and knowledge that few lawyers realize what a wealth of historical and legal background it has. Its history has been neglected in large part as well by institutional historians who have preferred to deal with larger questions of governmental and legal development. The result of this double neglect is seen in the fact that there are but few books in foreign languages and, until the appearance of this volume, practically none in English, dealing in detail with the history of criminal procedure. In view of the vital importance of understanding the processes of development lying back of present practices and of comparing our methods of procedure with those of other countries, such lack of historical reference works is to be regretted. The appearance, therefore, of a comprehensive work such as this in the Continental Legal History Series, containing a survey of the historic forms and literature of European criminal procedure, even including England, is a most encouraging sign of legal-historical progress in America.

The work to which this is an Introduction, though mainly a translation of Esmein's "Histoire de la Procédure Criminelle en

[1] A.B. (McGill University); A.M., Ph.D. (Harvard University); Professor of History in the University of Missouri; author of "The Right of Sanctuary in England" (1903).

France,"[1] is made of broader application and greater value by the inclusion, in both the earlier and later parts, of portions of other treatises. The larger number of these additional and supplementary chapters are translated from M. Garraud's broad and scholarly work on French criminal procedure, a part of which forms the introductory chapter of our volume. This is an excellent general discussion of the *accusatory, inquisitorial,* and *mixed* types of procedure in criminal cases. The second chapter, however, draws on another work, that of the learned German legal historian of over half a century ago, Professor Mittermaier, the author of a well-known history dealing with German criminal procedure. From this work we have a concise and scholarly account of the Roman criminal procedure in which the various processes and practices of the Roman legislative system of procedure are described and the somewhat accusatorial character of the Roman system is brought out. The presence of inquisitorial features in later imperial procedure is noted, and we get a good general idea of the extent and character of the Roman background to later criminal procedure. The third chapter is also from Mittermaier's work and describes primitive Germanic criminal procedure with sufficient fulness and detail for the purposes of a general survey. The difference that is frequently apparent between French and German research and scholarship is well brought out by comparing Garraud's chapters with those from Mittermaier. The former has decided superiority of style and organization, while the latter excels in exactness and in proofs and references. Both these accounts are of great interest and value to students of the history of law.

Part One of the main work is devoted to the history of criminal procedure in France from the twelfth to the seventeenth centuries and Garraud is again drawn on for an introductory section. This describes and comments on the general features of the evolution of French criminal procedure and is a useful and valuable survey. It connects the past and present in a clear and interesting manner by showing how the criminal procedure in France to-day is of a mixed type rather than strictly inquisitorial and is the result of a long process of legal evolution and special legislation. Such a well-organized and philosophical introduction is of especial importance in a work intended for English and American readers

[1] Histoire de la Procédure Criminelle en France et spécialement de la procédure inquisitoire depuis le XIIIe siècle jusqu'à nos jours, par A. Esmien, professeur agrégé à la faculté de droit de Paris. Ouvrage couronné par l'académie des sciences morales et politiques. Paris, 1882.

who may not be familiar with the peculiar characteristics of contemporary procedure in France. The meaning and importance of Esmein's more detailed account of the criminal jurisdiction of Old France (which is a better rendering of "L'Ancien France" than "Ancient France") is better appreciated and understood after knowing the present status.

The reader, having been furnished with a broad background of Roman and early Germanic criminal procedure and a perspective of general development from ancient times to the present, is prepared to follow the interesting story of the evolution of criminal procedure in France and other European countries from the later Middle Ages to the present. Professor Esmein's work, with some slight omissions and a number of important additions, furnishes an excellent basis for such a survey. Like many French and English monographs of great merit, Esmein's study was first presented as a prize essay in competition for the Bordin Prize in 1880. The subject proposed for competition was: "To make clear the history of the criminal Ordinance of 1670; to seek out what has been its influence on the administration of justice and on the legislation which followed it to the close of the eighteenth century." Esmein, who has then merely *agrégé* in the Faculty of Law at Paris, won the prize, by the unanimous decision of the judges, with an essay entitled: "Histoire de l'Ordonnance de 1670 et de la procédure inquisitoire en France." The young author ventured to go beyond the letter of the subject proposed by giving the historical and legal background to the Ordinance of 1670 and by carrying his treatise on criminal procedure in France beyond the limit of the eighteenth century up to his own time. This did not infringe on the spirit of the subject, however, but made Esmein's work of broader legal and historical value, for, as he says in his original preface: "The presentation of the history of a Law that has passed away should not merely tell how it was promulgated, applied, and later abrogated: it is necessary, in addition, to seek out the origin of the legal ideas it contained and to ask oneself if it has not transmitted something of value to the modern legislation that has followed it." With this spirit and viewpoint it is little wonder that Esmein produced a study of permanent value, and that the essay crowned by the Academy of Moral and Political Sciences should become the basis for the broad and scholarly work on the history of criminal procedure that we have in English translation in this volume.

Historical students will regret to some extent the omission in this volume of the first or introductory section of M. Esmein's work consisting of two chapters on the early jurisdictions of France, because these chapters contain an interesting account of an historical-legal character of the seigneurial and royal justice of France, in the later Middle Ages. But their place has been well taken by the broader survey from Garraud already referred to and students of History can always go to Esmein's original work for the special information in the omitted chapters.

The first topic dealt with in the translation from Esmein, therefore, is that of early procedure in France, which was thoroughly accusatory in character, in connection with the feudal courts. Beaumanoir and the various collections of feudal customs, together with the leading modern authorities of France and Germany, are used as sources for this excellent treatment of the more important features of feudal procedure. The transition from the accusatory form to the inquisitorial is next brought out, and special emphasis is laid on the influence of the Church and on the growth of the royal power in bringing about the change. The introduction of torture to extort confessions and the appearance of the secret examination are noted as important factors in the new system.

The next step is the organization and control of criminal procedure by royal ordinances which began with the ordinances of 1498 and of 1539. The latter ordinance was especially important and evoked some spirited opposition on account of its arbitrary and severe character. Under the influence of these ordinances all other forms of criminal procedure either tended to disappear or were abolished. It was only natural that the seventeenth century in France should witness a tendency on the part of the strong monarchical government towards an elaborate codification of criminal procedure along inquisitorial lines. This was accomplished under Louis XIV in the form of the great Ordinance of 1670.

The Ordinance of 1670 was the result of many discussions and conferences on the part of the royal ministers, especially Colbert, and the leading jurists of the time. Like the Magna Charta, the Ordinance contained little that was really new, being a codification of the criminal procedure that had gradually developed during the three centuries previous to its enactment. It marked, therefore, the culmination of the process of transition from the oral and public accusatory system of the feudal period to the written and secret inquisitorial procedure of the early modern period. The result was that a code of criminal instruction was now definitely established which lasted down to the French Revolution and was rigidly followed in all its details of secret processes, variegated tortures, and cruel punishments by all the courts of justice in France. Back of it lay the royal authority, which could be exercised arbitrarily against the subject, and it is little wonder that the French reformers of the eighteenth century regarded such a system as mediæval and irrational. Instead they professed admiration of the English system of the public accusatory type which involved trial by a jury and gave the defendant the benefit of being considered innocent until he was proved guilty and did not subject him to torture and secret examination. Esmein's account of the actual workings of the Ordinance of 1670 is particularly full and interesting and includes valuable material as to how the ordinance was regarded by leading jurists, philosophers, and political theorists in the eighteenth century.

Accompanying this discussion is an interesting survey of the criminal procedure which had grown up in other European countries such as Italy, Spain, Germany and the Netherlands, and England. This survey has been made completer and more valuable in its English form by the author's careful revision and the introduction (for the purpose of this translation) of considerable additional matter, especially in connection with England.

The third and final portion of Esmein's work is concerned with the legislation in regard to criminal procedure of the revolutionary period and of the Napoleonic era leading up to the Code of Criminal Instruction of 1808. An interesting account of the attacks on the old procedure contained in the *cahiers* of 1789 and of the first attempts at reform which were made by the Constituent Assembly is given, and the contest that raged between the advocates of jury trial and the upholders of a modified inquisitorial system is well brought out. This contest finally ended in a compromise by which a mixed accusatory and inquisitorial system of procedure was put into effect as a result of lengthy debate and discussion on the part of Napoleon's Council of State and of the leading jurists of the empire. The conclusions reached were embodied in the great Code of Criminal Instruction of 1808, which has served as the basis of modern criminal procedure in France although frequently modified by subsequent legislation. In this code the influence of the Ordinance of 1670 and of earlier criminal procedure is clearly seen in connection with the preliminary and secret examination by the magistracy, the severity of the restrictions on the defendant in a criminal case, and the system of written testimony and instruction. On the other hand, the influence of the reform element in favor of jury trial is seen in the provision for public trial and jury decision, in the recognition of the courts of Cassation and of Assize, and in the provisions for allowing the accused person better facilities for defense. To further reform the criminal law of France an elaborate Penal Code was compiled and promulgated by imperial decree in 1810. Both the Code of Criminal Instruction and the new Penal Code went into full effect on and after January 1, 1811, after a reorganization of the French judiciary had been made.

The detailed account given by Esmein of the adoption and workings of the Code of Criminal Instruction is well worth careful study. This is especially true of the chapter dealing with the discussion on the adoption of the jury as a part of the procedure. There were a number of able and influential men who opposed jury trial, and Napoleon himself was against it, but in the Council of State there was a strong sentiment for its retention which finally triumphed. The Grand Jury or Accusation Jury was abolished, however, and its functions transferred to a special tribunal. But, on the whole, as Esmein observed: "In the great and long drawn out contest between procedure by juries and the Ordinance of 1670, the former gained a decisive victory. Posterity ought to give recognition to the men who, in the Council of State of the Empire, were able to resist the hardly disguised wish of the Emperor, and whose courageous efforts resulted in the retention of the jury in our laws." The student of history will find this phase of Napoleonic history ably treated and will gain added respect for the members of the Council of State.

The chapter on the question of the retention of the jury, though especially interesting to English readers, is really not more important than the long and detailed discussion on the incorporation of a large part of the Ordinance of 1670 and of the special legislation of the early part of the Revolution into the new code of procedure. It is impossible to go into this matter at all fully in this introduction, as it would involve a special description of modern French criminal procedure; but attention might be drawn to the mingling of the old formal ideas of inquisition and written evidence with the more liberal tendencies represented by *Rehabilitation* and *Revision*, which are ably discussed.

The chapter on criminal procedure in France since 1808 brings our knowledge of the subject up to date along topical lines of development. The progress in legislation of legal character is noted; the changes or modification in the procedure preceding the actual trial are treated of; the important changes in connection with the preliminary examination are discussed and outlined in connection with the Laws of 1856, 1863, and 1865; the various projects of reform up to 1880 are taken up; and, in conclusion, the history of recent legislation affecting criminal procedure is recounted, especially the changes made by the Law of 1895 and introduced in the closing years of the last century.

Following the long survey of the history of criminal procedure in France, taken mainly from Esmein, the reader's attention is directed to a broad discussion on criminal procedure since 1800 in other countries of the world. This is a valuable and well-organized review of the whole field of modern criminal procedure taken from Garraud's work (already several times referred to). It forms a fitting conclusion to a volume devoted to European criminal procedure, emphasizing, as it does, the classification to systems and the internationalism of modern legal ideas. Information and viewpoint are admirably blended, and the adoption of a comparative method of treatment is justified by its results. Much the same can be said of the two scholarly appendices, A and B, both taken from Garraud's work. Appendix A is an interesting survey of the literature of criminal procedure from the Middle Ages to the present. The writers are organized as belonging either to the age before the Code of 1808 or after, and are further subdivided in accordance with their special characteristics, contributions, or nationality. Appendix B represents an admirable general sketch of the history of the continental European system of evidence. This is clearly organized into ethnic, religious, legal, and scientific phases of development or evolution, and into different systems and methods of proof, leading up to the present-day dominant but erroneous idea that the only convincing proof is "Jury Proof."

From such a volume as this, so comprehensive in its contents and so comparative in its methods, English-speaking students of law and history can derive much of value. To see how criminal procedure has originated and developed out of Roman, Teutonic, and Christian elements and ideas, how out of the practically uniform accusatory procedure of the feudal age in the various countries of western Europe there grew two divergent systems, those of England and France, one marked by the juries of indictment and trial, the other by secret inquisition, torture, and severity, is in itself fascinating. But even more interesting and significant than the story of the divergence of these systems is the story of their gradual reconciliation in the newer criminal procedure of Europe of to-day. The so-called *mixed* type of procedure adopted by the leading continental European states is a recognition of the value and importance of the trial jury as an institution, of publicity in court proceedings, and of giving the accused person a better and juster defense against possible unwarranted conviction. The acceptance by continental jurists and governments of these principles of Anglo-Saxon procedure does them honor as well as furnishes them with a system of procedure probably containing the best features of both the old systems.

Perhaps after reading or looking over this volume the thought may arise that America could benefit by imitating to some extent the mixed type of criminal procedure now in use on the continent of Europe. Even should such a reform not be possible, however, the American legal profession needs to be awakened to the fact that criminal procedure in the United States is half a century or more behind that of Great Britain and continental Europe. Instead of the swift and sure justice that accompanies the administration and procedure of the British courts or the careful and thorough investigation and well-organized prosecution and trial of the continental European tribunals, we have a procedure clogged by archaic technicalities, influenced by the wealth of the defendant or his friends, twisted by adroit criminal lawyers, and full of long delays, mistrials, hung juries, and dismissed cases.

The spirit of legal reform is everywhere present in the United States and will bring about important changes in criminal procedure. These should be based on broad comparative study of existing systems such as can only be gained from a work like this. Let the chapters from Esmein, Garraud, and Mittermaier that follow be read with care and attention, and a cosmopolitan and international viewpoint of criminal procedure is bound to result and to react beneficially on national prejudices.

University of Missouri,
Columbia, Missouri,
March 22, 1913.

INTRODUCTION TO THIS VOLUME

By William Renwick Riddell[1]

Common lawyers are apt to imagine that their science is something apart from the remainder of the realm of knowledge and thought, that the Common Law of England is something unique standing off by itself. To my mind the glory of the English Common Law is not diminished but enhanced by the recognition of the fact that it is not simply the creation of an isolated people, but is part of the juridical concept of the human race, and especially of nations with kindred origin. Speaking of a knowledge of law in the sense of knowledge of the sources and underlying philosophy of the law, as distinguished from a knowledge, however profound and accurate, of its existing precepts and their effect, the question may cogently be asked, "What do they know of English law who only English law know?"

And this applies not less to procedure than to substantive law.

This book contains a fascinating story of the evolution and development of Criminal Procedure on the Continent — an evolution and development which is of great interest both in its similarity to and in its difference from what appears in the history of the English procedure.

The first thing perhaps, which will strike the reader in this book, is the gradual but constant progress away from technicality and form.

Goldwin Smith used to say that to expect the lawyer to reform legal procedure would be to expect the tiger to abolish the jungle. He was giving a literary form to a thought underlying innumerable statements about lawyers — which lawyers have generally treated with the good-natured contempt which actuated the peasant to permit his wife to beat him, "It pleases she and don't hurt I." But the gibe is wholly unjust. The further back we go in the history of procedure the more technical we find the procedure — originally the procedure must be without "faute" —

[1] Justice of the Supreme Court of Ontario (Appellate Division).

and all the amendments have been the work of lawyers. I have before me a manuscript book of precedents for criminal indictments in the handwriting of a Judge who left our Bench about half a century ago. An indictment for murder covers three pages of foolscap. Nowadays it would not take three lines. The course of evolution has not in all cases been rapid, but it has always been in the same direction. To see and appreciate that this is so, not only in English-speaking countries but elsewhere as well, is to give the lawyer a higher estimate of human nature and of his profession.

The particular instances in which the procedure on the Continent agrees with that in England are not few, and are always interesting. The differences are equally so. In Rome, under the late Emperors, the Senate frequently asserted a jurisdiction over crimes, and by a summary procedure. This is quite analogous to the jurisdiction asserted by the Star Chamber, acting, as it not unfrequently did, not as a statutory body under 3 Henry 7, c. 1, but under the original common law jurisdiction of the Privy Council, and by a procedure quite as summary. The jurisdiction so exercised in England proved of great value to the country, although the Court itself got into disrepute and was abolished.

The great respect paid to trial by ordeal, and then its complete disappearance, are noticeable in France, as in England. The ordeal by fire or water was not peculiar to the Germanic races, but was perhaps more generally resorted to by them than by other peoples. Its final disappearance in France preceded by some centuries its disappearance from English jurisprudence. So, too, the wager of battle, which, at least in theory, lasted till a comparatively recent period in England, surviving for centuries the ordeal, but which became obsolete on the Continent very much earlier than in England. The same remark applies to compurgators.

One everywhere sees the evil case of him who had been taken in the act and consequently was more than half guilty.

The importance of an accused person putting himself "on the country" — a Canadian petit jury is still charged, "upon his arraignment he hath pleaded not guilty, and for his trial hath put himself upon his country, which country you are . . ." — is shown by the means taken to compel it, *e.g.* the "prison forte et dure" which, corrupted into "peine forte et dure" by English judges, had such a ghastly history. Giles Cory was not a solitary instance.

Another result of a refusal by an accused to put himself upon his country — *i.e.* outlawry — died a slow and lingering death.

Then consider the refusal of counsel to the prisoner, for which a theory was invented that the Judge was counsel for the accused. This it would have been difficult to persuade those to believe who were tried before Jeffreys and his like. The "State Trials" are witnesses to the falsity of the doctrine. But this was quite as reasonable, and displayed quite the same touching confidence in human nature, as the proposition that the Judges shall take care that the tortured are not crippled by their torturers. The torturers took the same care in this regard as Jeffreys did for Alice Lisle.

The wretched prisons, "cloacæ of infection," were universal, and neither Voltaire nor Howard brought about their complete abolition; and jailers' fees were too long an added infliction upon the unhappy mortal charged with crime.

The value of hearsay evidence, of presumptions, of confessions; the necessity of two witnesses,—all these have been matters of controversy in all civilized countries.

The arguments used a hundred years ago in France against the jury system are the same as those which influenced the Japanese jurists at a much more recent date. No doubt Britain — Home Country and Colony — the United States, all English-speaking countries, will go on with their firm faith in the jury system as the "palladium of civil liberty" — though it is being more and more felt that, however it may have been in the past, at the present time the jury has no more to do with the safety of civil liberty than the original Palladium had with the safety of Troy, and would be equally ineffective in a real crisis. And no doubt the "foreigner" will continue to wonder as did the French Canadians who, when in 1760–1763 the English law was introduced into Canada, marvelled that the English should leave the determination of their rights to tailors and shoemakers rather than to their Judges. But the jury in criminal matters seems to have made its way, even if jurors need not everywhere be unanimous.

All nations have gone through, or are going through, a stage in which there are imaginary crimes — witchcraft, sorcery; New England unhappily was no exception. It is but the other day that such crimes died out on this Continent — died an unnoted imbecile death.

These chronicles show that good sense constantly makes its appearance amid the most exigent technicality. The accused is not to be called upon to answer anything but the exact charge contained in the "indictment." He is to be confronted with the witnesses against him. Free men are to have free access to the courts. Indignation is expressed that sometimes officers take notes only of what the accused says and write it out afterwards; (the Music Hall jest represents the London Police Magistrate as saying to an accused, "Have you anything to say? You are not required to say anything, but if you do, it will be taken down, altered, and used in evidence against you on your trial").

The capital presentation in this work of the history of English law could not easily be excelled in the space — it shows the extreme care taken to be accurate.

I do not intend to analyze the book, much less to pick out the plums; the gold seeker is best satisfied to find his own nuggets. But I cannot refrain from calling attention to the *vox clamantis in deserto* of Pierre Ayrault, of La Bruyère, of Dupaty. They were forerunners and prototypes of our own Samuel Romilly. Into his soul entered the terrible wrongs of the criminal, real and supposed; and the strain of his heroic labors to right those wrongs had no small part in overthrowing a mind as fine and subtle as it was noble and humane. Those were men of whom their world was not worthy — who are but now coming into their own.

To the lawyer who is a mere tradesman, desiring only to make money out of his trade and caring for nothing else, a perusal of this book would be worse than useless. All such *βάναυσοι* are warned off this ground. *Procul o procul este, profani.* But fortunately the profession of law is a liberal and a learned profession, not a mere trade — there is more in it than meat and raiment, than money-making — and the sympathies and interests of the true lawyer reach far beyond bread-and-butter.

I envy the student of legal history, and especially him who makes the study of legal history a recreation from an arduous practice of his profession, his first perusal of this book. He will find much to wonder at, much to condemn, much to approve, in the practice, past and present, on the Continent. He may find lessons for his own country, what to follow, what to avoid. He will with difficulty conceive of anything which has not been at least touched on before; for "there is no new thing under the sun." Even in the old, old Roman law "the people exercised a great influence . . . through the appeal to the people against the decrees of the magistrates."

AUTHOR'S PREFACE TO THIS TRANSLATION

By A. Esmein

This book is the first published work of mine. It was composed between 1877 and 1880; I began it at Douai and finished it at Paris. It received the prize, in a competition, from the Academy of Moral and Political Sciences, of which to-day I am a member.

I am very glad to see it translated into English; for I am an admirer and friend of the Anglo-Saxon race. I am glad to see this translation published in the United States, the greatest democracy of modern times, which has set us an admirable example in its magnificent efforts to develop among its people the highest intellectual culture.

Although this book first saw the light thirty years ago, in 1882, I can still let it go into this new edition almost in its original form. Neither the labors of French and of foreign scholars, nor my own later studies, have given me reason to change its conclusions on any material points. Nevertheless, in this new edition, I have given it a thorough revision, taking into account the critical editions of early texts appearing since 1882; so that the work now represents a brief, but (I am convinced) a faithful, account of French criminal procedure and its history to the present day. I have entirely rewritten the pages concerning the origin and development of the "processus per inquisitionem" in the Canon law, — the subject of a lecture course of mine at the School of Higher Studies. I have also rewritten the portion devoted to the history of criminal procedure in England, in the light of the admirable researches of Pollock and Maitland, Thayer, and Holdsworth.

Paris,
April, 1913.

PRELIMINARY TOPICS

CHAPTER I [1]

THE DIFFERENT TYPES OF CRIMINAL PROCEDURE

§ 1. **The Three Types of Criminal Procedure.** — The history of civilization, in its organization and procedure for the repression of crime, presents a limited number of variant types. These succeed each other in a chronological order corresponding very closely to the logical order of their appearance. Three fundamental types of procedure are, in effect, distinguishable, — the *accusatory* type, the *inquisitorial* type, and the *mixed* type. The criminal law of almost every nation has begun with the accusatory procedure, and has changed to the inquisitorial procedure.[2] An evolution in an opposite direction, however, is now apparent; everywhere there is a tendency to restore the essential safeguards of the accusatory system, *publicity* and *confrontation*. The only institution of the inquisitorial system which has defied criticism and which is probably more powerful and general than ever is that of the *public prosecutor*.

§ 2. **The Accusatory System.** — The accusatory system has two leading features. It agrees with the primitive idea of the penal action, which is, primarily, but a sham fight between two combatants, to which the judge puts an end by deciding against one or other of the parties. It implies, at the outset, the mixture of two procedures, criminal and civil, which, both induced

[1] [This Chapter I = § II of Professor GARRAUD's work on "French Criminal Procedure." For this author and work, see the Editorial Preface. — ED.]

[2] Primitive laws gave to the procedure the effectual form of a combat. As always happens, this simulation began as a reality, and it is by no means rash to affirm that the first methods of litigants were those which are nowadays the last arguments of the vulgar — blows. See *Beaudouin*, "La participation des hommes libres au jugement dans le droit français" (Revue historique du droit, 1887–1888, pp. 246–279); *Ihering*, "Esprit du droit romain," vol. I, p. 122, note 33.

by private action, originally pursue their course in the same forms, before the same judges, and seek to attain the same satisfactions. Little by little, no doubt, the difference between the ends aimed at leads, notwithstanding the identity of the parties engaged, to the gradual differentiation of the penal proceeding from the civil. In the accusatory system, however, the difference between these two actions is never absolute, and there is a continual reaction of punishment upon indemnity and of indemnity upon punishment.

The following principles form the basis of this system of procedure:

(1) The *accusation* is freely exercised by *every citizen;* but there is no penal action without an accuser, who takes the initiative in it and the responsibility for it. In this respect, however, the setting in motion of the procedure belongs, originally, to the injured party; later on, when the necessity for and the interest of society in repression become felt, and as the penal law breaks away from the civil law, there is recognized, in each member of the group to which the injured party belongs, the power to begin the prosecution in the name of the collective body. This is the system of the *popular accusation.*

When this period of judicial civilization is reached, it becomes obvious that the accusation is a social function. Permanent and official organs, however, have not been created to exercise that function. This evolution of juridical conceptions is the point of departure of the breach which will continue to widen between the criminal and civil procedures. Society is obviously interested in the institution and prosecution of criminal actions. Neither the victim of a wrong, nor his fellow citizens, without the aid of public constraint, have the power to prevent the malefactor, emboldened by impunity, from very soon committing new crimes. The exercise of the social or public action is therefore justified in criminal matters; though it would be useless or superfluous in civil matters. It is undoubtedly useful from a social point of view that the rights of property be respected, contracts fulfilled, and injuries indemnified; but the surest way to attain these results is to leave private individuals free, giving them access to the tribunals, there to debate and have their rights acknowledged.[1] The civil action is therefore carried on in

[1] The difference between the penal and the civil action in this respect has been well put in relief by *Tarde,* "Penal Philosophy," *Howell's* trans. "The Criminal Science Series," Little, Brown, & Co., Boston, 1912, pp. 423–429.

the name of private interest; the penal action in the name of the general welfare. In the first, the initiative of the action should belong exclusively to the party who complains of a personal wrong; in the second, to the representative of the general public. This distinction becomes fundamental in every system of procedure. Whenever this evolution is accomplished, criminal procedure presents the following characteristics: Detection and prosecution of wrongful acts by the representatives of society; Trial by the representatives of society; Public punishment. Before, however, attaining this conception, which is that of civilized nations, many halting places are successively passed by.

(2) Primitive customs have a minimum of exigency and of ideal; they are satisfied with avoiding, as far as possible, recourse to brute force. They are regarded as having gained a great victory over the instinct of individual vengeance when they have laid upon the offended party the obligation to respect certain forms and certain delays in the exercise of his right, and have constrained him, in case of doubt, to submit to an arbitrage.[1] The *judge*, originally, is really the *umpire of a personal combat;* he must be chosen, or at least accepted, by both parties.

We also find, among almost all the nations which practised the accusatory system, either the principle of trial by the peers of the accused, or the absence of a procedure by default.

(3) The first of these institutions, *trial by the peers of the accused*, by the men of his tribe and of his caste, has always been looked upon, in primitive societies, as the best guaranty of impartial justice. It brings the case before unbiassed arbiters, who try it without appeal from their decision, guided only by their reason and conscience. Of the two questions which present themselves in the penal action, one, that of ascertaining if the accused is the perpetrator of the crime, is in the nature of a question of fact; the other, that of ascertaining to what extent he is morally responsible for it, is a question of degree of culpability. Popular judges are able to decide both questions. Their solution really requires no special juridical learning.

(4) The necessity for the *personal presence of the parties* arises, originally, from the very nature of the action, which is a feigned combat. Every combat presupposes, in effect, the presence of two combatants. It matters little that this was but a symbol. The form prevails over the fact. Later on, another idea is joined with the first, and gives to this rule of primitive law a new jus-

[1] *Sumner Maine*, "De la codification d'après les idées antiques," p. 13.

tification. The judge is an arbitrator, and must be accepted, at least tacitly, in order to be regularly vested with his power. The great concern at this period is to constrain the accused to submit to trial; the outlawing of the reluctant defendant is the forcible procedure by which it is sought to achieve this purpose in default of any direct means of compulsion and in view of the impossibility of passing sentence. If the accused does not appear he is not sentenced, but is treated as an outlaw.[1]

(5) The judge, in the accusatory system, cannot proceed on his own initiative, either in taking jurisdiction, or in obtaining proof. His rôle consists in replying to the questions which are presented to him, examining the evidence brought before him, and deciding upon that evidence. He is present as a second in the duel. He superintends the combat, that it may be fair throughout. He announces who is the victor. But at no moment of the proceedings does he take an active part, either to prosecute or to inquire. The trial has thus three essential characteristics; it is confrontative, oral, and public. The adversaries are brought face to face in a contest which takes place in broad daylight. Each of them produces at his discretion his means of proof. The proceeding resembles a duel with equal and fair weapons.

(6) The proceedings employed to discover the perpetrator of a crime and to prove his guilt are in perfect harmony with the prejudices, or, if you will, the beliefs of the period.

The chief effort of the prosecution is directed towards the establishment of the very act. In primitive procedures capture in the act appears, indeed, to be the normal hypothesis of repression; the sentiment of vengeance which inspires the penal system is, in this case, stronger; the culpability, which it is necessary to establish, is then less doubtful. Except in the case of capture in the act, if the accused does not confess, it is for him, by an inversion of the proof, to show his innocence by taking the exculpatory oath and sustaining it by the number of oath-helpers which custom demands. This is the normal method of proof. It constitutes a right for the accused. But it may be set aside in certain cases and then *ordeals* are brought into play, by which appeal is made to the judgment of the deity. These ordeals are of two kinds. In some, only one of the parties takes an active part, usually the accused. To instance the most widespread, there is the ordeal of branding, that of boiling water, and that of cold water. In the others, both parties play an

[1] See *Molinier*, p. 18; *Du Boys*, "Histoire du droit criminel des peuples modernes," vol. I, p. 122.

active part, as in the judicial duel and the ordeal of the cross.[1] This system is by no means peculiar to the Germanic customs; it is characteristic, not of one definite race, but of a certain stage of civilization.[2] In the mythological stage of the human mind the deity was invoked upon the question of guilt or innocence just as it was invoked as to the fate of a battle. In this respect there is a connection between beliefs and legal institutions. The same attitude of mind which allows of divination by auguries and sorcerers leads to the practice and the diffusion of the criminal examination by ordeals [3] and the judicial combat.[4]

The accusatory system, precisely because it symbolizes and regularizes the primitive combat, comes first in the juridical history of civilization. Its origin is to be found in the eastern legislations. It is seen to take a precise form in those of Greece and Rome, then decline and disappear, with liberty, in the latter days of the Empires. After the fall of the Roman Empire, we find it employed in crude and clumsy forms, in the Germanic and feudal customs; and while, in modern times, it has disappeared from the European continent, it continues to exist in England and the United States.[5]

[1] In France the ordeals by boiling water, branding, and cold water, frequently resorted to under the Merovingians, become infrequent from the beginning of the second dynasty.

[2] The exculpatory oath and the ordeals are found in Greek antiquity (*Esmein*, "Mélanges," p. 240 *et seq.; Sophocles*, "Antigone," verse 264); among the Hindus ("Laws of Manu," translated by *Loiseleur-Deslongchamps*, vol. VIII, pp. 109, 413–416). This system is still in force among a large number of barbarous races (*Köhler*, "Studien über Ordalien der Naturvölker," in Zeitschrift für vergleichende Rechtswissenschaft, vol. V, p. 368 *et seq.* and vol. IV, p. 365 *et seq.*). See on the nature of ordeals in the customs, *H. d'Arbois de Jubainville*, "Études sur le droit celtique," vol. I, p. 50.

[3] See on this point, *Tarde*, "Penal Philosophy," *Howell's* trans. "Criminal Science Series," p. 430; *Esmein*, "Cours élémentaire d'histoire du droit français," p. 98.

[4] *D'Arbois de Jubainville* (*op. et loc. cit.*) has pointed out, however, that the conventional duel of the Celts, like that of the ancient Romans (the Horatian combat), and those in the "Iliad" (the duel between Ajax and Diomedes), and the epic of Thebes, is inspired by a very different conception from the judicial duel of the Middle Ages. Like the latter, it has a place in litigious matters, but the idea of divine justice is absent from it. Neither the Celts nor Homer's heroes, nor the Horatii or the Curatii, looked for the intervention of the divinity for the triumph of the right. To them the duel was merely an imitation of private war.

[5] *Cf. Seymour-Harris*, "Principii di diritto e procedure penale Inglese" (Bertole's translation), Verona, 1898; *Fournier*, "Code de procédure criminelle aux Etats-Unis de New York; Introduction sur la procédure criminelle aux Etats-Unis" (Paris, Larose, 1893). But there is a public prosecutor in the United States. The insecurity and impunity resulting, in a country new and composed of such diverse elements, from the English system of prosecution, which leaves repression to the initiative of the citizens, has taught the United States the necessity of committing to a special functionary the duty of prosecuting repression.

To England, from the end of the 1700s, Europe was to go (by a kind of ancestral reversion) to seek for and recover the type of this archaic procedure, to which were to be sacrificed some of the best creations of French genius, such as the public prosecutor.

§ 3. **The Inquisitorial System.** — The system of procedure called *inquisitorial* is more scientific and more complex than the accusatory system. It is better adapted to the needs of social repression. Its two predominant features are, the *secret inquiry* to discover the culprit, and the employment of torture to obtain his confession. But this type of procedure embraces a number of kindred institutions, which cannot be separated, because they throw light on and coördinate each other.

(1) The detection and prosecution of the culprit are no longer left to the initiative of private parties. The State proceeds "ex officio" to perform this double duty. It creates organs to investigate as well as to accuse. The institutions which correspond to these necessary phases of the penal action undoubtedly do not spring up in a day; their origin is as obscure as their development is uncertain. It is not proposed here to deal with anything more than the final stage of the juridical evolution; the change in the nature of the trial ("instruction"), and in that of the arrest.

(2) An interesting phenomenon of the social and political evolution appears first in the function of the judge. That which was the right and function of everybody becomes the right and function of a few; the power to try has a tendency to become specialized. It tends also to become mandatory. The primitive arbitrator changes character. The judge, appointed by the ruler and no longer chosen by the parties, is imposed on, and no longer proposed to, the delinquent. He becomes the representative of the ruler, who alone has the right to administer justice. His nature, therefore, changes in a double sense. He is an *officer of justice,* vested with a social function, and chosen, because of the scientific nature of the penal action, from among those who have studied the laws, the legists. He is also a *permanent functionary,* charged with the trial of all causes of the same kind. At first itinerant, the judges are subsequently settled in certain districts, which thus become seats of justice. This results, by means of their decisions, in the creation and development of a body of criminal sciences. At first, the customs are collected; then, fixed by being written down; then text-books of legal practice are compiled and serve as guides to the professional men; and thus the

science is established in the course of the development of the spirit of observation and criticism.

(3) The judge's investigation is not limited to the evidence brought before him. The magistrate proceeds of his own accord and according to certain rules, with the inquiry ("inquisitio"), that is to say, with every search for evidence allowed by the law. This inquiry, *written* and *secret*, is not confrontative. The open duel between the accuser and the accused is replaced by the insidious attack of the judge.

(4) A new method of examination, more cruel perhaps, but more logical, than the ordeals, *i.e.*, that of torture, enters the higher courts of justice and filters through these to the lower tribunals. The confession of the accused having acquired a preponderating influence, the method "par excellence" of extracting this proof is now seen to be torture, *e.g.*, by the wooden horse, the boot, or the water. Torture is an institution of Roman origin. Under the Republic, no doubt, and at the beginning of the Empire, Roman citizens escaped it. The only persons exposed to it then were the slave when he was accused (or simply called to court) and the provincial.[1] But in the early days of the Empire the custom was begun of subjecting to this process of examination the Roman citizen accused of treason. Then torture comes to be of such general application that the handbooks recommend judges not to begin the examination by that, but first to collect the evidence.[2] It is, therefore, not surprising that the diffusion of torture coincides, in modern history, with the revival of the half-forgotten Roman law by the criminalists of the Belogna school. The transformation of the procedure by the substitution of torture for ordeals really begins to manifest itself from the end of the 1100 s. Since that time, no country of Europe has escaped the contagion.[3] At the end of the 1300 s torture had become a general custom. It was, to some extent, one of the fundamental institutions of the old criminal procedure.

Two institutions, destined to limit the power of the judge, that of the appeal and that of "legal proofs," have their origin in the inquisitorial procedure, of which they form two characteristic features.

[1] *Esmein* ("Cours élémentaire d'histoire du droit français," p. 36) observes that "antiquity never admitted the testimony of the slave without controlling him by torture in the giving of it."

[2] L. 11, C. IX, 41.

[3] See *Tarde*, "Penal Philosophy," *Howell's* trans., "Criminal Science Series," p. 435. *Cf. Molinier*, "La torture" (Toulouse), 1879. Extract from the "Recueil de l'académie des sciences, inscriptions et belles-lettres de Toulouse."

(5) The *appeal* is the right to bring anew before a higher judge the cause already decided by the lower judge. The conception of the appeal is foreign to the idea of justice done by the peers of the accused. It is, at first, repugnant to the popular idea of judicial infallibility. If the first judge can be wrong, why not the second? It implies, moreover, a hierarchy of tribunals: while popular judges should be supreme, each within the limits of his cognizance. Thus the appeal, as we understand it nowadays, did not exist under the Roman Republic; it made its appearance under the Empire. This method of recourse was unknown either to the Germanic or the feudal procedures, both essentially based on popular customs.[1] But with the reconstitution of the sovereignty and the hierarchy for the benefit of royalty, the appeal was introduced into the secular jurisdictions under the growing influence of the Roman law and the Canon law.

(6) The inquisitorial and secret procedure led to the organization of a system of "legal proofs" as a necessary counterbalance, in the interest even of the defense. The judge, to convict, must have before him certain kinds and quantities of evidence, defined by law; but, on the other hand, if he has this evidence before him, he must of necessity convict. His personal belief is of little consequence on either hypothesis. This system, by making conviction more difficult, tends, as a fatal result, to weld more firmly the fetters of criminal procedure. There is here a double movement, which in certain respects aggravates, and in others ameliorates, the situation of the delinquent.

The inquisitorial system is contained, in embryo, in the latest institutions of the Roman Empire. It agrees well with a centralizing and despotic power. Torture, as a proceeding for detection and proof, was especially resorted to at this period; and later, the theatre of the contagion which was to pervade all Europe was a corner of Italy, whence, about the middle of the 1100s, the resuscitation of the Roman law brought disturbance as well as a new ideal into all the feudal tribunals.

The Church was able to furnish the secular courts with a lesson and a model, in the methods of its ecclesiastical tribunals. By its example it paved the way for the substitution, consummated in the 1500s, of the inquisitorial procedure for the accusatory procedure in every country of Europe.[2] In the latter half of the 1200s

[1] The appeal for denial of justice, "défaut de droit" and the appeal for wrong judgment, "faux jugement," are institutions peculiar to feudal procedure and are analogous to the modern appeal merely in name.

[2] This system, originally employed for prosecutions for heresy, after-

the influence of the Roman law and of the Canon law led to the formation of this new procedure, which renounced the Germanic tendencies, and took its inspiration almost exclusively from these, the two learned legal systems of Europe.

Each of these two types of procedure, the accusatory type and the inquisitorial type, has its good qualities and its defects; neither contains, in itself, the safeguards necessary for the administration of criminal justice. In the accusatory procedure, the detection and the prosecution of offenses are left wholly to the initiative of private individuals — an initiative which may slumber through their inertia, fear, or corruption. The chances of impunity flowing from this system are still further enhanced both by the publicity which exists in all the phases of the procedure, and by the necessity which compels the judge to limit his investigation entirely to the evidence furnished him by the accuser. But, on the other hand, the inquisitorial procedure has very serious defects; under it, the prosecution and the detection of offenses are intrusted exclusively to the agents of the State; there is the atmosphere of secrecy and consequently of suspicion, in the midst of which the trial proceeds; and finally, there is the absence of any real confrontation between the prosecution and the defense.

Thus progress, in the path of juridical civilization, consists in borrowing from each of these types of procedure its best elements, and in forming a mixed type. One part of this composite type is taken from the inquisitorial system, the other part contains all the safeguards and good qualities of the accusatory system.

§ 4. **The Mixed System.** — This mixed type is characterized by the following features; they are to be found in the majority of the European systems of procedure, but the French Code of Criminal Examination of 1808 (the influence of which has been so great in Europe) systematizes them for the first time.

(1) The judges of guilt have no initiative in the proceeding; they cannot take cognizance themselves, of their own accord. It is, therefore, necessary that an accusation be brought; but this right of accusing is committed to special functionaries who thus act as *public prosecutors* and to whom the parties should, on principle, be merely auxiliaries.

wards for all crimes, became, under the name of "procédure à l'extraordinaire," the system of common law in force in the royal jurisdictions for the prosecution of serious crimes until 1789. See *Faustin Hélie*, *op. cit.*, vol. II, Nos. 206, 207, and 208; *Léo*, "Histoire de l'inquisition au moyen age" (translated by *Salomon Reinach*, Paris, 1900), book 1, ch. IX to XII t. I, p. 399 *et seq.; Tanon*, "Histoire de l'inquisition," *passim.*

(2) The *judgment* is rendered by magistrates and jurors. The method and conditions of the share of both of these in the administration of criminal justice vary, however, in the different countries.

(3) The proceeding is divided into two phases, the *preliminary examination*, intrusted to magistrates, and resulting in a preparatory decision, and the *final trial* before the court, which gives its judgment in the proceeding. The first has a double characteristic; it is neither confrontative nor public. The second admits both principles of confrontation and publicity.

(4) The judges are not called upon to state the *evidential basis* of their judgment. And although the search for and the furnishing of the evidence are subject to legal rules, its probative value is not measured beforehand and the outcome of the charge depends upon whether the judges are or are not thoroughly convinced.

Like every eclectic system, this procedure demands, in its application, a coöperation of effort and hearty support which it appears sometimes to have lacked. On the one hand, the magistrates, the professional men to whom the initiative and direction of the action were given, have manifested for the coöperation of the private citizens a sentiment of extreme distrust; and this has gone on increasing since 1810 at a rate which, for some years, has pointed to a return to the system of solely professional magistrates. On the other hand, with the desire of the magistracy to recover all its powers, there has unfortunately coincided the dislike of the majority of citizens for civic duties, and the steadfast wish to avoid them. Jury duty has been considered a bore by the very people best fitted to fulfil it. This state of affairs is not peculiar to France. It is apparent in every country into which this mixed system of procedure has been carried.

CHAPTER II[1]

ROMAN CRIMINAL PROCEDURE

§ 1. **General Characteristics.** — In every nation, the history of its criminal procedure stands in close relation to the evolution of its political conditions and the development of its views in regard to punishment. Wherever there has come into being a free constitution and an interest in public affairs, there has been an increasing demand that certain dangers to the freedom of the citizen be done away with, — namely, those dangers which frequently exist in the criminal procedure, because of those who wish to usurp power and would abuse the right of prosecution in order to attain political advancement. The more punishment bears the earmark of being a satisfaction of the party who has suffered a wrong, the more will the *accusatorial* procedure tend to predominate. But when the view becomes more prevalent, that punishment is necessary for the public interest as a means of upholding the law, *inquisitorial* methods gradually increase. The truth of these remarks is apparent in the criminal procedure of Rome.[2]

[1] [Chapters II and III=Chapters XIII and XV of Professor MITTERMAIER'S "Progress of German Criminal Procedure." For this author and work, see the Editorial Preface. — ED.]

[2] In regard to the Roman criminal procedure, the following writers may be consulted: *Sigonius*, "De judiciis" (the second and third books deal with the "publica judicia"); *Brissonius*, "Oper. minor," p. 32; *Ferratius*, "Epistol." (Patav. 1699); *Ayrault* (Ærodius), "L'ordre, formalité et instruction judiciaire, dont les anciens Grecs et Romains ont usé en accusations publiques" (Paris 1575, 1598). (Ayrault was himself "Criminal-lieutenant" in France. See *Niceron*, "Mémoires," tome XVII, p. 327. In regard to his life and his work, "Le Droit," 1884, No. 269, and as to the character of his work, see *Laboulaye*, "Essai," p. V.); "Lectii de public. judic." in *Otho* "thesaurus," I, p. 67; *Mathæi*, "De criminibus," especially the edition by *Nani* (Mediol. 1803); *Van der Hoop*, "De his qui antiquitus apud Roman. de crim. judic." (Lugd. 1723), in VIII Band of *Meermann*

Everywhere in the Roman criminal procedure there appears the peculiar characteristic that crimes are dealt with in certain categories.[1] Each category had its distinctive tribunal and rules of evidence, which varied with changing political conditions. The procedure in "perduellio"[2] was fundamentally quite different[3] from the procedure in "parricidium."[4] And again in cases in which judgment was passed against the accused with the formula "sacer esto"[5] there was also a special kind of procedure.

§ 2. **Early Tribunals.** — The judicial proceedings were either in the court of the kings,[6] who often passed judgment with the assistance of a council ("consilium"), — or before the quæstors[7]

"thesaurus," p. 608. Saxii "De ordin. judic. public. apud Romanos" (Traj. 1784); *Madihn*, "Vicissit. cognition. crim. apud Romanos" (Hal. 1772); *Invernizi*, "De publicis et crim. jud." (Rom. 1787); *Heyne*, "De judic. public. rat. et ordin. apud Romanos" (Goett. 1788); *Renazi*, "Diatr. de ord. et forma judic. crim." (at close of volume V of his "Elem. jur. crimin."); *Broquet*, "quinam fuit apud Romanos in crim. publ. procedendi modus" in Annal. Acad. (Gandav. 1820); *Schmiedicke*, "Histor. proc. crim. rom." (Vratislav. 1827); *Kennis*, "De crim. perduell. regum ætate" (Lovan 1828); *Rosshirt* in the "Archiv des Criminalrechts," Bd. XI No. 1, and No. 14; *Geib*, "Geschichte des rom. Criminalprocesses" (Leipzig 1842); *Platner*, "Quæst. de jure crim. Roman." (Marb. 1842); *Lebastard Delisle*, "De l'administration de la justice crim. chez les Romains" (Paris 1841); *Osenbruggen*, in the introduction to the work, "Ciceros Rede für Milo" (Kiel 1841); *Féréol Rivière*, "Esquisse historique de la législation criminelle des Romains" (Paris 1844); *Laboulaye*, "Essai sur les loix criminelles des Romains" (Paris 1845); *Hélie*, "Traité de l'instruction crim." (Paris 1843), Vol. I, pp. 34–173.

1 *Mittermaier*, in "Archiv des Criminalrechts" (1843), p. 153.

2 *Kostlin*, "Die Perduellion unter den röm. Königen" (Tübingen 1841); *Geib*, "Geschichte," p. 61.

3 It is certain that the same crimes, *e.g.*, murder, were under different political conditions, sometimes dealt with as "perduellio" and sometimes as "parricidium," *e.g.*, in the trial of the Horatii. *Rubino*, "Unters. über röm. Staatsverf," p. 490; *Kostlin*, p. 10, 57; *Wöniger*, "das Sacralsystem," p. 244.

4 In regard to the wider significance of "parricidium," see *Festus*. *Meister*, "Urtheile und gutachten," p. 461. Also *Diek*, "Historische Versuche über röm. Crim.," p. 9; *Dirksen*, "Vers. zur Kritik der Quellen des röm. Rechts," pp. 284 and 337; *Luden*, "uber Versuch des Verbr." p. 59; *Osenbruggen*, "Das altröm. Parricidium" (Kiel 1841).

5 *Abegg*, "De antiquiss. roman. jur. crim." p. 44; *Dirksen*, "Civil Abhandl." p. 102; *Rosshirt*, in "Archiv etc." XI, p. 2 e; *Platner*, "De crimin. jure antiquo Roman." (Marsburg 1836), p. 26. Also see *Kostlin*, "von Mord und Todtschlag" (Stuttgart 1838), Part I, p. 59; *Rubino*, p. 475; *Kostlin*, "Von der Perduellion," p. 127; *Platner*, "Quæst. de jure crim. Roman," p. 27.

6 *Kennis*, "Diss." pp. 34–41; *Dirksen*, "Civil Abhandl." p. 100; *Burkhardt*, "Die Criminalgerichtsbarkeit in Rom bis auf die Kaiserzeit" (Basel 1836); *Kostlin*, p. 20; *Geib*, p. 14; *Rubino*, p. 211; *Laboulaye*, p. 80; *Hélie*, I, p. 35.

7 These early quæstors were not permanent officials but were specially appointed for the particular case. L. 2. No. 23. D. De orig. Juris. *Dirksen*, "Uebersicht der Versuche zur Kritik der XII Tafeln," p. 617 and especially p. 654; *Invernizi*, p. 31; *Kennis*, p. 48; *Rosshirt*, in "Archiv etc."; *Burkhardt*, pp. 6, 8, and 9; *Zacharia*, "Sulla," pp. 147, 148. More

(often the "quæstores parricidii"),[1] — or before the "duumviris perduelliones,"[2] who were themselves a special kind of quæstors. Popular courts had jurisdiction under the kings[3] only in so far as a case could be referred to the people through appeal ("provocatio").[4] After the expulsion of the kings the jurisdiction belonging to them passed to the consuls,[5] who often availed themselves of the coöperation ("consilium") of the senate.[6] There was in the Twelve Tables the well-known provision[7] that the people in the popular courts and in the "comitia centuriata" should pass judgment upon a complaint brought against a Roman citizen.[8] Thus also in the "comitia tributa," which gradually extended its power, there arose the custom of deciding crimes that had a political significance.[9] The people exercised a great influence over criminal proceedings through the appeal to the people against the decrees of the magistrates ("provocatio"),[10] — a right confirmed by many laws.[11]

§ 3. **The Quæstiones.** — There would often be appointed by the people, or by the Senate,[12] "quæstiones," as commissioners for the trial and decision of particular crimes.[13] The many inconveniences of an appeal to the popular courts and the increase of crimes brought about a change in the nature of these "quæstiones." They became standing tribunals for the trial and decision of crimes that were of frequent occurrence. Each "quæstio perpetua" established for this purpose was created by a special statute ("lex")[14] which specified the crime to which it had appli-

correct views are found in *Geib*, p. 52. *Cf.* with *Lebastard Delisle*, p. 9; *Rubino*, p. 322.

[1] *Geib*, p. 51.

[2] *Schmiedicke*, p. 16; *Kennis*, p. 43. The correct view in *Geib*, p. 59; *Köstlin*, p. 102; *Laboulaye*, p. 84.

[3] *Geib*, p. 30.

[4] *Wöniger*, "Das Sacralsystem," p. 239; *Hélie*, I, p. 37.

[5] *Livius*, II, 5. L. 3. No. 16. D. De orig. Juris.; *Ivernizi*, p. 20; *Schmiedicke*, p. 31; *Geib*, p. 22.

[6] *Cicero*, "De legibus," III, 19; *Dirksen*, "Uber die XII Tafeln," p. 645; *Schmiedicke*, p. 42.

[7] *Geib*, p. 39.

[8] *Geib*, p. 32; *Férol*, p. 11.

[9] *Geib*, p. 35. *Cf. Platner*, pp. 49–65.

[10] *Burchardt*, p. 4; *Huschke*, "Die Verfassung des Servius Tullius," p. 584; *Geib*, p. 152; *Wöniger*, "das Sacralsystem," p. 265.

[11] L. 2. No. 16, D. De orig. Juris.; *Sigonius*, "De jud," II, cap. 4; *Van der Hoop*, in *Meermann* "thesaurus" suppl. vol. p. 617; *Wirsinger*, "Resp. ad quæst. de differentia inter delicta, dolus et culpa" (Bruxelles 1824), p. 99.

[12] *Geib*, p. 48; *Laboulaye*, p. 112.

[13] In regard to "quæstiones" held for crimes for which no punishment was provided by a special statute, see *Platner*, p. 12, etc.; *Geib*, p. 68; *Laboulaye*, p. 126.

[14] *Burchardt*, pp. 17, 19; *Bach*, "Histor. juris." p. 80; *Schmiedicke*, p. 124; *Rosshirt*, in "Archiv etc." XI, pp. 373, 382; *Zachariä*, "Sulla," 2 Hft. p. 143. There were such "quæstiones" in regard to the crimes of

cation and a certain procedure appropriate thereto. The number of these "quæstiones perpetuæ" steadily increased.[1]

Along with these standing criminal courts, the popular courts, however, in which the entire people passed judgment, continued to exist.[2] There often existed even in the time of the Republic "quæstiones extraordinariæ"[3] for cases for which as yet no "quæstio perpetua" existed; or perhaps, on account of some peculiar developments of a case, a special commission would be appointed.[4] Since the magistrates presiding over the "quæstiones" were regularly some one of the prætors,[5] it came about that the prætor whose turn it was to preside over the "quæstio" was called "quæstor" or "quæsitor."[6] In addition, one finds early mention of a "judex quæstionis,"[7] who,[8] however, since he sat instead of the prætor, and was invested by him with the presidency ("præsidium") of the criminal court, had the same authority that the prætor would have had, if he had presided.[9]

"repetundarum, ambitus, majestatis, and peculatus"; see *Ferratius*, "Epistol." lib. I, epist. 15; *Rosshirt*, in "Archiv," p. 404; *Cicero*, "Brutus," cap. 27; *Birnbaum*, in "Archiv," VIII, p. 656. But see *Heineccius*, "Antiq. jur. rom." (Haubold's edition), p. 768; *Klenze*, "Ad leg. Serviliam prolegom." p. xii. See also *Geib*, p. 170. *Féréol*, p. 18.

1 *E.g.*, "quæstio de falso, de sicariis, de parricidiis"; see *Hugo*, "Rechtsgeschichte," pp. 316, 633; *Livius*, I, 26; II, 35; XLIII, 8, 18; *Cicero*, "Pro Milone," 3; Especially *Van der Hoop*, "De his, qui antiq." cap. V.

2 *Cicero*, "Pro Milone," 6. Also a "nova quæstio," *Cicero*, "Pro Milone," 5, 6; *Cicero*, "In Verr." I, 42; II, 25; "Philip." II, 9. See also *Cicero*, "Attic." I, 13, 14, 16; *Rosshirt*, p. 395; *Köstlin*, "Die Lehre von Mord," I. Thl., p. 97; *Burkhardt*, p. 20; *Geib*, p. 216.

3 *Geib*, p. 219. As to whether the Centumviral courts also passed judgment "de criminibus," see *De Tigerstroem*, "De judic. apud Roman." (Berol. 1826), p. 216; *Huschke*, "Servius Tullius," p. 586; *Geib*, p. 233; *Féréol*, p. 34.

4 *Birnbaum*, in "Archiv," VIII, pp. 674, 679; IX, pp. 399, 412; *Platner*, "Quæst." p. 85.

5 *Cicero*, "In Brut." cap. 27; *Cicero*, "Pro Cœl." p. 13; "Pro Cluentio," 53; *Klenze*, p. 19; *Geib*, p. 178.

6 *Cicero*, "In Verrem," II, c. 10; *Virgil*, "Æneid," VI, vers. 432; *Cicero*, "In Vatin." c. 14; "Pro Fontejo," c. 6; "Pro Plancio," c. 17; *Schmiedicke* on page 116 has the wrong view. For better view, see *Geib*, p. 184. In regard to the meaning of "quæstor," see especially *Laboulaye*, p. 45; *Hélie*, I, p. 59.

7 *Cicero*, "Pro Cluentio," c. 54; "Pro Roscio," c. 4; "Cæcina," c. 10. L. 1. pr. and No. 1. D. "Ad leg. Corn. de sicar." L. 81. D. "De judic." *Köstlin*, "Lehre von Mord und Todtschlag," I, p. 99; *Osenbruggen*, "Oratio," p. 35.

8 *Sigonius*, "De judic." II, 5; *Ayrault*, "Ordre etc." p. 233; *Ferratius*, I, 4; *Van der Hoop*, "De his, qui antiq." p. 630; *Cremani*, "Element. jur. crim." vol. III, p. 40. See also *Schulting*, "Jurisprud. antej." p. 728; *Invernizi*, p. 98; *Birnbaum*, in "Archiv," IX, p. 356; *Rosshirt*, in "Archiv," XI, pp. 380–383, 390; *Zachariä*, p. 154. In the "Collatio leg. Mosaic et rom." Tit. 1, No. 3, there is a reference to the "prætor judexve quæstionis." *Zachariä*, II, 158.

9 *Geib*, pp. 188–193. *Cf. Féréol*, pp. 21, 22. In regard to the "judex quæstionis," see *Laboulaye*, p. 327; *Hélie*, I, p. 60.

It is also certain that the senate had a criminal jurisdiction in cases of conspiracy and also in cases of crime committed by foreigners. In these matters, the senate either undertook the investigation itself, or delegated it to a commission.[1]

§ 4. **The Judices.** — The rendition of judgment was in the hands of the "judices." The rules determining the class and rank from whom these were chosen reflect the contemporaneous status of political freedom.[2] In the beginning only senators were the judges. Later, after many changes, the knights ("equites"), then again both the knights and senators, and finally, persons of lower rank possessed this privilege.[3]

These "judices" were chosen each year, but the numerous statutes referring to the subject reveal a great diversity as to their number.[4] From among these "judices," just as is the case with modern juries, those passing judgment in each case were first designated by lot, and by the exercise of right of challenge ("recusation"). This ever increasing right of challenge belonged both to the accuser and the accused. Just as the crimes varied, so there was a diversity as to the number of judges necessary for a valid criminal judgment.[5]

§ 5. **"Judices" compared with Modern Jurors.** — It is improper (although many have done so [6]) to regard the modern English and French jurors as analogous to the Roman "judices."[7] The last mentioned rendered a general verdict as to the guilt of the accused without a separation of the questions of fact and law. But the

[1] *Dirksen*, "Civil Abhandl." I. Thl., No. 2, p. 135; *Rosshirt*, in "Archiv," XI, p. 31; *Geib*, p. 217.

[2] *Sigonius*, lib. II, cap. 6; *Krebs*, "De jud. rom. decir." (Lips. 1744). Here belong many of the "leges judiciariæ," especially the "lex Servilia." *Bach*, p. 61. *Haubold*, "Instit. rom. priv." p. 94. *Klenze*, "Diss." In regard to the "leges judiciariæ," *Laboulaye*, pp. 196–322. To this the "decuriæ judicum" also refers. *De Tigerstroem*, p. 163. *Zachariä*, p. 156, and p. 159 in regard to the changes which Sulla introduced. See especially: *Geib*, p. 213; *Laboulaye*, p. 263; *Hélie*, I, p. 61.

[3] Correctly treated in *Geib*, pp. 193–202. *Cf. Osenbruggen*, "Rede für Milo," p. 34.

[4] Here also belongs the "lex Servilia." See *Ascon*, "In Cicero Or. in Verr." c. 6; *Nes*, "De judiciis judic. jurator" (Traject. 1804), p. 15; *Rosshirt*, in "Archiv," XI, p. 385; *Osenbruggen*, p. 36; *Geib*, p. 307; *Laboulaye*, p. 354.

[5] *E.g.*, the "lex Servilia" required 50; according to *Cicero*, "Pro Cluentio," 30 were at one time necessary; according to "Orat. in Pison." cap. 40, 65 were necessary; and according to *Cicero*, "Epist. ad Attic." IV, 15, 28 judges were necessary. See especially *Geib*, p. 207.

[6] *Pentingal*, "An inquiry into the use and practice of juries among the Greeks and Romans" (London 1767), 3 vols.; *De Blankensee*, "De judic. jurat. apud Græcos et Rom." (Goett. 1812). See also *v. Oppen*, "Geschworne et Richter," p. 9; *Lebastard*, p. 25.

[7] *Geib*, p. 315; *Mittermaier*, in "Archiv" (1844), p. 151.

modern jury makes this separation, and (at least the French jury) has to pass judgment according to its innermost persuasion,[1] without any regard for rules of evidence. However, it cannot be denied, that the Roman "judices" and the modern jury are similar in this, — that both institutions rested upon the idea of popular courts, and that the "judices," like the jury, did not constitute a permanent tribunal, but were chosen by lot [2] for each particular case.[3] Also the extensive right of challenge (recusation), which belonged to the accused in respect to the "judices,"[4] as used against modern jurors, is a ground of similarity in both institutions. At least this was so in so far as there predominated therein the idea that the accused must submit only to judges whom he of his own free will acknowledges are wholly impartial.

§ 6. **Roman Procedure Accusatorial in its Nature.** — Roman criminal procedure, in accordance with the spirit of the Roman criminal law and the ideas prevailing in Rome, was regularly based upon the principle of a *formal accusation,* — not merely in the sense that only on the basis of a formal accusation could a criminal prosecution take place, but also in the sense that there was an issue only between the accuser and the accused, and that this issue was limited to the formal allegations of the accuser, who was obliged to furnish the evidence necessary for his case.[5]

Inquisitorial elements gradually developed in criminal procedure during the period of the Republic, when for the prosecution of the guilty in particular cases, extraordinary "quæstiones" would be appointed.[6] The procedure taking place before the "quæstors" and before the "pontifices" [7] had many peculiarities pointing to inquisitorial influences. Yet the foundation of procedure always remained accusatorial.[8]

[1] *Van der Does de Bye,* "Histor. judic. jurat." (Lugdun 1821), p. 29. In regard to the significance of the Roman jurors, *Laboulaye,* p. 337.

[2] "Sortitio." See *Ayrault,* p. 245; *Cicero,* "In Verrem," XI, 15; *Geib,* p. 308.

[3] There were special provisions for special crimes. Herewith in the "lex Licinia," were connected the "judices ædilitii." *Cicero,* "Pro Planc." 15, 17; "Pro Murena," 13; *Ayrault,* c. 1, p. 254.

[4] The reason for the challenge (causa recusationis) was not given. *Ayrault,* p. 240. The statute ("lex") also provided the disqualifications in respect to each crime. See *Cicero,* "Pro Cluent." 53; "In Vatin." c. 2. In regard to the influence of the "lex Licinia" see *Geib,* p. 313.

[5] *Ayrault,* "Ordre etc." p. 281; *Geib,* p. 98; *Laboulaye,* p. 134; *Hélie,* I, p. 70.

[6] *Geib,* p. 102; *Hélie,* I, p. 120.

[7] In regard to the procedure in the prosecution relative to the Bacchanalia, *Geib,* p. 107.

[8] *Mittermaier,* in "Archiv" (1843), p. 287.

In the popular courts the right to bring an accusation belonged only to those magistrates[1] who could call the "comitiæ" together and transact business with them,[2] while any citizen could bring an accusation before the "quæstiones."

Everywhere in the Roman institutions, there is apparent the effort to protect[3] the freedom of the citizen against the malice, plots, and indiscretion of the accuser, and at the same time an attempt to protect the interests of the State against the corrupt withdrawal of an accusation, through collusion or some partiality towards the guilty. The first attitude explains the laws relative to the "calumnia" of the accuser,[4] and the necessity of the "subscriptio in crimen."[5] The second gave rise to the provisions relative to "tergiversatio"[6] and "prævaricatio"[7] to which the "senatus consultum Turpillianum" refers.[8] The Romans also had the custom[9] (still used in modern English procedure) of using one of the guilty parties,[10] to whom immunity had been promised, as a witness against the others, *e.g.*, in crimes against the State. It is not settled to what extent there existed in the time of the Republic special officers whose duty it was,[11] in their official capacity, to investigate crimes and bring prosecutions, nor to what extent the "quadruplatores"[12] were such officers.

1 *Rosshirt*, in "Archiv etc." XI, p. 397; *Geib*, p. 100.

2 Private persons were obliged to bring their actions through the magistrate. As to the later law, No. 1, Inst. "De publ. jud." But *cf.* L. 30. Cod. "Ad leg. Jul. de adult." *Burchardi*, "Rechtssystem der Römer," p. 217; and in "Neues Archiv etc." VII, p. 465.

3 *J. van Renesse*, "De coercitione accusatorium in Oelrichs" (diss. belg.), vol. I, Tom. II, pp. 561–632.

4 The "lex Remnia" was important. See *Brencmann*, "Lex Remnia sive de legis Remniæ exitu cum diss. de fatis calumn." in *Otto*, "Thes." tom. III, p. 1561. Also *J. de Bye*, "De delicto calumniæ in public. judiciis." (Lugd. 1790); *Geib*, pp. 124, 291.

5 L. 3. No. 2. 7. D. "De accus." L. 24. D. "Ad leg. Corn. de falsis." L. 2. Cod. "Ad SC. Turpill." L. 5. Cod. Theod. "De accus."; *Klenze*, "Ad leg. Servil." p. 13; *Birnbaum* in "Archiv etc." IX, p. 361. See *Brencmann*, c. 1. p. 1635; *Bye*, "Diss." pp. 4–16.

6 L. 1. pr. D. "Ad SC. Turpill." See also: *Cicero*, "Pro Flacco," c. 20; "pro Plancio," c. 19.

7 *Cicero*, "In partit." 36. L. 1. No. 6. D. "Ad SC. Turpill."

8 *Nordkerk*, "De lege Petronia," c. IV, 3. 4.

9 Called an "index." *Ascon.* "In Verrem," c. 11; *Cicero*, "Pro Cluentio," c. 7; "In Catil." IV, 3; *Tacitus*, "Annal." IV, 28; *Invernizi*, p. 60; *Geib*, p. 105.

10 *Ayrault*, p. 291.

11 *Adam*, "Handbuch der römischen Alterthümer" (Translation), I, p. 552, refers to *Cicero*, "Pro Rosc." 20; "De legibus," II, 47; and *Plin.* "Epist." III, 9. But on the contrary, see *Winssinger*, "De diff. inter etc." p. 102.

12 As to "quadruplum" (fourfold), *Livius*, III, c. ult; *Ascon.* "In Divin." c. 7; *Cicero*, "In Verr." IV, 8; *Invernizi*, p. 80; *Geib*, pp. 106, 257.

§ 7. **Effect of Lack of a General Criminal System.** — The modern view of a criminal system embracing every variety of crime was unknown to the Romans.[1] Each law contained special provisions relative to the formal accusation, the proof, and the prosecution of the particular crime to which that law referred. Accordingly in each "quæstio" there could only be a trial and judgment in respect to that one crime, towards which the formal accusation in pursuance of the statute was directed.[2] This was important in cases where there was a question relative to a concurrence of crimes.[3]

The "Leges Juliæ Judiciariæ"[4] seem to have contained general provisions only in regard to single points relating to the appointment of judges and kindred subjects. In the majority of institutions having to do with procedure, one is obliged to distinguish whether the procedure came before the "quæstiones" or before the "comitiæ," — and if the latter, whether it came before the "comitia tributa" or before the "comitia centuriata." There is also the question whether the "judices" might apply only the penalties which the statute provides, or whether they might consider mitigating circumstances, — a question to be answered differently according to the kind of prosecution under consideration.[5] In the "quæstiones," the "judices" were strictly bound to the literal application of the statute.[6]

§ 8. **Acts Preliminary to Trial.** — The separation of procedure into a trial and a preliminary investigation existed in so far as the formal public session at which, under the direction of a "quæsitor" in the presence of the "judices," the case would be tried and decided, was preceded by a procedure in which the formal accusation would be first taken up, the evidence brought together, and an opportunity for preparation afforded the accused.

This separation of the preliminary investigation ("præjudi-

[1] *Ayrault*, "Ordre et formalité," pp. 5, 932; *Hugo*, "Röm. Rechtsgeschichte," p. 634; *Diek*, "Hist. Versuche über röm. Crim." p. 29. See also: L. 3. No. 5; L. 13. 18. D. "De testibus."

[2] *Geib*, p. 361.

[3] *Wafflaer*, "De concursu delictor." (Lovan 1823), pp. 33, 34; *Savigny*, "De concurs. delict. formal." p. 110; *Von Feuerbach*, "Ueber das Geschwornengericht," p. 227; *Plank*, "Die Mehrheit Rechtsstreitigkeiten," p. 95.

[4] *Bach*, "Histor. jur." p. 350; *Brissonius*, "Oper. minor." (edit. *Treekell*), p. 95. In regard to the appointment of judges under the later laws, see *Geib*, p. 207.

[5] *Besserer*, "De indole juris crim. Roman." II, pp. 22–49; *Rosshirt*, "Entw. der Grundsätze des Strafrechts." p. 71; *Geib*, p. 207.

[6] *Kostlin*, "Von Mord und Todtschlag," p. 194.

cium accusationis,"[1] "ordinatio causæ")[2] is explained by the fact that only that individual was designated "accusatus" or "reus"[3] against whom an accusation had been lodged as a foundation for the ensuing investigation in chief.[4] Thus the trial (in the modern sense) had to do with "crimen"[5] or "reatus."[6]

In popular courts, the accusation seems to have been immediately published by the magistrate. However, in the earlier period, there was only an announcement of the accusation, for which the day of hearing was set by the magistrate, who at the same time summoned the accused.[7]

The long intervals, the opportunity for the accused to attempt to influence the people, the requirement that the accusation be repeated three times[8] (with the necessary result that the people in the meantime became familiar with the matter to which the accusation referred) also constituted a kind of preliminary investigation.[9] Yet it is incorrect to think that there was that collecting of evidence by officials, which obtains in our time, or that there were hearings from which the accused was excluded. Such acts would be contrary to the nature of the accusatorial procedure and inconsistent with the conception that no attention was paid to procuring a confession.

A taking of security to insure the due appearance of the accused was necessary. Under some circumstances he could be temporarily imprisoned.[10]

§ 9. **Preliminary Investigation.** — In the "quæstiones perpetuæ"[11] various acts which were performed in regular order and preceded the formal arraignment in open court may be taken as corresponding to a preliminary investigation. The first of these acts was: the "postulatio rei,"[12] the formal prayer of the ac-

[1] *Quinctilian*, "Declam." 319.
[2] L. 1. Cod. "Ad. SC. Turpill." *Birnbaum*, in "Archiv etc." XI, p. 353.
[3] L. ult. Cod. "De accusat." "Archiv etc." IX, p. 352.
[4] Proof of this lies on the fact that in the classics a distinction is made between "postulo," "defero," and "accuso." See: *Forcellini*, "Lexicon," voce: "accusare," and *Cicero*, "Pro Roscio," c. 5. 10; "In Verrem," III, 16. L. 38. No. 10. D. "Ad leg. Jul. de adult." L. 3. Cod. "De plagiar." See also *Ayrault*, "Ordre etc." p. 303. In regard to the Roman preliminary investigation, see *Hélie*, I, p. 59.
[5] "Neues Archiv etc." IX, p. 340. [6] L. ult. D. "Ad leg. Jul. majest."
[7] "Dies dicebatur" *Cicero*, "De harusp." c. 4; "In Div. Verr." c. 21; *Quinctilian*, "Declam." 302; *Geib*, p. 116.
[8] *Cicero*, "Ad famil." XVI, 12; *Livius*, III, 35.
[9] In regard to the character of these preceding acts, see *Laboulaye*, p. 138.
[10] *Geib*, p. 117. [11] As to their character, see *Laboulaye*, p. 183.
[12] *Cicero*, "Ad Quinct. fratr." III, ep. 1; *Plautus*, "In Bacho," III, 3, 45; *Ayrault*, p. 305; *Brissonius*, "De formulis," p. 367; *Besserer*, p. 15; *Birnbaum*, in "Archiv etc." IX, p. 359; *Rosshirt*, in "Archiv etc." IX, p. 389; *Geib*, p. 266. L. 7. pr; *Laboulaye*, p. 342.

cuser to the presiding officer of the "quæstio" for permission to bring an accusation against some certain person, whereupon the presiding officer investigated the facts submitted by the accuser, and according to the circumstances granted or refused the permission. If he granted the permission, there ensued the "nominis," and also the "criminis delatio"[1] whereby the accuser made a formal and definite accusation,[2] which revealed the nature of the act, and the person of the accused. This regularly took place in the presence of the accused.[3] Thereupon followed the "inscriptio nominis"[4] ("subscriptio") or "criminis" as the formal notation of the accusation in a kind of court register, with the names of the accuser (who now formally declared himself as such) and the accused.[5] To this indictment ("libellus accusationis")[6] the accuser must limit himself in the ensuing trial.[7] The fact that the "magistratus" could sometimes refuse to place the name of the accused on the register[8] shows that he made a preliminary investigation of the accusation.

It was an established legal principle that more than one accuser could not prosecute the same accused;[9] thus a preliminary determination ("divinatio")—as to who might bring the complaint—was necessary.[10] It also appears (at least as a general rule) that one could not bring a charge against more than one person at a time in a "quæstio."[11] There is no mention of a preliminary investigation undertaken by the "magistratus" for the purpose of collecting evidence, or questioning certain persons; although an "inquisitio" is mentioned,[12] which seems to indicate such a

[1] In the old authorities, these two acts are often not clearly distinguished. *Cicero*, "Pro Cœl." 3; "Pro Cluentio," 8; "Divin." 20. L. 18. No. 9. D. "De quæst."; *Ayrault*, p. 306; *Birnbaum*, in "Archiv etc." IX, p. 358; *Geib*, p. 267; *Laboulaye*, p. 344.

[2] The "professio crimin." in L. 5. Cod. Theod., "De accus.," contains an example.

[3] *Geib*, p. 270.

[4] *Cicero*, "Pro domo," c. 20. L. 3. 7. pr. D. "De accus."; *Birnbaum*, p. 359 (*cf.* p. 263). In L. 3. D., referred to, a formula is given.

[5] *Geib*, p. 281.

[6] L. 2. No. penult. D. "Ad. leg. Jul. de adult." L. 2. D. "De accus."; *Birnbaum*, in "Archiv etc." p. 359, note 496.

[7] *Ayrault*, pp. 308–312.

[8] *Cicero*, "Divin." VIII, 8; *Laboulaye*, p. 346.

[9] *Ayrault*, p. 819.

[10] The others, however, could support the chief accuser ("subscriptores"). *Cicero*, "Div." 20; *Gellius*, II, 4; *Geib*, p. 268; *Cicero*, "Div." 15; "Pro Muren." 24; "Ad Div." VIII, 8; *Birnbaum*, in "Archiv etc." IX, p. 361; *Geib*, p. 322.

[11] L. 12. D. "De accusat." L. 16. Cod. "De accus." See *Ayrault*, pp. 327–332. Relative to the course of the preliminary procedure, *Osenbruggen*, "Rede für Milo," p. 37. (Kiel 1841).

[12] *Cicero*, "In Verrem," IV, c. 4; "Pro Murena," c. 21; *Plinius*, "Epist." III, 9; V, 20.

preparation of the evidence. The "interrogatio" mentioned in the classics was also carried on by the accuser without the inquisitorial coöperation[1] of the "magistratus."[2] Here the accuser, by means of questions put to the accused, produced the exact foundation necessary for his complaint. However, the view that the criminal procedure was preëminently a reflection of the civil procedure, and that the "magistratus" must always first allow the filing of the complaint, before it was formally prosecuted, makes it seem probable that it was not until after the permission of the "magistratus" to allow the "judicium"[3] had been obtained, that the accuser made a formal complaint.

§ 10. **Trial.** — When all these preliminary acts had been finished, the indictment of the accused was complete, and there was, as it were, a joinder of issue.[4] The accused became "reatus"[5] or "crimen,"[6] and he would forthwith be placed in the list of persons against whom the filing of complaints had been allowed. Then as soon as the day of hearing ("dies") had been set by the "magistratus," there began the regular trial ("judicium publicum"), technically called "quæstio" or "crimen."[7] Herein every action was taken with the greatest possible publicity, and there is no trace of written pleadings. There is apparent in everything the greatest solicitude for the defense of the accused, — who, if he so desired, could choose a representative to defend him ("patronus," "advocatus").[8] The presence of the accuser, who prosecuted the complaint, was an essential condition of the beginning of the public trial,[9] and he could not be represented by an attorney ("procurator").[10] Nothing can be found indi-

[1] *Ayrault*, "Ordre etc." pp. 420–424. The "interrogatio ex lege" (*Brissonius*, "De formulis," p. 471; *Besserer*, "Diss." p. 15) refers to the accuser. *Rosshirt*, in "Archiv etc." XI, p. 390. As to the nature of this "interrogatio," *Geib*, p. 273. It seems that the "inscriptio," referred to above, came next after the "interrogatio." *Geib*, p. 281.

[2] That there was a more summary procedure against a criminal who had been caught in the act, see *Hugo*, "Rechtsgeschichte" p. 534 (based on passages in "Appian de Bello civ." 2 II, 6); *Nagell*, "De flagranti crimine" (Groning 1828).

[3] L. 25. D. "Ad SC. Sillan."

[4] "Litis contestatio." Also as to "crimen," there is mention of "contestari crimen." L. 15. No. 5. D. "Ad SC. Turpill." L. ult. Cod. "de jure fisci." It is to this that the "receptio nominis" refers. *Geib*, p. 283.

[5] L. 9. No. 1. Cod. "De bon. proscript."; L. ult. D. "Ad leg. Jul. majest."

[6] *Birnbaum*, in "Archiv etc." VIII, p. 438.

[7] *Ayrault*, "Ordre, etc." p. 316; *Hélie*, I, p. 76.

[8] *Geib*, p. 320.

[9] L. 13. "De public. judic."; L. 15. Cod. "De accus."; L. 15. 17. Cod. Theod. "De accus."

[10] *Ayrault*, p. 478. The accuser also at times had with him his "patron," who supported him in the "deductio." *Ferratius*, "Epist." I, 6; *Rosshirt*, in "Archiv etc." XI, p. 392.

cating a uniform procedure for the opening of the trial.[1] Apparently the accuser, after a statement of the complaint, and often also after an opening speech, outlining the accusation, began with the production of witnesses.[2] This speech, and also the speech relating to the defense, preceded the taking of evidence. There is nothing to indicate that the presiding "magistratus" participated in the examination of the accused.[3] This would hardly accord with the spirit of a criminal procedure in which the burden of proof rested entirely upon the accuser. Moreover, there is nothing calculated to bring about a confession, — although of course, in case of a confession, the accuser rested his case, and need adduce no further evidence.[4] There is nothing to indicate, in cases where the accused immediately made a complete confession in open court, that the "quæstio" could be dispensed with, and judgment be entered immediately.[5] On the contrary, it seems rather as if judgment could not be entered against a "confessus" until after a formal trial. It is, however, true that in the earlier periods, there was no official examination of the truth of a confession. One hears nothing of the accused being compelled to plead to a complaint.[6] It is, however, conceivable that the accused damaged himself by a stubborn and inexcusable silence and strengthened the suspicion against him.[7]

The mention made of the "interrogatio" of the accused[8] has reference, both to the questioning by the accuser, and also to the questions which the accused in this production of evidence[9] could put to the accuser. In the time of the Republic, a free man would never be subjected to torture.[10] This would be applied only to

[1] L. 20. Cod. "De his, qui accus. non poss." mentions "Expositio criminum atque accusationis exordium." Also in regard to the different forms, see *Brissonius*, "De formulis."

[2] *Geib*, p. 318. Pompey, however, sought to reverse this arrangement, but the change introduced by him was not of long duration.

[3] *Ayrault*, "Ordre, etc." p. 479.

[4] *Cicero*, "In Verrem," V, 64; *Sallust*, "In Catilin." c. 52. Later the reliability of a confession was put to proof, and other evidence made use of. L. 1. No. 17. 27. D. "De quæstion." *Cf.* L. 8. Cod. "Ad leg. Jul. de vi," and *Niccolini*, "storia del principii per l' instruzione delle pruove," pp. 244–249.

[5] *Geib*, "De confessionis effectu in processo crimin. Romanorum" (Turic 1837); *Geib*, "Geschichte," p. 275.

[6] *Geib*, "Geschichte," p. 138.

[7] L. 8. Cod. "Ad leg. Corn. de falsis."

[8] *Ayrault*, p. 490.

[9] *Ayrault*, p. 479.

[10] *Grupen*, "Diss. prælim. observat. jur. crim. de applicat. torment." (Han. 1754); *Reitemeier*, "De orig. et rat. quæst. per tormenta apud Græc. et Rom." (Goett. 1683); *Westphal*, "Die Tortur der Griechen und Römer," (Leipz. 1785); *Wasserschleben*, "Hist. quæst. per torment." (Berol. 1836), No. 75.

slaves, if they were produced as witnesses, and even then with certain restrictions varying according to the character of the statutes ("leges").[1] A witness was examined by the party who had caused him to be summoned. If this party was the accuser,[2] then in the course of the evidence for the defense, the accused (or his attorney) could also put questions to the witness, — especially questions tending to discredit his testimony.[3] In like manner the accuser could interrogate witnesses advanced by the accused. Taken as a whole, the examination of witnesses was often similar to the system of direct and cross-examination which obtains in England.[4] The various statutes ("leges") dealing with the different crimes also varied in respect to the admissibility of witnesses.[5]

There is nothing to indicate that the "magistratus" could in the course of the "quæstio" put to a vote any matter relating to a single question,[6] *e.g.*, the admissibility of some of the grounds of discrediting witnesses. It has already been noted that the special speech in defense of the accused preceded the taking of evidence.[7] The extent to which the speakers availed themselves of all the subtle arts of oratory[8] is explainable when one considers that, especially in the popular courts, the people, not being bound by rules of evidence, easily confuse the office of the pardoner and the judge.[9] Moreover, in the "comitia," no postponement of judgment ("ampliatio") took place, and there could be only an immediate acquittal or conviction.[10] At the end of the trial there were no special closing arguments, such as obtain in the modern French procedure. The accuser and the accused, however, could expose briefly the weak points of the opposing argu-

[1] *Cicero*, "Top." 34; "Pro Milone," 22. L. 1. Cod. "De quæst."; *Geib*, "Geschichte," pp. 138, 330, 348.

[2] In the later period, the "magistratus" appears to have also asked some questions. L. 3. No. 3. D. "De testib."

[3] Passages concerning the methods of taking evidence, in *Brissonius*, "De formulis," p. 476. As to the examination, see *Geib*, p. 390.

[4] This principle of publicity seems to have been violated in the matter of the "recitatio" of the statements of absent witnesses. L. 3. No. 3. D. "De testib." See also *Brissonius*, p. 476. As to the extent to which written depositions were in use, see *Geib*, p. 342. As to the manner of the examination in Roman law, see *Laboulaye*, p. 367.

[5] L. 3. No. 5. D. "De testib."

[6] *Ayrault*, p. 515.

[7] *Ascon.*, "Cæcin." 4, distinguishes four kinds of "defensores."

[8] *Cicero*, "Orator." I, 8. *Quinctilian*, "Inst." II, 16 and 17. See also *Cicero*, "Pro Sextio," 69. Here belongs also the "laudatores" (used as witnesses of character). *Rosshirt*, in "Archiv etc." XI, p. 393; *Geib*, p. 344.

[9] *v. Feuerbach*, "Betrachtungen über Oeffentlichkeit und Mundlichkeit" (Giessen 1824), I, p. 269. *Geib*, p. 103.

[10] *Geib*, p. 148; *Laboulaye*, p. 377.

ment, and reënforce their own favorable testimony.[1] The vote was taken in the "comitia" in the same manner as upon any other question presented to it for its consideration: On the other hand, in the "quæstiones perpetuæ," the vote was taken by ballot,[2] without questions being put to the judges, and without any separation of matters of law and fact. The verdict was rendered by a majority vote, and was at once made public, — except that in cases where "not proven" ("non liquet") was the verdict of the majority, the decision could be postponed ("ampliatio").[3] In the time of the Republic, the individual against whom judgment had been rendered could avail himself of an appeal ("provocatio") to the people, who kept watch over the administration of justice by the magistrates.[4]

§ 11. **Changes under the Empire.** — Under the emperors,[5] the gradual destruction of civic freedom necessarily affected the old Roman criminal procedure, while Christian ideas, due to the spread of Christianity, tended toward the protection of the innocent, and the promotion of justice.[6] Yet the despotism of numerous emperors resulted in their use of the criminal procedure as the tool of their power.[7] The distinction between the judicial and executive powers gradually disappeared as the emperor united in himself all functions of government. Consequently the old popular courts ceased to exist. Although the "quæstiones perpetuæ" still remained, yet their original significance was materially changed. The civil and criminal powers were united in one officer.[8] The "præfectus urbi"[9] and the "præfectus prætorio"[10] were the regular magistrates for the administration of criminal justice. A system of permanent courts was established.[11] Not infrequently the emperors took upon themselves the decision of

[1] These were the "altercationes," *Quinctilian*, "Institut." VI, 4. *Geib*, p. 326.; *Laboulaye*, p. 363.

[2] As to the manner of voting, *Geib*, p. 364.

[3] *Ascon.*, "In Verrem," III, "De prætur. urb." c. 9; *Erhard*, "De ampliat. judicor. publicor." (Lips. 1793). For the distinction of the "comperendinatio," see *Geib*, p. 369; *Spies*, "De comperendin." (Lips. 1728); *Ferratius*, "Epist." I, 9; *Geib*, p. 372. As to the forms of verdict, see much in *Brissonius*, "De formulis," p. 480.

[4] *Wöniger*, "Das Sacralsystem," p. 288. *Cf. Geib*, p. 387.

[5] As to the changed spirit of procedure, *Laboulaye*, p. 387.

[6] L. 22. Cod. "De episcop. audient." is important.

[7] *Faustin Hélie*, in the "Revue de législation" (1844), pp. 339, 349. Proof of many milder provisions introduced into criminal procedure.

[8] *Haubold*, "Instit. jur. rom. priv." p. 91; *Féréol*, p. 46.

[9] Tit. Dig. I, 12; *Malblank*, "Conspectus rer. judiciar. Roman. German." (Norimb. 1797), p. 59, and especially p. 62; *Geib*, pp. 399, 439; *Hélie*, I, p. 133.

[10] *Malblank*, p. 56; *Geib*, p. 431.

[11] *Niccolini*, p. 188.

criminal cases,[1] or delegated the investigation thereof to a special officer. The senate frequently asserted a jurisdiction over crimes, especially over all crimes against the State,[2] or conferred jurisdiction upon some officer.[3] The "quæstiones perpetuæ" probably ceased to exist as early as the first century A.D.; at any rate there is no trace of them after the time of Caracalla.[4] The "judex quæstionis,"[5] although existing until a late period, was really nothing more than a commissioner appointed by a magistrate.[6] With this decline of the ancient "quæstiones" and the popular criminal courts, there disappeared also the voting "judices." Consequently, the "judicium publicum"[7] entirely lost its old significance, and was finally abolished by special statute. The number of "crimina extraordinaria"[8] increased until at last all criminal courts could, from the standpoint of the ancient law, be regarded as "extraordinaria" inasmuch as the "cognitio" now also regularly belonged to the magistrate.[9] The "præfectus urbi," the "præfectus prætorio," and the "præsides" did not regard themselves as bound by the old statutes ("leges"), and thus there developed in their criminal courts a new procedure ("extra ordinem").[10] In the courts of the officers above mentioned, the controlling factor was a certain council ("consilium"),[11] the judges of which were chosen by the magistrates, and paid by the State.[12] These, however, did not vote, as did the old "judices," thus leaving it to a decision of the majority, but merely handed down their judicial opinion.[13]

The old name "judicium publicum," although used in a sense

[1] *v. Feuerbach*, I, p. 270; *Dirksen*, "Civil Abhandl." I, p. 175; *Geib*, p. 420; *Laboulaye*, p. 429.

[2] Their jurisdiction was not however limited to crimes against the State. *Geib*, pp. 398, 412; *Laboulaye*, p. 413.

[3] *Dirksen*, p. 189; *Rosshirt*, "Geschichte und System des deutschen Strafrechts" (Stuttgart 1838), I, p. 188.

[4] *Schulting*, "De recus. judic." cap. VII, Nos. 1 and 2. See also L. 13. D. "De pœnis." L. 15. No. 1. D. "Ad SC. Turpill." As to the different views in regard to the abolition of the "quæstiones," *Geib*, pp. 394–397; *Hélie*, I, p. 127.

[5] L. 1. No. L. D. "Ad leg. Corn. de sicar." See also *Birnbaum*, in "Archiv etc." IX, p. 420; *Geib*, p. 396.

[6] *Schulting*, "Jurisprud. antejust." p. 728.

[7] L. 8. D. "De publ. judic."; *Geib*, p. 402.

[8] *Hugo*, "Rechtsgeschichte," p. 878; *Geib*, p. 404; *Platner*, "Quæst. de jure crim. Roman." p. 85.

[9] L. 1. D. "De offic. præf. urb."; L. 1. ult. D. "De pœn." See also *Birnbaum*, in "Archiv etc." VIII, pp. 676–679.

[10] *Geib*, p. 406.

[11] This consisted of the so-called "assessors."

[12] *Geib*, p. 442.

[13] *Geib*, p. 447. This brought it about, that the accused no longer had his former right of challenge. *Geib*, p. 600.

other than the original, was still applied to the criminal courts, when "levia delicta de plano" were being tried and decided.[1]

From the rules which in the case of most crimes were prescribed by the statutes ("leges"), there appears to have developed gradually a kind of procedure evolved from court custom,[2] which was based upon publicity.[3] Oral pleadings remained the rule, but even at this time, records of proceedings were kept and written testimony [4] of absent witnesses read.[5]

The fundamental form remained that of the *accusatorial* procedure. Hence a "libellus accusationis" was still necessary; [6] and on the part of the accuser there existed, as before, the "subscriptio in crimen." [7] But the nature of the underlying principles had already suffered considerable change. Through the development of the power of the State, the tendency towards centralization,[8] the gradually spreading influence of Christianity,[9] and a changed conception of punishment, there were necessarily introduced into criminal procedure more inquisitorial elements.[10] The judge in his official capacity[11] had to take a more active part in the discovery of the truth, even in the procedure based upon an accusation. The accused was now subjected to torture,[12] and the usual examination on the part of the magistrate [13] might now be directed more towards the procuring of a confession. Because of this growing official activity in the discovery of crime,[14] and the duty laid upon certain special officers of ridding the province of dangerous characters,[15] there necessarily developed a new procedure, governed by considerations of criminal jurisprudence and a regard for the exigencies of a system of police. Inasmuch as

[1] L. 6. D. "De accus."

[2] *Ayrault*, p. 531; *Geib*, p. 509.

[3] *Rosshirt*, "Geschichte und System des deutschen Strafrechts" (Stuttgart 1838), p. 189. As to the development of the new procedure, *Laboulaye*, p. 409.

[4] Apparently with the purpose to furnish the appeal judge the requisite information. *Geib*, p. 503. The use of writing brought about changes in the preliminary investigation that were much to the disadvantage of the principle of publicity. "Revue de législation" (1844), p. 341.

[5] It appears from L. 3. No. 3. D. "De test." that Hadrian attached no weight to such evidence. *Geib*, p. 633; *Hélie*, I, p. 146.

[6] L. 3. D. "De accus."

[7] L. 2. D. "Ad S.C. Turpill." L. 10. Cod. "Qui accus., non poss."; *Brissonius*, "De formulis," p. 469.

[8] *Hélie*, p. 163.

[9] *Hélie*, p. 173.

[10] *Geib*, p. 515. *Cf. Mittermaier*, in "Archiv etc." (1843), p. 433.

[11] L. 22. Cod. "Ad leg. Cornel. de falsis."

[12] *Hohbach*, "Beiträge zum Strafrecht," p. 2; *Geib*, p. 617.

[13] *Geib*, p. 614.

[14] "Publicæ sollicitudinis cura" as in L. 1. Cod. Theod. "De custod. reor."; *Geib*, p. 527.

[15] L. 13. D. "De officio præs."

minor officials, similar to our police, came more and more to be appointed for the searching out of dangerous characters, and the discovery of crime ("agentes in rebus,"[1] "irenarchæ,"[2] "stationarii"[3]) there arose, in cases where these officials[4] reported the crime, new methods for the institution of proceedings, which differed from those of the old accusatorial procedure.[5]

Many changes took place in the ancient forms, although the old names were retained; *e.g.*, the "nominis delatio."[6] Many of the old procedural steps seem to have been united into one.[7] Many of the early methods of procedure were changed by the now greatly developed power of the magistrate.[8]

The criminal procedure of the period of Justinian[9] retained everywhere remnants of the ancient forms,—of the accusatorial procedure, of publicity, and of oral pleadings. But the old spirit which gave significance to these institutions had vanished. Everywhere new forms arose. There even developed a certain theory of evidence,[10] since the accuser, in making out his accusation, and the judges, came to be directed by certain rules of evidence, developed through custom or decreed by the emperors.[11] It cannot, however, be authoritatively stated, that in order to mete out special punishments, more stringent requirements in the way of proof were exacted.[12] The extended jurisdiction of the magistrate also brought it about, that in cases where one act constituted more than a single crime, he was not bound as formerly by the allegations of the accusation, and moreover, in the infliction of punishment, the judges exercised a certain discretion.[13]

[1] *Ammian Marcellin*, XV, 3; *Augustinus*, "Confess." VII, 6; Cod. Just. lib. XII, Tit. 20–24.

[2] L. 6. D. "De custod. reor."; Tit. Cod. X, 75.

[3] L. 3. 4. D. "De fugitiv."; L. 1. D. "De offic. præf. urb."; L. 1. Cod. Theod. VIII, 5.

[4] The "advocatus fisci" (*Spartian*, "Vita Hadrian." c. 20; *Meister*, "Einleitung in den peinl. Proz." I, p. 179) cannot be regarded as a public accuser.

[5] *Mittermaier*, in "Archiv etc." (1843), p. 433.

[6] *Geib*, p. 548.

[7] *E.g.*, the "nominis delatio" and the "inscriptio," *Geib*, p. 558.

[8] *E.g.*, as to the questioning of witnesses. It appears from L. 3. No. 3. D. "De test.," that the emperor Hadrian proposed questions. This was gradually extended. *Geib*, p. 631.

[9] See for details, the criminal cases preserved by *Agathias* (translated by *Degen*), "Neus Archiv etc." VII, No. 22.

[10] *Post*, in the "Lehre vom Beweise." See also *Geib*, p. 610. Also the value attached by the Romans to circumstantial evidence will be discussed later.

[11] In regard to the later Roman procedure, see *Rosshirt*, "Zeitschrift für Civil- und Criminalrecht," 2d. Hft. p. 178.

[12] As might appear from L. 16. Cod. "De pœnis." But see *Geib*, p. 649.

[13] *Geib*, pp. 652–659.

Chapter III

PRIMITIVE GERMANIC CRIMINAL PROCEDURE

§ 1. **General Characteristics.** — In the Germanic law the development of criminal procedure [1] stands in close relation to the change of view as to punishment, and to the political conditions of the German nation. Not until the conception arose of the existence of crimes which were committed directly against the civic community, did the criminal procedure acquire a significance similar

[1] For the history of German criminal procedure the following may be consulted. *Gebauer*, "Vestigia juris german. ante." (Goett. 1766). Disp. 14, 15, 16; *Weisand*, "De re German. judiciar." Viteb. 1773); *Hofmann*, "De orig. progressu et natur. jurisprud. crim. ger." (Leipzig 1722); *Malblank*, "Geschichte der peinlichen Gerichtsordnung" (Nurnb. 1783); *Malblank*, "Conspectus rer. judiciar. röman. German." (Norimb. 1797); *Heineccius*, "Elem. jur. German. tum vet. tum hod." (Hal 1736), tom II, Tit. III; *Hauschild*, "Gerichtsverfassung der Deutschen" (Leipz. 1751); *Kopp*, "Nachrichten von der Verfassung der geistl. und Civil-Gerichte in Hessen." 2 Thle. (Cassel 1769); *Henke*, "Geschichte des peinlich. Rechts," 2 Thle. (Sulzbach 1809); *Meyer*, "Esprit, origine et progrès des instit. judiciaires" (la Haye 1819), (vol. VI, also the first part); *Rogge*, "Uber Gerichtswesen der Germanen" (Königsberg 1820); *Raepsaet*, "Analyse raisonnée hist. et critiq. de l'origine et progrès des droits des Belges." (Gand. 1824, 1826), 3 vols. For a description of the criminal procedure under the French kings, see "Théorie des loix politiques de la monarchie françoise" (Paris 1792, 8 vols.), in vol. VII, pp. 1–186, or in the new edition (Paris, 1844, by *M. de Lazardière*), vol. II, p. 97, vol. III, p. 1, and vol. IV, pp. 29, 200. There is also much in certain passages of *Bodman*, "Rheingauische Alterthümer"; *Feuerbach*, "Betrachtungen über Oeffentlichkeit und Mundlichkeit," (Giessen 1824); *Eichhorn*, "Rechtsgeschichte"; *v. Savigny*, "Geschichte des römischen Rechts."

The following are also important. *Maurer*, "Geschichte des altgermanischen und namentlich altbaier., öffentlichen, mundlichen Gerichtsverfahrens" (Heidelberg 1824); *Frieberg*, "Das altdeutsche Gerichtsverfahren" (Landshut 1824); *Buchner*, "Das öffentl. Gerichtsverf. in bürgerl. und peinl. Saachen" (Erlangen 1825); *Steiner*, "Über das altdeutsches imbes. altbaier. Gerichtswesen" (Aschassenburg 1824); *J. Burchardt*, "Diss. hist. de judiciorum criminal. formis olim hodieque" (Basil. 1823); *Vos*, "De judiciis Drenthinorum antiq." (Groning 1525). In regard to the Middle Ages, see *Cannert*, "Bydragen tot de kennis van het oude Strafrecht in Vlaenderen" (Ghent 1835); *Rosshirt*, "Geschichte und System des deutschen Strafrechts" (Stuttgart 1838); *Wilda*, "Das Strafrecht der Germanen" (Halle 1842); *Unger*, "Die altdeutsche Gerichtsverfassung" (Gött. 1842); *Pardessus*, "Loi salique" (Paris 1843), p. 567 *et seq; Hélie*, "Traité de l'instruction criminelle" (Paris 1836), I, p. 179.

to that of to-day.[1] The civic community, in the case of crimes committed against individuals, so long as the vengeance of the family prevailed, took cognizance of a crime only so far as those limits to the exercise of vengeance which custom had established were transgressed,[2] and in case of crimes which were deemed breaches of the peace, enforced the collection of the fines, or made effective the punishments incurred.

A fundamental principle of the old order was the separation of the judicial power from the executive and ministerial power. The ministerial power, resting in the hands of the princes, laid the foundation for the "comes." [3] This latter was the officer appointed by the king, who presided over the popular courts,[4] in which crimes of a graver nature were tried. He guided the trial, and saw to the execution of the formal sentence.[5] Along with the "comes," the "missi dominici" [6] were also important because of their supervision of officials and of the administration of justice, and of their duty of searching out secret crimes, and also because of the authority granted to them to organize a court themselves [7] and preside over the same.[8] The organization of society, under which every free man, whenever he heard of a crime, was bound at once to take steps for the keeping of the peace, shows that crime was universally regarded as a breach of the peace and likewise shows how the attempt was made to suppress vengeance. It explains also how, little by little, this peace preserved by the people became a peace preserved by officers.[9]

[1] As to its development, see *Wilda*, p. 169.

[2] *Wilda*, p. 160; *Waitz*, "Deutsche Verfassungsgeschichte," p. 193.

[3] *Marculf*, "Form." I, 8; "Capit." 779, Art. 21; "Théorie des lois politiques," tom. VII, p. 35; *Savigny*, "Geschichte des röm. Rechts," I. Thl., p. 222; *Meinders*, "De judic. centen." cap. III, No. 18; *Grimm*; "Rechtsalterthümer," p. 752; *Pardessus*, "Loi salique," p. 571; *Unger*, p. 152.

[4] "Capitul." III, a. 812, c. 4.; "Cap." 815. c. 3. Only in the great "placitis," where the "comites" presided, was there a criminal court dealing with the graver class of crimes; this was not the case in the court of the "centurius," where only minor crimes were tried. However, if the "comes" himself sat in the "judicium centenarium" graver crimes would be taken up. See *Rosshirt*, "Geschichte," p. 11; *Montesquieu*, "Esprit des loix," XXX, 18. But on the contrary, see *Le Grand de Laleu*, "Recherches hist. sur l'administration de la justice crim. chez les Français" (Paris 1822), p. 53.

[5] *Meyer*, "esprit." vol. I, p. 355.

[6] *Gregor*. Turon. V, 29; *Marculf*, I, 11. See the two treatises by *de Roy* and *Muratori*, printed in Baluz. Capitular. regum Francorum; *de Kock*, "Diss. de potestat. civil. episcop." p. 29; *Bluntschli*, "Rechtsgeschichte von Zürich," I, p. 38.

[7] "Capit." IV, 55.

[8] "Capit." III, 812, No. 8. *Muratori*, "Diss. de missis dom." p. II, cap. III, and V. See also *Wigand*, "Das Vehmgericht," p. 36.

[9] The old Swiss statutes and actions are interesting. See *Schauberg*, "Zeitschrift für ungedrückte Schweizerrechtsquellen," I, pp. 20–35.

§ 2. **The Judicial Power.** — The judicial power was exercised by the people. They met in the great popular courts, which were regularly held, and rendered judgment; in the beginning in full assembly,[1] although at an early date[2] the custom arose of choosing a certain number from the most experienced and oldest men of the community. These were the so-called "Schöffen."[3] Charles the Great found this system of "Schöffen" already established. He confirmed and improved it in this respect,[4] namely: That for the great popular courts, which were regularly held, the presence of all the free men of the Gau was required, while the presence of these "Schöffen" was required for both the ordinary and extraordinary courts. Only in the last named, would the "Schöffen" in a certain number[5] suffice for a valid judgment. Other free men, however, were not excluded from the court. In criminal cases, especially, the judgment seems to have been passed in the general popular courts.[6] Charles the Great extended this system of "Schöffen" over his newly conquered territories.[7] So far as criminal procedure, at least, is concerned there is no indication that judgment was passed only as to the facts. On the contrary, there seems to have been passed a final judgment either of conviction or acquittal.[8]

[1] *Pardessus*, p. 565; *Unger*, p. 143.
[2] VII "Scabini" are mentioned in "leg. Sal." tit. 60. Ripuar. 32.
[3] Passages in "Théorie des loix polit." tom. VII, p. 203.
[4] *v. Savigny*, "Geschichte des röm. Rechts." I, p. 195. However, see *Meyer*, "Esprit." vol. I, p. 396; *Maurer*, "Geschichte," p. 66; *Le Grand de Laleu*, p. 63; *Wigand*, p. 280; *Rogge*, "Gerichtswesen," p. 66; *Grimm*, "Rechtsalterthümer," p. 774; *Unger*, p. 169; *Pardessus*, p. 576; *Lehuerou*, "Hist. des institut. caroling." p. 382. Also in regard to the "Scabini Rachinburgi," see *Thomas*, "der Oberhof zu Frankfurt," p. 9; *Sachse*, "Histor. Grundlagen des deutschen Staatslebens," p. 295.
[5] As to the number of "Schöffen," see *Unger*, p. 281; *Hélie*, I, p. 195.
[6] This appears from "Capit." 801. Art. 27. cap. III. of 812, cap. 4. Cap. I, 810. See also "Théorie des loix," VII, p. 50; p. 204; *Bouquet*, "Rer. Gall. Script." III, p. 533. Also "Capit." 813, cap. 13; *Bluntschli* "Rechtsgeschichte," I, p. 37; *Falk*, "Gerichtsverfassung von Schleswig," pp. 83–86; *Hélie*, I, p. 254.
[7] In regard to the Italian States, *Troya*, "Della condizione dei romani vinti dai Longobardi," p. cccli; *Gregori*, Introduction, "degli statuti di Corsica," p. lxxxix. A document dealing with the Lombard "Schöffen," in *Troya*, l.c. p. clxx.
[8] *Eichhorn*, "Rechtsgeschichte," No. 75. But *cf. Rogge*, p. 68; *Maurer* p. 106; *Biener*, "Beiträge," p. 120. In regard to the separation of questions of fact and law, see *Birnbaum*, in the "Zeitschrift für ausl. Rechtswissenschaft," I. Thl. p. 160; II. Thl. p. 436. There is considerable uncertainty in regard to the "sagibarones," especially as to whether they expressed an opinion on points of law. *Birnbaum*, in "Zeitschrift etc." I, p. 151; and in "Archiv etc." XIV, p. 203. *Pardessus*, p. 274, regards them as representatives of the "comes." See also *Unger*, p. 197; *Maurer*, p. 19; *Beuker Andræ*, "De orig. juris. fris." p. 417; *Lehuerou*, p. 380. *Hélie*, I, p. 197; *Thomas*, p. 11; *Sachse*, pp. 287–293.

In the Frankish period,[1] it is impossible to say definitely to what extent a duty was incumbent upon the court, or particular officers,[2] especially the "Schöffen," to inform upon the crimes known to them personally, when no accuser appeared.[3] It does appear, however, that in the assemblies convened by the "missi"[4] there was a duty of censure incumbent upon certain "Schöffen" as in the "Sendgerichte."

In many places the great criminal folk-courts disappeared. They persisted longest, however, in the so-called "ungebotenen Dingen"[5] or in the inferior courts of justice,[6] in which each free man had to appear, and where, after a questioning of all present in regard to the crimes which had been committed in the course of the year, certain ones were censured. Later this duty of censure, in most places, ceased to have reference to the graver class of crimes.

The trial and decision of capital offenses still always took place before the land courts,[7] or in the grain exchange,[8] or else before the courts of the Gau,[9] or the parish.[10] In all these courts, "Schöffen"[11] (as lay assessors) or judges[12] had already come to pass judgment instead of the whole people; although frequently this was not the case,[13] and then a so-called "collaudatio sententiae"[14] would take place. In the place of the old "comes" there

1 "Capit. Carol. Calv." tit. XIV, cap. 4. "Capit." 828. No. 3. *Beiner*, p. 132.

2 "Cap." I, 802. c. 25, because of the expression "juniores." There is some controversy as to their construction; *Wigand*, p. 284. *Beiner*, p. 130. But see *Unger*, p. 402.

3 *Unger*, pp. 403–406.

4 "Capit." 828. in Pertz III, p. 328.

5 They were so called in the "nassauische Landesordnung" of 1498. Art. 76, 80.

6 See also the Würtemburg "rüggerichtordnung" of 1495; *Eberhard*, in *Pitts*, "Repertorium für peinl. Recht," I, p. 45. It is certain that in many countries the customs referring to the "Rügen," passed from the "Sendgerichte" to the courts of the Sovereign. *Unger*, p. 408.

7 *Buchner*, p. 137; *Grupen*, "Diss. prælim. observat. jur. crim. applicat. torment." (Han. 1754), p. 445; *Grupen*, "Discept." p. 576; *Kopp*, "Hessische Gerichtsverordnung," I, p. 270.

8 *Maurer*, p. 168.

9 References in *Grupen*, "Discept." p. 667.

10 Important passage in *Verhanderlingen der Genoothschap*, "Pro excolend. jur. patrio," I, p. 369.

11 "Sachsenspiegel," I, 62; "Schwabenspiegel," I, 75; "Kaiserrecht," I, 7; *Maurer*, p. 106. There is a collection of references dealing with the institution of the "Schöffen," in *Dreyer*, "Nebenstunden," p. 157; *Raepsaet*, "Supplement à l'analyse de l'origine des Belges," p. 134.

12 References to the effect that there were seven "Schöffen," in *Dreyer*, p. 142.

13 *Maurer*, p. 180; *Bluntschli*, "Rechtsgeschichte," I, p. 37.

14 "Sachsenspiegel," II, 12; *Falk*, "Gerichtsverfassung von Schleswig," p. 84.

came into existence, with similar prerogatives, certain judges and other officials, such as the public administrators ("Pfleger") and bailiffs ("Drosten"). That the presiding judge could not himself pass judgment remained a general rule everywhere, even in the 1400s.[1]

§ 3. **Trial by Battle, Ordeal, Compurgators.**—The more society rested upon the foundation of the old family and community relation, the more easily in an age of simple and primitive ideas could the conception prevail[2] that the mere accusation made by a free man created a definite and established suspicion against the accused.[3] This accusation of its own weight was equivalent to a challenge to the accused and his family. Thus every criminal action between the accuser and the accused was, as it were, a "casus belli" between both families or bands to which the two men belonged.[4] Consequently every free man against whom an accusation was brought either availed himself of this right of feud and a battle took place,[5] or else, in an imitation of this right of feud, summoned his relatives as security, who in a body[6] as vouchers,[7]

[1] *Warnkönig*, "Flandrische Rechtsgesch." III, p. 265. As to the changed position of the judges, *Unger*, p. 323.

[2] As to the use of the rack in the Frankish period (applied only to slaves), *Hélie*, I, p. 225.

[3] *Rogge*, p. 212; *Wigand*, "Vehmgericht," pp. 373, 386; *Evers*, "Ältestes Recht der Russen," p. 136.

[4] This explains the circumstance that both the accuser and the accused and their families appeared before the court. *Dreyer*, "Nebenstunden," p. 49.

[5] As to trial by battle, see "Leg. Saxon." XVI, No. 1; "Baiuv." XI, 4; XVI, 1; "Aleman." tit. 84; "Théorie des loix politiques," vol. VII, p. 17; *Rogge*, p. 206; *Hélie*, I, pp. 240–280.

As to the Middle Ages, see "Sachsenspiegel," I, 48 and 63; "Schwabenspiegel," I, 228; *Hauschild*, pp. 52, 106; *Kopp*, I, p. 479; *Meyer*, "Esprit." vol. I, p. 323. Likewise family feuds to-day persist among people who have few legal institutions, as among the Montenegrins, of which, see an example in "Le Droit" of Feb. 1839, No. 32.

[6] *Grimm*, p. 860; *Schildener*, "Beiträge zur Kenntniss des germanischen Rechts," pp. 34–73; *Luden*, "Deutsche Geschichte," III, p. 397. The "Théorie des loix politiques," vol. VII, p. 13 (on p. 45 is a collection of references to "preuves") calls them "preuves negatives." See also *Rogge*, p. 136. There were two kinds of "compurgatores." This appears very clearly from the "Leg. Walliæ" (*e.g.*, lib. 1. cap. 10. No. 47), "sacramentum minus et majus." In the first they stated on oath, "se credere, juramentum esse verum." Here they must all be unanimous. In the case of "majus," it depended on the majority. See *Wotton*, in "Præf. ad leg. Walliæ"; but also see *Hickes*, "Diss. epist. zum thesaur. linguar." p. 35.

In regard to compurgators, see *Abegg*, "Histor. pract. Erört." pp. 47–65; *Gaupp*, "Das alte Gesetz der Thuringer," p. 299; *Pardessus*, "Loi salique," p. 624; *Hildenbrand*, "Die purgatio canonica," p. 10; *Waitz*, "Deutsche Verfassungsgeschichte," p. 210; *Sachse*, p. 312; *Hélie*, I, p. 229. As to the different numbers of those who took oath, *Gaupp*, p. 305.

[7] *Schildener*, "Uber die religiöse Gemeinschaft der alten Mittschwornen" (Greifswalde 1833 and supplement 1835).

stood beside him with their testimony and furnished evidence that an accused at whose side there stood so many feud companions did not wantonly refuse a settlement, and then the community prohibited the plaintiff from raising a feud.

Many passages seem to sustain the assumption [1] that the privilege of securing an acquittal by means of this oath did not belong to the accused absolutely, but was dependent upon judicial permission.[2] The arrangements were various in kind.[3] It was an important difference whether those who supported the accused with their oath were not necessarily chosen only from among the relatives of the accused,[4] or whether the accuser chose from among the relatives of the accused those who should give oath together with the accused.[5] A restriction, which must be regarded as developed under the influence of Christianity, was that only those could support the accused with their oath who had a conviction of his innocence.[6]

The "Hardes" or "Stocknasn" [7] and the "Neffninger" [8] existing in Norse law, and employed for the settlement of disputes through their oaths, were fundamentally developed from the "Kionsnafn" (compurgators). Later they were definite men chosen by the people for the entire year; while the "sandmanner" [9] already were regularly appointed and permanent judges. Under the conditions at that time existing there could be no production of evidence [10] in the modern sense. Everywhere there can be

[1] *Pardessus*, p. 625.

[2] Especially, if the accuser could plead a "probatio certa."

[3] *Wigand*, "Vehmgericht," pp. 387–391; *Schildener*, "Guta-Lag," p. 170. As to the meaning of the word "electi," *Pardessus*, p. 627.

[4] *Stirnhoek*, "De jure Sueonum vet." p. 105; *Rosenvinge*, "De usu juram." II, p. 50.

[5] *Rosenvinge*, l.c. II, p. 158. Here belong the "Kionsneffninge" of tho "jutischen Lovbuch." *Rosenvinge*, "Grundriss der dänischen Rechtg." p. 244. As to "Folgeeid," "Deedeid," see *Verhanderllngen der Genoothschap*, "pro excolend. jure patrio," vol. V, p. 64.

[6] *Phillips*, "Englische Reichs- und Rechtsgeschichte," II, p. 259. In regard to restrictions in the statutes, *Pardessus*, p. 629.

[7] They were twelve assessors appointed by the chief bailiff, for the decision of single cases, having to do with the graver kind of crimes, and they rendered their verdict by majority vote. *Falk*, "Gerichtsverfahren." p. 94.

[8] Also called "nominati." They passed judgment as to the lesser offenses, but were appointed for the entire year. *Rosenvinge*, "De usu juram," l.c. II, p. 7; *Rosenvinge*," Grundriss," pp. 146–232. See also *Rogge*, p. 242; *Paulsen* in the "Zeitschrift für ausländ. Rechtswissenschaft," I, p. 484; *Falk*, p. 95. See also the article by *Repp*," Historical treatise on trial by jury" (London, 1832). Seo also "Deutsche Vierteljahrschrift," 1844, I. Hft. p. 216.

[9] "Jutisch Lowbuch," II, c. 1; *Rosenvinge*, p. 231.

[10] *Rogge*, p. 93; *Weigand*, "Vehmgericht," pp. 371, 385; *Cropp*, "Heidelberger Jahrbücher," 1825, No. 41, p. 669.

noticed the influence of the idea that the revelation of secret crimes may be left to the direct intervention of the Deity,[1] who would surely bring the truth to light and would not suffer the innocent to perish.

In close relation with this idea there stood the conception of the ordeal,[2] in so far as those who by good fortune had endured an ordeal could appeal to the protection of the gods, and to their certain manifestation that they regarded him as innocent, and stand acquitted of the accusation.[3]

There is no uniformity in the various folk laws in regard to the relation of the compurgators to the ordeal and the judicial trial by battle.[4] The earlier the ideas of the production of proof by witnesses came to prevail and the conception was gained that the testimony of two witnesses was required for a judgment,[5] the more would the old institutions be done away with.

The theory of proof, in so far as one can thus designate the means of conviction based on rules consisting in custom, was determined[6] by: (*a*) the kinds of crime which were under consideration, — since in the case of certain crimes,[7] on the existence of certain conditions, and certain testimony, there would be an immediate judgment; (*b*) by the circumstance whether or not the act was premeditated;[8] (*c*) by the trial by battle, — since, according to many statutes, the proposal of battle by the accuser precluded the accused from his defense by oath; (*d*) by the reputation of the accused, — since he who was of bad reputation had no claim to the right to stand acquitted upon his oath.[9]

[1] References in "Théorie des loix politiques," vol. VII, p. 16; *Meyer*, "Esprit," vol. I, p. 311.

[2] *Dreyer*, "Abhandl." III, p. 1269; *Maier*, "Geschichte der Ordalien," (Jena 1795); *Hof*, "Von den Ordalien" (Mainz 1784); *Grupen*, "Observat." IV; *Hauschild*, p. 187; *Schildener*, "Guta-Lag," p. 160; *Rogge*, p. 195; *Rosenvinge*, "Grundriss," p. 143; *Wilda*, in the "Hallische Encyclopadie," under the word "Ordalien."; *Pardessus*, p. 632; *Sachse*, p. 455.

[3] *Hildenbrand*, "Purgatorio," p. 16.

[4] In some countries, it appears that the accuser could defeat the use of compurgators, if he immediately proposed that both he and his opponent submit their cause to the doubtful outcome of trial battle, and only under exceptional circumstances could he require that the accused undergo an ordeal, *e.g.*, by fire. *Gaupp*, "Recht der Thuringer," p. 316. *Pardessus*, p. 632, that the method depended upon the proof which the accuser could produce.

[5] "Théorie des loix politiques," vol. IV, p. 200.

[6] *Albrecht*, "doctrina de probat. secund. jus. germ. med. ævi." (Regiom. 1825).

[7] *E.g.*, in case of rape.

[8] If the wrongdoer was not caught in the act, he had an advantage in the matter of acquittal through the intervention of compurgators.

[9] As to the procedure against the individual who contumaciously refused to appear, see *Bluntschli*, I, p. 205; *Cropp*, "Beiträge," II, p. 388.

Part I

HISTORY OF CRIMINAL PROCEDURE IN FRANCE FROM THE 1200s TO THE 1600s

INTRODUCTORY;[1] GENERAL FEATURES OF THE EVOLUTION

§ 1. **The Three Sources of French Criminal Procedure and its Evolution.** — French criminal procedure, the broad features of which we now propose to sketch, sends its roots deep through the three successive strata, Roman, Germanic, and Canon law, upon which all our juridical institutions are planted.

The first element in its history is the Germanic element. Down to the 1200s the procedure is very much more uniform than the law. It is public, oral, severely formal, and rarely makes use of the proof by oath-helpers or by battle. The ancient ordeals, by boiling water, branding, cold water, in favor under the Merovingians, soon fell into disuse. Such is the first phase. Under the pressure, however, of various causes, the accusatory procedure of the nations of the Germanic race becomes inquisitorial, written, and secret, taking its inspiration from the two learned legislations of Europe, the Roman law and the Canon law. An ordinance of St. Louis (which is usually attributed to 1260, but which is probably of earlier date) helps this movement by substituting, in the domains of the crown, the *procedure by inquest* or jury ("enquête") for the proof by *wager of battle.* The king could not put "coustumes ou ban" in the territory of his barons without their consent. The seignorial jurisdictions also show themselves averse to this substitution, and the nobles persist in demanding to be tried according to the ancient rules. But the citizens ("bourgeois") and the peasants ("vilains") readily enough accept

[1] [This introductory Chapter and Title I = §§ IV, III, and VI of Professor Garraud's "French Criminal Procedure." For this author and work, see the Editorial Preface. — Ed.]

these innovations, which proscribe the duel and replace the wager of battle ("en champ clos") by oral or written pleadings. The municipal jurisdictions of the rural communes and the towns, and all the jurisdictions of the south, eagerly adopt this procedure, which revives very ancient traditions, going back probably to the Gallo-Roman epoch.

The two procedures, accusatory and inquisitorial, so different in origin and character, also remain in opposition during the latter half of the 1200s and the first part of the 1300s. This is the transitional period, during which the plastic force of custom is acting. The evolution, begun in the 1200s, is accomplished in the 1500s. The Ordinance of 1539, proclaimed by Francis I at Villers-Cotterets, upon justice and the shortening of actions, definitely fixes the rules of the inquisitorial procedure in France. The Ordinance of 1670, which was the Code of Criminal Examination of the "Old Régime," merely systematized the method already sanctioned, making it precise in its details and even aggravating its severities.

From this time on, criminal procedure becomes crystallized for nearly a century. But the new and critical spirit preceding the Revolution has theoretically condemned this system as offering no safeguard to the accused. The philosophers look to England; they admire her judicial as well as her political institutions. It is the English criminal procedure, especially the jury, which the Constituent Assembly will endeavor to acclimatize in France; and it is that procedure which the Law of 16–29 September, 1791, and the Code of Offenses and Punishments of the 3d Brumaire, year IV, will successively organize.

But the same causes which, in the 1200s and 1300s, had brought about the substitution of one system of procedure for the other, operate anew; the need of reorganizing State authority is felt, of strengthening the system of repression, weakened amidst the troubles of the period, caused by civil and foreign wars. The Ordinance of 1670 again becomes the ideal of many minds; there is a desire to put it once more in force. Then a compromise is effected, and although the ancient procedure is not entirely revived in the Laws of the Consulate and of the Empire, the best part of the provisions of the Ordinance, and even some of its severities, pass into the first part of the Code of Criminal Examination, the second part retaining the accusatory procedure and the institution of the jury. This Code of 1808 has become, for the whole of Europe, a type on which many legislations are modeled. It therefore typifies an essential phase, and is a landmark in the historical evolution of the laws of procedure.

§ 2. **Double Tendency; Safeguards of the Accused; Social Protection; Classic and Modern Schools.** — From that time a double movement is apparent. There is a tendency to eliminate, by means of revision, the excessive severities which French procedure has inherited from the Ordinance of 1670, and to introduce into the preliminary examination the safeguards which it lacked. There is a desire to open the chambers of the examining judge, if not to the public, at least to certain authorized persons; to allow the presence of counsel during the examination; to recognize in the prisoner and his counsel, from this initial phase of the prosecution, the right to challenge and criticise the measures taken to arrive at the discovery of the truth. Protests against the secrecy of the examination seem general, and rebellion sets in against this practice of our old procedure, as dangerous for the judge as for the accused, which, as the English jurist Stephen expresses it, "poisons justice at its source."

But, on the other hand, the part played in the trial by the intervention of the jury, though in other times considered too restricted, seems nowadays to be almost excessive. There is a sincere demand for a justice less impressionistic; more scientific. To this ideal, it is thought, we might sacrifice that inveterate respect which has everywhere existed until recent times for the institution of the jury.[1]

There is, in this double movement, the expression of a ceaseless strife between the two tendencies which in these days divide the domain of the criminal sciences. The *Classical School* is above all individualistic, demanding new safeguards in favor of the accused, a continual control over the criminal authorities, the diminution of arbitrariness, and the increase of liberty. The *Modern School*, which is above all collectivist, desires to strengthen the "social defense," to deprive the prisoner of those safeguards which are summed up in the "presumption of innocence," to substitute for a humanitarian procedure a scientific procedure, to transform the penal action into a clinical examination and the judges into expert specialists, who must have a very special education in matters of psychology, anthropology, and criminal sociology.[2]

[1] See *Jean Cruppi*, "La Cour d'assises de la Seine" (Revue des Deux-Mondes, 1895, vol. IV, p. 39).

[2] *Ferri*, "Sociologia criminale" (4th ed.) 79–84, pp. 777–826; *Garofalo*, "Criminologie," pp. 387–397. See, but in a somewhat different direction, *Cruppi*, "La Cour d'assises," p. 130 *et seq.* and p. 281 *et seq.*

At the time when we write, and notwithstanding the evident progress of socialism and collectivism, it seems likely that the tendency, in matters of criminal procedure, is no longer to arm the social power in the strife against criminality, but much more probably to protect the prisoner against the abuses of social power. It is in this direction that the reforms, so numerous and so characteristic, of which criminal procedure in France and abroad has been the object, have been pointed within the past fifty years.

§ 3. **Features of Contemporary Procedure; Unity of Civil and Criminal Justice.** — The French system belongs to the mixed type. The present judicial organization and procedure are governed by four fundamental ideas.

The *unity of civil and criminal justice* in France means that the same tribunals take cognizance of both civil and criminal matters. This unity has its expression, 1st, in the person of the keeper of the seals, supreme head of both jurisdictions; 2d, in the justice of the peace ("juge de paix"), who has various civil functions, and who, in criminal matters, is at once officer of judicial police and police judge; 3d, in the attorney-general ("procureur général") and the "procureur de la République," who occupy the position of public prosecutors in both jurisdictions. This unity is made effective, 4th, in the Tribunal of First Instance, which furnishes the examining magistrate ("juge d'instruction"), and forms the correctional tribunal of the first stage; 5th, in the Court of Appeal, whose two branches, the correctional branch and the arraignment branch, act in criminal matters, and whose members take part in the trial of crimes, by presiding and by directing the jury.

This unity of civil and criminal justice imports merely an *organic unity*, and not a *unity of procedure*. The separation of civil and criminal procedure is an essential principle of the French legislation. Each of these procedures has its special code. This work being devoted to the criminal procedure, we shall study the details of the judicial organization only as they relate to that procedure. We shall take for granted a knowledge of the French judicial organization.[1]

The unity of civil and criminal justice is broken by the institution of the jury, which calls upon private citizens to take part in

[1] Reference may be made, on this point, to *M. Garsonnet's* "Traité théorique et pratique de procédure" (2d ed., 1898–1904, 8 vols. 8°, revised and corrected by *Charles Céygar-Bru;* 3d ed., 1912). Vol. I, down to page 473, is devoted to judicial organization.

the trial of crimes. In civil trials there is no jury,[1] except in matters concerning expropriations for public purposes, where citizens are summoned, in case of disagreement, to fix the indemnity due to the person deprived of his property.

§ 4. **Division of Official Functions.** — This organization is governed by the *principle of the division of labor.* The operations of criminal justice necessitate the organization of separate authorities to exercise the functions of *arrest, examination, trial,* and *execution.* And the law ordains that, by reason of incompatibility, the agents who exercise one of these functions cannot, unless in exceptional cases, encroach upon other functions. The authorities who unite in administering the criminal law are practically four, 1st, the *officers of judicial police,* charged with investigation, and examination preliminary to the charge; 2d, *courts of examination,* who, upon complaint made, decide on the arraignment or indictment of the accused and on the propriety of arrest and trial; 3d, the *trial court,* who decide on the issue, that is, on the guilt of prisoners and those accused, and pronounce the punishments; 4th, the *officers of the public prosecution,* whose duty is to invoke, by filing a charge or requisition, the action of these different authorities and also to see to the execution of their decisions.

The functions of the *judicial police* and of the *public prosecutor,* which consist chiefly in taking active measures, are performed by *individuals,* placed under the orders and supervision of a hierarchy of superiors. The functions of *judging,* which consist in deliberating and trying, are usually confided to *collective bodies,* whose decisions may be modified or quashed, but who do not have to take instructions from any one as to their manner of carrying out their duty. The officers of judicial police and of public prosecution are dependent on the executive, which can remove or dismiss them "ad nutum." The judges, on the contrary, are, in general, irremovable.

The official criminal procedure has three successive stages: it is begun by the *filing of a charge;* it is continued by an *examination;* and it is ended by a *judgment.*

(1) Before the criminal law can be applied, the perpetration of the wrong must be discovered. The authorities must therefore

[1] In the sitting of 30th April, 1790, after long debates and at the instance of Thouret and Tronchet, the Constituent Assembly decided against the establishment of the civil jury desired by Duport. Since then, the question has been taken up from a scientific point of view; but from a practical point of view it may be regarded as abandoned. See *Garsonnet, op. cit.* vol. I, § 3, pp. 83–88.

investigate into the commission of crimes and misdemeanors, secure, if necessary, the accused persons, and hand them over to the courts. The officers having this duty are the *judicial police.* This body is distinct from the *administrative police,* which has for its object the maintenance of order and especially the prevention of crime. The judicial police forms part of the judicial system. It investigates the offenses which the administrative police has not been able to prevent. It paves the way for and facilitates the action of the tribunals of repression. Its intervention precedes the first stage of the public prosecution. The law has organized the judicial police, but it has abstained from placing upon its action formalities of procedure which might cramp it. In this respect the preliminary and official inquiry, conducted by the police, must be distinguished from the magisterial examination ("instruction") properly so called, belonging to the judicial function. But as the purpose of the two institutions and the working of the two mechanisms are identical, we find, in fact, the police doing the work of examination and the examining judge doing police work.

(2) The public prosecution is intrusted, in its entirety, to officers who fulfil, along with various duties, the functions of the public prosecutor. They are charged with doing all the acts necessary to secure the infliction of a punishment upon the perpetrator of an offense. The victim of the offense, in whom is recognized the exclusive right to demand civil reparation for the injury suffered, has access, to obtain damages, to criminal tribunals either by way of intervention or of suit. But the civil action can only be tried, by these courts, accessorily to the criminal charge. This is the fundamental rule which limits the right of the injured party.

(3) The case, however, is not always brought before the criminal courts without other preliminary examination than that made officially by the agents of the judicial police. On a charge of crime invariably, and of misdemeanors optionally, a *magisterial examination preliminary to the formal charge* is always had. This duty is performed by certain special judicial officers called magistrates of examination ("instruction") who either authorize the charge or quash it. This examination is in the hands of the State's attorney and the examining magistrate. The former has the right to investigate and prosecute crimes and misdemeanors committed in his district; but he has no power, in ordinary cases, to do anything towards collecting the evidence, or ordering the arrest and detention of accused persons. These powers belong to the examining magistrate. The latter, however, has not the

right to initiate the charge of his own accord, that is to say, to begin the examination without being requested by the State's attorney. Still, this rule of the separation between the functions of examination and the functions of prosecution has a notable exception in cases of flagrant crimes or misdemeanors, or other cases of that nature. In these the State's attorney may himself begin the examination without waiting for the judge, and the latter may open it without being first requested by the State's attorney.

The preliminary examination had, until recently, three features derived from the inquisitorial procedure; it was *secret*, and *written*, and *not confrontative*. One of these characteristics, and the most open to criticism, the last-mentioned, has been very much modified by the Law of 8th December, 1897, especially in the stage of the preliminary examination which takes place before the examining judge in *ordinary cases*. Two important reforms have been brought about which have entirely changed the aspect of the procedure of examination. The first is the duty of the judge, at his first interview with the accused, to warn him of his right to make no statement except in presence of his counsel. The second is the presence and aid of counsel in the interrogatories and confrontations, to whom must be communicated the chief documents of the charge and who may have access to the evidence in the case.

The preliminary examination is not meant to serve as a foundation for the verdict of the judge who will decide as to the guilt of the accused. It merely allows the examining judge to determine whether there is ground for a formal charge, and, in that case, to decide upon the jurisdiction. The accused is not, in fact, immediately brought before the court which is to acquit if he is innocent and to condemn if he is guilty. The welfare of society and the interest of the accused demand that the appearance of the latter in court shall not take place until the accusation rests upon sufficient grounds. The law confers on certain authorities, intermediate between the officers charged with the examination and those charged with the trial, the investigation of the charges and the determination of the jurisdiction. These authorities, performing the functions of *magistrates of examination*, are the examining judge (above-mentioned) as a first step, and the court of arraignments as the second. This procedure of arraignments, which is obligatory in felonies, involves a measure of delay, which is probably not compensated for by the safeguards which it gives the accused. Nevertheless, it has passed into a great number of codes; and it is only in the last third of the 1800s that the obligatory and absolute principle of the control of the accusation by the judicial power has been breached and abandoned by the Austrian code of procedure in 1873 and the legislations which are inspired by it.

(4) When the prosecution has arrived in the trial court proper, the procedure changes character and borrows its essential features from the accusatory system. The three principles of *confrontation, orality,* and *publicity* govern the proceedings. The memoranda of the police and the record (" dossier ") of the preliminary examination cannot be used as evidence (*i.e.*, can be used only in a subsidiary way), for it is upon the oral, confrontative, and public testimony that the judge forms his " sheer belief " (" conviction intime "), the only proper basis of his verdict.

§ 5. **Division of Criminal Jurisdictions.** — The division of the criminal jurisdictions and authorities corresponds to the division of offenses into three groups, " crimes," " delicts," and " contraventions" (C. p. Art. 1). There are three categories of courts for the trial of criminal prosecutions: the assize courts, which try crimes; the correctional tribunals, for delicts; the police tribunals, contraventions. Each of these tribunals is invested with full judicial power for the repression of the offenses which are allotted to it; each exercises, with reference to these offenses, a complete ordinary jurisdiction. The other three classes of officers of repression perform their duties before these three classes of tribunals — the officers of charge, of examination, and of execution.

§ 6. **Jurisdiction over all Kinds of Persons and Offenses.** — These officers act *in regard to all kinds of persons and all kinds of offenses.* There are not two systems of justice: one, the common law; the other, privileged exceptions. One of the most odious institutions of the Old Régime, the special tribunals, for a short time resuscitated by the law of 16 Pluviôse, year IX, by the Code of Criminal Examination of 1808, and by the institution of the provosts' courts ("cours prévôtal") of 1815, exist only as a historic memory: article 54 of the Charter of 1830 made their return impossible. No doubt soldiers and navy-seamen, so long as they are subject to the duties of their station, hold an exceptional position, and their offenses belong to the jurisdiction of the military tribunals; but this is, in a way, the common law of the army, through which every citizen passes nowadays. There is even a question of the abolition of these exceptional jurisdictions in time of peace.

TITLE I

THE CRIMINAL JURISDICTIONS IN ANCIENT FRANCE

§ 1. **Phases of Judicial Organization of Ancient France. Union of Civil and Penal Justice.** — In ancient France, the organization of penal jurisdictions has passed through three successive stages; but, in every epoch, one feature in common is notable, namely, the union of civil and criminal justice, both administered by the same tribunals. This unity corresponds at first with the unity of the civil and criminal procedures; then, when the jurisdictions become differentiated, this results from the substitution of professional judges for popular judges, and from the conception of a single justice, emanating from the same source and administered in the name of the king.

In the barbarian era, the nations of Germanic race preserve their popular organization. Justice is administered by the chief ("rex, princeps, dux, comes, grafio," etc.) with the coöperation of the free men of the tribe ("boni homines, rachimburgi, pagenses," etc.) in temporary and periodical assemblies ("mallum" or "placitum"). The chief summons the assizes, presides over the assembly of the men who judge, receives the verdict without taking part in rendering it, and causes it to be executed. Thus, according to a rule which appears to have its foundation in customs prior to the invasion of Roman Gaul, it is the *men* who pronounce the judgment, and not the *chief*. A few "rachimbourgs" may compose the tribunal. Nevertheless, plenary assemblies are not uncommon.[1]

[1] I need not go into the sources. They will be found analyzed, with ability and minute care, in "l'Histoire des institutions politiques et administratives de la France," by *Paul Viollet* (1890, 8°, Larosse and Forcel) vol. I, pp. 307–312.

In the feudal period and during the Middle Ages, justice is, in a measure, diluted; it is everywhere, — in the family, the school, the king's palace, the municipalities, and around the feudal chieftain. From this results a two-sided fact, which sums up, at this epoch, the history of the judicial organization. This is the incessant conflicts of jurisdiction, "the daily bread of business,"[1] which arise between all these kinds of justice. This struggle between the tribunals for the extension of their jurisdiction is a struggle in which the royal justices will end by absorbing all the others, in the same way as royalty will end by absorbing the feudal system. The chief justices are four,— the royal, seigniorial, municipal, and ecclesiastical justices. The great division which governs this organization is that of the *secular jurisdictions* and the *ecclesiastical jurisdictions*.

§ 2. **Division of Courts of Justice. Secular and Ecclesiastical Jurisdictions.** — 1. Among the secular jurisdictions there are chiefly three kinds, the *seigniorial*, the *royal*, and the *municipal* courts.

(1) The right to administer justice was looked upon, at a certain period of history, as a patrimonial right. That is one of the characteristic features of the feudal system. The lord had thus jurisdiction over the fiefs and manors of his domain, in virtue of his supreme ownership of the land. The numerous seigniorial justices were originally divided into high and low justices ("alta, magna, major justitia"; then called "justitia sanguinis, sanguis"; in Normandy, "justitia ensis, placitum spatæ; minor, bassa justitia"); later will appear an intermediate grade, the middle justice ("media justitia"). This classification, which appears in the second part of the Middle Ages, had especial importance from the repressive point of view. The high justice in reality took cognizance of the more serious crimes, — murder, rape or violation, "avortes" or "encis" (that is, blows, etc., upon a pregnant woman causing abortion), and arson.[2] Unpremeditated homicide ("occisio") and the mutilation of a limb were ranked by the Parlement among the cases of high justice. In those provinces which did not recognize the middle justice, the low justice had, among its attributes, all that was not within the jurisdiction of the high justice. It has always been rather difficult to state precisely the cases of middle justice, when that is distinct from the high and low justices.

[1] *Viollet, op. cit.* t. 2, p. 453.

[2] See the enumeration of these cases of high justice in *J. Desmares*, "Decisions," 295. Compare *Becquet*, "Traité des droits de justice," chap. 2, in "Œuvres," Geneva 1625, vol. III, pp. 3–7.

Originally exercised by the lord himself, assisted, when a vassal was concerned, by the peers of the latter, the right to administer justice was delegated to officers, who took, according to locality, the names of "*baillis*" or of "*prévôts*."[1] This evolution answered a double purpose; it diminished the number of judges, and it made them a select body, giving them the character of officers.

(2) At the beginning of the feudal system, the king only exercised his jurisdiction over the fiefs and manors of his own domain: and there, he administered justice by the same authority and under the same conditions as a lord justiciar. Like the feudal chieftain, he put in his place, to fill this office, officers whom he invested with an authority at first temporary, afterwards permanent. Originally these were the *provosts* ("prévôts"); later, perhaps because of a need for concentration and surveillance, superior officers were created; they took the name of *bailiffs* ("baillis") in the north and the centre, and of *seneschals* ("sénéchaux") in the south of France.[2] The duty of these functionaries was to hold solemn assizes in the towns of their jurisdiction. They received all complaints against the royal officers and reversed their judgments; later still, the more serious offenses, those which were called *royal causes*, were reserved for them.

Finally, in the last phase of the royal jurisdictions, was the "Parlement," the outcome of two institutions, distinct in law, but blended in fact: the *King's Court* and the *Court of Peers*. The "Parlement," held at first at fixed periods and by sessions, became gradually a sedentary body. For a long time, royalty had only one "Parlement," that of Paris; the provincial "Parlements," all of later creation, appeared successively from the 1300s to the 1700s.

(3) The citizens of the communal and aldermanic towns, when prosecuted in criminal matters, could only be tried by their municipal courts, that is to say, by their peers. We know little of these courts.[3] On the one hand, the customs and books of customs furnished only meagre information as to these jurisdictions, which were little in sympathy with the royal and manorial officers or the jurisconsults. On the other hand, although the organization of these courts was apparently drawn from a uniform type, their

[1] The composition of courts of justice, however, varied according to the provinces and the times. See *Viollet, op. cit.* vol. II, pp. 461–465.

[2] See on royal bailiffs *Beugnot's* Preface in vol. I, to the edition of "Les Coutumes de Beauvoisis" by *Phillippe de Beaumanoir* (Paris 1842).

[3] See *George Testand*, "Des juridictions municipales en France, des origines jusqu'à l'ordonnance de Moulins" 1566 (8°, 1904, Paris).

jurisdiction varied from one commune to another. The radical fault of these jurisdictions, in the majority of the towns where they acted, was the union in the same hands of the administrative and judicial power. At Toulouse, for example, — and the organization of that town was by far the most usual, — the consuls or "capitouls," who had, in great measure, the government of the town, formed, after 1283, a civil and criminal court. This court was presided over by the "viguier," representing the count; but this presidency, purely honorary, did not give even a deliberative voice to those who filled the office.

§ 2. The *ecclesiastical* jurisdictions, the *courts Christian,* as they were then called, had a double source of jurisdiction, *personal* and *real.* The privilege of clergy, which comprehended all grades of the regular clergy and all those of the secular clergy down to the lay clerks, gave to those whose right it was to invoke it the privilege to be tried by these tribunals. To this jurisdiction belonged also the cognizance of certain crimes, committed by any person; for example, those of heresy, sorcery, adultery, and usury. If, however, these jurisdictions tried all these cases, they did not always pronounce the sentence. It was a principle of the Canon law that the Church could not shed blood, and consequently could not inflict capital punishment. In cases where the crime of which they claimed the cognizance entailed the last expiation, the Church delivered over the culprit to the secular arm, which passed the sentence and caused it to be executed.

The judge was usually the bishop. Like the lords, and probably before them, he delegated his right, first to the archdeacon, then, from the 1200s, to a special dignitary called the "*official.*" The ecclesiastical jurisdictions consequently took the name of "officialités."[1] The learned hierarchy of the Church permitted the organization of a series of appeals, from the official to the archbishop, from the latter to the primate, then, finally, to the Pope, as head and supreme judge of Christendom.

§ 3. **Development of the Royal Jurisdictions.** — These jurisdictions were all in existence down to the end of the 1700s. But, while the ecclesiastical, seignorial, and municipal jurisdictions gradually lose their importance, the royal jurisdictions flourish, develop, and end by almost absorbing the others. How is this transformation accomplished? What is the position of the several jurisdictions in the 1600s and 1700s?

[1] See the masterly work of *Fournier*, "Les officialités au moyen âge," 1880, now unfortunately out of print.

1. The royal jurisdictions developed, like royalty itself, because of usurpations of which the legists[1] made themselves the active and persevering instruments. Setting out from the idea that the king represents the public welfare, as he is the "keeper of the kingdom," [2] the officers and jurisconsults of the crown argue from this that the king has a preëminent right of justice throughout the whole kingdom. They were thus led to contrive various means gradually to lessen the jurisdiction of the secular and ecclesiastical courts for the benefit of the royal courts.

The first of these means was the institution of so-called *royal causes*. In the 1200s the causes of which the king claimed cognizance in his barons' territories because they "concerned" him are already very numerous. A jurisconsult of the end of the 1300s devoted twelve large pages to their enumeration.[3] The list of royal causes is always being augmented and will never close. The Roman law furnished to the legists their best weapons in this strife; for this right, which they construed for the benefit of royalty, is typical of the imperial Roman law. Very soon they began to lay down, as a principle of public law, that all justice emanates from the king. From the end of the 1200s they affirmed that all the secular jurisdictions are held from the king in fee or secondary fee.[4] His barons received from him the seisin of the rights of justice, but the king held them of no one.

The practical consequence of this theory was the introduction of the *appeal*. The feudal system had never entertained the idea of submitting anew, to a superior judge, the litigation already decided by the first judge. It did not recognize inferior and superior judges. All the feudal courts, within the limits of their cognizance, were superior courts (of last resort). There were, in the feudal procedure, but two ways of recourse: the *appeal for error in law*, in which the litigant complained of a denial of justice; and the *appeal from false sentence*, a kind of barbarian appeal, consisting in wager of battle by the litigant against the peers

[1] Or lawyers trained in the Roman law, then at the height of its influence under the Renascence.

[2] *Beaumanoir*, XXXIV, 41. See, however, the formula in the 1300s in the "Grand Coutumier," Book IV, ch. V, edited by *Charondas le Caron*, 1598, p. 323. "Generally speaking, there is but one justice which emanates from God, of which the king has the control in this kingdom."

[3] *Bouteiller*, II, 1. Compare Ord. 8th October, 1371 (ord. V, 428) reproduced in the "Grand Coutumier de France," Book I, ch. III, p. 90 *et seq.*

[4] See *supra*, note, and *Beaumanoir*, XI, 12, Book 1, p. 163 of the *Beugnot* edition, "For every secular jurisdiction in the kingdom is held of the king in fee or secondary fee."

who sentenced him. The appeal, in our sense of the word, is in time admitted from the seigniorial to the royal courts, when judgment had been rendered against the common custom, or when the vassals or undervassals did not do as they should.[1]

Finally, a right of prosecution was recognized in the king which his officers made use of to a great extent: that is to say, the king could summon before his courts all persons in regard to any matters, except those claiming the court or jurisdiction of their lord. But if the party summoned has tacitly accepted the royal justice either by acknowledging the rightfulness of the demand or by denying it, he can no longer apply to another court. The litigation must be finished where it is begun.

The jurisconsults of the crown in another way employed various means to restrict the jurisdiction of the ecclesiastical tribunals. Under the vague and elastic idea of the crime of treason or sedition ("lèse-majesté") they caused to be included among the "royal causes" various offenses formerly brought before the courts Christian; but, especially, they weakened, by the creation of causes called "privileged," the import of the privilege of clergy. In very serious cases which deserved a punishment less severe than the canonical punishments, the clerks were tried by the royal judges, unless the latter were forced to give them up to the Church. The list of these privileged causes, like that of the royal causes, always continued to grow.[2]

The municipal jurisdictions, the criminal at least, usually survived the supremacy of the communal towns. They offered few dangers, since the royal power had indirectly laid hands upon the nomination of the municipal officers.

2. In thus extending the sphere of their action, the royal jurisdictions completed their organization: on one side, the old tribunals are seen to become modified and developed; on the other, tribunals of exception to appear.

(*a*) Down to the last days of the old monarchy, the provosts constituted the usual judges of the first stage; the bailiffs and seneschals, originally itinerant, subsequently become sedentary, always constituted the second stage of the royal jurisdictions. The bailiffs, high officers of the crown, delegated their powers to inferior officers who were called lieutenants of bailiwick. To the *criminal lieutenant* fell the trial of criminal causes; he became the judge in criminal matters for all the cases transferred because of

[1] *Beaumanoir*, XI, 2, 3.
[2] See *Muyart de Vouglans*, "Inst. crim." 3d part, p. 34 *et seq.*

their gravity from the provosts' jurisdiction. At first he tried alone; later, he was assisted by assessors, who took the title of counsellors. But it was always he who made the criminal examination, and from this point of view he was, under the old system, an essential part of the machinery of repression.

In the reign of Henry II there were created seats of a special importance called *presidials* ("présidiaux"). By an edict of November, 1551, that prince ordained that, in the chief bailiwicks and seneschals' jurisdictions there should be a presidial, composed of at least nine magistrates, including the civil and criminal lieutenants, general and particular. These tribunals, so far as criminal, were not distinguished from other bailiwicks except that they could take cognizance of " prévôtal " cases.

In the Parlement of Paris, the personnel of which was always growing, a special branch called the Tournelle was established to try criminal cases. The ordinance of 28th October, 1446 (Arts. 10 and 11), is the first which mentions it as distinct from the other branches.[1] It is composed of secular counsellors, chosen from the Grand Chambre and sitting in the little tower of St. Louis, la Tournelle, from which it takes its name. The Grand Chambre itself pronounces the judgments prepared by these counsellors. In 1515, Francis I constituted this group of judges a special branch. But its composition never was autonomous, — in this sense, at least, that, by a rule of rotation, the counsellors passed from a civil to a criminal branch, so that even with this organization, the unity of civil and penal justice was always the dominating principle.

The provincial Parlements came into existence one after the other with the development of the political power of royalty and the territorial extensions caused thereby. Several of these Parlements did in fact no more than continue the old supreme courts of the large fiefs united to the crown.[2]

The Parlement of Paris, throughout its successive transformations, remained, up till recent times, the Court of Peers. All the peers of France had the right to sit there, and they could only be tried by the Parlement.

Besides their ordinary functions, the Parlement of Paris and certain other provincial parliaments, those of Toulouse, Rouen,

[1] *Pardessus*, "Essai sur l'organisation judiciaire," p. 163.

[2] The Exchequer of Normandy, become "Parlement," had, in 1519, a criminal Chamber, Tournelle, in imitation of Paris. In 1491 a criminal Chamber or Tournelle was installed at Toulouse, "so that criminal justice may be administered as at Paris."

and Bordeaux, took part in the administration of justice by Great Days, a kind of solemn and temporary assizes, held, in a province, by commissaries chosen by the king. The Great Days always had as their object the repression of serious and persistent general disorders, and of exactions made by the local authorities.

(*b*) Besides ordinary jurisdictions, tribunals of exception were created. They were of two kinds: 1st, some had jurisdiction of criminal causes only incidentally to the matters which constituted the chief object of their establishment; such were the provost of the Mint ("Hôtel des Monnaies"), the "Cour des Monnaies," and the Admiralty judges; 2d, others had a chief criminal jurisdiction; such were the provost marshals and the military judges.

TITLE II

THE PROCEDURE

CHAPTER I[1]

THE ACCUSATORY PROCEDURE OF THE FEUDAL COURTS

§ 1. **Introductory.**—The forms of civil and of criminal procedure in the feudal courts were identical. This is a feature generally characteristic of primitive systems of law; and the feudal customary law had borrowed it from the law of the Frankish epoch. The criminal law itself had doubtless undergone many changes since the Frankish epoch. The system of pecuniary compositions, for example, had for the most part disappeared; offenses were punished, according to their gravity, either with very severe corporal punishment or with fines by which the baronial courts profited. But the criminal procedure had remained accusatory in the strictest sense of the word.

§ 2. **The Accusation.** — The action belonged to the injured party alone, or if he was dead, to his kindred. This is a principle as to which the contemporary sources are in unanimous agreement: "It is not lawful for any one to bring an accusation except for himself, or for his kindred, or for his liege lord."[2] "No one is heard if he be not connected with the deceased by blood relationship, or if she be not his wedded wife."[3] "The next of kin may prosecute for murder or homicide, and if the next of kin be a minor or aged, the nearest of kin after him, or other relative on

[1] [This Chapter I and the entire remainder of the book (except Part IV and the Appendix) = Part I, Title II, and Parts II and III of Professor ESMEIN'S "History of Criminal Procedure." For this author and work, see the Editorial Preface. — ED.]

[2] *Beaumanoir*, LXIII, I, "Trés-ancienne coutume de Bretagne," ch. 96 (Bourdot de Richebourg).

[3] "Livre de Jostice et de Plet," XIX, 3, § 1, 2.

whom the kindred shall agree, may do so. And if peace be made, a minor may recommence the suit on coming of age. But if the proceedings have been brought and completed, no other proceedings can be brought or commenced."[1] Jean d'Ibelin takes great pains to enumerate, by way of limitation, those who may bring an accusation on account of murder.[2] And there can be no criminal action in the absence of an accuser. The criminal action being, therefore, merely a contest between two private parties, and only distinguished from the civil action by certain differences in detail due to the different nature of the circumstances involved, it is evident that it was unnecessary to create for it a special procedure.

The procedure was public, oral, and formal. The hearing was usually held in the open air, at the gate of the castle or at the public meeting-place of the town. The parties had to appear on the day fixed in the summons ("semonce"), unless they could invoke some one of the numerous excuses recognized by the feudal procedure. They could not be represented; the impossibility of representation in a court of justice was, according to ancient principles, more rigorously maintained in criminal than in civil affairs.

The accuser made his complaint orally without omitting any necessary words or making any mistake ("faute"), which would have permitted his adversary to have the complaint declared null.[3] The accused was obliged to answer on the spot; silence on

[1] "Grand coutumier de Normandie," ch. LXX; the following extract from the text permits the *man* to pursue for his master: "If any stranger (*i.e.*, in blood) make an accusation of homicide in this form: 'I complain of R. who has feloniously assaulted and killed Q. my lord in my presence: and while I was defending him he shed this blood and caused this wound.' Then he should show the blood and the wound to the judge in presence of knights who can bear witness to it. Should the other offer to defend himself, battle should be waged, as aforesaid. In this way murder and homicide can be sued by a stranger (in blood)." — "Summa de Legibus" (Tardif edition), c. LXIX. The idea of *private vengeance* is apparently always uppermost.

[2] Chap. LXXX *et seq.* Although *Jean d'Ibelin* admits spiritual as well as carnal relatives and even other persons (on foreign soil the bonds thus somewhat relaxed tighten again) he none the less upholds the principle according to which the pursuit belongs to interested parties alone.

[3] See fully on this formal aspect of the old procedure *M. Brunner's* noteworthy study, cited above: "Wort und Form in altfranzösischen Process." Modern writers, moreover, are not alone in noticing and commenting upon the matter: "Fabrefort . . . pleading a cause concerning a duel, and having proposed for Armand de Montaign against Émery de Durefort that he should prove his fact by his body on the battle-field, without expressly saying that the proof should be made by the combat of his party, was in danger of being drawn into the combat himself, and was ridiculed by the assembled company, so *formal* was then the procedure in such causes." *Loysel,* "Pasquier, ou dialogue des avocats," edit. Dupin, Paris 1844, p. 40.

his part would have been equivalent to a confession, and in primitive systems of law a confession is the best proof.[1] The defense could only consist of a denial exactly meeting the complaint in each particular, refuting it word for word, " de verbo ad verbum "; and this requirement was preserved for a long time, except in civil matters, where at an early date a general answer " en gros " was permitted.[2]

§ 3. **The Theory of Proof.** — The proofs were the same as in civil matters, and were derived from the usages of the Frankish epoch, feudalism merely giving the preference to those which best suited its own circumstances and allowing the others gradually to fall into desuetude.

But although the exculpation by the *oath-helpers* became rare, the exculpation by the oath of the defendant alone continued to find numerous applications, both in civil cases and in those for minor offenses. The latter mode of exculpation is the " deraisne " (" disraisina ") of the old Norman customary law.[3] Beaumanoir calls it " Le passer par loi," [4] and the " Très-ancienne coutume de Bretagne " contains a very curious application of it criminally.[5]

In the 1200s the ordeals (the " purgatio vulgaris " of the Canon law) are rarely any longer in practice; they were condemned by

[1] *Beaumanoir*, speaking of the confession, says, "This proof is certainly the best and clearest, and the least expensive of all," XXXIX, 2 (Salmon, No. 1146). As to the necessity for an immediate answer, see *Beaumanoir*, VII, 10; XXX, 94 (Salmon, Nos. 246, 915); "Livre de J. et de P." II, 14, § 6; *Jean d'Ibelin*, ch. LXI.

[2] "Livre de Jostice et de Plet," XIX, 2, § 1; *L. Delisle*, "Échiquier de Normandie," No. 113; "Grand coutumier de Normandie," ch. LVIII *et seq.; Jean d'Ibelin*, chs. XCI, XCVII, C, CIV; *Brunner*, *op. cit.* p. 706 *et seq.* *Cf. Britton*, Book 1, ch. XXII, "concerning Appeals," No. 7: "And as to the defense, the appellee may defend himself in this manner. 'Peter who is here defendeth all the felonies, and all the treasons and contrivances, and compassings of mischief against the person' of such an one, or such an one, according as he is charged, word by word. And we will that in these appeals, it shall be more necessary for the appellor to set forth the words orderly without any omission, that his appeal may stand, than for the defendant in his defense; and in every felony we allow the defendant to defend the words of the felony generally, without treating him as undefended." *Britton* (F. M. Nichols' edition, 1865), vol. I, pp. 101, 102.

[3] "Summa" (Tardif edition), c. CXXIII.

[4] Ch. XXX, 86 (Salmon, No. 912).

[5] (*Planiol* edition), c. 102, p. 145: "If he is not taken in the act or in pursuit, or if the fact is not notorious, as said, and for the reason that he has lived in the country a year and is of good repute as one who goes to monastery and market and he is not seized or arrested because of crime, he can say in case the judge wishes to proceed against him that he is not bound to wait for testimony by the custom in a case in which he could be put to death and that he prove himself to be of good répute. In the event that it cannot be judicially proved against him to a certainty, he shall take his vassal's oath that he did not do the deed [and this done] the custom decrees that he go freed and acquitted."

the Lateran Council of 1215. But before that time they played an important part in Normandy, as is proved by the fact that they were widely practised in England,[1] into which country they had been carried from Normandy. According to the "Summa de legibus"[2] they were there resorted to when a woman was accused, and also when a man was accused by a woman or incriminated by "the law." These last words doubtless point to the practice which we shall later on note in our own common law as that according to which the person on whom the "infamia" was laid because of an offense committed, had the burden of exculpating himself, "sese purgare." We find a passage in the "Assises de Jérusalem," however, which sanctions the ordeal only when it is accepted voluntarily and without restraint by the party under suspicion.

In the "Cour des Bourgeois," chapter CCLXI treats "dou juice portare":[3] "Be it known that neither the bailiffs nor the sworn men shall cause any man or any woman either to bear law forcibly. But if the man or the woman be accused of any crime imputed to him or her, and he or she voluntarily offer to bear law, reason commands and judges that he or she cannot retract the offer, but is held to bear (law) in spite of himself if he who

[1] *Thayer*, "A Preliminary Treatise on Evidence at Common Law," pp. 7–16; *Holdsworth*, "A History of English Law," I, p. 142; *Pollock and Maitland*, "History of English Law," II, pp. 596, 597.

[2] C. CXXVI, No. 2: "Olim mulieres causis criminalibus insecute, cum non haberent qui eas defenderit jussio (judicio) se purgabat et homines per aquem vel jussium cum justicia vel mulieres in criminalibus eos impetrabant; et quoniam hujusmodi ab ecclesia catolica sunt abscissa inquisitione frequenter utimur."

See *Brunner*, *op. cit.* p. 719 *et seq.* The most remarkable use of the exculpatory oath is the "deresne" of the old Norman custom; "Summa," II, c. XVIII, § 2. "Est enim disresina super injuria a querulo exposita coram justiciario purgatio per sacramentum querelati et coadjutorum suorum in curia facienda." It was only admitted in trivial causes, the "simplices querelæ." *Cf.* "Assises de Jérusalem": Inferior court, ch. CCXXII: "In the case of a man who is mortally wounded, if any one appear in court and complain of any one who he says has done this wrong, and he who is accused of it appears and says 'that (he did it) not as God wills' and he demands an assize and is granted an assize in the presence of the sheriff and sworn men, he swears upon the holy scriptures that he did not do it himself, or cause it to be done, or consent to the act, or know any one who did it, he is thereupon acquitted, since his judicial oath is received, as was demanded." *Kausler's* edition, p. 330.

[3] "Juice," equivalent to judicium, the branding which does duty as the judgment of God. "Summa de legibus Normanie," Tardif edition, c. CXXII, No. 2: "Sirendum est ergo quod hac probabilia quandoque per juramentum solius, quandoque per sacramenta duorum, quandoque quinque, quandoque sex, quandoque septem, in curia recipitur paicali." c. CXXXIV, No. 2: "Est autem disraisina purgatio super injuria coram justiciario a querulo exposita per sacramentum querelati et coadjutorum facienda."

charges the person with the crime wishes. . . . And if he will not bear law as the court tells him, reason judges that (the complainant be heard) as, since (the person accused) will not bear law, it is very clear that he had done that which is imputed to him; for if he had not done it he would not have distrusted the law, which is a just thing to all people who seek justice.[1]" We also find a curious application of it in the "Très-ancienne coutume de Bretagne;" but there the ordeal appears, by a singular reversion, as a "succedanæum" of torture.[2]

The judicial duel, the appeal to the divine judgment, aided by the oaths of both adversaries and decided by *battle*, has, on the other hand, a longer lease of life. It is the customary mode of proof, at least in cases of crime. In all serious crimes, for which the punishment was loss of life or mutilation, the accuser could proceed by "appeal"; that is, he could spontaneously and immediately challenge the accused to the judicial duel;[3] but in minor cases this direct challenge probably could not be given, and proof by witnesses would be necessary.[4] The appeal was, moreover, a very risky procedure, not only on account of its purpose, but also because the challenge had to be couched in certain terms (the words by which battle took place), and an error in the expressions used might specially aggravate the conditions of the combat.[5] It is, therefore, probable that the accuser, instead of pro-

[1] *Kausler* edition, p. 307.

[2] C. 101, *Planiol* edition, p. 144: "And if complete proof cannot be found and common repute or strong presumption is adduced against him [he ought to] undergo the ordeal 'jous' ('juice, judicium') or torture ('gehine') three times. And if he is able to endure the torture without confession, or the ordeal ('jous') should save him, it would certainly appear that God has worked miracles for him and he ought to be safe. Therefore the man [or woman] shall not be put to the ordeal 'joux' or the torture until proceedings have been taken against them in such way." It is surprising to find the "judicium ferri" in Brittany a century after the fourth Lateran Council, for the "Très-ancienne coutume" belongs to the first third of the 1300s; but I suspect that, particularly in the chapters treating of the criminal procedure, the author must have studied an earlier text, the data of which he applied, without regard to their appropriateness, to the law of his own time.

[3] *Beaumanoir*, LXI, 2 (Salmon, No. 1710).

[4] It is only "in regard to all crimes involving risk of loss of life or limb" that the ordinance of 1260 declares that henceforward proof by witnesses shall replace the proof by battle. *Cf. Beaumanoir*, XXXIX, 4 (Salmon, No. 1148); "Livre de J. et P." II, 18, § 1.

[5] *Jean d'Ibelin*, ch. CXX; *Beaumanoir*, LXI, 41; LXX, 5 (Salmon, Nos. 1264, 1972); "Abregé des assises de la cour des Bourgeois," part II, ch. XXXVI; "Grand coutumier de Normandie," ch. LXVIII; "Livre de J. et P." XIX, 33; "Établissements de S. Louis," II, 118; *Britton*, I, I, ch. 22: "An appeal is a plaint brought by one person against another in a set form of words with intent to convict him of felony." (*Nichols'* edition, t. I, p. 95); "Stylus Curiæ Parliamenti," CXVI, § 8.

ceeding by way of the "appeal," although that was available to him, could offer to prove the fact by witnesses, subject to the accused's right subsequently to falsify (" fausser ") these witnesses.

This testimonial proof was quite different from that known in the later systems of law; it was entirely formal. The witnesses proceeded to pronounce a formula which they sometimes merely repeated after the " avant-parlier " or advocate; this formula must state that they were eye-witnesses, and they confirmed it by swearing on relics.[1] Two witnesses, fulfilling these conditions, were sufficient to entail condemnation, and their oaths necessarily led to that result;[2] in such a system the witnesses could not be enumerated or their evidence weighed. These witnesses, produced on the day fixed by the decree which ordered the proof, from which no adjournment could be granted, testified at the hearing in open court and in confrontation with the parties.[3] This publicity was necessary, for one reason, to allow the accused to make use of a valuable right, that of *falsifying* or challenging the witnesses. He could, in effect, accuse them of perjury, and on that ground challenge them to the judicial duel. The action would then depend upon the outcome of that battle. This challenge had to be made, according to some authorities, before the taking of the oath; according to others, immediately thereafter; but it was certainly essential that all the actors in the drama should be present when it was made.[4] Seeing that the " garants," as the witnesses were called, risked their lives, they could not be compelled to testify. For other reasons a large number of persons were incompetent to testify; in this category were included all who were unable to fight, women, minors, and the clergy, for example, and all those social reprobates who were considered infamous.

The foregoing is a sketch of the leading features of the ancient accusatory procedure. It was entirely oral; writing played no part in it. Whether the proceeding chosen was by appeal or by

[1] "Grand coutumier de Normandie": "Witnesses in the secular court are those who testify to what the complainant has alleged in these words: 'I saw and heard it and I am ready to do what the court may decree.' . . ." *Cf. Jean d'Ibelin*, chs. 70, 77; *Beaumanoir*, XXXIX 57 (Salmon, No. 1200).

[2] *Beaumanoir*, XXXIX, 5; LXI, 54 (Salmon, Nos. 1149, 1762); *Jean d'Ibelin*, ch. 68.

[3] *Beaumanoir*, XXXIX, 78 (Salmon, No. 1222): "In such a case the proper course is for the witness to appear in open court for the purpose of testifying publicly, and there he may be challenged."

[4] *Jean d'Ibelin*, ch. 74; "Clef des assises de la Haute-Cour," 101; *Phillippe de Navarre*, ch. 10; *Geoffrey le Tort*, ch. 23; *Beaumanoir*, LXI, 55 (Salmon, No. 1762).

testimonial proof, it was an equal and public contest between two private persons.

But this system was notably barbarous and inadequate; and it was bound to leave many crimes unpunished. Very soon it came to be seen that the community and the State were sufferers from the offense as well as the private individual; and even before the advent of a new system this idea had stamped its influence on certain points of the procedure.[1]

§ 4. **Capture in the Act.** — Capture in the act ("taking with the mainour," etc.) was originally subject to special rules; we usually find it occupying a place of its own in primitive systems of law. Although the prosecution of crimes is not readily admitted in primitive times, that is because it was considered almost impossible to clearly convict an accused who denied his guilt. When he is taken in the act, however, the proof becomes clear and all hesitation vanishes. During the Middle Ages, when a person was taken in the act, an accuser is unnecessary and the wager of battle is not available. The justiciar, surrounded by his men, before whom his servants ("sergents") bring an individual taken in the act, judges him at once in the public presence, according to the testimony of those who have seized him.[2] We also know that, following the traditions of the Frankish epoch, the feudal procedure had originated a formal and ingenious way of preserving to the affair the character of a capture in the act for a certain time after its accomplishment. This was the arrest "by hue and cry" — the pursuit by "haro," "harou," or "hareu."[3]

[1] *Beaumanoir*, LIX, 7 (Salmon, No. 1673): "Malefactors not only transgress against the adverse parties and their kindred but also against the lords who are their protectors and justiciars."

[2] "It is not proper for any one to proceed against him . . . for such a deed which is so clear should be avenged by the judge officially, as long as no one proceeds against him directly." *Beaum.* VI, 12; LXI, 2 (Salmon, Nos. 208, 1710); "Livre de J. et P." XIX, 44, § 14. The "Assises de la cour des Bourgeois" has a curious chapter in connection with this point, ch. CCLIX: "If peradventure it happen that one man assault another and kill him, or a woman, and two vassals pass the spot and see him commit the offense and arrest him, as all vassals should hold and arrest (for) all the rights of their lord and all the wrongs done to him, and if they deliver him over to the court and they say faithfully in the court, before the sheriff and the échevins on the faith and homage which they owe to the king that they saw him commit this murder, reason judges and commands that it be adjudged that such person is attainted without battle and that it avail him not to say 'no, as God wills, he did not do it,' but he should be immediately hanged. For to this extent should the testimony of two vassals be equal to two sworn men or 'échevins' in such a matter." Edit. *Kausler*, p. 314.

[3] "Grand coutumier de Normandie," ch. 54; *Beaumanoir*, LII, 16; XXXIX, 43 (Salmon, Nos. 1571, 1187). The present-day text-books on English law still describe this procedure as the "arrest by hue and cry."

All this, however, gave but a limited scope to the public prosecution; an endeavor was made to go further. What was to be done in the case of the murder of a man who left no relatives? In such a case it was unreasonable to confine the accusation to the person injured or his relatives; and, according to certain writers on the customary law, it became the duty of the public authorities to intervene. "If it peradventure happen that a man or woman be slain and if this murder be imputed to any man and he who is dead have no relatives or friends (in blood) male or female who demand his death from him who killed him, reason judges that the king or the lord of the soil, or the lady of the town if it belong to her, is bound to demand his death by law and by assize, and the method is to assign a champion, if he (the person accused) deny this misdeed; for our Lord says in the Scriptures that the blood of the poor cried out to him for justice saying 'Lord God, avenge the blood of the poor.' And since this is said by our Father in Heaven, so should it be understood on earth by law that to the baron's court should be given earthly vengeance as is laid down by all commandments. And for this purpose his right is established to undertake these matters and to avenge the death."[1] "If the king impute to a man that he has killed another, he ordains that he be punished. To this the man may reply, 'I will not answer, as it is not law, since one should not answer for such a deed when no one complains except you.' It is asked, What says the law? And the answer is: If such man as the deceased had children or descendants or near relatives who were able to avenge their relative, the suit is theirs, not his lord's. But if the man or woman who is killed have no relative who can avenge him or her the king can pursue and administer punishment; the corporal punishment of such person belongs to him who *seized* him."[2]

§ 5. **Arrest on Suspicion.** — There was still another situation. If the victim or any of his relatives were still living and made no complaint, the barons' court had no cognizance of it. But in course of time a right was ascribed to it. Although the public authority could not, in its own name, press for the application of the punishment, it was at least granted power to seize the male-

See *Stephen's* "Commentaries on the laws of England," Book IV, p. 351 (edit. 1873).

[1] "Assises de la Baisse Cour," ch. CCLXVII, p. 324 (edit. *Kausler*).

[2] "Livre de J. et P." XIX, 45, § 1; *cf. ibid.* § 2: "It is asked if an answer shall be made to him when he (the injured party) makes no complaint. The reply is in the negative, since he is alive against whom the offense is said to have been committed."

factor and invoke the necessary proceedings by the interested parties. Numerous texts lay down this principle.[1] But this did not furnish a final solution of the difficulty; and from this provisional state there were two ways out.

According to the logic of these old institutions, the action of the public authority in seizing the person on suspicion was but a means preliminary to accusations. So we find in texts of the most diverse origin a procedure of the following nature. It is the duty of the lord to announce by sound of trumpet that he holds such and such a person on suspicion of such and such a crime, and to call upon the victim or his relatives to constitute themselves accusers. If after a certain period and several publications, usually made at three assizes, no one appears, the prisoner is liberated on bail, or, according to other writers, he is imprisoned for a year and a day. If no accusation shall have been brought within that period, he is finally set free and acquitted. "The lord should allow him to go, and he is acquitted of this murder, so that he is no longer bound to answer any one who accuses him thereof."[2] The following is a very clear summary of this procedure. "No one shall be arrested on suspicion for such deeds involving corporal punishment if the grounds of the suspicion are not clear or reasonable. And if any one be arrested on suspicion he can be held forty days. And if within the forty days no one appear to accuse him he shall be liberated on bail, body for body. And this bail shall last for three periods of forty days each. If no one appear to accuse him his surety will be freed; it may be that if any appear to accuse him within a year and a day, such person will be heard, but not afterwards."[3] This was merely a stimulant to

[1] *Jean d'Ibelin*, ch. 85: "The lord shall cause search to be made for him who is charged with the murder, if he is his subject, and apprehend him, and put him in his prison." "Compilatio de Usibus Andegaviæ," § 7: "Custom and law is that no man be arrested without 'plaintif' (accuser) if he be not arrested on the spot or apprehended by judges on suspicion. A murderer can properly be arrested without accuser when he has slain the man, for the blood cries out. This was shown us in the killing of Abel by his brother Cain, to whom God said: 'Cain, the voice of Abel thy brother's blood, whom thou hast killed crieth unto me from the ground." "Livre des Droiz," § 334: "A judge should not apprehend anybody without accuser or without present misdeed, or on suspicion. But he may properly apprehend the murderer when he has slain a man, for the *blood* complains." "Livre de J. et P." XIX, 26, §§ 5, 12; "Etab. de S. Louis," II, 16; *Beaumanoir*, XL, 14; XXX, 90 (Salmon, Nos. 1236, 917).

[2] *Beaumanoir*, XXX, 90 (Salmon, No. 917); *Jean d'Ibelin*, chs. 35, 85; "Livre de J. et P." XIX, 26; "Compilatio de usibus Andegaviæ," § 24; "Livre des Droiz," §§ 252, 387.

[3] "Livre de J. et P." XIX, 26, § 12. According to some writers, final release took place on the expiry of the time for publication. *Beaumanoir*, XXX, 91 (Salmon, No. 918).

private accusation; it was not prosecution in the name of the State.[1] This practice was even employed to give immunity to whomsoever had committed an act which might give rise to a criminal prosecution on the part of the victim, or, if he was dead, on the part of his relatives, and it was doubtless for this reason that it survived as long as it did. He delivered himself up to the lord, who, by means of a procedure regulated by custom, made public the facts and gave an opportunity to possible accusers to come forward. If the prescribed period expired without any accusation being brought, the perpetrator of the deed had nothing further to fear, as prosecution was no longer possible. The "Très-ancienne coutume de Bretagne," which calls this procedure "finporter," doubtless because it "put an end" to the whole matter, gives full details of it.[2] We also find the same practice in the "Livre des usages et anciennes coutumes de la comté de Guynes" in 1344.[3] In the latter instance the procedure is blended with that of the inquest by the country, "enquête du pays," (of which we shall treat in the next section),[4] probably in order to make it more decisive and efficacious. This is called "putting oneself to law" ("se mettre à loi"), a term which is often used in certain Flanders' texts to denote the action of a man who by this means exposes himself to accusations with the real object of securing himself against any possible accusation. It is only to be supposed that the person who thus spontaneously exposed himself to prosecution did not do so unadvisedly or without first taking due precautions. This procedure was most frequent in the case of homicide by misadventure. The "Livre des usages de Guynes" gives as an example the killing of a man in an archery contest; and one text recommends the perpetrator to compromise at once with the interested parties.

§ 6. **The Inquest by the Country.** — There was another alternative. The prisoner might agree to be judged without any

[1] In certain provinces, this procedure could be invoked by the person under suspicion; it was then said that he put himself "to his law" ("à loi"). See "Ancien coutumier de Picardie" (*Marnier's* edition), LV (p. 47). "In law, Andrieu the knight, Jehan and Henri brothers, who put themselves to law in the court of Poitieu at Abbeville and were allowed to do so on suspicion of the killing of Colart Hurtant, and summoned several times by wager of battle any who wished to charge them on account of the said suspicion, to appear and do right and law upon them; and no one appeared against them or offered . . . released and absolved of the said suspicion."

[2] (*Planiol's* edition), c. CI, CII, p. 142–145.

[3] (*Taillar and Courtois's* edition, Saint Auer. 1856), p. 144 *et seq.*

[4] *Esmein*, "L'acceptation de l'enquête dans la procédure criminelle au Moyen Age" in "Revue générale du droit, de la législation et de la jurisprudence," 1888, p. 14 *et seq.*

accuser, under a certain procedure called by the texts the "inquest by the country" ("l'enquête du païs") — "When any one is arrested on suspicion of a serious offense . . . he may be asked if he will submit to the inquest into the matter."[1] The assent of the prisoner was absolutely necessary. "Be it known that no one is condemned by inquest unless he submits thereto."[2] It is true that very strenuous means of persuasion were used to obtain this assent: "He ought to be arrested by the judge and imprisoned for a year and a day with very little to eat and drink, if within that time he does not submit to the inquest by the country."[3] The old "Coutume de Bourgoyne" (1279–1360) also says (Art. 13, "Enqueste"): "Inquest made against any one for crime is null unless he puts himself on inquest."[4] The "Livre des coutumes notoires demenées au Chastelet de Paris" warns against inadvisedly putting oneself on inquest: "No one should put himself on inquest if he can help it, for he may put himself in very great danger, since everybody cannot be friendly to him; but he can properly authorize the judge that he, under God and on his soul, inquire and cause inquiry to be made by his liege vassals, and this can be done where there is no complainant."[5] The effect of acceptance of the inquest by the accused was decisive; it was conducted both for and against him, and, as Beaumanoir says, it "ended the quarrel." According to its result the man was acquitted or condemned.

What was this inquest? It was a kind of proof by witnesses, but very different from the common law testimonial proof before described. It was, moreover, no new thing. It had existed in the Carlovingian period under the name of "Inquisitio."[6] The fact that, in France, it was very soon merged with the testimonial proof introduced by the Ordinance of 1260 makes it rather difficult definitely to ascertain its features from the texts of the 1200s. The "Grand Coutumier de Normandie," however, gives a detailed description of it.[7] "Those people who are likely to know about

[1] *Beaumanoir*, XI, 14 (Salmon, Nos. 1236–1238).
[2] "Livre de J. et P." XIX, 45, § 1; "Ancien coutumier de Picardie," p. 52.
[3] *Cf. Beaumanoir*, XXXIV, 21 (Salmon, No. 1042).
[4] *Charles Giraud*, "Essai sur l'histoire du droit français au Moyen Age," vol. II, p. 291.
[5] *Mortet's* edition, § 61, p. 71.
[6] See *M. Brunner*, "Die Enstehung der Schwurgerichte," particularly chapter VI.
[7] Ch. LXVIII. The Latin text according to the "Somma" is as follows (II, ch. II, § 13): "Si autem de multro facto nullus sit qui sequelam faciat aut clamorem, si publica infamia aliquem super hoc fecerit criminosum, per justiciarium debet arrestari et firmo carcere obersvari

the offense shall be summoned without delay, to the number of twenty-four at least, such as are not suspected (of bias) from like or dislike . . . the most capable and the most honorable in the place where the offense was committed." The bailiff is to bring them singly before four knights and commit their statements to writing; then "the accused shall be brought forward and he shall be asked if he wishes to object to ('saonner') any of the swearers, who shall be pointed out to him."[1] Finally, the swearers are called up together and what they have said is read over to the accused by the judge. "And they shall acknowledge that they have so sworn; and upon that judgment shall then be pronounced with the advice and on the opinion of the assistants of the court."

In England this institution played a leading part, as we shall later see; it gave birth to the jury in criminal matters. Although it proved barren in France, owing to its somewhat unfavorable environment, it is none the less the same institution as that which attained such a splendid development on the other side of the Channel.

A few of our old texts, however, show the "jurée du pays" in what seems to me to be a different application, and call to mind the "jury de dénonciation;" this operated in the 800s, as the Capitularies show, and survived, without any real interruption, in the ecclesiastical procedure, where, as we shall presently see, it culminated in the "inquisitio generalis." It was also the anti-

usque ad diem et annum cum penuria victus et potus; nisi interim super hoc inquisitionem patrie se offerat sustinere. Quam si sustinere voluerit sollicitudo justiciarii debet procurare quod omnes illi, quos de multro aliquid scire præsumpserit vel ipsius aliquam noticiam habere, de quocumque loco fuerint, coram se certo die et loco faciat convenire et hoc subito et inopinate, et causa propter quam eos faciat submoneri celetur, ne parentes criminosi eorum prece vel precio corrumpant sacramenta; et ab eis unoquoque per se vocato, coram IIII^or militibus non suspectis, utrum criminosus illud multrum fecerit inquiratur diligenter. Et auditis dictis eorum et inscriptis, et si sufficiens *seonium* super aliquem miserit dictum ejus pro nullo debet reputari et a *jurea* debet removeri. Et si sufficiens non fuerit seonium nihilominus ulterius procedatur. § 14. Hujusmodi jurea fieri debet per XXIIII^or homines ad minus legales quos nec favor nec odium a jurea debeat amovere. . . . § 18. Post hoc autem coram ipsis juratoribus et aliis in publico convocatis dictum eorum coram reo debet per justiciarum recitari et per juratores confiteri quod ità juraverunt. Et super hoc debet fieri judicium in continente et judicium factum sine dilatione adimpleri, et quod XX^ti eorum juraverint observetur. Et si aliqui eorum se nescientes dixerint tot debent juratores apponi, si possunt inveniri, quod per sacramentum XX^ti eorum veritas rei eluceat inquisite." (*Tardif* edition, c. LXVII, No. 11.)

[1] According to Beaumanoir, the time for requiring the person put to the inquest to offer his objections was at the very beginning, before any of the "men" had been heard. (XL, 14, Salmon, 1236.)

type of the "inquisitio," from which sprang the English "grand jury." The "Très-ancienne coutume de Bretagne" places the matter in this light: "When a serious offense is committed in a district . . . it is the judge's duty to cause to *be sworn certain people of the district* — men, women, and children, who are competent to take oath — and to ask them [where they were] [1] the day and night the offense was committed. And if the judge find the people of a house constantly changing, he can arrest them, and also if he can find through third parties that suspicion points to any one, in order to enable him to find the cause for the suspicion, he shall proceed against him according to the custom in such cases. And then the judge shall cause him to be interrogated and asked who he was and where he dwelt, and with whom he ate, and what food (such people) ate, and who they were, and other words and like matters, without question or notice of the deed, but only so that the discrepancy be discovered." [2]

To return to the inquest "accepted" by the accused. In 1887 M. Zucker, professor in the Prague University, in a very interesting monograph full of ingenious criticisms, put quite another interpretation on it.[3] He does not think that the inquest by the country, accepted by the accused, antedated the "aprise," of which we shall speak presently, and which is the official prosecution, the "processus per inquisitionem" of the Canon law. According to him, the only object of the accepted inquest was to make an action without an accuser possible; it was merely a detail of the "aprise," a plea in defense put into the hands of the person against whom the "aprise" was directed, and who could use it to avoid a prolonged detention or take advantage of a justificative fact.[4] But this opinion is too inconsistent with the data furnished by a comparison of all the texts. Beaumanoir in particular shows conclusively that the "aprise" and the inquest are two different procedures; that the judge only resorted to the "aprise" when the accused did not accept the inquest and that

[1] It seems to me that the bracketed words added by the editor should be omitted.

[2] *Planiol's* edition, ch. CXIV, p. 154. The question of the "jurée du païs" is also discussed in chapter CXVI, p. 155: "and if it is so that any person complain that he has been robbed of anything, whereby either man or woman ought to suffer death if the fact were proved against them, should he who complains swear by the saints that he does not know whom to accuse, the judge shall *make the 'jurée' and the inquest,* as he is called upon to do for serious offenses."

[3] *Dr. Alois Zucker,* "Aprise und loial enquête, ein Beitrag zur Feststelling des historischen Basis der modern Voruntersuchung", (Vienna, 1887).

[4] *Op. cit.* pp. 85, 86, 88, 89, 97 *et seq.,* 100, 101, 110, 111.

his powers were not the same in both cases.[1] It was undoubtedly possible, with the consent of the accused, to shift from the opened "aprise" to the inquest, and it might be very much to the advantage of the accused to give such consent after having at first refused it, since the accepted inquest might effectively secure him against a serious peril. For a long time during the 1200 s and 1300 s it shielded him from the "question," — the torture — introduced into the "aprise," and that would make it a likely course for him to take. In effect, the only reason for the introduction of torture into the "aprise" was that it was often essential to have the confession of the accused in addition to the other proofs obtained before capital punishment could be inflicted; on the other hand, whatever testimony might have been obtained, the accepted inquest permitted the judge, if he was convinced, to pronounce the full sentence. The judge, on his side, seeing his powers increased by this acceptance, naturally tried to obtain it even while the action was in progress. I have tried to make all this clear, with the aid of numerous texts, in my study upon "L'acceptation de l'enquête dans la procédure criminelle au Moyen Age." [2]

§ 7. **Detention pending Trial and Bail.** — In this old procedure, which, though restricted in scope, was logical, detention pending trial played an important part. The arrest was styled the "prise," [3] but it was attended by the liberation on bail or "récréance," [4] and from this point of view the old customary law was liberal enough. The "Livre de Jostice et de Plet," treating of bail, commences as follows: "When a man is imprisoned or any chattel is held, the method of giving back or liberating on bail. — This proclamation is made for the purpose of preventing oppression by the lords and felonies by those who seize the goods of others." [5]

The maxim that liberation on bail is not granted when a crime for which the penalty is the loss of life or limb is concerned is, however, found in books on customary law of diverse origin.[6]

[1] "Coutumes de Beauvoisis," *Salmon's* edition, Nos. 1186, 1235–1238, 1244.

[2] "Revue générale du droit, de la législation et de la jurisprudence" (1888).

[3] *Beaumanoir*, ch. LII, "des Prises."

[4] "Récréance" means causing the person arrested to give security to again put himself at the disposal of his captor on a specified day, or at any time on the summons of the "Seigneur" who caused his arrest. *Beaumanoir*, LIII, 2 (Salmon No. 1583): "If any one desire to have bail ('récréance') in any matter, he should give sureties for the bail. For according to the custom of the secular court, there is (can be) no bail without sureties."

[5] XIX, 26, § 1..

[6] "Etablissements de St. Louis," II, 5: "Bail should not be allowed in matters involving risk of loss of life or limb or where blood has been shed.

In such cases the security given by a surety or bail ("plege") was not considered to offer a sufficient safeguard. The personal sureties certainly bound themselves most rigorously "body for body, property for property," according to the old formula which was long kept up. But this was not pushed to its logical end. The punishment which the defaulting criminal had incurred was not inflicted on his bail. The latter was merely mulcted in pecuniary damages, which were, however, sometimes very heavy.[1]

It would nevertheless appear, from a mere consideration of the sources, that an evolution took place in this respect. Here is a noteworthy passage from the "Etablissements de St. Louis." "If it should happen that the person liberated on bail should flee, and should not appear at the term fixed for his appearance, the judge should then say to the sureties: You have bound yourselves that such and such a man shall appear before us on such and such a day (specifying these) and he was accused of such and such a great offense and he has fled. For this reason I will that you be proved and sentenced to suffer whatever punishment the fugitive would have suffered. Sire, they say, do not do this, because in becoming bail for our friend, we but did our duty. And therefore the sureties may be fined a hundred sous and a 'denier' and released. And this fine is called 'Relief d'home,' and the judge should therefore take great care not to take bail for any who are accused of such grave offenses as murder or treason, because such sureties could not suffer any other fine than that we have mentioned."[2]

Ibid. II, 7. "In the secular court bail has no place in adjudicated matters, nor in cases of murder, treason, rape, blows delivered on a pregnant woman to cause abortion, ambush on roads, robbery, larceny, fire-raising." *Cf. ibid.* I, 104. *Beaumanoir*, LIII, 2 (Salmon, No. 1583): "Release on bail should be allowed in all cases of arrest except those for crime or where there is suspicion of crime involving possible loss of life or limb, unless the fact is known or proved." "Livre de J. et P." XIX, 26, § 6: "But if I am arrested for a matter involving corporal punishment is bail or restoration of goods proper should any one complain against me? Neither bail nor restitution is proper." *Cf.* "Compilatio de Usibus Andegaviæ," § 47. "Très-ancienne coutume de Bretagne," ch. XCVII, *Bourdot de Richebourg*.

[1] *Beaumanoir*, XLIII, 24 (Salmon, No. 1332): "A surety cannot lose his life for becoming bail, although he may have pledged himself body for body for any one held for serious case of crime to return and stand trial on a certain day and if he who is bailed should flee; in such a case the surety is at the mercy of the 'Seigneur' when he has lost all his property." The surety is usually sentenced to a fine of a hundred sous.

[2] "Etablissements de St. Louis," I, 104. The "Livre de Droiz," § 763, is to the same effect: "It is commonly held that if any one become bail to the court for a man who is held for a crime in general terms and without declaring or specifying that he undertakes that the man shall submit to a specified punishment, the court cannot, under the customary law, impose a penalty of more than a hundred sous. If any one become bail

From another point of view there were good reasons why a lord should not readily liberate on bail a person accused of a crime; in doing so he ran a great personal risk. "If the man allow bail in the case of a crime where he is not entitled to do so he puts himself in two dangers, and the first is a greater peril than the other; for if he who was bailed departs without returning on the day when he ought to stand law, he who allowed the bail loses his justice, it being no excuse that he took sureties. For the sureties cannot be sentenced to death on account of their becoming bail: but the malefactor could have been if he had not been allowed bail. The second peril to the man when he allows bail in a case where he should not do so is that if the count knows that he has unduly allowed bail or he should find the accused when he wishes him he can arrest him without giving court or jurisdiction to him who allowed the bail. In this case, however, the latter does not lose his justice, but he loses the jurisdiction of and the vengeance for the offense. And he can allow the bail in such a way as to lose his justice although it is customary to allow such bail where he makes the bail against the prohibition of the lord, for his disobedience in allowing injudicious bail ("fole récréance") is interpreted as an injury to his justice."[1]

But the rule under which liberation on bail was not allowed in cases of crime involving "loss of life or limb" has its exceptions. First of all, on the occurrence of a crime, an accusation might be brought by the party interested, when, as we know, the procedure most frequently began directly by an *appeal*, or challenge to the judicial duel.[2] In such a case, detention pending trial was the rule; but, strange as it may appear, this was applied to the accuser as well as to the accused.[3] This is explained, first, by the general character of the accusatory procedure, the object of

for a man held on a criminal charge 'body for body, and property for property,' as it is expressed, it is to be understood that as to his body he shall suffer the same punishment as he (the person bailed) would and as to property the same civil punishment. And many are able to discover in this reasonings to the contrary." *Cf. Beaumanoir*, LVIII, 18 (Salmon, No. 1658). See *M. Tanon*, "Registre criminel, de la justice de Saint Martin des Champs au XIVe siècle," preface, pp. lxxx, lxxxi.

[1] *Beaumanoir*, LVIII, 18 (Salmon, No. 1658).

[2] *Beaumanoir*, LXI, 2 (Salmon, No. 1710).

[3] *Beaumanoir*, LIII, 4 (Salmon, No. 1585); "Etablissements de St. Louis," I, 104; "Somma de Legibus Normaniæ," II, 2, § 2: "Primo autem capiendum est vuadium defensoris, et post ea vuadium appellatoris, et de lege deducenda plegios debent tradere, *uterque tamen in prisonià ducis mancipandus est.*" "Très-ancienne coutume de Bretagne," ch. 104: "And if there be an accuser, he should be imprisoned as well as the other, for both parties should be punished alike."

which is to maintain an absolute equality between both parties.[1] Another explanation is, that the accuser, should he get the worst of the combat, forfeited his life and his property.[2] The duel was like a two-edged sword, which was bound to strike one or other of the combatants. This rule of mutual imprisonment lasted, in France, as late as the accusation by formal party.[3] It was not confined to the cases where the duel was the method of proof chosen or enjoined by the customary law. But that particular case had one distinctive feature. If wager of battle had been given, even where the most serious crimes were in issue, both parties might be set at liberty on sufficient bail, for it was very essential that the adversaries should prepare themselves for the combat. "In case of crime this liberation on bail shall be made but in one case,— when wager of battle is given in serious cases by one party against the other; in such a case, if the parties bind themselves by sufficient sureties ('pleges') that they will return on the day fixed, liberty on bail shall be accorded to them, so that they may be able to prepare themselves for proceeding as the case requires." [4] The "Grand Coutumier de Normandie" gives the same solution in a somewhat different form. After saying that both accuser and accused must be imprisoned, it adds that they may be confided to the care of trustworthy persons, whom it calls the living prison ("vifve prison").[5] But here again the treatment of both adversaries must be equal. Liberty on bail cannot be granted to one party without at the same time granting it to the other. The "Etablissements de St. Louis," after saying that "the judge shall hold the persons of both in equal imprisonment, if one is not

[1] This sense of equality caused the imprisonment of both parties in the feudal appeal. Under the Roman system of "judicia publica" it had led to the abolition of detention pending trial. See *Geib*, "Die Römische Criminalprozess bis auf Justinian," part 2.

[2] *Beaumanoir*, LXI, 11 (Salmon, No. 1718): "He who is defeated loses his life and whatever he possesses of whatever lord he hold it." See "Très-ancienne coutume de Bretagne," ch. 104, quoted above, and ch. 96. "For if it is decided that the accuser has not made out his case he shall be convicted of his accusation, and shall be punished in the same measure as the other would have been if he had been found guilty."

[3] As regards Germany compare the "Carolina," Art. 12 *et seq.*

[4] *Beaumanoir*, LIII, 4 (Salmon, No. 1585), *cf.* LVIII, 18; (Salmon, No. 1658).

[5] "Somma," II, 2, § 2: "Per justiciarium tamen his quod necesse fuerit ad duellum debet inveniri, et utrumque, si voluerit *vive prisonie* poterit committere dum tamen bonos de ipsis habuerit, qui eos ita fideliter cutodiant, quod vivos vel mortuos ad diem duelli terminatam reddant, et ad duelli deductionem habeant preparatos." And both may be bailed "en vifve prison" if they so wish, provided they are faithfully delivered to good guardians who will give them up dead or alive on the day appointed for the battle, armed for the fight if they are alive."

more troublesome than the other," calls him a "fole justice" who shall allow one of them to be set free on bail, while the other is held.[1]

In this respect the powers of the judges were at first very restricted; but they continued to expand. The "Livre de Jostice et de Plet" allows the judge a wide latitude: "If it is asked whether restoration (of goods) or liberation on bail is proper where two are arrested on account of an offense of which one of them accuses the other, the answer is that the matter is in the judge's discretion. And if it is asked whether one of them may be liberated on bail and the other held, the answer is, no; no advantages can be given to one more than to the other, nor can one be relieved more than the other."[2] This discretionary power was bound to have a greater development in the royal jurisdictions than elsewhere in the absence of the feudal responsibilities.

Another situation might present itself besides that of an accusation by formal party. The lord could, as we have said, *apprehend* ("prendre") and imprison the person suspected of crime, and, in order to give rise to accusations, make his arrest public at three assizes, or after such other delay as the customary law provided. This imprisonment was limited to a year and a day, for, after the lapse of that time, no accusation was any longer possible. But could the imprisonment be terminated sooner? The writers on customary law generally admit that at the expiration of the periods for publication, the accused had the right to demand to be set at liberty on furnishing bail.[3] Some, it is true, maintain that the detention should continue.[4] Still others hold that the final *release* ("delivrance") should take place immediately after the expiration of the delays.[5]

A last hypothesis presents itself. The person *arrested* ("pris") by the lord may consent to submit to the inquest by the country. Ought he then to be liberated on bail? That is probable; cer-

[1] I, 104; *cf. Beaumanoir*, LIII, 4 (Salmon, No. 1585).

[2] XIX, 26, § 9.

[3] "Compilatio de Usibus Andegaviæ," § 24; "Livre de J. et P." XIX, 26, § 12. Ordinance of 1315: "The suspicion may be so great and notorious that the suspected person, against whom the denunciation shall be framed, ought to be detained in the abode of his seigneur and there remain a space of forty (days) or two or three at the most, and if that terminate without any one accusing him of the deed, he shall be bailed ('ostagez')." (Ord. I, p. 358.)

[4] *Jean d'Ibelin*, ch. LXXXV.

[5] See *Beaumanoir*, LVIII, 20 (Salmon, No. 1660); XXX, 90 (Salmon, No. 917).

tain texts seem to hold the opinion that liberty is a matter of right when there is no formal party: "If the judge imputes to me that I have been concerned in the deed done, for which death is the penalty, and no one claim aught of me save himself, by right he shall not seize my property, but my body; but in justice he shall liberate it on bail, body for body." [1]

The net result of what we have stated is that liberty on bail was a matter of right except where an offense had been committed which might entail the loss of life or limb. Of all this old theory, although it is mainly allied with the feudal system and the judicial duel, two ideas continued to prevail in the following period. These are, first, that bail ought to be allowed in the case of minor offenses, and, second, that it ought to be refused in the case of serious crimes.

§ 8. **Procedure by Contumacy.** — The old law came to recognize a procedure of contumacy, which constitutes a point of departure for our legal system so far as that relates to the doctrine of default, although the procedure has completely changed its aspect in the course of its successive transformations. The old criminal procedure, in common with all formal procedures, admitted of no judgment by default. An accuser and an accused must be present from the beginning to the end of the action. A means was found, however, of insuring that justice should take its course despite all resistance on the part of the recalcitrant. As in the Germanic practice, the procedure by contumacy resulted, not in a condemnation for the act struck at by the prosecution, but in the outlawry of the person guilty of contumacy. Every safeguard given by the law was withdrawn from the person who refused to submit to the law. That was only logical. The veritable flood of summonses and delays connected with the procedure vary somewhat according to the different customs, but this variation does not prevent the ascertainment of its main features.

The procedure of contumacy was called "*forbannissement*" — banishment, or outlawry. The sentence of "forbannissement" could only be pronounced at the assizes, and the procedure could only be followed for serious offenses, which we shall find called later on "le grand criminel." [2] The ancient "Coutume de Nor-

[1] "Livre de J. et P." XIX, 26, § 5.

[2] "Livre de J. et P." XIX, 37, § 4: "It is asked for striking a man, or for insult or drawing blood or causing bloodless wounds, causing contusions without death or mutilation and he flee, if he ought to be banished? And the answer is, No. — § 5. Then it is asked if he be charged with murder, or theft, or rape, or homicide, or dismemberment, or if he have taken from the other by force, or if he do not appear to make his peace and if he

mandie" probably exhibits its purest type. Three summonses to three successive assizes are necessary: "*Criminalem autem dicimus actionem de qua convictus aliquis membris vel corpore condemnatur. Si quis autem crimen, quo secutus est, confessus fuerit in publico, sui judicium protulit damnamenti. Diffugiens autem hujusmodi criminosus ad tres primas assisias contumax debet vocari. Est autem assisia militum et virorum certo loco et certo termino XL dierum spacium continente, per quos de auditu in curia judicium et justitia debet exhiberi. Ad quartam autem recitatis ejus criminibus et subterfugus facto ab his judicio debet forbanizari publicè sub hac forma: Nos forbanizamus Petrum propter mortem Luce, quem occidit, ex potestate ducis; ità quod si quis eum post elapsum hujus assisiæ invenerit ipsum vivum vel mortuum reddat justiciario, vel si non poterit clamorem patriæ qui dicitur harou clamosis vocibus debet excitare.*"[1] This is all quite clear; — the outlawry and the delays, consisting of four periods each of an assize. These four periods will always be found, and the last term will always be of an assize or forty-day duration ("quarantaine"). "Be it known that before a man shall be outlawed, he shall be caused to be summoned for three specified days, eight days apart, and if he do not appear within (that time) his nearest relatives shall be sent for and told to have him on a day fixed. And if he clear himself by proper excuses he shall be heard; if not, the space of forty days shall be allowed to elapse from that time, and if within that time he do not appear he shall be banished."[2]

According to the "Etablissements de St. Louis" the fugitive is summoned "that he appear within seven days and seven nights to acknowledge or defend, and he shall be caused to be summoned in open market-place . . . shall be caused to be summoned anew for judgment that he appear within fifteen days and fifteen nights . . . then within forty days and forty nights, and if he do not appear then he shall be caused to be banished in open market-place."[3] According to Beaumanoir there were different periods of delay according to whether a peasant or a gentleman was concerned: "If he is a vassal he shall be summoned by three fortnights, at the third fortnight to the provostship. And if he do not appear within the three fortnights, at the third fortnight it shall be proclaimed that he appear at the first assize thereafter . . . and if he do not appear at that assize he shall be banished."[4]

flee, should he then be banished? And the answer is, Yes; for such things involve corporal punishment and peril of his eternal salvation."

[1] "Somma," I, 23, §§ 5, 6.

[2] XIX, 37, § 9.

[3] I, 26.

[4] LX, 5 (Salmon, No. 1695).

For the gentleman there were three provostship summonses and then three assize summonses; it seems as though there were here two systems superposed: "If he be a gentleman he shall be summoned to appear in law of the sovereign by three fortnights to the provostship; and if he do not appear he shall be summoned for three consecutive assizes thereafter, between which assizes shall elapse the space of at least forty days, and if he do not appear within the last assize, he shall be banished."[1]

This procedure of contumacy could be followed whether there was a party plaintiff, or merely *suspicion* and action by the lord justiciar. In either case there was disobedience of the seigniorial summons.

The person banished was really without the law; his murder went unpunished, and all were forbidden to shelter him: "When a man is banished from the court by any of the count's men no other man may or shall shelter him, but shall seize him if he find him upon his land, and shall acquaint the count that he holds such outlaw . . . whoever shelters him knowing of the banishment, his house shall be torn down and the penalty is in the discretion of the court according to what he is worth, and also punishment of imprisonment."[2] Moreover, these terrible threats were not the only means of constraint employed to bring about the appearance of the person accused of contumacy. His property was confiscated by virtue of his outlawry,[3] and that was sequestrated by the lord from the beginning of the procedure, namely, from the first default.[4]

The most distinctive feature of this form of process was that it resulted in making, not a condemned person, but an "outlaw." It soon lost this characteristic. Resistance to the law was construed as a kind of confession; hence the outlaw was looked upon as "attainted and convicted" of the crime, for which he ought to

[1] *Beaumanoir*, LX, 6 (Salmon, No. 1695); XXX, 99 (Salmon, No. 930).

[2] *Beaumanoir*, LXI, 21, 23 (Salmon, Nos. 1728, 1730). Banishment, however, was not and could not be decreed except from the territory subject to the jurisdiction of the lord justiciar (*Beaumanoir*, LXI, 22, Salmon, No. 1728); but Beaumanoir points out a curious procedure (LXI, 21, Salmon, No. 1728), the object of which was to extend its effect to the whole jurisdiction of the lord paramount.

[3] *Beaumanoir*, LX, 9 (Salmon, No. 1698).

[4] *Beaumanoir*, LXI, 10 (Salmon, No. 1717): "For fear of the risk consequent on delay the count shall set guards upon him whom he has summoned . . . and double daily until he appear to prevent his loss." "Livre de J. et P." XIX, 37, § 8: "In the first place he shall cause him to be summoned at his dwelling where he is expected to return . . . and if he do not appear his goods shall be seized and shall remain in the judge's possession." *Cf.* "Ancien coutumier de Picardie," LIV (p. 46).

suffer the usual punishment if he should be captured and given up to the lord. Beaumanoir and the "Livre de Jostice et de Plet" are the first to formulate this new idea.[1] From their time onwards the procedure by contumacy will always contain a combination of these two ideas of outlawry and condemnation for the deed under prosecution.

Was the outlawry, with its terrible consequences, final and irrevocable? When the outlaw was seized, or when he presented himself willing to purge his contumacy, as it was later phrased, could he demand to be tried confrontatively? The logical answer was, No. Originally, outlawry, being the punishment of the disobedience and not of the crime, was final, or at least could not be recalled except by him who had decreed it. The recall was a discretionary decision, not the result of any method of recourse.[2] This recall involved the exercise of a kind of right of the crown, as in the enfranchisement of a serf, and to grant it the baron required the assent of the superior suzerain.[3] Moreover, the *letters of recall* might nullify all the consequences of the outlawry and contain a complete pardon, or they might merely open up the possibility of a new judgment. This is very clearly illustrated by Beaumanoir: "If the outlaw be recalled by the sovereign for any cause of pity, as I have said above, he shall have everything belonging to him which was held on account of the suspicion of the offense, whether in the hands of the court or of others, for he who is acquitted in the court of the sovereign cannot be condemned in the court of the subject. But it is otherwise if the count recall his outlawry on petition or on entreaty or in his discretion for cause of pity, for in such recalls the subject shall not give up what he holds of the out-

[1] *Beaumanoir*, LX, 9 (Salmon, No. 1675): "Whoever is accused of any of the aforesaid matters and it happen that by the custom of the county he is outlawed, and he is rearrested after the outlawry, he has forfeited his life and effects and is judged as if he had notoriously done the deed of which he was accused." *Ibid.*, XXX, 12 (Salmon, Nos. 834, 835): "He should be judged according to the misdeed for which he is outlawed." "Livre de J. et P." XIX, 37, § 7: "And if he is arrested soon after the outlawry he is condemned for the deed." "Ancien coutumier de Picardie (Anc. cout de Ponthieu et Vimeu, XIV)," p. 131: "If he defaults he ought to be convicted of the crime of which he is accused."

[2] *Beaumanoir*, LXI, 24 (Salmon, No. 1731): "If the count withdraw his outlawry from any reason of mercy; if, for instance, he has heard that he who was outlawed, was, at the time when he was accused and outlawed, in foreign lands or on a pilgrimage, and it is evident that he was ignorant of the accusation and of the outlawry . . . or if the count has since felt certain that he did not do the deed for which he was outlawed, it were a work of mercy to withdraw such manner of outlawry."

[3] *Beaumanoir*, LXI, 26 (Salmon, No. 1733): "The man who has caused any outlawry in his court on account of crime cannot for any reason withdraw it without the consent of the count."

law's on account of the offense if he does not purge himself of the offense by judgment, in the same way as if he was accused and freed himself from the accusation or submitted to inquest and was freed by the inquest; then, indeed, it would be proper that he should have his own in whosever hands it was." [1]

But akin to these principles another idea grew up. There was a tendency to allow the "outlaw-condemned" ("banni-condamné") to prove his good faith, and to attack judicially the sentence of outlawry. The "Livre de Jostice et de Plet" for this purpose provides a last delay of pardon: "Be it known that if any one remain in a state of outlawry for forty days he is outlawed merely; and if he appear within the next three assizes and make his excuses that he shall and will suffer law, he shall be allowed to do so. And if he do not appear within the three assizes he shall be condemned for the deed of which he is accused." [2] The "Etablissements de St. Louis," without fixing any period of delay, declares that if the outlaw appears and pleads his good faith "then the judge shall receive his oath on what he wishes to declare and he who desires to accuse him shall have his defense." [3] There are here the elements of a future development; but the primary idea is not destined to disappear for some time; and in the procedure for default which the Ordinance of 1670 will organize, we shall see pardoning decisions and methods of recourse concurrently in operation.

Such was our very old criminal procedure. In so far as it was logical in its imperfection, it embraced in reality two distinct elements. One of these belonged to the past and was very soon to disappear without leaving any traces; the other, on the contrary, contained the germs of new institutions, and we shall show how it changed its aspect to conform to the changing conditions.

[1] *Beaumanoir*, LXI, 25 (Salmon, No. 1732).

[2] XIX, 37, § 10; *cf.* "Ancien. cout. de Picardie," XCVIII (p. 88).

[3] "Etab." I, 26. Judging from a passage in the "Livre de Jostice et de Plet" it would appear that the effects of the outlawry could not be wiped out by lapse of time, XIX, 37, § 12; "Cefroi de la Chapele (says) that the bailiffs of Orléans caused a man to be outlawed on proclamation and report that he declared that he had killed a man. And he was summoned at his domicile by command of the king for the space of forty days, and neither appeared nor sent nor lodged a defense and for this he was outlawed and suffered the outlawry without appearing for fifty years, during which time the court did not summon him. At the end of that time he came to the bishop of Orléans and declared that he belonged to his jurisdiction, lying down and rising on his land, which was the case. The bishop had the power to withdraw this outlawry. And it was decided that he would not withdraw (it) because he had not come sooner to allege his privilege nor had the law required him, and he was given up to the bishop to whose jurisdiction he belonged. The bishop caused him to be tried and decided that he should be hanged."

CHAPTER II

THE ORIGIN OF THE INQUISITORIAL PROCEDURE AND ITS GROWTH DURING THE 1200s AND 1300s

§ 1. **Introductory.** — In the harsh and inadequate procedure which we have described, the pursuit of offenses was the affair of private individuals. It was only in rare instances that public authority could intervene in an efficacious manner; except in the case of capture in the act, all it could do was to seize the culprit and await the pleasure of the injured parties in bringing the accusation, or the culprit's consent to the inquest.

It was impossible for such a state of matters to last. We shall therefore see a regular official prosecution make its appearance in the 1200s and rapidly develop, simultaneously with the substitution of inquests for the old methods of proof. But before studying this movement in the works of our old writers, it is necessary to explain briefly what was the criminal procedure of the ecclesiastical courts. Its influence upon the transformations which we purpose to describe is undeniable. This is not due to the fact that the Church had created its own system of procedure in every detail. On the contrary, most of the different elements of which it made use it borrowed from secular institutions. It imbued these, however, with a new spirit and lost no time in substantially altering them. It is sometimes said that the inquisitorial procedure of ancient France is merely the result of a borrowing from the Church. That, as we shall make clear, is not precisely correct; but it is none the less true that the Church was the first authority which changed from the accusatory to the inquisitorial procedure. And having been the first to effect this evolution, it very naturally furnished a model to France and the neighboring nations which inspired a similar movement under the impulse of similar requirements.

§ 2. **The Ecclesiastical Criminal Procedure.** — The system of repression in force was manifestly inadequate. It was essential that an unfettered and effective official prosecution should be created, and the Canon law laid the foundation for this by instituting, at the end of the 1100s, the inquisitorial procedure, the "processus per inquisitionem."

The Canon law had originally recognized only the accusatory system in criminal matters, influenced in this respect both by the Roman law and by Germanic custom. In the 800s, however, it made a step forward. When, by reason of a crime committed, any one had been pointed out as suspected by public opinion, and this "mala fama" or "infamia" was established by the judge, the Canon law had admitted that this gave a certain right of action against the "infamatus." This did not allow the judge to bring witnesses against him and condemn him if he should be convicted, but the accused was obliged to exculpate himself from the crime imputed to him. This exculpation was effected, according to the circumstances of the case, by the oath of the "infamatus" supported by compurgators, "co-swearers" ("purgatio canonica"), or by ordeals ("purgatio vulgaris"). If he refused, or failed, he could be condemned as convicted of the offense charged against him.[1] These methods of proof the Canon law had borrowed from the Germanic customs, although it may at first have spontaneously adopted a similar method, allowing, in certain cases, a suspected person to exculpate himself by his own oath, but without "co-swearers."[2] In the procedure introduced in the 800 s, if the "infamatus" refused to exculpate himself, or failed in the "purgatio," he was considered convicted of the crime and could be condemned accordingly. Out of this procedure grew, by evolution, the inquisitorial procedure.[3]

At least as early as the 800s the Canon law had also opened another way. It had permitted notorious ("notoria") crimes to be prosecuted and condemnation pronounced by the judge without the necessity of an accuser; whence the maxim "notoria

[1] C. II, qu. 5; X, "de purgatione canonica," V, 34; X, "De purgatione vulgari," v. 35.

[2] Chaps. V, VI, VIII, IX, C. III, qu. 5. *Hildebrand*, "Die purgatio canonica et vulgaris," 1841; *Richter-Dove*, "Lehrbuch des deutschen Kirchenrechts," § 226; *Löning*, "Geschichte des deutschen Kirchenrechts," II, pp. 496, 503.

[3] *Hincmar de Reims*, "De presbyteris criminosis," c. XVI.

accusatore non indigent." But this rule was not of very much practical use on account of the difficulty which existed in determining what constituted "notorium."[1]

The Canon law did not yet admit of an official prosecution properly so called; and it gave as the chief reason for this that the judge (a different person as prosecutor was not thought of) would be at once judge and accuser.[2] This was the doctrine of Yves de Chartres (end of the 1000s and beginning of the 1100s);[3] and it was also that of Gratian (first half of the 1100s).[4] It is that taught by Rolandus, the future pope Alexander III, about 1150,[5] and Bernard of Pavia in his "Summa decretalium," written between 1191 and 1198.[6] But in the final years of the 1300s a new form of criminal action made its appearance, the "processus per inquisitionem," which is really an official prosecution by the judge.

This procedure is distinguished from the earlier form of which I have spoken and in which the "infamatus" was compelled to exculpate himself. The difference is clearly shown by the fact that the judge cannot proceed except upon the "infamia precedens"; but, on that being established, he can summon or arrest the accused, bring witnesses against him, and condemn him if proof of his guilt is furnished by this means. Other striking features corroborate this view.

But it is apparent that this change was not brought about by custom, but by legislation. It was introduced by the decretals of Pope Innocent III. The first to come under notice is of date 1198.[7] Then a series is found in rapid succession, in 1199,[8] 1206,[9] 1212.[10] At last, in 1215, the fourth Lateran council solemnly confirms the principle.[11]

[1] Cc. 15–17, C II, qu. 1.

[2] *Panormitanus* upon c. 7 X, "de accusat." V. 1, No. 7: "Judex non est loco partis . . . non fungitur duplici officio, quia aliquis debet esse accusator, alius judex."

[3] *Yves de Chartres*, Ep. CXIX, CVIII, CCVI.

[4] Dictum upon c. r. C. IV, qu. 4.

[5] "Summa magistri Rolandi," *Thaner* edition.

[6] In the "Compilatio prima decretalium" of *Bernard of Pavia* the title devoted to criminal prosecutions bears only the heading "De accusationibus," while the corresponding title in the Decretals of Gregory IX (V. 1) is entitled "De accusationibus, inquisitionibus et denunciationibus." The doctrine contained in the "Summa decretalium" corresponds to that of the cited title of the "Compilatio prima."

[7] c. un. X. "Ut ecclesiæ vel beneficia sine diminutione conferantur," III, 12.

[8] c. 10 X, "de purg. can.," V, 34; cc. 31, 32 X. "de simonia," V. 3.

[9] c. 17 X, "de accus.," V, I.

[10] c. 21 X, "de accus." V, 1.

[11] c. 24 X, "de accus." V, 1.

[For the text of these decretals, and their bearing on the same movement as later influencing English law, see *Wigmore*, "Treatise on the System of Evidence," § 2250 ("History of the Privilege against Self-crimination"). — TRANS.]

At the same time, and even in the same texts, the theory was put forward that it was essential to discard the standard objection that the judge would become judge and party too. It was got rid of in two ways. In the first place, texts of Holy Scripture were invoked, which had nothing to do with the question except as showing that God or His prophet spontaneously intervened to inquire into human excesses.[1] Symbolical interpretation applied this power to the ecclesiastical judge. On the other hand, we have seen that the "inquisitio" could not proceed unless the "infamia" had in the first place been established against the "inquisitus;" it was said that as this was equivalent to an accusation brought from without, and in a manner personifying this establishment, it took the place of an accuser. This theory was destined to become classic.[2]

It was not, as has often been said, the struggle against the heretics which led to the introduction of this official prosecution. A special application of it was undoubtedly made to heresy in the "inquisitio hæretica pravitatis" (as to which I shall have something to say later), that is, the right to proceed "per inquisitionem" against heretics, delegated to certain special commissioners, usually selected from among the Dominicans or the Franciscans. The earliest case of inquisition thus delegated (of which we know) took place in 1227. The decretals which were the basis of the procedure "per inquisitionem" are sometimes directed against heresy among the clerks, but most frequently merely against clerical abuses. It was for the repression of these abuses generally that the papacy felt the need of a more strenuous mode of prosecution.

The evolution of the "inquisitio" from the "infamia," leading to the obligatory "purgatio," is attested by other characteristics than the persistence of this essential condition, the preliminary establishment of this "infamia." In the first place, if the "inquisitio" did not lead to a conclusive result, if it did not furnish sufficient evidence against the accused, he could be compelled to exculpate himself by the "purgatio canonica"; this was a late return to the old system.[3]

[1] cc. 30 X, "de simonia," V, 3; 17, 24 X, "de accus." V. 1.

[2] *Panormitanus* upon C. 2. X, "de accus." No. 7: "Nota quod in inquisitione judex non tenet hanc partis, sed infamia est loco accusatores seu denunciatoris"; and upon C. 17 X, "deacons," No. 6: "De occultis non fit inquisitio ubi non processit infamia quia defuit veras et fictas accusator."

[3] *Hostiensis*, "Summa," Lyons edition, 1517, p. 409: "Si omnes testes dicunt cum (inquisitum) innocentum non suspenditur non purgatione oneratur infamia nisi ad tollendam facti." But see, as to the "accusatio," C. 6 X, of "purg. can." V. 34.

On the other hand, one of the most formal and, at the same time, most odious features of the procedure "per inquisitionem" is that the "inquisitus" was not only compelled to reply to the interrogatories of the judge, but he must also reply on the faith of his oath, after having taken oath to tell the whole truth.[1] This rule goes back to the earliest days of the procedure "per inquisitionem." It appears to be quite contrary to the original principles of the Canon law, holding that nobody in "forum externum" should be compelled to incriminate himself. But a reply to this objection was looked for in the earlier system upon which the "inquisitio" was grafted. According to that system the "infamatus" was obliged not only to exculpate himself by his oath, but also to furnish "co-swearers"; in the "inquisitio" only his own oath was required, and this was a lesser requirement. This justification was put forward by the future Innocent IV in very precise terms, and it became classic.[2] It was, however, merely a sophism. The formal method of the "purgatio canonica" and the replies to dexterous and imperative interrogatories were very different things.

The Canon law, however, ameliorated one characteristic of the procedure "per inquisitionem" which had operated unfavorably to the accused. Its construction of it was that, even if a conviction were obtained, the heavier punishments which a successful "accusatio" would have involved could not be inflicted in an "inquisitio," but only the lesser punishments. Thus, when the prosecution was against a clerk — as at first was always the case — and he had been found guilty and incapable of continuing in his ministry, he might be deposed, deprived of office ("ab officio"), but not degraded.[3] It must, however, be added that if the confession of

[1] *Esmein*, "Le serment des accusés dans le droit canonique," in the Bibliothèque de l'Ecole des Hautes Etudes (Mélanges), Vol. VII, 1896, p. 257 *et seq.*

[For the bearing of this on English legal history, see *Wigmore*, "Treatise on the System of Evidence," § 1815 *et seq.* — TRANS.]

[2] "Commentaria Innocentii quarti pontificis maximi super libros decretalium," Frankfort edition, 1570, p. 246, upon c. 2 X, "de confessis," II, 18: "Quod probo sic. Potest ei indici purgatio ubi per sacramentum suum et purgatorium potest negare se crimen commisisse. Multo fortius antequam indicatur purgatio, potest ab eo quærere an crimen commiserit. Sed tamen non præcisa cogam eum respondere, sicut nec præcisa cogitur se purgare; sed, si non responderit sicut si se non purgaverit suspendetur, vel alias procedetur contra eum: quia videtur vanum purgare de simplia verbo qui se purgare debet multorum juramento." *Cf. Panormitanus*, upon c. 2 X, "de confessis," Nos. 16, 19.

[3] c. 24 X, "de accus.": "Criminalis accusatio sed capitis deminutionem, id est, degradationem intenditur. Sed cum super excessibus suis quidam fuerit infamatus, ita ut clamor ascendat qui diutius sine scandalo tolerari non potest, absque dubitationis scrupulo ad inquirendum et puriendum ejus excessus procedatur, si fuerit gravis excessus, etsi non

the accused was supported by the testimony furnished in the "inquisitio," the doctors admitted, as in the case of "notorium," that the condemnation to the full punishment could be pronounced.

The procedure "per inquisitionem," as it came to be described, met with very natural resistance in other directions. Texts there are which show us the "infamati" whom the judge wished to prosecute according to this method, invoking the earlier law and essaying to exculpate themselves by the "purgatio canonica." Others show them invoking the custom followed under the secular law and demanding that the judge should continue to hold them prisoners and fix a term within which accusers, if any, should be invited to present themselves, liberation or the "purgatio" to follow in the event of no such appearance.[1] None of these objections was allowed to prevail.

The procedure "per inquisitionem" had a special form and a somewhat different application. This was the "inquisitio generalis," otherwise called "preparatoria" or "ordinaria." Its purpose was, not to establish the "infamia" of a single specified person, but it was applied to a society or community of people which it compelled to disclose whether it had in its midst any individuals defamed by reason of offenses or misdemeanors; it called for informations and revelations. It was especially serviceable in the work of inspection and reformation of monasteries. It had a peculiar and very ancient origin.

Under the Carlovingian monarchy an actual jury of denunciation, "jury de dénonciation," is seen to be in operation. It appears both in the secular courts, where the texts show it first from the beginning of the 800s, and in the ecclesiastical courts. There it is grafted upon older institutions (which probably served the party to attain the same end), namely, the diocesan synod and the bishop's "visitatio." Considering only the ecclesiastical aspect, we have precise information on the subject from Reginon, who

degradetur ab ordine ab administratione tamen amoveatur omnino." As to the effect of the supplementary confession, see the Decretalists upon the above-cited chapter 24.

[1] *Gofodus*, "Summa decretalium de accus." Lyons edition, 1519, p. 199: "Quid si superior velit inquirere, reum autem dicat! Nolo ut inquiras sed profigas terminum accusare volentibus et, accusatore deficiente paratus sum me purgare. Nunquid audietur reus an judex? Videtur quod reus quia quod reus petit ordinarium est, quod diut judex extraordinarium et judex potius ordinario quam extraordinario jure precedere debet. Puto potius inquirendum quia purgatio sequitur inquisitionem." *Cf. Hostentius*, "Summa, de inquis." Lyons edition, 1517, p. 408; *Durantis*, "Speculum," p. 33.

wrote in the first third of the 900 s,[1] and Burchard de Worms, who wrote in the first third of the 1000 s.[2] The ecclesiastical judge, the bishop, in his visits to the places where his jurisdiction lay, convoked all the members of the clergy and also the faithful. From among the latter he chose a certain number of men and made them swear to denounce those whom they knew to be guilty of offenses or certain named public trespasses; these were the "juratores synodi." Those whom they denounced were under the necessity of exculpating themselves, according to the nature of the case, by the "purgatio canonica" or by the "purgatio vulgaris" on pain of being convicted.

This institution never disappeared from the ecclesiastical organization, although the performance of its duties was often suspended in the midst of feudal disorder. The fourth Lateran council plainly had it in view for the denunciation of heretics.[3] Other texts show the old procedure discharging its duties anew in the "visitationes" of the bishop or the archbishop.[4]

The effect of these obligatory denunciations in the olden days had been to force the denounced parties to the "purgatio canonica" or "vulgaris," but when the procedure "per inquisitionem" was once established these naturally gave place to it. The judge who had made the "visitatio," in a parish or in a monastery, and had admitted testimony for the persecution, could proceed against the accused by hearing witnesses against him, who might be either those who had testified in the "inquisitio generalis," or new witnesses. The change is well shown by the description given by Durantis of the "inquisitio generalis." He puts it forward as the natural instrument for the use of the bishop in his "visitatio," when he "inquires of the clerks as to the laymen, and of the laymen as to the clerks and laymen"; much the same thing is seen in Regino's book as regards the 900 s. Without speaking of "juratores synodi," Durantis also says that the bishop would do well "secrete cum aliquibus de parochia fide dignis inquirere."[5] We have, besides this, direct proof of the evolution in the "Registre de

[1] "Libri duo de synodalibus causis," *Wasserschlaben* edition.

[2] "Burchardi Wortmatencis ecclesiæ episcopi decretorum libri vigorati," Migna Patrol. lat. t. CXL, p. 536 *et seq.* The interrogatories, eighty-eight in number, will be found in Book I, c. 90–95.

[3] C. 9 X, "de hæret." V. 7; c. 29 X, "de accus." V. 1.

[4] A very close application, which will hereinafter be made use of, is furnished by the "Registre de l'officialité de Cerisy" (1314–1457), published by *M. G. Dupont.*

[5] *Durantis*, "Speculum," Book III, part 1, "de inquisitionibus," § 3, Frankfort edition, 1592, p. 30: c. 1, § 4, VI, "de cons." III, 20; *Panormitanus* upon c. 7 X, "de test. cogend," II, 21, No. 5.

l'officialité de Cerisy."[1] In the 1300s the official of the abbey, who had succeeded to the jurisdiction of the bishop within a certain radius, still made his "visitationes" in the old way, with the convocation of the faithful and the procedure of denunciation by the "testes synodales"; this was called "Inquisitio," "Inquisitio generalis," "Inquester," "Informatio."[2] According to the earliest accounts the effect of the synodic denunciations was merely to submit the denounced persons to the "purgatio canonica."[3] But, starting from the year 1320, examples of the "purgatio" are no longer to be found. The "inquisitio generalis," as a consequence of numerous decisions, then always gives place to the "inquisitio specialis" against the denounced person, the synodic denunciation being equivalent to an "informatio." But these applications, showing the affiliation, are, generally speaking, rare and exceptional after the 1200s. The "inquisitio generalis," which is very frequently used and practised, and which has its roots in the domiciliary visits to the monasteries, is directed against regular and secular societies; it consists in "inquirere de capite et de membris."[4]

The "inquisitio" led to the "denunciatio," the charge by the judge upon the denunciation of a private individual. The "denunciatio" had no doubt been mentioned at an earlier date; even Gratian alludes to it in his exposition of criminal procedure;[5] but he appears to have used the term as synonymous with "accusatio." Even at a very early date a procedure was known in the Canon law which survived and was expounded by the Decretalists according to the traditionary law upon C. 13 X, "de judiciis." This was called "denunciatio evangelica" or "caritativa," because it was based upon certain passages of scripture (Math. xviii, 15–17). It was, to all intents and purposes, a procedure of repression, originating in the denunciation of one Christian against another. This might have resulted in a real mode of criminal procedure and it looks as if the old-time doctors had made attempts in that direction; but their efforts were fruitless, and the "denunciatio evangelica" was ultimately considered as of no further

[1] "Le registre de l'officialité de Cerisy" (1314–1457), published by *M. Gustave Dupont* (extracted from the "Mémoires de la Societé des Antiquaires de Normandie").

[2] "Registre de Cerisy," Nos. 25, 26, 73, 96, 138; "inquisita," 110, 121; "Inquisitio loco visitationis," 43; "Informare," 215.

[3] "Registre de Cerisy," Nos. 5b, 20a, 25e, f, 84d.

[4] *Durantis*, "Speculum, de inquis." §§ 2, 3, p. 30.

[5] c. 47, C. II, qu. 7, and Dictum upon c. 20 C. II. qu. 1; *Hostiensis*, "Summa," p. 406; *Panormitanus* upon c. 13 X, "de jud." II, 1, No. 45.

efficacy than to allow of the application of the "censuræ" or "pœnæ medicinales" and not of that of real and personal punishments, "pœnæ vindicativæ." It was a means of discipline, not of criminal repression.

Once the "inquisitio" was established, however, the judge, instead of proceeding of his own accord, "ex mero officio," could proceed with the inquest, "inquirere," upon the denunciation of a private individual. This was at first done as a matter of fact, but by and by it came to be done as a matter of law. The person who formally made the denunciation was naturally one who was interested in the prosecution; he was even one who could have brought an "accusatio." This he did not do, preferring to set in motion the "inquisitio" of the judge by means of a denunciation; but the fact remained that it was in his interest that the action was brought. Doctrinally he was called the "promovens inquisitionem," and this "inquisitio cum promovente" was governed by special rules which ascribed to the denunciator an active part; so much so as at first to tend to assimilate this particular application of the inquisition to the "accusatio." Chief among these rules are the following.

We have said above that the "inquisitus" was obliged to take the oath "de veritate dicenda"; but this was originally imposed upon him only when the judge pursued "ex mero officio," not when there was a "promovens," "sed ibi adversarius habet probare ea qua denunciavit." But this distinction was subsequently done away with, and the taking of the oath was enjoined in both cases. This was only logical, seeing that in the procedure of "accusatio" it was imposed even upon the accused.[1] In the second place, when there was a "promovens," the rule was that the "informatio" must first of all be established by formal proofs, which it was for the "promovens" to furnish. It will be seen later on that when the judge prosecuted "ex mero officio" the same necessity did not arise. But in the former case it resulted in the accused being allowed not only to dispute these proofs, but also to meet them with contrary proofs, in establishing his "bona fama" by witnesses.[2]

But doubts were raised as to the application of the rules of the "accusatio" in regard to one main point. The unsuccessful accuser could be condemned, as calumnious, to the punishment of retaliation, that is, to the punishment which he had claimed for

[1] c. 18 X, "de accus." V. 1. *Panormitanus* upon c. 16, *ibid.* No. 2.
[2] *Panormitanus* upon c. 19 X, "de accus." V. 1.

the accused, and for this purpose he had first of all to submit to the "inscriptio in crimen"; should the "promovens" be treated in the same way in this respect? One thing was undeniable, namely, that if he had made the denunciation in bad faith and calumniously, he ought to be punished "extraordinem," with a "pœna extraordinaria." But should the "inscriptio in talionem" be imposed upon him? It seemed that it should not, because in the "inquisitio" the judge was, in law, the sole prosecutor.[1] This idea, however, was far from becoming the fixed general opinion, which was, rather, that when punishment was possible, the "inscriptio in crimen" was necessary. It was argued that the "promovens" was, as a matter of fact, the equivalent of the accuser.

The denunciation took very simple forms; it could be made orally and by the voice of a third person, a "procurator." There were those, even among the academical Canonists, who likened it to the "denunciatio evangelica," declaring that it equally entailed, in effect merely, the "correctio" of the culprit, and that although it often resulted in the infliction of a "pœna vindicativa," that was when the disorder was such that order could not be otherwise restored.[2] This would explain the characteristic noticed above that the "inquisitio" did not authorize the same severe punishments: "nutius punitur per inquisitionem."

But the essential difference between the two kinds of "denunciationes" is that any one, without distinction, could make the one ("evangelica"), while only those entitled to bring the "accusatio" could make the other ("judicialis").[3]

The net result of what we have said, however, is that the "denunciatio judicialis," as understood, had become a particular form of criminal action, and the "inquisitio," properly so called, only existed when the judge proceeded in the matter "ex mero officio." [4]

A new organ of the machinery of the ecclesiastical judicature, the "promotor," was the inevitable outcome of the theory of the "promovens inquisitionem." This titular officer of the officialities was nothing other than a functionary charged with the duty of denouncing offenses to the judge and "promovere inquisitionem,"

[1] c. 16 X, "de accus." V. 1.
[2] c. 16 X, "de accus." and *Panormitanus* upon this chapter, No. 2.
[3] *Durantis*, "Speculum, de accusat." p. 24.
[4] *Panormitanus* upon c. 24 X, "de accus." No. 21: "Proprie processus inquisitionis est quando judex facit ex officio suo puro et mero nemine deferente et impetrante inquisitionem: sed quando fit ad denonciationes alicujus tunc est proprie processus per viam denunciationis. Propter hoc facit quia, ex quo denuntiat et eligit viam quasi extraordinariam, debent præmonnisse quia forte inquisitus se conescisset."

against the culprits. His function, moreover, was one of progressive growth. Its origin is found in the commissions and temporary and extraordinary delegations made by the judge in the course of the procedure of "inquisitio." When he proceeded "ex mero officio" he was bound frequently to appreciate the arduousness and difficulty of his task, and he then appointed a capable person to play the part of promotor or "promoveur" in a specified case. This was a material and moral assistance to him, and appears to have furnished an answer to the objection which regarded the judge as being at the same time judge and party.

It is upon chapter 53, X, "de testibus" II, 20, that the old-time doctors base this practice. Innocent IV had already shown it to be prevalent and attempted to deduce therefrom doctrinal consequences. In his time the character of such a "promotor specialiter a judice deputatus" had not yet been altogether determined. In particular, it was asked if, once he had been brought into a particular "inquisitio," he could not be recalled or a substitute appointed, and whether he could lodge an appeal from the judgment. He was, at all events, already styled "Minister inquisitionis"; but Hostiensis states that he was not in reality a party to the action and that the litigation should not be conducted with him.[1] The function was nevertheless destined to become consolidated and grow into that of a titular office. But no mention is yet found of a titular "promotor" in the "Liber practicus de consuetudine Remensi," which belongs to the end of the 1200s or the beginning of the 1300s, although elsewhere unmistakable and interesting traces are found of the usage of "promotor specialiter delegatus a judice."[2] An influence was bound to be exercised in the development of the office by the king's "procuratores," or lords justiciar, who make their appearance about the end of the 1200s. From 1274 we find a "procurator episcopi Parisiensis,"[3] as to whom we shall have something to say elsewhere. In the "Registre de l'officialité de Cerisy" the promotor appears from the year 1338.[4]

The details of the "processus per inquisitionem" were settled

[1] "Vox loquando iste non est vera pars, sed quasi pars similitudine quia talis nullum libellum offert nec litem contestatur."

[2] "Liber practicus de consuetudine Remensi" (in the "Archives législatives de la ville de Reims" published by *M. Varin*), Nos. VIII, p. 43. Cc. LXXX, c. 269, p. 210.

[3] *Tanon*, "Histoire des justices des Eglises et communautés ecclésiastiques de Paris," p. 341.

[4] "Registre de l'officialité de Cerisy," Nos. 204 b, 334, 338 c, 269, 288 c, 386, 414 b.

at an early date, and afterwards remained almost unaltered. They were, in fact, succinctly laid down by the fourth Lateran council.[1] In the canonical common law they even allowed a sufficiently extensive liberty of defense to the accused. The "inquisitio" naturally began with the establishment of the "infamia." But when the "inquisitio" was made "ex mero officio" no particular form was prescribed for this institution. The judge assured himself concerning it and informed himself in this respect ("sese informabat") as far as his pleasure and ability went; in case of appeal, however, it became necessary to justify in regard to it before the superior judge.[2] But it was otherwise when there was a "promovens." In order to prove the "infamia" he had, first of all, to produce witnesses, who were heard by the judge, or more frequently by a deputy of the judge or merely by a notary, in the absence of the accused, who, moreover, had not yet appeared. This gave rise to the first opportunity of defense offered to the accused. When he was summoned he was entitled to require that he be made acquainted with the testimony by which he was "infamatus," and he could then dispute it.[3] It was asked if the "inquisitus" could not himself bring witnesses to prove his "bona fama." It was a natural thing to allow this, but it was also a delicate matter, to prevent the testimony of one set of witnesses contradicting that of the other. The judge was generally allowed to choose between the different affirmations "propriis auribus se informans."[4] Unless there had been an "inquisitio præcedens de infamia," it was necessary in all cases for the "inquisitus" to claim, otherwise the irregularity was waived.[5]

The accused was then summoned, unless he had been "captus" at the outset. He appeared before the judge and was made acquainted with the offenses imputed to him. This was done in either of two ways. If the "inquisitio" was brought "ex mero officio," the judge drew up "articuli," comprising the different charges upon which the "inquisitio" was to rest, and these he was required to communicate to the accused, giving him a copy of them and granting a delay sufficient to allow him to examine them.[6] If there was a "promovens," he was obliged, in the same way as a plaintiff in a civil action, to draw up a "libellus"

[1] c. 24 X, "de accus." V. 1.
[2] c. 19 X, "de accus." V. 1, and *Panormitanus* upon this chapter.
[3] *Panormitanus*, "Practica," c. 150.
[4] *Panormitanus*, upon c. 19 X, "de accus." No. 10.
[5] c. 2 VI°, "de accus." V. 1.
[6] *Durantis*, "Speculum, de inquis." p. 36.

and the "litiscontestation" intervened, the accused taking part.[1]

The examination began with the interrogation of the accused by the judge, who could repeat it as often as he pleased. The accused was compelled to reply, and we know that he was bound to reply under oath. The difference at first recognized in this respect between the "inquisitio ex mero officio" and the "inquisitio cum promovente," disappeared at an early date.[1] If he pleaded guilty, that was, in effect, sufficient to authorize his condemnation,[2] and if he pleaded not guilty, the judge or the "promovens" produced evidence, mainly testimonial, against him.

In the "inquisitio" in its first form, two distinct sets of witnesses were, by law, heard, one to the "infamia" and one to the guilt. When the "inquisitio" was made "ex mero officio," the testimony establishing the "infamia" was not, for the most part, formal testimony. In all cases the testimony received in the preliminary inquiry (or examination), "super infamia," was inadmissible against the "inquisitus" for the purpose of proving his guilt, and there were necessarily two successive and separate inquiries, even when the same persons testified in each.[3] But this rule was not absolute; it was subject to exception in the case of proof of the "corpus delicti" in notorious offenses unless the culprits were known,[4] and in the "inquisitio generalis," directed against a society or a community,[5] where the "inquisiti" could be condemned upon the testimony of the witnesses originally heard and without new inquiry.

The witnesses whose allegations could entail condemnation were heard in secret and out of the presence of the "inquisitus." This, however, was not a characteristic peculiar to the "inquisitio"; it also existed in the action "per accusationem" and in civil causes. Liberty of defense, as it was then understood, was in force. In the first place, on the termination of the inquest, the "inquisitus" received the depositions of the witnesses. He

[1] *Durantis, ibid.*, p. 34; *Panormitanus*, "Practica," c. 150.

[2] *Durantis*, "Speculum, de inquis." p. 34: "Post hoc interrogabitur; quod si confessus, bene, procedat ad pœnam. Si vero negaverit, tunc inquisitur inducat testes."

[3] *Durantis*, "Speculum, de inquis." p. 32: "Si enim reciperentur testes simul super crimine et super infamia, sæpe is qui inquisitionem prosequitur, ut sic ad probationem criminis admitteritur de quo quis infamatius non est, quod esse non debet;" — p. 33: "quid si inquisitor potuisset inquirere de infamia et de criminibus? Responde: Non servaretur ordo juris, Nam infama inquisitio præcedere debet veritatis cognitionem nec debet processus tali permixtione confundi."

[4] *Innocent IV*, upon c. 23 X, "de elect." I, 6.

[5] *Panormitanus*, upon c. 22 X, "de accus." No. 2.

not only got the witnesses' names but also a copy of the depositions themselves.[1] He had the right to have such witnesses interrogated anew and to produce against them his objections to their admissibility and his replies to their testimony.[2] He could even freely plead excuses and justifications and bring witnesses in support of these allegations.[3] Finally, the old texts contain no restrictions as to the assistance of a counsel.[4]

It is true that the procedure of the "inquisitio" allowed torture, but it was the torture of the "accusatio" and practised under the same conditions. The Canon law had permitted it by virtue of the predominating influence of the Roman law. No trace of it is to be found, to be sure, in the procedure of the ecclesiastical courts of the Frankish monarchy,[5] and the "Decretum" of Gratian contains the opposite theory, which bars and repudiates torture.[6] That is also the doctrine reproduced in the "Summa" of Paucapalea, while that of Etienne de Tournay (between 1165 and 1177) only recognizes the application of the torture to slaves and false witnesses (p. 221). The instrumentality by which the influence of the Roman law in this direction was augmented and sanctioned is to be found in certain passages borrowed from the ancient ecclesiastical Fathers who lived in the days of the Roman Empire, and who spoke of the torture which they saw in practice every day in a civilized country as if it were a natural and normal thing.[7] Johannes Teutonicus, who compiled the glossary to Gratian's "Decretum," also approves, in his teaching, of torture, and he adopts all the applications made of it by the Roman laws.[8] The great doctors of the 1200s, including Innocent IV and Durantis, entertained no doubts as to the legality of this method of examina-

[1] c. 26 X, "de accus." V. 1. *Durantis*, "Speculum, de inquis." p. 32: "Et dabitur ei facultas defendendi se et dabuntur ei nomina testium et dicta eorum sunt ei publicanda et de iis copia facienda, ut se defendere possit et proponet exceptiones et replicationes tam in principali quam contra testes."

[2] *Durantis*, "Speculum, de inquis." p. 33: "Item potest opponi contra testes inductos et replicari et contra dicta eorum. Unde cum testes contra eum producentur, protestetur quod possit opponere in personas eorum et dicta; et formet interrogationem et judici porrigat ut secundum Uno, testes interroget, secundum Rolandum."

[3] cc. 18, 19 X, "de accus." V. 1. *Durantis*, "Speculum, de inquis." pp. 28, 34, 35.

[4] *Panormitanus*, "Practica," c. 150, p. 30: "Advocatus inquisiti quibus modis prospicere possit suo clientulo."

[5] It is hinted at only in one pseudo-Isidorian passage (c. 4, C. V. qu. 5), which speaks of the torture administered to accusers and witnesses, and which aims at the protection of the bishops against accusations.

[6] C. XVI, qu. 6, under the headings of "Cause" and "Torture."

[7] c. 1 C. XV, qu. 6; c. 1 C. XII, qu. 5.

[8] Gloss upon C. XV, qu. 6, *q.v.*

tion. Certain formal texts, having the force of laws, also admitted it.[1] In the "inquisitio hæreticæ pravitatis" the legislation was particularly precise.[2]

We have said that the canonical procedure "per inquisitionem" in its broad features remained throughout much as it had been at its beginning. It underwent sundry important modifications, however, the consequences of which were more severely felt in the secular than in the ecclesiastical courts. One of these was the abolition of the distinction, formerly so well defined, between the "inquisitio super forma" and the "inquisitio super veritate." The first "informatio" had a double purpose; but a practice was introduced by which, at least whenever the "inquisitus" demanded it, the witnesses heard in the information must be examined anew.[3] This was the "repetitio tertium," equivalent to our re-examination of the witnesses.

Another was the limitation placed upon and the final abolition of the right of the "inquisitus" to have full knowledge of the depositions produced against him and to learn the names of those who had made them. Already the doctors of the 1200s asked whether it was invariably necessary to acquaint the "inquisitus" with the names of the witnesses. Some of them would not permit it when it might be attended with danger. Innocent IV left it to the judge's discretion.[4] The fact was noted that c. 26 X, "de accus." expressly mentioned the "dicta testium" only and did not speak of the "nomina." One of Boniface VIII's decretals unreservedly suppressed the names in the "inquisitio hæretica pravitatis."[5] A further step had to be taken. Letters of the popes Pius IV and Paul III generalized the principle.[6] We shall find that with us the practice ceased in the secular courts in the course of the 1300s. It was maintained that this safeguard was replaced by another, the *confrontation*, that is, the bringing

[1] C. 1. (Alex. III) X, *de deposito*, III, 16; "Nam judicibus dedimus in mandatis ut idum iniquum *sub questionibus* ad rationem ponant." Flagel lation in particular appears to have been employed as a means of torture, c. 4, X, *de raptor*: "Poteris . . . etiam flagellis adficere ea tamen moderatione adhibita quod flagella in vindictam sanguinis transire minime videantur." One passage would seem to have a general application, c. 6, X, *de reg. juris*, V. 41: "In ipso causa initio non est a quæstionibus inchoandum." It is true that some read "questibus" instead of "quæstionibus." But that text is taken from a letter of Gregory I, and merely reproduces a Roman rule in regard to torture, Book 1, par. D. XLVIII, 18; L. 8, § 1, C. IX, 41.

[2] *Clement*, 1, "de hæret," V. 3.

[3] *Guazzini*, "Tractatus ad defensionem inquisitorum," Venice, 1649, "defensio," 25 V, pp. 15, 19.

[4] *Panormitanus*, upon c. 26, "de accus." V. 1.

[5] c. 20 VI°, "de hæret." V. 2.

[6] *Guazzini*, *op. cit.* "defensio," 24, II, p. 3 *et seq.*

face to face of the accused and the witness, when the deposition of the latter was read over to the former. The confrontation was not unknown in the canonical procedure, but it was not required as a matter of right and the proceeding was quite valid without it. It was, however, very frequently employed, as it was, as a matter of fact, an excellent method of examination. It was, moreover, held in law that it cured all defects of the summons, — even the lack of summons,[1] — and that it was equivalent to the "publicatio processus."[2]

Such is the inquisitorial procedure of the common law. But, for the general mass of humanity, who had little knowledge of the history of the law, it received a special and world-famous application in the *Holy Inquisition* itself. Created in the 1200s to quell the great heresies of the Waldensians and the Albigenses, this was in very active operation in the south of France for about a century. It had two especially distinctive and peculiar features. In the first place, its judges were not the ordinary ecclesiastical judges, but special delegates of the Pope, usually drawn from among the Dominican and Franciscan friars, who constituted special tribunals of Inquisition. In the second place, though its procedure followed, in effect, the "processus per inquisitionem," or Canon common law, as we have described it; yet the Holy Inquisition employed the most drastic rules of the Canon common law. We have already referred to the text which sanctioned the withholding of the names of the witnesses from the "inquisitus"; the aid of counsel, if not wholly prohibited, was at all events rendered more difficult and its allowance surrounded with precautions; and, above all, witnesses considered incompetent on principle were held to be admissible and were heard. The first of these characteristics lost much of its importance through the decrees passed by the Council General of Vienna in 1312, but it never altogether disappeared. Associated in the pursuit and the judgment of heretics were the Inquisitor and the bishop, the "judex ordinarius." Each of these functionaries maintained an independent initiative in the pursuit and the summons; but all the important steps of the procedure had to be taken in unison.[3]

Elsewhere, from the 1300s onward, the Holy Inquisition has a local history of its own with each of the important European nations. In France it soon lost its importance; at the end of the 1500s it is in rapid decline and on the way to ultimate total

[1] *Guazzini, op. cit.* "defensio," 20, c. 19, II, p. 315, 317.
[2] *Guazzini, op. cit.* p. 318, No. 7. [3] *Clement,* 2 "de hæret." V. 3.

desuetude. The pursuit of heresy became a *royal and privileged cause*, the cognizance of which belonged to the royal jurisdictions, except when the king pleased to confer it upon the ecclesiastical authority, which sometimes happened in the course of the complex and changing legislation of the 1500s against the Protestants.

But we may leave at this stage the "Inquisitio heretica pravitatis," for the great influence exercised upon the development of French law cannot be attributed to that institution, but to the "inquisitio" of the Canon common law.

§ 3. **The "Aprise" or Official Inquest. Its Appearance in the 1200s.**—We have pointed out above that in the 1200s the official prosecution made its appearance in the secular jurisdictions under the name of "aprise."

How did this come about? Down to that time the inquest ("enquête") was only possible if the man arrested *on suspicion* submitted to it of his own free will; though an indirect and very strenuous means of constraint was often employed, "the close ('dure') prison with little to eat and drink." Was it not simpler, more in accordance with the dignity of the law, to decide that all consent should be dispensed with, that the judge should have the power to open the inquest in all cases, and if it should be conclusive, apply the punishment? Such a development was the logical outcome, and the old jurists found in the theory a judicial basis.

In case of a capture in the act, it was always admitted that the malefactor could be punished without a formal accusation, solely on the testimony of those who had seen him commit the misdeed.[1] It was thought that a fact which would be sworn to by many witnesses and which would, therefore, be a matter of public notoriety could be held to be a capture in the act; and that the judge could then of his own accord hear the witnesses and pronounce the punishment.[2] This was called "l'aprise," in low Latin,

[1] "Livre de Jostice et de Plet," XIX, 44, § 14: "Those who are arrested for present misdeed and immediately brought into court go by inquest . . . in case of denial: because it is recognized that misdeeds known to have been done ought to be punished."

[2] "If he who is arrested on suspicion of an offense will not stand the inquest into the fact, the 'aprise' is the appropriate procedure; that is to say, the judge should of his own accord make an 'aprise' and inquire whatever he can ascertain concerning the deed, and if by the 'aprise' he find the *fact notorious among a large number of people*, he can properly pass judgment upon the 'aprise.' And he should be able to ascertain the fact so clearly by the 'aprise' that the prisoner can be judged. But before he can be sentenced to death by the 'aprise,' it is proper that the fact should be clearly ascertained by at least three or four witnesses, so that the sentence shall not be based *solely upon the 'aprise' but also upon notorious fact.*" *Beaumanoir*, XL, 15 (Salmon, No. 1232).

"aprisio." Beaumanoir explains the word in this sense that "the judge is the wisest as to the necessity (of the case) that he has opened up."

According to him, this would be merely a kind of police inquiry which could only entail a condemnation if it approached the semblance of an establishment of a capture in the act.[1] But this theory was too subtle and too inadequate to last long. The "aprise" ought to be, as far as its effects were concerned, exactly similar to the inquest: but the similarity was not very striking. For a fairly long time the sufficiency of the "aprise" to sustain the ordinary and normal punishment of the offense was denied.[2] Several texts only allowed of the outlawry of the guilty person in such a case. "Les Etablissements de St. Louis" expressly says so: "If any be of evil report by proclamation or by public rumor, the law should seize him and inquire ('enquerre') into his acts and his mode of life at the place of his abode, and should he be found on inquiry guilty of any act involving capital punishment, he should not be condemned to death if no one accuse him, or when he is not taken in the act and there is no avowal. But if he will not submit to inquest, then the judge should make it and banish him, should he appear guilty on the facts and as he shall find by the inquest which he shall have made of his own accord."[3] "Le Livre des Droiz et Commandements de Justice" is no less

[1] He contrasts the "aprise" with the inquest "which brings the quarrel to an end." XL, 16 (Salmon, No. 1233). — See as to the "aprise" the "Registre des Grands-Jours de Troyes," quoted by *Brussel*, "Usage des fiefs": "Cum non appareret sufficiens, accusator . . . inquesta seu aprisio facta est," vol. I, p. 227. — "On the advice of knights, esquires, and certain other gentlemen . . . caused him to be arrested and imprisoned . . . and on the aforseaid information and advice caused an 'aprise' to be held upon the fact and suspicion of the said murder." In Beaumanoir's eyes the word "aprise" is really the translation of the term "informatio" and "aprandre" is the equivalent of "se informare." Fundamentally, therefore, he copies the Canon law as far as he can. *M. Zucker*, "Aprise und loial Enquête," pp. 93, 96, holds, on the contrary, that the term "aprise" comes from "prisio," "prise," the fact of the seizure and imprisonment of a person. But that is not reconcilable with the passage quoted from Beaumanoir. "Prise par suspicion" is doubtless frequently mentioned, but that is because the capture and the imprisonment almost always accompany the "enquête" or the "aprise."

[2] This is a feature which we have noticed in connection with the "inquisitio" of the ecclesiastical courts.

[3] II, 16; *cf. Beaumanoir*, LXI, 20 (Salmon, No. 1727). The text of the "Etablissements," in order to permit of this official prosecution, expressly refers to the Roman law: "For it is one of the duties of the provost and every loyal judge to cleanse his province and his jurisdiction of all wicked men and women according to the law written in the Digest "de receptatoribus" . . . and in the law "Congruit" in the Digest "de officio Præsidis" . . . and so he may put him to the inquest and if the inquest should prove him guilty, the judge should condemn him to death, if it be one of the cases above mentioned."

clear, although it belongs to a later epoch. "Of bad report and official action of the court; how malefactors may be punished, on proclamation, or on public report and bad repute:—To wit, he may apprehend him and inquire into his actions, at the place of his abode; and if he finds him guilty he should not therefore condemn him to death when he is not taken in the act or on avowal or when he has refused the inquiry; but he can clearly banish him according as he shall be found guilty. But several well advised deny this so far as regards the banishment."[1]—"Also, another proof which the old law calls 'inquisitive,' that is to say, when an information is laid or any official inquest ('enqueste') in any matter or offense, and witnesses are brought, but he who is under suspicion is not tried of his own free will, or taken in the act, or submits to the inquest by the country ('du païs') of his free will, such inquest shall not be the basis of his apprehension and detention for the purpose of making him stand trial."[2]

The "aprise" was undoubtedly introduced into the secular jurisdictions principally in imitation of the procedure of the ecclesiastical courts; that will be clearly apparent in the ordinances of the 1300 s which regulate the new inquest in a very clear fashion, though in few words, and which reiterate the principles and the terminology of the Canon law.[3] The first ordinance which mentions it in any precise way calls it an institution of the countries of written law. This Ordinance of 1254 is designed "for the reform of the customs in Languedoc and Languedoïl."

It contains a double text in Latin and in French. The Latin text, designed for the provinces of the South, contains an article, 21, couched in these words: "Et quia in dictis seneschaliis secundum jura et terræ consuetudinem fit inquisitio in criminibus volumus et mandamus quod reo petenti acta inquisitionis tradantur

[1] § 328.

[2] § 476, *cf. Boutaric*, "Actes du Parlement de Paris," decree of 1259 (No. 345); it concerned a real royal violation of the law; the culprit is to be kept in prison until he has paid the penalty of his crime against the king. "Salva tamen eidem vitâ suâ, membris suis et hereditate sua, quia non supposuit se isti inqueste." No. 4372; Decree of 1315; the guilty person is condemned to death: "it was proved against him that he had accepted the 'enquête' presented to the bailiff."

[3] On the influence of the Church in the domain of the procedure see *M. Glasson*, "Les sources de la procédure civile française" (Nouvelle Revue historique du droit français et étranger," 1881, p. 413 *et seq.*). *M. Stintzing* ("Geschichte der deutschen Rechtswissenschaft," 1880, p. 27) points out that by reason of the exegetic plan exclusively followed in the Universities, "the criminal procedure in so far as it was connected with the civil procedure was, especially for the canonists, a subject which they had to expound from the second book of the 'Decretals.'"

ex integro." [1] Is not the conclusion possible that the criminal inquiry before reaching the North would have taken root as a normal institution in the South, where the inquisition against the heretics had first made its appearance?

But the "aprise" found a basis of support elsewhere than in the Canon law. It is nowadays accepted that in the time of the Frankish monarchy, under the Carlovingians, another procedure held its place side by side with the strict and formal common law. In this procedure, which was styled "per inquisitionem," the judicial duel, the exculpatory oath, and the formal testimony had no place. In principle, the king alone, by virtue of his sovereign authority, had the right to proceed by inquisitions personally or by delegates. The person commissioned to inquire ("inquirere") assembled together a certain number of men belonging to the district, and, on the faith of their oaths, took their declarations upon the point in litigation; he then pronounced the sentence in accordance with their allegations. This description of regalian right did not belong to the judges except by virtue of a commission from the sovereign; but when fiscal rights were concerned the procedure was always "per inquisitionem," and the churches and monasteries obtained by privilege the employment of this procedure in the actions in which they were interested. It was also employed in actions in which widows, orphans, and the indigent, "homines minus potentes," figured. But in the Frankish period the inquisition was rarely employed except in civil matters.[2] This right of causing inquest to be made ("en-

[1] Ord. 1, p. 72. The editor points out that, in the French text, Articles 20, 21, and 22 are wanting.

[2] See upon all these points the noteworthy works of *M. Brunner*, "Die Entstehung der Schwurgerichte," ch. VI, pp. 84–126 (1871). — "Zeugen-und-Inquisitions-Beweis des Karolingischen Zeit." (1866). In the capitularies instructions addressed to the "missi" are sometimes found, which charge them to inquire ("inquirere") when a crime has been committed. But it appears that once the "inquisitio" was made, the action could proceed to its termination only in one of two ways; either an accuser presented himself, or the accused purged himself by his oath or by the ordeals. See especially "Capitulaire de latronibus," Ann. 804 (Pertz I, 129); chapter I is in very general terms: "Ut ubicumque eos repererint diligenter inquirant et cum discreptione examinant, ut nec hic superfluum faciant, ubi ita non oportet, nec prætermittant quod facere debent;" but chapter 2 provides for the presence of an accuser and the judicial duel; chapter 3 speaks of ordeals. See also examples of official prosecution in the laws of the barbarians. Lex Burg., LXXXIX (*Walter*): "*De reis corripiendis.* Gundebaldus rex Burgundionum omnibus comitibus . . . præceptionem ad eos dedimus ut si quos caballorum fures, aut effractores domuum, tam criminosos quam suspectos invenire potueritis, statim capere et ad nos adducere non moretur. Futurum ut is qui capitur, et ante nos adductus fuerit, si se innocentem potuerit adprobare, cum omnibus rebus suis liber abscedat, neque calumniam pro eo quod ligatus aut captus est movere præ-

querir") was retained by royalty in the Middle Ages. It exercised it when its civil or feudal interests were at stake. The "Livre de Jostice et de Plet" contains an important chapter which in this respect reproduces the principles of the Frankish period.[1] Book XIX, Tit. 44: "§ 1. If the king claims from any one heritable or moveable property, taken from him or due to him, he wins or loses by inquest. . . . § 3. If any one beats or maltreats one of the king's officers of the law while in the performance of his duty, that is a matter for inquest. . . . § 7. If any stranger take a prisoner of the king's, together with other things belonging to the king, by main force, that is a matter for inquest. . . . § 11. Whoever makes raids by force of arms and carries away and destroys, that is a matter for inquest. . . . § 13. He ought to make inquest who knows to do it; and should make inquiry as to all the particulars of the dispute, and the witnesses cannot be falsified."[2] But that did not apply to criminal matters; the consent of the accused was at that time necessary, as we have seen, before the inquest ("enquête") could proceed. This reasoning, then, must be adopted; since the king is directly interested in the repression of crime, why not employ the inquest in this case as in all cases where the king's interests are concerned? This is a strong argument; and it happens that in the same chapter of the "Livre de Jostice et de Plet" in which we read that old maxim "none shall be put to the inquest to lose life or limb"[3] we see the inquest admitted in criminal matters:

"If injury is caused to a poor person who cannot prosecute his rights, either by himself, his goods, or his friends, such matter should proceed by inquest; for such matters are not allowed to come to naught because of such poverty. And if he claim for an

sumat. Si vero criminosus inventus fuerit, pœnam vel tormenta suscipiat, quæ meretur . . . et non solum in eum tantum pagum, ubi consistit, liceat persequi criminosum; sed sicut utilitas aut fides uniuscujusque habuerit, etiam per alia loca ad nos pertinentia non dubitent hujusmodi personas capere, et judicibus præsentare, ut præfata scelera non liceat esse diutius impunita." — *Lex Wisigoth*, Lib. VI, tit. 5, l. 14: "Si homicidam nullus accuset, judex mox ut facti crimen agnoverit, licentiam habeat corripere criminosum, ut pœnam reus excipiat, quam meretur."

[1] The title is: "What matters should be dealt with by inquest."

[2] In civil matters, the inquiry was introduced on a great many points into the ordinary procedure, in order to dispense with the "battle." This was done, for example, in matters of sasine ("Livre de J. et P." XIX, 44, § 6), of partition (*ibid.*, § 10), and wills (*ibid.*, IV, 4, § 1). Chapter 44 of book XIX sets out with a maxim very propitious to the extension of the inquiry. *Johanz de Beaumont* says: "Chamberlains of France should see to it that battles should be avoided as far as possible and that lawsuits should be brought to an end; this concerns a right common to all.'"

[3] XIX, 44, § 4.

offense involving capital punishment it is not a matter for inquest, except it happen that the king should grant conditional absolution." [1] And a little further on: "If the man or the woman who is killed shall have no relative or friend who can avenge him or her, the king can prosecute and punish according to what is ascertained in the 'aprise,' without capital condemnation." [2] — "The king can make an inquisition by reason of evil notoriety on keepers of brothels, thieves, doers of malicious mischief, rioters, and those who are accustomed to commit other mischief, and punish at his pleasure, without capital punishment, so that honesty do not suffer; if any one is feared on account of his cruelty or excesses, punishment ought to be administered without delay." [3]

In this way the inquest by the country ("enquête du pays") was bound to become merged in the "aprise." But the probability is that the right of causing an inquest to be made ("faire enquérir") was at first exercised by the king alone as a kind of right of the crown. The "Olim" books, which offer numerous examples of criminal inquests, do not fail to note that they were held "de mandato domini regis." [4] Even at a fairly late date the right of inquest was still refused to the inferior courts of justice: "No mesne lord can release a felon without the assent of the baron, but the cognizance belongs to the baron; nor can he cause inquest to be made ('fere enqueste'), which appertains to high justice." [5]

§ 3 *a*. **Same: The Denunciation.** — The "aprise" led to the *denunciation*. Many people were bound to shirk an "accusation." Its danger was apparent as long as the judicial duel remained in existence, and later, the courts, following the

[1] XIX, 44, § 8. [2] XIX, 45, § 1.

[3] XIX, 44, § 12. The "Livre de Jostice" also takes notice of the ecclesiastical inquisition, I, 3, § 7: "The king by advice of his barons makes the following 'établissement' or law; when a man shall be suspected of heresy, the ordinary judges should request the king or his court to make the 'aprise' in regard to the case. He should be apprehended and imprisoned. Afterwards the bishop and the prelates of the place, that is, the Church officials, should hold an inquisition upon his case and inquire of him concerning his faith. And if he is condemned by their judgment and holy Church takes what belongs to it, the king afterwards takes possession of the prisoner and causes his execution, and all his goods belong to the king, except his wife's dowery and his heritage."

[4] See for example vol. I, pp. 213, 394, 482, 544, 619, 768. See *Pardesssus*, "Organisation judiciaire," p. 107: "The court (of the king) appears in very early times to have given to the proof by witnesses or by written documents the preference over the judicial combat, and I firmly believe that, when Saint Louis, by the ordinance of 1260, prohibited this combat within his domains, he but generalized a custom which his court had for a long time practised."

[5] "Etablissements de St. Louis," II, 35. Probably the only object of this text, even in its concluding words, was to limit the right of low justice.

principles of the Roman law, still declared that the defaulting accuser could be condemned to the punishment of the talon. It is important to remember that before the ecclesiastical courts the injured party could rest satisfied with denouncing the misdeed to the judge, who then prosecuted officially; and this convenient procedure now came to be employed before the secular jurisdictions. But at the outset, as in the case of the "aprise," before the denunciation could be effectually made, the fact must be sworn to by numerous witnesses, — it must be tantamount to a taking in the act.[1] This restriction was bound very soon to disappear and the denunciation to be always admitted. The complainant, however, did not necessarily lose all his interest in the action: he often remained a party to it,— as in the case of the "promovens inquisitionem" of the Canon law,— with the object of obtaining a pecuniary reparation for the damage which he had suffered; this gave rise to the appointment of the civil party. The following passage of the "Livre des Droiz" contains a very accurate description of the new forms of the criminal procedure: "The law declares that there is a difference between accusation, inquisition, and denunciation. '*Accusation*' is when any one accuses another of crime and constitutes himself a party; it is proper in such case that he give security and submit to the punishment known to the law as 'ad pœnas talionis.' '*Inquisicion*' is when the judge makes inquiry of his own accord and brings suit 'quod fama præcedat,' according to law. '*Denonciation*' is when any one informs against another in any matter, for the purpose of having restoration of his chattel, in which case he should aver that he does not seek criminal recourse against the party, but merely restoration of his chattel."[2]

The "aprise" and the denunciation were not introduced without meeting with strong opposition. When the person prosecuted was a serf ("homme de poeste") there was little trouble; but when the matter concerned a gentleman having the right

[1] *Beaumanoir*, LXI, 2 (Salmon, No. 1710): "But there is indeed another way besides the accusation; for before the accusations are made, if he who desires to accuse wishes, he may denounce to the judge that this misdeed has been done in the sight and to the knowledge of so many reputable men that it cannot be hidden; and upon this he ought to act as a good judge would, and inquire into the matter although the party does not wish to submit to inquiry. And if he find the misdeed open and notorious, he may sentence him according to the misdeed. For it would be an unjust thing if any one had killed my near relative openly or before a large number of people, if it behooved me to fight in order to obtain vengeance. And so in those cases which are mentioned one may proceed by way of denunciation."

[2] § 942.

to trial by his peers according to the old forms, with accusation and battle, the "aprise" constituted an attack upon the privileges of the feudal subject. The aristocracy resisted, and numerous traces of this strife remain. The most curious document reflecting this is the account of an action brought against one of Saint Louis' "men" ("hommes"). This narrative, reduced to writing by the Confessor who wrote a life of the king, presents a vivid picture of this old quarrel, and we may be pardoned if we quote it almost in its entirety. "As my lord Enjorranz, lord of Couci had caused three young gentlemen to be hanged . . . because they were found in his forest with bows and arrows [1] . . . the said abbot [2] and certain female relatives of the said persons who had been hanged carried complaint of their killing before our gracious king; who caused the said Enjorranz, lord of Couci to be summoned before him, since it was his duty to make adequate inquest ('enqueste suffisant') as should be done in such a case; and he then caused him to be arrested by his knights and officers and brought to the Louvre, and put in prison and there held in a room, unfettered. And one day while the said Enjorranz, lord of Couci was thus held, our said gracious king caused the said lord of Couci to be brought before him, with whom came the king of Navarre, the duke of Burgundy, the count of Bar, the count of Soissons, the count of Brittany, the count of Champagne, my lord Thomas, then archbishop of Rheims, and my lord Jehan de Thorote, and also all the barons of the kingdom.[3] Finally it was proposed on behalf of the said my lord of Couci before our gracious king that he desired to take advice, and then he went apart with all the beforesaid noblemen . . . and when they had consulted a long time they returned before his gracious majesty and the said my lord Jehan de Thorote [4] in behalf of the said Enjorranz, lord of Couci urged that he ought not to and would not submit himself to inquest in such case, such inquest touching his person, his honor, and his property, and that he was ready to defend himself by battle, and denied absolutely that he had hanged the aforesaid youths or caused them to be hanged. And when our gracious king had patiently heard the determination of the said my lord Enjorranz, lord of Couci, he replied that in the affairs of the poor, the churches, and of those deserving of commisera-

[1] They had committed a hunting offense.

[2] The three youths belonged to the retinue of an abbot.

[3] This is an assembly of peers called together to judge one of their number.

[4] He plays the part of "avant parlier."

tion it was not proper thus to proceed by law of battle; for it was difficult to find any who would combat for such manner of people against the barons of the realm, and he said that a new procedure could not be adopted different from that followed in former times by our ancestors in similar cases. And then his gracious majesty related how his uncle, king Philip, because my lord Jehan, then lord of Soilli, was said to have committed a homicide, caused an inquest to be made against him and held the castle of Soilli for twelve years, although the said castle was held of the king by immediate homage. Then his gracious majesty refused the said request and straightway caused the said lord of Couci to be arrested by his officers and brought to the Louvre and there held under arrest . . . and then his gracious majesty adjourned his court and the aforesaid barons departed thence amazed and abashed. And that same day, after the said reply of his gracious majesty, the count of Brittany said to him that he ought not to maintain that inquests should be made against the barons of the realm in regard to matters which concerned their persons, their property, and their honor. And his gracious majesty replied to the count: 'You did not speak thus in former times when the barons who held of you by immediate homage brought before us their complaints against yourselves and offered to prove their cause of action in a specified case by battle against you. You then answered before us that you should not proceed by battle but by inquests in such cases, and that battle is not the lawful way.'—He added that, since the said lord of Couci had not submitted to the said inquest he could not, according to the customs of the kingdom, judge by inquest made against him by which he could punish him personally. But as he knew well God's will in this case, he would not allow his noble birth or the power of any of his friends to prevent him from administering full justice upon him. And finally his gracious majesty, by the advice of his counsellors, sentenced my lord of Couci (to a fine) of twelve thousand livres of Paris." [1]

[1] "La vie de St. Louis" by Queen Marguerite's confessor. "Recueil des Historiens des Gaules et de la France," Vol. XX, pp. 113, 114. The demands of the barons are renewed with added vigor on the death of St. Louis. When Queen Blanche convoked them for the coronation of her son, they laid down their conditions: "Maxima pars optimatum ante diem præfixam petierunt de consuetudine Gallicana omnes incarceratos et præcipue comites Flandrensem Ferrandum et Bononiensem Reginaldum a carceribus liberari, qui in subversionem libertatum regni jam per annos XII arctiori custodia in vinculis tenebantur. Petierunt insuper quidam eorum terras suas sibi restitui quas pater ejus Ludovicus et avus illius Philippus multo jam tempore injuste detinuerant occupatas. Adjiciunt

Here the protests of the barons and the manner in which St. Louis laid down the new doctrine are portrayed with a lifelike touch. But royalty could not overcome everywhere and at once this obstinate resistance of the old system of law. In the 1300s we find, on the contrary, a number of documents which half yield to it. Two ordinances of 1315 (Louis X) recognized the privileges of the aristocracy of Burgundy and Champagne in this respect. The king decides upon the protest which has been made to him: "The first matter submitted to us is as follows. First, that in case of crime it shall not be lawful to proceed against the said nobles by denunciation or upon suspicion, nor judge or condenm them by inquests, unless they submitted thereto; although the suspicion might be so great and so notorious that the suspected parties against whom the denunciation should be made ought to remain in the custody ('en l'hostel') of his lord for a period of forty days, or two or three such periods at the most, and if within that time no one should accuse him ('l'approchoit') of the deed, he should be liberated on bail ('ostagez'); and if an accuser present himself ('en faisant partie') he should be entitled to have their defense by wager of battle. We allow them, if the person be not so infamous or the deed so notorious that the lords should have recourse to some other remedy. And as to the wager of battle, it is our will that it be made use of as has been formerly done."[1] And the following provision is made in regard to the nobility of Champagne: "Art. 13. Also, when any gentleman of Champagne was arrested on suspicion in case of crime he should be heard as to his sufficient reasons and defenses and held prisoner for a certain time, and if any one should appear who accused him ('feist partie contre li') he was entitled to defend himself by wager of battle if he did not desire to submit to inquest. And to this end he should be released from prison, if he had not been arrested in present misdeed ('en présent meffet'). It is our will and purpose that every one arrested for a criminal matter be heard as to his sufficient reasons and that justice be done him in the matter, and if any 'aprise' be made against him, that he be not condemned or judged by that 'aprise' alone."[2] Finally, Bouteiller also shows that the nobility of Artois enjoyed the same privileges:

etiam quod nullus de regno Francorum debuit ab aliquo jure suo spoliari nisi per judicium XII. parium." Math. Paris, "Historia Major Anglorum" (ann. 1226), *Wats.* edition Paris, 1644, p. 231.

[1] "Ordonnance rendue sur les remontrances des nobles de Bourgogne, des Evêchez de Langres, d'Autun et du Comté de Forès" (Ord. I, p. 558).

[2] Ord. I, p. 575.

"Be it known that according to the customs of Artois and several places, a gentleman who does not submit to inquest should not be put nor be compelled to put himself (to inquest) if he does not request it. And if that should be done without his knowledge and consent, he should not be prejudiced thereby if he does not voluntarily ratify it." [1]

§ 3 *b*. **Same: The Secular Inquisition in the 1300 s.** — The inquisitorial procedure, however, constantly gained ground. It made especial progress in the energetic hands of the royal officers. Some traces of this progress are still discernible. In 1347 King Philip of Valois decides upon the demand of the inhabitants of Lyons against the king's counsel. The former complained: "quod passim et indifferenter judex ordinarius inquirit de omnibus criminibus sine accusatore vel denunciatore, qui persequitur legitime, cum tamen consuetudo dictorum civium sit, sicut asserunt, quod solum in criminibus furti, incendii et proditionis inquisitio fieri debeat, et non aliter nisi post denunciationem et accusationem ut suprà." The king merely ordains that this custom be proved by witnesses.[2] In 1363 King John confirms the privileges granted to the inhabitants of Langres by their bishops, by which the official prosecution is limited only in a certain degree:[3] "We declare and ordain that neither we nor any of our said officers shall be entitled to proceed against the said inhabitants nor arrest any of them officially, except in criminal cases where person and property are at our disposal, and the certain committing of the deed be notorious and against a person of bad fame and repute or strongly suspected of the said deed. . . . But our spiritual officers shall be entitled to proceed officially against those inhabitants, according as the law allows them." The "Très-ancienne Coutume de Bretagne" retains distinct traces of this development: ch. 113. "Whoever commits an offense against minors or those under the protection of justice or the Holy Church, women or men of feeble condition, as to property or person, or

[1] "Somme rurale," I, Tit. 34, p. 224.

[2] Ord. II, p. 258. In a certain number of town charters lists are found limiting the crimes for which proceedings "per inquisitionem" could be taken. See "Consuetudines Tolosæ" rubric "de inquisitionibus" *Bourdot du Richebourg* (IV, 2, p. 1044). "Cout. de Limoges" (in Latin), *ibid.*, p. 1149.

[3] The inhabitants made the following complaint: "It is deplored by us and our said officers that it is declared that no matter what be done, neither we nor our said officer can proceed officially against them in a criminal case, nor arrest for such an offense, if the said resident male or female be not taken in present misdeed or be not prosecuted by party, or the fact be not *notorious*, both by their privileges and customs above mentioned and by certain decision already made on the subject by our bailiff."

against those who come or go to church or market, or on pilgrimage or (to attend) their lord's term days or for fire or water at home or abroad, on the sea or the highway, who are on their way from house or from market or to market town or whatever the offense may be the law can proceed against such offenders on denunciation of party." [1] — ch. 114. "When a serious offense is committed in a district, such as murder or burning of houses or property or highway robbery or despoiling of churches, or of ships, or other serious offenses, it is the duty of the judge to cause the people of the district to be put on oath in regard to the matter, men, women, children, and servants, who are capable of taking the oath, and to demand of them where they were on the night or the day that the offense was committed, and if the judge find that the people of a house are changeable, he can arrest them: and if he can find from others that any one is suspected, he shall proceed against them as should be done according to custom." — ch. 115. "And also justice may and shall proceed with all action where the blood of man or woman has been shed by violence." [2]

Although the accusation, as we have already pointed out, by no means disappeared,[3] the accusatory procedure, as we have described it, underwent important modifications. The wagers of battle began to disappear. The ordinance issued by St. Louis in 1260, at the Parlement of the Octaves of Candlemas, was the point of departure of this transformation.[4] This is the celebrated "Établissements le roy" of which Beaumanoir speaks so often in his chapters on *proofs, inquests*, and *wagers of battle*. "We prohibit all battles within our domain . . . and for battles we substitute proof by witnesses," said the king. This resulted

[1] *Bourdot de Richebourg*, IV, 1, p. 227. It will be noticed that the majority of the matters struck at call to mind those in which, at the Frankish period, the procedure was "per inquisitionem" in civil matters.

[2] *Cf.* ch. 102, p. 225: "And if he is not captured in the act or on pursuit, or if the fact is not notorious, as the saying is,—for the reason that he has been dwelling in the district for five years, and is of good repute, as one who goes to church and market, and has not been arrested for crime, he may say, in case the courts wish to proceed against him, that under the customary law he cannot be compelled to submit to proof by witnesses against him."

[3] According to certain texts, this was even the only way open to certain parties, since everybody was not allowed to denounce: "Coutume de Bragerac," Art. XXII: "Item si quis vilis conditionis et parvi status voluerit denunciare contra hominem bonæ famæ et boni status, non suspectum de contentis in denunciacione predicta, talis denunciatio minime recipitur. Si vero eum accusare velit directe, ad hoc erit admittendus, dum tamen criminosus et captus accusans non existat." *Bourdot de Richebourg*, IV, 2, p. 1016.

[4] Ord. I, 86; *Isambert*, I, 283.

in the suppression of the *appeal* or direct challenge to the judicial duel and the challenging ("faussement") of witnesses for perjury. The consequence was that a goodly number of persons hitherto incapable of testifying became competent witnesses.[1] But that was not all. The king also changed the method of taking the testimony. The new method was very much more intricate and required much more learning than the old, and writing played a great part in it. It was copied from the practice of the ecclesiastical courts, and it also borrowed some of the features of that inquest of which we have formerly spoken. The witnesses, summoned by order of court,[2] no longer appeared in open court, but before certain delegates of the judge, who were called inquirers ("enquesteurs") or auditors.[3] They questioned the witnesses separately and "artfully" ("subtilement"). This, it will be seen, is far removed from the old formal testimony. The parties were not present at this examination. They were present only at the taking of the oath by the witnesses; at which time they were obliged to state their grounds of objection to the competency of the witnesses if they had any to urge, or at least reserve them.[4] The examiners reduced the depositions to writing, and these writings became the principal document in the action; moreover, both parties, accused as well as accuser, had access to it; "the auditor should hear them (the witnesses) separately and anon make public;"[5] — "then he shall judge of the matter according to the testimony of the witnesses published to the parties."[6]

The accused could produce witnesses on his side. The sentence was pronounced in open court, after a debate in which both parties or their counsel addressed the court.

It will be seen that the forms of the accusatory procedure and those of the official prosecution or the prosecution on denunciation tended to borrow from each other and even to become merged.

[1] *Beaumanoir*, XL, 37 (Salmon, No. 1259).

[2] As they no longer ran any risk, they could not thereafter refuse to testify.

[3] *Beaumanoir*, XL, 12 (Salmon, No. 1234). These were practitioners or experts, "prud' hommes" and occasionally the judge's assistants, officers of the court, and others.

[4] *Beaumanoir*, XL, 18, 28; XXXIX, 27, 28 (Salmon, Nos. 1240, 1251, 1170, 1171).

[5] "Etablissements de St. Louis," I, 1.

[6] Ord. of 1260, Art. 4. The most elaborate precautions were taken to have this important document accurately worded and preserved. The inquirers must be "at least two lawful and capable persons" and each time the inquest was closed, the document must be closed and sealed. *Beaumanoir*, XL, 2, 27 (Salmon, Nos. 1225, 1250). Here we find already the "sacs" of later days.

But this was still merely a tendency. The king had not been able to force upon the lords justiciar the procedure which he introduced within his own domains. It took time for the inquest to gain ground and supersede the battle; it forced its way on its own merits alone.[1] The judicial duel did not disappear all at once and forever, even within the royal domains. In 1306 Philip the Good readmitted it into all accusations involving capital punishment except theft, where the crime had been committed "so secretly and quietly ('en repos') that it would have been impossible to convict the perpetrator by witnesses."[2] But it was an institution doomed to extinction. In Bouteiller, the wagers of battle appear as something unusual and adventitious; and Loysel says later, "All battles and combats are now probibited, and the king alone has the power to decree them."[3]

§ 4. **Torture.** — Although the judicial duel was kept up for a rather long time, and although Philip the Fair temporarily re-established it within the crown domains, this was, according to the Ordinance of 1306, because of the great difficulty in producing the two eye-witnesses required by the old customary law to sustain condemnation. But practice ere long introduced a new method of inquiry, as powerful as it was odious, namely, torture.

Torture is out of place in a purely accusatory procedure and in a free country; the accuser and the accused are two combatants who fight in broad daylight and with equal weapons. So at Rome, as long as the procedure remained strictly accusatory, torture was never made use of against a freeman. Although it did play a great part in criminal actions, that was when it was necessary to make a slave speak, either as an accused or as a witness; in the olden days the idea was universal that the slave only told the truth when under the influence of pain.[4] An exception to this rule was made by the law "Julia Majestates," which decreed that when the crime of high treason was concerned all accused persons without distinction might be put to the torture. As the criminal procedure underwent modification and the accusatory principle lost ground, the employment of torture was, ere long, admitted as

[1] "Établissements de St. Louis," I, 24; *Beaumanoir*, XXXIX, 21; LXI, 15, 16 (Salmon, Nos. 1165, 1722, 1723): "When king Louis abolished them (the wagers) in his court, he did not abolish them in the barons' courts."

[2] Ord. I, p. 435; *Isambert*, I, p. 831. See "Stylus Curiæ parlamenti," ch. XVI.

[3] "Inst. Cout.," VI, 1, max. 30.

[4] See *Geib*, "Geschichte des römischen Criminal prozesses bis auf Justinian," p. 348 *et seq.*; and our study on the "Délit d'adultère à Rome" (Nouvelle Revue historique, 1878, p. 416 *et seq.*).

a normal mode of proof in accusations or suits relating to serious matters, when strong presumptions already existed against the accused. But, except in actions for high treason, the "honestiores," that is, all those belonging to the upper classes of society above the rank of decurions, were by law exempt from torture.[1]

The system of private accusation which the barbarians brought with them did not recognize the employment of torture any more than did the old Roman procedure. When the "Leges" were drawn up, however, a place was found in a certain number of them for this cruel method of examination; these were the law of the Bavarians,[2] that of the Burgundians,[3] the law of the Vizigoths,[4] and even the Salic Law.[5] This was, of course, a borrowing from the Roman institutions;[6] but few of these laws sanctioned torture except in the case of an offense ascribed to a slave, and to that extent the borrowing is comprehensible. The Germanic law gave to the aggrieved party a right of action against the master of the delinquent slave,[7] with this proviso, that the owner could not undertake the defense of the "servus."[8] The latter was at that time obliged to defend himself; but he was not acknowledged to have the same rights as a freeman; he could not purge his fault by oath supported by co-swearers; he had to undergo the ordeal of fire or boiling water.[9] Was it not surer and simpler, without being more cruel, to subject the slave to torture, then, as did the Romans? So it was decided by the "Leges" cited above, precautions being taken, at the same time, for the indemnification of the master should the slave tortured prove to be innocent.[10] The law of the Burgundians subjected, not only

[1] *Geib, op. cit.* p. 615 *et seq.*

[2] *Merkel,* "Text. primus," Tit. IX, § 19. *Pertz,* "Leges," II, p. 306 (*Walter,* VIII, 18).

[3] Tit. VII, XXXIX, LXXVII (*Bluhme* edition). *Cf.* CVII, 3.

[4] L. VI, Tit. I, ll. 1–3.

[5] Tit. XL (*Merkel*).

[6] No manuscript version of chapter XL of the Salic Law contains any "Malberg glosses."

[7] *Cf. Wilda:* "Strafrecht der Germanen," p. 650 *et seq.*

[8] *Ripuar.*, Tit. XXX: "Si servus talis non fuerit, unde dominus ejus de fiducia securus esse possit, dominus . . . sine tangano loquatur et dicat: ego ignoro utrum servus meus culpabilis an innocens de hoc extilerit." *Walter,* I, p. 171.

[9] *Ripuar.*, XXX, § 1 (al. 31): "Quod si servus in ignem manum miserit et læsam tulerit, dominus ejus . . . de furto servi culpabilis judicetur." Lex Frision, III, 6: "Servus autem ad judicium Dei in aqua ferventi axaminet." *Walter,* I, 356.

[10] The Salic Law permitted the slave to be subjected to torture a second time, XL, 2: "Si confessus non fuerit, ille qui eum torquet, si adhuc voluerit ipsum servum torquere etiam nolente domino, pignus domino servi dare debet sic servus postea ad suppliciis majoribus subditur." *Bajuv.*, VIII, c. 23, § 1: "Si quis servum alienum injuste accusaverit, et innocens tormenta pertulerit . . . domino simile mancipium reddere non

the slave, but also the husbandman ("originarius, colonus"), to torture,[1] and in a peculiar provision, it even condemned to it the stranger ("advena") who came to seek refuge with a Burgundian. It is true, as the text shows, that such "advena" was strongly suspected of being a fugitive slave.[2]

The law of the Visigoths goes farther. More thoroughly impregnated than any other with Roman law, it allows torture even when the accused is a freeman, in default of other proof. Its system is most peculiar in other respects. It conforms the method to the accusatory principle. If the accuser cannot otherwise prove his accusation, he must claim the application of torture by an "inscriptio trium testium subscriptione roborata;[3] he must besides lay his complaint before the judge secretly and in writing, the confession made under torture being of no avail when the accused knew of what he was accused.[4] The accused is safeguarded in other respects. If he comes out of the ordeal victorious, his accuser is put at his discretion.[5] Moreover, a gentleman could not be tortured except for the most serious crimes "in caussis regiæ potestatis, vel gentis, aut patriæ, seu homicidii vel adulterii," and upon the accusation of a person of his own rank. The freeman of inferior station could also be put to torture for a theft or other offense, provided the value involved exceeded the sum of five hundred solidi.[6] Should a less sum be involved, the judge must subject the accused to the ordeal by boiling water, and if that did not show his innocence, he could then torture

moretur." *Cf. ibid.*, §§ 2, 3. Burg., VII, LXXVII. Lex Wisigoth, Book VI, Tit. I, l. 5.

[1] Burg., Tit. VII.

[2] Burg., XXXIX, § 1: "Quicumque hominem extraneum cujuslibet nationis ad se venientem susceperit, discutiendum judici presentet, ut cujus sit, tormentis adhibitis fateatur."

[3] Lex Wisigoth, Book VI, Tit. I, l. 2: "Quod si probare non potuerit . . . trium testium inscriptio fiat, et sic quæstionis examen incipiat." (*Walter*, I, 537.)

[4] *Ibid.*: "Accusator omnem rei ordinem scriptis exponat, et judici occulte præsentata sic quæstionis examinatio fiat . . . quod si accusator, priusquam occulte judici notitiam tradat, aut per se aut per quemlibet de re quam accusat per ordinem instruxerit quem accusat, non liceat judici accusatum subdere quæstioni, cum jam per accusatoris indicium detectum constet ac publicatum esse negotium."

[5] *Ibid.*: "Qui subditur quæstioni, si innoxius tormenta pertulerit, accusator ei confestim serviturus tradatur; ut salva tantum anima, quod in eo exercere voluerit, vel de statu judicare in arbitrio suo consistat." The remainder of the text also delivers up to the relatives of the accused the accuser who (he being the director of the torture) shall have caused the death of his victim in the torments.

[6] *Ibid.*: "Inferiores vero humilioresque ingenuæ tamen personæ, si pro furto, homicidio, vel quibuslibet aliis criminibus fuerint accusatæ, nec ipsi inscriptione præmissa subdendi sunt quæstioni, nisi major fuerit caussa quam quod quingentorum solidorum summam valere constiterit."

him.[1] It might also be possible to find in the law of the Burgundians a provision subjecting freemen to torture; but the text dealing with this is rather obscure.[2]

When the feudal system was evolved, torture, the use of which, as we shall show, had by no means wholly disappeared along with the judicial organization of the Roman empire, had no place in the accusatory and public procedure which brought the fief owner (" homme du fief " or " miles") before his peers. But is it quite certain that it was never employed when the justiciar or his provost arraigned before them those bondsmen and peasants who could not appeal from their sentence except to God?[3] Beaumanoir speaks of it in one passage rather in an appreciative way; but there is no mention of torture in Pierre de Fontaines. The " Livre de Jostice et de Plet," which, as we know, follows the order of the Digest, reproduces no provision under the title " de Quæstionibus," and its Book XX, which corresponds with Book XLVIII of the Digest, is one of those in which its unknown author lays completely aside the Roman law, to the influence of which he so often bows, to follow the purest and most archaic customary law. On the other hand, the "Assizes of the Court of Bourgeois of Jerusalem" contains two passages in which torture figures, and where it is mentioned as a well-known institution. One of these deals with the case of a dead man whom a person has buried at the home of the latter; public rumor reveals a crime: "And if it be known by public rumor that he had been killed, justice demands that the body shall be disinterred to ascertain how he met

[1] Lex Wisigoth, Book VI, Tit. I, l. 3: "Quamvis parva sit actio rei facta ab aliquo criminis, eum per examinationem aquæ ferventis a judice distringendum ordinamus, et dum facti temeritas patuerit, judex eum quæstioni subdere non dubitet."

[2] Tit. LXXXIX (*Walter*): "Gundebaldus rex Burgundionum omnibus comitibus . . . præceptionem ad vos dedimus ut si quos caballorum fures, aut effractores domuum, tam criminosos quam suspectos invenire potueritis statim capere et ad nos adducere non morentur. . . . Si vero criminosus inventus fuerit pœnam vel *tormenta* suscipiat quæ meretur." *Cf.* Bluhme edition, Tit. CVIII, and the note. (*Pertz,* "Leges III," 577.)

[3] In the first edition of this work I said: "*M. Beugnot* in the 'Glossaire' accompanying his edition of *Beaumanoir* gives the word 'gehine' (torture) without referring to any passage in the book and we have not been able to find any place where it is mentioned." But M. Salmon in his "glossaire" refers, at the word "gehine," to No. 1996 of his edition (CLXIX). *Beaumanoir* relates the strange and interesting story of a woman who caused her husband to be beaten to death by two ribalds and impudently tried to charge them with it before the judge; but the latter discovered the fraud; "then accused her of two lies which she had told and imputed the deed to her, and as soon as he determined to put her to the torture ('engehine') she confessed the whole truth and was burned." It is true that in this case there was only the threat of or presentment to the torture.

his death. And if it is seen or ascertained that the deceased had been strangled or killed by violence, the court is then bound to try these people by the drinking ordeal or torture so that it may ascertain the truth of this misdeed. And if he has killed him by violence,[1] it is right that all who were concerned in the misdeed should be buried head downwards without other injury."[2]

The other text deals with the case of a man whom two knights swear they surprised in the act of committing murder. Both men being relatives of the victim, their testimony is not sufficient to entail condemnation, in the absence of a confession, but it is sufficient to cause the accused to be put to the torture "*by water*" without having recourse to the accusatory procedure. "The evidence of two liege men should be equivalent to that of two sworn men ('jurés') and it is a matter for trial by the assize because the deceased is not related to the liege men. For if he were related reason judges that the prisoner should not be hanged if he did not acknowledge it. But it is quite reasonable that he should be put to the torture by water until he acknowledge the truth and as soon as he shall have acknowledged it, he should then be hanged. But if he acknowledge nothing under the anguish that he has suffered for three days,[3] he should then be imprisoned a year and a day, to see if within that period he will submit to the ordeal, or if any one will appear who will prove him guilty of this murder. And if no one appears within the year and the day and he will not submit to the ordeal he should be released from prison and therewith acquitted of the murder without being required to answer any one who should desire to accuse him, because he has done all that was required of him."[4]

The Ordinances lay down and regulate the employment of torture from the 1200s. The Ordinance of 1254, Art. 21, ordains that torture shall never be administered upon the testimony of a

[1] There is either an error or a hiatus in the text at this point: the *Kausler* edition has the note, "Locus lacuna laborat."

[2] Ch. 285 (*Beugnot* edition, II, p. 216). *Cf. Kausler* edition, CCLVIII (pp. 338, 339). The text, after explaining that it concerns a person who has buried a man in his house, proceeds: "If it happen that a man or a woman inter in the town, a dead man or woman in his or her house," then after declaring that the place is confiscated to the good of the Church, he adds: "And the body be given up to the mercy of God and the proprietor of the land, since he who has done such misdeed cannot very well be heard to say whether he killed him whom he buried or whether the latter died a natural death."

[3] It should be noted that according to the law of the Visigoths, torture could also last for three days. Book VI, Tit. I, l. 2: "Per triduum quæstio agitari debet."

[4] *Kausler* edition, ch. CCLIX, pp. 314, 315.

single witness when the accused is a man of good fame. "Personas autem honestas et bonæ famæ, etiam si sint pauperes, ad dictum testis unici, subdi tormentis seu quæstionibus inhibemus, ne hoc metu vel confiteri factum vel suam vexationem redimere compellantur."[1] In 1315, the nobility of Champagne protest against the use of torture, and the king decides upon their grievances: "Art. 51. Also, Concerning the complaint that our officers and provosts go upon their property to summon private persons and their men before them, and that they put them to the torture contrary to their customs and rights. We will and ordain that our said provosts and officers cease from all the aforesaid things, in accordance with the strictest commands of the old ordinances on the subject."[2] But here again all protests were doomed to futility; in the 1300s torture was already in general use.[3]

What were the causes which permitted the establishment of this odious procedure?

In the first place, the energetic repression of crime was necessary. Royalty strove to satisfy this necessity, so at first torture appears most frequently before its jurisdictions.[4] The influence of the Roman law was predominant. Our jurists found, in the pages of the Digest and the Code, the custom of torture expounded by the great jurisconsults and regulated by the constitutions of the emperors. Such weighty authority was without doubt bound to cause partial forgetfulness of the odious nature of this mode of examination, of its cruel character; moreover, the people of these rude times were not likely to be too sensitive.[5]

[1] Ord. I, p. 72. This article is one of those found in the Latin text only and wanting in the French text.

[2] Ord. I, p. 575.

[3] [For another account of the history of torture, see Professor *A. L. Lowell's* article on "The Judicial Use of Torture," Harvard Law Review, XI, 293. Further citations on its history in England are given in *Wigmore*, "Treatise on Evidence," 1905, I, § 818, n. 7.—TRANS.]

[4] A passage in *Bouteiller* ("Somme rurale," I, 34, p. 229) shows that not all of the jurisdictions had the right to put to the torture: "Be it known that in the case of a court where the men judge according to their custom and law, they should not judge by confession by torture, for such judges have no authority to put or cause any one to be put to torture, and cannot judge if it is not confessed before them without any recourse to torture, or if it is not duly proved by witnesses. And so the usage of inferior courts ordains."

[5] Other authorities did not blink the terrible nature of torture. See in this respect a curious passage in the "Très-ancienne Coutume de Bretagne," ch. XCVII: "If he deny the deed, and be taken either red-handed or in pursuit or the deed be notorious among the people of the parish, it is proper that he submit to the inquiry and the "garentie" (proof by witnesses) . . . and if it cannot be completely proved and common report or strong presumptions are found to be against him, he should have or-

A last cause was that torture filled a blank in the official prosecution, the "aprise," as we have described it. The "aprise," as we have said, could not form the basis of a capital sentence unless it contained testimonies so numerous and so conclusive that the fact could be regarded as notorious. Failing that, the confession of the prisoner was indispensable. That confession the judge must strive to obtain by every means, and to obtain it, seize whatever method, effective albeit cruel, was open to him. That consideration was decisive of the question; this is shown by the fact that when the prisoner accepted the inquest he could not be put to the torture; the practical effect of such acceptance was that a condemnation could be reached without recourse to torture. "Be it also known," says Bouteiller, "that when the prisoner submits to inquest he should never be put to the torture; for that would be to do him wrong and injustice. For torture should not take place except when the offense is such that proof cannot be brought or found and the offense is always presumed when information makes it clear." [1] This similarity between the rigorousness of the proofs and the use of torture is destined to form a vicious circle within which our old criminal procedure will revolve throughout its whole future existence.

Torture was introduced along with a rule which had the appearance of palliating its atrocity and which appears to have been recognized from the very beginning; the confession obtained was not held to be legally valid unless it was ratified after the pains inflicted had ceased. An Ordinance of the month of April, 1215, enacted in response to the complaints of the nobles of Champagne, reads as follows: "As it appears that our officers, against the ancient usages and customs of Champagne, endeavor to put to the torture the nobles of Champagne taken on suspicion of crime although they are not taken in the act nor in thorough knowledge of the fact. . . . We grant and ordain and forbid any nobles to be put to the torture, if the presumptions of the misdeed be not so

deal or torture three times. And if he can endure the torture or the ordeal without confessing he shall have saved himself (*and it will be evident that God performed miracles for him*), and he should go unscathed concerning the deed and it should be adjudged that he be acquitted and released." (*Bourdot de Richebourg*, IV, 1, p. 214.) — As in the passage in the "Assises" and that in the law of the Vizigoths quoted above the text speaks here of torture *on three occasions*.

[1] "Somme rurale," I, 34, p. 224. The same rule is found in the "Coutume de Bragerac," Art. 17 (*Bourdot de Richebourg*, IV, 2, p. 1015): "Item si burgensis sit accusatus de capitali crimine non manifesto, esto quod informatio adprehendat illum aut vehemens suspicio, dum tamen dictum crimen non sit notorium vel manifestum, *et velit se supponere inquestæ de dicto crimine, in isto casu non erit quæstionandus.*"

great that it is proper to do so by right and reason or the misdeed would remain unpunished, in which case it shall be henceforth forbidden and we hereby forbid that any one be condemned or judged on account of the said torture, *if he does not persist in his confession for a sufficient time after the torture.*" [1] This rule was maintained. "We have spoken of the voluntary confession, which is the third kind of proof held to be essential; for as to the involuntary confession made while under torture, that may very well constitute proof if the accused persists in it after the torture; otherwise, should he not persist, it forms rather a presumption than an essential proof." [2] But the palliation was more apparent than real. The judge, according to the "Très-ancienne Coutume de Bretagne," could repeat the torture three times. The accused who retracted after the torture naturally exposed himself to a fresh administration of it.

§ 5. **The Public Prosecutor.** — In the 1300s the official prosecution was already armed almost cap-à-pie; then appeared its principal medium, the *public prosecutor.*

The king's procurators and the procurators fiscal of the lords were originally merely men of business. The feudal procedure was, as we know, oral and formal, and like another formal procedure, that of the "Legis Actiones," it did not acknowledge the principle of representation in courts of law.[3] So far down as the 1200s even, no one could be represented in suing ("demandant") [4] civilly any more than criminally. The king and the sovereign lords were exceptions to this rule; they could sue by procurator ("demander par procureur"). This is the origin and primary meaning of the maxim "In France no one pleads by procurator save the king." The king and the nobility had, therefore, procurators entitled to prosecute their rights either before foreign jurisdictions or their own courts. These were advocates, practitioners in whom they placed their trust, and who were originally distinguished from their fellows only by having more illustrious clients. But it was predestined that these procurators of the king and the nobility should become real functionaries, and that was what practically did happen.

[1] *Isambert,* "Anciennes lois françaises," III, p. 90. *Esmein,* "L'acceptation de l'enquête dans la procédure criminelle au Moyen Âge," p. 9 *et seq.*

[2] *Bodin,* "De la démonialité des sorciers" (Antwerp edition, 1593), Book II, ch. III, p. 349; *cf. ibid.*, pp. 357, 358.

[3] [For the full history of this principle, as seen in Norman, French, English law, see the translation of Professor *Brunner's* essay, "The Early History of the Attorney," in the Illinois Law Review, II, 257. — TRANS.]

[4] *Beaumanoir,* IV, 2 (Salmon, Nos. 137, 138).

Besides their procurators, the king and the nobles had also certain advocates, who remained for a long time mere advocates, before being provided with a real office: "Be it known that the official advocate shall rank highest in the court of the lord he represents, as does the king's advocate in the royal courts. And be it known that where there is an official advocate for any lord he never can act as an advocate against that lord, even although he should receive no compensation or payment from the said lord. Law wills, however, that the official advocate may, at the will and with the permission of his own lord, act as counsel for any other lord, provided that it be not against his lord or against the cause which had been formerly pleaded on behalf of his lord." [1]

One of the most important duties of the king's procurator or fiscal was the superintendence of the prosecution of certain offenses: fines and forfeitures, the fruit of penal sentences, were one of the chief sources of revenue of the king and the nobles. The appellation of procurators fiscal, which was applied to the procurators of the seigniorial courts of law, still exists as a souvenir of this conception. Ere long another interest of a higher order was added to this original duty. Justice to all is the duty of the justiciar, and he is directly interested in the prosecution of crime; it is therefore his procurator's duty to secure its repression as far as possible. The procurator certainly could not constitute himself accuser as could an injured party, but it was in his power to instigate the judge to take cognizance. The above is a general view of the origin and original functions of the king's procurators; it is essential, however, to go more into detail, and in this respect the Ordinances are our best sources of information.

The king's procurators do not appear in any of the customary lawbooks of the 1200s; but, after 1302, Philip the Fair regulates their duties in terms which carry the conviction that the institu-

[1] "Somme rurale," II, 2, p. 671. *Loysel;* "Pasquier." "There was at that time (1380) no official king's advocate, but one of the attorneys general of the Court was chosen for the defense and protest of the rights and causes of the king, as occasion arose. This is shown by the Registers of Parlement of 18th February, 1411, where mention is made of one M. Jean Perier, canon of Chartres, who spoke as king's advocate, and also by the decrees and proceedings of M. Jean le Coq called Gally, who lived much later, namely, in the time of Charles VI, when he and several other advocates were employed to plead for the procurator-general, which prevented their pleading for the parties. . . . From which we gather two facts, one being that the titular office of king's advocate is modern inasmuch as the ordinary attorneys pleaded for the procurator-general, and the other that the king's advocates also pleaded for and advised the parties, when the king had no interest in the matter; and this is corroborated down to the time of Louis XII in regard to the pleading, and down to that of Francis I in regard to the consultations." (*Dupin* edition, pp. 23, 24.)

tion had already existed for quite a long time. That king wills particularly that they take a general oath, as in the case of royal functionaries, and that when they act in his name, they take the oath of calumny (" de calumnia ") like other parties.[1] He also forbids them to take up the causes of others, except in certain cases. We recognize here the king's counsel themselves. A reaction sets in, however. In 1318 the king's procurators are for a time suppressed in the districts following the customary law, and the duties they performed return to the bailiffs.[2] The cause of this suppression was probably the opposition of these districts to the new criminal procedure in which the procurators already played an important part. So we find the town of Lyons in 1347 demanding to be relieved of the king's procurator for a like reason.[3]

But such resistance was fruitless. In all the courts of the 1300's we shall see the king's procurators acting as an acknowledged power. The " Registre criminel de la justice de Saint-Martin des Champs," published by M. Tanon, which covers the period from 1332 to 1357, several times mentions the " procurator of our lord the King ";[4] and Jean Desmares ascribes to him a very clearly defined rôle.[5] As for the procurators of the nobles, their existence could not cause any trouble. That of Saint-Martin appears frequently enough in the " Registre criminel."

How do the procurators gain entrance into the criminal procedure? Not by appearing as direct accusers, — by constituting themselves parties; although we find some traces of such a con-

[1] Ord. I, p. 368: "Art. 15. Volumus insuper quod ipsi procuratores nostri jurent secundum formam infra scriptam.— Art. 20. Cæterum volumus quod procuratores nostri, in causis quas nostro nomine ducent, contrà quascumque personas jurent de calumnia sicut predicte persone. Et si contingat ipsos facere (substitos) substitutis satisfaciant et non partes adversæ, immo procuratores nostri de causis alienis se intromittere aut litteras impetrare non præsumant, nisi pro personis conjunctis ipsos contingeret facere prædicta." It is apparent that from this time the procurators are exclusively the king's agents. *Cf.* Ord. 1303, Art. 18 (Ord. I, p. 399).

[2] Ord. of 1310, Art. 29: "All procurators shall be withdrawn except those in places where the written law is followed." (Ord. I, p. 657.)

[3] Ord. of 1347, Art. 2: "Item super procuratore regio quem petunt removeri a civitate Lugdunensi cives prædicti, ordinamus seu providemus quod dispositio istius remotionis promittitur ad regem. Interim tamen in civitate Lugdunensi dictus procurator nullas inquestas promovebit, nisi illas quæ sibi mandatæ fuerint a seneschallo promoveri extrà civitatem Lugdunensem nec aliquas causas in dicta civitate nomine regis agitabit nisi primorum hereditates regis contingant." (Ord. II, p. 258.)

[4] 9th December, 1337 (p. 107); 1st July, 1339 (p. 153); 7th December, 1340 (p. 153); 4th September, 1343 (p. 198). All these cases dealt with difficulties as to jurisdiction arising between the royal judge and the judge of Saint-Martin.

[5] Decisions 89 and 150.

ception,[1] that would appear too contrary to the old principles, which required that one must have a direct interest before he could accuse. It is into the official inquest that they insinuate themselves, slipping in through an opening provided for them by the procedure "per inquisitionem" of the Canon law. We have seen that, according to the Canon law, the judge could be instigated to use his power by a denunciator, who could remain party to the action, producing his witnesses and furnishing his evidence; that is called "promovere" or "prosequi inquisitionem." This is the part which the procurator will play; he is the denunciator of all crimes, and intervenes in all prosecutions, whether he appears alone or in conjunction with a private individual.[2] His function, according to the Ordinance of 1347, cited above, is "promovere inquestas fieri." From the contemporary viewpoint, it is the judge who authorizes the king's procurator to act, not the latter who prompts action by the judge:[3] "Ordinance of 1350, Art. 15. Also, let no one be accused officially without sufficient information made under order of court by a party not suspected. And before the procurator begins his action or joins with the party, let the said information be seen and advised upon by the bailiff or other sufficient person acting on his order."[4] In the "Registre criminel de Saint-Martin" the official procurator appears several times, playing a part similar to that described.[5]

[1] *Jean Desmares*, 89: "The king's procurator in a criminal accusation in the bailliage of which he is procurator is not obliged to subscribe himself on pain of retaliation, 'secus de alus.'"

[2] *Biener*, "Beiträge," pp. 200, 201. The Church had also its official "promoters"; but they were of later creation and were copied from the "procurators" of the secular jurisdictions. See *M. Fournier*, "Les officialités au Moyen-Âge."

[3] Ord. of 1338, Art. 7: "Statuimus etiam prohibentes ne quis procurator regius partialiter se admergatur in causa quacumque nisi prius a judice, coram quo lis pendebit, in judicio, partibus præsentibus et auditis, mandatum expressum." (Ord. II, p. 124.)

[4] Ordonnance contenant plusieurs règlements en faveur des seigneurs et habitants de Normandie, à cause d'une imposition accordēe au roi. (Ord. II, p. 407.)

[5] p. 74 (18 October, 1336): "The said defaults with the prosecution of the said misdeed have been prosecuted so far by our promoter and procurator, as to the denunciation and claim made to our mayor of Saint-Martin by the said August." — p. 69: "Jehannette the haberdasher surrendered by the lieutenant of the provost and the king's procurator who held her prisoner." — pp. 187, 188 (30 September, 1842), an accused is acquitted "by action tried between the procurator of the Church and the said Jehan." — *Cf.* 223, 224. An agreement takes place upon a question of jurisdiction "between Master Pierre Martin, clerk and procurator of the Church of Saint-Martin des Champs of Paris of the one part and Jehan de la Bretesche, bailiff of Saint-Denis of the other part." M. Tanon very judiciously observes that at the period covered by our register the king's procurator did not appear to fill "the part in the prosecution of all crim-

But the farther we advance, the more important the action of the king's procurator becomes. We have already quoted a curious passage from Jean Desmares in this respect. Here is another of his decisions: "Also, when any high justiciar has had the prosecution and the first cognizance in his court, the pleading is bound by litiscontestation against any one amenable to his jurisdiction in regard to offenses . . . if there have been no privilege or defenses violated or other thing which could give the cognizance of the cause to another judge: in that case it is proper for the plaintiff to prosecute his action and his claim before that judge in the court in which it was commenced, notwithstanding that the plaintiff, *with the concurrence of the king's procurator*, demand that the cause be remitted to the court of the sovereign." — "When it happens," says Bouteiller, "that any one commits an offense in regard to which no one constitutes himself a party except the king's procurator by prior information,—for no one is brought into court except by summons on the request of the king's procurator,—if the person summoned should object, saying that he desires to be treated and judged by men ('hommes') or by complaint or prior commission . . . the king's procurator shall dispute this and say that the bailiff should judge him and take jurisdiction of the case, because *the king is the only party plaintiff* and it is on prior information. It was, however, declared by decree of Parlement in the year 1377 that the bailiff either alone or with such counsel as seemed good to him could and should take jurisdiction, since the king alone was interested and there had been prior information."[1]

We shall see the maxim that the king's procurator is a real accuser established later on, and that this title belongs to him alone; but some vestige of the original idea always remains; to the very last the judge has the power to take cognizance of the offense himself.

In the "Registre criminel du Châtelet de Paris," which runs from 6th September, 1389, to 18th May, 1392,[2] king's procurator Andrieu or Andry le Preux constantly figures; mention is also made of the king's attorney-general in the Parlement,[3] and the king's

inal matters which necessarily belonged to him later or in common with all the procurators fiscal." (Pref., p. lvii.)

[1] "Somme rurale," II, 1 (p. 653); *cf. ibid.*, I, 34 (p. 221). "Who may constitute himself formal party in denouncing, either by formal action, or officially at the request of the procurator or by the judge's official right."

[2] "Registre criminel du Châtelet de Paris" . . . published for the first time by the Society of French bibliophiles. 2 vols. Paris 1861.

[3] I, 301.

advocate.[1] For the most part, Andry le Preux is merely mentioned as figuring among the "preudhommes," who composed the council of the provost or his lieutenant, but a phrase appears from time to time indicating the rôle of public prosecutor. A judgment of 6th November, 1391, shows information made "by command of the honorable and learned master Jehan Truquan, lieutenant of Mons. the provost of Paris, at the request of the procurator of our lord the king at the said Châtelet against Jehannin Pelart . . . (of) which information the said prisoner desired to prosecute inquest."[2] The determinations of the accused and those of the king's procurator are reported several times: "The above named prisoner, Jehan Pelart, and also the said king's procurator, desire to prosecute their rights by the inquest hereinbefore made and written."[3]—"The inquest and process herein above written, by which the said king's procurator and prisoner have both desired to prosecute their rights, were seen, examined, and read word for word."[4] Finally, we find several oral requisitions by the king's procurator or fiscal reported;[5] one passage containing an abbreviated formula would seem, if it were set out at length, to recognize in the public prosecution the right which he will undeniably have later on, thanks to the rule of "further inquiry" (*post* p. 238).[6]

Simultaneously with the determining of the public prosecutor's rôle, rules for the official prosecution are laid down and embodied in the royal Ordinances. Like the "inquisitio" of the Canon law, this procedure necessarily embraces two parts, the information and the inquest. First of all the information must be made to the judge or his delegate,[7] since no one could be prosecuted

[1] I, 36, 74, 268, 373; II, p. 6: "The procurator at Chartres of our lord the king." The promoters or official promoters of the official are also mentioned several times. I, 84, 246, 255.

[2] II, p. 352, 4. [3] II, 356. [4] 16th January, 1390–1391, II, p. 26.

[5] 24th March, 1391–1392, "Gerart de Sanseurre was taken from the prison of the said Châtelet and brought before the aforesaid . . . who it was said and maintained by such procurator was an idler and a vagabond, without means or employment, etc." (II, 456). — 2d September, 1390 (II, p. 2): "Jehannin le Fournier . . . was taken from the prisons of my lord the duke at Tours . . . and was brought to trial in open hearing . . . and was there, by the procurator of said my lord the duke . . . accused of being of the condition and a confederate of certain prisoners who went up and down the land."

[6] 25th August, 1390 (I, 443): "Exculpated brother Pierre le Brun and the prior of the Jacobins, who were prisoners, because they had been accused at Chasteaudun, etc. And on account of this, done upon this advice of the aforesaid and others, the said prior and brother Pierre have been released from the said prisons, etc. Regarding the present, etc. Reserved for the king's procurator, etc."

[7] Sometimes the king's procurator proceeded with the information himself, not by order of the judge, but by virtue of a commission contained in royal letters. See Ord. of 1344, Art. 7 (Ord. II, p. 215).

officially "unless prior secret information against the said person be first made and advised upon." [1] The judge must deliberate upon this information with his counsel, and should he find that it contains sufficient charges, the real confrontative action then begins. In determining their essential features these two divisions of the action have not been invariably clearly separated.[2] Certain texts, however, leave nothing to be desired in the way of precision. We shall content ourselves with citing two chapters of the "Coutume de la Ville et Septène de Bourges": "Ch. XXXIX. *The mode of procedure against any accused of a criminal offense.* Proceedings must be taken against any one who is accused either by accusation or by denunciation in criminal cases, or in any important civil case in which the king may be greatly interested, as offenses done and attempted, villainies and wrongs on privileged persons, and on the king's burgesses within his domain, villainies done to officers of court or other important cases which demand immediate punishment. After secret information made by trustworthy people, above suspicion, if it be sufficient to show the guilt of the accused, his person and goods may be seized, and an inquest proceeded with, he being summoned, and by the inquest justice shall be done, and the arrest is always understood should the case require it. . . . Ch. XLI. *The difference between information and inquest.* There is a difference between information and inquest. The information does not carry condemnation. The inquest justly made, the party, being summoned to the hearing of the testimony and to see it judged and published, is thereby acquitted or condemned; and it is quite reasonable that the defendant should have first answered the 'articles' on his oath." Plainer language is impossible. It is evident that the "inquest" required the reappearance of the witnesses heard in the information, if not for the reiteration of their depositions before the accused, at least for the purpose of taking the oath in his presence. This reappearance could, however, be dispensed with if the accused waived it. It was then said that he consented that "the information be equivalent to inquest." This is a

[1] Ord. of 1363 (Ord. II, pp. 664–665); Ord. of 1350 (Ord. II, p. 400).

[2] See a note of *De Laurière* (Ord. III, p. 159): "The distinction which should here be drawn between the information and the inquest is that the former should be made by the judge officially, before any proceedings are taken against the person who is impeached in court as a criminal; the judge should determine after consideration of this information whether there is cause shown for an action against him or not. If such action be brought the judge then directs an inquest to be made."

formula found more than once in our "Registres criminels" of the 1300s.[1]

At this stage all the important features of the inquisitorial procedure have been already settled. Before going further it may be well to give a general sketch of the criminal procedure as it was known and practised in the 1300s and 1400s. Here we have sure guides. On one hand, Bouteiller's work, which, as we know, had a great success; on the other, the "Registre criminel de Saint-Martin des Champs," which shows us a criminal tribunal in action during the first half of the 1300s, and the "Registre criminel du Châtelet de Paris," extending from 6th September, 1388, to 18th May, 1392.

§ 6. **Final Changes. The "Ordinary" and "Extraordinary Procedures."**—According to Bouteiller, who aims at a systematic exposition, the criminal judge could take cognizance in four ways: "by denunciation, by present misdeed, by accusation of formal party ('partie formée') and by public report, of which inquest and prior information is made."[2] We shall go over these four methods with him, altering somewhat the order he has selected.

1. The *accusation of formal party* is the ancient accusatory procedure. "By formal party every judge who may and shall take cognizance of criminal cases, may and shall allow any man, lawfully competent, to become party against the accused and undertake and carry on the cause by close prison."[3] The principle of equal combat between the two adversaries always requires the imprisonment of the accuser as well as the accused. According to a rule borrowed from the Roman law, the accuser who was worsted was obliged to suffer the punishment which he had demanded. "In several places and according to the written law it is a dangerous matter to form party criminally against any one. For according to the written law he who fails therein incurs the same punishment that he would have been satisfied to have the prosecuted party sustain. This is called by the learned the punishment of retaliation."[4] This very harsh rule was, however, more honored in the breach than in the observance. A remission of the punishment was granted to the unsuccessful accuser on a petition directed by him to the court. This was called "praying for total pardon and remission." A severe punishment was inflicted in the case of calumnious accusation alone.

[1] "Registre criminel du Châtelet," II, 354. "Registre criminel de Saint-Martin des Champs," pp. 57, 83.

[2] "Somme rurale," I, 34 (p. 221).

[3] p. 222.

[4] *Bouteiller*, "Somme rurale," p. 222.

The accusation, burdensome and harsh, was a relic of the past. From the 1300s its use was infrequent. In the "Registre de Saint-Martin des Champs" we find but two certain examples of formal party, one on 7th October, 1332,[1] and the other on 14th January, 1338.[2]

2. On the disappearance of the accusation, the *denunciation* came more and more into use. It took place "when any one did not wish to make or form party against any one for a crime; he can always denounce him to the court and *offer to produce or name witnesses*."[3] The judge was by no means bound to prosecute. He first of all considered whether he ought to place confidence in the denunciation. If he decided to act, he proceeded with the information in the first place, then summoned or caused the arrest of the accused, and the action took its course. As Bouteiller clearly indicates, the denunciator was usually party to the action; he pointed out the witnesses and attended the inquest. He was in reality an accuser who kept in the background and from motives of personal interest left the chief part to the judge acting in his official capacity. By a natural enough phenomenon a part of the rules of the accusation were applied to the denunciation. The punishment of retaliation and the obligation to remain in prison were alone spared to the denunciator. All this is shown by the "Registre criminel de Saint-Martin." In that the denunciations are so frequent that it is useless to count them; it is by their means that the action usually begins.[4] The forms of denunciation differ in some degree. Sometimes it is said that the procedure is "on the request and denunciation" of such and such a person.[5] Sometimes the denunciation "denounces to us the deed as a matter for the court and prays us to do what is right

[1] "Brought into our prison by the men of the provost of Bondis, Jehannin de Saint-Soupplet, butcher, on the accusation made by Jehannin le Bouchier . . . because he accused the said Saint-Soupplet in judgment, declaring that he had stolen his wood . . . and that, besides, he was a murderer, and that so he would prove . . . and that on the aforesaid accusation the said provost had put and held him in prison. — Also, this day brought by the said provost's men the said Jehannin . . . accusing the prisoner" (pp. 25, 26).

[2] "Jehanne de Montargis, wife of Thomas Lenglais, and Colin Piquart held in our prison by the mayor for the reason that on trial before the mayor the said Jehanne said, maintained and affirmed on oath against the said Colin . . . and the said Jehanne offered to prove what is said" (p. 117).

[3] *Bouteiller*, p. 221.

[4] See pp. 10, 16, 19, 27, 31, 32, 34, 41, 48, 57, 63, 67, 68, 81, 82, 84, 89, 93, 94, 98, 102, 114, 116, 124, 132, 139, 143, 145, 166, 167, 173, 174, 178, 203, 207, 209.

[5] pp. 167, 173, 174, 185, 186.

and just therein."[1] Or again, "He requests that we will administer the law and do justice for him in the matter."[2] The denunciation is made to the judge, but it is usually repeated in public court in presence of the accused.[3] The denunciator is called upon to furnish witnesses, and he must prove his cause of action;[4] should he subsequently declare that he demands nothing from the accused, or if he fail to furnish witnesses, or abandon, the consequence would appear to be the acquittal of the person prosecuted.[5]

One judgment seems even to import into the procedure of denunciation the release or "deliverance," which was formerly pronounced when, an accused being held prisoner, no accuser appeared within a certain time: "3d May, 1332. Released Godefroy Lalement after VIII days imprisonment. . . . Acquitted in regard to the contumacies which he impetrated against the denunciation by the council of the assizes the Sunday after Saint-Nicholas of May."[6] It might appear from the following that calumnious denunciation was punished: "He says in judgment and on oath that he had caused their imprisonment without cause, and that he repented of it and compensated them" (p. 102).

The blending of the accusation and the denunciation which takes

[1] p. 114. [2] p. 188.

[3] pp. 32, 34: "And it is denounced to us by our said mayor of St. Martin, in the manner aforesaid, in the presence of the said Jehan (the accused)" (p. 188). — In one case, the denunciator is wounded and cannot be brought to the place where the court is held; the judge in such a case goes to him and receives his denunciation before witnesses.

[4] p. 105: "It was sufficiently proved by Marie, wife of Jehannin de Trambley," the denunciatrix; — action of Sedille Lenglaiche "for the reason that Estienne the painter had denounced against her . . . acquitted by action tried between her and the said Estienne (4 May, 1345)."

[5] On 23d February, 1338, Endelot de Picardie denounces against Guillaume Damours, mason, that he had ravished her: "The said Endelot denounced the aforesaid crime, and asserted on oath the said denunciation to be true, and which the said Guillaume denied completely. — And this done, he immediately required and summoned the said Endelot, if she had any witnesses by whom she could inform us of the truth of the said fact, that she should name and produce them, which she swore and affirmed on her oath that she had not. . . . And to fully inform ourselves of the said case we grant day to the said Endelot on Thursday next. — Acquitted because she never prosecuted her denunciation." 22d December, 1332: "Guillot le Pelletier was put and held in our prison on the denunciation of Richart . . . who has been acquitted by party and therefore delivered from prison and set at liberty by the court" (p. 31). — 26th November, 1336: "Sedilon la Franquette . . . held in our prison on the denunciation of Guillot . . . delivered because he withdrew and claimed nothing of him" (p. 81). — 13th October, 1338: "Michelet le Lièvre and Catherine his wife denounced to Autel Labbé mayor of Saint-Martin against Guillot de Soissons . . . delivered from prison because party did not wish to claim anything of him" (p. 145); *cf.* pp. 200, 203; *cf.* "Registre criminel du Châtelet de Paris," I, 309.

[6] pp. 10, 11; *cf. M. Tanon, ibid.*, note 1.

place here is by no means a casual commingling; from this is destined to spring a very original institution, — that of the civil party. From this time, it must be noted, the injured party is allowed to act in a civil suit, for the purpose of obtaining reparation, without bringing the criminal action: "In a criminal case," says Jean Desmares in his decision 58, "which seeks for a civil reparation, only two defaults are sufficient, but the facts must be proved; and in that seeking a criminal reparation, four are essential, and the applicant need not prove his facts." We also read in the "Registre de Saint-Martin": "3d May, 1332. This day Thomasette de Piront made civil demand against Marote de la Mare, wife of Richard Lenglais, and Huete de la Mare, her sister, saying that in the stews of the said Marote she had delivered her purse into the care of the said Huete, and lost, from its contents, the half of XXIII pieces of white 'maille,' and seeking solely for the restoration of her lost chattel. Imprisoned. The said sisters released after VIII days imprisonment to this date." [1] These prosecutions for civil purposes are often found in the "Registre du Châtelet." The parties then took great care to limit their demand "protesting and declaring only civil reparation is sought." [2] — "Pierre des Moulin, master of arts . . . makes express protest and calls the aforesaid parties present in witness that he intended to say, he did it not for any injury, but to tell the truth, and also that he only looked for civil reparation." [3] — "These scholars protesting that they sought for civil reparation." [4] — "Guillaume Certain . . . by manner of denunciation and for civil issue says and reports to the said Mons the provost." [5] The object of these reservations and protests is to make it plain that, although parties to the action, the denunciators do not formulate a real accusation, from the consequences of which they recoil; they also show that this distinction is still a novelty and that mistakes might be made.

3. The case of "*present misdeed*" ("présent meffait") is the ancient procedure of capture in the act; "by present misdeed may and shall be understood that the judge may and shall officially take action against the delinquent and convict him of the deed and sentence him to capital punishment solely of his own accord, without other denunciation or prior information; if he deny and the case be easy of proof, the judge or official procurator shall offer to prove it, and, this proved, punishment

[1] p. 11. [2] I, 213. [3] I, 310. [4] I, 138.
[5] II, 275. See II, 89, a sentence which awards to the civil party his conclusions.

shall follow, and if proof of it be not quite clear, since the case is of present misdeed, the judge may and shall put him to the torture to ascertain the truth." [1] The "taking in present misdeed" occurs very often in the "Registre de Saint-Martin." [2] Even the old customs are found to be faithfully preserved. The clamor of "harou" is mentioned several times, and it is often said that the criminal has been "taken on chase and proclamation." [3]

4. Finally, the proceeding by "*common report*" is the ancient "aprise": "by common report may be summoned into a secular court by prior information, or otherwise by bruit and notorious report, as where any one may be so noted in the district as a murderer or highway robber, that it is clear and known to all that he is so: in such case prosecution of the crime may be made by the judge officially without other party, or by office, or by the procurator officially, and the judge may do it officially at his request." [4] The action must always begin by information, except in the accusation by formal party, and in the case of capture in the act, where the matter is urgent. This is an important point, and it is a characteristic feature which the later law will enforce with still greater strictness. In the "Registre de Saint-Martin" the official charge is very frequent. It goes under its ancient name of "arrest on suspicion." The two parts of which it is composed, the information and the inquest, are clearly indicated in several passages; [5] in several others care is taken to state that the capture of the prisoner has not taken place until after prior information.[6] Sometimes, however, only the inquest is mentioned, without any

[1] *Bouteiller*, p. 222.

[2] pp. 38, 58, 63, 64, 73, 77, 92, 93, 99, 104, 124, 130, 134, 136, 138, 142, 151, 156.

[3] "Brought them into prison, and also because their neighbors in the street raised the hue and cry upon them, they having fled" p. 115. — "Captured them in hot pursuit and on the hue and cry of neighbors," p. 141. — "That when she cried *harou* he had put her hood over her mouth, in order that her cries should not be heard" (p. 47). — "Our officers arrested him at night with candles burning in pursuit and on hue and cry" (p. 71). *Cf.* "Registre du Châtelet," I, 410. "*Harou* the murder," II. 63; "*Harou* the fire."

[4] *Bouteiller*, p. 223.

[5] "6th November, 1341. Acquitted by the council by the *inquest, information* and report of the sworn men made upon the aforesaid case, by the mayor" (p. 184). — "Delivered from prison by the *inquest* and *information* which has been made by the mayor of the said town of Bouffemont and elsewhere" (p. 185). — "Acquitted of the fact and of his murder by our council by virtue of the *information* and *inquest* made by the mayor upon it" (p. 189). — In many cases, it is true, one of the two only is indicated.

[6] "6th April, 1337: Jehannin Leuffaut of Paris brought by Robin the jailer and Croz who arrested him . . . for the reason that we were sufficiently informed that he had beaten Jacquemin de Soissons to the effusion of blood" (p. 93). — "On 18th January, 1338, Jehan de Florence Lom-

question of information;[1] under either hypothesis we may say that the information alone exists, replacing the inquest and so performing a double function: it is true that in the one case it takes place with the consent of the accused himself, and that in the other the result is favorable to him.[2]

When the judge takes cognizance, two ways present themselves to him, and we find two forms of procedure, the "*ordinary*" and the "*extraordinary*." This is a leading distinction, the importance of which will constantly continue to increase: "Also, Be it known that there are actions ordinary and extraordinary."[3] The "ordinary" procedure took its course in public; it knew nothing of the employment of torture, and it allowed the accused an unfettered defense. In the "extraordinary" procedure, on the other hand, torture was allowed; secrecy very soon began to find its way into it, and the defense was bound to be thereby more and more trammelled. This was, unfortunately, the procedure of the future. And this duality is found almost everywhere else in Europe at this period.

When must one or other of these ways be taken? The "ordinary" procedure was always followed when there was accusation by formal party: "And it should be known that, according to some, if the prisoner is arrested on accusation by formal party and put to his law he should not afterwards be put to the torture, but should be tried by ordinary action."[4] The parties respectively brought their witnesses, who were heard by the examiners ("enquesteurs"); the inquest was immediately communicated to the accused; the advocates or defendants argued on both sides in open court, and on this the sentence was based. Pierre Ayrault will be found as late as the 1500 s describing this form of procedure, then extinct, but whose disappearance was regretted by his strong intellect and great heart: "I have read," he says, "among the criminal actions brought more than six score[5] years ago by master Jean Belin, lord of Doinart and Foudon, my grand

bart, brought by command of the mayor and by information made by P. de Chivry our tabellion, for the reason that it was proved and found by the said information that he had beaten and struck basely blows causing contusions" (p. 115).

[1] p. 24; 200.

[2] "14th June, 1336. Ydre de Laon . . . delivered by imprisonment and by information that she agreed to inquest" (p. 57). — "12th November, 1336; Pierre Terlait, resident of Saint-Martin is given up to the court of the monastery by the provost of Paris who had arrested him on suspicion; delivered by information made by R. Pié de Fer examiner of the Châtelet de Paris" (p. 83). See above.

[3] *Bouteiller*, "Somme rurale," I, 34 (p. 223).

[4] *Ibid.*

[5] This takes us back to the middle of the 1400 s.

uncle, that by ordinance a time was granted to the party to bring witnesses for the prosecution and to the accused to do the same in his defense, provided in the latter case he had by his answers brought forward some fact in justification or extenuation. It seems to me (or I am deceived with antiquity) that nothing could be more equitable or just . . . The whole action took place at one time, and as in a single picture, the truth for both parties was presented before the judges."[1] In a system in which the denunciator and the accuser were so nearly assimilated, such as that which we have noted in the "Registre de Saint-Martin," this rule was bound to be followed even in case of denunciation.

The "ordinary" procedure had to be adopted even in the official prosecution when the individual prosecuted accepted the inquest: "If the doer be then arrested and desire to submit to all inquests, in all such cases he shall be admitted to ordinary action and shall only be treated on accusation of party or officially, and by proofs, without any torment of 'question' whatsoever, and without threats made, and shall always have reasonable imprisonment and facility for the conduct of his whole cause."[2] This is confirmed by a passage from the "Livre des Droiz et Commandemens de Justice": "If any be suspected of any criminal matter and the law pursue him as guilty, he shall be apprehended and punished according to the degree of the misdeed, and if he who is accused knows nothing of (the matter) he shall request the court to proceed against him in regard to the said offense, for the purpose of being acquitted of the deed. And the mode of action should be such that the judge may declare the fact in judgment by way of demand against him and lead finally to punishment should he confess; and if he denies (it) he should offer to make such proof of it as shall be reasonable. And he who is accused should allege his reasons and justifications and undertake proof thereof as is meet. And on this follows the allegation of the facts and the granting of authority to either side to bring his witnesses and make his inquiries, and then other lawful procedure. And the proceedings shall be conducted with greater deliberation and more leisurely in such cases, than in others."[3] In the "Registre de Saint-Martin" we find a certain number of cases where the criminal expressly submits himself to inquest.[4]

[1] "L'ordre et formalité et instruction judiciaire," Book III, Art. 2, No. 50.

[2] *Bouteiller*, "Somme rurale," II, 3 (p. 765).

[3] § 943.

[4] "23d August, 1332; Robin Fleurian . . . has submitted in our information to inquire into the request above mentioned" (p. 23). — "The

In contrast with the "ordinary" procedure is the "extraordinary" procedure. Its very name is awe-inspiring; and it will be said of it that it owes the name to the fact that the normal rules of law are no longer observed.[1] Bouteiller already gives a sufficient idea of the powers which it allows to the judge: "Also, the extraordinary action shall be used and brought in all other cases, especially in great and heinous crimes which are denied, and which have been committed secretly. And the judge shall not hesitate to bring the extraordinary action and to learn the truth daily, without any intermission, by information or otherwise."[2] The "extraordinary" action allowed torture. "If the person in question be found anyway suspected by strong presumption, he (the judge) may and shall put him to torture according to his physique, for one person can stand more severe torture than another, and the judge should by all means take care that he does not torture the man so that he thereby loses life or limb, for that is at the peril of the judge and his agents, also that he refrain from torture by fire, which is forbidden by the king; and if by dint of torture he will say nothing nor confess the first time, the judge can repeat it the second day, and even the third and fourth if he sees that the case requires it, and if there be such great presumption and the prisoner be a man of high courage."[3]

Another feature erelong distinguished the "extraordinary" procedure. The depositions of the witnesses were not produced to the accused. Everything was hidden from him for the purpose of removing from him the means of evading the prosecution. Originally, conformably to the principles of the Canon law, the "acta inquisitiones" were produced to the accused, both in the official inquiry and in that which took place upon the accusation of a party. This communication was ordered by the Ordinance of 1254, Article 21: "Et quia in dictis seneschaliis secundum jura et terræ consuetudinem fit inquisitio in criminibus, volumus et mandamus

men of Saint-Martin arrested him at Noysi and consigned him to close prison. He submitted to inquest concerning this matter, and the inquest was made by the men of Saint-Martin concerning this misdeed; it could not be proved against the man" (p. 225). — "The barber of Anet and his son arrested on suspicion of murder . . . were brought to Paris and personally to Saint-Martin for this matter; they submitted to inquiry and the inquest was made against them upon this matter by the men of Saint-Martin" (pp. 228, 229).

[1] *Damhouder*, "Practica criminalis," Pars. III, quæstio 103, No. 21: "Nonnunquam proceditur ordinarie et secundum juris ordinem et aliquando extraordinariè, id est, juris ordine non servato." It is true that the law mentioned here is the Roman law.

[2] *Bouteiller*, "Somme rurale," I, 13 (p. 765).

[3] *Ibid.*, I, 34 (pp. 228, 229).

quod reo petenti acta inquisitiones tradantur ex integro."[1] An Ordinance of 1338 grants to the parties in a general way the right to attend at the hearing of the action which took place before the assembled bench.[2] But gradually the tendency grew to refuse production of the documents to the accused: "Certe jure canonico et civili judex ex officio potest procedere infamia præcedente . . . de hac facienda est inquisitio, quam judex non tenetur parti ostendere nisi velet."[3] — "Although in the Parlement no publication of witnesses is made either in civil or criminal causes, yet publication of the names and testimony of the witness is made in the Châtelet, and in criminal causes as to the names only and not of the testimony, and for this reason; if publication were made of the testimony in criminal causes, when the guilty defendant knew that the crime was proved against him, he could flee, and thus offenses would remain unpunished and he could encompass the death, annoyance, and obloquy of those who had testified against him."[4] This secrecy, which recalls the proceedings of the "inquisitio hæreticæ pravitatis," became one of the distinguishing features of the "extraordinary" procedure: "Be it known that where one is to be put to the torture on prior information which shows genuine and strong suspicion of the crime for which he is imprisoned, which crime he does not deny, the said information and crime shall be shown to the counsellor of the Court before the prisoner is put to the torture and the prisoner shall be heard as to why he denies the crime contrary to the information laid against him, *without the information being shown to him,* it shall, on the advice and order of the counsellors of the Court, be declared that the prisoner be put to the torture."[5]

It is to be noted that, even though it should have proved impossible to obtain the confession of the accused by torture, he could not on that account be fully acquitted: "If by torture he will say nothing, nor confess, and is not convicted by witnesses, if it should happen that, on suspicion, he be imprisoned for a long time and by 'exclamasse,'[6] to ascertain if any will appear against him, and if for a long time none appear, the punishment of imprisonment which he shall have undergone and suffered shall be the penalty

[1] Ord. I, p. 72.

[2] "Statuimus et mandamus relationes processum tam civilium quam criminalium amodo fieri coram seneschallis et judicibus aliis . . . in præsentia partium litigantium si ad id voluerint interesse." (Ord. II, p. 125.)

[3] *Joannes Faber*, "ad Instituta, tit. De publicis judiciis."

[4] *Jean Desmares*, 262.

[5] *Bouteiller*, "Somme rurale" I, 34 (p. 229).

[6] Proclamation by public hue and cry.

for the bad presumption, and then he should be released at the discretion of the judge on pain of being attainted and convicted of the matters with which he is charged and of which he is presumed guilty, and no other release ('delevrance') shall be made by the judge, for if he be freed absolutely, it would seem that he had been held prisoner without cause."[1]

In this "extraordinary" procedure we already find the prototype of the 1500s and 1600s; the information as a starting point; then the order "à l'extraordinaire" decreed by a judgment; the application of torture, also decided by judgment; and, lastly, something resembling the "further inquiry" ("plus amplement informé"). It still, however, offered the accused a certain number of safeguards which were subsequently to disappear. The publicity of the hearing still remained. Originally, as we have said, the pleadings were made in the open air, but that state of matters necessarily disappeared along with the old feudal customs. "The vestiges of it," says Ayrault, "are still at the doors of churches, castles, markets, and public places where the benches of the judges still remain. They have begun to deride the open air judges, now that they have erected courts of justice and court-rooms to judge in. But that shows that formerly the greatest judged there very well."[2] Publicity, however, still existed within the court-rooms, somewhat restricted, it is true. To quote Ayrault once more: "The actions of the late master Jean Belin, lieutenant-general of this jurisdiction, which we have mentioned, usually note that seven or eight named by him, besides himself and his clerk of court, were present at the examination, and he adds, 'and several others,' to show that admittance was open to all who desired it."[3]

This publicity is likewise shown in the "Registre criminel de Saint-Martin des Champs"; it extended to everything which took place at the trial, that is, except the information or the inquest made before the commissioners or examiners ("enquêteurs") and the torture administered in secret. The clerk of court of Saint-Martin is careful to specify the principal persons present,

[1] *Bouteiller*, "Somme rurale," II, 13 (p. 765); *cf.* I, 34 (p. 229). — This principle is often applied in the "Registre de Saint-Martin"; it speaks of a man "delivered by imprisonment" (pp. 57, 64). — "Delivered by long imprisonment and by being beaten with rods" (p. 67). — Sometimes only a penalty was inflicted on the unconvicted accused; it was then said that he was delivered by penalty; when he could not pay, however, the matter was ended by his being set at liberty under the formula "Delivered by poverty" (pp. 77, 95, 99, 100, 101, 102).

[2] "L'ordre, formalité," etc., Book III, Art. 3, No. 56.

[3] *Ayrault, op.* and *loc. cit.*, No. 71.

always adding at the end of the list "and several others." That it was indeed a veritable public and not merely chosen assistants is shown by the fact that the names of artisans abound and that women are often designated.[1] Publicity is particularly proved for the following documents: first, the denunciation, which must be repeated at the trial,[2] then the reports of physicians or midwives, which play an important part,[3] the release of prisoners on bail,[4] the confessions made at the trial and the sentences which follow thereon.[5] Publicity is also the rule for the judgment on declinatory pleas and confessions from foreign jurisdictions,[6] for the reading of royal letters,[7] and the exhumation and examination of bodies.[8]

Liberation on bail is still practised very extensively, according to the "Registre criminel de Saint-Martin." It does not appear to have ever been a matter of right, but it seems that the judge could always grant it; in fact, we find it granted in very serious cases, such as theft, where capital punishment was involved.[9] The sureties pledged themselves, according to the old formula, "body for body, property for property"; they were as a rule only answerable for the appearance of the accused;[10] they sometimes also undertook to pay the amount decerned for.[11] In one case the prisoner, instead of furnishing sureties, gave in pledge "two anvils of the value of LX sols of Paris";[12] latterly, they were sometimes liberated without bail.[13] The pecuniary sufficiency of the sureties was, besides, not the only security had against the accused who was set at liberty; failing his appearance he was as a matter of course declared attainted and convicted.[14] This presumption of guilt arising from flight is one which was to remain a long time in our law.

Rigorous as the "extraordinary" procedure was, it for a long time allowed the accused to defend himself. Before sentence he could plead his cause or have it pleaded for him; and he could also allege facts in justification and prove them by witnesses. In this respect there must originally have been a considerable laxity, for

[1] See, in particular, pp. 20 and 28. [2] pp. 35, 41, 42, 114, 124, 167.
[3] pp. 13, 19, 20, 22, 29, 35, 36, 45, 46, 48, 64, 106, 109, 112, 117, 127, 133, 139, 170, 171, 173, 181, 188, 189.
[4] pp. 30, 31, 33, 34. [5] pp. 26, 51, 174.
[6] pp. 39, 40, 47, 50, 52. [7] p. 62. [8] pp. 148, 197.
[9] See 29th March, 1332, p. 4; 12th April, 1332, p. 6; *cf.* pp. 3, 4, 5, 6, 14, 15, 22, 28, 32, 33, 34, 37, 40, 127, etc.
[10] The formula is then: "Sureties for his appearance before us each day for which we shall summon him."
[11] p. 127. [12] p. 34.
[13] "27th January, 1328: Released Jehanne de Montargis, on himself." It is true that Jehanne was an accuser in formal action.
[14] See pp. 4, 6.

we even find the following in the "Pratique" of Masuer: "If the accused, being imprisoned, offer to prove his defenses, he should be allowed to do so before proceeding further, provided he can do it easily; and this is reasonable, especially as irreparable injury and damage is involved." [1]

In Bouteiller's time the "extraordinary" procedure appeared only as a last resource; it gave place to the "ordinary" procedure when there was a formal party, and even when the accused, prosecuted officially, submitted to the inquest. To this extent, though it was not lawful, it was almost tolerable. This state of matters could not last, and the exception was found to become the rule. The prisoners could refuse to accept the inquest; it might be to their advantage to do so, for it is quite possible that, in conformity with the early spirit of the institution, eye-witnesses were not at that time essential. That would give an opportunity for the "extraordinary" procedure. But it must frequently happen that the testimonial proof did not furnish sufficient evidence of guilt, either in the accusation by formal party or in the accepted inquest. Would not the judge feel an almost irresistible temptation to employ even torture to extract the confessions which he believed to be necessary? That is exactly what happened, as Bouteiller himself acknowledged by reversing all the rules and distinctions which he had laid down. After saying that torture is not allowed when there is a formal party, he adds: "Should the judge consider the case as one of murder and the prisoner be so cunning that nothing can be learned by the testimony and the case is 'prima facie' made out, then the judge shall have power to put to torture if that be possible without doing harm." [2] To the same purpose he specifies a number of serious cases where the person under suspicion is not permitted to exculpate himself ("se mettre à purge"),[3] and where the "extraordinary procedure" should be compulsory: "Several cases do not allow of purgation, such as murder, arson (of houses), violation of women, highway robbery, . . . treason, heresy, unnatural offenses . . . by purgation all

[1] "La Pratique de Masuer," done into French by *Antoine Fontanon*, new edition by *Pierre Guénois*, Paris 1606 (Book XXXII, No. 14, p. 589). The translator, *Fontanon*, carefully points out in a note that this is the old law. "In regard to what is said in two different articles as to the accused being allowed to prove and verify his justifications and defenses, and that restoration should be made of his goods seized on his giving bail, that has since then been somewhat changed."

[2] "Somme rurale," I, 34 (p. 223).

[3] This is doubtless the same procedure as that indicated in the "Ancien coutumier de Picardie" by the expression "se mettre à loy." See above, p. 64.

would escape, because when a man is 'put to purgation' he cannot be tried by any but an 'ordinary action,' and *the above-mentioned cases should be tried by 'extraordinary' actions.*"[1] This movement was undoubtedly brought about in great measure by the learned system of "legal proofs"[2] which found its way into jurisprudence. This system had been borrowed from the law-doctors, especially those of Italy, who, in turn, had found its first germs in the Roman law, and had developed them to a great extent. Very clear or "open" ("bien apertes") proofs were necessary; "according to the law, proofs in criminal matters should be as clear as the sun at noonday to show cause." In default of the accused's confession, certain proofs, the nature of which was determined beforehand, were essential to base a condemnation; and a desire to obtain the confession at all hazards was the inevitable consequence. Very soon it made no difference whether the accused accepted the inquest or not; the "ordinary" or the "extraordinary" procedure was followed according to the greater or less gravity of the crime. So strong is the influence of an old usage, however, that to the last the custom was kept up of asking the accused if he wished to put himself upon the witnesses.[3]

At first sight it would appear as if the "Registre criminel de Saint-Martin" made no distinction between the two forms of procedure. Nowhere does it specifically mention the "extraordinary" or "ordinary" actions; but it substantially shows that there is a difference between the cases. Whenever a matter so serious as to warrant the infliction of capital punishment is in question, we find one or other of the following formulas: — "Action tried — crime: action tried — criminal action."[4] When, on the other hand, the data of the information do not reveal a serious crime, or when the report of the physician ("mire juré")

[1] "Somme rurale," I, 34 (p. 223).

[2] [See *post*, Part II, chap. III on the system of "legal proofs." TRANS.]

[3] See *Dupaty*, "Mémoire pour trois hommes condamné à la roue," Paris 1786, p. 20. — "Réquisitoire" of Louis Séguier, to demand the suppression of Dupaty's "Mémoire," pp. 30, 31: "It is true that the final question put to these prisoners substantially demands *whether they wish to trust to (the evidence of) these witnesses*, and that they replied, 'Yes, if they tell the truth.' *This question is a formal one in all our first interrogatories;* from none is it omitted. It does not assume either complaint made, information ordered, or witnesses heard. It can neither mislead, deceive nor surprise the prisoners."

[4] pp. 43, 66. Note by *M. Tanon:* "A similar statement is met with in the majority of capital cases. Its principal object is to indicate the inquisitorial procedure adopted by the judge in serious criminal cases. Bouteiller calls 'extraordinary' action that which is adopted in *serious and heinous crimes.*" See pp. 78, 81, 121, 169, 177, 180, 186, 187, 188, 219–221.

states that the victim is "not in danger of death or loss of limb" it is observable that the parties plead civilly.[1] This does not mean that the case is a purely civil one, as we would express it nowadays, for a penalty is often inflicted,[2] but merely that there is no occasion for a criminal punishment, and that the proceedings will be by "ordinary" action ("procès à l'ordinaire") and will follow the rules of civil procedure, which were originally also those of criminal procedure. The "Registre" contains a passage which expresses this very clearly: "Information is made of it and converted into civil and has expiated the offense against our safety."[3] The Ordinance of 1670 will contain thé same phraseology.[4]

The "Registre de Saint-Martin" does not specify the employment of torture in so many words; but it must be noted that the details of the proceeding are not stated, and that nearly all those who undergo capital punishment after action brought, are declared "to have confessed." In one particular case, moreover, the clerk of court expressly states that the confession has been obtained without torture: "Jaquet, son of Jehan Duderot, aged nine years or thereabouts, detained in our prison, for the reason that he confessed, without constraint or terror of *torture* ('*gehine*')."[5] Sometimes proceedings are employed to obtain a confession which call to mind the threat of torture, — the mere presentment, "présentation," — practised in later times.[6]

[1] p. 35: "Sent out of crime — acquitted civilly." — p. 76: "And pleaded civilly, are released next day." — p. 127: "They proceed." — p. 94: "Reported the peril suffered by duchess Emmeline; criminal denunciation; — civil, they proceed." — p. 116: "Crime reported, civil."

[2] p. 82: "Civil — by penalty." — p. 83: "Crime — reported — civil and penalty." — p. 93: "Civil — penalty."

[3] p. 97.

[4] Ord. Tit. XX, Art. 3: "If it should appear before the confrontation of witnesses that the matter should not be prosecuted criminally, the judges shall receive the parties in ordinary action. And for this purpose they shall decree that the informations be converted into inquests." See *Jousse* upon this article: "This is called civilizing a (criminal) process or remitting the parties to civil remedies. It may, however, be said, all things being considered, that this procedure does not put an end to the criminal action; but that from that time that action merely ceases to be prosecuted by the extraordinary method, and commences to be prosecuted by the ordinary method."

[5] p. 51. See Introduction, pp. lxxxviii to xci.

[6] "And subsequently the Saint-Martin people brought them back to Noisi, and brought them by force and made believe that they would hang them. And they would nowise confess the said murder, and because it was not quite clearly proved against them, the Saint-Martin men banished them at Noisi in the court of Saint-Martin perpetually and on pain of the gallows, from all the Saint-Martin land" (p. 229). The men concerned had submitted themselves to inquest, and probably this stratagem was employed against them because they could not be tortured according to the rules laid down. See *M. Tanon*, p. xcix: "They were allowed to submit to inquest. If they did the effect of the inquest was

Finally, an examination of the state of the decisions of the earliest provostship of France as it existed at the end of the 1300s is a matter of interest to us, as those decisions would inevitably serve as an example to other provostships.

There is not, in the "Registre criminel de Châtelet de Paris," which, as we know, covers the period between 1389 and 1392, a solitary case of real accusation, that is to say, by formal party. The term accusation [1] appears often enough, but it is quite apparent that these are in reality nothing other than denunciations. It is always the court which prosecutes officially; most frequently, it is true, it acts on the request of those interested; in such cases their complaint goes under different names, "denunciation, request, pursuit, clamor" ("dénonciation, requeste, pourchaz, clameur"); fundamentally there are always denunciators. It is noteworthy that, judged by the rules laid down above, the action does not always originate in a perfectly regular manner. According to these principles every official prosecution, save in the case of capture in the act, should, in practice, begin by an information. In the "Registre" the action sometimes opens by an information, which the clerk of court has transcribed; [2] in other cases, an information is indicated but not produced; [3] usually, it is upon a mere denunciation of party that the judge proceeds and has the accused arrested; [4] sometimes the party himself directly causes his arrest by an officer of the court.[5] From this point of view the denunciation retains all the efficacy of the ancient accusation; we may add that, when this proceeding is followed, the rule is that the denunciator shall affirm his complaint on oath, in open court, in confrontation with the accused, thus allowing the prisoner a first opportunity to defend himself.[6] Detention pending trial

to determine their acquittal or condemnation, and recourse to torture was not allowed."

[1] Certain passages seem even to faithfully reproduce the old-time distinctions; II, 279.

[2] See, for example, II, pp. 20, 441, 352; *cf.* I, 523.

[3] I, pp. 330, 382, 406; II, 239, 525.

[4] See, for example, I, 376. One might be tempted to believe that in these numerous cases a preliminary information has always existed, without any mention being made of it, but for the fact that sometimes order to inform is given after the arrest and the first interrogation. See I, p. 256; II. p. 77.

[5] I, p. 14; *cf.* I, 212, 365.

[6] I, 158, 173. 175, 344, 365, 393; II, 6, 7, etc. This is a feature which we have already remarked in the "Registre de Saint-Martin des Champs." *Cf.* "Coutume de Bragerac," Art. XII (*B. de Richebourg*, IV, 2, p. 1014): "*Item* aliquis Burgensis non debet capi nec arrestari pro aliquo crimine, nisi in flagranti seu recenti crimine, aut de dicto crimine fuerit publice diffamatus, aut denunciatio fiat contra eum de dicto crimine; qui quidem

exists in all cases without exception;[1] and not a single example of release on bail is to be found here.

A minute inspection of the action, however, reveals the constant employment of the two most odious methods of examination known to the "extraordinary procedure," namely, the oath of the accused and torture. The accused is invariably made to swear that he will tell the whole truth; he swears "upon the holy Gospels, upon the salvation of his soul and the share which he hopes to have in heaven that he will speak the truth concerning that which is asked of him."[2] As for torture, the instances in which it is not inflicted upon the accused are extremely rare. It matters little that he has declared his acceptance of the inquest in the clearest fashion,[3] and that there are eye-witnesses;[4] and even when he has confessed, the judge is authorized to employ torture if he suspects that the accused has committed other misdeeds besides those he has confessed. The following passage well illustrates the spirit which animates this system of jurisprudence: "The said provost asked of the said councillors present what was proper to be done with the said prisoner and if his confession was sufficient to warrant the punishment of death. All of them were of opinion that, as to the present (misdeed), it was not advisable that the

denuncians debet jurare ante captionem dicto bajulo . . . dictam denunciationem se scire vel credere fore veram, et hoc etiam tenetur facere coram parte denunciata antequam dictus denunciatus respondeat dictis propositis contra ipsum."

[1] There is a regular entry of prisoners in the jail book, I, 202; however, all are not treated alike; some receive solitary confinement; others are imprisoned together; II, 285. Sometimes they may communicate freely with the outside, I, 245: "Was confined in the prison called 'la Fousse' so that any one might talk with him"; sometimes, on the contrary, such communication was forbidden; II, 83: "The wife of the said Hays had gone to the said Chastellet to confer with her husband, and she had a great quantity of florins in a purse which she carried, of which she had offered the jailor two florins, if she could speak to her said husband; with which the jailor would have nothing to do."

[2] Where Jews were concerned the Jewish custom was followed in administering the oath, II, 44: "Joesne d'Espaigne and Salmon de Barselonne Jews . . . after they had been made to swear according to their law, by putting the hand upon the head, that they would tell the truth . . . acknowledged and confessed." *Cf.* II, 132. The oath of the accused is also required by Chapter XLII of the "Coutume de la Ville et Septène de Bourges," above cited.

[3] I, 285: "Says that concerning the aforesaid matters he relies upon the opinion and common report of the said country . . . asked whether concerning the common report of his condition and actions and also of the said accusation he will trust and believe in the testimony and depositions of Adenat le Brebiat, Jehan Beautas and Perrinet Beautas, who were present for this purpose in judgment before the said prisoner, said on his oath, yes, be the result death or life, and that he knows and acknowledges these to be men of good life, report and credit;" he is tortured, p. 287. — *Cf.* II, 361, 381, 407, 448.

[4] II, 81, 85.

condemnation of the said prisoner should be proceeded with, the pilfering which he was known to have done being so small, but they decided that the prisoner should again be put to the torture several times, in order to ascertain more plainly the other crimes and offenses by him done, committed, and perpetrated."[1] It appears that up to a certain point two institutions, subsequently distinguished, the preparatory torture and the preliminary torture, were then blended. The judgments decreeing torture are usually based upon the discrepancies in the accused's statements and upon the inferior character and suspicious nature of his station and condition.[2]

The judge of the Châtelet knew, moreover, how to vary and grade the torture according to the constitution of the accused persons and the necessities of the cause. It was usually the torture of water which was employed, and it seems that sometimes the accused was forced to drink, and sometimes water was thrown upon him;[3] for this purpose he was stretched naked upon a wooden horse, to which he was bound.[4] A gradation was imported into the tortures by having two patterns of wooden horse, "the little and the big horse."[5] There were other kinds of torture of a more formidable description, — that of the "pelote,"[6] and probably that of the "courtepointe."[7] Some-

[1] I, 207. *Cf.* I, 463: "Notwithstanding the said confession he was caused to be put to the torture twice on the succeeding day, to ascertain and inquire if he knew anything more of the said poisonings than he had confessed, or if he knew any others who were accessories ('consentans') or guilty."

[2] See I, 196: "Considering her condition of life, which is that of a sinful woman and of little reputation." In one case where torture is not administered it is declared that the accused is "a respectable man, not suffering or in want of money, because he is well and decently clothed" (II, 28). *Cf.* "Coutume de Bragerac," *Bourdot de Richebourg*, IV, 2, p. 1015, Art. XVI. "Si captus fuerit dictus Burgensis pro crimine capitali publico vel manifesto et sit talis conditionis quod ipsum oporteat qustionare."

[3] I, p. 145: "And before water shall be given him to drink or any be thrown upon him." — I, 179: "When he has been given a little to drink." On nearly every page expressions like these appear: "Then water will be given him to drink." — "Then a little water should be thrown upon her."

[4] "Was stripped naked, put and bound to the rack." Such expressions are of constant occurrence. See, for example, I, 264: "The said Marguerite was stripped, bound to the rack by the hands and feet."

[5] See, for example, I, 207: "This prisoner was put to torture upon the little and big wooden horse." — 248: "Was tortured upon the little horse and when it was desired to put him on the big horse he earnestly implored that he be set free."

[6] I, 212: "Was brought back again and put to the torture of the 'pelote.'" — II, 54: "Because he would confess nothing he was put to the torture of the 'pelote.'"

[7] II, 203: "Was stripped quite naked, put, bound, and stretched out to the torture of the 'courtepointe' upon the little horse."

times the severities were moderated, and they tortured "mildly" ("doulcement").[1]

It is apparent that the torture could be repeated indefinitely; its repetition had no other limits than the judge's pertinacity or the accused's strength of resistance.[2] It was a terrible method of examination; but it must be acknowledged that it usually succeeded in extorting the truth from very questionable characters amenable to the tribunal of the provost of Paris. As a general rule, from the moment they are put to the torture they commence a general confession of the most unedifying description; the list of thefts and murders lengthens indefinitely under the pen of the clerk of court. If we remember the state of insecurity and the depredations revealed by the "Registre criminel," we can understand the stern and harsh attitude of the men of that time towards accused persons. But, on the other hand, torture sometimes lends its formidable aid to the prejudices of the period and stamps with its approval the most regrettable errors. In an action for sorcery, when under torture for the fourth time, a woman finally confessed that she had seen the devil and had heard him speak. "And then . . . appeared before her an enemy in guise and condition of the enemies acted in the Passion plays, except that he had no horns. He spoke these words; 'What wantest thou?' . . . And she who speaks said to him . . . and she who speaks saw the said enemy depart through an open window of her room; and on leaving the said house, this enemy made a great noise, as of a whirlwind, of which she who speaks was in very great fear and trembling." [3]

Constitutions there are, however, robust enough to endure these sufferings, and their owners escape with their lives whatever the judge may do. Thevenin de Braine was put to the torture four times without confessing anything; so then "taking into account the nature of his constitution which is that of a perverse man of obdurate and wicked disposition, whose offenses, by him

[1] I, 241: "Were of opinion that . . . this prisoner should be mildly put to the torture."—II, 523: "Except that, in consideration of his age, he was only once treated and tortured and that mildly."

[2] Margot de La Barre is tortured four times (I, 330, 333, 335, 353). Regnault de Poilly "in order further to learn the truth from his lips was tortured five times on so many different days" (I, 432).

[3] This proceeding deals with witchcrafts vaguely reminiscent of the second idyll of Theocritus. A courtesan, Marion l'Estatée, is really smitten with her lover who is about to get married. Through the instrumentality of an older friend, Margot de La Barre, she causes artless harmless spells to be cast upon him. Marion was tortured three times and Margot four; both were burned alive.

done and committed, could not be ascertained by his confession, though when any one commits crime, and does not call witnesses he should do so (confess); and considering that he has been formerly banished for offenses done and committed by him and acquiesced in the said banishment . . . and that he is an incorrigible man . . . deliberated and were of opinion that the said Thevenin de Brayne should be forever banished from the kingdom of France on pain of the gallows." [1]

Before the confession obtained by torture could serve as a foundation for a condemnation it must besides be adhered to without torture. So the "Registre" states that each time the sufferer, benumbed with cold, worn out, and bruised, is led to the kitchen of the Châtelet, he is there warmed and strengthened; [2] he is then interrogated anew on trial without other constraint than the faith of his oath. If he retract, the confession obtained by torture goes for nothing. It is true that the prisoner naturally reckons on being put to torture again; there are, however, those who withdraw their confession each time and thus escape death.[3]

The above are the sad features which mark the procedure of the Châtelet de Paris, but it must be said that there are less sombre sides to the picture. The "Registre criminel" shows that the accused could introduce his defense freely enough. We certainly never see it conducted by an advocate; but the prisoner could scrutinize the testimony produced against him and offer his justification. As we have said, the action often did not commence by an information, as the rule required. In such case, if witnesses are to be heard, they are frequently brought into court and testify in presence of the accused, who has every facility for contradicting

[1] II, 147; *cf.* I, 163: "Considering . . . that the said prisoners have acknowledged and confessed as little as possible, (also) their condition and the punishment of imprisonment suffered by them, deliberated and were of opinion that these prisoners should be revolved in the pillory in the market place, the cause of their judgment being there proclaimed, and after that banished from the town, sheriffdom, and provostship of Paris forever." — I, 506: "Considering that this Berthand is a wandering man, and his condition, that it were well he should be tortured once more, and if he confessed nothing further than is stated above, that he should be drawn in the cart to the court of Paris, where his left ear should be lopped off, and he should (then) be banished forever from the said town of Paris and a radius of ten leagues around."

[2] The usual formula is: "So was put out of this (torture) and brought to be warmed in the kitchen in the customary manner"; occasionally something more is said, I, 167: "After he had been very thoroughly warmed, clothed, and refreshed." — II, 373: "After he had been well and leisurely warmed." — I, 324: "After he had been fed, warmed, and refreshed, was again brought back into judgment."

[3] Process of Joesne d'Espaigne, II, 33–36; he is merely "banished from the kingdom." *Cf.* I, 438 *et seq.*

them.[1] When there is an information, several passages show that the accused is conversant with it.[2] If the second part of the action, the *inquest,* is entered upon, we find in several places that the mode of proceeding already outlined by Beaumanoir is followed; the witnesses are brought face to face with the accused and take oath before him, so that he may present his grounds of objection, but they testify out of his presence, before the examiner ("enquesteur") alone.[3] But according to the traditionary principle, the prisoner is made acquainted with the depositions, which are read to him: "He demanded and requested that upon the deposition of said Marion, which was read to him, she should tell the truth."[4] — "After the deposition (of) Gieffroy Olivier, read to him verbatim, agreed with and relied on everything for or against him or said of him."[5] Sometimes a request of the accused that the witness testify anew in his presence is granted. "Macete, wife of Hennequin de Reuilly . . . requested if she wished to rely upon what the said witch would say and testify for or against her, says on her oath No, and that she would willingly hear her speak, and for this (reason) . . . the said mons. the provost causes to come and attend in judgment the said Jehanne de Brigue, who is said to be a witch . . . in the presence of the said Macete."[6] Moreover, for the purpose of avoiding any difficulty, it also happens that after the information, instead of proceeding with the inquest in the form above described, the witnesses may be made to testify in open court in presence of the accused: "By the opinion of the said councillors it was said . . . that Margot . . . and

[1] I, 134: "Which prisoner, having heard the depositions hereinbefore written, made in his presence by the said Gilet and David, was asked," etc. — I, 303: "Before further proceedings shall be taken against the said prisoners, the said knight shall be despatched . . . on a day fixed, to be examined upon the said matter, in the presence of the said prisoners." — I, 313 (the following relates to certain herbs found in the possession of the accused, and which are supposed to be poisonous): "For this purpose, Richart de Bules, herbalist, was summoned into his presence . . . to whom were shown the herbs above mentioned."

[2] I, 407: "Denied having even . . . spoken the words mentioned in the information." — I, 260: "As to the words contained in the said information declared to have been spoken by her, she knew nothing of them."

[3] See, especially, II, p. 20 *et seq.;* four depositions are quoted; in the case of each witness it is said that he has been sworn in the presence of Charlot de Couvers (the accused) . . . heard and examined in the absence of the said Charlot: "they are interrogated, as in Beaumanoir, concerning the facts of the rescript hereinbefore written."

[4] I, 264.

[5] I, 415; *cf.* II, 290, 347.

[6] II, 320; I, 350: "Asked if . . . she would rely upon and believe in what the said Ancel should say and depone. The said Margot said, Yes, provided that she heard him speak and that he took the oath in her presence. And for this purpose the aforesaid Ancel was summoned, who . . . said and testified in presence of the said Margot."

Jehennette of Blé, examined in the said information, should be anew made to swear, and be heard and examined in presence of the said prisoner. And, this done, and immediately the said women were summoned into court, the depositions of whom the said prisoner . . . referred to; (and) who were examined and testified in presence of the said prisoner." [1]

If the law is severe it still endeavors to administer even-handed justice. The accused has the opportunity to prove his innocence; [2] from the moment when he invokes some justificative fact, such as alibi, every effort is made to facilitate his proof of it. If uncomplicated facts only have to be verified and the witnesses to be heard are at hand, the judge has them immediately examined into; [3] or an examiner is sent from the Châtelet to secure the testimony.[4] "On hearing the confession of which prisoner, the said master Nicolas Bertin was ordered to repair to this lady of Fymes and ascertain from her whether or not the said prisoner had told the truth." [5] Or a regular information might even be opened; "Ordered the said master Jehan Soudan that he should commune with and examine the said Ancel Gohier and such others as he might see as should seem proper, to ascertain if the alibi offered by the said Margot was true or not, and that he should report what might have been done in this matter next day or as soon as might conveniently be done." [6] The accused had only one recourse against sentences to torture—the appeal to the Parlement. The appeal, composed of one word, stayed the execution of the interlocutory decree. It is brought several times in the "Registre criminel," but at the same time it is noticeable that the Parlement always affirms the decision of the Châtelet.[7]

Although the main features of the criminal procedure, as we have just sketched it, were already settled, it was still, on certain points, changeable and uncertain. Greater precision was essential.

[1] II, 81.

[2] Let us say, in passing, that in one instance the question of challenge to the judicial duel arises in the "Registre"; that was the case of a poor girl, of whom we have spoken before, and who no doubt had heard gentlemen talk (of it) I, 344.

[3] II, 345: "Jehan Vilete, door-keeper, was ordered by the said lieutenant to go speedily to the said rue de la Vennerie and cause to come all the women living there engaged in the business of binding hemp, to be examined by the said lieutenant in respect of what is said." —I, 411: "It is ordered that the said Gieffroy Olivier shall be sent for and made to come into the presence of the said prisoner."

[4] II, 232; I, 404; II, 361: "The said Master Dreue d'Ars is commanded to journey to this lady and examine her . . . as well and assiduously as possible."

[5] II, 411. [6] I, 346. [7] I, 334; II, 143, 144, 299, 415, 428.

To accomplish this, we find the "récolement," or re-examination of witnesses introduced. According to an old custom it was not the judge himself, but a special delegate, who heard the witnesses in the information and reduced their depositions to writing. It was usually an officer of the court and sometimes a practitioner who laid the information, with the assistance of a notary; sometimes the courts kept special functionaries charged with this duty, who bore the old name of "*enquesteurs*." "The king's procurator and the civil party cause information to be made of the crime committed by a sergeant royal or of the lord high justiciar, (to act) with whom is summoned a notary royal or of the secular court; and in some places the order of the judge is taken to do this; in others that of the 'enquesteur' of the jurisdiction to which the report is to be made; in others the 'enquesteur' only is empowered to conduct the information, which is unreasonable and leads to a multiplicity of parties; in other places the order of the judge is not taken."[1] These customs were very inconvenient, as they placed the most important interests in the hands of an inferior officer. In order to rectify these inconveniences it was provided that the judge ought himself to hear the witness anew. This was the "re-examination to confirm": "The witnesses examined by the judge," says Ayrault, "are not subject to confirmation unless the cause be removed from him, as from a judge suspected."[2] This, moreover, assumes that the aforetime division of the action into *information* and *inquest* had become a dead letter, and that the inquest, as we have described it, had fallen into desuetude; it had undoubtedly always been admitted that, whether the accused assented to it or not, "information should be tantamount to inquest." The information will ultimately tend to absorb the rest of the action. Simultaneously with the introduction of the confirmation, as the accused, in the "extraordinary" procedure, received neither copy nor knowledge of the information, the custom was begun of confronting him with each witness separately. This was the least that could be done, and it was at this moment that the accused must prefer his objections (to the witnesses) if he had any to offer. As to producing witnesses on his side, this was probably forbidden soon after this period, at least unless by authority of the judge after the witnesses for the accusation had been heard, re-examined, and confronted.

[1] *Imbert*, "Pratique," I, III, ch. 2, No. 2 (edition of 1604); *cf. Ayrault, op. cit.*, 1, III, Art. 1, No. 40. Although the authors cited belong to the 1500s, the customs they describe go back to earlier times.
[2] *Op. cit.*, Book III, Art. 2, No. 38.

Under such a system, all that remained of the ancient accusatory procedure must necessarily vanish. The accusation by formal party died out in the 1500s, without being suppressed by law: "It is to be noted that formal parties are not allowed in France to-day, Be it known that any one may be arrested and imprisoned for an offense, without prior information, provided he who constitutes himself formal party will submit to imprisonment like the other." [1] — "This was undoubtedly done until not long ago, and such accuser was called formal party, but this is no longer the practice. And I certainly have never seen it happen but once: this was a case of two unknown foreigners who had no sureties. . . . I allowed it in their case because they were unknown and proposed it themselves." [2] Henceforward we shall find but one real accuser, the king's procurator or those of the lords; the punishment is inflicted in the public interest, and no longer to satisfy a private thirst for vengeance. "We have two kinds of accusers," says Imbert, "those who prosecute the interest of the king and the common good, who are called king's counsellors, that is, the advocate and procurator of the king or of the lords, possessing high justice; they seek for corporal punishment and suitable and pecuniary penalty against the delinquent; the others demand reparation of their civil interest, which they have suffered because of the offense committed upon their persons and to their property and do not seek for corporal punishment by our practice, although they might, according to common law, be able to seek for corporal punishment and reparation of their interest." [3] The injured individuals did not quit the action altogether; they remained in it, as we said when speaking of the denunciation, for the purpose of claiming damages. From the above comes the constitution of the civil party, one of the most original features of our criminal procedure. The injured person is to all intents and purposes a party to the criminal action; he brings witnesses; it is really he who originates the cause by requesting from the judge permission to inform, "faire informer," as the phrase will run as long as the ancient law exists. The steps in the procedure are taken in his name and at his expense.[4] Besides, the public prosecutor is not, as a matter of fact, the prin-

[1] *Imbert*, "Pratique," III, ch. 1, Nos. 11, 14.
[2] *Ayrault*, *op. cit.*, Book III, Art. 1, No. 15.
[3] *Imbert*, "Pratique," II, ch. 1, No. 3.
[4] "Most frequently the king's procurator and the civil party are claimants together, and then the civil party bears the whole expense of the criminal process." *Imbert*.

cipal party, but a *joint party.*[1] The constitution of civil party ("partie civile") is in reality a combination of formal party ("partie formée") and of the ancient *denunciation* by the injured party; henceforward it will be totally distinct from the denunciation, where the private individual is merely the instigator of an action in which the official prosecutor figures alone.

[1] "The king's procurator is forbidden by the Ordinances to *join* with any civil party, without prior information." *Imbert,* "Pratique," III, ch. 1, No. 3.

CHAPTER III

FRENCH CRIMINAL PROCEDURE UNDER THE ORDINANCES OF THE 1400s AND 1500s

§ 1. **Introductory.** — We now enter upon a period of change and formation. In this development, which so materially changed the criminal procedure, the judicial practice of the royal courts was the agency whose influence was especially felt. It was, indeed, practically the only factor; the legislative power, that is, the royal power, had only intervened to affirm, in some short provisions of the Ordinances, rules already recognized and admitted. That duality of forms which divides the criminal procedure into "ordinary" and "extraordinary" process, the keystone of the whole edifice, was established by the jurists and by actual practice. But when the evolution had been completed and the system had attained its full development, royalty stepped in to embody it in statute law. Several famous Ordinances at the end of the 1400 s, and during the first half of the 1500 s, are declaratory of already settled rules of the customal law. They particularize various points on which the practice was wanting in exactness, or erroneous. If they introduced some new severities, it may be said that, even in that respect, they but hastened what practice would have ultimately effected, and probably generalized what it had introduced in some particular place. Of these Ordinances, by far the most important are those of 1498 and 1539.[1]

§ 2. **The Ordinances of 1498 and 1539. The Criminal Action in the 1500 s.** — The principal purpose of the Ordinance of 1498,

[1] The lengthy Ordinance of 1507 (*Isambert*, XI, p. 464 *et seq.*) is merely an adaptation of earlier ordinances, to suit Normandy; in regard to criminal matters in particular, Article 184 *et seq.* are merely repetitions of Article 106 *et seq.* of the Ordinance of 1498.

so far as it concerns our subject, was to distinguish clearly the "ordinary" from the "extraordinary" procedure, and to point out how one or other of these might be chosen, and what forms were to be followed in either case. First of all an information must be laid, a document which was kept secret from every one except the king's procurators.[1] "After deliberation on the said informations, a 'dictum' shall be made in writing, signed by him who shall have seen and reported them, which shall contain the provisions as to personal citation, arrest, etc."[2] If occasion required, citation or capture was the next step; then came the interrogations,[3] which, along with the informations, were at once communicated to the king's procurators,[4] so that they might file their charges. From this point the procedure became bifurcated: "Article 108: And it shall be decided whether the procedure shall be extraordinary, or if the parties shall be heard." If the latter method was decided upon, the parties "shall be heard in trial in open court before an order for further hearing shall be made, and that done the said parties shall be heard by our said bailiffs, seneschals, and judges, or their lieutenants, as shall appear proper;"[5] that is to say, the procedure was to be by inquests ("enquêtes") and pleadings according to the old forms.[6] A quicker procedure could, however, be followed. The king's procurator or the party might declare that they would take law by the confession of the accused: "they shall lodge their motions in writing only, to which the accused who pleads guilty can reply in extenuation only, and that being done, justice shall be administered as is proper."[7]

If, on the contrary, the "extraordinary" procedure was decided upon, the ordinance goes on to specify its two distinctive features,

[1] Art. 120 (*Isambert*, XI, p. 367); Art. 96 *et seq.* (p. 362).

[2] Art. 98 (p. 362).

[3] Art. 106: "Let all those imprisoned, arrested, or summoned to appear personally, be examined with all speed by our said bailiffs, seneschals, and judges, or their lieutenants, and let the matters be despatched summarily and conclusively, our advocate and procurator and the parties (civil parties) being heard."

[4] Art. 107: "Nothing being shown or communicated to the parties."

[5] Art. 107.

[6] Art. 119: "The parties are summoned confrontatively and by inquests."—Art. 118: "The cause shall be tried publicly." *Cf.* Ordinance of 1493 (*Isambert*, XI, p. 241), Art. 84: "And in regard to the cases of prisoners and those summoned to appear personally, or others who desire to come into court, we will and ordain that our said advocate, who shall plead our cause, shall read over at length the charges, informations, and confessions, and adopt the appropriate conclusions, so that the delinquents may acknowledge their offenses, and that it may serve as public example."

[7] Art. 109; *cf.* Art. 108.

secrecy and the employment of torture. "Article 110. In regard to prisoners and others accused of crime, where it is necessary to institute criminal action, the said action shall be conducted as diligently and secretly as possible, so that none shall be apprised, in order to avoid the subornations and forgeries which might be made in such matters, in the presence of the clerk of court ('greffier') or of his assistant, without summoning the jailor, officers, clerks, or attendants, or any others who have not taken the oath to us and to justice."[1] As to torture, the Ordinance of 1498 contains certain provisions which are in reality an amelioration of the earlier practice. It first of all provides that the judgment which decrees the torture shall be rendered after a serious deliberation;[2] and it expressly forbids a repetition of the torture in the absence of fresh evidence.[3] Bearing in mind the practice vouched for by Bouteiller and the "Registre du Châtelet," this may be considered a substantial improvement. The official report had also to be drawn up, containing "the form and manner of the said torture, and the quantity of water administered to the said prisoner, and how often, if at all, the torture has been repeated,[4] the interrogations and the replies, with the persistence of the prisoner, his constancy or variation, and on the day after the said torture the said prisoner shall be interrogated anew away from the place of the said torture to test his persistence, and everything shall be written down by the said clerk of court."[5] There is no doubt that the accused's only knowledge of the charges was

[1] Art. 110. It follows from the text and also from Article 108 that the decree which sent the action to the extraordinary procedure was not given in court and the parties heard.

[2] Art. 112. "And the said proceedings (having been) taken with all diligence as aforesaid, down to the 'question' or torture, our said bailiffs, seneschals, and judges, or their lieutenants, shall cause the said torture to be deliberated upon in the council chamber or other private place by notable and literate men, not suspect nor favorable, and who have not been of counsel to the parties, our advocate and procurator being present or summoned." This is the very same Council which we have seen in the "Registre du Châtelet." The Ordinance of 1498, speaking in another article of torturing "ear-cropped men, outlaws, and vagabonds," still mentions the *judgers*: "Art. 94. . . . Without in any way departing from the customs, usages, and laws observed in certain places of our kingdom, where the custom has been to judge the said criminals with the aid of *judging men*."

[3] Art. 114. "We forbid our bailiffs, seneschals, and judges to repeat the said 'question' or torture on the said prisoner without new facts supporting presumptions."

[4] Consequently, it was possible to put the accused to the torture several times in the course of the same sitting. What was forbidden was to recommence it after that sitting had ended.

[5] Art. 113. The accused was thus given twenty-four hours for meditation after the torture.

through the confrontations spoken of in Article 111;[1] but, on the other hand, it would appear that he was allowed to plead his defenses from the outset, and such proof of these as was conformable to the practice at that date was immediately taken: "Article 111. Then shall be made all necessary progress with fullest informations, confirmations, or confrontations of witnesses, or with the proof of alibi, or any other fact that there may be, if admissible, for or against the prisoner, as diligently and secretly as possible, in such a way that none may be apprised." Finally, the sentence of condemnation was pronounced in presence of the accused.[2] If "by the extraordinary action, duly carried out, nothing shall have been learned, and it shall be necessary to hear the parties and admit them to ordinary action, our said bailiffs . . . shall order the parties to be heard by the council on a certain day, on which the prisoner shall be brought into court and the matter tried publicly."[3] As to liberation on bail, it seems that that was only allowed when the "ordinary procedure" was followed.[4] It will be seen that the Ordinance of 1498 is notable inasmuch as it contains a description of the entire procedure. It is important particularly in respect of its provision for absolute secrecy in the "extraordinary" action. Henceforward there is an express law, repudiating publicity, traces of which we have found in the practice of the 1300's and the 1400s. The public is barred from the court-room of the criminal tribunals, to which they will not regain entrance for a long time.

But the most important Ordinance in regard to criminal matters was that promulgated by Francis I at Villers-Cotterets in April, 1539, on justice and the shortening of trials. Modeled upon

[1] But see the Ordinance of April, 1510, relating to the amendment of the laws, etc., promulgated as a result of the assembly of the Nobles held at Lyons (*Isambert*, XI, 575 *et seq.*), Art. 47: "In order to obviate the abuses and inconveniences which have heretofore resulted from the judges of the said districts of written law having conducted the criminal actions of the said districts, as well as the inquests, in Latin, we have ordained and hereby ordain that henceforth all criminal actions and the said inquests . . . shall be done in the vernacular and the language of the district, so that the witnesses may hear their depositions and the criminals the proceedings had against them."

[2] Art. 116: "Our said bailiffs, seneschals, and judges, or their deputies, shall pronounce sentence in open court or in the council chamber, that being within the prison house, according to the lawful customs of the district, to which place of court-room or council chamber the said prisoner shall be brought and the said sentence pronounced upon him in the presence of the clerk of court, who shall record it in the book of sentences."

[3] Art. 119.

[4] Art. 119. An Ordinance of the month of October, 1485, relating to the provostship of Paris (*Isambert*, XI, p. 147 *et seq.*), contains interesting information about the prisons.

another Ordinance previously promulgated for the reform of the style of Brittany, this work of Chancellor Poyet, who afterwards suffered under the stern law which he himself had brought into existence, definitely settled the rules of criminal procedure in France. Very soon people even came to believe that it had originated all that it dealt with. On the other hand, the Ordinance of 1670 will do nothing more than take the system which that of 1539 had organized and particularize it in its details, at the same time often increasing its severities. It is therefore useful to pause here long enough to explain this system, elucidating the text of the Ordinance by the comments of the authors who commented on it.

This criminal procedure is, in the first place, distinguished by a certain number of salient and characteristic features. In every prosecution, the king's procurator or that of the lord is, in future, a party. He is doubtless only a joint party, but from this time onwards the principle exists that the criminal examination requires the united action of two magistrates, the procurator who claims or petitions and the judge who conducts the examination. The action is divided into two parts of very unequal duration, the examination and the judgment. The first, of inordinate duration, comprises all the search for evidence which will make up the record, and this is the province of a single judge. He is "the criminal judge" according to the law books, which always speak of him in the singular number, that is, the criminal lieutenant or the seigniorial judge. It is not until everything is in readiness that the accused appears before the entire bench, if there is one, and that tribunal has for its enlightenment only the written proceedings and the last interrogation of the accused. Everything is in writing; and everything is secret, both examination and judgment; and in the majority of cases the latter is not evidentially grounded.

The following is the whole course of a prosecution. Formerly, except in the case of capture in the act, where the culprit is seized and interrogated immediately, the information was the first step in all criminal procedure.[1] This is undertaken either upon the complaint of the civil party, who obtains permission to lodge information,[2] or of the lord, who, advised by a

[1] Unless the offenses in question were so trivial that the injured party could at once proceed with the ordinary action.

[2] Every complaint on the part of the injured party is necessarily a constitution of civil party (or private prosecutor); no distinction is made between the two.

denunciation or otherwise, petitions the judge; or by the spontaneous act of the judge, who can always take action ex officio. That is a right kept up by the Ordinance of 1539 (Art. 145). The witnesses cited by the civil party, or by the public prosecutor, are heard separately and privately, either by the judge or by special officers called examiners ("enquêteurs"), or more frequently by a mere officer of the court assisted by a royal notary.[1] The deposition of each witness had to be transcribed "ad longum," but it seems that it was necessary to read it over to the witness and require him to sign it.[2] The employment of these inferior officers in such an important act was a great evil; "there is no man in such good standing as to escape at the hands of these officers and notaries . . . and they make the information serious or trivial according to the party's wish, not according to what the witnesses really say."[3] The Ordinance of 1539 tolerates this practice. "The judges," says Article 145, "*shall inform or cause information to be made.*"[4]

The information or inquiry made and submitted to the criminal judge, it devolved upon him to communicate it to the king's procurator, to require his conclusions, which were given in writing (Art. 145): "the information having been made and communicated to our said procurator, and his conclusions considered, it shall be his duty without delay to return the said information, without taking any fee therefor." It does not appear that there was any communication to the civil party. According to the conclusions, the judge allowed the matter to drop or issued the decree, that is, the order which required the appearance of the accused. The Ordinance of 1539 was vague in this respect. "Such lawful provision," it said, "shall be decreed as shall meet the necessity of the case." (Art. 145.) But judicial practice had

[1] *Imbert*, "Pratique," III, ch. II, Nos. 2 and 3. *Cf.* "Le style de la cour de Parlement," by *Philbert Boyer*, latest edition, revised after the author's death in 1610: "It shall be necessary to deliver the said request (to have a commission to cause information to be made) to a clerk of the criminal court, who shall thereupon draw up the commission, addressing it to the judge or examiners of the districts or to the head officer of court upon this request. Which information shall be made in the presence of a respectable deputy, who has taken the judicial oath."

[2] *Imbert*, III, ch. XIII, Nos. 13, 14.

[3] *Ibid.*

[4] Sometimes "monitories" were decreed. These were orders by the temporal judge, affixed to the church doors and read after mass, enjoining all the faithful to tell the curé what they know about the crime; the curé took the depositions and sent them under seal to the criminal judge. This practice recalls those denunciations which the faithful already made on oath in the "judicia synodalia"; it was probably in these that the monitories originated.

introduced two kinds of decrees, that of personal summons and that of bodily arrest, "prise de corps."[1] The "personal summonses should be executed like the ordinary summonses in civil matters, except when the accused is a man who is feared and accustomed to resist arrest, and if it be dangerous to summon him personally or at his domicile, the judge orders and permits him to be summoned by public proclamation by sound of trumpet at the market place or elsewhere, wherever there is a concourse of people nearest to his residence."[2] The effect of the decree of personal arrest was to put the accused in a state of detention pending trial: "according to the common law the apprehension of a person in his residence was not allowed, but nowadays one may apprehend him in his residence provided it be in the day time and not the night time, and with 'records' (special kinds of witnesses), and not with a great assemblage of people and by main force; and provided nothing in the house be destroyed or carried away; but if the doors are closed they may always be broken open."[3] The decree of bodily arrest could only occur in serious offenses; "great prudence in this respect is required on the part of a judge," says Imbert, "to avoid issuing a warrant of bodily arrest unless in case of public crime and even then only in serious matters." The judge, however, was not bound by what the commentators wrote; the exceptions to this rule were numerous,[4] and individual liberty found in these rules but a slender safeguard.

The accused, whether he appeared or was arrested, must be interrogated by the judge "immediately, carefully, and assiduously."[5] The interrogation took place "in the house of the said judge or in the criminal court-room set apart for the purpose," and this art of interrogating was a great one, too often cruel and treacherous. It put the accused at the mercy of the judge. He was compelled to reply without having the aid of a counsel and without having had any knowledge of the information.[6] He also swore that he would tell the truth. This odious formality was, however, not imposed by any law, but was the result of a custom

[1] *Imbert*, III, ch. II, No. 3. [2] *Ibid.*, III, No. 1. [3] *Ibid.*, V, No. 2.

[4] It was possible to commence with the decree not only in the case of taking in the act, but also in the case "of a non-resident poor person who had no personal effects, or where the offense was such that it was probable that he would conceal whatever chattels he possessed . . . then it was lawful to arrest without information and to make it afterwards" (*Imbert*). This is the same practice which we have seen in the "Registre criminel du Châtelet"; see *supra*, p. 135.

[5] Ordinance of 1539, Art. 146. [6] *Ibid.*, Arts. 146 and 162.

already very old, as we have said. Imbert is explicit on this point: "The judge," he says, "must first make him swear to tell the truth and then interrogate him."[1] All the replies were reduced to writing: "It is essential that the clerk of the court transcribe, under the judge's direction, everything that the judge shall say and state to him." If the accused had confessed in his interrogation, this document was communicated to the king's procurator, who considered whether he wished to take law upon it, that is, to demand judgment, without more formality. If he was of that opinion, which, according to the theory of evidence then in force, did not happen in serious cases, the interrogation was communicated also to the civil party. Both these parties then gave their conclusions in writing and these were communicated to the accused "that he might reply to them by way of extenuation only."[2] From this point, nothing more remained to be done than to appear in order to receive sentence. If, on the contrary, the parties did not wish to take law on the interrogation, which always occurred when the accused pleaded not guilty and sometimes when he confessed, there was a ruling to the extraordinary action, or to the ordinary action. For this purpose the judge, always acting alone, rendered an interlocutory decree. Prior to the Ordinance of 1539, the three parties to the cause, including the accused, stated their demands at the hearing, either orally or in writing.[3] "The joinder of issues," says Imbert, "takes place when, after the hearing of the prisoner, the parties appear before the judge, and the prisoner pleads, by coming personally to be heard and his statement communicated to the king's advocate and procurator and demands to be acquitted or at least to be granted ordinary action and released on bail . . . and the complainant civil party objects and demands that the accused be proceeded against extraordinarily by confirmation and confrontation of witnesses and to receive during the action provision of sustenance and medicaments. And in such places as the court of Parlement, the king's advocate pleads the fact of the accusation contained in the information and moves that it be tried extraordinarily as is said; and in other places they submit their motions at the termination of the hear-

[1] L. III, ch. X, No. 2. The Latin text prior to the ordinance is no less clear: "Judex ergo primum ad nudandam veritatem reum jurejurando adigit." Boyer's "Stile" reads: "Then the commissary has the accused brought before him and makes him swear to tell the truth" (p. 238 recto).

[2] Ordinance of 1539, Art. 148; *cf.* Ordinance of 1498, Art. 109.

[3] See, however, what is shown in the Ordinance of 1498, *supra*, page 137, note. *Imbert's* text, quoted above, appears to show that on this point the law was not rigidly followed in actual practice.

ing."[1] This was the time for the accused to present his defense with some advantage, especially if he had the aid of a counsel, although the information had not been communicated to him.[2] But the Ordinance of 1539 (Art. 162) "abolished all the forms, usages, and customs by which accused persons had been accustomed to be heard in judgment for the purpose of ascertaining if they should be accused and for that purpose to have communication of the facts and circumstances covering the crimes and offenses of which they were accused, and all other things contrary to what is hereinbefore expressed." Henceforth, therefore, only the motions of the public and private prosecutors were submitted to the judge in writing; the accused was no longer allowed to speak. Conformably to the Ordinance of 1498, however, when the judge decided upon the 'ordinary' procedure, he must first hear all the parties in judgment; Article 150 adds in effect, "unless the matter was of so little importance that *after the parties were heard in judgment* it was proper to order that they should be received in ordinary action." Save in this very rare case, the judge ruled that the action would be "extraordinary," and he fixed a day to proceed with the confirmations and confrontations of witnesses.[3]

The witnesses were subpœnaed afresh for the confirmation; "the judge first causes the witness whom he is about to examine to swear to tell the truth, and if he is in doubt whether or not the testimony is false he will require him to state what he knows of the subject of the accusation, which he will briefly summarize to him, without informing him of the contents of his deposition con-

[1] *Imbert* "Pratique," III, ch. X, No. 6.

[2] See "Notice sur les archives du Parlement de Paris" in *Boutaric's* "Actes du Parlement." "The existing registers of the end of the 1400s and those of the 1500s down to the year 1529 belong to the category of pleadings. After a lapse of several years, the first register which appears in the ordinary series is one of those of the council of November, 1535, to November, 1536. Registers of pleadings are no longer found after that period and all are of the council down to the end of that century. It is not correct to say, as Chancellor *Séguier* does in his 'Mémoires sur le Parlement de Paris,' that the Tournelle did not hold hearings at the time of its establishment. The contrary is shown by the very terms of the edict of April, 1515, making it permanent. It was no longer so under the Villers-Cotterets Ordinance of August, 1539, which forbade advocates to act in criminal matters (Vol. I, p. 227)."

[3] Ordinance of 1539, Art. 151; *Imbert*, III, ch. XII, No. 1. The ordinance itself provides that, on the expiry of this delay, the action will be tried on the documents extant, except for the granting of a second delay, for good cause shown; but Imbert informs us that "the said ordinance is not followed, as the royal and other judges still grant three or four delays as before, which is a cause of much vexation to the unfortunate prisoners."

tained in the information, and if he sees that he states substantially what is contained in that deposition, he will cause it to be read to him by the clerk of court, and after that he will demand of him on the oath which he has taken if it contains the truth, and will write down in what respect he confirms and in what he corrects his first deposition." [1] Immediately after that came the confrontation of the witnesses with the accused: "And if he persists and charges the defendant, the said witness shall be immediately confronted with him, that is to say, the judge shall have the defendant brought before him in presence of the witness, and they will both be made to swear to tell the truth, and afterwards interrogated whether they know each other well, and if the defendant is he of whom the witness speaks in his deposition and confirmation." [2] The confrontation had a double purpose, first, to allow the accused to state the objections which he might be able to urge against the witness, and in the second place, to enable him to directly contest the charges brought against him. This is the first and only time the opportunity to do this is offered to him. The Ordinance of 1539, going farther than the former practice, decided that at that moment, before the reading of the deposition to him, the accused must offer all his objections. "Art. 154. Before the reading of the deposition of the witness in the presence of the accused, the latter shall be asked if he has any objections against the witness there present, and enjoined to state them promptly, which it is our will that he be bound to do, otherwise they shall not be afterwards received, and of this he shall be expressly warned by the judge. . . ."—"Art. 155. The accused shall no longer (after the reading) be allowed to state or urge any objections against the said witness." That was putting the knife to his throat. The actual practice, however, was rather less severe; it allowed the accused to demand time to lodge his objections.

The reading of the deposition was then proceeded with: "Should he urge no objections (to the witness) and declare that he does not wish to urge any, or demand time to state them or submit them in writing, the judge shall read the deposition of the witness in the presence of the defendant and the witness; and he shall demand of the witness, and afterwards of the defendant, if it contains the truth, and shall cause their answers to be written down." [3] The confrontation, very inadequate as it was as a means of defense, since it took place in secret and without the aid of a counsel, yet offered some help to a capable and intelligent accused. He

[1] *Imbert*, III, ch. XIII, No. 9. [2] *Ibid.* [3] *Ibid.*, No. 10.

might by his remarks induce the witness to retract or contradict himself. The witness ran no risk in retracting; "The witness is not bound by his confirmation and confrontation to stand to his deposition as reduced to writing in the information, and may with impunity vary and change his deposition."[1] Were all the witnesses confronted? It would appear that the Ordinance only required confrontation in the case of the witnesses for the prosecution who stood to their testimony at the confirmation; "however," says Imbert, "some judges of wide experience confront all the witnesses, both those of the prosecution and those who are not."

Up to this point the accused had taken only a passive part in the action. He had, in short, had the privilege of examining, at the time of the confrontation, the witnesses brought by the public and private prosecutors; but he had not had the opportunity to summon any witnesses on his own behalf; he had not been able to prove his innocence directly. Was he ever to have the opportunity to do that? On this point a most astounding and sadly ingenious theory was put forward. It was not admitted, in a general way, that the accused could bring any witnesses to prove that he was not guilty. In effect, from a purely logical point of view, there was no need to prove a negative fact such as non-culpability; and according to the theory of legal proofs the thing was, not to convince the judge, but to produce specific evidence. If the fact was not "legally" proved by the witnesses brought by the prosecution, any proof on the part of the accused was said to be useless. If, on the contrary, the action should establish, by the requisite proofs, that the crime had actually been committed and that the accused was the perpetrator of it, he could only rebut the testimony by means of the objections which he had urged, or prove that these witnesses were suborned, or, finally, offer certain positive facts, which formed his justification. These facts — called "justificatifs" — were of two kinds; some proved the innocence of the accused indirectly, but beyond dispute. Such were, the "alibi," or the production of the person who was believed to be dead, or the production of a prior sentence pronounced against the real perpetrator of the crime.[2] Others, without rebutting the facts established in the action, deprived the act of all criminality; for example, legitimate self-defense, or insanity of the doer of the act at the time of its occurrence. Objections to the wit-

[1] *Imbert*, III, ch. XIII, No. 12; but he asks (No. 14) if the witness who has signed his deposition can still change with impunity.

[2] Several of these facts were, subsequently, sometimes offered as *peremptory exceptions to the accusation.*

nesses and justificative facts, therefore, were the only defenses left to the accused. It is evident that his proof must always be in support of some fact distinct from that proved by the prosecution. But that was not all. He could not produce this proof until all the proof of the prosecution had been produced; and even then he encountered obstacles. We have seen that he was obliged to state his objections to the witnesses at the time of the confrontation; as for his justificative facts, he was bound in practice to urge them from his first interrogation; "if he has any justificative facts he must state them in the said confession;"[1] he could then produce them in the course of the examination ("instruction") each time he was brought before the judge, or even without that, by a request addressed to the latter. But to produce them was not all-sufficient; it was still necessary, in the case of the justificative facts, as well as in the case of the objections, that the judge should allow him to prove them.

The whole process, information, interrogation, confirmations, and confrontations,—all the documents, in short,—were communicated to the king's procurator: "If he find that the accused has pleaded any peremptory facts conducing to his acquittal or innocence, such as "alibi," or any lawful and admissible facts concerning objections, he shall require the accused promptly to name the witnesses by whom he intends to prove the said facts . . . failing which he shall move for torture or final sentence."[2] On that motion the judge decided. He could always disallow proof of the justificative facts by ruling them to be inadmissible. Assuming, on the contrary, that he had admitted proof of the objections and justificative facts, a final obstacle still presented itself. "Then shall be drawn up," said the Ordinance, "admissible facts, if any there be, for the defense of the accused either by way of justifications or objections, which he (the judge) shall show to the said accused and shall order him to name promptly the witnesses by whom he intends to sustain the said facts, which he shall be bound to do, otherwise they shall not afterwards be received."[2] If the

[1] *Imbert*, III, ch. X, No. 4.

[2] *Imbert*, III, ch. XIII, No. 15; Ordinance of 1539, Art. 157. "If the accused were permitted to present their justificative facts from the start, the decree granting this permission, fatal to the public welfare, would constitute a title and an assurance of immunity for them; they would, on the pretext of bringing their proofs, indirectly evade those which might convict them; and by weakening the strength, authority, and weight of the evidence, they might often render the court powerless to prove either the crime or the innocence, without having even proved their justificative facts." *Séguier*, "Réquisitoire de 1786."

[3] Art. 158.

accused shall have been able summarily to indicate all his witnesses, how were they brought before the judge or the examiner? They were "heard and examined 'ex officio' by the judges or their clerks and deputies,"[1] in the absence of the accused. It was the prosecutor who directed the inquest for the defense; the witnesses, however, not being subject to objection. The official report of this information was added to the record of the action.

Whatever the result of the examination might be, the next step was to call for the motions of the public and private prosecutors, and to bring the matter before the assembled bench; "when the process is complete, the judge orders that it be communicated to the king's counsel so that they may lodge their motions thereon within three days."[2] But this mass of waste paper relating to proceedings at which no one except the examining magistrate had been present, was not to be submitted to the court without anything to facilitate their comprehension of it, and therefore a report was made upon the process by a judge. This institution of "reporter" is an essential part of the written procedure. It is always found in its wake.

The conclusions or motion of the public prosecutor, instead of being final, that is, leading to the infliction of a punishment, could only lead to the application of the preparatory torture. "The judge places the whole matter before the council, and if the offense in question is so nearly verified and proved that only the confession of the defendant is lacking, and the crime is heinous and such that, if proved, it would warrant a severe corporal punishment, the judge shall cause the matter to be deliberated in some private place by influential and literate men, not suspect or favorable, who shall not have been of counsel to the parties, the king's advocate being present or summoned."[3] In this case the Ordinance of 1539 provided that the torture be administered immediately, except in the event of appeal (Art. 164). Nothing, however, was prescribed as to the manner of its administration, and the methods thereof were as varied as they were odious. Hippolytus of Marseilles took the pains to enumerate forty methods of torture in Italy, and they were apparently no less numerous in France. "According to the provisions of the law, the judges should not use for the

[1] Ordinance of 1539, Article 139. [2] *Imbert*, III, ch. XX, No. 1.

[3] *Imbert*, III, ch. XIV, No. 1. These "expert and learned" men, styled in Latin "causidici," are the practitioners with whom the judges of that period still surrounded themselves, and who were the successors of the judges of the feudal period. *Cf.* Ordinance of 1498, *supra*, page 147, note 2.

torture anything but cords. Nevertheless, in various provinces, the judges and provost-marshals use other instruments, such as fagots, water for 'l'avallement de la serviette,' vinegar, oil poured down the throat drop by drop, eggs cooked in the embers and applied under the armpits, sometimes intolerable cold, hunger, or thirst induced by the manducation of excessively salt food given to the accused without anything to drink; others by tightly compressing the fingers either in the end, or in the cock of an arquebus or pistol, or binding them with little strings or packthreads between various little sticks called 'gressilons'; others by the bundle of cord, others by the pump, and others in different ways. See 'Hippolytus of Marseilles in commen. super tit. de quaestion. in l. I, ubi ponit quatuordecim species tormentorum diversas.' — But everything depends upon the decree of the judge."[1] Nevertheless, the practitioners seem to have placed great faith in witchcraft and drugs, by means of which accused persons endeavored to make themselves insensible to torture. Damhouder's narrative, as an ocular witness of and actor in one of these dramas, must be read to give some idea of what aberration the human intellect can be capable of.[2] The official report of the torture was drawn up; but next day the accused was interrogated anew, to see if he adhered to his confessions. This was in conformity with the earlier law, but it had become a mere formality: "Inasmuch as there be many so cunning and wily that they will totally deny whatever they have confessed under torture when they are interrogated the next day, the custom has been to stop with the confession made under torture, if it be probable, and conform to or approach the contents of the informations."[3]

When the torture had been administered, or if at the outset the conclusions of the public prosecutor had been final, "the entire criminal process so made shall be submitted by the judge for deliberation by the council of his court, as before said, in presence of the advocates and king's procurator, to take counsel as to what is to be done, and the clerk of court shall transcribe the opinions and deliberations." Then an interrogation of the accused usually took place before the whole court which was to judge him.[4] But

[1] "Le procès civil et criminel," by *Charles Lebrun de la Rochette* (Rouen 1616), Part 2, p. 140.

[2] *Damhouder*, "Praxis," ch. XXXVI, No. 21 *et seq.* *Lebrun de la Rochette*, "Le procès civil et criminel," Part 2, p. 144 *et seq.*

[3] *Imbert*, III, ch. XIV, No. 6.

[4] *Imbert* says nothing about the accused being interrogated before the entire assembled bench. This final interrogation, although very important, was altogether discretionary.

at no time had the accused the help of a counsel; the Ordinance expressly declares, Art. 162, "in criminal matters the parties shall in no wise be heard by counsel or agency of any third person; but they shall answer by their own word of mouth for the crimes of which they are accused."

The deliberation upon the judgment might occur in various ways. When there was only a council ("conseil") of practitioners assisting the judge, he merely took their opinions, which were not binding upon him; but when there were counsellors or assessors, it seems that the question was decided by the mere majority opinion alone.[1] In this case, the judges, according to Ayrault, gave their opinion orally or by ballot. "These are formalities which depend on ordinances or the practice of the companies. Different courts use different methods. Provided that everything in the process is seen, no error is made in pursuing either course."[2] Already the custom was introduced into the higher jurisdictions of not assigning a reason for the judgments. "It should be understood that in a criminal judgment it is necessary particularly to declare for what crime the accused is condemned, and that the Court of the Parlement of Paris does so, at least usually; the royal judges do not, however, regard this rule; thus they put in their judgments the clause, — for the punishment and reparation of the crimes of which he is found guilty in the action."[3]

Even when the procedure had become secret, the judgments had for some time been pronounced publicly, or at least in presence of the accused; but this last trace of publicity also disappeared: "The said Ordinance (of 1498), Art. 116, states that if the prisoner is condemned to death, or other corporal punishment, the judge shall pronounce sentence in open court, or in the council chamber where the prisoner shall be brought, and the sentence shall be read to him in presence of the clerk of court, who shall record it in the books of sentences . . . but this formality is not adhered to nowadays, as the judge sends his decision to the clerk

[1] "The judge puts the criminal process with the said motions to the vote of eminent advocates of his jurisdiction not suspected or favorable. And although by the Ordinance of King Louis XII, Art. 115 . . it is said that the clerk of court should write down the opinions of those taking part in the deliberation, this was not invariably done; for the clerk is not present at the said deliberation unless when there are counsellors whom the judge is compelled to summon to the judgments of the actions, and to decide according to the majority opinion of the said counsellors." *Imbert*, III, ch. xx, No. 4.

[2] "L'ordre et formalité," etc., III, Art. 4.

[3] *Imbert*, III, ch. xx, No. 6.

of court, who communicates it to the prisoner in the doorkeeper's room, where he has the prisoner brought." [1]

The accused had been kept in jail throughout the whole of these proceedings. In the 1300s we have said that liberation on bail was granted freely enough, but it was necessarily excluded by the general character of the new procedure. In this respect again the Ordinance of 1539 sanctions a severity formerly unknown: "Art. 152. In matters subject to confrontation accused persons shall not be released during the delays which are given for the purpose of making the said confrontation." It was, therefore, only when the action was put on the ordinary rôle that liberty on bail was allowed (Art. 150). Very soon we shall find Ayrault protesting against the maxim which made detention pending trial a rule without exception. Certain indications, however, show that the provisions of the Ordinance on this point were not always respected; "in trivial matters involving no corporal or criminal punishment," says one who lived at the end of the 1500s, "the judges are accustomed to release accused persons on bail or on their juratory bail, or even in the custody of a sheriff's officer or officer of court. It might be said against this that the Ordinance forbids it and that criminals should not be released until the confirmations and confrontations have taken place, and that this would be an obstacle in the way of prosecution, and that it would be impossible to obtain proof of a crime, which would consequently go unpunished; but the obvious answer, based on common sense, necessary and peremptory, is that when the Ordinance was drawn up, false witnesses were not so abundant as at present. This is in common and daily evidence, to such an extent that there are as many and more sentences carried out on false witnesses than for all other crimes. I say this not only from the horror and detestation of this abominable crime of perjury, or because I desire the introduction of a new (system of) practice; but because it is necessary to use new remedies to cope with the increasing maliciousness of the evildoers." [2]

Thus, little by little, the safeguards of the defense disappeared. The procedure had become absolutely secret, not only in the sense that everything took place beyond the range of the public eye, but in the sense that no production of documents was made to the accused. The aid of counsel and the freedom to summon witnesses for the defense had been taken away from him one after

[1] *Imbert*, III, ch. xx, No. 3.
[2] *Boyer's* "Stile," 1610 edition, Part IV, Title 12, p. 239.

the other. Submitted to skilful, and often treacherous, interrogations, he was in a terrible plight; it might even be said that after the Ordinance of 1498 his position became more desperate; and the Ordinance of 1539 sanctioned new severities.

The appeal was, however, always open in criminal prosecutions; and for a long time it was always taken before the royal judges. Imbert, who still recognized a certain recourse, "ressort," from the seigniorial judges in civil matters, recognizes none in criminal matters.[1] The Ordinance of Crémieu of 1536, confirming a usage already established, gave to "appellants from corporal punishment" the right to pass over the middle judge, and go directly from the lower judge to the supreme court, provided they formally expressed their desire to do so (Art. 22). The Ordinance of 1539 went farther. In Article 163 it provided that in future all appeals, in criminal causes, should "be taken immediately and without intermediary step to the supreme court, for whatever cause it may be appealed." This perhaps went beyond the equitable limit; therefore a "Declaration" of 21st November, 1541, determined that the foregoing provisions should apply only "to appeals from sentences and judgments of torture and other corporal punishments, such as civil or natural death, scourging ("fustigation"), mutilation of members, perpetual or temporary outlawry, condemnation to public works or services." In criminal as in civil matters, the appeal had, in general, to be made immediately the sentence was pronounced; but even in civil cases this was only nominal, for letters "of relief" were easily obtained, which permitted subsequent appeal; in criminal matters it was a matter of right; "when the accused is a prisoner, he always appeals as of course."[2] It even appears that the person condemned to a corporal punishment was not under the necessity of raising ("relever") his appeal; "when the accused is condemned to corporal punishment, he is brought with his process before the court or before the middle superior judge." Appeal could be lodged, not only from final sentences, but also from all the decisions of the judge, decrees, rulings to the "extraordinary" action, sentence of torture, etc. The appeal had, usually, a suspensive effect.

We have not spoken of the procedure by contumacy since we described its earliest forms. It had been very greatly modified.

[1] The order was, 1st, the seigniorial judge or the royal provost; 2d, the bailiff or the seneschal of the province; 3d, the Parlement (*Imbert*, III, ch. xx, Nos. 1–7).

[2] *Imbert*, IV, ch. I, No. 1.

In particular the periods of delay had been changed; in this respect no difference between the gentleman and the humble plebeian was now recognized. The "Registre criminel de Saint-Martin des Champs" contains several cases of procedure by contumacy, all of them of the same nature. There was a first summons given on three consecutive days, the accused being summoned by oral proclamation by one or more officers of court.[1] Then came four more fortnightly summonses, only the first three of which appear to have been strictly required;[2] on the last default came outlawry. The following are two cases in which this procedure was followed, complete and in detail: "In the year LII (1352) Girart de Neelle . . . was duly summoned by Philipot de la Villette and Jehan Lefournier, our officers, at his residence, and on the people of his house and his neighbors, the said summons being served for suspicion of the murder of lord Guillaume des Essars . . . on three days to personally appear, to wit, on the Sunday following Saint Denis, and on the succeeding Monday and Tuesday (14, 15, 16 October), on which days he was held in default, and on each of these summonses he was summoned for each of the said days in judgment by Girart la Souris, our officer, and because he was summoned to appear for our rights and those of the mayor and the court, once, twice, thrice, and the fourth in full, to wit, for the first forty days, on Wednesday before Saint Luke the Evangelist (17 October) in the year 1352, on Wednesday before All Saints (31 October), for the second, on Wednesday following Saint Martin in winter (14 November), and on Wednesday before St. Nicholas (5 December), on which days he was held in default and did not come or appear to take law for the said crime: he was outlawed forever on pain of the gallows as use is."[3] — "10–12 January, 1352. . . . Jehan Millon was put in default on suspicion of the murder of the deceased Symon de Cappeval . . . and since he, Jehan Millon, was summoned to the rights of the court and mayor of the said place, to wit, three times on pain of outlawry: and at the place and in the accustomed manner, to wit, for the first forty days the Sunday after Epiphany (13 January) for the first; on the Sunday after the Conversion of Saint Paul (27 January) for the second; on the Sunday when 'Reminiscere' is sung (17 February) for the third, and on the

[1] pp. 32–74: "Perrin-Duport on three day oral summons by Phelipot Malgars and Colin de Montmartre," *cf.* p. 85.

[2] "Was summoned to appear for our rights and those of the mayor and the court, once, twice and thrice and the fourth and last" (pp. 211, 212).

[3] pp. 311, 312.

Sunday when 'Lætare Jerusalem' is sung (3 March) for the fourth, on which days he was held as in default, the said Jean Millon was banished from all the lands of my lord of Saint-Martin on pain of the gallows." [1]

From that time there are two phases in the procedure by contumacy: first, a summons on three days in close succession, then three or four summonses at intervals of a fortnight. But the proceedings were too long, and the Ordinance of 1539 shortened them. It contains two articles on the subject. "Art. 24. In all civil or criminal matters where four defaults have been usual, two, well and duly obtained by summons served personally or at the domicile, shall be sufficient, except that the judges may 'ex officio' add a third if the said summonses have not been served personally and they see that the matter can be so arranged." [2] — "Art. 25. In criminal matters on the first default made upon personal citation let arrest be made, and if there be two defaults it shall be ordered that, failing apprehension of the defaulter, he shall be summoned on three short periods with attachment and seizure of his property, until he has obeyed." These texts were not very clear, but the practice was plain enough. First, a single default or two defaults were declared, then the decree issued against the accused. This either ordered his arrest, or took the form of a merely personal citation: "Where there has been only personal summons the proper course is to wait for two defaults before proceeding by summons on 'three short periods' and by attachment; but if there be arrest, the clause of 'three short periods' and attachment may be included in the same decree." [3] There was not entire harmony as to what was the delay indicated by these "three short periods." According to Imbert it was essential "that there should be an interval of three full and complete days, as to the first two . . . and the last and third period must consist of a week or other sufficient period of time according to the distance between the places." But, according to Boyer, "the said summonses at three short intervals should be distinct and separated

[1] pp. 213, 214. Sometimes the "Registre" does not give the whole of the procedure. Thus in the case of one called Guillon, the defaults for the three consecutive days of the first summons only are mentioned, viz. the 30th and 31st December and 1st January (pp. 32, 33). The same thing occurs in the case of one named Perrin Dupont (pp. 74, 75); on 20th January, 1337, the default of Jehannin de Senlis on three days is noted (p. 85); then on 21st January, 1337, is added, "By Pons the Mayor, Jehannin de Senlis, default for the first day for the specified offense on the preceding Sunday," and that is all; *cf.* p. 133. Evidently there are omissions here.

[2] *Cf. Jean des Mares*, 58.

[3] *Imbert*, II, ch. III, No. 5.

by the same writ with such a sufficient interval between them as ten or eight days at least; some maintain that the procedure requires only three days, although by the law 'ad peremptorum ff. de judiciis' it is essential that ten days intervene."[1]

Contumacy resulted in a real and final condemnation; henceforth, moreover, the charges were proved before it was pronounced. This idea, although contrary to the Roman laws, is thoroughly admitted: "Although, according to the civil law, final judgment cannot be pronounced against one guilty of contumacy in criminal matters, in this kingdom we adopt a contrary custom, which is in accordance with several Italian statutes, by which the person guilty of contumacy is regarded as if he had confessed the offense of which he is accused."[2] In theory, to entail this condemnation letters from the sovereign were necessary; but the idea of regarding the judgment as capable of being purged and annulled by the appearance of the condemned person grows and will soon triumph. Imbert points out that the judgment can be attacked by way of appeal, and, although he observes that "letters" are then necessary, it is evident that these are mere matters of form: "If, therefore, the accused do not personally appear, judgment of contumacy is pronounced against him, but he can always appeal from the judgments of contumacy, and in that case shall have royal letters, directed to the first royal judge who has given the judgment, by which he shall be commanded to allow him (the accused) to be within the law, notwithstanding the judgment of contumacy, which shall be annulled by the said letters on reimbursing the expense thereof."[3] Boyer goes farther; he supposes that by the accused's appearance the judgment *ipso facto* falls.[4] Traces of the

[1] *Boyer's* "Stile," p. 234.

[2] *Imbert, loc. cit.; cf. Constantin,* "Commentaire sur l'ordonnance de 1539," p. 56: "Bartolus . . . dicit valere statutum vel consuetudinem, quod judex condemnet et procedat contra contumacem, quæ consuetudo viget in toto regno Franciæ." — The clause of execution was incorporated into the decree: "Si pris et appréhendé peut être." (If taken and arrested may be.) See *Bornier,* Ordinance of 1670, Title 17, Art. 15: "This clause . . . was probably a matter of the old style, for in former times the sentences rendered for contumacy were executed personally on those sentenced if they were found . . . as it was only inserted 'ad terrorem' and was not practised in France it was very properly repealed by the Ordinance."

[3] Ch. IV, p. 663.

[4] "The person in default can always purge himself of the accusation, although the said decree has been issued and executed, and to do this he is obliged to give himself up as a prisoner in the prison of the Court of Justice, and on that being done the record of the registers of the imprisonment for the pursuit of the accusation upon the examination of the action must be produced, otherwise he shall be released as hereinafter mentioned." "Stile," p. 236.

original idea will, however, subsist for a long time; Serpillon points out that the question was still in dispute and was determined by a decree in 1635.[1]

In this procedure, the seizure of the effects of the rebel, the origin of which we have traced to the feudal period, was carefully regulated; this was the *attachment* ("annotation"). It took place after the summons at three short intervals had been served.[2] The Ordinance of Roussillon (Art. 80) declares that if accused persons do not appear within a year after the seizure, "their property attached and seized shall belong absolutely to whomsoever has right to it." This feature was borrowed from the Roman law, and added to the old procedure of contumacy, which up to that time had been wholly common law. The Ordinance of Moulins (Art. 28) went further; it ordains that if the judgment carries confiscation or fine, persons guilty of contumacy "shall forfeit not only the income of their property, but also the ownership of all their effects awarded by the law. And the civil parties shall retain their adjudications without power of redemption, and we and our seigniorial justices what shall have been awarded to us and them by fine and confiscation." The text added that the king could grant letters to "allow the condemned persons to come into court and to exculpate themselves after the said period and to remit the severity of this our Ordinance." Letters of pardon again appear in the procedure of contumacy. It was generally considered that this law had repealed the provisions of the Ordinance of Roussillon. The Ordinance of 1670 will do no more than bring together these principles, and develop and in some respects perfect them.

§ 3. **Protests against the Ordinance of 1539. Constantin, Du Moulin, and Pierre Ayrault.** — We have seen how and by what disintegration of the old forms the system sanctioned by the Ordinance of 1539 was slowly built up. It is not so easy to understand the unopposed acceptance of this procedure by the nation; still, it is an undeniable fact that the Ordinances which are the subject of our study coincide in point of time with the meetings of representatives of the country who could make the voice of the people heard. This, however, is capable of explanation. This procedure, due in great measure to the practice of the royal judges,

[1] "It was formerly a matter of doubt as to whether the appearance of one condemned to death annulled the contumacy. This was the subject of a conflict of opinion which was decided by a decision of the Court of Assize of the month of June, 1633." "Code criminel," p. 851.

[2] Ordinance of 1539, Art. 25.

had grown with the growth of royalty; it rested upon a sentiment of inherent infallibility and stern protection, which royalty had borrowed from the Church, and which constituted its principal strength. The people, emerging from the anarchy of the Middle Ages and from the great wars against the English, torn ere long by the devastating religious wars, felt above all else the need of security and peace.[1] The new Ordinances furnished a better assurance than any other law for the repression of crime. For this reason, they were willingly accepted and almost popular. The Ordinance of 1539 was not, however, passed without protest on the part of the jurists; both feeble and eloquent voices were raised against the severities which it introduced.

The first undoubtedly to criticise it was a Bordeaux lawyer, called Jean Constantin, who wrote in the year 1543.[2] His commentary is in Latin. His was not a great intellect, and Néron gives him small praise in the preface to his collection.[3] He was, in truth, an honest man, who had no love for provost-marshals, a thing often observable in those days.[4] He displays an undigested erudition, stuffed with texts from the "Corpus juris" and the works of Italian doctors, whom he quotes at every turn, piling citation upon citation between the different parts of a single phrase. But that was the fashion of the time, and Constantin deserves our passing consideration. He represents the unadulterated doctrine of the Italian doctors, and he certainly shows that, if France had borrowed literally certain points of its criminal doctrine from these doctors, — the theory of proofs, for example, — it had given to the inquisitorial procedure a shape and direction of its own and a severity unknown to the Ultramontanes. The expressions themselves

[1] Leaving judicial documents out of the question, every page of the "Registre criminel du Châtelet" shows the brigandage and the state of insecurity under which France suffered at the end of the 1300 s.

[2] "Commentarii Johannis Constantini, in jure licentiati curiæ que Parlamenti Burdigalensis advocati, in leges regias seu ordinationes de litibus brevi decidendis recenter editas," P. 248: "Hoc anno millesimo quadragesimo tertio."

[3] "A commentary on this ordinance appeared ten years after its publication written in Latin by *Jean Constantin*, advocate to the Parlement of Bordeaux. The great copiousness of this work cannot be denied, but if the useless matters are eliminated and the large number of quotations with which it is swelled are cut down, substantially little is left." "Recueil de Néron," preface, Paris 1720.

[4] "Isti intrunculatores et judices maleficiorum quos præpositos marescallorum nominamus, et qui eis tallia officia committant, qui cum deberent esse literati viri, sunt ignari, et omnium honorum litterarum expertes, tiranni vindicatores sibi et suis complacentes, pereant a cæterorum commercio et exterminentur tales tyranni et homicidæ et eorum officia bonis viris et litteratis committant" (p. 237).

had sometimes changed their meaning in passing into France, and Constantin gives a curious example.[1] In the name of the law-doctors he protests against the severities of the Ordinance.

Commenting upon Article 162, he inveighs against the exclusion of advocates: "Practicam antiquam quæ hic tollitur et aboletur meminit Angelus in suo tractatu maleficiorum . . . ubi dicit quod ipse reus vel ejus advocatus potest interrogatoria facere."[2] Commenting on Articles 157 and 158 he shows what slender resources the law leaves to the accused for his defense: "Quomodo potest allegare reus aliquid ad suam defensionem si sibi non detur copia testium et totius processus? Ideo quæro, numquit facta et completa inquisitione, testes et totus processus debeant publicari et de his fieri copia ipsi reo."[3] Farther on he launches into a long dissertation, citing all his authorities, and coming to the conclusion that the law-doctors admit, in general, the production of documents, that it was even a matter of right whenever there was a party "promovens inquisitionem." As to the provision which bars the proof offered by the accused at any time during the action, and allows only that of justificative facts, Constantin not only declares it odious, but absolutely refuses to allow it. As to article 158 he says: "De severitate hujus articuli satis patet ex suprà dictis, maxime in articulo CXLVI ubi habes quod istæ ordinationes, quæ excludunt reum a defensione ante sententiam, sunt omnino contrà jus commune . . . licet Angelus dicat talia statuta excludentia reum a defensione valere, ego limito hoc esse verum si reus petat calumniose se admitti ad defensionem, alias secus, . . . quia confesso et condemnato datur defensio; ergo multa magis non confessus nec condemnatus, volens de innocentia sua probare, admittitur quandoque ante sententiam, si videas eum hoc calumniose non petere, ut puta quia hoc tempore, de quo loquitur ordinatio nostra, non habebat probationes et postea reperit vel alia modo constat de sua innocentia."[4] As to article 162, rejecting the confrontative judgments

[1] "Judices maleficiorum in senatu Burdigalensi hoc anno millesimo quingentesimo quadragesimo tertio consedentes, qui, cum me ad se accessissent quod quemdam furem sententia torquendum dixissem, et ipsi suo arresto cum suis furtis absolvendum, quæsiverunt inter alia quid erat ordinariè procedere; qui, quum dixissem quod secundum formam et ordinem juris, subridebant dicentes, quod imo procedere ordinarie erat sine confrontationibus et extraordinarie per confrontationes, et quia usus non eram confrontationibus in processu illius furis dicebant me errasse in facto et in jure, et allegabant advocatus et procurator regius l. *Ordo, ff. De publiciis judiciis;* quod plusquam asininum est et tantis viris indignum; sed quia coram ipsis non audebam aperte loqui, ideo tacui: nam aliam esse formam et ordinem juris in criminibus et aliam horum statutorum nemo est qui nesciat" (p. 248).

[2] p. 288. [3] pp. 281, 282. [4] p. 284.

formerly allowed, he is still more forcible. "Nota quod dixi articulo CXLIX quod debet assignari terminus reo ad suam defensionem faciendam; alias non debet damnari. . . . Ita dicit Bartolus, et Imola . . . quod hanc practicam servat totus mundus, qui quidem terminus tollitur his ordinationibus ut dicto articulo constat. Ergo non servamus illam practicam quam servat totus mundus, juris et justitiæ ignari; quare dico quod non valet tale statutum per quod tollitur defensio quæ est de jure naturali . . . cum jus naturale jure civili tolli non possit, et quod judex, ipso non obstante, potest præfigere terminum ipsi reo ad suam defensionem faciendam . . . alias poterit lædi innocens, quod non esse debet."[1] All this, even when disencumbered of the citations with which it is burdened, certainly offers few fine phrases. But although the style is poor enough, the ideas are none the less noble on that account.

Constantin was not the only practitioner to find fault with the pitiless severities of the Ordinance: here and there in Imbert are to be found short remarks in the same spirit. But louder voices were raised. First there was that of Du Moulin, who commented on the Ordinance of 1539 in a grotesque style, in a clumsy Latin mixed with French. Several of his indignant and curt remarks have survived the ages as lasting protests. He tried first to put as favorable an interpretation upon the text as possible. As to Article 155, which does not give the accused any delay to allege his objections, he says: "Si hoc verbum (delay) referatur ad singula et sic ea excludendo, esset barbarica iniquitas; ideo debet intelligi quod implicet non distributive sed collective. Ita quod judex possit dare dilationem modicum arbitrio suo, et sensus est quod verba non excludent aperte dilationem dari, quod est favorabile."[2] In the same fashion he repudiates the literal interpretation of Article 157, ordering the accused immediately to name his witnesses for the proof of the justificative facts.[3] Two of his outbursts in particular have remained famous, that upon article 158, where he brands the name of Poyet with that epithet of infamy which never left it: "Vide tyrannicum opinionem illius impii Poyeti";[4] the other, on article 154, which does not require

[1] pp. 291, 292. [2] "Recueil de Néron," vol. I, p. 250.

[3] *Ibid.*, p. 251: "*Nommer* intellige quâcumque demonstratione, quia non semper innocens scit nomina eorum per quos probabitur absentia allegata; *faits justificatifs:* etiam de facto vidi *à Mascon* 1550 *reçu* post 21 menses et dicere etiam variando quæ nova facta *estoient venus à sa mémoire et nommer tesmoins pour ce prouver* et ad requestam *du procureur du Roy* et tantum non vocato accusatore."

[4] "Recueil de Néron," vol. I, p. 251.

the judge to verify the witnesses for the defense: "Vide duritiem iniquissimam per quam etiam defensio aufertur, sed nunc judicio Dei justo redundat in authorem, quia major pars judicum voluit hanc servare constitutionem hoc mense octobris 1544. Sed est perniciosissima consequentia." [1]

But louder still than Du Moulin speaks another, who cannot be too highly eulogized, Pierre Ayrault. He had a great intellect and a large heart. In his chief work, "l'Ordre, formalité et instruction judiciaire," we still obtain valuable information on Roman criminal law; and this learned work is written in an admirable, fervid, and glowing style. Rising high above his contemporaries, he showed to a nicety the dangers of the criminal procedure to which France was given over. We may be permitted to quote the chief passages in which he fights for a cause, which, though for a long time lost, could never perish, and demands orality in the trials and publicity and liberty in the pleadings.

His first concern is to point out the fundamental defects of the system which he attacks, namely, its secrecy, the undue importance attached to written documents, and the immense power left in the judge's hands. "Justice," he says, "is treated like sacred mysteries, which are imparted only to the priest.[2] . . . In olden days at Rome and in Greece all this examination ('instruction'), confirmation, confrontation, and judgment took place with open doors and publicly, in presence of the people and of all the judges and parties concerned. In no other respect is our practice more contrary than in this, for so rigorous is our requirement that criminal actions be examined apart and in secret that we will not judge them if any other than the judge and his clerk of court should have been present. Whence this difference? Are right and reason different factors in republics where the people take part in the administration from those existing in States dependent on one single person? We in France have certainly not thought so for a long time. . . . It is not, therefore, political difference which causes this variance between secret and open examination. . . . In private it is easy to twist the evidence, to intrigue or browbeat. The court-room, on the contrary, is the bridle of the passions, the scourge of bad judges. But, while this public examination serves as a curb for bad judges, it gives good judges an inconceivable sense of security and freedom. The innocent will never be clearly acquitted or the guilty justly punished, and there will always be some cause for com-

[1] "Molinæi opera," vol. II, p. 792.
[2] "L'ordre et formalité," etc., Book III, Article 3, No. 21.

plaint, if their trial has not been conducted and considered publicly. That head with more eyes, more ears, more brains than those of all the monsters and giants of the poets, has more strength, more energy to penetrate straight to the conscience, and lay bare on what side the right lies than our secret examination."[1] "Is it reasonable to credit what one judge and a hired clerk report as to the testimony of ten or twenty witnesses? . . . Such depositions do not show either what is said by the deponent or how he says it. It is the concoction of an officer, a searcher, or an examiner, even, forsooth, of a judge, if it has been taken by one, who all make the witness say what seems good to them. Nothing can be said in reply, though there may be ever so great a contradiction in the terms, and the very first assertion which the witness has made use of in deponing exists no longer when we come to our confirmations and ordinary confrontations. I have oftentimes heard the late lord lieutenant-general of this jurisdiction, a very well-informed man, say that the witnesses might be likened to clocks. Just as we can make the latter strike any hour we want, so the witness, according to the way he is examined, and the terms used to embellish and clothe his narrative, testifies for the prosecution or the defense; . . . for this reason he declared that nothing was so harmful in the trial to which we are accustomed as the introduction into it of the methods and functions of the hearing of witnesses. On the report of an examiner and inquisitor the judge gives credence to men whom he has never seen, and if perchance he causes their re-examination, they usually tell another tale, or else say, 'Let them read me my deposition; I stand to what is written therein.'"[2]—"The mouth lies most when it is closed tight from fear of falling into a trap, but our gestures and outward expressions, whether we wish it or not, speak, and speak the truth, in one way or another."[3]

The oral and public procedure has never been better defended, or in better language. Ayrault paints with no less vigorous a brush the terrible power of the examining magistrate and the helplessness of the defense. "I insist that the best feature which the criminal examination of the ancients possessed was that this act of interrogating the parties depended upon themselves or their advocates and not upon the judges. . . . The method has been so thoroughly changed, and ours is so radically different, that if any other

[1] "L'ordre et formalité," etc., Book III, Article 3, Nos. 58, 59, 60, 63, 64.

[2] *Ibid.*, Book III, Article 3, No. 38.

[3] *Ibid.*, Book III, Article 3, No. 64.

than the judge should now interrogate the accused, or if he should do it in the presence of the party, the whole proceeding would be null. . . . Depriving the parties of that option of interrogating, hearing, and examining their witnesses, we have put the matter in the judge's hands to such an extent that the unfortunate parties appear to-day with their hands tied, and blinder than those who write in midnight darkness. . . . Nowadays, when all the functions which rested with the parties and their lawyers center in him (the judge), he must proceed with so much guile and finesse, if he would drag the truth from the lips of a criminal, that it is very hard to say whether these artifices should be dubbed justice or chicanery."[1]

The system of objections and justificative facts appears particularly intolerable to Ayrault's honesty. "The testimony would be much better rebutted by timely debate, argument, and refutation than by blame and reprehension of the person giving it. But since we are on the subject of objections, let us see, for the sake of argument, if the ordinance introduced by Chancellor Poyet, providing that the accused must plead them before having heard the testimony of the witness, and that after the reading they should no longer be admissible, is just and equitable. . . . The same officer even ordered that no witnesses should ever be brought by the accused except his relatives, neighbors, and fellow-citizens. . . . How can the accused know at the very moment whether or not the witness is bribed or has been incited against him; his relatives, his friends, his solicitors and attorneys themselves cannot find that out so soon; how can he do it from his prison? The device of alleging objections before the reading has resulted in the accused persons being constrained to object at all hazards, and in the majority of their objections being matters of course . . . the ignorant especially need protection . . . everybody does not understand the ordinance, no matter what notification has been given of it. Does this not look like the establishment of such a formality that not to object before or after will deprive one of life or honor? . . . Many unfortunate accused persons, who do not know A or B do not know either to object or challenge.[2] All the foregoing emboldens me to say that

[1] Book III, Article 3, Nos. 21 and 22. These inconveniences are noticed by *Imbert* (III, ch. X, Nos. 2 and 3), who gives wise advice to the interrogating judge and censures the practices of crafty magistrates.

[2] *Imbert* likewise makes a protest in this respect: "Which ordinances," he says, "are extraordinarily severe (and their author has met the fate of Perillus); for it is very harsh and severe to make an unfortunate prisoner languishing under an imprisonment of a year or six months instantly

I do not clearly understand what induced the said Chancellor Poyet to abandon that excellent and straightforward mode of proceeding, where both parties bring their evidence at the same time, for that which he has introduced of granting an interlocutory judgment to inquire as to justificative facts and objections, the former method having been an invariable rule hitherto. Whence comes this contrivance of not allowing the accused to bring his evidence until that of the prosecutor is brought and settled? . . . Is there justice in the fact that one party labors and strives to bring his evidence after the other is all ready? . . . A duel fought on the understanding that one should fire all his shots first and the other afterwards would be neither just nor seemly. In the trials now in vogue the judgments are arbitrary and the assessors are prone to accept what they are primed with rather than what is proved, the accused are in danger of seeing themselves condemned in spite of and without regard to their justificative facts and objections. In short, is it proper to judge an action after looking at but one side? . . . There remain in this ordinance two matters, which we ascribe to the said lord chancellor Poyet, so far removed from the old time forms as to throw doubt upon his equity; it is declared that the accused shall name his witnesses immediately and that not he but the king's procurator shall cause their appearance. What does this signify? The prosecutor is to have ample time to make his investigation, but the accused is to divine at once what witnesses can vindicate him! And a third party, and not he, is to bring those whom he names for his defense; his innocence will thus depend upon the fidelity or faithlessness, the diligence or indifference of another. Is there any king's procurator as concerned about the vindication of the accused as the accused himself?" [1]

Ayrault also inveighs against the abuse of detention pending trial and of the monitories ("monitoires"). After having praised the practice of release on bail in a magnificent passage, and lauded the ancients for having permitted it, this is what he says

cite his said witnesses, and not to allow the prisoner nor another for him to speak to the witnesses who may come to testify on his behalf, and that the king's procurator, who is an adverse party, should cause their appearance, not to mention the fact that they will probably be delivered into the charge of an officer of the court who is practically for the party adverse to the prisoner. And on this account it would be well to somewhat ameliorate the said ordinances" (III, ch. xiii, No. 16). The proof of the justificative facts and the objections to the admissibility of the witnesses is here the matter in question.

[1] *Ayrault*, Book III, Article 3, Nos. 50–52.

of sudden arrest: "It may nowadays be almost ranked as the regular procedure. It oftentimes happens, I know not how, that what is the finest and most reasonable thing in theory is very unprofitable in practice. It has been necessary, in order to safeguard the public, to discard the traditions of freemen and treat all as sworn enemies, rogues, and slaves, for whom prisons, tortures, and gibbets have been invented. All our other reasons may be as plausible as you like; yet so harsh is our practice, that experience shows us that if the accused are not kept in prison, it is impossible to convict a single one; there is no witness who dares testify, no judgment which can be executed."[1] — "Nothing is so common nowadays as to resort to the monitories and ecclesiastical censures to obtain proof and revelation of crime prosecuted or to be prosecuted before us. Have we any criticism to make upon the ancients because, to gain these same ends, they implored from their pontiffs such imprecations and maledictions? . . . I think not . . . To entice the witnesses by bribery or by fear of being punished by God or man was a thing they never did. As it is a crime for the accused to bribe the witnesses on his behalf, so should it be for the prosecution to coerce them, or bribe them. The ancients, after all, were more careful about their religion than we are. The public is not so deeply interested in the charging and proof of a crime as to injure itself by the profanation and pollution of holy things."[2]

We may be pardoned for having multiplied these quotations; it was useful to show that in our country the sentiment of true freedom remained in some exalted hearts, at a time when it was most lacking in our institutions. It is not quite correct to say that "when the royal Ordinances altered the form of criminal actions, to substitute the written examination for the traditions of the old oral procedure, no voice was raised to recall the individual safeguards."[3] The fact is, however, that the protests which were made found public opinion indifferent. The bitter plaint of Pierre Ayrault, which to-day commands our admiration, then fell on empty ears: "Vox clamantis in deserto." The country

[1] *Ayrault*, Book III, Article 2, No. 30. It is strange that this is the only word of blame to be found in Ayrault for this horrible institution of torture. Compare *Imbert* on detention pending trial: "Although it may be somewhat arbitrary, it would nevertheless be well to designate expressly by Ordinance the offenses for which an order for arrest could be granted, so as to restrain the license which many judges usurp on this point." Book III, ch. II, No. 4.

[2] *Ibid.*, Book III, Article 2, No. 31.

[3] *M. G. Picot*, "Histoire des États-Généraux, vol. IV, p. 254.

thankfully accepted everything that helped to check the disorders from which it had suffered so long. "Towards the end of the Middle Ages," says M. Picot, "after the terrible Hundred Years' War, which had shaken France to its very core, royalty realized that the nation's greatest need was internal order. The whole country was then obviously enamoured passionately of safeguards which bade fair to shield it from the violence of the strong hand." And the movement which had transformed the criminal procedure in France was at the same time making headway among the neighboring continental nations; there its force was irresistible.

§ 4. **The Criminal Procedure and the States-General of the 1500s.** — Whenever the nation chose to speak by the mouths of its representatives, either in the States-General or in the convocations of Notables, it approved of the revolution effected in its criminal procedure. On rare occasions, the Third Estate, actuated by the vague instinct of freedom which never left it, and the Nobility by a sentiment of jealous independence, raised objections on certain matters of detail. As time went on, satisfaction with the new procedure became more marked and it struck its roots more vigorously and tenaciously. This approval of the secret and inquisitorial procedure by the States-General has been demonstrated at different periods. Attorney-General Séguier recalled it in 1786, in a celebrated speech before the Parlement of Paris, in which he discountenanced the desires for reform. "One remarkable thing," he said, "which we should not forget, the great Ordinances of the kingdom have in common. The Ordinance of Villers-Cotterets is dated 1539, that of Orléans 1560, that of Moulins 1566, and that of Blois 1579. They all belong to the same century; the aim of all is the reformation of the law. The three last mentioned were issued in answer to the complaints, laments, and protests of the three estates of the kingdom . . . and in all these solemn laws, in which, if I may be permitted to say so, the nation demanded justice from its sovereign, there is no complaint against the form of procedure, nor against the barbarity of the Ordinance of Francis I. Can it be pretended that the whole nation assembled in deliberation upon its affairs has been blind enough not to demand, in this respect, the reform of a fantastical system of law which is also contrary to natural law?"[1] Later, at the time of the drawing up of the Code of Criminal Examination, when the "prévôtal" jurisdictions were introduced into our judicial system, under the name of "Special Tribunals," those who drew up the Code re-

[1] pp. 240, 241.

called that the States-General of the 1500s had approved of this institution. "It will be sufficient for the purpose of the debate to observe that a special institution, analogous to that which we now propose to you, reëstablished in every part of France by Francis I at the beginning of the 16th century, was recognized, demanded by the States-General held at Orléans, Moulins, and Blois, and sanctioned and reconstituted in the celebrated Ordinances issued in answer to the protests of these States."[1] The only mistake made by Séquier and M. Réal was in deeming the attitude of the States-General to be a vindication of the procedure of the Ordinance of 1539.

It is of interest to examine more minutely the exact language of the Estates; which M. Picot's excellent "Histoire des États-Généraux" has made an easy task.

In the Estates of 1560, the Nobility merely insisted that the king's procurator should be "bound to disclose the informer on pain of being liable in his own individual name." The Third Estate and the Clergy demanded an increased activity in the use of public prosecution, and the Ordinance of Orléans (Art. 63), embodied this desire in the law.[2] The Third, however, protested against the provision which "compels accused persons immediately to allege their objections to the witness, which is a great hardship, and often results in the innocence of many being imperilled." It urged that the judge should be empowered to grant a delay. The king's Council replied that "the Ordinance shall be observed."[3] The greatest concern of the Estates centred upon the provost-marshals; while the Third demanded and obtained for certain royal courts concurrent jurisdiction with the provost,[4] all three orders were unanimous in their demand for speedier and more effective action by the marshalcy.

In 1576, at Blois, the Third Estate desired that the accused should be "regularly informed of the name of the informer against him before any confrontation."[5] This desire was destined to be ignored; but not so another, likewise preferred by the Third, to the effect that "all those who shall investigate crimes by information shall be bound to examine the witnesses as to the full truth of the fact, as much for the defense as for the prosecution of the accused." It was considered that enough had been done for the defense by thus handing over its care to the conscience of the

[1] "Exposé des motifs du titre VI, livre II, du Code d'Instruction Criminelle," by *M. Réal* (Leiré, vol. XXVIII, p. 47).
[2] *M. Picot, op. cit.*, vol. II, pp. 169, 170. [3] *Ibid.*, vol. II, p. 171.
[4] Ordinance d'Orléans, Article 72. [5] *Picot, op. cit.*, vol. II, p. 528.

judge. It was at bottom a purely formal satisfaction, and the provision was inserted in the Ordinance of Blois (Art. 203), and was subsequently incorporated in the Ordinance of 1670 (Title V, Art. 10). A more important matter, also prescribed by the Ordinance of Blois, was that the judges were obliged to ask the witnesses if they were "relatives, kinsmen, domestics, or servants of the parties, and to mention the fact at the commencement of their depositions, on pain of nullity and damages to the parties."[1] But what was wanted more than anything else was an acceleration of the public prosecution and in the service of the marshalcy: "A perusal of the 'Cahiers,'" says M. Picot, "clearly shows that the deputies were charmed with the Ordinance of 1539. . . . The information by itself seemed to them fitted only to terrify evildoers and consequently to reassure peaceable people. So they refrained from criticising the secret examination."[2]

At the new Estates of Blois, in 1588, the foregoing questions still less troubled the minds of the deputies; "neither the Clergy nor the Third concerned themselves with the criminal examination."[3] The Nobility demanded the acceleration of the proceedings; they manifested a desire to revive accusation by individuals, as opposed to the action of the public prosecutor, proposing a provision, which, moreover, has passed into our laws, providing for the forfeiture of all right "against the widows, heirs, or assignees of the victims of homicide who did not prosecute the murder or manslaughter in the person of their husbands or relatives."[4]

The mission of the Estates of the Ligue of 1593 was exclusively political, and criminal legislation was not the concern of that assemblage, the immortal satire on which is contained in the "Ménippée." The Assembly of Notables, held at Rouen in 1596, was likewise without influence in this matter.[5]

It was at the Estates of Paris of 1614, and at the Assemblies of Notables of Rouen (1617) and of Paris (1626, 1627), that the representatives of the country were able to give expression to their opinions for the last time before the drawing up of the Ordinance of 1670. Public opinion showed itself still more favorable to the secret and inquisitorial procedure: "a whole generation of the legal profession were trained under the mysterious customs

[1] *Picot, op. cit.*, vol. II, p. 528. The Nobility had desired "that prisoners released for want of evidence should not be liable to arrest after the expiration of one year from the date of the decree ordering the further inquiry."

[2] *Ibid.*, vol. II, p. 530.

[3] *Ibid.*, vol. III, p. 184.

[4] *Ibid.*, vol. III, p. 184.

[5] *Ibid.*, vol. III, pp. 257, 323.

of the written examination, and the indolence of injured parties had gradually accepted the initiative on the part of the magistrate, which spared the citizen the care of defending himself, and substituted the protection of the State for individual action."[1] Even in the "Cahiers" we find the expression of views tending to aggravate still more the hardships of the procedure. It is at the request of the Third Estate that the Ordinance of 1629 will be found expressly to forbid entering pleas at the outset of the criminal proceedings (Art. 112), lest the lawyers and the procurator-general should perchance by mere hint designate the witness clearly enough "to give the accused the opportunity to prepare themselves and bring forward objections and have recourse to stratagems against the witnesses for the prosecution."[2] All three orders insisted upon a single judge conducting the information with the assistance of his clerk or "greffier."[3] This, it is true, was chiefly from motives of economy; the same impulse moved the compilers of the Ordinance of Moulins to provide (Art. 37) "that henceforward a single commissary and not two shall be appointed to attend to the examination of actions; always in the presence of his clerk of court or assistant, the whole on quadruple penalty." The Third Estate also concerned itself with "dilatory 'incidents'[4] and evocations,[5] commonly used for the purpose of evading the punishment of crimes; it demanded that it should not be possible to suspend the examination under diverse pretexts, and that the judge should not stop until the moment when he pronounced the final sentence."[6] Some alleviations were, however, demanded. The Nobility "persisted in demanding that the attorneys-general, being parties, should be compelled to name the informers at the beginning of the action."[7] The Third Estate wished that "the interrogation of the accused should take place within twenty-four hours after his arrest."[8] The jurisdiction of the provost-marshals received the attention of the deputies; they proposed that their "jurisdiction, which is a pure abuse, be restricted to disorders committed by the military."[9]

The complaints of the Estates of 1614 and of the Assemblies of Notables which followed resulted in the publication of an Ordinance. In 1627 Michel de Marillac gathered around him a certain

[1] *Picot*, vol. IV, p. 61.
[2] *Ibid.*, vol. IV, pp. 61 and 187.
[3] *Ibid.*, vol. IV, p. 64.
[4] Facts emerging in the course of a case constituting a claim depending upon the principal claim.
[5] "Evocation" is the calling of a case from one court to another.
[6] *Picot*, vol. IV, p. 64.
[7] *Ibid.*, vol. IV, p. 60.
[8] *Ibid.*, vol. IV, p. 61.
[9] *Ibid.*, vol. IV, p. 65.

number of State's Councillors, and the complaints of the deputies were considered. An Ordinance was made, comprising a large number of articles, many of which were devoted to the administration of the law and to the procedure; but it was by no means a detailed and systematic codification. It was registered by the Parlement of 15th January, 1629. But this "Code Michaud," as it was called, was rarely observed in practice.

In the 1600s, as we shall see, public opinion demanded no reforms in criminal law; it was not even hinted that the procedure which was followed could possibly be bad. But the need was ere long felt of a Criminal Code, precise and detailed, which should settle all the details and do away with the irregularities and divergencies in the administration of justice. The time of the Fronde had been one of severe distress. Crime, the inevitable offspring of evil days, had increased; and at the same time, by a phenomenon invariably observable in the midst of political troubles, the administration of justice had become less exact and less energetic. Five years after the death of Mazarin, Denis Talon was able to say "that the number of evil doers had grown to such an excess on account of the impunity with which crime was committed, that soon all security of public liberty will have ceased to exist."[1] In 1665, the "Great Days" of Auvergne, of which Fléchier has left us a very interesting account,[2] showed in a startling fashion the disorders and scandals which tarnished the administration of justice. It was also the case that, although for a long time the broad features of the procedure had been settled, no general law had regulated its details. The inexactitude and diversity of the systems of judicial practice were also an evil which continued to be more and more keenly felt: "The evil," according to one of the compilers of the Ordinance of 1670, "has come to such a pass that in the same Parlement several maxims have changed two or three times within thirty years, and even at the present day they are construed differently in the different chambers of the same Parlement."[3] Nothing but a general law could provide a remedy. Such a law was also called for to correct another abuse. The criminal proceedings being entirely written, a multitude of formalities and useless productions were introduced into it, which had the effect of retarding the progress of actions, and

[1] Quoted by *M. Pierre Clément*, "Lettres, papiers et documents de Colbert," vol. VI, Introduction, p. xxxix.

[2] "Grands-jours d'Auvergne," *Chéruel*.

[3] "Lettre d'Auzanet à un de ses amis." See *Pierre Clément*, "Lettres et documents de Colbert," vol. VI, App. p. 397.

inevitably ended in the excessive increase of the expense of the proceedings.

The Monarchy had emerged triumphant from the recently ended strife, which it had waged for centuries, first against feudalism and then against the nobility; the Fronde had been the final convulsion of the opposed forces. Henceforward unopposed, royalty strove to establish that absolute and centralized government which left such a marked imprint upon France. The time was favorable for a reform of the laws. Whenever, after secular struggles between rival forces, a nation arrives at a stage which seems to it final, and which in reality should assure it of a long period of stability, it feels the need of recasting and unifying its laws. A desire is felt to unite into one harmonious whole the rules of law which have been in slow process of formation and to disencumber them of their heterogeneous elements. That was the kind of work imposed upon the government of Louis XIV. A fact which clearly shows that there was a real need for such an undertaking, one of those ideas which "are in the air," as we say to-day, is that two eminent men, Lamoignon and Colbert, simultaneously formed the conception of a codification of the laws, and separately commenced the first labors to attain that end.

Part II

HISTORY OF CRIMINAL PROCEDURE IN THE LATE 1600s AND THE 1700s

TITLE I[1]

THE FRENCH ORDINANCE OF 1670

CHAPTER I

THE DRAFTING OF THE ORDINANCE OF 1670

§ 1. **The Project of a Codification; Colbert, Pussort, and Louis XIV.** — Louis XIV, in several passages in his Journal and his Memoirs, speaking of the Ordinances dealing with the laws promulgated during his reign, claims as his own, not only the glory of the execution, but also the original conception.[2] Those around him strove, indeed, to persuade him that he was the real achiever of the enterprise, and posterity seems to have been of that opinion, since it has given the name of "Code Louis" to the collection of these Ordinances. It is, to-day, thanks to modern research, possible to assign to each his share in the work. In the account which we shall now give, the Ordinance of 1667 and that of 1670 must be considered together; both are parts of the same work, executed by the same hands.

The credit of the undertaking belongs to Colbert and his uncle, Pussort. Even in the 1700 s legal scholars had come to believe this, although all they had to go upon were the minutes of the meetings between the members of the Parlement and the State councillors. Speaking of the criminal Ordinance, they called Pussort "the chief compiler of that law." Colbert and Pussort were both men capable of carrying out such a work successfully. Colbert's strength of will is well known, and Pussort was as energetic and able

[1] [The order of the author's chapters in this Part has been slightly changed, to make the development clearer for the purposes of this volume. — ED.]

[2] "Mémoires de Louis XIV" (*Dreyss* edition), vol. II, pp. 156, 224, 368.

as he. Saint-Simon, who had no love for him, yet speaks of him in these terms; "M. Colbert was a self-made man; his ability had stood him in good stead . . . he was very wealthy and very avaricious, morose, exacting, and bore a fierce and discontented expression which reflected his disposition, and the sternness of which aroused fear . . . withal a man of great integrity, a vast ability, keen insight and very hard-working, invariably taking the lead in all the important commissions of the Council and in all important internal affairs of the kingdom." [1]

Colbert's plan is shown by a document in his own handwriting, found among his papers.[2] It is a "list of the royal ordinances promulgated by our kings for the regulation of law, police, finances, and military affairs of the kingdom." This list, intended for the king, runs from the reign of Saint Louis to the year 1626; it concludes with this résumé: "It clearly appears from all these lists that, since the time of Charlemagne, who drew up the Capitularies which comprise the regulation of all ranks of his kingdom, and those of his son Louis le Débonnaire, no king has labored of his own accord to put into a single code all the Ordinances of the kingdom; that all our great kings, Charles V, Charles VII, Louis XII, Francis I, and Henry IV, immediately they were at peace, and even often during war, have made Ordinances concerning justice and other matters; that Henry III alone had the conception of reducing the whole into a single Code, which work he intrusted to president Brisson, who compiled the Code Henry, never put in force; keeper of the seals Marillac had the same fate, with the result that this great work has been reserved in its entirety for Louis XIV." The date of this memorandum is unknown, but it can be asserted that as early as 1661 the industrious Pussort was already at work on the realization of Colbert's project: "I have scratched the surface of the work which I suggested to you on the matter of the ordinances;" he wrote to Colbert on 6th September, 1661, "but I recognize that it is a work of enormous extent and entailing delicate handling. I shall continue to work upon it when I have nothing more pressing on hand. If you have need of me and my work, both are at your disposal." [3] The codification of the ordinances was in itself an immense work, even without comprising in it the unification of the civil law; so, down to 1665, Colbert's plan appears to have slumbered.

[1] "Mémoires," *Chéruel* edition, vol. I, p. 325.

[2] "Lettres, papiers, et documents de Colbert," edited by *M. Pierre Clément*, vol. VI, App. p. 362.

[3] "Lettres, etc., de Colbert," vol. IV, App. p. 368.

The prime minister wished the new work to be a direct work of royalty. It was a maxim of ancient law that the legislative power resides in the king and in him alone.[1] The great Ordinances of the 1400s and the 1500s had doubtless often been issued after convocations of the States-General and after Reports from the deputies; but in a legislative sense they none the less emanated from the king alone. The "Coutumes" had been drawn up by delegates and representatives of the three orders, but they had only become written laws by royal promulgation. This point was indubitable. But in order to accomplish his legislative task the king must surround himself with counsellors and compilers; for the Ordinances concerning justice it seemed natural to consult the Parlements; and Colbert did not want to do this. We find among his papers an autograph draft "upon a way to put the Parlement in its proper sphere and to strip it for ever of the powers by which that body has attempted to hamper the State, by wishing to take part in its administration."[2] The minister, like his royal master, did not wish to associate the Parlement officers with the glorious enterprise which he meditated; he wished to ask assistance only from State councillors and eminent lawyers, famous members of the bar. "None of these great works," he said later, "can very well be accomplished except by means of the State councillors, and of the Masters of Requests."[3]

Colbert probably communicated his project to the king in the year 1664 or 1665, easily finding a way to make the communication as if the conception had spontaneously occurred to His Royal Highness. He says as much in an important memorandum of 15th May, 1665: "The plan which the king signifies that it is his intention to carry out for the judicature of his kingdom is the greatest and most glorious which a king could conceive. . . . His Majesty, recognizing perfectly the two duties of kings, the first, the duty of protection, and the second, the duty of administering justice to his subjects, and having already so completely accomplished the former . . . he at the same time recognizes his desire to perform the latter with the same success. . . . He has not left it to us to say by what means that is to be accomplished, having said in a few words all that the deepest meditation of the

[1] Even as late as the 1700s the lawyer Barbier reëchoes the tradition upon this point: "Every king," he says, "since he possesses full power, may change and repeal the laws of his predecessors, as the latter have done with the laws and customs made before their time" ("Journal," vol. VII, p. 281).

[2] "Lettres, etc., de Colbert," vol. II, VI, p. 15.

[3] *Ibid.*, vol VI, p. 8.

ablest men living could contrive upon the subject in several years." [1]

§ 2. **Memorials of Members of the State Council.** — Colbert first of all advised the king to have the leading members of the State Council submit Memorials upon existing abuses and the remedies to be applied to them. This was one way of acquiring useful information and at the same time finding out the most capable of the councillors.[2] These Memorials were furnished and they are still in existence in the "Bibliothèque Nationale." [3] Colbert does not seem to have had a very high opinion of the work; in fact, he has left an "epitomized abstract" of these Memorials, in which these words often recur — "nothing in general, either in proportion to the plan or the king's greatness." Pussort's Memorial alone is carefully analyzed.[4] But we need not allow Colbert's valuation of these curious and unpublished documents to prevent our cursorily dwelling upon them. Pussort's work is undoubtedly far superior to the others; it is notable not only for the consistency of the ideas, but also for the excellent style in which it is written, and the dignity of the sentiments which he expresses. But the other Memorials can show us what projected reforms were striven after; in particular, we shall see what the councillors thought of the criminal law, and what abuses they had in view to correct.

The Memorials, taken in the aggregate, show that the councillors understood by the reform of justice rather the reform of the magistracy than that of the law. The diversity of the "Coutumes" was no doubt complained of, and a codification of the provisions scattered through the Ordinances was considered a useful work; but the most essential matter was to insure the exact observance of the laws. In this respect Pussort well expresses the general opinion: "France is credited with the best and wisest Ordinances in Europe, but it probably has the reputation of a worse administration of them than in any other country; the forethought displayed has been so accurate in every particular that Your Majesty will find little to add to that. But it is in regard to the methods of administration of these provisions that we require the whole weight of your

[1] "Lettres, etc., de Colbert," vol. VI, pp. 5, 6.

[2] "It seems that the first thing that His Majesty should do is to choose such persons as are capable of undertaking such a great work; and that is apparently what he has prudently resolved upon in ordering all those of his council to give him their opinions, so as to be able to choose, with a knowledge of the case, the number of persons whom he would select to serve him on such a great plan" ("Lettres, etc., de Colbert," vol. VI, p. 6).

[3] "Bibliothèque Nationale Manuscrits: Mélanges Clérambault," No. 613.

[4] "Lettres, etc., de Colbert," vol. VI, p. 21.

authority, as we have to struggle against either the nature of the climate, or habit so old and firmly intrenched that it has almost become a second nature." [1] The Code Michaud in particular receives his approval as being worthy of being adopted. "I am of opinion that we should especially adhere to the later Ordinances, among which is that of keeper of the seals Marillac, which, it must be acknowledged, has been drawn up with great care and in a spirit of zeal and justice." [2] — "which, although very excellent and judicious, has not been received with the approval due to it, and has not been practised nearly enough in the Parlements, although they would find it hard to state their reasons for this." [3]

The councillors exhibit a genuine ardor for the reform of the magistracy; they, above all, reproach it with ignorance and venality, the inevitable results of the sale of offices and the system of *judges' fees*. "All kinds of persons are appointed indiscriminately," says Pussort, "minors just out of college whom the law has not considered capable of defending themselves in the least important matters touching their interests without the intervention of a guardian, to be the judges where the lives and property of your subjects are at stake, and to give their opinions upon the most important matters of the State, ignoramuses who but for the help of their wealth would have remained among the rank and file of the people, to decide, without any attention, questions which have perplexed the most enlightened doctors, and to see through what human malice and guile have most artfully disguised; corrupt men and those bred in the midst of the debauchery and the prostitution of justice brought about by their ancestors or by themselves, to discharge for your majesty the greatest and most sacred of all the duties of his crown." [4] — "The greatest evil which the age has introduced into courts of justice and which breeds and perpetuates chicanery and litigation is that petty and sordid sale of offices which is ever on the increase; it is a poison which insidiously spreads among the most elevated parties and threatens the ultimate destruction of the spirit of justice." [5]

[1] "Mélanges Clérambault," No. 613, p. 443. *Pussort* explains the causes of this disorder: "The cause of this bad administration is primarily the characteristic bent of the nation. It has a love for novelty, provided it finds there honor and virtue as well, but it has not enough phlegm in its constitution to enable it to stick to its choice, being instantly carried away by the appearance of something else more specious" (p. 411). We shall often find these ideas subsequently repeated in less happy terms.

[2] "Mémoire de d'Aligre," p. 5.

[3] "Mémoire de la Maugrie," p. 277. [4] p. 406.

[5] "Mémoire de Barillon de Morangis," p. 33; *cf.* "Mémoire de Boucherat," p. 84.

The councillors advocate measures which are at first sight astounding in their temerity. They demand safeguards in the shape of assurances of the learning and character of the magistrates; some of them, at least, demand the suppression of the sale of offices and of judges' fees,[1] and even of the irremovability of magistrates. In this respect, it is true, it is public sentiment which speaks; we are reminded of the Fronde. "It will be necessary to modify the Ordinance of Louis XII, confirmed in the late evil days of his reigning majesty, providing that appointments to judicial offices shall only take place on death, resignation, or forfeiture. . . . But as the offices are in the gift of the king and as he is free from venality, it is right that they should be revocable at his pleasure."[2] Pussort, who, for the time being, only asks for the reduction of the number of judicial officers by one fourth or one fifth, is, on the whole, of the same opinion. "It is the judicial offices alone, the disposal of which the kings, having deprived themselves, first by the venality which they have introduced, and latterly by the establishment of the Paulette, have freed from their particular dependence, and have deprived themselves of the only means which they possessed of being able to reward the meritorious. . . . If this means had been in use we would not have seen the sovereign companies of judges indiscreetly engaging in the cabals and strifes which have disquieted this kingdom, and the leaders would not have failed to make the counsellors remember their duty; and if the presidents had been blind enough to disregard their duty to their king, their honor, and the offices they filled, they would have found all the chief officers of their courts in action. These, possessing virtue, courage, and ambition, would have been glad to take advantage of such a favorable opportunity to mount by their services into the positions for which their chiefs had proved themselves unworthy."[3]

Another very bold proposal, which will come up again in the debate upon the Ordinance of 1670, and is found in several Memo-

[1] "The best expedient would be completely to do away with the sale of offices and let the king have the absolute disposal of them, filling and vacating them in favor of those possessing the requisite qualifications" ("Mél. Clér." No. 613, p. 625). In regard to judges' fees, see the following pages. The foregoing is taken from a Memorial which begins at folio 609 of the volume, and whose author's name we have not discovered. Following the title there is only the statement, "This Memorial was brought before Monseigneur at Saint-Germain on 19th June, 1665." D'Estampes also proposes in very positive terms the abolition of the sale of offices and judges' fees, p. 191; *cf. Pussort*, p. 418. *Boucherat*, p. 62.

[2] "Mémoire de d'Estampes," p. 107.

[3] *Pussort*, pp. 428–431.

rials, aims at the suppression of the seigniorial and ecclesiastical courts. Pussort refers to "the great number of jurisdictions existing in the kingdom, which breeds four kinds of evils, — the multiplication of jurisdictions, conflict between them, increase of litigation and annoyance to his majesty's subjects. The true remedy for this disorder would be to unite all the seigniorial courts, secular as well as ecclesiastical, with the royal courts, of which they are the offspring." [1] — "The suppression of all the seigniorial courts of the kingdom is due to the dignity of the king, and the establishment of royal courts in those places where they may be deemed necessary, for it is indecorous to royalty that the judges appointed by individual lords, and who are in most cases peasants, incapable of performing any duties, who dishonor the name of judge and bring justice into contempt, should be set up as judges of the property, the honor and the lives of the king's subjects. The right of taking life, that is to say, high justice, the distinguishing mark of sovereignty, belongs to the King. . . . In ancient times private individuals were never found in the enjoyment of this right . . . and even to-day in all the European states it is unheard of that this right of appointment of judges should be in any other hands than those of the sovereign power. That is the invariable rule in Italy, Spain, England, Venice, and elsewhere except in Germany." [2] Councillor Lemaistre de Bellejame merely proposes to keep criminal justice in the hands of the royal judges.[3] De Sève asks that, if within three days after the crime, the seigniorial judges have not informed, the royal judge should have the precedence.[4] Deshameaux desires that "the officers of the middle and low courts of justice should not be entitled to any other jurisdiction than that of tenures, quit-rents, and other seigniorial rights."

While, however, they always have in view the reform of the magistracy, the authors of the Memorials are of opinion that it is also necessary to remodel and recast the Ordinances. It is desired "to establish a fixed and uniform procedure throughout the kingdom," [5] "to lay down general maxims as to the courts," [6] "to codify all the Ordinances which his majesty desires to be kept

[1] p. 445. [2] "Mémoire sans nom d'auteur," pp. 615, 616.

[3] This is what he says of the ecclesiastical jurisdictions: "The jurisdiction of the Church is not in the best condition. The action is examined mechanically, judges' fees and commissions are taken, no criminal actions are brought unless there is a party who advances the cost, impunity reigns in it, and all this is due to the sale of the offices of official, promoter and clerk of court II" (p. 49).

[4] "Mémoire de Sève," p. 485. [5] "Mémoire de Boucherat," p. 75.

[6] "Mémoire de d'Estampes," p. 117.

and observed within the kingdom,"[1] "to prescribe a uniform procedure and practice."[2] But a question which necessarily presented itself was, how to proceed with this codification?

It is remarkable that the States-General naturally occur to the councillors. They do not accept the idea of a convocation of the States, but they for the most part think it their duty to raise the point, if only to reject it. "An assembly of the States-General of your kingdom might be suggested to your majesty, but they contain such a large number of deputies that the diversity of opinions would destroy their good intentions. The late king of glorious memory called to his assistance private assemblies of leading men in 1617 at Rouen, and in 1626 at Paris, composed of prelates, the chief members of your nobility, and officers of your sovereign courts whom he selected along with those of his council, by whose advice a new Ordinance for the reform of justice was drawn up . . . and the Ordinance of 1629 was issued after the assembly of leading men of 1629. . . . Your majesty could, if he wished, form his Ordinance upon the Memorials and opinions which your majesty has ordered us to prepare without the great hindrance of either assemblies of States or of leading men."[3] Mesgrigny also refers to the States-General.[4] Pussort himself mentions them, but only to treat them haughtily: "It must be agreed that the reformations of the States-General, which are the highest and noblest aims of royal foresight, are incompatible with the turmoil of civil war and variances between sovereign and subjects: at such times the rebels never fail to demand reforms which will give color to their revolt and to take advantage of opportunities to weaken the royal power, and kings never fail to grant them so as to show their regard for the public welfare as well as to disperse the clouds. But such reforms are never enforced; that is neither the purpose of those who asked for them nor of the grantors, and probably one of the reasons (besides those which I have mentioned before) why there are no regula-

[1] *Pussort*, p. 117.

[2] "Mémoire sans nom d'auteur," p. 494. One of the Memorials (p. 646) proposes even to establish a uniform civil law, one general and sole coutume; but other councillors think that the "Coutumes" cannot be changed (*D'Estampes*, p. 117); and *De Sève* designates them as "laws established by the general consent of the people under the authority of the kings, which are for the most part as old as the monarchy, and are called 'Coutumes,' among which I would rank what is in some provinces of France called written law, seeing that the authority of its decisions is not derived from the Emperors, but from the people who have voluntarily embraced them, as Procopius has written" (p. 465).

[3] "Mémoire de la Maugrie," p. 227.

[4] p. 376.

tions in France which have been fully put into operation is that a careful examination shows that they have originated in the midst of the turbulence of civil war, and it may be said that the sound of the cannons has drowned the protest of the laws." [1] In the debate in the State Council, the word States-General will also be heard,— with what effect we shall see.

The majority of the Memorials agree in giving the judicial officers a share in the reform. "This matter is most proper for discussion by officers of the courts of justice, daily engaged in the examination and report of actions, who, better than any others, know the abuses and stratagems of the litigants and those who conduct them." [2] "It is essential to have the advice of the chief officers of the Parlements." [3] It was desirable "that the first presidents and attorneys-general should be caused to convoke the Parlements in a body or by deputies to consider general maxims and that Memorials be sent to his majesty within six months at latest." [4] "His majesty should have a preliminary conference with the principal officers of his sovereign courts of Paris, who are aware of the particular abuses which are committed there and in the bailiwicks and inferior courts, upon which it is said they are even now at work." [5] "It seems proper . . . to advise the Parlements and other sovereign companies of judges to choose from among these bodies or their deputies not more than four or six of their leading men (a greater number would cause confusion) to revise the Ordinances and make a compilation of those which are not observed." [6] Pussort alone, in pursuance of his fixed ideas, draws up a very precise plan in which the magistracy plays no part. "This work," he says, "which is of great extent, can and should be the business of several individuals, among whom the matters can be distributed according to their abilities and the particular knowledge which the duties they have performed have enabled them to acquire. I am satisfied that six men would be sufficient for the success of this work, and that a less number would cause delay, and a greater number lead to confusion. I think that it would be advisable that they should give up all other occupations and even retire to some country retreat, out of the reach of everything that could distract their attention, so that, by applying themselves entirely to the work, they could accomplish it with the greatest despatch and accuracy. These six individuals should work quite separately,

[1] p. 422. [2] *D'Aligre*, p. 4. [3] *Barillon Morangis*, p. 31.
[4] *D'Estampes*, p. 117. [5] *La Maugrie*, p. 277.
[6] p. 493; *cf.* "Mémoire de Mauroy," p. 355.

and report to each other once a week on what they had done. I would have this assembly headed by a man of merit, ability, and eminence, who would supervise the work, distribute the subjects, preside at the meetings, and report to your majesty on the more important matters on which it would be necessary to take your majesty's orders."[1] We shall see by and by what success Pussort's plan had.

What do these Memorials show us upon criminal procedure, the subject of our special interest? They assert in this respect that the Ordinance of 1539 is a perfect model, and its development is all that is required. "This Ordinance has disentangled all the confusion which existed in the examination of criminal proceedings, arising from the fact that formerly there was no precise rule for the examination of such actions, so that it often happened that, for want of a valid examination, crimes remained unpunished, or were sometimes too severely punished, or the fact was not sufficiently proved, or the proofs were lost owing to the length of the procedure."[2] — "Criminal justice, the usual subject of their (the judges') neglect, must not be omitted, and for this I see but little help, since *it rests with their conscience alone*. As to the forms, there is nothing to add to the articles of the Ordinance of 1539 dealing with criminal proceedings, except to insist that they be given effect."[3] This procedure is by no means considered too severe; on the contrary, if there is any cause of complaint, it is rather on account of its exceeding mildness, and some of the harsher rules which the Ordinance of 1670 will contain, are indicated in these Memorials. "Impunity for crime is the greatest of all disorders met with in the administration of justice, and it springs from the favorable and lax interpretation put by the judges, from time to time, upon the Ordinances which have been issued on this matter."[4] — "The accused should not be allowed to communicate with any one before their interrogations, nor should they be allowed any counsel before the confrontation of the witnesses, provided that take place within a month or two at the latest, according as the judges may order after the imprisonment. After that time the accused should have counsel, without prejudice, however, to the safety and custody of prisoners as that has always been seen to; unless a crime against the State is concerned, where secrecy is important, in which case they should neither have communication nor counsel without the order and permission of

[1] *Pussort*, p. 447.
[2] *Boucherat*, p. 62; see also *D'Estampes*, p. 118.
[3] *De Sève*, p. 485.
[4] *Pussort*, p. 400.

the judges." [1] "The criminal matters which have been handled for some years past have shown that the Ordinances have not, in all respects, provided the necessary forms for the examination of criminal actions, such as in the matter of decrees to hear right, advice to give to the accused free or face to face, the making of permissible distinctions. . . . It appears that the persons condemned by contumacy are treated too favorably by the Ordinance, which grants them five years within which to have themselves rehabilitated." [2]

These documents above all reveal betrayals of trust and abuses, such as appear at the Great Days of Clermont. Pussort speaks "of the assistance which influential persons who have been accused have received from officers of the long robe by the intrigues which they have practised with them, so that it is rare to see the punishment of a crime of any description, but a very common occurrence to see those who have brought the actions ruined and annoyed by the excessive expenses of the proceedings." He mentions "those criminal societies aided by the authority of the magistrates and put, to some extent, under the protection of the laws." [3] — "Nothing is so dangerous as to countenance rebellions against justice, the sheltering of criminals in the houses of the great, to deprive the officers of the law of the liberty of making their seizures and executions, so that justice remains unobeyed. An usher with his rod carries the authority of the prince." [4] The abuse of costs and the rapacity of the judges are denounced.[5] At Rouen the proceedings are communicated to the king's counsel only for the purpose of giving their final conclusions; [6] at Toulouse judges' fees are exacted for decrees rendered for contumacy "which prevents alike the acquittal of the innocent and the punishment of the guilty, against the spirit of the Ordinance, which, in order to facilitate both, has taken especial care to burden criminal proceedings with few judges' fees." [7] In particular that serious abuse of inquiries made by the incompetent or people of bad character is mentioned. "I am forced to tell your majesty of a mischievous custom which is practised in some présidials. . . . In order to increase practice and chicanery, they establish clerks in the cities and market-towns of their jurisdiction, who, at a price, distribute commissions to make inquiry into crimes and offenses, addressed to the chief royal officer of court, which are entitled of the Prési-

[1] p. 525. "Mémoire sans nom d'auteur."
[2] p. 646.
[3] p. 400.
[4] *Barillon Morangis*, p. 30.
[5] *Boucheral*, p. 73.
[6] *Ibid.*, p. 83.
[7] *Ibid.*, p. 84; *cf. Barillon*, p. 75.

dial, of the lieutenant-general or of the criminal lieutenant, and as these commissions are delivered to all and sundry without cognizance of the cause, it very often happens that the guilty informs against an innocent party, and carries the information to decree; the innocent party is arrested, which occasions many wrongs." [1] The Councillor of Sève points out a double defect in the procedure: on the one hand, there was a tendency to follow the "extraordinary" procedure, even for very trivial offenses; on the other hand, even in case of serious crimes, if no civil party appeared, the prosecution was very often neglected.[2]

But by far the most defective institution was that terrible "prévôtal" jurisdiction, the name of which remains with sad significance. Some of the Memorials treat this subject with remarkable spirit. "It would be expedient for the well-being of justice to abolish the small marshalcies, or unite them with the large ones existing in the cities where there are présidials. For the small marshalcies work incredible ruin among a poor populace; the provost lives in one locality, the lieutenant in a market-town, and the assessor in still another place. As they have no archers they commission jailbirds, and arrest poor peasants, whom they think may have some property, under the pretence that they have stolen or have carried firearms, and imprison them in private jails until they have extorted money from them. I omitted to mention that if your majesty does not abolish the petty marshalcies, he should at least abolish the assessors, who cause more mischief than the rest, because, being graduates, they are better acquainted with the tricks of chicanery." [3] D'Estampes also declares that the provosts do not do their duty, because the archers are not paid, and he would have the acceptance of money from the parties expressly prohibited.[4] Mesgrigny and D'Estampes both demand that the provosts should bring the proceedings "immediately and without delay," and that they should be obliged to announce to the accused whether they are going to try them "prévôtally" or in the last resort, "at the first interrogation, so that the accused may not be surprised and may be able to plead his declinatory pleas and objections to the jurisdiction, which should be decided in the accustomed manner according to the Ordinances . . . the defenses being different when he is to be

[1] *D'Estampes*, p. 382. [2] p. 485.

[3] *Mesgrigny*, p. 283; *cf.* a letter from the bishop of Tarbes to Colbert, of 21st May, 1664. ("Correspondance administrative sous Louis XIV," vol. II, p. 133.)

[4] p. 132.

tried in the last resort from what it is when there is an appeal."[1] Both agree in desiring to prohibit the superior judges from taking jurisdiction of appeals from provosts, vice-bailiffs, and vice-seneschals;[2] which is at first sight astonishing on the part of men who did not approve of this jurisdiction; but Mesgrigny states the reason for this view. "Since the Ordinance of 1629, there has been a Declaration which ascribes to provost-marshals the power to try subject to appeal, which is a very bad institution, for the provosts abuse it, and when an enemy desires to injure a domiciled citizen, and even a titled gentleman, it is to the provosts that he applies."[3] One thing appeared to be absolutely necessary, to fix strictly the still vague jurisdiction of the provosts.[4] This the Ordinance did; but it was necessary to return to the matter again in the following century.

We have lingered a long time over these Memorials; but these unpublished documents appeared to us to possess some interest. They contain a greater freedom of speech than will often be found in the debate in the State Council or in the Conferences.

§ 3. **Colbert's Plan; the Council of Justice; its Preliminary Labors.** — Colbert adopted in its entirety the plan proposed by Pussort. In the memorandum which he prepared upon the Memorials he makes this statement: "Concerning the codification of all the Ordinances, — to appoint six capable persons with a president, who shall retire into the country to compile the Code of all the Ordinances to be observed and put into effect throughout the whole kingdom."[5] He then addresses to the king that Memorial of 15th May, 1665, of which we have spoken above. In that he shows clearly from the outset that an extensive codification is proposed. "As all His Majesty's thoughts and actions are in proportion to the magnitude of his intellect, we have been sufficiently impressed by the fact that in undertaking this enterprise he does not wish to follow the example of his predecessor sovereigns who have been contented with making some collections of Ordinances, the enforcement of which they did not greatly exert themselves to insure. His Majesty having informed us that he wished to bring together into a single body of Ordinances everything necessary to establish the judicial practice in a fixed and certain way and to reduce the number of judges . . . it only remains for us to explain our views according to the command which His Majesty

[1] *D'Estampes*, p. 133.
[2] *Ibid.*, p. 132; *Mesgrigny*, p. 382.
[3] p. 383.
[4] *Barillon Morangis*, p. 76.
[5] "Lettres, etc., de Colbert," vol. VI, p. 21.

has been pleased to give us, on the methods that may be practicable to accomplish these great aims."

The plan which Colbert now proposes is, as has been said, that which was followed later for the drawing up of the Codes which govern us to-day. It is in two parts: a discussion in the State Council of the plans prepared by the committees or sub-committees; and, at the same time, to facilitate the labor, an extensive inquiry opened throughout the whole country among the appropriate bodies.

First of all, "a Council of Justice" is constituted, composed of the ablest members of the State Council. "Its sitting must be appointed to take place on a day fixed, once a week or every three days, and at the same time the division of the subjects must be made, namely, the examination of the whole collection of the Ordinances to find out all the changes which will have to be made. For this matter, which is the greatest and the most extensive of all the work, it will be necessary to appoint four or six of the ablest State Councillors, who will take with them the four or six ablest advocates of the Parlement, who will together compose a separate committee, under the leadership of the dean of the State Councillors. — It will also be necessary to keep this matter separate from that of the distributive civil justice. — In each of these matters two State Councillors and two advocates will work; to examine, in the assembly of the whole twelve, what shall have been decided by the four, and immediately to submit the whole, well digested, to the King's Council." Colbert is not contented with sketching this wise division of labor and assigning to each his share; he goes on to point out the spirit in which the work should be done. This is what he says of the criminal procedure: "To examine everything which concerns the system of criminal justice of the kingdom, as being the most important, *to cleanse it from all chicanery,* and to take care to establish sure methods, while protecting and safeguarding the innocent, for promptly arriving at the punishment of criminals." We shall see how Colbert was understood.

For the *inquest,* of which we have spoken, it was necessary, "at the first sitting, to choose eight masters of requests of as high a degree of ability and probity as may be, to go to assist in all the Parlements of the kingdom": they were to receive "an ample instruction"; and in the stated meetings they were to collect the complaints and observations which they would report to the Council of Justice. For the purpose of facilitating the reports, certain members of the Council must be designated to receive the communications of such and such of the masters of requests on their mission, "to correspond with all the masters of requests making their circuits in the provinces; to report to the council on all the disorders which they should find in the matter of justice, to allow of the immediate application of the remedies which should be found appropriate, and to submit immediately to the special meeting of the six whatever should concern the drawing up of the Ordinance." This was done, at least partly;[1] but we do not have the results of this vast inquiry. Louis XIV no doubt refers to it when, in "his 'feuillets' for 1667," he mentions, while speaking of the drawing up of the Ordinances, the "Memorials sent from other Parlements."[2]

The Council of Justice, proposed by Colbert, met for the first time in the Louvre, on 25th September, 1665. The great work then began, and was to be continued without interruption until its complete achievement. The entire history of these discussions is not known. Although the official minutes of the Conferences held later between the members of the Council and the delegates from Parlement were published in good season and served as a basis for the interpretation of the Ordinances, for a long time nothing transpired as to the sittings of the State Council. An official report of these sittings was, however, drawn up, and a manuscript of the "Bibliothèque Sainte-Geneviève" contains a portion of it, entitled, "Délibération du conseil de la réformation de la justice." This document, which was brought to light and used for the first time by M. Francis Monnier,[3] has been published in its entirety by M. Pierre Clément in his "Lettres, mémoires, et instructions de Colbert."[4] It is, however, unfortunately only a fragment; it contains the official reports of only three sittings. On the other hand, we possess a very interesting letter from the advocate Auzanet to one of his friends upon the reform of justice. This is the

[1] On the last folio of No. 613 of the "Mélanges Clérambault" we find a note dated 2d October, 1665, containing the names of "masters of requests chosen to serve in the departments," with remarks upon each of them.

[2] "Mémoires" (*Dreyss* edition), vol. II, p. 252. Colbert, moreover, collected the documents. We find in the month of September, 1665 (the day of the month not appearing), a note in which he requests M. de Gomont, an eminent lawyer, "to make a draft or plan of the course the king may and ought to take for the reform of the justice of his kingdom." "Lettres, etc., de Colbert," vol. VI, p. 12.

[3] "Guillaume de Lamoignon et Colbert, Essai sur la législation française au XVIIe siècle," 1862. (Extracted from the report of the Academy of Philosophical and Political Sciences.)

[4] Vol. VI, App. p. 369 *et seq.*

testimony of one of the chief actors, but its extreme brevity shows that the author did not wish altogether to tear the veil from these mysteries.[1] Both these documents relate chiefly to the drawing up of the Ordinance of 1667; nevertheless, as the plan adopted at the beginning was followed to the conclusion, it is not entirely useless to examine them briefly.

The first sitting of the Council of Justice was held, as we have said, on 25th September, 1665, "in His Majesty's cabinet after mass."

Those chosen to compose the council were MM. Voisin, de Villeroy, Colbert, Hotman, Chancellor Séguier, de Machault, de Verthamon, Poncet, Boucherat, and Pussort. Chancellor Séguier appeared in the great enterprise for the first time; till then Colbert had conducted everything, and the Chancellor was so little acquainted with what was proposed to be done that he made a number of mistakes during this first sitting.[2]

The sitting opened with a speech by the king. He announced that he desired the reform of justice, "which he was resolved to prosecute assiduously, and that the Council which he had that day assembled was not for one year or for several, but that he intended to employ it and summon it around him as long as he lived." The Chancellor, after having lauded the king's resolution, said that it would be proper to begin with matters concerning the ecclesiastical state; "he assigned these matters to the members of the Council who sat on his left." The king appeared to be displeased; "although matters did not turn out either according to the plan, or to the liking of the king, His Majesty, with extraordinary moderation, allowed the Chancellor to make this assignment;" then, searching in the pockets of his close-coat, "he drew from among several Memorials and papers one written by himself, which he said he had composed while at Villers-Cotterets to explain his intentions upon the principal points of the object of the meeting."

[1] "You have frequently requested me to acquaint you with the details of everything that took place in all the meetings which have been held for the reform of justice, but I have neither been able nor permitted to gratify your wish, because of the secrecy which has been imposed; but since time reveals the most private occurrences, and this matter has now been made public, I am at liberty to gratify your curiosity and will explain the causes of this assembly and the orders which have been given and followed on this subject." "Lettres, etc., de Colbert," vol. VI, App. p. 396 *et seq.*

[2] "Colbert has the king's ear, and he has become the real chancellor, reforming, at the same time, every department of the administration. . . . Séguier presides over all the reform committees, but it is Colbert's inspiration which governs these boards." "Le chancelier Séguier," by *M. René de Kerviler*, p. 379.

What Memorial was this? Had the recollection of the Ordinance of 1539 inspired the king at Villers-Cotterets, or was this merely the report drawn up by Colbert? This much is certain, that Louis XIV first of all proposed two of the measures pointed out by his minister; reforms in the State Council, and the sending of masters of requests through the provinces. Thereupon the meeting terminated.

The second sitting was held on 11th October, 1663, again at the Louvre. MM. d'Estampes, de Morangis, and de Sève figured in the Council for the first time; M. Poncet had dropped out. This time they proceeded to determine on the course to be followed. Colbert had also prepared a speech, the original of which we have among his papers, but which, it seems, was never delivered; in it he insists upon the idea that it is nothing short of a codification that the king desires.[1]

Hotman, being the youngest, spoke first; he appeared to be thoroughly conversant with Colbert's plans; he pointed out that it was not a matter of making really new laws, but of reforming the old laws, emphasizing the fact that "the criminal jurisdiction has not enough laws and regulations . . . and that is why such a lengthy and divergent style of procedure is observable in criminal matters, where the toleration of recent times has introduced so much laxity that it seems absolutely necessary to provide against this by definite regulations which shall confirm and fix firmly all the forms." He proposes to his majesty "to divide the duties among the individuals whom he has assembled"; he also demands a wide inquiry. "The commissioners will look for the means of accomplishing their task in the opinions which they will bring back from the provinces, namely, in criminal matters, in the opinions of the criminal lieutenants and former king's attorneys, judges, and assessors in the marshalcies."

M. Voisin, who was the next speaker, proposed to follow the Code Henry and employ commissioners. M. Pussort stated that Justinian had "in a similar project, utilized ten years' assiduous application of twelve of the ablest and most experienced jurisconsults," and that consequently "he could not give a reasoned opinion offhand." M. Boucherat said that "as the reform of the Ordinances was of unlimited extent and deserving of the forethought and application of a great king, it could not be resolved upon or undertaken without long and arduous study; that the kings who preceded His Majesty had sometimes convoked the Estates,

[1] "Lettres, etc., de Colbert," vol. VI, p. 14.

and sometimes eminent individuals who had been met by the leading officers of the Council and of the courts of the kingdom; and that, while he thought that His Majesty's project deserved much consideration, it could not be resolved upon on the spot." [1] It is strange to hear the word States-General, which we have already found in the Memorials. Boucherat apparently wished that body, which more or less directly represented the country, to have a share in the work; this man, whom Saint-Simon treats very cavalierly,[2] here gives utterance to the most enlightened thought. MM. de Morangis, de Sève, and Le Tellier are also seen to share his opinion. This was bound to displease Colbert very much, but M. de Verthamont returned to the plan of working simply by commissioners; then the report would be made in presence of the king so that "the decision should be resolved and established by the great intellect with which God had endowed His Majesty. This he did not say from a spirit of flattery, but from the public knowledge of all His Majesty's subjects as well as foreigners, who were obliged to acknowledge that God had endowed him with an extraordinary intellect and a genius which raised him above other men." He did not stop there, but went on to make comparisons, which he apparently thought very ingenious, between Justinian and Louis XIV. This had the effect of restoring the king to good humor. M. de Machault was of opinion "that it would be sufficient to take the lectures on the Ordinances, and the Code Henry, or the Ordinance of M. de Marillac, add omitted matters, strike out superfluous matter, and in a short time put things in a state of perfect law."

Then came Colbert's turn to speak. He began by extolling the king; then he proceeded clearly and briefly to explain the plan which ought to be followed, which we already know. Then everybody rallied. The king asked the Chancellor for his opinion, and he spoke next. "The task of the reform of the laws was a sovereign prerogative; all the opinions and even the regulations of the courts could have no force of law, the form of which must be stamped with the character of the prince." He approved the assignment of the matters to councillors assisted by advocates, and suggested that the conferences to prepare what should be submitted to the king's council should be held at his home. The king stated that this was what he had resolved upon; but he set

[1] "Lettres, etc., de Colbert," vol. VI, p. 374.

[2] "It is difficult to understand how M. de Turenne manages to execute the duties of his office, simple as they are." "Mémoires," vol. II, p. 217.

aside the idea of conferences at the Chancellor's: "in all matters of business he had invariably wished that the matters should be brought before him without intermediary, so that he might learn freely and more naturally the sentiments of all who transacted his affairs. This he could not do if, before speaking in his presence, they should be in agreement and with uniform ideas." Such sentiments from Louis XIV are not surprising. The Chancellor then made to the king proposals for the assignment of matters; but "the king, rising, said that he would confer with him in private, and that the matter deserved some discussion."

On Monday, 13th October, Colbert, by the king's command, sent to the Chancellor the list of commissioners chosen. It was drawn up beforehand, for it is found attached to the Memorial of the month of May, which we have mentioned before; and it had undergone hardly any change. We find: "for justice (to be subdivided into civil, criminal, and police), MM. de Verthamont, Colbert, Pussort, Voisin, Caumartin, Le Pelletier de La Reynie; M. Hotman to act as secretary.—Advocates who should act on the said reform: MM. Auzanet, l'Hoste, Senior, de Gomont, Raguenau, Bellain, and a sixth to be afterwards appointed."[1] The useful work was about to commence; but here we find a considerable hiatus in our documents. We have only the official report of a single sitting of the Council of Justice, that of Sunday, 25th October, 1665. The discussion related to the Articles which subsequently composed Title I of the Ordinance of 1667, upon the observance of the Ordinances. On this point the king and Colbert were insistent. It was necessary to check the power of the Parlements and render of no avail the right of enrolment. Lamoignon said of the Ordinance of 1667, "that it commences by threats against the Parlements and all the sovereign companies of judges." An interesting debate took place in the Council of Justice; it was declared that the ecclesiastical courts should, on the same principle as the others, be subject to the laws of the State, and that the title of "Sovereign courts" as applied to the Parlements must be abolished. Louis XIV intervened in his usual high-handed way. "The king has said that during his life protests may be made without fear, because he knows well how to reject the useless and disorderly and give consideration to those which are respectful and reasonable." But all this takes us far from our subject.

[1] "On the 16th of the same month of October, the king appointed M. Foucault, 'greffier' of the Chamber of Justice, to work in the capacity of lawyer." "Lettres, etc., de Colbert," vol. VI, p. 377.

The conferences of the commissioners and advocates, however, had begun; Auzanet's letter, above quoted, shows us their nature. In October, 1665, probably soon after the 13th, M. de Verthamont, who was to be president of the committee, "sent letters to the advocates requesting them to meet at the Chancellor's." They attended, gowned, and were received by Séguier, who apprised them of what was wanted of them. "A few days after, the commissioners having met at M. de Verthamont's, the latter took his seat at the upper end of the board or table, in the president's chair: on his right were M. Pussort, State Councillor, also in a speaker's chair, then MM. de Caumartin, and Le Pelletier de La Reynie, masters of requests, and MM. l'Hoste, de Gomont, and Foucault, advocates; and on his left were MM. Voisin and Hotman, masters of requests, MM. Auzanet, Ragueneau, and Bellain, advocates." This is a verbal photograph of the meeting. This stickling on questions of etiquette, which is shown by several passages in Auzanet's letter, is destined later on to cause a little ill feeling in the first conferences with the parlement officers.

At first there were two sittings every week; then, as the king was at Fontainebleau, only one day was fixed; and they met at Essonne, "so that the State Councillors and the masters of requests, on one hand, and the advocates on the other, could each come halfway." In the course of the work, M. de Verthamont died, and the meeting place was changed to Pussort's. "M. l'Hoste having been appointed director of hospitals, his place was left unfilled, and the number of commissioners was thus reduced to nine." Subsequently, Colbert came to this Council, "the secretary of state," says Auzanet, "to whose care the king intrusted the order, administration, and the most important functions of the State;" he did not wish to preside and "in spite of all entreaties he was contented to take a second place."

The observance of the Ordinances was the first thing to occupy the Council's attention, and the articles which were discussed at the Council of Justice on 25th October were presented as having been elaborated by the commissioners. As a matter of fact, they had never touched them. "This matter did not remain long in doubt," says Auzanet, "for at the following meeting, the king acquainted us with his wishes on the matter and sent the eight articles which constitute the first title of the Ordinance of 1667." As to the remainder, they proceeded in the following manner. It would appear from a passage in the official report of subsequent conferences published by Foucault in 1709, that Pussort first of all did one preliminary piece of work. "From among the commissioners of the Council, M. Pussort was selected to draft the articles upon reform. That great man worked on this with much care and exactness; his work was inspired by that quick perception and that inviolable attachment to justice which were universally acknowledged to be the most admirable of his sublime qualifications." Then the subjects were assigned "to each of the lawyers to work upon by himself, for the purpose of dividing the subjects into articles and putting the articles in order. And after the reading of the whole title to the meeting, each article was considered separately, lodged, and agreed upon by a majority vote, and although very often the opinions had been diverse, nobody exhibited the slightest jealousy or eagerness to impose his opinion, but everything passed with the most laudable good feeling and good nature."[1] This settled, the articles were submitted to the Council of Justice. "After we had settled the articles among ourselves, they were submitted to the king's Council, where, in His Majesty's presence, those which were considered just were authorized and the others amended or rejected." The lawyers did not attend these discussions, for, Auzanet adds: "at several junctures the king did our company the honor of adopting its opinion upon matters proposed, which were dealt with directly and had to be settled in the Council, in his majesty's presence."

§ 4. **The Parlement's Share.** — The Ordinance upon the civil procedure was, however, completely elaborated. "After our meetings had continued for fifteen months," says Auzanet, "it was found that there was sufficient matter for an initial volume, and to warrant its execution." Nothing more appeared to be necessary than to publish this work, when the Parlement all at once reappears upon the scene. New conferences are about to take place, but this time delegates from the Parlement of Paris figure alongside of the State Councillors and the masters of requests. What is the meaning of this unforeseen occurrence? Auzanet, in reporting the fact, merely says that the king "thought fit" to have it so. Louis XIV himself explained his position upon this point. "In regard to the general regulation of justice, of which I have already spoken, a considerable number of articles having been drawn up in the form which I desired, I did not wish longer to deprive the public of the benefit which it awaited from them; but I did not consider it fitting either to send them to the Parlement as they were, at the risk of some chicanery happening

[1] *Auzanet*, "Lettres, etc., de Colbert," vol. VI, p. 399.

to them there, which would have vexed me, or to carry them out at once myself, in case it might some day be alleged that they had been passed upon without thorough investigation; that is why, taking a middle course, which would obviate both objections, I caused all the articles to be read over at my Chancellor's, in the presence of deputies from all the Chambers and commissioners of the Council; and, when some reasonable objection was raised in the conference, it was immediately brought before me, to be dealt with as I should see fit. After such discussion I finally proceeded personally to cause the Edict to be published." [1] These scruples and fears are very unlike the monarch who so recently treated the Parlement's right of protest in such a high-handed manner. The cause of the fact has, moreover, been sought for elsewhere, and this is what was found.

First president Lamoignon, almost at the same time as Colbert, had been impressed with the necessity of codifying the laws. Not being able to handle such an enterprise, his sole aim was to settle the controverted points in the jurisdiction of the Parlement of Paris. He purposed to employ on this work magistrates and also lawyers, and among the latter the very Auzanet whom we have seen not long ago also chosen by Colbert. Such a mark of esteem coming from opposite quarters was the highest encomium on this man; and it is through him that we learn what happened. "M. de Lamoignon, First president of the Parlement of Paris, impatient of the conflict of opinion in his company of judges, and aware that I had previously begun some memoranda upon a part of these doubtful questions in order to apply the necessary remedy, ordered me to recover these memoranda and add to them whatever I should deem proper, which was done; after which M. the First president, having obtained the consent of the king to his purpose, held three or four meetings of some twelve lawyers in his house and took their views upon the first articles. Two deputies from the Grand Chambre and a like number from each of the Chambers of Inquests also met in his house on other occasions, in whose presence, the said articles and the opinions of the lawyers having been read, several articles were resolved upon and the remainder left in abeyance. But the progress made was so unsatisfactory that M. the First president came to the conclusion that he would never achieve his purpose by this means, and discontinued the meetings." [2] Lamoignon did not, however, entirely abandon his

[1] "Mémoires pour 1667" (*Dreyss* edition), vol. II, p. 224.
[2] *Auzanet*, "Lettres, etc., de Colbert," vol. VI, pp. 397, 398.

plan; he insisted on Auzanet continuing his work, and also employed another lawyer in the Parlement, Bonaventure Fourcroi. "This task lasted over two years, during which time two meetings were held every week, one of these privately, attended by the two lawyers and M. de Brillac, councillor in the Grand Chambre, and M. Le Pelletier, president of the Inquests, to arrange the subjects and formulate the articles, and the other in presence of M. the President, to judge of and resolve upon the articles according to his opinion. . . . Here the initial work ended, awaiting its publication under public authority." [1] As we know, it never saw the light of day; all that survived of it were the "resolutions of president Lamoignon."

Lamoignon's enterprise, which, it must be said, had been directed upon the most difficult part of the legislative system, the civil law, came to nothing. The President must, however, have felt very keenly being excluded from the great official work after having been authorized by Louis XIV, according to Auzanet, to attempt something similar. His great wisdom and loyal character led him straight to the king; but, with great acumen, he had the appearance of not knowing what had taken place without his cooperation. He proceeded to make to Louis XIV a proposal similar to that which Colbert had made and succeeded in getting adopted; at least that is what we gather from his biographer, Gaillard. "Colbert had commissioned Pussort with a task for the reform of justice. His design was not to acquaint any one with the Ordinance, and to publish it by the sovereign authority alone, enacting it in a 'bed of justice.' M. de Lamoignon, apprized of this design, approached Louis XIV, and proposed to him, as a way of making his reign illustrious, this idea of reforming justice, after the finances. The king said to him, 'M. Colbert is even now employing M. Pussort on this task; see M. Colbert on the subject and act in concert with him.'" [2] Astonished at the confidence which the king had placed in the First president, Colbert saw his plans go awry. "Then began conferences, of which the official report has been published, the modification of a number of articles showing how necessary these conferences were." [3] Is this strange statement quite in accordance with the truth? Lamoignon's stratagem and Louis XIV's reply may be doubted, but one thing appears to be certain, that the First president did go to see the king, and the

[1] This took place before 1665.
[2] "Vie du président de Lamoignon," quoted by *M. Pierre Clément.* "Lettres, etc., de Colbert," vol. VI, p. 14.
[3] *Ibid.*

latter, probably remembering the encouragement which he had previously given to the head of the Parlement of Paris, ordered the new conferences; it is highly probable that Louis XIV was, at the same time, very glad in this way to avoid any obstacle to the enactment.

However that may be, "on 24th January, 1667, the king sent a message on the subject to the Parlement, and especially to the First president and the attorney-general, commanding the First president and the other presidents of the Parlement, four councillors of the Grand Chambre, and five former presidents of the Chambers of Inquests with the oldest members of these chambers, the former president of Requests of the court of justice and the oldest member of the first chamber and the lawyers and attorneys-general to meet continuously at the Chancellor's to confer with him and the commissioners of the Council by whose advice the articles had been drawn up." This much is shown by the official report of the conferences, but it was not the Chancellor who had been the means of bringing about this decision; it is even almost certain that he was not informed of it until everything was in readiness. The letter sent to him by Secretary of State Guénégaud is in the following terms: "My lord, I have, by order of the king, written to the Parlement of Paris, informing it that His Majesty, considering it inexpedient to publish the articles of the Ordinances which he has caused to be codified for the reform of justice until they have first of all been seen and considered by you and any members of the Council and by several of the chief officers of the Parlement appointed by His Majesty, the First president should hold meetings at your house immediately and as often as possible, so that they may give His Majesty their opinion upon the whole, of which I think your lordship should be notified, so that you may know what is being done in this matter." [1] The conferences began on Tuesday, the 26th January, at the Séguier mansion. Fifteen sitttings were held to begin with, the last of which took place on 17th March, 1667. There were nine commissioners of the Council, including the Chancellor, twenty-nine deputies of the Parlement, including the First president, the attorney-general and two solicitors-general.[2] M. Joseph Foucault was the clerk of the assembly. A weighty and dignified discussion ensued in which especially shone Pussort in the defense of the articles as his own work, and the First president. After the termination of the discussion, the various articles, the

[1] Letter quoted by *M. de Kerviler*, "Le président Séguier," pp. 385–386.
[2] "Procès-verbal de l'Ordonnance de 1667," p. 4.

modification of which had been demanded, were submitted anew to the King's Council, which made its final decision. We learn from Auzanet how the finishing touches were ultimately given to the civil Ordinance. "Seeing that the articles which had been compiled by different persons were found to be couched in different styles, the king appointed MM. Morangis, Pussort, and Boucherat, State councillors, and M. Hotman, master of requests, and myself, the only practitioner, to put the Ordinance in shape, by reducing it to a uniform style and arranging the titles in their proper order. This occupied seven whole weeks, five and sometimes six sittings being held each week; and finally, in April, 1667, the first Ordinance was drawn up in the form in which it appears to-day, brought before the Parlement of Paris and published in the presence of the king sitting in his Parlement on the 20th of the same month." [1]

§ 5. **Discussion of the Ordinance; Lamoignon and Pussort.** — Although our narrative is the story of the drafting of the civil Ordinance, it is also that of the drafting of the criminal Ordinance. Both were parts of the same task. The organism which produced the former produced the latter and by the same work. Here the details of the preparation of the articles by the commissioners and of the debates in the Council of Justice are much less numerous. Auzanet, at the end of that letter of December 1st, 1669, the whole of which we shall very soon have quoted piece by piece, states that the elaboration of the criminal Ordinance began in May, 1667, and had not ended at the time when he wrote. "In the month of May, 1667, the same commissioners, reduced in number to nine, have continued, as they still continue daily, to labor on the said matters in the manner aforesaid, to make and compile other Ordinances when his majesty shall deem fitting." This preliminary work was not completed until the middle of the year 1670. New conferences with the deputies of the Parlement then began. The official report shows that they were really a continuation of the conferences of 1667: "On 6th June, 1670, the king's commissioners and the deputies of the Parlement met at the Chancellor's house, at 3 P.M. and held their sitting in the lower gallery in the same order and arrangement they had followed since the conference of the year 1667." The composition of the assembly differed somewhat from that of 1667; it was as follows: I. Commissioners of the council: Chancellor Séguier, MM. d'Aligre, de Morangis, d'Estampes, de Sève, Poncet, Boucherat, Pussort, Voisin, Hotman. II. Deputies of the Parlement: the First president, presidents

[1] "Lettres, etc., de Colbert," vol. VI, p. 400.

Maisons, Novion, Mesmes, Le Coigneux, de Bailleul, Molé de Champlastreux, de Nesmond. III. Councillors of the Grand Chambre: MM. de Catinat, du Brillat, Fayet, de Refuges, Paris, Royault. IV. Deputies of Inquests: MM. Potier de Blanc-Mesnil, de Bermond, de Bragelone, Maudet, de Fourcy, Faure, Le Pelletier, Le Vasseur, Maupeou, Malo. V. Deputies of Requests of the Court of Justice: MM. Chatron and Leboult. VI. MM. de Harlay, procurator-general; Talon and Bignon, first and second attorneys-general.

There were only seven conferences, the last of which was held on Monday, July 8th, 1670. After a revision in the Council of Justice, the Criminal Ordinance was "issued at Saint-Germain-en-Laye in the month of August, 1670, then registered at Paris in Parlement, 26th August, 1670." The official report of these conferences, like that of the conferences of 1667, was published soon after. At first a number of manuscript copies were put in circulation, and two printed editions of it appeared during the 1600s. But in 1709 a new quasi-official edition of it was published "by the associates chosen by His Majesty for the printing of his new Ordinances." The heading "by authority of the king" shows that this publication was made by Foucault, State councillor, and of the Privy Council, and that he reproduced a manuscript which had been delivered to him by "his father, Foucault, Secretary of State and Director of the Finances." The latter was the secretary of the conferences of 1667 and probably also of those of 1670.[1]

We possess sufficient information to enable us without difficulty to summarize the discussion. Three men, two in particular, take part in the first draft; these are Pussort, president Lamoignon, and attorney-general Talon. Pussort and Lamoignon, who have already fallen foul of each other in 1667, are this time true adversaries, maintaining at the same time the most unassailable dignity: there is no article on which they do not speak. Pussort represented the spirit in which the new law had been drawn up, according to Colbert's views. Their chief desire had been to disencumber the procedure of the complexities and quibbling which clogged it, to strip it of all parasitical growths, to lessen its length and its cost. It was also desired to have a strong and certain instrument of repression, without interfering too much with the rights of the defense.

Lamoignon showed himself in a double aspect. High-spirited and noble-hearted, he protested against the severities of this terrible

[1] This is the edition which we invariably cite.

procedure; he alone in this assemblage spoke in the name of humanity, as the following age accepted it; and in this respect he far outdistanced his contemporaries. He protested against the compulsory oath of accused persons, against the provision refusing them the assistance of counsel, and against the article punishing as for perjury the witness who contradicts himself at the confrontation. Finally, although he inveighed less vigorously against torture, it is none the less a great distinction for a magistrate of the 1600s to have said "that he saw strong reasons for its abolition, but that was only his own private opinion." [1]

Lamoignon had, on the other hand, professional loyalty and respect for tradition in the highest degree; and this conservative leaning led him to oppose a certain number of articles which nevertheless realized an advance. This caused him to defend the seigniorial jurisdictions, the suppression of which was threatened by one provision. These were, however, most frequently particular courts; but to abolish them would have meant "despoiling the lords of the principal part of their property, without which their lands would have lost all their value, it being certain that the nobility had nothing but the preservation of their jurisdictions at heart, since there is nothing which distinguishes them in a greater degree from the rest of the king's subjects." [2] He protested against the necessity imposed of interrogating the accused within twenty-four hours of his arrest,[3] and against the admirable provision that the judgments in the first instance shall be rendered by three judges at least and those of the last resort by at least seven.[4] Here is apparent the magistrate whose chief anxiety is promptness of service. The articles reducing the rights and emoluments of the judicial officers above all aroused protests from the First president; he spoke in favor of the clerks of court,[5] the king's procurators,[6] even of the jailers.[7] Here, as in the case of the seigniorial judges, he defended the rights of property. "These are offices which they have dearly bought, and which comprise the greatest part of their property."

Talon spoke often and very authoritatively; but his remarks were much less trenchant. Sometimes he supported Pussort and sometimes the First president; he showed all the characteristics appropriate to magistrates of the public ministry. Although he was a magistrate, he was at the same time "the king's man." The other magistrates and councillors, including even the Chan-

[1] "Procès-verbal," p. 222. [2] *Ibid.*, p. 15. [3] *Ibid.*, p. 151. [4] *Ibid.*, p. 246. [5] *Ibid.*, p. 82. [6] *Ibid.*, p. 108. [7] *Ibid.*, p. 135.

cellor, played an unimportant part. Of these, MM. Boucherat and de Novion spoke most frequently, usually on matters of detail. If we are to believe Saint-Simon, de Novion was certainly a man capable of grasping details: "He was neither unjust nor dishonest like his grandfather the other First president de Novion; but he knew nothing of his profession except the petty technicalities, in which he was as proficient as the ablest attorney; outside of that obscure science he could not be depended upon."[1] The neutral rôle of MM. de Harlay and Bignon is matter for surprise. They were really men of great merit. Saint-Simon also speaks of them. "Descendant of these great magistrates, Harlay had all their weight, which he exaggerated to the point of cynicism, affecting indifference and modesty. . . . He was learned in public law, and well grounded in the various systems of jurisprudence; he ranked with the most conversant in Belles-Lettres, and was well read in history."[2] — "Bignon was a magistrate of the old school in respect of knowledge, integrity, and modesty; worthy of the name he bore, so well known in the legal profession and in the republic of letters, and he had, like his father, enjoyed a wide reputation as attorney-general."[3]

After having been discussed in these conferences, the articles, as we know, again passed through the hands of the Council of Justice. Sometimes the comments which had been made in the name of the Parlement were taken into consideration, but more frequently they were ignored. It is to prove a matter of subsequent regret that President Lamoignon's advice was not listened to with more respect.

[1] "Mémoires," vol. XIV, p. 216.
[2] *Ibid.*, vol. I, p. 136.
[3] *Ibid.*, vol. I, p. 392.

CHAPTER II

THE PROCEDURE UNDER THE ORDINANCE OF 1670

§ 1. **Introductory.** — We have no intention of making a commentary on the Ordinance of 1670; but it is essential briefly to indicate the novel features which it introduced and for that purpose to take a bird's-eye view, as it were, of its chief provisions. As it contains both jurisdictional rules and rules of criminal procedure properly so called, we must adopt that division of the subject.[1]

§ 2. **Jurisdictional Rules.** — From the 1200s a continuous movement took place, as we have seen, impoverishing and despoiling the seigniorial and ecclesiastical jurisdictions for the benefit of the royal jurisdictions. In order to arrive at this result the jurists had gradually changed the old rules of jurisdiction; apart from the appeal, their principal inventions had been the jurisdiction of the court of the place of the offense, the theory of precedence, and the theory of royal causes. Let us see what form these had taken in the new law, now that royalty was irrevocably victorious.

I. The jurisdiction of the court of the place of the offense was finally triumphant. It was even the only competent court (Tit. I, Art. 1); the court of the accused's domicile and that of the place of capture were discarded. President Lamoignon, in the debate, protested against this provision, showing the difficulties which would result from it in practice, but the article was retained. Pussort said, "It was of importance that the court should be ascertainable with certainty."[2] This jurisdiction was not, however, exclusive of all others. If the complainant had brought the

[1] We shall cite the principal Commentators of the Ordinance according to the following editions: *Bornier*, "Conférence des nouvelles Ordonnances de Louis XIV," 1703 edition. — *Jousse*, "Commentaire sur l'Ordonnance criminelle," 1766. — *Muyart de Vouglans*, "Institutes du droit criminel," 1757 edition; "Instruction criminelle," 1762. — *Rousseau de La Combe*, "Traité des matières criminelles," 1769 edition. — *Serpillon*, "Code criminel," 1767 edition. — *Pothier*, "Procédure criminelle," *Bugnet* edition.

[2] "Procès-verbal," pp. 4–6.

matter before another judge, and the accused did not demand its transference before the reading of the first deposition, at the time of the confrontation, the action went on.

II. Article 11 of Title I enumerated the royal causes assigned to the bailiffs, seneschals, and presidial judges, "exclusively to our other judges and those of the lords." We know that all the Ordinances up to that time had made a similar enumeration, having invariably finished it with the words "and all others appertaining to the royal right." This clause was omitted for the first time. It was no doubt considered useless to retain this weapon, now that the strife was at an end. Lamoignon urged the replacement of these words in a long speech; this is a proof of that conservative spirit which we have remarked in the First president. Pussort replied that the king's intention had not been to extend his power, he being sole master, but to decide all disputes; "The edict of Crémieu specified five or six royal causes and added 'and others,' but that is a matter of form." Lamoignon, here more royalist than the king's men, returned to the charge and won his case; the list ended with the words: "and other causes explained by our Ordinances and regulations."

III. As to the precedence of the royal judges over those of the seigniors in the matter of jurisdiction, the plan contained an Article which completely ruined the seigniorial courts. "Our judges," it said, "shall take precedence of the inferior and non-royal judges in their jurisdiction if they have made inquiry and 'decreed' the same day;" the seigniorial courts have in future only those causes which have escaped the vigilance of the royal officers, or which the latter disdained. The First president here still constituted himself the energetic defender of the past; it was, according to him, a question of absolute justice and propriety. Pussort supported the plan; he pointed out that the greater part of the seigniorial judges were "incapable," that the administration of justice was burdensome on the seigniors themselves; he finally vehemently claims the rights of royalty. "The real property of (criminal) justice, which is called 'jus gladii,' is a right of taking life over the king's subjects, lying, properly speaking, in the hands of His Majesty, who communicates it to his officers."[1] But royalty had not the temerity to abolish the seigniorial judges completely. Two modifications were introduced into the Article: precedence was given only to the bailiffs and seneschals, and not to all the royal judges; a term was fixed for the lord's judges, before the arrival of which precedence

[1] "Procès-verbal," pp. 15–17.

could not intervene.[1] Pussort had admitted the first compromise and rejected the second; both figure in the final working of the article.

As between the royal judges themselves, the provosts might have precedence taken of them by the bailiffs "three days after the crime was committed";[2] the traditionary provision was also adopted according to which the provosts took no jurisdiction of the crimes of the nobility.[3]

IV. The Ordinance dealt with the appeal at length in Title XXVI; but upon this point Royalty had won such a decisive victory over the seigniors that it did not deem it necessary to register it formally. The appellate judges were always royal judges; in the second instance the courts of the seigniors never intervened. "It is only the criminal lieutenants of the bailiwicks and royal seneschals who have the right of criminal jurisdiction. This is decided by Article 22 of the edict of Crémieu, and still more clearly by the Article of the Ordinance which speaks only of bailiffs and royal seneschals; with the result that the judges of the lords who have appellate jurisdiction in civil cases of some other judges, have not the same right in criminal proceedings." [4]

V. The ecclesiastical jurisdiction had gradually lost ground, thanks to the theory of the *ordinary misdemeanor* and of the *privileged case*. The ordinary misdemeanor could be retained by the secular judge, as long as it was not required to be transferred; and in that case only the bailiffs and royal seneschals had jurisdiction, to the exclusion of the seigniorial judges.[5] The secular judge was not divested of the privileged cause. It was settled by the Ordinance of Moulins that the secular judge should hold the ecclesiastical accused until the action had been brought against him and concluded; only, he must thereafter hand him over to the ecclesiastical judge so that the latter might try the common misdemeanor covered by the privileged cause.[6] This successive intervention gave rise to much trouble. An endeavor was made to unite both actions in one; this was settled by the edict of Melun of 1580 in Article 22. "The examination of actions against ecclesiastical per-

[1] This is a delay of 24 hours, Tit. I, Art. 9.
[2] Tit. I, Art. 7.
[3] Tit. I, Art. 10.
[4] *Serpillon*, "Code criminelle," p. 1139.
[5] *Muyart de Vouglans*, "Inst. crim." Part III, pp. 50, 51.
[6] "We ordain that our officers shall examine and judge in all cases the privileged offenses among ecclesiastical persons, before relinquishing them to the ecclesiastical judge, which relinquishment shall be made on condition of their being imprisoned for the punishment of the privileged offense, where it shall not have been satisfied, for which the Bishop's officers shall answer in case of release."

sons in privileged causes shall be made conjointly by ecclesiastical and royal judges; and in that case the said royal judges shall go to the bench of the ecclesiastical jurisdiction." But the only result of this joint examination, prolific of jarring and conflicts, was to effect a compromise between the rights of royalty and the old immunities of the Church. Now that royalty was passing a new law, would it remove this difficulty? This it tried to do, and the first draft contained two articles which retained the ecclesiastical judges' jurisdiction only for purely ecclesiastical offenses. This was very reasonable and was what the States-General had asked several times; but it was not allowed to pass, royalty yielding to the Church as it had yielded to the seigniors. In this case also it is Lamoignon who appears in defense of the past. "He was obliged to represent to the king that both articles intrenched on clerical privilege to a great extent and seemed almost to destroy it. . . . This clerical privilege, however, is universally recognized wherever there are catholics, and it might be said that this general custom is an adjunct of the altar." [1] And he reviewed the history of the Church's immunities, calling to mind that this privilege "had the sanction of possession during fourteen hundred years"; he begged "His Majesty to make the reflections he might find necessary." Pussort then rose in favor of the reëstablishment of the rights of the civil authority. "The king's intention is not to restrict the ecclesiastical jurisdiction, but to regulate it. . . . The discipline of the spirituality is left absolutely to the ecclesiastical judges. . . . The article, it is true, is contrary to the practice, but it is in conformity with reason; . . . it is not decent that a royal magistrate should act as the assessor of another judge . . . therefore the article is just." [2] It could not have been better put, but Pussort invoked reason, an authority whose reign would not arrive till a century later, and he had the opposition of all-powerful tradition. Talon came to the rescue of the First president. Being a "king's man," he began by doing homage to royalty. "It is true," he said, "that this privilege is a favor which monarchs have granted to the clergy, actuated by pious motives and by the respect which they have for the sacredness of their ministry . . . so it is indubitable that it is in the prince's power to revoke or restrict a privilege granted by his predecessors;" but he moved for the maintenance of the immunity; "it is sufficient if this privilege is placed within limits; in this way the bad effect which it had at some junctures would be rectified, and the complaints which the

[1] "Procès-verbal," pp. 44, 45.

[2] *Ibid.*, pp. 46, 47.

bishops and all the clergy in the kingdom and even the Pope himself would not fail to make if a single feature of a privilege based upon the constitutions of the Roman emperors, renewed by Charlemagne and affirmed by fourteen hundred years' possession were withdrawn, would be avoided.[1]" This formidable opposition, as Talon points out, gave the king, who, in the Council of Justice, had seemed to rely very much on these articles, matter for reflection. They were suppressed and replaced by a text which maintained the *status quo:* "Art. 13. Nothing in the preceding article shall derogate from the privileges which the clergy have been accustomed to enjoy." As, however, the Ordinance did not regulate the joint procedure, it was necessary to make a kind of separate Code for this purpose. This was the object of several Laws; first of all the Edict of February, 1678, expanded the principles contained in the Edict of Melun, incorporating in it but one restriction by way of sparing the feelings of the Parlements; then came a Declaration in July, 1684, the general Edict of 1695 upon the ecclesiastical jurisdiction, and finally a Declaration of February 4, 1711.[2]

VI. The Ordinance did not deal with the jurisdictions of the cities, mayors, échevins, consuls, etc., and did not modify their rights in any respect. Everywhere they had mere police matters; that was what the States-General had asked for them at Orléans,[3] and it was granted to them by the Ordinance of Moulins, Arts. 71 and 72. Those authorities, however, which took the cognizance of civil actions from the municipal jurisdictions, left to them that of criminal actions, with which they were already invested. But the majority of the cities, taking them individually, lost the high justice. Royalty, however, did not invariably succeed in these usurpations, and we possess a curious document of the very time of Louis XIV, which gives us a view of one of these little dramas. This is a letter from Colbert to Talon, dealing with a question of the suppression of the aldermanic courts in operation in Hainault. "It appears from what we hear from these frontier districts that nothing makes a worse impression upon the minds than the suppression of their aldermanic courts and the establishment which has been made of benches in the method in vogue throughout the kingdom, because they are informed that the majority of the officers only buy their offices to more easily make exactions from them."[4]

[1] "Procès-verbal," pp. 47, 48.
[2] *Muyart de Vouglans,* "Instr. crim." Part III, p. 70 *et seq.*
[3] *Picot,* "Histoire des États-Généraux," vol. II, p. 216 *et seq.*
[4] "Lettres, etc., de Colbert," vol. VI, p. 2.

Colbert, therefore, comes to the conclusion that the offices must be redeemed and the old order of things reëstablished. Here the old communal spirit of the people of Flanders was encountered; and in a certain number of cities of the south the same opposition was met. The result was that in a great number of cases, if not as a general rule, "the cities have retained a right of trial in criminal matters down to the time of the Revolution. Strange to say, royalty had taken from them the civil jurisdiction and left them the criminal jurisdiction." [1]

The jurisdiction of the royal judges was thus settled in opposition to the other jurisdictions. But we have seen that a certain number of courts of exception figure among the royal courts. The Ordinance merely left the majority of these to the existing laws, but it selected for special treatment the most important of these jurisdictions, that of the provost marshals.

We know how the "prévôtal" jurisdiction, originally purely military, had gradually extended its sway; it was a formidable weapon in the hands of royalty, with which to put down the disorders which disturbed the public safety, but it was a terrible tribunal. These "men of arms" tried summarily, harshly, and there was no appeal. It was considered good enough for those amenable to their jurisdiction, whom Imbert calls "the provost marshal's jail-birds; these were in former times the vagabonds and especially 'the armed men roaming over the country and eating honest men's poultry.'" [2] The States-General, however, had often complained of the disorders which this jurisdiction brought in its train.[3] The new Ordinance ought at least to regulate it in a precise way; this was the object of a part of Title I and of the whole of Title II. Article 13 of Title I really extended the jurisdiction of the provosts, and it did not pass without opposition.[4] President Lamoignon declared "that it might be affirmed that the greatest abuses met with in criminal justice have originated with these officers . . . who oppress the innocent and discharge the guilty. The majority of them are more to be feared than the thieves themselves." This constituted such a great evil that the defenders of the institution

[1] *Laboulaye*, Revue des cours littéraires, year 1865, p. 723.
[2] *Imbert*, Book II, ch. V, No. 4.
[3] *Picot.*, *op. cit.*, I, 447; II, 135, 172–175, 529, 530; IV, 63–65.
[4] Besides the offenses committed by vagrants and excesses by the soldiery, it was the duty of the provosts to try "unlawful assemblies and thefts upon the highways, nocturnal thefts in the towns, sacrileges accompanied by breaking in, premeditated murder, sedition, popular tumults, and coinage of false money, whatever the station of the perpetrators might be."

themselves are compelled to acknowledge it. "The provost marshals," says Pussort, "being men of no uprightness of life, their bad conduct has brought them into very great disrepute." Talon for his part says that "as neither the officers nor their archers have any fees to live on, there are no malversations to which they have not given themselves up; they perform no duty unless they hope to get some emolument from it." Finally, president de Novion adds "that this was not for the purpose of establishing the public safety but of extending the power of the provost marshals."[1] Royalty, however, desired the preservation of this jurisdiction, and the discussion was restricted to matters of detail; the list of "prévôtal" cases which the draft contained was passed with very few exceptions.

While maintaining the "prévôtal" jurisdiction, the safeguards which had been contrived by judicial decisions to regulate and curb it were also retained and increased. First, The provosts must necessarily have their jurisdiction passed upon by the presidial in the jurisdiction in which the capture took place "within three days at latest, although the accused has put in no declinatory plea."[2] Second, Within twenty-four hours of the capture, the accused must be interrogated by the provost in the presence of the provost's assessor, who was a graduate in law; and it was necessary to declare to the accused at this first interrogatory that it was intended to try him "prévôtally." Third, The jurisdictional judgments could not be rendered by less than seven judges, like all the other "prévôtal" decrees, whether preliminary, interlocutory, or final.[3] Fourth, When crimes, "prévôtal" by their nature and not by the character of the person, were concerned, the provosts had no cognizance of them if they had been committed in the cities where the provosts resided. This provision was an indication of the true character of the institution. The provosts, "road watchmen," had been created to beat the country in increasing circuits; the old Ordinances were very strict in that respect. "Going up and down the country, they will not stop in one place more than a day, unless for necessary cause (Orléans, 68; Moulins, Art. 43)." To call upon the provosts to try the crimes committed within the towns of their residence would have been to invite them to reside there continuously. Fifth, Minute precautions were taken to avoid disorders and malversations;[4] in particular an inventory must be made of everything found upon the captive, and that had

[1] "Procès-verbal," p. 28 *et seq.*
[2] Tit. II, Art. 13; see also Arts. 19, 20.
[3] Tit. II, Arts. 18, 24.
[4] See Tit. II, Arts. 10, 14.

to be done "in the presence of the two inhabitants nearest to the place of capture, who shall sign the inventory." [1] Sixth, The right of precedence over the marshals was given, or rather confirmed, to the presidials. In "prévôtal" cases the latter had jurisdiction "preferably to the provost marshals, criminal lieutenants of the short robe, vice-bailiffs, and vice-seneschals, if they had issued decree either before the latter or the same day;" in order to give final judgment they had to observe all the rules we have just laid down. The ordinary judges, in a "prévôtal" case, could only inquire and decree in case of capture in the act, and were obliged to refer the case to whom it might concern.

The Ordinance of 1670 was not destined to be the last word of the old law upon this matter: in 1731 (5th February), a royal Declaration was issued upon "prévôtal" and presidial cases. It contained thirty articles and was much better drawn up than the corresponding titles of the Ordinance. It for the first time clearly distinguished the cases which were "prévôtal" by the character of the persons from those "prévôtal" by the nature of the crimes. It was also more lenient than the old law on several points.[2] Gentlemen not previously condemned were excepted from the "prévôtal" or presidial jurisdiction in the last resort. If we have dwelt at some length upon the "prévôtal" jurisdiction, it is not merely because of the important place which it occupies in the Ordinance and in the ancient French social life; but also because we shall see it reappear at the commencement of the 1800s, soon after to disappear for ever.

We may note, in concluding this explanation of the principles of jurisdiction, that the clergy, gentlemen, king's secretaries, and officers of judicature had the right to be tried in the "Great Chamber of the Parlement and not in the criminal Tournelle . . . on appeal only, and provided they petitioned for a reference (to the Great Chamber) before the voting began in the Tournelle." [3]

§ 3. **The Procedure.** — The Ordinance left the procedure to rest upon the rules established by the prior judicial practice. In future, and more than ever, it can be truly said that there is but one true accuser, the king's procurator or that of the seignior: the private prosecutor could only ask for damages. The last traces of the old accusatory system had not, however, yet disappeared. For offenses which did not merit corporal punishment, the intervention of a settlement between the injured and the guilty parties suspended and even put an end to the public action

[1] Tit. II, Arts. 9, 11. [2] See Arts. 17 and 20. [3] Tit. I, Arts. 21, 22.

also.[1] Title III speaks of *accusers* at the same time as it speaks of *denouncers;*[2] and the law always places private individuals in the first rank in the prosecution of crimes; "If there is no civil party, the actions shall be prosecuted at the instance and in the name of our attorneys or of the attorneys of the seigniorial courts."[3] The public prosecutor would seem not to make his appearance except following and in the absence of complainants; but this is only an empty appearance; or rather whatever reality there is in this presentation of the matter is from a fiscal point of view; if there is a civil party, it is he who bears the cost of the action; if not, it is the king or the seigniorial judge.[4] In other respects the theory of the civil action in the shape in which it has come down to us was finally settled in its broad details; it is in annotating the title on *Complaints* that our old authors have made that subtle and deep study which may still serve as a model for us to-day.

I. The Ordinance clearly distinguishes denunciations from complaints. The denouncers address themselves to the king's procurator; they write and sign their denunciation, or the clerk of court writes it out in their presence; subsequently, if the accused is acquitted, they can be sentenced as calumnious or imprudent; but they do not figure in the action. The act makes an innovation in regard to complaints. They can be made by request addressed to the judge, who shall answer them (Art. 1). This is the old request for permission to inform. Or again, they may be written by the clerk of court in the judge's presence; but they must always be addressed to the judge. Faithful to the spirit of reform in which it was conceived, the Ordinance rejects in this matter sheriffs, officers of the court, archers, and notaries. But here is something which possesses novelty and importance. Down to that time every complaint, being the request for a permission to inform, by the very fact of its being made, constituted the complainant a civil party, imposing on him the heavy burden of costs. Private individuals were, therefore, naturally reluctant to ask the judge to take cognizance; they remained inactive or constituted themselves denouncers to the king's procurator, who did not always act. The Ordinance declares that "the complainants shall not be deemed civil parties unless they so declare formally by the complaint."[5] It does more; formerly

[1] Tit. XXV, Art. 19.
[2] Tit. III. "Des plaintes, dénonciations, et accusations."
[3] Tit. III, Art. 8. [4] Tit. XXV, Arts. 16, 17. [5] Tit. III, Art. 5.

one did not become a civil party except by a complaint; his intervention in the course of the action was not thought of. Henceforth it could be accomplished in a "subsequent document which could be drawn up at any stage of the action." Finally, as a last favor, the civil party was allowed to abandon "within twenty-four hours and not afterwards"; and in case of abandonment he was not held liable for costs subsequently accruing. These were innovations enough for one single article. They were excellent, and so president Lamoignon said. "The article," he said, "is new, but it appears to be excellent." [1] The judge having taken cognizance, he proceeded first of all to establish the "corpus delicti," and the Ordinance contains very judicious provisions as to the official reports of the judges and the reports of physicians and surgeons.[2]

II. Title VI of this act, which had so far adhered to the chronological order of events, was devoted to inquiries, the chief part of the action. The principle of the *secrecy* of the procedure was rigorously followed: "The witnesses shall be heard secretly and separately." [3] — "The clerks of court are hereby forbidden to communicate the inquiries and other secret documents of the action." [4] These provisions seemed so natural that they did not give rise to any criticism. But alongside of this traditional severity the Ordinance contained admirable reforms in matters of detail. The custom of causing "an officer of court and a notary" to make the inquiry was entirely abolished. Henceforth the deposition is to be written "by a clerk of court in the presence of the judge." [5] — The witnesses must, before testifying, "produce the writ which has been served upon them to testify, of which mention shall be made in their depositions." This was a way of insuring obedience to the rule that the witnesses should only be brought by the public prosecutor or by the civil party; [6] to prevent witnesses for the accused being insinuated into their number, production of the citation must be made necessary.[7] — Everything was devised so that the information, so important a document, should be true and unaltered; the oath to be administered to the witnesses, the questions to be put to them, the reading of the depositions, the prohibition of interlineations, the necessity for the ratification of

[1] "Procès-verbal," p. 66.
[2] Tits. IV and V.
[3] Tit. VI, Art. 11.
[4] Tit. VI, Art. 15.
[5] Tit. VI, Art. 9; *cf.* Art. 6.
[6] Tit. VI, Art. 1.
[7] This provision has been incorporated in the Code of Criminal Examination (Art. 74), but it has not the same value, the accused being always able to summon to the hearing the witnesses for the defense.

erasures, the material effect of the register (Articles 5, 9, 11, 12), — all these provisions were prescribed on pain of nullity.

The witness fee was fixed by the judge (Art. 13). The commissioners' draft added that payment of it should be made by the hands of the clerk of court, forbidding the parties to give anything in addition; but the First president observed "that the witnesses were sometimes at a distance; and if the parties were not careful to see that they came, and to pay their travelling expenses, they would neglect to appear." The words "by the hands of the clerk of court" were struck out, and the parties were merely forbidden to give anything in addition to the fee taxed. Lamoignon had helped to retain an abuse.

The monitories followed the informations (Title VII). The judges decreed permission to obtain them, and the official was obliged to obey. This was also possible "even though no proof had been begun, or on refusal of the witnesses to testify;" this was excessive, especially as it was said that the judgment which would intervene on attachment, if there should be any, would be executed notwithstanding "appeal even as from abuse." Lamoignon observed "that the examination of an action is not begun by a 'monitory';"[1] but everything was passed.

III. If the information contained charges, it resulted in an order which had always to be given upon the motion of the king's procurator.[2] The draft of the act provided that "neither judges' fees nor commissions" could be claimed for these motions. Lamoignon protested, Pussort vainly argued, "that the king's purpose was not to diminish the emoluments of his officers, but rather to curtail the actions, by depriving them of the opportunity of claiming decrees too readily and too causelessly."[3] The provision was suppressed.

The Ordinance allowed three kinds of writs, that of summons to be heard, that of personal citation, and that of arrest. The first, which we have not found in Imbert, had been introduced by judicial decision. It was milder than the personal citation, inasmuch as it did not entail, as the latter did, the prohibition of exercising all functions.[4] In order to choose between these different writs, it was necessary to take into account the nature of the crimes, the proofs, and also the persons. A warrant of arrest could not be granted against a resident "except for corporal or ignominious punishment." The writ of summons for hearing was,

[1] "Procès-verbal," p. 74.
[2] Tit. X, Art. 1.
[3] "Procès-verbal," p. 108.
[4] Tit. X, Arts. 10 and 12.

on default of appearance, converted into a writ of personal citation, and that, in the same circumstances, into a warrant of arrest,[1] at least if the accused did not plead a hindrance or excuse in the forms prescribed by Title XI. These were the "essoins of accused persons," and this is the last time that this description of dilatory exception, formerly so important in the feudal procedure, will appear in our laws in the proper sense of the term.[2]

Writs could not be granted without a prior information. That was the general rule, but it was subject to many exceptions, not only in the case of capture in the act, but also on other less favorable hypotheses. "Arrest may be decreed on notoriety alone for duelling; on the complaint of our procurators against vagabonds, and on that of the lawyers for crimes and domestic offenses." [3]

The warrant of arrest placed the accused in a state of detention pending trial; and an order of the judge was always necessary for release (Art. 23). But release on bail was not always possible in the "extraordinary" action.[4] After the interrogation, however, if there had originally been only a personal citation, and the warrant of arrest had only been issued in default of appearance, the accused could be released (Art. 21). This provision was very severe, and paid little regard to individual liberty. At the same time, it was more precise than any of the earlier Ordinances, and contained several safeguards. The king's procurators were obliged to send twice a year to the attorneys-general a "statement signed by them and the criminal lieutenants of the entries in the jail-book and detainers made during the preceding six months in the prisons of their jurisdiction, which had not been followed by a final judgment, with the dates of the warrants, jail-book entries and detainers, the name, surname, designation, and residence of the accused, and the title of the accusation in brief and the stage of the procedure." [5] This was an admirable provision,

[1] Tit. X, Arts. 3 and 4.

[2] If he who was personally cited should appear, he could not be imprisoned unless new charges were brought up (Art. 7); or "by secret deliberation of our courts, it has been resolved that he shall be arrested on his appearance, which cannot be ordered by any other of our judges." — This "retentum" well illustrates the spirit of this procedure, which often plays with the accused to the very end.

[3] Tit. X, Art. 8; *cf.* Arts. 5 and 6. — The decrees could be issued by the examining judge alone. Bornier, it is true, considered them as null "when they were rendered by a single judge without the opinions of any others" (p. 348); but the prevailing opinion was to the contrary. "The decrees are usually rendered by the examining judge." *Jousse*, "Comment," p. 187. — "The contrary usage sufficiently proves that Bornier's idea does not conform to the rules." *Serpillon*, "Code crim." p. 532.

[4] Tit. XV, Art. 12.

[5] Tit. X, Art. 20.

and it undoubtedly inspired articles 249 and 250 of the Code of Criminal Examination.

After dealing with the warrants the compilers of the Ordinance naturally turned their attention to the policing of the prisons. This they did in Title XIII. The prisons of the 1600s and the 1700s were atrocious places: "Dare to descend for an instant into these gloomy dungeons, into which the light of day never penetrates, and gaze on the disfigured features of your fellow-creatures, bruised by their chains, half-covered with some rags, poisoned by an air never renewed, and apparently impregnated with the poison of crime, eaten alive by the same vermin which devour the corpses in their graves, hardly kept alive with some coarse food sparingly distributed, kept in a constant state of terror by the groans of their unfortunate comrades and the threats of their keepers."[1] These are the words of a magistrate in an opening address and the poignant truth is apparent under the rhetorical amplification. Voltaire said later: "A prison need not resemble a palace, but no more is it necessary that it should resemble a charnel-house. It is a common complaint that the majority of the jails of Europe are cloacæ of infection, which spread disease and death, not merely within their precincts, but throughout their neighborhood. Daylight there is none, and the air is stagnant. The prisoners communicate to each other only their tainted exhalations. They suffer a cruel punishment before they are tried. Charity and good policy ought to suggest a remedy for such inhuman and dangerous negligence."[2]

The Reports of 1789 furnish irrefutable testimony to the same effect. The Third Estate unanimously demands that "the prisons be made safe and healthy, that they do not impair the health of the prisoners, and that hospitals be instituted."[3] — The same protests appear in the Reports of the Nobility: "the prisons," says one of them, "are in an inhuman and indecent state."[4] The Clergy are equally vehement: "let the prisons, where too often the innocent suffer side by side with the guilty, cease to be, against the spirit of the law, a *seat of horror and infection;* let the poor wretches at least have fresh air, and wholesome and sufficient sustenance; let the prison hospitals be aired and so equipped that they may be of service to the sick."[5] These are incontrovertible facts.

It must not, however, be thought that the legislatures and the

[1] *Servan,* "Discours," etc., p. 14.
[2] "Idée de la justice et de l'humanité," Art. xxv.
[3] *Prudhomme,* "Résumé des cahiers," III, pp. 588, 173, 174.
[4] *Ibid., op. cit.,* II, pp. 152 and 411. [5] *Ibid., op. cit.,* I, pp. 163 and 357.

magistrates of ancient France showed themselves indifferent to the fate of the prisoners. This harsh discipline and these sufferings appeared to them natural and necessary. But, on the other hand, numerous precautions were taken to prevent peculation and vexations on the part of the jailers. Certain court practices touched upon the matter. Thus the Tournelle of the Parlement of Paris held a sitting annually on the day before Ascension to listen to the grievances and inquire into the lot of the prisoners.[1] The Parlements frequently made regulations for the police of the prisons of their jurisdiction. That of the Parlement of Paris of 1st September, 1717, is celebrated and very extensive. The compilers of the Ordinance were inspired by the same sentiment. In Title XIII we find few provisions concerning the penitentiary question, as we would call it nowadays. The sexes must be separated (Art. 20); the turnkeys shall visit the prisoners every day in their dungeons, and must report those who are sick, so that they may be visited by physicians and if need be transferred to rooms (Art. 21); the prisoners must be given "bread, water, and straw in good condition, according to the regulations" (Art. 25). That is all. Nearly all the other Articles are directed towards the repression of the peculations of the keepers. They disclose serious disorders and above all a shameful venality (Arts. 2, 6, 7, 9, 15, 19, 10, 11, 14, 18, 22, 28, 30, 33). The jailers are constantly forbidden to take money for the performance of their prescribed duties. The king's procurators or those of the lords are commanded "to visit the prisons once a week to receive the complaints of the prisoners" (Art. 25).[2]

IV. The accused, whether summoned or arrested, must be interrogated by the judge. This was an act of the greatest importance. We shall see that in the majority of cases, in the absence of the accused's confession, the heavier sentences could not be pronounced. The art of interrogating was therefore a very valuable qualification of the examining magistrate, in this secret procedure. The authors of treatises on criminal law laid down a series of rules on this subject which have become standard, the

[1] "On Ascension Thursday the Parlement holds its sitting at the Châtelet for the prisoners. The last appointed president, at half past ten o'clock, goes to Châtelet with the councillors of the Tournelle. The hearing ceases on their arrival, the civil lieutenant leaves his place, and while the Parlement holds the hearing, the criminal lieutenant, the king's procurator, and the criminal lieutenant of the short robe are on the bench of the king's people, so that they may be able to answer should there be any complaint against them." *Barbier*, "Journal," II, p. 328.

[2] Compare Article 610 *et. seq.* of the Code of Criminal Examination.

fruit of experience and study. The remarks with which Jousse prefaced Title XIV of the Ordinance remain the most judicious of these short treatises, which are somewhat reminiscent of the manuals of the confessional.

A slight amelioration was introduced into the practice of the interrogatories, which had to be begun within twenty-four hours from the imprisonment at the latest; but the severe rules introduced by judicial practice and the Ordinances were retained and even aggravated. The interrogation must take place secretly, before the judge and his clerk. The oath introduced by custom was expressly imposed upon the accused (Art. 7).

A memorable discussion is known to have occurred on this point during the preliminary conferences. President Lamoignon showed all the nobility of his great heart, and gave voice to the opinions of the old magistrates whom he cited as precedents. He strove with all his power to have the necessity for the oath done away with. He pointed out that it was only a mere custom, which was introduced, "like those things neither the origin of nor the reason for which were well known." He recalled the sanctity of the oath. "If it is obligatory, it will infallibly invite the accused to commit an additional crime, and to add to the untruth which is inevitable at such junctures a perjury which could be avoided. If it is not obligatory, it is taking the name of God in vain." — "In France it is universally said that it must be done in this way without inquiring into the reason for its being done; for none of the nations from whom we have taken all our good maxims has so practised it." He pointed out "that the civil law, far from sanctioning it, was undoubtedly opposed to it, and that there is not the slightest trace of it even in the Canon law before that was confounded with the formalities of the Inquisition." He observes that the "Carolina" (of Charles V of Germany) does not speak of it, nor had it made its way into the Netherlands at least. He finally invoked the tradition of the old French magistracy. "No one is bound to condemn himself out of his own mouth," President Lemaître had said; and De Thou, "whose memory is held in such high esteem in the courts of justice and elsewhere . . . in interrogating a person accused of a named crime would never make him take the oath, because there was no Ordinance compelling the judges to exact it from the accused, and he would not invite him to a manifest perjury." [1]

Pussort attempted a refutation of this vigorous reasoning;

[1] "Procès-verbal," pp. 153, 159.

but his efforts were feeble. "The arguments which have been advanced cannot be admitted, as it is in no case permissible to do evil to attain the greatest good; natural law when opposed to that of Christianity must naturally give way to it, nobody doubting that death is preferable to a mortal sin . . . the use of the oath is very old, and was observed before the Ordinance of 1539 . . . and the use of it is much more solemn, inasmuch as it has been established without law; . . . it is not entirely useless; . . . timid consciences are to be found which the fear of perjury might force to acknowledge the truth." M. Talon supported Pussort. He maintained "that in Spain, Italy, and, it might be said, among all the nations of Europe, the oath was administered to the accused before they were interrogated. . . . This obstacle," he said, "having been raised, it was absolutely necessary to make it the subject of an article in the Ordinance." Lamoignon, who really remained unanswered, asked that the king be consulted. The king retained the article.

But to command a thing to be done is not the same thing as having it done. What was to be done if the accused refused to take the oath? The Ordinance had foreseen the probability of an absolute refusal by the accused to answer.[1] It provided that action should then be brought against him as a voluntary mute.[2] After being called on three times to reply, and after three warnings of the consequences of his silence, the judge proceeded, recording, whenever there was occasion for the appearance of the accused, that he refused to speak. All the proceedings were, however, valid, and even if the accused should subsequently wish to reply, nothing was reopened, not even the confrontation. This very rigorous procedure, more severe than that followed in the case of contumacy, furnished a means of indirectly forcing the accused to the oath. He who was willing to answer, but without taking

[1] Title XVIII, concerning the deaf and dumb and those who refuse to answer.

[2] A person present was not allowed to figure as a contumax. "There was formerly a contumacy, the party being present, when the examination was against voluntary mutes, but that form of procedure was disapproved by resolution of the Parlement of Paris of 1st December, 1663." *Serpillon,* "Code crim." p. 900. — "Formerly a curator was appointed for voluntary mutes, but the Ordinance has thought fit to abrogate this usage, and to deprive them of an aid of which they showed themselves unworthy." *Muyart,* "Inst. crim." 1st part, p. 684. — "The practice of the Châtelet has changed at different times as to the form of bringing an action against voluntary mutes; formerly a curator was assigned to them, but the inconvenience of this, due to the necessity of recommencing the procedure when the accused offered to reply orally, was recognized." *M. Talon,* "Procès-verbal," p. 217.

the oath, was put in the same position as a voluntary mute. So Jousse decided. After speaking of the voluntary mute he adds, "it is the same if the accused refuses to take the oath, as sometimes happens."[1] And Serpillon, while protesting against this practice, appears to declare it. "He who answers, saying that he does not wish to take the oath, cannot be considered as such (a voluntary mute). He does not refuse to answer, he does not remain silent, and no punishment is pronounced against him who refuses to take the oath. It is, however, true that MM. the commissioners of the Parlement of Paris, in the proceedings against the infamous Damiens, on 8th February, called upon that accused three times to take the oath, which he refused to do; which proves their custom in that respect."[2]

The aid of counsel was once more prohibited by the Ordinance. The accused must always answer personally. This applied not only to the first interrogation, in which case it could be easily understood, but throughout the whole course of the examinations, whether before the criminal lieutenant, or before the assembled bench. If, however, a crime not capital was concerned, "the judges might, after the interrogatories, permit consultation with whomsoever they pleased," without there being any question of a defense being turned into a speech at the bar. If, on the contrary, a capital crime was concerned, all consultation was forbidden, "notwithstanding all customs to the contrary, which we repeal, except for the crimes of peculation, extortion, fraudulent bankruptcy, theft by clerks or partners in financial or banking affairs, in regard to which crimes the judges may order, if the matter requires it, that the accused may communicate with their clerks after the interrogation." Such was the plan proposed. Although it had all the appearance of imposing a less absolute prohibition than that of the Ordinance of 1539, it really went beyond the latter, the somewhat vague language of which left a certain power to the judges. Lamoignon here again raised his voice in favor of the accused. "This Article forbids the judges to assign counsel to the accused, even after the confrontation. This is new and very hard on the accused." Taking up the cause of free defense, his language seems antedated by a century. "If counsel has saved some guilty persons, it might also happen that innocent persons might perish for lack of counsel. — No evil which could happen in the administration of justice is comparable to that of causing the death of an innocent person, and it would be

[1] "Comment," p. 384.

[2] "Code crim." p. 902.

better to acquit a thousand guilty. — This counsel which has been granted to the accused is not a privilege accorded either by the Ordinances or by the laws. It is a liberty obtained from natural law, which is older than all human laws. — Our Ordinances have deprived accused persons of so many advantages that it is highly just to preserve to them what they have remaining. — If our procedure is compared with those of the Romans and other nations, it will be found that the latter are not so rigorous in this respect as in France, especially since the Ordinance of 1539. — It might be ordered generally that the judges should not grant counsel to accused persons except for crimes of a complex nature, but it would appear to be exceedingly dangerous to specify particularly what these crimes were, and by so doing exclude all others." [1]

In opposition to Lamoignon, Pussort anew constituted himself the advocate of inflexible repression. "Experience taught that the counsel which was granted deemed it an honor, and thought themselves at liberty with a clear conscience, to secure the impunity of the accused by any method." He was bold enough to recall the action of Chancellor Poyet to mark the import of the Ordinance of 1539. "It is true," he said, "that the silence of the Ordinance has been variously interpreted. . . . It has given the judges the opportunity to use it in various ways, some refusing (counsel) entirely, others granting it in all kinds of accusations, and still others only in certain cases. . . . We know how fertile these kinds of counsel are in finding openings to frame conflicts of jurisdiction, how they often scheme to discover nullities in the proceedings and to give birth to an infinitude of side issues. An accused is refused nothing, and it is necessary to read all the documents of the action, as well those which lead to his acquittal as those for his conviction. Provided, therefore, he has the means of employing enough advocates and furnishing the costs, expedients are not wanting to make the action go on forever. It is therefore peculiarly in the interests of the wealthy and of impunity that counsel is granted." [2] Here, as an eminent criminal law-writer has remarked, Pussort found himself in opposition to a truth taught by experience. By a logical necessity, it must be that the written and secret procedure, overburdened by formalities before it can deserve the name of procedure, offers to chicanery an admirably tilled soil.

M. Talon proposed a compromise. He wished that counsel should be excluded in a general way "in causes which depend

[1] "Procès-verbal," pp. 162–164. [2] *Ibid.*, pp. 164, 165.

solely on witnesses," but that they should be granted, also generally, and without proceeding to a dangerous enumeration "in accusations in which documents are produced for the conviction of the accused and where he is able to produce them in his defense." He cited as examples the trust-entails of children and wished the addition of the clause: "and others of the same nature." The article passed, after being modified by the addition to the cases in which counsel for the defense would be permitted "the trust-entails of children and other crimes where personal status is involved." [1] It was considered that enough was done to safeguard the rights of the defense by inserting in the text this reservation: "It is left to the sense of duty and the good faith of the judges to investigate before giving judgment whether there is any error in the proceedings." This was the same idea which prompted the declaration that the testimony in the inquiry should be taken "for the prosecution and for the defense." Under this system the judge in a manner played the part of Providence. He is infallible, and defends the accused at the same time that he prosecutes him.

All the formalities of the interrogation were, however, minutely and carefully regulated.[2] The interrogation was at once communicated to the public prosecutor and the civil party (Arts. 17, 18), who, if there was a confession, could take law immediately, that is to say, ask for judgment, but only, as we shall explain later, if the crime did not merit corporal punishment. The accused in the same circumstances could ask to take law on the charges, which were then communicated to him. On either hypothesis there were requests addressed to the judge by the prosecutors and answers on the part of the accused (Art. 20). If it was not appropriate to take law in this way, the civil party and the public prosecutor presented their motions in law asking for a ruling to the "extraordinary" action. The accused could also present a request to be received in "ordinary" action; but this "civilizing" of the action was only allowed when the offense entailed merely a pecuniary punishment.[3]

V. The ruling to the "extraordinary" action resulted in an order stating that the witnesses heard in the inquiry were "heard anew, confirmed in their depositions, and, if necessary, confronted with the accused." [4] By whom was this important judgment to

[1] Tit. XIV, Art. 8. [2] See Arts. 9, 11, 13, 16.

[3] The effect of Tit. XX, Art. 3, of the Ordinance was that the conversion to the "ordinary" action could take place even after the ruling to the "extraordinary" action, provided it was done before the confrontation.

[4] Tit. XV, Art. 1.

be rendered? "By the judge," said the Ordinance. It seemed logical to conclude from this that the judge of examination alone was meant. Besides, he alone had so far appeared upon the scene. Jousse, however, no doubt taking into consideration the immense power which would thus be put into the hands of one man, was of the contrary opinion "that this order should be rendered in the Chamber, as a judgment on the merits, by three judges if the judgment is subject to appeal, and by seven when it is final."[1] But he was alone in this opinion. "In the bailiwicks and other jurisdictions subject to appeal, the examining judge may alone render a judgment of confirmation and confrontation.—It is matter for surprise that M. Jousse, so conversant with this fact, should have observed upon this article that the ruling to the 'extraordinary' procedure should be rendered by three judges if it is subject to appeal. That is contrary to the authorities which he cites, since they only speak of the last resort, which implies that the criminal lieutenants can, alone, render them to the 'ordinary' procedure, as a multitude of rulings have decided. Besides, it is the custom of all the courts of the kingdom that the examining judge by himself renders the judgments to the 'ordinary' procedure. It would be tedious to cite the regulations in refutation of this error."[2]

The confirmation was necessary in order that the deposition should constitute a charge against the accused; but in the inspection ("visite") of the proceedings, on the contrary, the depositions of the witnesses for the defense were read although they had been neither confirmed nor confronted, in order to be noticed by the judges.[3] Consequently, it was asked if there was any necessity for confronting all the witnesses; that appeared to be more just; however, it was usually decided that only those for the prosecution ought to be confronted.

The confrontation was the first opportunity that this merciless procedure gave to the accused to acquaint himself regarding the charge, until this time kept a secret from him. But the Ordinance rendered this resource almost entirely illusory. Originally, the object of the confirmation had been to allow the judge to check the inquiry which had been made by a mere officer of the court, assisted by a notary. Now it was of no more use for this purpose, the judge always making the inquiry himself. The confirmation was made a means of clinching the testimony so as to render all argument at the confrontation useless. "The witnesses," said Article

[1] "Comment. sur l'ord. de 1670," p. 296.
[2] *Serpillon*, "Code crim." p. 690.
[3] Tit. XV, Art. 10.

11, "who, from the time of the confirmation, retracted their depositions, or changed them in essential particulars, shall be prosecuted and punished as false witnesses." Lamoignon, for the third time, protested on behalf of the defense. "It may be dangerous to enact so strict a law, because sometimes an accused could put a witness right on important points and bring to his recollection the truth of a fact which had escaped him. That could sometimes be done in good faith, both on the part of the accused and of the witnesses, and the accused's situation would be rendered much worse if the witness were not allowed to retract at the confrontation without being treated as a criminal. . . . Everything is against the accused down to the confrontation; for it is then that he commences to realize his position and to become acquainted with the nature of the crime and of the proof. That is why it is more fitting to leave the matter in the judge's discretion; he is able to perceive whether the contradiction which occurs between the deposition, the confirmation, and the confrontation of the witness savors of bad faith or is clearly the result of want of knowledge."[1] Better sense could not be uttered; but Pussort said "that so far it has been considered an invariable rule, established by the authors and sanctioned by usage, that no man who has taken two oaths in the presence of the court can change with impunity; . . . that the article had been considered necessary for the public safety, and, far from being productive of perjuries, it would, on the contrary, from the necessity which it would entail upon them of confirming their testimony at the confrontation whether it were true or false, compel the witnesses to be circumspect and not to give their depositions without reflection . . . and that, besides, the essential circumstantial clauses of the article cover everything." The power of certain preconceived ideas is truly astonishing. After having resolved upon the article as Pussort wished, this provision was inserted: "If the accused discovers in the witness's deposition some contradiction or circumstance which could clear up the fact or prove his innocence, he can require the judge to call upon the witness to acknowledge it." This has to-day almost the appearance of a jest.

Although the confrontation could hardly any longer be of use to the accused in contesting the depositions, it was still useful for the pleading of his objections to the witnesses; but the rule introduced in 1539, according to which he was bound to plead his

[1] "Procès-verbal," p. 178.

objections immediately and prior to the reading of the deposition, was retained;[1] he was not allowed to plead them afterwards. That passed without remark. It was a point which had been admitted for a long time. Care was merely taken to declare expressly that the accused could "at any stage of the action plead his objections to the witnesses, provided they were proved by writing" (Arts. 20).

VI. When the informations, interrogations, confirmations, and confrontations were finished, the action was said to be examined ("instruit") and passed from the hands of the examining judge into those of the reporting judge, whose duty it was to analyze the proceedings and to exhibit the results to the whole assembled bench. But first of all the record was intrusted to the king's procurator, so that he might make his final motions.[2] This he was bound "to do immediately." These motions might claim the pronouncement of the penalty, but they might also claim the application of torture or the proof of justificative facts. They were "lodged in writing and sealed," and were not to be opened until later, after the report. They must not "contain the reasons upon which they were based."[3] At this point the report intervened, "When the action has been completely examined, and the king's procurator or fiscal, after having taken communication of it, has sent it back to the clerk of court's office with his motions, sealed, the process shall be remitted to one of the judges, who makes the report of it to the assembled bench."[4] This was extremely important. No doubt the documents of the proceedings were read before the councillors; but how were these magistrates, coming into the matter for the first time, to obtain a thorough knowledge of it? They judged by the report. The reporting judge must therefore "give his opinion first. This is the invariable custom in all the courts, and the reason for it is that the reporting judge is presumed to be better acquainted with the facts of the action than the other officers."[5] The fact that the reporting judge had such great authority made the choice of this magistrate a matter of importance; but it was not a point determined by the Ordinance. In the bailiwicks the criminal lieutenants reported the actions. "They have the right," says Serpillon, "founded on the Edict of May, 1553, to report all the actions in their jurisdiction." He also cites an Edict of 1537 and a multitude of decrees and regulations, which

[1] Tit. XV, Arts. 15 and 16.

[2] Tit. XXIV, Art. 1.

[3] Tit. XXIV, Art. 3.

[4] *Pothier*, "Instr. crim." p. 466.

[5] *Serpillon*, "Code crim." p. 1052.

show that the question of judges' fees was always involved.[1] But, on the other hand, the criminal lieutenant was the examining judge; and the action was thus almost entirely confided to his discretion. This was an abuse which the Ordinance of Blois had aimed at suppressing;[2] but as it only spoke of the Parlements, its provision was not applied to the jurisdictions trying cases in the first instance. It is surprising that those who drew up the Ordinance, usually so solicitous in settling the details of the administration of justice, passed over this point in silence.

No one except the judges was present at the inspection ("visite") of the process, or at the report. Even the "king's people" were expressly excluded.[3] Before proceeding to the judgment, however, the accused was made to appear for the purpose of undergoing another interrogation. This was the first time that the magistrates, with the exception of the examining judge, saw him or heard him speak. When the motion of the public prosecutor demanded corporal punishment, the final interrogation had to take place upon the "sellette" or prisoner's seat.[4] In other cases, it took place "behind the bar of the court-room . . . the accused then stand publicly behind the railing forming the bar."[5] The Ordinance does not mention any necessary formalities other than interrogations upon the prisoner's seat. The abuse had also insinuated itself into several jurisdictions not to hear the accused when there were no motions for corporal punishments. A royal Declaration of the 13th April, 1703, suppressed this abuse. "It never was the spirit of our Ordinance of 1676," it was said, "to deprive accused persons in any case of their natural right to plead orally, nor to take from the judges the means they possess of enlightening themselves regarding the circumstances of actions prosecuted 'extraordinarily.'" The accused must always he heard either upon the prisoner's seat or behind the bar.

It might happen, however, that the examination of the action was not finished. "When, after the inspection of the process and the final interrogation of the accused, the judge comes to the conclusion that the proof is not sufficiently full, and that he is still in doubt as to the judgment which it should entail, then it may happen that these doubts are met by strong presumptions, which

[1] *Op. cit.*, p. 1230 *et seq.*

[2] Art. 130: "The criminal actions brought or examined before the Parlements in the first instance, cannot be reported by him who shall have made the confirmations and the confrontations, and examined the said actions."

[3] Tit. XXIV, Art. 2.

[4] Tit. XIV, Art. 21.

[5] *Serpillon*, "Code crim." p. 682.

arise against the accused in such a way as to make him appear rather more guilty than innocent, and that nothing is wanting for his conviction but his own confession. In this case torture can be ordered. . . . Or, again, it may happen that these doubts make the balance swing in the prisoner's favor, as when he has, in his final interrogation and his confrontation set forth certain facts or furnished certain objections to the witnesses, the proof of which would completely show his innocence. In this case the judge shall, at the request of the accused, or even of his own accord, choose from among these facts or objections those which appear to him to be the most relevant, in order to make them the subject of an inquiry which he shall order by a special judgment, and which is called admitting the accused to his justificative facts." [1] Let us examine both sides of this alternative.

VII. There were more than one variety of this torture, the lamentable progress of which we have related. Looked at from the point of view of intensity of the pain, it is divided into *ordinary torture*, and *extraordinary torture*. The judge always had full power to stop with the first, or to go on to the latter.[2] Looked at from the point of view of the function which it fulfilled, there was the *preparatory torture*, which was used to extort from the accused the confession of his crime, and the *preliminary torture*, which was administered to *condemned persons* to compel them to disclose their accomplices. It is of the preparatory torture that we now speak.

The Ordinance regulated the circumstances under which recourse could be had to torture. It required that the "corpus delicti" be established; and that there should have already been "considerable proof." [3] The decrees sentencing to torture were appealable as a matter of right.[4] The accused, interrogated before being tortured, must be interrogated immediately after, so that it could be seen if he stuck to his confessions. An important point was that "whatever new proof appeared, the accused could not be put twice to the torture for the same fact;" [5] and, if he had been released and entirely withdrawn from the torture, he could not again be put to it." [6] These provisions somewhat alleviated this horrible proceeding; but as a counterbalance the Ordinance sanctioned the torture under reservation of proofs, which had been introduced by judicial decisions, and of which we shall speak later. All this

[1] *Muyart de Vouglans*, "Inst. crim." p. 390.
[2] This calls to mind "the little and the great horse" in the "Registre criminel du Châtelet."
[3] Tit. XIX, Art. 1.
[4] Tit. XIX, Art. 7.
[5] Tit. XIX, Art. 12.
[6] Tit. XIX, Art. 10.

passed without encountering any opposition. It was a natural thing at that period. Lamoignon and Pussort, surprised, no doubt, to find themselves in agreement, both spoke against the preparatory torture, but without pressing the matter, and as if merely to salve their consciences. Pussort declares "that the preparatory torture had, in his opinion, always seemed useless, and that if it was desired to do away with the practice of an ancient custom, it would be found that it is rare that it has drawn the truth from the mouth of a condemned man."

The president "said that he saw great reasons for doing away with it, but that was only his individual opinion."[1] Lamoignon, however, had something more practical to propose. No fixed rule existed as to the mode of administering the torture; the usages of the companies of judges were the only law. Was it not urgent to put an end to all arbitrary action in this respect? "It is to be wished that the method of administering the torture be uniform throughout the whole kingdom, because in certain places it is administered so harshly that he who suffers it is unfitted for work and often remains a cripple for the rest of his life." To that Pussort made this astounding reply: "It was difficult to make torture uniform; . . . the description which it would be necessary to make of it *would be indecent* in an Ordinance; . . . but it is implied in the article that the judges shall take care, when they cause it to be administered, that the persons condemned to it are not made cripples."[2]

Nothing was therefore settled in this respect, and the practices differed as in the past. We find in Muyart de Vouglans the following concise description of the most frequently used methods: "In the Parlement de Paris, the torture is administered in two ways, by water and by the boot." The Parlement, by decree of 18th July, 1707, gave a detailed memorandum in regard to torture, which comprises twenty-three articles. This is a very curious document, wherein everything is provided for.[3] This regulation was adopted in many jurisdictions, but in certain others the old methods were adhered to, "In the Parlement of Brittany it (torture) is administered by squeezing the thumb or the fingers or a leg of the patient with iron machines called 'valets.' . . . In the Parlement of Brittany the naked feet of the sufferer are placed together (he being seated), and attached to a chair in front of a fire. . . . In the Parlement of Besançon, torture

[1] "Procès-verbal," p. 225. [2] "Procès-verbal," p. 224.
[3] See in *Serpillon*, "Code crim." p. 930 *et seq.*

is administered in two ways. The sufferer, whose arms are tied behind his back, is raised into the air by a pulley attached to his bound arms; . . . for the extraordinary torture, a large iron or stone weight is attached to the large toe of each foot, which, when he is raised, remain suspended from his feet." [1] Serpillon, on his side, describing the torture by boiling oil, as it is administered in the Autun presidial, adds, "I do not know of any other court in the province which practises this cruel torture, which is said to have been in vogue of old throughout all France." [2]

As to the preliminary torture, the Ordinance merely declared that "it could be decreed by the judgment."

The old rules as to justificative facts were retained and more explicitly laid down than they had ever been before. "Judges" were "forbidden, even in the courts, to order the proof of any justificative facts, or to hear the witnesses to arrive at such proof, until after the inspection of the process." [3] Nothing could be admitted to proof except "the facts chosen by the judge from among those which the accused shall have set forth in the interrogations and confrontations," and the latter must immediately name the witnesses, who were subpœnaed at the request of the public prosecutor and heard without being seen by the accused. The helplessness of the defense is apparent; it was, however, necessary that the claims which the civil party presented to the judges and the documents relating thereto be communicated to the accused. "A copy of them shall be delivered to the accused, otherwise the claims and documents shall be rejected." [4]

VIII. The next thing was the pronouncement of the judgment. The Ordinance repeats the traditional provisions commanding the judges to give criminal matters the preference over civil causes and forbidding them to try important cases "of an afternoon." [5] But they also contained new and important provisions. In all the jurisdictions where sentence was passed subject to appeal, the sentence must be pronounced by three judges at least "if there are so

[1] *Muyart*, "Inst. crim." p. 403. [2] "Code crim." p. 967.

[3] Tit. XXVIII, Art. 1.

[4] Tit. XXIII, Art. 3. It was asked whether communication of the depositions of the witnesses upon the justificative facts ought to be made to the accused. See *Poullain du Parc*, "Principes du droit français," vol. XI, p. 374. "Article 8 only orders the communication of the inquest to the public prosecutor and the civil party, which leaves room for the belief that the accused cannot demand its communication. This, however, is not an information, but an inquest; and since the civil party ought to have communication of it, it appears unjust to refuse it to the accused. The silence of the Ordinance is not negative of this communication, although it gives rise to a considerable difficulty on the point."

[5] Tit. XXV, Arts. 1 and 9.

many on the bench, or graduates in law, who shall go to the place where the court sits, and where the accused is imprisoned, and who shall be present at the final interrogation."[1] This was an admirable reform, especially considering what manner of judges those of the seigniors were. Lamoignon, however, made some opposition. He still defended the interests of the seigniorial courts. He even wished that it should not be required that the assessors always be graduates in law; "in the minor jurisdictions there might be counsel of good sense and fit to be officers who are nevertheless not graduate." But Pussort successfully replied: "Too great precautions cannot be taken when the lives and honor of the king's subjects are concerned, especially if it is considered that gentlemen might be amenable to the judges of the seigniors, who are all inexperienced and who might easily be bribed."[2]

As to judgments in the last resort, they must always be rendered by seven judges, whether in the case of judgments of examination or judgments on the merits. In default of judges, resort was had to graduates.[3] The accused always had the benefit in the event of a divided court, and the most severe judgment could not be passed in the case of a sentence in the last resort except by a majority of two votes (Art. 12). Montesquieu called the last-mentioned provision a divine law.

The Ordinance fixed a scale of punishments, so as to make it clear what the most severe sentence was.[4] This was very important, in view of the system of arbitrary punishments which governed the ancient law. It is to be noted that torture figured as a punishment in this enumeration, whereas elsewhere it was settled that it was only a method of examination. The real truth of the matter had to be acknowledged. The benefit which this article appeared to insure was not, as a matter of fact, very great. This list of punishments was not complete. Many others were recognized by judicial practice. A perusal of the old authors makes this readily apparent.[5] They were divided into corporal and afflictive punishments, punishments merely afflictive, degrading punishments, and slight punishments which were not degrading.

The Ordinance did not require that the judgment recite the facts found as its basis. The inferior judges, however, "must

[1] Tit. XXV, Art. 10. [2] "Procès-verbal," p. 246. [3] Tit. XXV, Art. 11.

[4] Art. 13: "Next below the punishment of natural death the most severe are those of torture with reservation of proofs in their entirety, the galleys for life, perpetual outlawry, torture without reservation of proofs, the galleys for a term, the lash, the 'amende honorable' and temporary outlawry."

[5] See especially the enumeration given by *Jousse*, "Comment." pp. 208–211.

state the basis of the condemnation or that of the acquittal. Thus, whenever that is lacking (*i.e.* that they do not state the basis) the Parlement or other court annuls the sentence or the judgment; nevertheless it pronounces what is the same thing as the sentence. But the Parlements and courts are not bound by this formality. The decree merely rehearses that the accused is condemned for the crimes are named in the charge." [1]

The old provisions as to the payment of costs were retained. If there was a civil party to the action, they were borne by him; if there was not, by the king or by the seigniors. The accused was never directly condemned in the costs, although the civil party had recourse against him; and when the king paid the costs of the action, a penalty was pronounced against the accused, which constituted a kind of set-off.

The decrees of condemnation had to be executed on the same day they were pronounced. Only in the case of women big with child was the execution delayed until their delivery. The sacrament must be offered to those sentenced to death.[2]

If the accusation was found to be baseless, it would seem that judgment of acquittal should always be pronounced; but that was not the case. When condemnation did not take place, three solutions were possible: *acquittal, putting out of court,* and "further inquiry." Acquittal was the pure and simple rejection of the accusation, and gave the accused the right to proceed for damages against the civil party. The "out of court" was a less complete acquittal: "when the accused is not discharged acquitted, but merely sent out of court, he cannot claim damages, not, being completely absolved. This kind of judgment leaves the accused under suspicion; he escapes through lack of proof." [3] This kind of judgment was, however, allowed only in the supreme courts.[4] Lastly, the "further inquiry" was merely a provisional acquittal; "this last appears to be the safest and most regular of all, as being the most conformable to the spirit of the Ordinance, and it should take place when there are not enough proofs to condemn, and still enough to prevent acquittal."[5] It was either for a time or indefinite: "the 'further inquiry' for a time is given for crimes which are not absolutely atrocious or the presumptions of which are slight; it also takes place in all cases where there is no other party than the king's procurator or that

[1] *Rousseau de Lacombe,* "Mat. crim." p. 437.
[2] Tit. XXV, Arts. 23 and 24.
[3] *Serpillon,* "Code crim." p. 409.
[4] *Ibid.,* "Code crim." p. 1069.
[5] *Muyart,* "Inst. crim." p. 362.

of the seigniors, and where it would have been proper to put out of court, if there has been a civil party . . . the indefinite 'further inquiry,' on the contrary, is only pronounced in serious cases and where the presumptions are strong. The effect of this is to cause the accused always to remain 'incerti et dubii status,' and the public prosecutor can, if new proofs are discovered, again take up the prosecution against him . . . it is the punishment, not of the crime, but of the presumptions and of the strong indications, not purged."[1] It seems that any one once taken in the coils of this procedure must of necessity leave behind him something of his honor and his liberty.

IX. The Ordinance devoted an entire title (Title XXVI) to *appeals* ("appellations"), and here it was apparently generous. The accused could appeal from all the judge's decisions, not merely from the judgments on the merits, but also from the preliminary and interlocutory judgments of examination.[2] In the case of a condemnation to an afflictive punishment, the appeal was taken directly before the courts; in other cases it was taken to the bailiwicks or to the courts "at the choice and option of the accused." For certain very serious condemnations to corporal punishments, the galleys, perpetual outlawry, the "amende honorable," the appeal was *a matter of right* and the cause was necessarily brought before the courts.[3]

The appeal might offer some resource to the accused. The procedure was not necessarily secret nor the aid of counsel absolutely forbidden. It appears, at least before the Ordinance of 1670, that one distinction must be made. If a sentence entailing afflictive punishment or torture was involved, the action on appeal was continued in the same forms as in the first instance and without counsels' speeches. The other appeals, on the contrary, and especially those from the decisions of examination, were judged in the same form as the civil appeals;[4] if the appellant chose the oral procedure, the "oral appeal,"[5] instead of the written procedure, as he was entitled to do, they were judged in court and upon counsels' speeches. The Ordinance of 1670 ratified this practice. Article 2 of Title XXVI declares, in effect, "that appeals from permission to inform, decrees, and all other examinations shall be brought in the hearing of our courts and judges." But it was sought to restrict this provision, which had only been pre-

[1] *Muyart*, "Inst. crim." p. 363.
[2] Tit. XXVI, Art. 1.
[3] Tit. XXVI, Art. 6.
[4] "Pratique de Boyer," pp. 117, 119.
[5] *Ibid.*, pp 220, 221.

scribed to accelerate the judgment of appeals upon the measures of examination. "The appeals from judgments of examination, or preliminary judgments," says Muyart de Vouglans, "should be brought before the courts and judges at public hearing. Consequently, the appeal from *interlocutory judgments*, which are not mentioned in this article, should, like that from final judgments, be judged in the chamber with closed doors and be subject to judges' fees, in the same way as those in written actions."[1] This power was, moreover, rendered almost illusory by the article of the Ordinance which provided that "no appeal can prevent or retard the execution of the decrees, the examination, and the judgment."[2] If the action was judged with sufficient celerity on the merits, the incidental appeal was judged at the same time and in the same form as the appeal upon the merits.[3] Here, however, one door was open to the defense. It was possible to plead his cause, not upon the merits, but upon an incident; only, he must not delay, and credit and money were necessary for this. "In the lower criminal courts, and in the debates created by various incidents relative to appeals and certain acts of examination, the counsel's speech will, erelong, be admitted. President Séguier also remarked that the Tournelle has granted hearing 'subsequently and for a very long time.' The 'feuilles d'audience' prove this custom."[4]

The only safeguard which the accused found in the procedure of appeal from final judgments in the actions sent to the criminal side was the higher standing of the magistrates. There was no real argument. Attorney-General Séguier is compelled to acknowledge "that the Ordinance limits almost all the appeal procedure to interrogating the accused upon the prisoner's seat or behind the bar."[5] — "This interrogation in the court is the time

[1] "Inst. crim." p. 832.

[2] Tit. XXVI, Art. 3.

[3] *Serpillon*, "Code crim." p. 1141: "This article does not indicate that the appeals which it mentions shall be adjudged at the hearing; it only provides that they may be brought there; this leaves the judge at liberty, when a final judgment has intervened in the court of first instance after the appeal, to judge by writing in case of appeal. It is proper then to decide not only upon the examination, but also upon the appeal from the final judgment rendered, on a consideration of the documents. Although that rule is not observed in the jurisdiction of the Parlement of Paris, we in Burgundy are accustomed to follow it."

[4] "Notice sur les archives du Parlement de Paris," by *A. Grün*, in *Boutaric*, "Actes du Parlement," vol. I, p. 227. — There was, however, a tendency to restore the inferior criminal courts to the purely written procedure: "In Burgundy, minor crimes are often tried by written proceedings" (*Serpillon*, p. 977). We note, conversely, that there was still trial in court and pleadings when a monitory was issued and an objection was lodged to its publication.

[5] "Réquisitoire de 1786," p. 157.

for the accused to allege his complaints against the sentence, and consequently his justification. This is the reason that the clause, 'Heard the accused as to his reasons for appeal and crime imputed to him' is always put into the decrees."[1] In this respect, most of all, the reporting judge was all-powerful. It must not be forgotten, besides, that those accused of "prévôtal" and presidial crimes were tried in the last resort by the provost marshals or the presidials.

The prosecution, on its side, could appeal. "The king's procurators or procurators-fiscal may appeal 'a minima' from sentences which they do not consider to be in proportion to the kind and seriousness of the crimes, and in that respect do not conform to their motions."[2] The civil party could also appeal "on account of an inadequate award of civil reparation, civil interests, or damages." In those cases where the appeal was not a matter of right the different parties could make it, so long as the action had not undergone limitation, but waiver of this right and acquiescence in the judgment was allowed.

The appeal was, in general, suspensive (we refer to the appeal lodged, not to the period granted to make it). If a sentence of condemnation was involved, the execution of the punishments was suspended; but pecuniary punishments were executed provisionally, provided they did not exceed a certain amount.[3] Where decisions of examination were involved, on the other hand, the appeal was not suspensive; the only exception was when the execution of the decree would have caused irreparable damage, as in the case of sentences to torture. The custom of "decrees forbidding the continuation of the examination" was not totally abrogated; but it was restricted.[4] As to judgments of acquittal, in the case of appeal by the public prosecutor, the accused must remain in prison, and if "the appeal 'a minima' has not been lodged until after the prisoner shall have been released and freed from imprisonment at the time of the pronouncing of the judgment, the prisoner shall be bound to be in readiness at the time of the judgment of the action."[5] If the civil party alone had appealed, the appeal proceeded as in a civil action. In regard to details, the Ordinance minutely regulated the procedure as to the appeal; it also restricted the right of evocation of the courts.[6]

[1] "Réquisitoire de 1786," p. 159.
[2] *Rousseau de Lacombe*, "Matières crim." p. 481.
[3] Tit. XXV, Art. 6.
[4] Tit. XXVI, Art. 4.
[5] *Rousseau de Lacombe*, "Mat. crim." p. 480.
[6] Tit. XXVI, Art. 5.

X. A final recourse might be available to the condemned person, but it was not mentioned in the Ordinance, for the reason which we shall state. This was the recourse to the king's council, the application for a writ of error. The judgments of the supreme courts were final and, on principle, could not be attacked. They might, however, be annulled, thanks to a theory which plays a great part in ancient law, and of which we shall have to speak very soon, that of *justice reserved.* All justice resided in the king and emanated from him. In delegating its exercise to his officers, he none the less retained the plenitude of it within himself, and could quash decisions, including those of the supreme courts.[1] But the appeal could only be based on a violation of the law. "It is equally permissible to claim the quashing of a judgment when it has been rendered contrary to the provisions of the Ordinances and the customary law. The reason of this is that the supreme courts are no less under the obligation to observe the laws than the inferior judges."[2] Attorney-General Séguier, in one of his addresses to the court, which we have quoted several times, explains the doctrine at length. "The legislature has not forgotten that the dignity of the magistracy does not shield it from the deceptions and weaknesses common to human nature. It has recognized, probably by personal experience, that to err is human, and that even the most careful of men may make mistakes, without being subject to the accusation of bias or betrayal of his trust. The law, the guaranty of the rules made by itself, jealous, at the same time, of the forms which it has sanctioned, and in which alone it recognizes its work, has, from an excess of precaution, thought fit to allow, after all the stages of jurisdiction have been exhausted, recourse still to the Sovereign himself, in cases where judgment has been rendered contrary to the provision of the Ordinances, and in all those where the prescribed forms have not been exactly observed. Every condemned man has thus a way of escape from the condemnation."[3] The application was brought before the privy council "consisting of the Chancellor, four secretaries of State, State councillors, and masters of requests, who serve in it by rotation . . . the masters of requests report the matters to the privy

[1] Before the theory of appeal to the court of cassation took shape, there existed another method of attacking the decrees of the supreme courts, namely, the *assignments of error*, which, moreover, lasted for a long time concurrently with the recourse to the court of cassation, and which the Ordinance of 1667 abrogated. See *Guyot*, "Répertoire," under "Cassation."

[2] *Guyot*, "Répertoire," see "Cassation."

[3] "Réquisitoire de 1786," p. 9.

council."[1] Refusal of the application followed, or quashing and remand to a new jurisdiction, according to the particular case. The procedure was settled in a definite fashion by the regulation of the Council of 28th June, 1738, the provisions of which, as we know, have partly passed into our modern legislation. In criminal matters, this regulation required the deposit of a penalty and the "mise en état," provisions which were adopted by our Code of Criminal Examination.

This was, to all appearance, a powerful weapon to place in the hands of the accused. These proceedings, written and bristling with formalities, were bound to be very often riddled with errors rendering them null, and memorials could be presented to the king's council, which were unfailingly published.[2] Yet, it amounted to nothing. The possibility of bringing this recourse was often the result only of royal favor. In effect, the appeal to quash, when brought, did not stay the execution of the judgment. In civil actions, it did not prevent the claim from producing its result, execution having no irreparable consequences. In criminal proceedings, the hand of the executioner had often intervened before it had been possible to reach the king's council. An additional favor of His Majesty was necessary before a quashing was possible, in the shape of an order from the sovereign staying the execution. "In civil actions, the judgment which is attacked is executed all the same; but in criminal matters, the extraordinary remedy of appeal to the sovereign should be preceded by a suspension of execution of the judgment, because it is not in the power of the magistrates to suspend the condemnation which they have pronounced."[3] This saving order intervened frequently. The last years of the absolute monarchy are not alone in offering frequent examples of it.[4] In order to obtain it, influential entreaties were necessary, or some happy chance, such as the passage of some

[1] *Guyot*, "Répert.," see "Conseil." He remarks that "no petition to quash can be brought before the council until it has been first communicated to the commissioners generally appointed for the investigation of claims in cassation."

[2] *Guyot*, "Répert.," under "Cassation." "No request may be distributed, nor consultation nor memorial printed relative to claims in cassation, before these claims have been ordered to be communicated. This is why advocates in the Council are forbidden to sign writings of this kind. The parties or their counsel can only distribute among commissioners or other judges their pleadings in manuscript."

[3] *Séguier*, "Réquisitoire," cited pp. 9, 10.

[4] See, for instance, "Correspondance administrative sous Louis XIV," vol. II, p. 184, dealing with sorcerers condemned to be burned alive; the courier arrives on the very day appointed for the execution; p. 190 deals with the case of a woman who was hanged and survived; *cf.* p. 206.

great personage through the province. Frequently, the messenger who bore the order did not, as in the old tales, arrive until the scaffold was already prepared.[1] The application for a writ of error was the only method of extraordinary recourse available against criminal judgments in the last resort. They could not, in effect, be attacked by the bill of review.[2]

XI. The procedure by contumacy which the Ordinance contains is that of the prior law, simplified and stated precisely. If it was found impossible to execute the warrant for the arrest of the accused, search for his person and an inventory of his property might be made. Then came a subpœna at a fortnight's notice, and a summons at a week's, by a single public proclamation; any other delay was forbidden.[3] Next, a judgment intervened upon the motions of the public prosecutor, ordering the confirmation of the witnesses, which was equivalent to confrontation. Finally, "the same judgment shall declare the contumax properly examined, make the award, and contain the condemnation of the accused."

The essentially revocable nature of the judgment of contumacy was clearly shown by the prohitition to insert the clause "If taken and apprehended can be." Instead of real execution, that being impossible, an execution in effigy was organized for capital punishment, for some other punishments posting up upon a list in a public place, or still others the service of the judgment at the accused's residence. This was a matter of great importance; it made the periods begin to run, at the expiration of which serious forfeitures were incurred.

At whatever period the condemned person might present himself,

[1] This is what we read in a Memorial which we shall examine later; "Come to your senses," the abbé said to him, "all is not lost; try to tell your story; the keeper of the seals is here;" [which was the case], "I shall have him present a request by a person having due credit at the French court. . . . The wisdom of the legislature, and the vigilance of the worthy chief justice sent to M. the Marquis of Belbœuf, procurator general to the Parlement of Rouen, the order to stay the execution. . . . It was time, for the orders were given and the execution fixed for the next day" (Mémoire de Lecauchois, pp. 7, 8, 11).

[2] The contrary would seem to result from certain testimonies of our old jurisconsults; see *Muyart de Vouglans*, "Institutes," p. 368. But that should be understood only in the case where the action follows the "ordinary" form, that of civil actions. *Jousse* explains it very well: "One can also appeal by bill of review against the decrees and judgments in the last resort rendered in criminal matters, although final, *when they have been rendered in public hearing*, and generally against all those of examination" ("Commentaire sur l'Ordonnance," p. 329). — *Guyot*, "Répert." Voce "Revision": "Letters of revision are in criminal matters very nearly what bills of review are in civil matters." *Cf. Dupaty*, "Moyens de droit," p. 67.

[3] Tit. XVII, Arts. 7–10.

as long as the action was not prescribed, the judgment by contumacy dropped as a matter of law;[1] but at the end of a year or of five years certain effects remained. At the end of a year, the accrued profits on the personal property of the contumax and the purchase price arising from the sale of his movables were finally lost to him; at the end of five years, "the pecuniary condemnations, penalties, and confiscations, were regarded as awarded after hearing, and ranked as if ordered by judgment."[2] Civil death was then incurred in a definite fashion if the punishment carried by the judgment was of a character to warrant it.

When the contumacy was purged, the confrontation of the witnesses with the accused was proceeded with, notwithstanding that it had already been declared in a judgment that the confirmation was equivalent to confrontation.[3] If, however, the witnesses had died, or if it was impossible to confront them, their depositions remained admissible; only a confrontation on paper was made, and the only possible objections to witnesses were those supported by documentary evidence. If the accused had been captured at the outset, and had escaped, but only since his interrogation, the action continued confrontatively, notwithstanding his absence.[4]

Besides the procedures which we have sketched, which were the normal ones, the Ordinance described several followed in exceptional cases. These were the actions brought against deaf and dumb persons,[5] those brought against communities, — cities, towns, villages, corporations, and societies; and, finally, the odious prosecutions which the ancient law sometimes directed against the corpse or the memory of a deceased person.[6]

§ 4. **Reserved Justice, and Letters from the King.** — Such were the rules of criminal procedure according to the Ordinance of 1670; but certain circumstances might interfere with it or stop its course.

In ancient France it was quite true to say that all justice emanated from the king. Although he had undoubtedly delegated its exercise to the judicial officers, he could intervene whenever he chose. This was the theory of *reserved justice;* and it gave rise to *letters of mercy* (" lettres de grâce ") emanating from the king, a generic term embracing numerous varieties. " Nothing was more worthy of the good-will of our kings than the reservation they made

[1] Tit. XVII, Art. 28.

[2] Down to that time the parties had been entitled to sue for payment of their damages, but on giving security (*Serpillon*, p. 870). This system was very simple and it obviated many difficulties which present themselves under the existing law.

[3] Tit. XVII, Art. 10.

[4] Tit. XVIII, Art. 24.

[5] Tit. XVIII.

[6] Tit. XXII.

of this power, at the same time that they intrusted to the magistrates the care of rendering justice to their subjects; it is equivalent to saying that the power of the latter is, above all, limited to pursue the crime, to pronounce the punishments and see that they are executed; but that the prosecutions, the condemnations, and the execution cease immediately it pleases the monarch to interpose his authority and to declare the crime and the accusation to be extinct."[1] That was not all. The king, as the depository of omnipotence, could not only stay the course of justice; but could also supplement his action in a mysterious way by means of "lettres de cachet." Let us examine these two kinds of letters a little more minutely.

The term "grâce," mercy, or king's pardon, according to Jousse, is a generic term embracing all the letters emanating directly from the sovereign power.[2] There were numerous kinds of them, and the Ordinance carefully specified them all, but they all belonged to two types. The first of these appeared after a sentence pronounced, for the purpose of staying its execution. The others, more forcible, stopped all procedure and even obliterated the crime. The latter corresponded to what we call to-day an act of amnesty, with this difference, that they were granted in the interest of a mere private individual.

The most important of the letters of mercy were those of *royal pardon* ("abolition"). "These are they which His Majesty grants for private individuals, accused of crimes which, according to the provision of the laws and ordinances of the kingdom, deserve capital punishment. They are only granted in rare cases and for weighty reasons, and are only given out in the office of the great seal." They usually intervened before the sentence; however, "as the king declares that he pardons the crime, no matter how it happened . . . they could be obtained even before the judgment of condemnation."[3] The *letters of remission* ("lettres de rémission") were of rather a curious character; they were granted for "involuntary homicides only, or those which had been committed under the necessity of a lawful defense of one's life." What was the necessity for these letters of remission when lawful self-defense excluded all culpability? The reason was that in France, at that period, "although the crime had been committed for reasonable

[1] *Muyart*, "Inst." p. 103.

[2] "Comment." p. 322. They were distinguished from *letters of justice* properly so called, like those of appeal, or of bills of review, which were, so to speak, mere formalities of procedure.

[3] *Muyart*, "Inst." p. 110.

cause and under the necessity of lawful self-defense, one could be punished for homicide in the absence of letters of remission." [1] For involuntary or accidental homicide, the same thing was allowed. At bottom this was nothing but a fiscal proceeding. There was also another kind of letters of remission. This was a reproduction of letters of royal pardon (" lettres d'abolition ") couched in different terms. The *letters of pardon* (" lettres de pardon ") were granted for those crimes " which do not involve the punishment of death, but which, nevertheless, cannot be excused." All these letters, which arrested the course of justice, constituted one of the plagues of the Old Régime, and the States-General had often protested against this abuse; [2] but it had not been able to obtain anything but the declarations contained in the Ordinances, by which the king renounced his right of pardon in the more serious cases. The Ordinance of 1670 contained an enumeration of this class of crimes.[3]

The other letters which remain to be mentioned did not intervene until after the condemnation. These were, first of all, the letters *to be at law*, " pour ester à droit," which were necessary to the contumax five years after the execution by effigy, in order to prevent the confiscation of his property; then the letters of *recall from banishment of the galleys*, " ban de galères," and the letters of *commutation of punishment*, " commutation de peine," similar to the letters of pardon in force to-day; the letters of *rehabilitation*, " réhabilitation," granted for the purpose of reinstating the condemned in his honor and his property; in them it is always presumed that he had satisfied the punishment, and paid the civil damages; they are obtained for those who have died as well as for living persons. " Finally came the *letters of rehearing* ' lettres de révision,' granted by the king for the reëxamination and new trial of a criminal action, either on account of defects of nullity in regard to form, with which it may be tainted, or because of the apparent injustice in substance which it contains. These perform the same duty in criminal actions as the letters in the form of a bill of review do in civil actions." [4]

Although all these letters constituted the exercise of *reserved justice*, they were, however, connected with the delegated jurisdiction in so far that they had to be enrolled and ratified, " entéri-

[1] *Rousseau de Lacombe*, p. 83; *cf. Muyart*, "Inst." p. 542. This was not quite in accordance with the theory which proposed to class lawful self-defense among the justificative facts. See *Jousse*, p. 495.

[2] See *Picot*, I, p. 121; II, 191, 555, 556; III, 186; IV, 84.

[3] Tit. XVI, Art. 4.

[4] *Muyart*, "Inst." p. 114.

nées," by the tribunals; to wit, by the courts, if gentlemen were concerned, and by the presidials and bailiwicks, if plebeians were concerned (Arts. 12 and 13). This ratification was not always a mere formality. In certain cases, the judges were required to make certain whether the letters "conform to the charges and informations," and if there was not agreement between them in this respect they proceeded with the judgments; "His Royal Majesty having been deceived, the crime which is then prosecuted is not the one which His Majesty has pardoned." It was the same in the case of the letters of royal pardon, remission, and pardon. If, on the other hand, the crime was heinous, or especially if it was one of those in regard to which the king had renounced his right of pardon, the tribunals could present protests, the courts to the king directly, and the other jurisdictions to the Chancellor. In the cases of letters of recall from condemnation to the galleys, commutation of punishment, and rehabilitation, they must be ratified "without inquiring as to whether they conformed to the charges and informations, except as regards the right of representation"; but as a guaranty of good faith, the decree or judgment of condemnation had to be attached "under the counter-seal of these letters." The Ordinance originated a kind of litigious procedure for the ratification of the letters, in which the private prosecutor and the public prosecutor took part. The letters of rehearing gave rise to a regular action. It was necessary, in order to obtain them, to bring an action before the king's council (Arts. 8–10).

The "*lettres de cachet*" constituted a very much more strenuous act of the royal power. They derived their name from their form. "This is a letter written by order of the king, countersigned by a secretary of State, and sealed with the king's seal."[1] They might contain all sorts of commands, and especially an order of exile or of imprisonment. "The king being looked upon as the fountain head of all justice, has the peculiar privilege of being able to dispose of the liberty and property of citizens without trial, at his own free will."[2] And it must be understood that it was not a matter of addressing these letters to courts of justice; we are here in the domain of the king's good pleasure. "This description of letter is carried to its destination by some police officer; . . . the person who is commissioned to deliver the letter makes a kind

[1] *Guyot*, "Répert." voce "Lettre de cachet." See *Mirabeau*, "Des lettres de cachet et des prisons d'État." A work composed in 1778, Hamburg 1782 (all the first part).

[2] *Laboulaye*, "Revue des Cours littéraires," year 1868, p. 9.

of official report as to the execution of his trust."[1] We are aware of the use to which royalty put this lamentable expedient. The criminal laws were silent on the point. A thing which is essentially arbitrary is not a subject for regulation. Protests were, however, often raised, and sometimes from high places. Malesherbes, especially, speaking for the Court of Accounts, once presented to Louis XV a protest of great force;[2] and the Parlement, in the strifes which disquieted the reign of that king and which recent researches have laid bare, come to the point of disputing the "lettres de cachet." In 1753 (April), while speaking of certain protests, the lawyer Barbier thus expresses himself: "Particular mention is made of the article regarding 'lettres de cachet.' This article goes the length of impugning the authority of all the ministers, and, besides, also attacks the king personally, as if it presumed that he would sign 'lettres de cachet' without knowing what he was doing, or that the ministers would have it in their power to issue them without consulting the king."[3] He says again, the same year: "The protest of the Parlement of Rouen has not yet been printed, but the Jansenists have spread the reasons for this protest through Paris. The reasons given cannot be the true ones, seeing that it openly attacks the sovereign authority. It is expressly said that the king is not entitled to make use of 'lettres de cachet' except in regard to his ministers and household officers, but not against any private subject; that if such an one is guilty or suspected of being guilty in any matter, the king should leave him to justice to be tried by the courts and according to law."[4]

Another manifestation of the sovereign power was the appointment by the king of commissaries charged with the trial of criminal actions, or the *evocations* which he made of them to his council. "In France a distinction is made between commissaries appointed by the king and those appointed by the courts and other judges. . . . The general commission is granted by letters from the chancellor's office and only the king can grant it. The king alone can grant extraordinary commissions, and these commissions must contain the extent and limits of the authority granted to the commissaries. Any description of private individual can be selected by the sovereign either to judge or to reverse. . . . The commissaries so appointed should publish their letters of com-

[1] *Guyot, loc. cit.*
[2] See *Laboulaye,* "Revue des Cours littéraires," 1864, p. 643.
[3] "Journal," VI, p. 368.
[4] "Journal," V, p. 415.

mission at the place where they intend to use them, especially when it is a question of doing some act of justice or of severity. If they do not do so, one may refuse to obey them. In the examination and judgment of the matters in regard to which they have been appointed, they are bound to act in conformity with the laws and Ordinances of the kingdom in the same manner as other judges. No appeal is allowed from a judgment of commissaries appointed by the king unless they have exceeded the limits of their commission. . . . When they are appointed for the trial of any criminal matter they may set aside their procedure if it is defective and order its recommencement. Extraordinary commissions, moreover, are considered a dangerous expedient. For that reason they are not readily permitted by the Parlements."[1] We know of what abuses royalty sometimes made this institution the medium, and the States-General frequently protested against it.

[1] *Guyot*, "Répert." voce "Commissaires."

CHAPTER III

THEORY OF PROOF

§ 1. **Proofs under the Customary Law.** — The criminal procedure which has been the subject of our study, that terrible mechanism which was gradually organized until it reached its utmost tension in the Ordinance of 1670, must, in order to be properly understood, be correlated with the theory of proof which was formulated during the same period. This theory is the system known in the history of law as that of *legal proofs*. Its chief essential is that, before the judge can condemn, he must bring together certain predetermined proofs; but, on the other hand, confronted with these proofs, he must, of necessity, condemn; in either case, his personal opinion goes for nothing. The leading maxim of the ancient law in this respect is that judgment must be rendered "secundum allegata et probata."[1] The judge may be likened to a harpsichord, responsive according to the particular keys which are struck. This tyranny of proof was invoked as a necessary counterbalance to the inquisitorial and secret character of the procedure, and it would appear as though such proof, "clearer than the sun at noonday," was required in the interests of the defense. But, on the other hand, the theory of legal proofs bound still more firmly the fetters of the criminal procedure by rendering the conviction of the guilty person more difficult to obtain; the double movement led inevitably in the same direction.

The system was of gradual growth. Its primitive elements were found by the bailiffs and provosts in the texts of the Roman law; but it was in existence in all its power at the time when the

[1] *Loysel*, "Inst. cout." Title on Judgments, rule 11. — "Nec præsumant judices judicare secundum eorum conscientias, ut faciunt Veneti juris et justitiæ ignari, sed solum secundum leges et jura et probationes sibi factas, licet aliud viderunt oculata fide, vel habeant in conscientia sua quantum sit probatum, nisi eis esset notum et judici." *Constantin*, "Comment. de l'Ord. de 1539," p. 238. — "It is not enough that the judge is as thoroughly convinced as any reasonable man could be by a collection of presumptions and facts leading to presumptions. This is a most erroneous way of judging, and is really nothing but the expression of a more or less *based* opinion." *Poullain du Parc*, "Principes du droit français," vol. XI, p. 112.

jurists took the place of the "men judgers," in the feudal courts. When a body of permanent magistrates has for a long period had the sole administration of the criminal law, the slow formation of a system of legal proof is inevitable; and on the improbable assumption of the disappearance of the jury from our system of laws, we might expect to witness the revival of this subtilty and casuistry, at present so remote.

The Ordinance of 1670 did not expressly state these minute and complex rules; but it took them for granted. Such a statement would have been inappropriate in a legislative statute; but notwithstanding the fact that they are only to be found in the books on doctrine and judicial practice, these rules had none the less the authority of regular laws. We shall briefly inquire into the introduction of these principles into our law, explain the theory as it developed in the 1600s and the 1700s, and show how it harmonized with the forms of the procedure.

(1) Although, in the feudal procedure, the proofs were of a rude nature — often rather irrational — their appreciation was easy; the judge, a mere spectator, had, as a general rule, only to establish one material fact. The confession was the most complete proof, even obviating the necessity for any further procedure; but neither force nor subterfuge was employed to obtain it. This feature the English procedure still retains. If the accused pleaded not guilty, recourse was had either to the judicial duel or to witnesses. In the former case, victory or defeat in the combat dispelled all doubt. In the latter, the testimony originally consisted of a set formula; there was no weighing of the evidence by the judge. Nothing could be simpler than such methods of proof, and their very simplicity made them acceptable to the uncultured intellects of the time, puzzled by the problem of proving and placing beyond all doubt a thing denied. The list of proofs did not, however, end with these. Presumptions were also recognized. These were, however, equally simple, rude, and, so to speak, formal. Thus, it was held that an accused prisoner who made his escape thereby acknowledged his guilt. "When any one imprisoned on suspicion of a crime makes his escape a presumption is raised so clear as to be equivalent to proof of the fact; for his flight raises such a strong presumption that he did not dare to stand law that he is punished for the crime if he is recaptured." [1] — "Those arrested, charged with or suspected of any offense, who make their escape or break bounds, and are seized

[1] *Beaumanoir*, XXXIX, 15 (Salmon, 1160); XXX, 13 (Salmon, 836).

beyond their bounds, are convicted of the offense for which they were arrested and punished according to the offense." [1] In the same way, repeated defaults, leading to outlawry, in the procedure for contumacy, are considered by the custumal law-writers as equivalent to an irrebuttable presumption of guilt.[2]

In the special proceedings which took place when the person under suspicion accepted the inquest by the country, the judge doubtless had a freer appreciation and a more delicate task; but we have hardly any information about this form of judgment, which was destined to disappear from our law at an early date.

When the Ordinance of 1260 suppressed the formal testimony produced in open court, the theory of proof was thereby altered. The judge had to weigh the deposition; but the old principle was retained, whereby two eye-witnesses agreeing upon the facts were required for a condemnation. The "aprise" in particular, augmenting, as it did, the powers of the judge, exercised a great influence upon the development of the theory of proof.[3] From the very outset there was an evident disposition to be very exacting as to the proof, but at the same time judicial practice strove to devise means of finding combinations of presumptive evidence which had been thus far overlooked. Presumptions were made the chief study.

Some of the ancient presumptions and the ancient proofs lost their force. This happened very soon in regard to the confession; alone and unsupported, it no longer constituted a complete proof. This was because it was not free and spontaneous, but extorted by skilful questionings, and it is a rule which allows of hardly any exceptions in the history of law that the confession does not constitute a complete proof against the guilty party except where it is absolutely voluntary. It would even seem, according to one authority, that at a certain period both confession and testimony were required jointly for a condemnation, but the passage in the "Livre des Droiz," making this assertion, should not be considered as going farther than to demonstrate the decreasing force of the confession among the methods of proof.[4] The pre-

[1] "Livre des Droiz," § 333.

[2] *Beaumanoir*, XXXIX, 16 (Salmon, 1161); XXX, 13 (Salmon, 836). "Livre des Droiz," § 331. This is the period when contumacy resulted in a condemnation for the offense and no longer in mere outlawry.

[3] See *Beaumanoir*, XXXIX, 12, 13, 14 (Salmon, 1157, 1158, 1159).

[4] § 644: "The law is that if a man is condemned to death by any court of law, he, or some of his lineage on his behalf, can appeal to the supreme judge. . . . And the law provides that if he who is condemned is not convicted *by confession and witnesses* his sentence is null and void; *and if there should have been confession without witnesses or witnesses without con-*

sumption of guilt flowing from contumacy also diminished, and it was in course of time held that the judge should not, in that case, necessarily pass sentence. The flight of the prisoner became no longer an insuperable imputation against him.

On the other hand, however, new presumptions, firmer and more subtle than the old, were introduced. Very few of these, it is true, were of such a nature as to ground a condemnation upon. Beaumanoir divides them into two classes, as follows: "Some can make the fact so clear that it is proven by the presumptions, and the others are so doubtful that they do not of themselves prove the offense." [1] Among the first he specifies several the force of which never diminished, — that, for instance, which consists, in the case of manslaughter, in the fact that two witnesses have seen the accused in flight holding in his hand a naked and bloody sword.[2] But others grew weaker, such as that which consists in the fact that threats were uttered before the crime. The utterer of the threats, when he denied them, was regarded as the perpetrator of the crime, "when a threat is made and, after the threat, the thing is done of which the threat gave promise." [3] Very soon this was nothing more than a "proximate presumption." But the number of presumptions strong enough to cause the condemnation of a man was exceeding limited, and whatever the number of other presumptions might be, they could not effect a condemnation. "No one should be punished on account of presumption alone, unless the presumption is very plain, as we have said before, although there may be many probable presumptions against the prisoner." [4]

fession, and *both of these should not have concurred*, the sentence shall be unlawful."

[1] *Beaumanoir*, XXXIX, 11 (Salmon, 1156).

[2] "They saw Jehan leave the throng carrying a naked and bloody knife, and heard the man who was slain say: 'He has killed me.' And in this 'aprise' it was impossible to prove this notorious crime except by presumption, for no one saw the blow dealt; nevertheless the said Jehan was sentenced and executed on that presumption." XXXIX, 12 (Salmon, 1157).

[3] *Beaumanoir*, XXXIX, 13, 14 (Salmon, 1158, 1159). — "Ancienne coutume de Bourgogne," Art. 53: "Also, if I threaten any one personally or as to his property and subsequently injury and damage happen to him, and I deny threatening him and he proves it, the judge shall have and hold as proven what has been done to the threatened person; and if I confess to having threatened him, and swear that no injury or damage has happened to him by me or mine, although I have threatened him, such threats will not avail him; and if after I have so sworn he offers to prove that injury and damage has happened to him through the said threats, he shall not prove it by witnesses nor by inquest but by wager of battle." *Ch. Giraud*, "Essai sur l'histoire du droit français," II, p. 278.

[4] *Ibid.*, XXXIX, 18 (Salmon, 1162).

Such a theory, marked probably by exaggerated scruples, could not have been other than worthy of approbation had it not been that the judge, finding his way barred by these accumulated obstacles, hit upon a means of surmounting them. This means, as we have already said, was torture. When there was but a single eye-witness testifying against the accused, or when a very strong, but not, according to the law, irrebuttable presumption existed, the court, placed as it was between the two alternatives, either to allow a man whom it thought guilty to escape, or to complete its proof at all hazards, did not hesitate to have recourse to torture.

The jurists thought to find, and, indeed, did, to a considerable extent find, these new principles in the texts of the Digest and the Code. At Rome, as long as the jurors of the "quæstiones perpetuæ" continued to be the judges, no very precise theory of proof was developed. The rhetoricians had merely distinguished a certain number of rules for the facilitation of the drawing up of pleadings and the greater assurance of oratorical success. But when the power of judging passed into the hands of permanent magistrates, a theory of legal proofs began to see the light of day, along with the principle of arbitrary punishments and the resource of appeal. This result was due to judicial practice, and the jurisconsults of the period contributed exclusively to the formation of the theory although it never attained perfect development.[1] It was very soon agreed that the confession should not constitute a complete proof unless it was supported by corroborative evidence.[2] The causes which could result in the rejection of evidence were determined, thus limiting the judge's unrestricted rating of the evidence; we even find traces of a classification of presumptions and the rudiments of a doctrine of written proof. The use of torture is also governed by settled rules, showing, on the one hand, that it is a resource which should only be employed on the failure of all others, and on the other hand, that forcible presumptions must be found before it is allowed.[3]

These are the principles which the authors of the 1400s and the 1500s set out in detail and in so doing developed and expanded; they constructed from them a theory which was certainly no more than "in gremio" in the Roman laws. This theory, for which

[1] *Geib*, "Geschichte der Röm. Criminalprozess bis auf Justinian," p. 611 *et seq.*
[2] Book 1, §§ 17, 27, D. 48, 18.
[3] Book 8, pr. Book 1, § 1. Book 18, § 2. Book 20, D. 48, 18.

thanks are due chiefly to the Italian criminal law-writers, imposed itself wherever the inquisitorial procedure was introduced. We find certain traces of it in Bouteiller, and the Ordinance of 1498 owes to it, among other provisions, one which is very remarkable. It declares, as we have seen, that if no result has been attainable by the "extraordinary," or criminal proceedings, the parties must be sent to the "ordinary" action, that is, to civil forms of action;[1] this is explicable if we consider that quite special proofs were necessary before pronouncing capital punishment, the normal aim and end of criminal proceedings.

(2) The system of legal proofs was thoroughly settled in the 1500s and the 1600s. It continued in vogue as long as the criminal procedure of the Ordinance lasted; that is to say, down to 1789. We shall attempt to describe it briefly, taking our information principally from Muyart de Vouglans, who has devoted Part VI of his "Institutes du droit criminel" to this subject, summing up and coördinating the theories of the law-doctors, or at least of those who had accepted French judicial practice.

Four methods of proof were recognized: witnesses, the confession, or vocal proof, written documents, or instrumental proof, and presumptions, or conjectural proof.[2] These are, to be sure, found in all systems of law; but these various modes might afford many combinations peculiar to the present system. What was wanted was a complete proof, sufficient to warrant a capital sentence. That was the hypothesis the criminal law-writers always put to themselves, capital crimes constituting, in their opinion, the very foundation of criminal law.[3] The rigor of the rules as to proof was not retained in regard to less grave accusations.[4]

[1] See above, p. 146 *et seq.*

[2] This is impliedly recognized in the Ordinance, Title XXV, Art. 5: "Actions can go to examination and judgment although there is no information, if there is otherwise sufficient proof by the interrogations of the accused or by authenticated documents or documents acknowledged by the accused, or other presumptions and circumstances of the action."

[3] "There being no law authorizing the punishment of innocent persons, a complete proof is essential before capital punishment can be pronounced, no matter what the crime may be, and such proof can be produced only according to the forms prescribed by the law. . . . Failing that, any judgment of condemnation is at least rash; and it may, in a sense, be said that such a judgment is unjust, even when the accused is really guilty." *Poullain du Parc*, vol. XI, pp. 112, 113.

[4] *Poullain du Parc*, vol. XI, p. 116: "In non-capital accusations, it is evident that such strong proofs are not required. . . . But when there are only strong presumptive facts, their force can only ground pecuniary punishments, unless the judge adopts the alternative of sending the case 'quousque,' that is to say, for 'further inquiry.'"

Our ancient authors proceeded, in the most logical way, to teach that two things must be proved to warrant the conviction of the accused person: 1st, that a crime had been committed; 2d, that the accused was the perpetrator of it.

Proof of the first point meant the establishment of the "corpus delicti": "De re priusquam de reo inquirendum."[1] This preliminary proof was already required by the old "coutumal" laws; but it was then of a rude and formal character; it was necessary to exhibit to the judge the wound or the corpse itself. "Be it known that in such proceedings, if the blood and the misdeed are not exhibited to the court and sufficiently ascertained, battle ought not to be waged in cases entailing death or mutilation."[2] In case of necessity, the judges visited the scene of the crime, in order to proceed "à la vue," — by what they saw, — which they immediately put on record. "In Saint Louis's time, assault could only be proved by the judges' inspection of the blood or the wound, judicially seen."[3] But at an early date this rude method gave place to inspection by professional people. In the "Registre de Saint-Martin," the "mire juré" (sworn doctor) and the "matrone jurée" (sworn matron) play an important part and make numerous reports.

Two kinds of offenses were distinguished in regard to the establishment of the "corpus delicti." The first were those which leave physical traces, "delicta facti permanentis"; homicide, arson, and robbery, for instance. In such cases the physical fact of the doing of the deed could be ascertained and the establishment of the traces that it had left became the judge's first duty. This was accomplished by means of the minutes of the magistrate, who proceeded to the spot; or, if the facts in question required technical knowledge, by means of reports by physicians, surgeons, and experts. No other proof was, as a rule, allowed,[4]

[1] *Muyart de Vouglans*, "Inst." p. 308.

[2] "Grand Coutumier de Normandie," ch. LXXV. Compare the language of the complaint in the "Livre de Jostice et de Plet," XIX, 9, § 1: "And saw the wrong openly." — *Ibid.*, XIX, 2, § 2: "And if any one accuse another of the murder of a man who is not found, it is asked what the law says of that? The reply is that there is no cause of action, nobody having been seen murdered, unless the murder has been actually witnessed, or the body of the slain man has been actually seen. It may be properly said that the murder of a man who has been thrown into the Loire and is not found has been witnessed.

[3] *Dupaty*, "Moyens de droit pour trois hommes condamnés à la roue," 1786, p. 117 *et seq.*

[4] *Muyart de Vouglans*, "Instit." pp. 308, 309: "This proof is so essential, that its place cannot be supplied either by the testimony of witnesses, or by mere presumptions and conjectures, whatever value these may otherwise have, not even by the accused's confession."

save in exceptional cases where such action was impossible.[1] This matter of minutes and experts' reports had been carefully regulated by the Ordinance (Tits. IV and V), and, strange to say, early judicial practice recognized the accused's right to demand a second inspection and report. "He is entitled to ask permission to have a second inspection made by other surgeons at his expense, which he easily obtains on his petition, provided he presents it within a few days after the first inspection."[2] In regard to those offenses which leave no lasting traces, "delicta facti transeuntes," slander, for instance, it was impossible to separate the establishment of the "corpus delicti" from the proof of guilt. In this case, certain authors, such as Jousse, declared that "the corpus delicti could not be proved at all"; others, including Muyart de Vouglans, stated that in such a case "proof of the 'corpus delicti' cannot be obtained otherwise than by the accused's confession added to presumptions and conjectures." But, fundamentally, these were merely different ways of expressing one and the same thing.

To establish the second point we have mentioned, namely, the guilt of the accused, the theory of proofs appeared to its fullest extent. The whole of the methods of proof, considered in regard to their value, were divided into three classes, *complete proofs*, *proximate presumptions*, and *remote presumptions*. Each of these classes comprised totally different methods. Only the complete proof was sufficient, unsupported, to ground a capital sentence. "When all the conditions laid down by the law are fulfilled, the proof is then deemed legal and complete, which is absolutely necessary to effect condemnation to capital punishment."[3] It could, however, be obtained, first, by testimony, second, by the production of documents, or third, by presumptions. Did the confession constitute a complete proof? That was not generally conceded.

[1] *Poullain du Parc*, vol. XI, p. 81: "It does not follow that the crime ought to go unpunished in every case where it is impossible to establish the 'corpus delicti.' But the judges should then proceed and judge with greater circumspection, because it may be that the crime is imaginary, as turned out in the case of Pivardière and in several others." p. 109: "When the 'corpus delicti' is not found, clear proofs are necessary of sufficient force as to make it possible, in a way, to say that the crime must have been committed."

[2] *Muyart de Vouglans*, "Inst." p. 226. It is true that the first inspection was often made at the request of the party prosecuting for civil amends before the judge took cognizance. The accused did not get production of the judge's minutes. *Poullain du Parc*, vol. XI, p. 90: "It is the invariable rule in Brittany that the accused shall not be summoned to the judge's minutes nor to the reports of the experts."

[3] *Ibid.*, "Inst. crim." p. 307.

First. Testimonial proof was naturally considered the proof "par excellence" in criminal cases, "it being impossible to prove the majority of crimes in any other way;" but numerous conditions had to be realized before this proof became complete. It was absolutely necessary that there should be *two witnesses* testifying to the same fact; that was the unquestioned tradition. "Testis unus, testis nullus," or as Loysel said, "Voice of one, voice of none." The testimony of a single witness was not regarded as being absolutely valueless, but it could not alone be the basis of a capital sentence;[1] "it is, generally speaking, certain that depositions of witnesses turning upon isolated and different facts can constitute no proof."[2] It was, besides, necessary that both witnesses should have been eye-witnesses, — "that they should have seen the accused committing the crime." *Hearsay* witnesses could never furnish a complete proof, whatever might be their number; nor those called "testes ex auditu proprio," who testified to "having heard the accused's threats and the cries of a person dying"; nor those styled "testes ex parte accusati," who claimed to have received from the accused the confession of his crime; nor "a fortiori" the mere hearsay witnesses, "testes ex auditu alieno."

That is not all. The witnesses had to make a decided deposition and give a reason for it. If they expressed themselves in qualified terms, as "I believe . . . if I am not mistaken . . . it might have been . . . if I remember rightly," they were called "vacillants" and "could not be used in criminal cases, such evidence not constituting even a presumption." The deposition must always have remained identical in every particular throughout the three examinations undergone by the witness, in the information, or preliminary inquiry, the confirmation, and the confrontation. We know, moreover, that the Ordinance had taken precautions to insure that at the confrontation at least no variation should be possible. Lastly, it was essential that the witnesses should be neither *incompetent* nor *objected to.* Although the use of the right of objection had been notably hampered in the procedure, judicial practice had, by way of counterbalance, multiplied the causes of objection: affection, fear, mortal enmity,

[1] A complete proof could not be drawn from the testimony of two isolated witnesses, that is, testifying to different facts, unless in the case of crimes "which are committed by repeated acts, such as incest, adultery, blasphemy, sodomy, peculation, concussion, usury, and theft." *Muyart de Vouglans.*

[2] *Muyart de Vouglans,* "Inst. crim." pp. 322, 323.

weakness from age and weakness of intellect, infamy, personal interest, relationship, and many other causes still, were all admitted. The list of persons subject to objection given by Muyart de Vouglans begins with relatives and ends with "paupers and beggars," whose testimony could be excluded in certain circumstances. When these two "raræ aves," the perfect witnesses, were met with, they inevitably entailed condemnation; the judge was bound thereby.

Second. Next to the testimonial proof came the written proof, much rarer in criminal cases — so rare, even, that certain law-writers maintained that it was an impossibility. Erroneous as this opinion is, it is comprehensible when we bear in mind that, in this system, there had to be direct evidence of the perpetration of the crime.[1] On a closer examination it was seen that there were certain crimes which could hardly be proved except by writing, "because they consist chiefly in the thought or the intent, such as heresy, confidence, plotting against the prince, usury, subornation of witnesses;" and others "where the testimonial and instrumental proof concur," such as forgery. In order that the writing, where it was thus admitted, should constitute a *complete proof*, it was first of all necessary "that it should be precise as to the fact of the crime; that is, in questions of insult, lewdness, subornation, or conspiracy, it was necessary that the facts should be expressly mentioned in the very document which it was proposed to produce against the accused. Consequently, if it was used only to draw inferences against the accused, it ceased from that time to be regarded as complete proof, and entered into the class of conjectural proofs."[2] In the second place, it was essential that the writing should be authenticated, or, if it was signed by the accused, that he should acknowledge it. This was implied by Article 5, Tit. XXIV, of the Ordinance of 1670. A verification of handwriting could never furnish a complete proof. "In effect," says Muyart de Vouglans, "in addition to the fact that the experts always explain themselves in a vague and uncer-

[1] *Muyart* recognized that there are numerous cases where testimonial evidence entirely excludes instrumental evidence, "as in the case of such crimes as slander, blasphemy, adultery, rape, or the coinage of false money." "Inst. crim." p. 327.

[2] *Muyart de Vouglans*, "Inst. crim." p. 330. — "It is essential that the document should *contain* and prove in a precise manner the fact in question, for if the passage does not expressly contain the crime or misdemeanor in question, and it is only used to draw inferences and deductions from, such proof can no longer be called complete documentary proof; it is merely a conjectural and imperfect proof." *Rousseau de Lacombe*, "Matières criminelles," p. 371.

tain manner in such phrases as, 'We believe, we consider,' everybody knows that their art is, of itself, subject to a multitude of errors." [1] — "If it is a private writing and requires to be judicially authenticated to be available against the accused, it is no longer properly a complete proof, since it is no longer the document which, by itself, proves the fact . . . so that it is nothing but a mere conjecture and a testimonial proof." [2] These qualifications were exceedingly reasonable; the art of the handwriting experts was uncertain, as it may be said to be still. In the draft discussed among the parlement officers and the commissioners in 1670, there was even an article in the following terms: "No sentence of afflictive or degrading punishment can be based on the deposition of experts alone, unsupported by other proofs, adminicles, or presumptions." [3] It was suppressed, upon the observation of M. Talon, that the judges "were only too circumspect in such matters, without there being any need to tie their hands." [4] But the theory remained, all the same, as it had been. In this system, the personal writings of the accused, even when he had acknowledged them, could never constitute full proof against him, for they could contain nothing more than an extra-judicial confession, and, as we shall see by and by, the judicial confession itself did not have that effect.[5]

Third. Complete proof could also result from *presumptions*, on condition, it must be understood, that the fact from which the inferences were to be drawn had itself to be sufficiently established, *i.e.*, by two eye-witnesses or by writing. Judicial practice had in fact kept some of these presumptions incontrovertible, as we have found them in the very ancient law; they were called *manifest and necessary* presumptions and they were often compared with the presumptions, "juris et de jure" of the civil law. The following is an example: "When in a case of manslaughter two witnesses not subject to objection testify to having seen the accused, with a naked and bloody sword in his hand, leaving the place where soon afterwards the body of the deceased has been found wounded by a sword blow." [6]

[1] *Muyart de Vouglans*, "Inst. crim." p. 330.

[2] *Rousseau de Lacombe*, "Matières criminelles," pp. 371, 372. *Cf. Poullain du Parc*, vol. XI, p. 191 *et seq.*

[3] This was Art. 15 of Title VIII.

[4] "Procès-verbal," p. 99.

[5] *Muyart de Vouglans*, "Inst. crim." p. 336. The Ordinance (Tit. IV, Art. 2; Tit. XIV, Art. 10; Tit. II, Art. 9) nevertheless provided that an inventory of the accused's papers should be made.

[6] *Ibid.*, "Inst. crim." p. 346. *Cf. Poullain du Parc*, vol. XI, p. 118: "The comparison of manifest presumptions with the presumption 'juris et de jure' does not appear to me to be warranted . . . evidence is very

The authorities were not in agreement as to the value as proof of the accused's confession made in court. Some of the most celebrated, Jousse, for instance, held to the ancient opinion according to which it was the proof "par excellence" and the most complete; "of all the proofs which can be had in criminal cases, the accused's confession is the strongest and most certain; consequently that proof is sufficient. . . . Such a confession is the most complete proof that could be wished for."[1] Jousse relied upon the authority of Bartolus, Paul de Castro, and Julius Clarus. He declared "that it could never be presumed, without subverting all the laws of nature, that a man would in cold blood accuse himself of a crime which he had not committed." He also cited in support of his opinion the formalities of the interrogations, so thoroughly regulated by the Ordinance, and asked if so much care would have been taken to obtain a confession, if it had not had a decisive value?[2] It was in reality these very formalities which prevented the ascription to the confession of its natural force. Jousse's opinion therefore remained a solitary one, and this was what was in general decided. In the case of a crime grave enough to entail capital or even merely afflictive punishment, the confession was not sufficient to ground such a sentence: "Nemo auditur perire volens;" it was essential that the confession should be corroborated by urgent presumptions or the deposition of a competent witness. That was Louet's[3] opinion, and, later, that of Domat[4] and of Duplessis.[5] The authors of the 1700s are no less

rarely admitted in rebuttal of the presumption 'juris et de jure,' while in criminal cases evidence is admitted in rebuttal of manifest presumptions." This evidence in rebuttal of which Poullain du Parc speaks consists, as he explains, of the justificative facts, lawful self-defense, for instance.

[1] *Jousse*, "Comm. sur l'Ordonn. de 1670," on Art. 5, Tit. XXV, Nos. 1 and 2.

[2] Jousse, however, only recognized the confession as a complete proof when the "'corpus delicti' is indubitable and properly verified by means of an inspection or an official report of the judge or by the deposition of witnesses." If, however, the crime was one of those "which could only be committed in the intention, such as heresy, in feelings not outwardly manifested . . . it being impossible to prove the 'corpus delicti,' the confession of the accused could not be sufficient to cause his condemnation." *Jousse*, p. 434.

[3] Letter C, No. 34.

[4] "Le droit public," Book III, Title I, "Concerning crimes and misdemeanors": "Although the accused acknowledges the crime (if it is a capital offense) the production of the evidence is not abandoned; for it would be unjust to condemn an innocent person on a false confession."

[5] "Réponse de Duplessis à Colbert sur le procès de la Voisin": "The bare confession by a criminal of his crime cannot effect his condemnation; but if, besides his confession, there is a single witness, that is sufficient. In the same way, if in addition to his confession there is some presumption, either real or arising from the deposition of even a single witness, that is sufficient for his condemnation." "Lettres, etc., de Colbert," vol. VI, App. p. 429.

explicit. "The confession from its nature cannot effect the condemnation to capital punishment; for that the concurrence of several other circumstances are necessary; . . . it must be accompanied by several weighty presumptions or the deposition of a competent witness." [1] — "The free and voluntary confession of the accused does not constitute a complete proof against him: 'Nemo non auditur perire volens.'" [2] Lastly, Serpillon disputes Jousse's opinion most respectfully, but at the same time most energetically.[3] If, on the contrary, a slight punishment was in question, it was admitted that the sentence could be grounded on the confession made in court, provided that the "corpus delicti" was conclusively established: "It is true that there are judgments which have sentenced the accused upon their confession alone, but to lighter punishments than the crimes deserved." [4]

The provisions of the Ordinance of 1670 were, however, perfectly in harmony with this theory. Article 5 of Title XXV provides "that criminal actions can be examined and judged although there are no informations, and if there is otherwise sufficient proof by the interrogations and by documents, either authenticated or acknowledged by the accused, and by the other presumptions and circumstances of the action." From this it is evident that to obviate recourse to testimonial evidence the culprit's confession was not, of itself, sufficient; it was still necessary to add to that the written proof or presumptions.[5] Article 17 of Title XIV provides that immediately after the appearance of the accused, and before proceeding further, "the interrogations shall be at once produced to our procurators or to those of the seigniors, to take law upon them or to make such motions as to them appear advisable;" and the authorities have always understood this provision to mean that if a crime meriting a severe punishment was in question, the motion, notwithstanding the confession, should not be for an immediate sentence. "If the crime should appear to him (the public prosecutor) to be a serious one, he moves for the criminal ruling of confirmation and confrontation; for in this case, even when the accused should have confessed to all the counts of the accusation on which he is charged, a full examination under the criminal forms is none the less necessary." [6] Finally, Article 19 of the same

[1] *Muyart de Vouglans*, "Inst. crim." p. 339.
[2] *Rousseau de Lacombe*, "Matières criminelles," p. 372.
[3] "Code criminel," p. 1012. [4] *Serpillon, loc. cit.*
[5] "Real presumptions which naturally appear from the thing itself and do not arise from the testimonial evidence are here spoken of." *Duplessis* ("Lettre à Colbert," above cited).
[6] *Serpillon*, upon this article.

Title XIV is also in perfect harmony with the whole of this theory: it permits the accused of crime "for which he will not be liable to afflictive punishment" to "take law" on the charges after the interrogation. This power remotely recalls the plea of "guilty" of the English procedure; it was serviceable to the accused, by permitting him to avoid the delays of a criminal trial. It is conceivable that it did not exist unless there was a confession, but the confession was not enough; it was still necessary that the crime should be one not punishable by afflictive punishment; otherwise the procedure had to be followed through to the end. Although the ancient authorities have sometimes attempted to explain this rule in other ways, it is quite conceivable that although admitted in serious crimes the confession did not by any means constitute a complete proof. The importance of the confession was, nevertheless, considerable; added to what was called a proximate presumption, it constituted a real and sufficient proof; and these proximate presumptions were of much more frequent occurrence than complete proof.

The *proximate presumptions* were also called *half-proofs.* This term, against which Voltaire's common sense afterwards protested, was not adopted by all the jurists;[1] but it was, nevertheless, in use, and not without reason, considering the system of which it formed a part. The proximate presumptions could not, by themselves, justify a capital sentence of the accused. Some of them were strong enough, however, to make it seem very difficult to forbear from inflicting upon the guilty person the chastisement he deserved. If the voluntary confession had been obtained, that would have been possible; in default of a voluntary confession, a *forced* confession had to be obtained, and this was done by means of torture. The principal effect of proximate presumptions in grave accusations was, therefore, to permit of the administration of torture. This is declared in the clearest manner in the 1500s, the 1600s, and the 1700s. "Where there shall have been neither full nor entire proof against the accused, but there shall have been half-proof of the crime by a witness of notable standing and not of mean station, testifying to the principal fact, which witness shall be free from any objection or suspicion what-

[1] "Several authors have defined the half-proof as a means of taking the false for the true." *Denisart,* "Half-proof." — "There is no such thing as half-proofs; several of the authorities deprecate this expression. It is a barbarous and fictitious term; this is proved by the fact that not a single text on law mentions it. Half of the truth cannot be discovered; there is no such thing as a half-truth . . . half-proofs are as impossible as half-men." *Serpillon,* "Code criminel," p. 1074.

ever, or where there shall be strong conjectures and presumptions at least equivalent to the said half-full proof, not avoided or diminished by the proof which shall have been produced 'ex officio' for the justification of the accused, sufficient for the administration of torture, (the judge) shall proceed to the judgment of torture."[1] — "It is clear that every presumption constitutes a half-proof which may be sufficient to warrant the administration of torture."[2] — "There are some crimes of a nature deserving of capital punishment, and it is in regard to these in particular that the presumptions may give cause for torture."[3] So that this theory, apparently so favorable to the accused, resulted in rendering torture almost inevitable; it became the indispensable corollary of this system of proof.

Another means of arriving at a capital sentence had been to *add the presumptions together*, and this was admitted by certain jurisconsults: "If there were two weighty presumptions, each proved by two witnesses, they could unquestionably constitute complete proof, according to their quality . . . if these presumptions were of such a quality that a natural connection existed between them, uncontradicted, and they all belonged to the class of proximate and weighty presumptions, it might be said that they proved each other, and that the incomplete proofs in regard to each fact should be cumulated so as to constitute a perfect proof, which should be sufficient for a condemnation."[4] But the sufficiency of these combinations was, in general, denied. "The half-proof is no more conclusive than a half-truth; and, for the same reason that two uncertainties cannot make a certainty, two half-proofs cannot constitute a complete proof."[5]

Although the proximate presumptions were not sufficient to base a capital sentence, they permitted the judge to inflict "certain afflictive, degrading, or pecuniary punishments,"[6] if he deemed them strong enough for that purpose. But care was taken to add that "before imposing a punishment not commensurate with the

[1] "Pratique de Lizet," 1577, p. 28.
[2] *Duplessis*, "Lettre à Colbert," cited above.
[3] *Muyart de Vouglans*, "Inst. crim." p. 351.
[4] *Duplessis, loc. cit.*
[5] *Denisart*, "Half-proof."
[6] *Muyart de Vouglans*, "Inst. crim." pp. 346, 351. *Poullain du Parc* (vol. XI, p. 115) even shows that the judge can in such case sentence to the galleys for life: "The preparatory torture under reservation of proofs is more severe than the galleys for life; and since it can be decreed upon considerable evidence (although insufficient to base a capital sentence), it must necessarily follow that the judge can sentence to the galleys, however atrocious the crime may be, upon considerable evidence, when there is not enough to warrant a capital sentence. For the same reason, if the evidence is less considerable, the judge can modify the punishment."

character of the crime, for the reason that the evidence, although considerable, was not sufficient to sustain a capital sentence, it was necessary that the judges should have exhausted all the means indicated by the Ordinances for the proof and the investigation of the crime." [1]

Attempts were occasionally made to maintain that complete proof of atrocious crimes was not necessary for the capital sentence: "In atrocissimis leviores conjecturæ sufficiunt et licet judici jura transgredi." "Such a barbarous and absurd idea," says Poullain du Parc, "has never been entertained in France. It is the badge of tyranny and cruel despotism. The more atrocious the crime, the more terrible should be the punishment; consequently, the evidence against the accused should be so much the clearer in proportion to the atrocity of the crime with which he is charged." [2] What facts constituted proximate presumptions? Here again the Ordinance furnished no details. It merely declared that torture could only be administered where the crime was one deserving of capital punishment, and where there was a considerable amount of evidence, which, however, "was not sufficient." [3] This necessarily left a wide discretion to the judges. "The Ordinance not having determined in the article . . . the nature of the presumptions and circumstances which it proposes should constitute proof in criminal actions appears to have left the matter in the discretion of the judges." [4] — "When the witnesses do not testify to having seen the blow struck, and they furnish nothing but presumptive facts, it being possible that some of the presumptions may be more weighty and conclusive than others, and that the judges may be more impressed by some facts than by others . . . the matter usually lies in the judges' discretion." [5] Certain rules were, however, laid down by precedent.

Among the half-proofs we find, first of all, the testimonial proof, or *imperfect* writing, the deposition of a single eye witness, or personal writing verified by experts, and also the *extra-judicial* confession of the accused, when it was denied by him, but proved "by two competent witnesses," or by his "diaries and household papers." [6] Then in this category of proximate presumptive facts a crowd of presumptions began to be marshalled. Muyart

[1] *Poullain du Parc*, XI, p. 116.

[2] *Ibid.*, XI, p. 110. *Cf. Dupaty*, "Mémoire" and "Moyens de droit pour trois hommes condamnés à la roue," *passim.*

[3] Ordinance of 1670, Tit. XIX, art. 1.

[4] *Muyart de Vouglans*, "Inst. crim." p. 347.

[5] *Duplessis*, "Lettre à Colbert," cited above.

[6] *Muyart de Vouglans*, "Instit. crim." pp. 336, 350.

de Vouglans divides them into general presumptions and presumptions peculiar to certain crimes. He enumerates sixteen belonging to the former class, some of which are very curious; we find among them, "the status of the accuser, whether or not he is a person of standing, or the head of a house, in regard to offenses committed by his domestic servants;" the "status of the accused, whether or not he is a vagrant or a non-resident." The presumptions peculiar to certain crimes are specified with great care; the nomenclature of some of them would be laughable, if we did not catch a glimpse of the torture lurking behind them. Thus we find ranked among the proximate presumptions of the crimes of *magic* and of *sorcery* the following things: "If there have been found in the accused's house books or instruments relating to magic, such as sacrifices, human limbs, waxen images transfixed by needles, the bark of trees, bones, nails, locks of human hair, feathers intertwined in the form of a circle or nearly so, pins, embers, parcel of embers found at the head of children's beds . . ., 2d, If he has been seen placing anything in a stable, and the cattle therein have soon afterwards died, 3d, If a document has been found upon him containing a compact with the devil . . ., 7th, If those living in intimacy with the accused have been seen to change their abode immediately after his arrest . . ., 8th, If he has the name of the devil constantly upon his lips, and if he is in the habit of calling his own children or those of other people by that name."[1] This was written in the 1700s! Muyart de Vouglans adds, it is true: "All these presumptive facts might, according to the authorities, be a reason for torture, but we shall see, in treating of this crime (sorcery), with what circumspection the judge ought to behave in such a delicate matter and one which the inordinate credulity of the common people might cause to degenerate into dangerous superstition."

All the proximate presumptions could, as a rule, be the occasion for the administration of torture, provided they were themselves proved, and for that a single witness was sufficient. For a large number of half-proofs, however, it was necessary to add *a remote presumption* at least, in order to justify torture. At this point a third class of presumptions made their appearance, under the name of *adminicles;* these had only a corroborative value.[2] This was a very slender safeguard, for very little was required to give rise to remote presumptions. Muyart de Vouglans gives

[1] *Muyart de Vouglans*, "Instit. crim." p. 353.
[2] See *Muyart de Vouglans*, "Inst. crim." pp. 346, 350, 351.

the following examples of them: "The changeableness of the accused's discourse, the tremor of his voice, his uneasiness of mind, his taciturnity, . . . the proximity of the accused's house to the place where the crime was committed, . . . the accused's feigning deafness, or to have lost his mind or his memory when he is questioned, . . . the accused's bad expression, or the ill name he bears."[1] The remote presumptions had to be proved by two witnesses, or by the judge's minutes.

Certain authorities, however, showed themselves to be more exacting. "It cannot be too often repeated, that several presumptions in combination are necessary to furnish a considerable proof, such as is required by this article of the Ordinance.[2] The majority of the authorities require three presumptions; but manifest presumptions must be distinguished from remote presumptions; the former furnish necessary inferences from a certain fact, . . . an example of a manifest presumption is the case of two competent witnesses who testify to having seen the accused leave a place where a murder has just been committed carrying a naked and bloody sword; this presumption would appear to be 'luce clarior.'[3] For a sentence to torture, however, other presumptions called remote are also required, such as prior threats, proven enmity and such like 'adminicles,' unless, at all events, the accused was a vagrant or a person of bad reputation."[4] Duplessis holds a similar opinion. "Three kinds of presumptions are usually distinguished, namely: 1st, General and remote presumptions, as from the general bad conduct of the accused, if he has been already arrested for similar crimes; these can have little more effect than to put the judges on inquiry and merely arouse their suspicion; 2d, Nearer presumptions, which, however, are not immediately connected with the act, as, in homicide, where the accused was the mortal enemy of the person slain, or where he threatened him or boasted that he would kill him, etc.; these are somewhat stronger, but they are in no ways conclusive, and do not constitute even a half-proof; 3d, Proximate presumptions, immediately connected with the act, as, where a man has been slain in a house or in a wood, and at the same time the accused has been seen to leave the house or the wood in flight, with naked

[1] *Muyart de Vouglans*, "Instit. crim." p. 350.

[2] Art. 1, Tit. XIV, specifying the circumstances under which the sentence to torture can be passed.

[3] The classification here, compared with that of Muyart de Vouglans, would seem to carry the various presumptions down a step lower in the scale. *Cf. Poullain du Parc*, XI, p. 119.

[4] *Serpillon*, "Code criminel," p. 912.

and bloody sword. . . . These facts raise thoroughly conclusive presumptions that the accused has committed the crime, but still they are not absolutely irrebuttable; presumptions of this description go under the name of 'full presumptions,' and they usually constitute half-proof."[1] When all is said, it must be acknowledged that it was difficult to indicate with sufficient certainty the evidence upon which torture would be administered. "The difficulty is to ascertain what evidence should be regarded as considerable. What might come under that description when applied to a vagrant or other bad character ought not to be so considered when the accused is domiciled and of good character; consequently nothing is so arbitrary or difficult to settle. It depends upon the place, the time, the status of the persons concerned, and a multitude of other circumstances."[2]

Remote presumptions, unsupported, permitted the judge to pronounce pecuniary punishments, or a "further inquiry"; he could also, if there was a party prosecutor for civil reparation, send the action to the civil side. "And where by the proceedings there has been neither full nor half-full proof, but merely some presumptions or conjectures less than the said half-full proof and not sufficient for the administration of torture, and a likelihood resulting from the proceedings that the complainant in a criminal case could more fully prove and verify the crimes charged by him against the accused in a civil action, in such a case, if the judge has done all that could and should be done to end the criminal action, he should refer the parties to a civil action."[3] — "When there are only strong presumptions, their force can determine nothing but pecuniary punishments, if the judge does not enter an adjournment 'quosque,' that is to say, for 'further inquiry.'"[4]

In the midst of these waverings and hesitations, one point remained certain and acknowledged on all hands, namely, that a sentence of capital punishment was impossible in the absence of a complete proof; and it was exceedingly difficult to procure one. Except where that had been obtained, it was essential to add to weighty presumptions the confession of the accused. To this end two powerful mechanisms were organized; one was the interrogation — subtle and secret — where the accused, without the opportunity of pleading any defense, was obliged to swear to reveal the truth, and by which the so-called voluntary confession was obtained; the other was torture, by which the *forced confes-*

[1] *Duplessis, loc. cit.*

[2] *Serpillon,* "Code crim." p. 911.

[3] "Pratique de Lizet," p. 28.

[4] *Poullain du Parc,* vol. XI, p. 116.

sion was extorted. That was the end and aim of the system of legal proofs; and in the supposed necessity for a confession must be found the real reason for the maintenance and continuance of torture. This is most explicitly stated by Muyart de Vouglans: "The reasons which appear to necessitate its authorization are based upon the fact that it being often impossible to obtain a full conviction of the crime, either by the depositions of witnesses or by documents, or by presumptions, which rarely concur in such a way as to constitute that proof, clearer than day, which is essential for a condemnation, there would be no less injustice in sending away absolved the person who is otherwise suspected of crime, than there would be in condemning him who is not completely proven guilty; not to mention the fact that the welfare of humanity demands that crime should not remain unpunished. It is for that reason that, in the absence of other means of arriving at this complete proof, we are obliged to torture the body of the accused." [1] Unsympathetic remarks such as these are not surprising, coming from Muyart de Vouglans, who invariably constituted himself the advocate of this odious procedure; but they expressed a logical necessity which imposed itself without discrimination on all. "In the perplexity in which the judges find themselves," says Poullain du Parc, "when they see very strong presumptions against an accused, and when all the means of proof are exhausted, they are driven to the resource of the preparatory torture." [2] And this is what Serpillon, who himself had begun to protest against torture, has to say: "About twenty-five years ago we were still *compelled* to sentence to the preparatory torture the notorious Auribaut, of the parish of Planché-en-Nivernois, accused of about a dozen crimes, the majority of which were murders on the highways. Without this not a single one of them would have been fully proved." [3] By what was Serpillon "compelled"? By the theory of legal proofs.

There might, however, remain to the accused one last resource. If he resisted the torments of the torture without confessing, the accusation was doubtless completely purged, and the strong presumptions which had made the administration of the torture possible were totally obliterated. But this last hope might prove to be a vain one; there was such a thing as *torture under reservation of proofs*. Then, although the accused, by dint of constancy, refused any confession, it was possible, nevertheless, by virtue of

[1] "Inst. crim." p. 341.
[2] Volume XI, p. 114.
[3] "Code criminel," p. 909.

the presumptions, to sentence him to some punishment other than death. The use of torture under reservation of proofs is of very ancient date. Imbert describes it in the following extraordinary language. After saying that there are criminals "so wily and malicious that whatever they have confessed under torture, they altogether deny when they are questioned next day," he adds: "For which reason, when the judge sees that there is not sufficient proof to justify corporal punishment, but merely pecuniary punishment, in order that he may not, by denying everything obtained by torture, elude the pecuniary punishment which he ought to suffer, he orders that the delinquent be put to the torture, without the presumptions resulting from the prior proceedings being purged on that account. For although capital punishment or other serious corporal punishment ought not to be based upon presumptions, even though unquestionable, pecuniary punishment and some slight corporal punishment can always be adjudged."[1] Would not the appropriate inscription above the doors of the criminal courts have been: "Abandon hope, all ye who enter here"?

[1] "Pratique," Book III, ch. XIV (p. 739).

CHAPTER IV

INFLUENCE OF THE ORDINANCE OF 1670 UPON THE ADMINISTRATION OF JUSTICE

THE purpose of the Ordinance of 1670 was to reform, not to make innovations. The principles which it sanctions were already in existence, and the severities which it registers, though new to all appearance, were, for the most part, already found in practice. Its influence, however, was very great. The appearance of a Code in a country is always a matter of the utmost importance. It is the law at one and the same time made uniform and transformed. Although diversity of the systems of jurisprudence does not wholly disappear, its influence is felt only in matters of detail. Change in the institutions by an imperceptible advance is no longer possible; scientific interpretation alone can tread these decreed paths, and can sometimes, in elucidating, develop the law. The Ordinance of 1670 is a real code; it is exact in its details, and it is also exact in its phraseology; this has stood the test of long experience. It was able to root itself firmly; the future had in store for it a life of a hundred and twenty years.

§ 1. **The Procedure regularized and stated precisely by the Ordinance.** — At the time Louis XIV caused the Ordinance to be drawn up the administration of justice was uncertain. Different systems of judicial practice sprouted like rank and hardy weeds. Abuses abounded on all sides: non-observance of the forms, which at that time constituted the sole safeguard of the accused; the disastrous influence of the inferior officers and agents on whom the judges devolved part of their duties; the high price of justice caused by the addition of abnormal gratuities to the regular large costs; this has all been shown by the authentic documents which we have analyzed.

The Ordinance of 1670 unified the forms of criminal procedure. Certain special usages it did undoubtedly respect, particularly those of the Châtelet of Paris, the situation of which, in the heart of the large city, justified certain privileges; but that very seldom happened.[1] Although differences did arise in the future, these were only in regard to points not provided for by the Ordinance, which, it cannot be denied, had sometimes passed over rather important matters in silence. We must not forget that it was silent as to the mode of administration of torture and as to the choice of reporting judges of criminal actions. The numerous regulations of the different companies of judges agreed upon between their officers or settled by parlementary decree might throw doubt upon the regular operation of our law;[2] but a close inspection will show that these deal either with questions of internal regulation, which no Code could provide for, or matters, such as that of royal causes, where an intentional uncertainty in the wording of the act had necessarily opened the door to arbitrariness.

The Ordinance absolutely prohibited the intrusting to officers of court, notaries and clerks of court, those duties, so important (informations and interrogations), which had been formerly handed over to them.[3] In the inferior courts assessors were prescribed for the judge. These were subjected, by means of reports addressed to the king's procurator, to a supervision, which it was sought to render effective.[4] The cheapening of actions was studied, by the suppression of a number of needless items of costs.[5] In numerous articles the Ordinance forbade divers functionaries, under severe penalties, to accept any perquisite to which they were not strictly entitled; and these prohibitions were addressed, not only to jailers and keepers of prisons,[6] and to clerks of court, but also to the judges.[7]

Pecuniary economies were also realized by other articles, the direct and chief aim of which was to expedite the procedure, by stripping it of useless writings with which it was encumbered: "We hereby abrogate the orders to 'hear law,' to deliver pleas in extenuation, reasons and pleas of nullity, responses to furnish pleas

[1] See Tit. I, Art. 29; Tit. II, Art. 28; Tit. III, Art. 3; Tit. XIV, Art. 14; Tit. XXV, Art. 9.

[2] They occupy over two hundred and thirty-two pages of Serpillon's "Code criminel" (from p. 1229 to p. 1463).

[3] Title III, Art. 2; Tit. XIV, Art. 2.

[4] Title X, Art. 20.

[5] See, for instance, Tit. VI, Arts. 9, 18; Tit. VII, Art. 7.

[6] Title XII, Arts. 19, 22, 29, 30, 33.

[7] Title XIV, Art. 16.

of obreption and to inform, to submit civil conclusions, and all other orders; we also abrogate the custom of lodging civil motions, notifications, inventories, objections, reasons for and pleas of nullity, or of appeal, complaints and answers, orders and foreclosures to produce or object taken in court or in the clerk's office."[1] The length of this list shows what relief must have been furnished. "All these ancient forms mulcted the parties in costs and occasioned indefinite delays, but this article has abrogated them, with the purpose of simplifying criminal procedure as much as possible."[2] In regard to the acceleration of the procedure the restrictions placed upon the misuse that was made of the orders to answer ("arrêts de défenses") must also be noted.

The Ordinance settled the formalities for the different documents with great precision. Henceforth the judges had a certain and methodical guide, and they could no longer invoke the authority of customs or the silence of the laws to justify their neglect. The better to insure the execution of its provisions, the legislature had, in the majority of cases, taken care to require that the observance of formalities be stated in the official reports. This is the safeguard to which every formal and written procedure has recourse. It is true that where there is secrecy in the proceedings it loses very much of its efficacy. The Ordinance sometimes inflicted severe punishment upon erring judges. It usually consisted in their suspension, or also of heavy penalties and an action for damages available to the injured parties. The system was very severe, and Lamoignon, the faithful defender of the magistracy, protested vigorously against these provisions, as he had already done when the Ordinance of 1667 was drawn up.[3] A special effort was made to have all the writings made regular and accurate. The prohibition against leaving interlineations and blanks, the compulsory authentication of erasures, and the signatures of officers and parties are recalled at every step. It was not considered that this was descending to insignificant details, but, on the contrary, acting in the highest interests; this must be so in every written procedure. It was even desired that each class of documents in the proceedings should be recorded in a separate record. "The Ordinance wishing to prevent confusion, a record or report was necessary upon which all the decrees and the order of examination should be written, as well as the motions of the civil party for reservation of final proofs.

[1] Title XXIII. [2] "Code criminel," p. 977.
[3] "Procès-verbal de l'Ord. civile," p. 476 *et seq.*

Separate reports are necessary for each interrogation, another for the confirmation of the witnesses, and another for the confirmation of the accused; as many reports of confrontation as there are accused persons are also necessary."[1]

It may safely be asserted that these various provisions of the Ordinance were beneficial. The procedure, regulated, accelerated, and freed from very heavy expenses, was purged of grave abuses. But, on the other hand, this precision of the law rendered impossible certain indulgences by the magistrates, which had been very valuable to the defense. Henceforth the courts, which, under the rule of the Ordinance of 1539, "granted counsel in all prosecutions," or "in certain cases," as Pussort put it, must be more severe; a strict law barred the lawyers from the criminal courts. From this time forward, the magistrates cannot imitate de Thou in his refusal to administer the oath to an accused "because he knew that no Ordinance compelled the judges to exact it from accused persons." Whatever might be their private opinion, judges must in future condemn as a perjurer the witness "who varied in some essential particular at the confrontation." But as judicial practice inclined to these extremes of its own volition, it must be owned that, on its appearance, the Ordinance of 1670 leaned to the side of leniency rather than that of severity. The abuses which it abolished would not have corrected themselves, and the severities which it sanctioned were imposed without the aid of the law.

§ 2. **Observance of the Ordinance.** — But how was the Ordinance observed in reality? It is rather hard to say. To determine with exactitude the influence exercised by the new code of criminal procedure, it would be necessary to have for the 1600s and the 1700s accurate statistics, and these we do not possess. We are not, however, absolutely destitute of documents. The "Correspondance administrative sous Louis XIV" contains a whole part devoted to justice. For another thing, the criminal law-writers of the 1700s sometimes make observations which are so much the more important in that they content themselves with interpreting the texts. Finally, the arguments which distinguish a certain number of criminal actions on the very eve of the French Revolution contain bitter criticisms and grave allegations. All this allows us to ascertain a certain number of facts.[2]

[1] *Serpillon*, "Code criminel," p. 733.

[2] The "Archives de la Bastille, documents inédits publiés et recueillis," by *M. François Ravaisson*, may also be very profitably consulted. A

Let us first of all glance at what concerns the unity and regularity of the forms of the criminal procedure. One of the chief aims, if not the chief, of the compilers of the Ordinance was to realize this unity. At first sight it would seem that they were successful. Shortly after the publication of the new law, Duplessis said, in a Memorial addressed to Colbert, which we have already quoted: "It is difficult to find any flaws in the procedure. The proceedings in criminal matters are very simple; the essentials are merely the information, the interrogations, the confirmations, and the confrontation, and the formalities are so thoroughly denoted by the Ordinance that it is not easy to make mistakes regarding them." [1] But this was really too eulogistic. Nothing was so complex as this written procedure, strewn with formalities. We can see at a glance the irregularities which were perpetrated and ere long the existence of local systems of judicial practice. On 17th June, 1687, the Chancellor of Pontchartrain writes to the Parlement of Rennes: "I have learned that several abuses have found their way into your court and into the bench of your jurisdiction, which, it appears to me, must be remedied, if they are established. . . . 1st. It is claimed that the royal judges as well as those of the seigniors, who sit in the jurisdiction of the Parlement, cause monitories to be published in all criminal actions which are brought before them, whatever proof there is of the crime either by the informations or by the interrogations of the accused, and that is done solely from the fear that the Parlement will quash their proceedings if they have been defective, which is declared to have happened very often. This custom is very mischievous and even very dangerous; . . . recourse to monitories was not introduced among us in extraordinary actions except in default of all other methods, when the truth cannot be otherwise arrived at. . . . Accused persons may take advantage of this method of obtaining a hearing of the witnesses for their defense and as to such facts as they deem appropriate. . . . 3d. It is alleged that you allow an accused without objection to undertake to prove falsehood in the depositions of the witnesses, which is very mischievous. Besides piling up the expenses and lengthening the trial of actions,[2] this would be tantamount to

large part of this, it is true, refers to a period prior to 1670. Side by side will there be found regular proceedings, interrogations, and official reports of torture, as well as letters and reports showing the part played by "lettres de cachet" all the time they were in use.

[1] "Lettres, etc., de Colbert," vol. VI, App. p. 422.

[2] *Cf. Poullain du Parc*, "Principes," vol. XI, ch. XIV, p. 350 *et seq.*

admitting the accused to his justificative facts before the inspection ('visite') of the action, which is expressly forbidden by the first Article of Title XXVIII of the Ordinance of 1670." [1]

The same Pontchartrain, on 28th September, 1710, expostulates vigorously with the magistrates of the city and borough of Furnes. He declares "that it is unprecedented to confrontatively condemn an accused without first hearing him, as expressly appears from Articles 5 and 15 of Title XXVI of the Ordinance of 1670, which provide that in such case the accused shall be remitted to the courts of the jurisdiction of the judges who tried him in the first instance, and that he be interrogated upon the prisoner's seat at the time of the judgment. It is not enough to produce there all the proceedings had against him, because it is thought that by the new interrogation, circumstances may be learned which may serve to acquit him or condemn him to more or less severe punishments." [2] Sometimes the courts also aggravate the severities of the law. On 6th August, 1679, Chancellor Le Tellier, writing to d'Aguesseau, steward of Languedoc, is compelled to state "that there is no impropriety in a witness, after having said in his deposition that he saw the accused in the action and having repeated this in his confirmation, stating his doubt, at the confrontation which is made between him and the said accused, whether he is the same person he intended to speak about." [3] The authors make equally grievous criticisms on Article 20 of Title X of the Ordinance, which commands the king's attorneys to send every six months to the attorney-general a statement of the jail-books with a statement of the procedings. Serpillon declares "that this is the worst executed article of the Ordinance, important as it is, in order that the superiors may be made acquainted with the proceedings that have been neglected and suppressed. . . . There have never, at any time, been any decrees regulating this subject." [4]

[1] "Correspondance administrative sous Louis XIV," vol. II, pp. 450, 452.

[2] "Correspondance administrative," vol. II, p. 489. *Cf.* for certain usages of the Parlement of Toulouse, *ibid.*, p. 484.

[3] *Ibid.*, vol. II, p. 215. This correspondence contains here and there curious interpretations of the usages. President de Lamoignon writes as follows to attorney-general de Harlay: "I have always understood that the Parlement never gives the reasons for its decrees in writing; that is only done in the provincial Parlements. Among several reasons which could be given for this difference there is one essential reason applicable at all times; this is, that the attorneys-general of the other Parlements express themselves in writing because they are far away; but that of the Parlement of Paris is close to the king and must orally account for all that His Majesty desires to be informed about" (p. 174).

[4] "Code criminel," p. 574.

D'Aguesseau, on his side, raised serious objection to the local customs, protesting "that in criminal matters the customary laws of the provinces themselves and, with greater reason, of their courts, should never prevail against the provisions of the Ordinance." At the end of the 1700s, the diversity of the systems of judicial practice in criminal matters is a matter of notoriety. "I must own that the defect of the wording which I object to is a practice in the Parlement of Paris and perhaps in other Parlements of the kingdom. In truth, other Parlements, and these are in the majority, adhere to the letter and spirit of the Ordinance, which imperatively enjoins upon them, they say, the setting out in writing."[1] "Several of the supreme courts allow the relatives of the private prosecutors to testify, and others, on the contrary, reject them; with the result that among the courts certain depositions are like the coinage among the nations; certain depositions are current in one court and not in another."[2] Poullain du Parc, in the volumes which he devotes to criminal law, frequently stops to state the particular practice of the Parlement of Brittany.[3]

This diversity of systems of judicial practice was, moreover, a natural and inevitable occurrence. The compilers of the Ordinances had certainly endeavored to avoid this result. Pussort had pointed out the evil in his usual clear and forcible manner. "There remains as a final remedy to withdraw from the sovereign companies of judges the liberty which they have usurped of construing the Ordinances. This is an encroachment upon the royal authority, to which alone belongs the making of the laws; from it should also come their interpretation. This right is one which was always reserved by the Roman emperors, so much so that the provincial judges were invariably obliged to consult them when some case occurred with them which had not been foreseen by the laws, or as to which the laws were not sufficiently explicit. The emperor Justinian, who compiled and reported what the emperors Julian and Adrian had ordained, gives an excellent reason for this. It is, he says, because God has intrusted the emperors with the government of men, so that they may reform whatever may be defective and prescribe limits and precise rules as to matters which come up for the first time and have not been provided for. This

[1] *Dupaty*, "Mémoire pour trois hommes condamné à la roue," 1786, p. 116; he is speaking of the drawing up of the final interrogation.
[2] *Ibid.*, p. 180; *cf.* "Moyens de droit," on the same subject, p. 36.
[3] See, for example, vol. XI, pp. 65, 350.

rule was followed by all the jurisconsults, who unanimously agreed that it was not within the province of the pretorian courts (with which the supreme courts in this kingdom are synonymous) to construe the laws upon any equitable pretext whatever, for two weighty and sufficient reasons. The first is that if this liberty was left to them they could, by their constructions, nullify the authority of the laws and erect themselves into legislators; the second is that if it were allowed, all the judgments would be arbitrary and dependent upon the whim, the caprice, the passion, and the interest of the judges, and there would be no certainty." [1] The Ordinance of 1667 also read (Title II, Article 7): "If in the judgments of actions which may be pending in our Courts of Parlement and our other courts, any doubt or difficulty arises as to the execution of any articles of our Ordinances, Edicts, Declarations, and Letters Patent, we forbid them to construe them; but it is our will that in such cases they adjourn, and learn from us what may be our intention." But this prohibition was bound to be vain. Pussort was striving against a kind of natural law, — a logical necessity,—and he was bound to be defeated.

§ 3. **Persistent Defects in the Administration of Justice. The Question of Money. The Written Procedure.** — Several causes in particular were bound to render the Ordinance ineffectual upon many points. The question of money ranked first. We already know from the Memorials of the State's Councillors what part judges' fees played, even in criminal matters, and in this respect nothing was changed,[2] with the exception of some economies which had been brought about. But that was not all. When there was no private prosecutor in the action, it was the seigniors in regard to their jurisdictions, and the royal tax-collectors in regard to the royal jurisdictions, who had to defray the expenses. But neither of these, the one more than the other, were disposed to put their hands in their pockets. From this it frequently resulted that for want of money the course of justice was stopped. In 1664 the attorney-general of the Parlement of Bordeaux wrote to Colbert: "It is impossible to compel the tax-collectors to defray the expenses necessary for the punishment of criminals

[[1] "Mélanges Clérambault," No. 613, p. 438 (Mémoire de Pussort).

[2] See "Lettre du chancelier Le Tellier" to Daulède, first president of the Parlement of Guyenne, 21st July, 1679. He states, among other things, that the reporters do not send the decrees to the offices of the clerks of court until after they have been paid their judges' fees ("Corresp. admin. sous Louis XIV," vol. II, p. 214). See also 11th June, 1664; letter from Steward Courtin to Colbert, describing the extortions of the judicial officers of Arras (*ibid.*, p. 136).

and to carry them through their appeal. They say that they have no funds, so that many heinous crimes remain unpunished.[1] In 1879, in Guyenne, the convicts' chains could not be loosened for want of money;[2] in 1707, a letter from the chancellor of Pontchartrain to the steward of Burgundy indicates similar inconveniences: "There are men condemned to the lash languishing in the prisons of Bourg en Bresse, because the tax-collector cannot be persuaded to send sixty livres to the executioner of Dijon."[3] In the growing disorder of the finances of the monarchy, these scandals showed no signs of coming to an end.

The question of money not only hampered the prosecutions, it often vitiated them. It interposed itself before the accused at every moment during the course of the procedure. Rousseau de La Combe observes as to Article 14 of Title X of the Ordinance: "All clerks of court, jailers, and the prisoner who had been longest in the prison (called the dean or provost) are forbidden to accept or exact anything from the prisoners in the shape of money, wine, or victuals in return for the initiation of the prisoner. This was called right of entry, or initiation. It was a mischievous custom, which the Ordinance has suppressed, corrected, and prohibited. The prisoner who would not bear this expense was even beaten and insulted, and even now it is very difficult to prevent this abuse."[4] In 1786 a former prison doorkeeper refers to this exploitation of prisoners as a natural thing: "It was necessary to pay the rent of a room to avoid having to share the straw with the vilest criminals, and to obtain the other usual necessities, without which the prison would be a terrible habitation, worse than death itself."[5] In this respect the Ordinance had been absolutely powerless; the sale of offices, from the highest to the lowest, and the lamentable financial system, were insurmountable obstacles.

The compilers of the Ordinance had endeavored to insure to accused persons the only safeguard of which the system adopted by them allowed, namely, accuracy and regularity in the record, and observation of the forms. But here once more they found themselves face to face with practical impossibilities. This written procedure was too minute and complex not to be capable of falsification, especially in the hands of inferior officers. Testimony as

[1] "Correspond. admin. sous Louis XIV," vol. II, p. 133.

[2] *Ibid.*, vol. II, p. 214. [3] *Ibid.*, p. 448.

[4] "Matières criminelles," p. 36. These customs were very old. See Edict of October, 1485, (*Isambert*, XI, p. 150).

[5] "Mémoire à consulter et consultation" for M. Lecardé, late clerk of court of the conciergerie of the Rouen courts of justice, against M. Lecauchois, advocate in the Parlement of Rouen, Paris, 1786, p. 22.

to the existence of abuses abound on the eve of the Revolution. Particularly in the case of the answers of accused persons and witnesses, it was undeniable that the transcription made by the clerk of court was very often but a faint echo of the spoken words. "Consider, I pray, that the translation by which the replies of accused persons in the lower courts are often reported is at times very incorrect. Here is an example of this in the present proceedings. The provost asks Simare if he had had no relations with Bradier. Simare, who does not understand what is meant by this phrase, replies in the negative. Bradier, however, is his brother-in-law. In answer to the next question, however, Simare admits having been at Salon with Bradier. Unfortunate people! they do not understand the questions asked of them and they, in turn, are not understood! You word your question and translate their replies. . . . Ah! the duty of the first judges, who alone interrogate, who alone translate and who alone draw up, is certainly a delicate one!"[1] Such a defect was really irreparable. And, again, it often happened that the writing out was not done on the spot. The clerk of court merely took notes and afterwards transcribed at his leisure. "I shudder when I call to mind that it is now customary in more than one court of the kingdom to take only notes of the depositions of the witnesses, or the answers of accused persons in the court-room, and to write them out afterwards out of court at leisure and to his liking."[2] All this was no doubt forbidden by the law; but human nature showed itself here, and nothing was easier when the accused and the witness could not sign their names.

The magistrates did not read the whole of these documents upon which their judgment was based. The reporting judge was heard, and faith was placed in him. "I find that four hours and a half at least were necessary for the mere reading of the proceeding, whence I calculate that it was impossible that this action could have been reported to the bench in three-quarters of an hour in the absence of the king's attorney-general."[3] Finally, the copies sent to the appellate judges were too often defective. "In all the supreme courts judgment is rendered only upon copies made and sent by a clerk of court and often by a deputy clerk of court, of the seigniorial jurisdiction. This makes one shudder. I could mention several examples of this where the

[1] *Dupaty*, "Mémoire pour trois hommes condamnés à la roue," p. 139.
[2] *Ibid.*, p. 66.
[3] "Mémoire justificatif" for Marie, Françoise, and Victoire Salmon, by *M. Lecauchois*, advocate of the Parlement of Rouen, Paris, 1786, p. 10.

copies were falsified. And yet we are asked to hold our tongues about our criminal Ordinance!"[1]

Official mistakes and violations of the rules laid down in the Ordinance were especially numerous in the inferior seignorial and royal courts. "His majesty's council is without doubt far from approving of this truly alarming system, which continually gets worse, owing to loose methods and lack of zeal, but the inferior judges must not be discouraged in their administration, and their number, already too small, further diminished by severities, however lawful these may be. . . . Complaint is raised from almost every side against the betrayal of trust of the inferior tribunals, and this clamor has been regarded in some quarters as seditious. No, it is by no means seditious. If it has been silent hitherto, that is because its utterance has been stifled for nearly two centuries."[2] It is no exaggeration to say that some of the trials laid bare "the mysteries of the inferior courts."[3]

§ 4. **Effect of Influence and Money upon the Enforcement of the Rigorous Provisions of the Ordinance.** — If the beneficent provisions of the Ordinance of 1670 were not always respected, neither were its rigorous rules always observed. One point in particular is to be noted. The Ordinance made secrecy of the procedure an inviolable rule. The accused must never be made acquainted with the charges, nor ever have counsel before his interrogation, and seldom after it. But it is easy to show that these principles yielded readily enough to two things, — potent at all times and especially then; these were, official influence and money.

Favor or money could procure communication of the documents either to the accused, or to their friends. Those who directed the administration of justice and those who expounded the Ordinance invoked in vain the prohibition contained in the law. On 25th July, 1677, the marquis de Seignelay writes to the lieutenant of the Admiralty court at Dieppe: "I have to inform you that the informations are documents which must be kept secret, and that you must not communicate (them) to any one without His Majesty's express mandate."[4] Here is some testimony gathered from the "Archives de la Bastille." A member of the

[1] *Dupaty*, "Mémoire," p. 232. See "Mémoire" for Catherine Estinès against the officers of the royal bench of Rivière, by *M. Lacroix*, advocate, Toulouse, 1786.

[2] *Dupaty*, "Moyens de droit," for Bradier, Simare, etc., Paris, 1786, p. 60.

[3] "Mémoire" for Catherine Estinès, p. 54.

[4] "Corresp. admin. sous Louis XIV," vol. II, p. 206.

judicature writes to Seignelay on 22d May, 1695: "M. de Pomponne gave M. the ambassador of Savoy a copy of the first interrogation. The latter gave consultations based upon that, on behalf of Colonna. He now asks me for a copy of the rest of the proceedings. . . . I have deemed it my duty to adhere to the rules and refuse it. M. de Pomponne having done me the honor to write to me that it was the king's wish, I have obeyed."[1] Another letter of 24th April, 1676, from an agent in the accused's interest, reads: "I have not been able to ascertain more exactly what Mainrot said in his interrogation upon the prisoner's seat, although I sent some one to the clerk of court. He would not let him see it, and said, when asked for a perusal of it, that he had orders to keep it secret."[2] "The Ordinance," says Serpillon, "provides that the witnesses be heard secretly, and Article 15 forbids clerks of court to make communication of the proceedings. There are, however, numerous contraventions of this rule, so strictly enjoined, and many officers who, in derogation of their official duties, communicate the proceedings to the parties, especially in petty crimes, under the impression that the prohibition relates to serious crimes only, while the Ordinance makes no distinction. Private prosecutors misuse it to suborn witnesses at the time of the confirmations and confrontations; the accused concocts replies on the knowledge he possesses of the depositions. In this way the truth cannot be discovered, justice is not administered, and crimes remain unpunished."[3] Jousse is no less to the point: "This prohibition of communicating the secret proceedings is badly enough observed in practice, and too often it happens that it is violated with impunity."[4]

At the end of the century, when greater freedom of speech prevailed, it was openly told how the thing was done. The clerks of court provided the documents, and the lawyers quoted them in their briefs. The forms were, however, respected in some briefs. In the brief of lawyer Lacroix on behalf of Catherine Estinès, the author often, in quoting from the deposition of a witness, makes use of the formula, "Such witness *ought* to have said." These surreptitious communications were, moreover, not usually complete. In 1786, Attorney-General Séguier was able to say in a celebrated address: "Everybody knows, and the jurisconsults themselves admit, that a criminal brief is nearly always only a collection of facts and circumstances furnished by the accused

[1] Vol. VI, p. 93. [2] Vol. VI, p. 184. [3] "Code criminel," p. 483.
[4] "Comment. sur l'Ordonnance de 1670," p. 165.

persons. Counsel almost invariably labor under the sad impossibility of verifying its accuracy. They are compelled to rely upon the statement of their clients."[1]

A curious debate, which took place in 1790 in the National Assembly, shows that, in later times, the practice under the Ordinance, as to the secrecy of the proceedings, had become somewhat divergent. The new law destined to take the place of the Ordinance, was being discussed. "Formerly," said *M. Rey,* "the confirmation of the witnesses was made in presence of the accused. The Magistrates, following the spirit rather than the letter of the law, even allowed communication of the charges." *M. Fréteau:* "In my capacity of judge I ought to state that this is not true. I have narrowly escaped expulsion from the Parlement of Paris for having given access to an indictment. Not only has the accused no such right, but no human means can confer upon him the privilege of becoming acquainted with the charges, and I must be permitted to deny, on behalf of the entire magistracy, the statement that your committee's draft is more absurd than the old Ordinances." *M. Goupil:* "And on my part I bear witness that in the Parlement of Rouen the accused were given copies of the charges whenever they asked for them. I have had in my office the charges of various proceedings, which I have quoted in italics in briefs. . . . It is not true that the Ordinance of 1670 absolutely prohibited this communication; it prohibited it only in the absence of an order of the judges. The Naval Ordinance drawn up in 1681 under the eyes of these same magistrates and in the same spirit did not forbid the judges' right to grant communication." *M. Rey:* "Communication was customary in the jurisdiction of the Parlement of Toulouse."[2]

It was equally possible to have a lawyer for counsel. The romances of the 1700s are not alone in showing us accused persons communicating with their counsel, even prior to the interrogation. Judicial documents also prove that this irregularity was not without precedent.[3] The aid of a counsel seems to have been a matter

[1] "Réquisitoire de 1786," against Dupaty's memorial, p. 14. At page 26 he points out that the author of the memorial "seems to have had cognizance of the procedure."

[2] Sitting of 28th October, 1790; Moniteur of the 29th.

[3] See "Archives de la Bastille," VI, p. 150. "I immediately afterwards went the same day to the most eminent advocate of the Parlement in criminal matters, called M. Beurey, to consult him upon the means that could be taken to prove the calumniousness of what Colonna has stated in his interrogation . . . but before explaining myself to him, having asked him if he had been consulted by any one in Colonna's matter, he

of right in all cases when, a delay being granted, the accused sought the reversal or review of the decree.[1] When the compassion or connivance of the jailers or keepers of the prisons was gained all difficulty vanished.[2]

But all this was a matter of solicitation and influence. It was always arbitrary, and sometimes the liberty of defense was bought for cash. It constituted a shocking inequality between rich and poor; that was to be acknowledged later on. "Our criminal Ordinance is strangely inconsistent. It is so distrustful of the enlightenment and the accuracy, of the remoteness and obscurity of the lower criminal courts, that it grants to accused persons the remedy of appeal to the supreme courts from all their judgments whatever; and in the meanwhile, by depriving the accused of counsel, it deprives them of every means of making use of the appeal. — What am I saying? They were able, these unfortunate people, to take advantage of the resources which the Ordinance grants to them; they could even have a counsel. How? By what means? Is it necessary to say how? If they had not been poor. Alas! yes. But for their poverty they would, like the rich, have had counsel; like the rich, they would have appealed; like the rich, they would have penetrated the secrecy of the proceedings either in the court-room, or they would have purchased it in the offices of the clerks of court; they would have presented petitions; they would have issued briefs. And, is it credible that the judges of Chaumont would have immured three *wealthy* men in their dungeons for a period of thirty months? What! Shall those laws, designed for the relief of the unfortunate in proportion to their misery, be used, on the contrary, to oppress those

told me that he had been consulted on behalf of the Marquis de Livourne along with another advocate called M. Lambin."

[1] *Dupaty*, "Mémoires," p. 221. "Arrived at the prison, I ask to see these three unfortunate men. I am shown into a room where I wait." — *Lecauchois*, "Mémoire" for the girl Salmon, p. 16: "Consider the obstacles I had to encounter in the course of the fifty to sixty hours of interrogation which I have had of this girl . . . what precautions I have had to take to draw from the accused, with the help of my discoveries from other sources, the information within her knowledge, under these argus eyes, without their learning anything. . . . Besides, I know of no law which ordains that the counsel for the defense shall not question his client or confer with him except in the presence of witnesses."

[2] In the case of the girl Salmon, Lecardé, keeper of the prison, receives six letters from the accused, after her transfer to another jail ("Mémoire" for M. Lecardé, pp. 6-9, 12, 15). See "Archives de la Bastille," VI, p. 159. "The day before yesterday, the said Rencontré, detained for two years in this town in the prisons and by order of M. the procurator-general of the Parlement, twice indicted and detained, went to drink with the jailer in a tavern outside the prison, where he made the jailer drunk, and escaped."

unfortunate, and in proportion to their wretchedness! What! shall the poor, the wretched, and, as arrogance calls them, the dregs of the nation, twenty millions of human beings, be reduced in the future to learn that they have a king only through the molestations of the tax-collectors, magistrates only by the sight of scaffolds, and to know of God only after their death!"[1] — "Are you men of influence not yet contented with your criminal courts of justice? Only look at all that has been done for you for more than two centuries, since the time of Poyet down to that of Pussort. It has bereft the defense of accused persons of all communication of the proceedings and all counsel, and solely to the prejudice of the masses, for *you* are rich. It has deprived the defense of the accused of the publicity which watches over the courts and keeps them solicitous; and this solely to the detriment of the masses, for *your* whole existence is so important and so valuable! It has curtailed for the defense, by more than half, the power to vindicate itself, and solely to the detriment of the people; for who would, in effect, dare to incriminate *you?* And, finally, it has stripped punishments of all moderation and proportion, and solely to the prejudice of the people, for all the judicial machinery of kings is often necessary to enable the justice of the laws to reach *you!*"[2]

§ 5. **Commentators on the Ordinance.** — A final effect of the publication of the Ordinance of 1670 remains to be pointed out. In the compilation of this code, the compilers furnished a solid foundation for criminal law. They laid a basis for learned commentaries, which did not fail them. The Ordinance made a scientific study of criminal procedure a possibility. Hitherto the practice had been explained rather than the laws expounded. In the works of the jurists the texts of the Ordinances only intervened at intervals, in support of the exposition; they did not constitute its true basis. A perusal of Imbert's treatise, for example, is sufficient to convince us of this fact. Thereafter an expounder of the law would take up the articles of the Ordinance point by point, to deduce all their consequences. The *commentaries* succeeded the *books of practice;* or at least the former held the chief place. The exegesis was not drawn from the Ordinance alone. Several works bore titles displaying an extensive synthesis — the "Code Criminel," or the "Institutes de droit criminel." This contributed potently to give to French criminal

[1] *Dupaty*, "Mémoires," p. 237.
[2] *Dupaty*, "Moyens de droit pour Bradier," etc., pp. 43, 44.

procedure that clearness and at the same time that severity ever unknown among the congenerous usages of neighboring countries.

This importance acquired by the commentators was by no means to the liking of Pussort, the chief author of the Ordinance. His wishes were utterly opposed to it, and he did not conceal his opinion on the subject. He advised the king "to forbid any one whomsoever to make any notes or commentaries upon the Ordinances, or any collection of decisions, under penalty for forgery, a fine of ten thousand livres and confiscation of the copies; the commentaries on the Ordinances and the reasonings drawn from the decisions only having the effect of weakening their authority under the specious pretexts of equity and of the weight of the matters judged." [1] But in this case once more Pussort was striving against an inevitable tendency.

The works of the criminal law-writers, especially those of Jousse and Muyart de Vouglans, were very soon incorporated with the Ordinance, so to speak. They were as much obeyed by the courts as the law itself. "Jousse wrote that, and Jousse is the spirit, the reason, and the judicial practice of the courts of the kingdom, yes, the very court practice. Did not the jurisconsult Meynard say in dealing with a question: 'the jurisconsults have ordained'? And they did in fact ordain, especially in regard to criminal justice. All the blanks in our criminal legislation, incomplete, disjointed, falling into ruins as it was, are, if I may say so, filled up by the maxims of the criminal law-writers." [2] — "Certainly not from the inferior courts is it worth while to demand or even to hope for the abjuration of all the barbarous maxims which the criminal law-writers have incessantly established in the criminal jurisdiction. For criminal law has been so far abandoned to the criminal law-writers by our monarchs, too much occupied for the most part in increasing their power to concern themselves with the happiness of their subjects." [3]

[1] "Mélanges Clérambault," No. 613, p. 453.
[2] *Dupaty*, "Mémoire," p. 156. [3] *Ibid.*, p. 227.

TITLE II

CRIMINAL PROCEDURE IN EUROPE GENERALLY

CHAPTER I

CRIMINAL PROCEDURE IN OTHER COUNTRIES

§ 1. **Introductory.** — The criminal procedure developed in France was not a purely national institution; on the contrary, it formed part of the common law of Europe. We can convince ourselves of this by taking a glance at the nations surrounding ours, — Italy, Spain, Germany, and the Netherlands. There also the same evolution took place; there also had the Canon law introduced the inquisitorial action and the Roman law exercised its influence. To the accusatory and public procedure had succeeded the written and secret examination. To the rude proofs of the feudal period had succeeded the learned doctrine of presumptions.

The French procedure, however, is distinguished from other kindred procedures by features peculiar to itself. Nowhere had the forms become better settled, or the rules more clearly and firmly established, and from this point of view Muyart de Vouglans could write without exaggeration: "It can be said to the honor of France that its practice in this respect has been brought to a degree of perfection which gives it a preëminent position among enlightened nations."[1] But, at the same time, nowhere had the severities of the system been more rigorously enforced, or the defense more rigidly hampered. For good as for ill, the system had been carried to extremes. One exception must be made, however, in regard to torture; this was resorted to by Italy and Germany especially with a harshness exceeding that practised in France. One institution in particular, that of

[1] "Lettre sur le livre des délits et des peines," p. 20.

the public prosecutor, distinguished France from the neighboring nations. Not that it was not also found abroad, but it had either been introduced by French influence, or it was imperfect and did not form, as with us, an essential part of the machinery of the procedure.[1]

In contrast to France, a new juridical world was making its appearance on the other side of the English Channel. England had preserved the accusatory and public procedure, and the liberty of defense of the accused. Developing elements which the other European nations had also possessed, but which they had allowed to perish, it had created the procedure by jurors, which then constituted a kind of anomaly, but which was destined to spread its powerful influence over the whole of Europe.

We shall endeavor in a few pages to point out some of the main features of the several systems.

§ 2. **Italy.** — Italy, under the dominion of the Lombards, had become familiar with the procedure and the criminal law of the Germanic customs, the "compositions," the private accusation, the oral and public trial, the exculpations by oath and the co-swearers ("cojurantes"), the ordeals, and especially the judicial duel.[2] But Italy was the country where the law of ancient Rome had developed, and where that of modern Rome had gradually been elaborated. More than any other country it was bound to feel the influence of the Roman law and the Canon law. It is proved to-day that the study of Roman law had never been interrupted. The Bologna school was not a revival. It was the new growth on an old tree, which had, for long, pushed forth but slender branches, but in which the sap had always been flowing under the bark.

Schools of law there had been in continuous succession, first at Rome, then at Ravenna, at Pavia from the first half of the 1000s, and at Verona at the same period. This brings us to the Bologna school, which, from the first half of the 1100s, attained such a high standard that "all that had gone before had soon fallen into oblivion." [3] The Bologna professors were, at the same time, men of business. "The Bologna school was not merely the initiator of a scientific movement. It also exerted an influence on the prac-

[1] *Biener*, "Beiträge zu der Geschichte des Inquisitionsprozesses," p. 208 *et seq.*

[2] See *Sclopis*, "Histoire de la législation Italienne," vol. I, p. 199 *et seq.*

[3] *M. Rivier*, "La science du droit dans la première moitié du Moyen-Age" (Nouvelle revue historique de droit français et étranger, 1877, p. 1 *et seq.*).

tice of law; for the 'glossatores' made it their study to apply the laws to the facts of life."[1] If they saw the accusatory system dominate in the "Corpus juris," they, at the same time, found torture there. They also found there the germs of that theory of presumptions which they were the first to build up, and which spread from Italy throughout Europe. In addition to these, the canonists built up the inquisitorial procedure, which was to be finally sanctioned by the papacy.

Statutory laws were also enacted. These were, originally, municipal statutes, the laws of free cities. "The cities, under the inspiration of the Roman and Christian principle, adopted high ideals and punished offenses according to their deserts and for the common welfare. In the constant revision of these statutes, the influence of the Roman law always continued to increase."[2] The same thing happened in regard to the Canon law, and gradually the inquisitorial procedure took its place alongside of the accusation. The judicial organization varied according to the cities, but two successive types of communal government were distinguishable. Originally the towns were governed by consuls.[3] The origin of this magistracy is doubtful. M. Pertile thinks that the consuls sprang originally from the council, with which the bishops surrounded themselves for the administration of their dioceses and temporal sovereignties.[4] To the number of two or three, according to the places and the times, they tried civilly and criminally, exercising the repressive jurisdiction in common.[5] They were, besides, assisted by a college of judges or a council of practitioners.[6] A revolutionary change afterwards took place in the government of cities, putting the power into the hands of one alone,[7] who presided over the courts of law as in the other departments of the administration; but the forms changed little in regard to the jurisdiction. "When the attempt is made to bind together more closely the political and civil forms, and the 'podesta,' the foremost magistrate of the republic, is called upon from without, it is requisite that he have judges with him, or counsellors be furnished for his assistance."[8] These counsellors, or assessors, were almost always learned jurisconsults, celebrated professors.

[1] *Pessina*, "Elementi di diritto penale" (3d edit., p. 51); *cf. Pertile*, "Storia del diritto Italiano," § 168: "The Glossators and their successors annotated and practised even the criminal law of the Pandects and the Code as if it were a living universal law."

[2] *Pertile, op. cit.*, § 168.

[3] *Ibid.*, vol. II, Part I, § 48.

[4] *Ibid.*, vol. II, Part I, p. 25.

[5] *Ibid.*, vol. II, Part 1, p. 25.

[6] *Ibid.*, § 49.

[7] *Ibid.*, § 40.

[8] *Sclopis, op. cit.*, vol. II, p. 293.

[8] *Ibid.*, vol. II, p. 113 *et seq.*

Among the old Italian laws those of Sardinia ought to be cited ("Carta di Logu"), settling "the rules of procedure; the accusation is here the rule, but the necessity of an 'inquisitio' is recognized, in the absence of accusers." [1] In lower Italy appeared the "Constitutiones Regni siculi," united with a Code by Frederic II in 1231. By these laws feudal and ecclesiastical courts of judicature were abolished and bailiffs and justiciars and the high court of the kingdom substituted for them.[2] Criminal law was, in particular, resuscitated from its Roman source, and the violences of private feuds and the judicial duel were abolished. The influence of the Roman law also made itself felt in the introduction of the inquisitorial procedure.[3]

But it was, in truth, the practice and the writings of the jurisconsults that brought criminal procedure to its perfect development. The procedure of the "inquisitio" rapidly took the lead, and put the old accusation in the background. We cannot give the long list of jurists whose works contributed to this evolution.[4] We shall merely cite several names which overtop the others and mark halting-places. About 1271 *Gulielmus Durandus* publishes his "Speculum juris." [5] A canonist, he describes the "inquisitio" chiefly according to the canon law, but shows that it had its place also according to the civil law: "leges . . . semiplene de inquisitione tractant, sed secundum canones plenius patet forma et natura inquisitionis et quando et qualiter in ea procedatur." *Albertus Gaudinus*, who died probably in 1300, admits the inquisitorial procedure as a common law institution: "hodie de jure civili judices potestatum de quolibet maleficio cognoscunt ex officio suo per inquisitionem. Et ita servant judices de consuetudine et ita vidi communiter observari, quamvis sit contra jus civile." [6]

At the beginning of the 1300s, *Bartolus* and *Baldus* describe and explain the "inquisitio." [7] In the 1400s, *Angelus de Gambilionibus de Aretio* in his "Tractatus de maleficiis" explains the inquisitorial proceedings at length, torture, and the theory of presumptions.[8] But it is chiefly in the 1500s that the Italian criminal law-writers shine with incomparable lustre. Italy seemed

[1] *Sclopis, op. cit.*, vol. II, p. 113 *et seq.*

[2] *Ibid.*, vol. II, p. 254 *et seq.*

[3] *Pessina*, "Elementi," pp. 46, 47.

[4] See *M. A. du Boys*, "Histoire du droit criminel de la France du XVIe au XIXe siècle, comparé avec cela de l'Italie," etc., vol. I, p. 125 *et seq.* — *Biener*, "Beiträge," Chap. IV; "Glossatoren und italienische Praktiker," p. 78 *et seq.*

[5] Upon Durand, see *M. Glasson*, Nouvelle Revue historique, 1881, pp. 417, 418.

[6] *Biener, op. cit.*, p. 96.

[7] *Ibid.*, p. 98 *et seq.*

[8] *Du Boys, op. cit.*, I, pp. 300, 311; *Biener, op. cit.*, pp. 106, 110.

then to be the home country of criminal law, as, strange to say, a similar movement appears to be again taking place in our own days. *Hippolytus of Marseilles,*[1] *Julius Clarus,*[2] *Farinacius,*[3] *Menochius,*[4] to mention merely the most celebrated jurists of that period, definitely establish the principles of criminal procedure and the system of legal proofs. *Hippolytus of Marseilles* makes a special study of torture, and *Menochius* of the theory of presumptions.

Along with the "inquisitio," which is approved almost without restriction, the accusation is still recognized; but it plays only a secondary and barren part.[5] The judge takes action either "ex officio" or "ad instantiam partis," and in the latter case we have the "inquisitio cum promovente," which we have mentioned several times. Clarus also carefully describes, along with the accusation, the "querela partis offensæ," which bears a strong resemblance to our civil action.[6] If a "delictum facti permanentis" is in question, the first necessity is the establishment of the "corpus delicti." This done, the judge proceeds with an "informatio," the purpose of which is to establish the "diffamatio." He hears the witnesses secretly and takes their depositions in writing. This first phase of the action is concluded by the drawing up of the "charta inquisitionis" or "libellus criminalis," a kind of indictment, which will be used as the basis of the subsequent procedure.[7]

[1] "Practica causarum criminalium" (Lugduni, 1528). See *Biener, op. cit.*, pp. 110, 112.

[2] "Sententiarum receptarum liber quintus" (Lyons, 1772).

[3] "Farinacii opera" (Duaci, 1618).

[4] "De præsumptionibus, conjecturis, signis et indiciis commentaria" (1628 ed.).

[5] *Jul. Clarus*, "Practica crim.," qu. 3, Nos. 6, 8, p. 416: "Sed certe quidquid sit de jure communi hæc omnia cessant ex consuetudine præsentis temporis; nam etiam de jure civili hodie in quocumque casu permissum est procedere ex officio et sic per inquisitionem . . . et consequenter hodie superflua est etiam illa practica quam tradit Alex. in apost. ad Bar. quod scilicet judex omnino statuat parti offensæ terminum ad accusandum, quo elapso poterit deinde, ubi pars non accusat, ex officio procedere, nec poterit postea pars etiamsi velit accusare impedire processum ipsius judicis inquirentis."

[6] Qu. 10, No. 1, p. 428: "Licet isti duo modi procedendi sc. ad querelam et ex officio videantur non modo diversi, sed etiam quodammodo incompatibiles, tamen consuetudo admittit quod super querela partis judex statim incipiat inquirere. Scias autem quod hæc querela multum differt ab accusatione; . . . si non esset via aperta judici ad inquirendum aliter quam per querelam, puta quia non præcederet denunciatio neque diffamatio neque aliquid ex his . . . non deberet judex procedere super hujusmodi querela, nisi haberet legitima requisita, licet contrarium plerumque observetur de consuetudine. . . . Si talis instigator prius querelavit et ad ejus querelam judex inquisivit, tenet locum partis et ideo est citandus."

[7] *Jul. Clarus*, qu. 7, No. 1, p. 424: "Facta denuntiacione, judex super ea assumit informationes et indicia et eis assumptis format libellum, sive

Then the accused is summoned or arrested and subjected to the "libellus"; he is obliged to answer regarding the points therein contained. If he pleads not guilty, the judge hears the witnesses anew, after they have taken the oath in presence of the accused.[1] Then comes the torture, if its administration is proper, and lastly the judgment. This written procedure takes place secretly.[2]

All this very much resembles the criminal action which we have described as conducted in France. In Italy we merely find more of the "libellus criminalis" and less of the confrontation.[3] It must also be borne in mind that the freedom of the defense was greater there, and the treatment of the accused less severe than with us. No doubt the accused was usually required to take the oath at the time of the interrogation;[4] he was not present at the deposition of the witnesses, nor could he even give in a list of questions to be put to them.[5] But he received communication of the written depositions, according to the old principles,[6] and was entitled to have witnesses heard in his defense. Only, he could not make use of these powers until he had answered the interrogation.[7] It must be noted, in particular, that the aid of advocates was allowed, and that the judges could even sometimes appoint them officially for the accused.[8] These defending counsel were not allowed to assist their client at the time of the interrogation;[9] and a copy of the

inquisitionem, in quo narrat quomodo propter denunciationem datam . . . intendit ex officio procedere, et ità communiter servatur in practica."

[1] *Jul. Clarus*, qu. 7, No. 1, p. 552: "Si neget, iterum examinant testes, eo citato ad videndum eos jurare, et valde graviter erraret judex qui, omissa tali repetitione testium, procederet ad torturam vel condemnationem; nam testes recepti ante litiscontestationem nullam fidem faciunt contra reum."

[2] See Sclopis, *op. cit.*, I, p. 208 *et seq.*

[3] It was not unknown, but it was not necessary.

[4] *Jul. Clarus*, qu. 45, No. 9, p. 551: "Magis est communis opinio quod deferendum reo juramentum de veritate dicenda."

[5] In that respect his treatment was similar to that of the private accuser. *Clarus*, qu. 23, No. 3, p. 457: "Consuetudo observat quod inquisitus vel accusatus nunquam dat interrogatoria testibus pro fisco deponentibus non etiam dat accusator interrogatoria deponentibus ad defensam: sed judex aut fiscalis eos interrogat, prout sibi videtur."

[6] *Jul. Clarus*, qu. 49, No. 3, p. 580: "Etiamsi contra aliquem procedatur per viam inquisitionis nomina testium contra eum productorum nec non et dicta ipsorum (competenter) publicanda sunt, ad effectum ut possit se ipsum defendere."

[7] *Ibid.*, qu. 45, No. 8, p. 551: "Consuetudo servat totum oppositum, quod sc. reus interrogetur et examinetur ante datas defensiones et copiam indiciorum."

[8] *Ibid.*, qu. 49, No. 11: "Dicit Blanc. quod ita quotidie servatur, quod scilicet judices dant advocatos carceratis."

[9] *Ibid.*, qu. 45, No. 11: "Quæro etiam, quando fit examen rei, debeant esse patroni causarum? Resp. quod de jure videtur dici posse quod sic; sed certe usus et curiarum stylus hoc non observat."

information was given them with some hesitancy;[1] but they were, none the less, a great help. Farinacius composed a portion of his works from the pleadings which, in the first part of his career, he had prepared in the defense of accused persons.

Did the institution of public prosecutor exist in Italy? There was originally another institution which must not be confused with it, which, however, partially answered the same purpose. The judges often had functionaries placed under them whose duty it was to denounce the crimes which came to their knowledge; but these inferior officers were really merely official denunciators. "Albertus Gandinus, Bartolus, Angelus Aretinus, and Hippolytus of Marseilles recognized these personages, whom they called 'syndici,' 'consules locorum et villarum,' 'ministrales,' 'officiales.' I find these officers mentioned in several statutes of Italian towns; in the statutes of Verona they are called 'jurati contratarum' and 'massarii villarum'; in the statutes of Roveredo, 'massarii,' 'jurati,' 'syndici villarum' and 'plebatuum.'"[2]

But there is also a question of a true "procurator fiscalis" in the authors.[3] "About the end of the Middle Ages Venice had a magistracy combining all the characteristics of a public prosecutor liberally constituted; it is the same thing as the 'avouerie' of the commune which existed in the 1200 s."[4] But, generally speaking, the institution was of imperfect development. That would, at least, appear from the following extracts from eminent authors: "In Italy, in the 1500 s, we find, more plainly than before, the inquisitorial procedure, with the participation of a 'procurator fiscalis,' particularly at Rome, Naples, and Milan.

[1] *Jul. Clarus*, qu. 6, No. 23: "Reus dicit judici ut priusquam ad alteriora procedat det ei copiam indiciorum quæ super diffamatione assumpsit. Angel. dicit quod cauti advocati hoc petunt, ut possint impugnare testes diffamantes . . . non video quomodo sit danda ejus copia reo petenti."

[2] *Biener*, "Beiträge," pp. 92, 93. The author remarks in a note that in Farinacius (Book I, tit. I, No. 17) they are called: "Antiani seu parochiani, qui statutis tenentur denunciare delicta commissa in eorum villis seu parochiis." But this may be a relic of the "testes synodales."

[3] *Julius Clarus* clearly distinguishes the three classes of personages who are entitled to invoke the inquisition. Qu. 10, No. 3, p. 428: "Scias igitur quod tria sunt genera eorum qui instigatores seu promotores inquisitionis appellantur. Aliqui enim id faciunt ex necessitate, vel saltem ex debito eorum officii, prout sunt advocati et procuratores, seu syndici fiscales, ad quos maxime pertinet instare assidue ut judices contra delinquentes inquirant. Alii vero faciunt ex præcepto sive deputatione judicum, qui solent deputare aliquem coadjutorem, qui loco partis seu fiscalis assistat inquisitioni . . . postremo aliqui id faciunt sponte quia comparent in judicis et subministrant testes et indicia contra reos inquisitos."

[4] *Sclopis, op. cit.*, p. 260.

But what this participation of the fiscal was cannot be determined without elaborate research, for which the authorities are usually lacking, since only local institutions are found. Julius Clarus himself, who, in his works, chiefly based upon the common law, gives such ample information as to the Milanese practice, makes only a passing mention of the procurators fiscal of Milan, because they did not constitute a common law institution. In short, it must be admitted that the fiscals were introduced into certain districts of Italy only from the end of the 1400s, and the principal cause of their introduction was the influence exerted upon Italy by France and Spain. Especially in the 1500s we find in Savoy the criminal procedure with a fiscal quite in the French form, which must be attributed to the influence exercised by France upon Savoy from the end of the 1400s." [1] — "The fiscals to which we find allusions made, in Julius Clarus for example, are not, properly speaking, public prosecutors; they intervene in support of the prosecution after the judge has taken office on denunciation or officially, but they have no initiative of prosecution . . . " it is only "when the inquisition has opened that they are admitted, as the private accuser or the complainant would be, to argue presumptions and to appear at the trial." [2] These observations are well founded, but they might profitably be more precise. It must be acknowledged, too, that Julius Clarus on several occasions plainly states that the procurator fiscal is truly party to the criminal action; [3] and although, on the other hand, the fiscal can primarily do nothing more than instigate the judge to open an inquiry, taking no active part until the latter has issued results, that is perfectly in conformity with the principles which govern the powers of the public prosecutor in France in the 1400s and the 1500s.[4]

§ 3. **Spain.** — Spain had been thoroughly imbued with Roman civilization, and after its invasion by the barbarians, it still had the law which, among the "Leges barbarorum," bears the

[1] *Biener*, "Beiträge," pp. 213, 214. [2] *Du Boys*, *op. cit.*, I, p. 322.

[3] *Jul. Clarus*, qu. 10, No. 4, p. 429: "Quæro numquid instigator sit citandus in causa inquisitionis? Resp. De advocato seu syndico fiscali nulli dubium est quin sit citandus; nam in quocumque judicio, in quo potest ex officio procedi, *fiscus est loco partis*."

[4] *Ibid.*, qu. 10, No. 6: "Tu scis quod hodie, nemine quærelante, *fiscus succedit loco accusatoris*. . . . Numquid debet eo casu fiscus querelam seu accusationem porrigere, super quâ judex deinde procedat? Resp. quod non, sed tantum proceditur ad informationem eo instante. Et ita se habet communis observantia omnium curiarum, et dicunt semper instare fiscum ut procedatur contra delinquentes, etiam si de hujusmodi instantia in actis non appareat; debet tamen prius esse aperta viæ judici ad inquirendum aliter quam per instigationem ipsius fiscalis."

clearest imprint of the Roman law. Certain usages also, which the rest of Europe were not to take up until the renaissance of Roman law, torture, for example, had never disappeared from Spain. Torture is found in the "Forum judicum," with some restrictions, it is true.[1] The "Fuero-Juzgo" also sanctioned the institution of delators, or informers, whom it even compensated,[2] but it maintained the accusatory system as a principle.[3]

The Mussulman conquest and the strife following it gave Spain a peculiar position in European history, and in the midst of these convulsions the Code of the Visigoths fell into oblivion. The majority of the people were ignorant of the existence of a "Fuero Juzgo," and had no rule of government except what they saw practised in other parts of the country. The only laws which governed the administration of the courts of justice were the good sense of some practical men, and the precedents made by judgments passed in similar cases.[4] "The Spanish feudal system was originated at that time, and with it the criminal procedure, which everywhere ruled in the feudal Courts, and of which the judicial duel was the principal expedient.[5]

Under the influence of the crown a considerable advance was made, namely, in the constitution of "Fueros." The towns in great numbers obtained charters insuring to them certain privileges and organizing their courts. Very soon this privileged right became a common right,[6] what the Spanish authors usually call the *foral* government ("gobierno foral").[7] The "fueros" date back to the 1000s, the 1100s, and the 1200s; two of the most celebrated were that of Leon, conceded by Alphonse V, and the "Fuero Viejo" of Castile. Generally speaking, the criminal

[1] See *supra*, p. 109. *Cf.* "Historia del Derecho Español," by *Don Juan Sempere* (Book II, chap. XIX, p. 95).

[2] Book VII, tit. 1.

[3] "Ni el conde ni el juez podien proceder de oficio en causa alguna criminal, como no constava por pruebas muy manifestas el autor de delitto" (*Sempere, op. cit.*, p. 40). See, however, as to the official prosecution, *supra*, p. 97, note 2.

[4] *Sempere*, "Historia," p. 132.

[5] *Ibid.*, "Historia," Book II, chaps. III to V.

[6] *Sempere*, "Aquellas cartas pueblas y al parer cartas privilegios fueron amplificando cosi insensiblemente los derechos y representacion del estado general."

[7] *Sempere*, "Historia," Book II, ch. VII *et seq.* — *Don Francisco Martinez Marina*, "Ensayo historico critico sobre la legislacion y principales cuerpos legales de Leon y Castilla" (Books IV and V). — "Historia de la legislacion y recitaciones del derecho civil de Espana, por los abogados Amalio Marichalar marquez de Montesa y Cayetano Manrique," 1861–1876, in particular, vol. II, p. 162 *et seq.*

law contained in them is that known at that period to the towns of other countries. We find in them the accusatory procedure, the oath of purgation, the ordeals by red-hot iron, but we also find the "informatio" of veracious witnesses. There, as in the French towns, we see the beginnings of the official prosecution in the inquest or "pesquisa," of which we shall treat immediately.[1]

Certain circumstances were, however, to give to the Spanish law a decisive direction. First of these is the ever increasing influence of the Church and the Canon law in Spain, leading to what the Spanish authors call the "nueva jurisprudencia ultramontana";[2] and in the second place is the renewed study of the Roman law, which was hailed with enthusiasm. "On the opening of the law schools at Bologna and other Italian towns in the middle of the 1100s, a great number of Spaniards flocked into these schools; down to the foundation of the University of Lerida in the year 1300 all the lettered men of Aragon were trained in Italy . . . the University of Valencia had been founded at the beginning of the 1200s, but it did not last long; afterwards that of Salamanca was erected, and the best-endowed chairs were those of the civil and canon law. It must be noted that in the teaching of the law, while there was but one chair of civil law, there were three of Decretals, which clearly shows the preponderance of the new ultramontane ideas at that time. . . . They increased so rapidly that very soon the laws, 'fueros', and national customary law were forgotten and set aside in favor of the new Italian maxims. In order to check this abuse, the Cortès of Barcelona, in 1251, demanded that the practice of the civil law and the canon law be absolutely proscribed in the civil courts."[3]

It was at this time that Alphonse X, the Wise, thought it necessary to settle the laws in new codifications. First to appear was the "Fuero real," or "Fuero de las leyes," "an excellent compendium of laws, concise, clear, and methodical, comprising the most important laws of the municipal 'fueros,' adapted to the Castilian customary law and to the 'Fuero-Juzgo,' whose rules were very often literally copied."[4] Book IV, and last, is devoted to criminal law, and it is not surprising to find there, side by side with the accusation, which forms the rule, the "pesquisa" or

[1] *Sempere*, p. 161. — *Alb. du Boys*, "Histoire du droit criminel en Espagne," pp. 54–130.
[2] *Sempere*, "Historia," Book II, ch. XVIII to XXII.
[3] *Ibid.*, "Historia," pp. 160–162. [4] *Marina*, "Ensayo," p. 277.

inquest, which is the prosecution "ex officio" and which takes the form which it was to bear everywhere in Europe.[1]

But the king meditated the promulgation of a more extensive and more detailed law. This was the Code of seven parts, the "Septenario" or "Siete partidas."[2] This work, commenced in 1256, was completed in 1263 or 1265. Such a codification, undertaken in the midst of the changes which Spain was then undergoing, was bound to be of a somewhat hasty character. "Frequent contradictions are met at each step in the confused mixture of so many systems of legislation, ecclesiastical, lay, feudal, foral, and royal."[3]

The criminal procedure is found in Parts III and VII. It was already fixed in its positive features. The law recognized three methods of prosecution, the accusation, still holding the first place, the denunciation, and the official prosecution. The last mentioned was made effective by the "pesquisa" or inquisition, which thus intervened in case of denunciation;[4] a brief description of it according to the "Siete Partidas" is as follows. "'Pesquisa' in romance language has the same meaning as 'inquisitio' in Latin and it refers to money matters. . . . The 'pesquisas' could be made in three ways. . . One, when a general 'pesquisa' is made as to a large territory, or as to any city or town or other place, the 'pesquisa' being made as to all and any of the inhabitants thereof. . . .[5] The second . . . when it is made as to the deeds of any who are traduced, or other indicated deeds the doer of which is not known; the third way is when the parties appear, praying that the king or the person having the power to judge order the 'pesquisa' to be made."[6] But the right to have the "pesquisa" made appears originally to have been a privilege of the

[1] Book IV, Tit. XX: "Accusationes y pesquisas."—See *du Boys*, *op. cit.*, pp. 175–185.

[2] See "Los Codigos Españoles concordados y anotados" (Second edition, Madrid, 1872–1873), vol. III.

[3] *Sempere*, "Historia," p. 276.

[4] These three methods are also those pointed out in the customary laws of Tortosa of the 1200s; see "Historia del Derecho en Cataluna Mallorca y Valencia, Codigo de las Costumbres de Tortosa," by Doctor *Bienvenido Olivier*, vol. III, p. 590 *et seq.*

[5] This is the "inquisitio generalis" of the canonists and the jurists.

[6] "Partida III," Tit. 17, ley. 1: "Pesquisa en romance tanto quiere dezir en latin como *inquisitio* et tiene a muchas cosas . . . las pesquisas pueden se fazer en tres maneras. La una quando fazen pesquisa communalmente sobre una gran tierra, o sobre alguna cibdad, o villa o otro lugar, que sea fecha pesquisa sobre todos los que y moraren, o sobre algunos d'ellos. . . . La segunda . . . quando la fazen sobre fechos senalados, que non saben quien los fizo. La tercera quando las partes se avienen queriendo que el Rey o aquel quel pleyto ha de judgar mande fazer la pesquisa."

sovereign power, as in France.[1] The inquisitors, or "pesquesidores," were always required to have a warrant from the king or the "Merino major," and, where towns and cities were concerned, from the person with right to try in these places. We also find inquisitors at regular stations.[2]

The "inquisitio" ought, in principle, to be made officially only to learn the truth regarding doubtful and hidden matters, of which certain persons are suspected of being the perpetrators, and are on that account defamed.[3] There ought to be at least two inquisitors, with a clerk ("dos pesquesidores a los menos e un escrivano").[4] They ought to be "God fearing men of good repute; for by their 'pesquisa' many may die or suffer other bodily punishment." [5]

The "pesquisa" takes place in secret. The inquisitors make the witnesses take the oath, "then they take each of them aside and examine them; then when they have examined them, and the witnesses have said that they have nothing more to tell, they ought to forbid them on the oath which they have taken, to reveal to any living being what they have said in the 'pesquisa.'" [6] On the conclusion of the inquiry they must be handed over to the judges ("e si deven la dar a aquellos que la ovieren de judgar").[7]

The accused is then summoned or arrested, and his interrogation is proceeded with; the judge makes him swear to tell the truth and has his replies written down by the "greffier," or clerk.[8] Torture

[1] "Partida VII," Tit. 16, ley. 2: "Si el Rey de su officio mandasse fazer pesquisa." *Cf. ibid.*, law 3. — As to the "justicia" of Aragon and his power of inquiry, see *Marichalar and Manrique, op. cit.*, vol. VI, p. 332 *et seq.*

[2] "Otrosi pueden poner pesquisidores los señores de algunos lugares honrrados, si han poder de fazer justicia en aquel lugar, do quieren fazer pesquisa. Otrosi pesquesidores y a que deven ser puestos para pesquesir en las cibdades e en las villas. Et estos deven poner aquellos que han poder de judgar o de fazer justicia con el consejo et con omes buonos señalados de cada collacion." "Partida III," Tit. 17, ley. 2.

Gloss: "Istos intellige eos qui de jure communi syndici, vel officiales jurati seu testes synodales dicuntur." There were not at that time inquisitors, properly speaking, but official informers.

[3] "Partida III," Tit. 16, ley. 3: "llamanlos (los lestigos) por saber dellos la verdad de las cosas dubdosas, que son mal fechas abscondidamente, de que algunos son infamados."

[4] *Ibid.*, Tit. 17, ley. 4. — Gloss: "Optima certe provisio si esset in usu!"

[5] *Ibid.*, Tit. 17, ley. 4: "Buenos omes que temon a Dios e de buena fama deven ser los pesquesidores, puesque por su pesquisa han muchos de morir o de sofrir otra pena en lor cuerpos."

[6] *Ibid.*, Tit. 17, ley. 9.

[7] *Ibid.*, Tit. 17, ley. 9.

[8] "Part. VII," Tit. 29: *De como deven ser recabdados los presos:* "E estonce el Rey o autel Judgador (que lo mande prender) deven *le fazer jurar* que diga la verdad de aquel fecho sobre que la recabdaron, et deve lo todo fazer escreir lo que dixere et andar adelante en el pleyto." — And the gloss: "Per istam legem est quotidie in practica quod accusato vel inquisito recipitur ab eo juramentum de veritate dicenda."

was extensively employed; "the old sages held it proper to torment men in order to learn the truth from them."[1] — "According to the 'Fuero-Juzgo' the judge ought not to proceed to the torture unless at the request of the party; the 'Partida' states that it is the magistrate's affair, and even obliges him sometimes to have the torture administered officially; the Gothic law restricts their procedure to serious and important cases, the 'partida' assigns no limit to it."[2] However, the "Partida," following the example of the Roman law, takes care to exempt certain classes of persons from the torture.[3] Torture was not a feature essential to the inquisitorial procedure, and it seems that as much should be said of the oath exacted from the accused.[4]

What latitude was allowed to the defense in the proceedings following the inquest? The accused ought, in theory, to receive communication and copy of the "pesquisa," so that he might have, against those who had testified therein, "all the objections that he had against other witnesses."[5] The text adds, however, that if the king, or his agent ordering the inquest to be made, sees fit, the names and testimony of the witnesses shall not be communicated to the accused.[6] The glossary, moreover, conclusively shows the origin of this provision: "Vide casum specialem, in quo non datur inquisito copia testium et nominum eorum; sic etiam *in causa hæresis* propter timorem futuri scandali subticentur nomina testium." According to the "Siete Partidas," the assistance of the defender, "personero," is forbidden in

[1] "Part. VII," Tit. 30, *de los tormentos.* "Porende tenieron por bien los sabios antiguos que fizieron tormentar a los omes, por que pudiessen saber la verdad ende dellos."

[2] *Marina*, "Ensayo," p. 390.

[3] "Partida VII," Tit. 30, ley. 2; Persons not tortured: "Menor de catorce anos, cavallero, fidalgo, maestro de las leyes o de otro saber, ome quo fuesse consejero senaladamente del Rey o del comun de alguna cibdad, o villa del Rey, los fijos dessos sobre dichos, mujer que fuesse prenada."

[4] See the gloss cited above, note 8, p. 299.

[5] "Part. III," Tit. 17, ley. 11: "Seyendo la pesquisa fecha en qualquier de las maneras que suso diximos, dar deve el Rey o los judgadores traslado della a aquellos a quien tanxere la pesquisa de los *nombres de los testigos et de los dichos*, por que se pueden defender a su derecho, diziendo contra las personas de la pesquisa o en los dichos dellos, et ayan todas las defensiones que aurian contra otros testigos."

[6] "Pero si el Rey o otro alguno por el, que mandassa fazer pesquisa sobre conducho tomado, estonce non deven ser mostrados los nomes ni los dichos de las pesquisas a aquellos contra quien fuere fecha la pesquisa, e esto mismo deve ser guardado quando las partes se avienen en tal manera, que se libre el pleyto por ella, e non sean mostrados los testigos nin los dichos d'ellos."

"Partida III," Tit. 17, ley. 11: The last words appear to allude to a practice recalling somewhat the *acceptance of the inquest* of the old French law; see upon this point the gloss: "Videbatur contrarium dicendum in causa criminali, ubi non potest renuntiari defensio."

criminal proceedings. The accused must conduct his own defense.[1]

There is no mention of the "procurator fiscal" in the "Partidas." But in the "Leyes de recopilacion," which appeared in 1566, in the reign of Philip II, there is a title bearing the heading "de los procuradores fiscales."[2] There exist several Ordinances of 1436, establishing procurators to act before the courts in the absence of other accusers, and fixing their duties. In the procedure of the Spanish Inquisitión in matters of heresy, we also find from the beginning, that is to say, at the end of the 1400s, a "promotor fiscal," whose influence is very extensive. This personage appears to have been created in Spain during the first half of the 1400s, and to have been imported into the Inquisition against heretics, which thus assumes the character of a state institution.[3] In all cases, there is, first of all, a preliminary examination; the fiscal cannot accuse before the fact of the crime and the presumptions have been made known by a denunciation or by public notoriety. Then the "libellus criminalis" is communicated to the private accuser or to the fiscal; the procedure then follows its course in the accusatory form.[4]

The "Siete Partidas" became, after some opposition, it is true, the general law of Spain. In criminal matters, the laws which followed it, the "Nueva Recopilacion" and the "Novissima Recopilacion," did no more than repeat, more in detail, the principles they had laid down.[5] The system of criminal procedure, without ever attaining the preciseness it had in France, presents the essential features which make it easily recognizable; it is the secret and written procedure, the hampered defense, and torture.[6]

[1] "Part. III," Tit. 5, ley. 12: "En pleyto sobre que puede venir sentencia de muerte o de perdimiento de miembro o de desterramiento de tierra para siempre . . . non deve ser dado personero, ante diximos que todo homo est tenudo de demander o defender se en tal pleyto come esta por si mismo e non por personero." *Cf. Marina*, "Ensayo," p. 367.

[2] Book II, Tit. 13.

[3] We leave altogether out of consideration the *Spanish Inquisition*, properly so called.

[4] *Biener*, "Beiträge," pp. 208, 209.

[5] *Marina*, "Ensayo," p. 434 *et seq.* *Sempere*, "Historia," p. 457 *et seq.* See "Novissima recopilacion," Book XII, Tit. 32: "De las causas criminales, y de modo de proceder en ellas y an el examen de testigos" (Los Codigos Españoles, vol. X). — The "Neuva recopilacion de las leyes," in the reign of Philip II; the first edition appeared 1569 by Alnala de Honares. See *Marichalar and Manrique, op. cit.*, vol. IX, p. 251 *et seq.* — The "Novissima recopilacion" is of the reign of Charles IV; it is dated 1806. See *Marichalar and Manrique*, IX, p. 533 *et seq.*

[6] These severities were accepted as in France. However, a protest of the Cortes in 1592 against excessive torture inflicted upon accused persons must be noted. See *Marichalar and Manrique, op. cit.*, IX, p. 318: "Cla-

§ 4. **Germany. The Netherlands.** — Germany preserved the old Germanic customs in its judicial organization for a long time. For the men of entirely free condition, we still find in the 1200s and 1300s the jurisdiction of the old "mallus legitimus" under the name of "Landgerichte"; criminal causes where only persons of quasi-servile condition figured, were tried by the Dizaine or "Zent." The old forms of the Germanic procedure were naturally maintained before these tribunals. In principle, there was no official prosecution; before a criminal trial could take place a complainant must present himself; "War kein Klager ist, darin soll och kein Richter sein;" where there is no complainant, there is no judge.[1] And the complaint could be made only by "parentes et consanguinei, swermach." The action was oral and public; the proofs were the oath with "cojurantes," the unilateral ordeals, and, above all, the judicial duel. The complainant and the accused must both be imprisoned, as in our old prosecution by formal party.[2] But there, as in our customary laws of the Middle Ages, the capture in the act played a very important part; it allowed a prosecutor to be dispensed with, and neither the ordeals nor the oath of purgation were then admitted. We find the clamor of "haro" under the name of "Gerüchte," or "Gerüfte." According to certain customs a kind of public prosecution was also known, called the "Rügegerichte." In the judicial assemblies, on certain days, it was the duty of the mayor, "Bauermeister," or the mere peasant, to denounce those known to them to be guilty of serious crimes, and that was sufficient to put the denounced person upon his exculpation.[3] This custom undoubtedly dated from the ecclesiastical and lay institutions of the Carlovingian period, which we have already described.[4]

Sometimes the judge constituted himself prosecutor; "when he had, of his own knowledge, the conviction that a person was

maron (the cortes) . . . contra el rigor de los jueces en aplicar el tormento a los processados, usando de medios crueles e unusitados, hasta el punto de que los reos, desperados de sufrirlos, se hayan levantando testimonios a si mismos y culpado a otros falsamente."

[1] *Haltaus*, "Glossarium Germanicum medii aevi." Anklaga.

[2] Upon all these points, see *Zoepfl*, "Deutsche Buchtsgeschichte," vol. III, § 131. — *Biener*, "Beiträge," p. 134 *et seq.* — "Sachsenspiegel," I, 63, § 2; III, 28. — "Schwabenspiegel," ch. 78, 79, 234.

[3] *Zoepfl*, *op. cit.*, vol. III, p. 432. — *Biener*, "Beiträge," p. 135.

[4] *Haltaus*, V° "Rügen" "specialissime publicare, indicare, denuntiare magistratui aliquid, deferre delictum vel excessum denuntiatione certa fideli, et jurata quæ pro fundamento sit inquisitioni et convictioni, ad eum finem ut magistratus mulctet aut puniat. In instrumento notarii anno 1457: Villani *de Synodo* sancte tanquam obedientes filii representare ibidemque excessus commissos contra ritum statutorum sanctæ matris Ecclesiæ publicare."

guilty, in default of other means of proof, he ought to affirm the guilt by oath, supported by 'cojurantes.'"[1] This resembles the curious institution of the "Besiebnen." This is what Haltaus says of it: "Deinde moribus datum erat libertati gentis nostræ ut maleficus in facto non deprehensus, semper, sive adesset accusator sive minus, per septem testes paris conditionis et status esset convincendus, *durch das Besiebnen.* Cum vero ægre tantus inveniretur testium numerus et magna esset pejerandi licentia, sæpe etiam maleficia transmitterentur impunita; his quoque in commodis, his malis quærendum erat remedium. Itaque non paucæ civitates sæculo XIV et sequenti impetrarunt per privilegium ut quemcumque major pars magistratus sub jurisjurandi sui obtestatione maleficum ex publica infamia affirmasset, is condemnaretur pro maleficio."[2] In this transformation we can see the first traces of the "inquisitio," hidden under the old forms and the old names. This disguise of foreign institutions appears in Germany more than once.

Very soon the institution becomes settled; the judges of different cities obtain the right to prosecute and judge "upon bad repute," "auf bösen Leumund." In 1258, for example, we find that the archbishop of Cologne could "contrà publice infamatos inquirere et judicare etiam nullo conquerente."[3] This is equivalent to the introduction of the "inquisitio" of the Canon law.

In the 1400s, the old state of matters is everywhere changed by the operation of a great work. The old courts, the "Schöffengerichtes," the "Landgerichtes," cease to be judicial assemblies. The populace, however, tired of the "pleading duty" joyfully accept the relief offered them. The task of the administration of justice tends to pass into the hands of the jurists and trained men. In the enfiefed seigniorial courts, the judges are functionaries appointed by the seigniors; beside them sit the judgers, the aldermen, similar to the council of practitioners whom we have found, in France, around the judge. The Carolina again mentions them in the 1500s.[4] The procedure, the

[1] *Zoepfl, op. et loc. cit.*, p. 437.

[2] Voce "Fæm." See the charters cited by *Haltaus;* he adds "habes lector, si non origines, at memoriam et veram indolem processus inquisitorii in Germania, jam inde a medio sæculi XIII, quem ex inquisitorio et accusatorio mixtum appellaveris."

[3] *Haltaus.* Voce "Fæm." — *Biener*, "Beiträge," p. 138 *et seq.* — Sometimes the judge also appoints a prosecutor officially (who is called "Klagen von Amtswegen"), especially where indigent people, the victims of a crime, are concerned. See *Haltaus*, Voce "Elendig"; *Biener*, "Beiträge," p. 140 *et seq.*

[4] Ch. 1: "Von Richtern, urtheilern und gerichtspersonen." See *Stintzing*, "Geschichte der deutschen Rechtswissenschaft," p. 61 *et seq.*

fruit of the Roman and Canon law, as developed by the Italian doctors, made rapid progress. At the beginning of the 1400s the "Klagspiegel," the success of which was so great, carefully describes, besides the accusatory procedure, the inquisitorial procedure. When the judge had established the bad repute ("Leumund, Geschrei"), he could bring the action officially, provided a serious crime was concerned. The employment of torture was allowed, when there were sufficient presumptions ("Warzeichen").[1] "The reason for the employment of torture, following the Italian example, was that, on one hand, ordeals and co-swearers were no longer believed in, and, on the other hand, it was not desirable to pass sentence upon presumptions alone, whatever their weight might be."[2] At the end of the 1400s, these principles, borrowed from the Italian doctrine, had triumphed in Germany, and were confirmed in several special laws, such as the "Wormser Reformation" of 1498, and the "Tiroler Malefizordnung" of 1499.[3]

But these changes were not accomplished without giving rise to grave abuses. This procedure, as we have seen, with its complex theory of proofs, was a delicate and difficult tool to handle. Now, all the culture possessed by the German judges and aldermen often consisted of the lessons of local practice. They had no way of imbibing the necessary knowledge from the learned books containing it. Most frequently, incapable of combining and weighing the value of presumptions, they found themselves sorely perplexed. In the fear that they had not got together a complete enough collection of evidence, they employed torture to extort a confession, no matter what presumptions had been already obtained. At the end of the 1400s general complaints are raised against the bloody and arbitrary justice administered in Germany.[4] In 1498, in accordance with a decision of the "Reichs-Kammergericht," the emperor officially appoints a doctor of law as president of each seigniorial court. But the best remedy for these disorders was bound to be a written law, simple, clear, and detailed enough to serve as a faithful guide to the magistrates. We therefore see an important legislative movement take place

[1] *Stintzing, op. cit.*, p. 43 *et seq.;* 609.

[2] *Zoepfl, op. et loc. cit.*

[3] *Stintzing, op. cit.*, p. 610.

[4] *Ibid.*, p. 610 *et seq.* See especially p. 611: "Es war der Ausdruck des Allgemeinen Nothstandes, als des Kammergericht dem Reichstage zu Lindau 1496 eine Vorstellung übergab, in der es hiess dass ihm täglich die Klagen gegen Fürsten, Reichstädte und andere Obrigkeiten vorgebracht würden, das sie Leute unverschuldet ohne Recht und redliche Ursache zum Tode verurtheilen und richten liessen."

in this direction, the principal agent of which was an eminent man, Johann, Freiherr of Schwarzenberg and Hohenlandsberg.[1]

Schwarzenberg was not a learned man, but a statesman, and a man with the talent for popularizing scientific knowledge. After a stormy youth, we find him in the service of the bishop of Bamberg, whose chief functionary, "Hofmeister," he became. In this position he shared in the administration of justice, and conceived the idea of a reform of the criminal procedure. This idea culminated in the compilation of an Ordinance, the "Bambergische Halsgerichtsordnung," which Bishop Georges published in 1507 with the force of law. Schwarzenberg accomplished his work successfully by surrounding himself with learned and devoted collaborators. In the same way he had Cicero translated and published, although himself ignorant of Latin.[2] The Ordinance appeared in the form of a book of practice, with diagrams ("Figuren und Reime").

Schwarzenberg afterwards passing into the service of the margraves Casimir and George de Brandebourg, a new adaptation of the Bamberg Ordinance was made, under the name of "Brandenburger Halsgerichtsordnung." But it was expedient to undertake a larger work, which would give a Criminal Code to the Empire. The proposal had been made and accepted at the diets of Fribourg (1497–1498) and Augsburg (1500) to draw up a single criminal Ordinance for the whole Empire, the work being committed to the care of the government of the Empire, assisted by the "Reichs-Kammergericht." The matter, however, hung fire, and it was only at the diet opened by Charles V at Worms in January, 1521, that a decided step was taken. A commission was appointed to draw up the Ordinance, and a first draft was presented by it in the month of April. The commissioners had, naturally enough, taken the already celebrated "Bambergensis" as a basis for their work.[3] The diet of 1521 delegated to the government of the Empire the care of submitting the prepared draft to a revision.[4] The enterprise was, however, still destined to

[1] Schwarzenberg's life, as well as the legislation due to or inspired by him, have been the subject of interesting studies. *Weissel*, "Hanns Fr. v. Schwarzenberg," 1878. — *Güterbock*, "die Entstehungsgeschichte der Karolina," 1876. — *Brunnenmeister*, "die Quellen der Bambergensis," p. 1879. — *Stintzing*, "Geschichte der deutschen Rechtswissenschaft" (ch. 14), 1880. Stintzing summed up the researches of his predecessors. More recently Josef Kohler and his associates have made elaborate researches into the history and influence of Charles V's criminal statute: "Die Carolina und ihre Vorgangerin," ed. *Kohler* and *Scheel*, 3 vols., 1902–04.

[2] *Stintzing, op. cit.*, pp. 613, 716 *et seq.*

[3] *Ibid.*, pp. 621, 623.

[4] Schwarzenberg was connected with the Imperial government from 1521 to 1524 (*Stintzing, op. cit.*, p. 623).

slumber for a time. In 1524 a new draft was presented to the diet of Nuremberg, but not discussed. A third was, in 1529, submitted to the diet of Spires, and finally debated at that of Augsburg in 1530. It was not, however, finally adopted, owing to the opposition of certain States, which refused to renounce their special customary laws. At last, in 1532, at the diet of Regensbourg, the final vote was obtained, thanks to the insertion of a clause, called "salvatorische Clausel," guaranteeing to each State the maintenance of its good and ancient customary laws.[1] On 22d June, 1532, thirty-five years after the work was first undertaken, the States announced to the Emperor its completion.[2] The Ordinance was promulgated as a law of the Empire by Charles V on 27th June, 1532, under the title of "Keyser Karls des fünften und des heyligen römischen Reichs peinlich Gerichtsordnung." Erelong it was usually called "Constitutio criminalis Carolina," or merely the "Carolina."[3]

These laws are not learned Codes, their aim being to furnish a convenient guide to practitioners of little education. They mingle the criminal law and the criminal procedure, and the most part of their provisions are devoted to explanation of the theory of proofs and presumptions, that complex machinery, complex especially for uncultivated intellects.[4] The law formulated by them is, however, that created by the united action of the Canon law and the Roman law. A very remarkable thing is that they contain, upon many points, the outward forms followed according to the old Germanic custom; but these forms are, in a way, nothing more than the scenery, and the real drama takes place behind the scenes.

The Carolina, which we select as a type of these kindred laws, still expounds at length the rules of the accusatory procedure.[5]

[1] The following is the clause: "Doch wollen wir durch diess gnädige Erinnerung Kurfürsten, Fürsten und Ständen an ihren alten wohlhergebrachten rechtmässigen und billigen Gebräuchen nichts benommen haben." — "In spite of that," says *Stintzing* (p. 627), "the Carolina was promulgated as a real Imperial law, the mandatory force of which was independent of the will of the States; but the 'salvatorische Clausel' assigned it a subsidiary place; it made it subsidiary to the local law, although, when the work was undertaken, it was intended to establish an absolutely inverse relation."

[2] *Stintzing, op. cit.*, pp. 621, 625.

[3] It is often cited as: "C.C.C.," the "Bambergensis," the "Brandenburgensis." The Carolina is to be found, along with its various preliminary drafts, in the following edition: "Die peinliche Gerichtsordnung Kaiser Karl's V. nebst der-Bamberger und-Brandenburger Halsgerichtsordnung," edited by Heinrich Zoepfl, second edition, 1876, and in the monographs cited by Josef Kohler, above cited.

[4] *Stintzing* says of the Carolina: "It is at once a Code and a textbook, very like the Institutes of Justinian." *Op. cit.*, p. 629.

[5] "Carolina," Art. 11 *et seq.*; "Bamb." Art. 17 *et seq.*

We find in it the imprisonment of accuser and accused according to the old principles, the bail, the promises of proof on the part of the accuser. On the other hand, but few articles are devoted to the official prosecution; but in those texts addressed to the practitioners, it has the first place in the order of the articles.[1] It expressly appears, moreover, with its traditional characteristics; this is the case where "jemandt eyner übelthat durch *gemeinen leumut* berüchtiget oder andere glaubwirdige anzeygung verdacht und argkwonig, und derhalb durch die oberkeyt von ampts halben angenommen wurde."[2] Whether accusation or inquisition is concerned, the witnesses are heard by commissioners in the well-known form of the inquest, and the testimony is taken down in writing.[3] Complete proof can only result from the confession, or the testimony "of two or three competent and credible witnesses."[4] In the absence of such proof, recourse must be had to torture, and pains are taken to explain in detail what presumptions are sufficient to cause torture to be administered.[5] It seems, besides, that the confession obtained by torture cannot be dispensed with. Thus torture will be made use of even when a manifest fact is in issue, as where a thief is captured in the act, in possession of the stolen property, and this "so that in regard to such public and undeniable facts the final judgment and the punishment may be prosecuted with the least possible expense."[6] According to the "Bambergensis," art. 80, even when there was sufficient proof, the culprit should nevertheless be tortured to extract a confession;[7] but the Carolina does not contain this monstrous provision (art. 69).

In regard to the final act of the judicial drama, the "entlich rechttag," the Carolina has preserved the traditional forms and solemnities.[8] "On the day appointed," says the old text, "on

[1] "Carolina," Arts. 6–10: "Annemen der angegeben übelthetter von der oberkeyt und ampts wegen." — "Bamb." Arts. 10–16.

[2] *Ibid.*, Art. 6.

[3] *Ibid.*, Art. 6.

[4] *Ibid.*, Arts. 70–87; "Bamberg." Arts. 81–90; "Carolina," Arts. 65–68; "Bamberg." Arts. 77–79.

[5] *Ibid.*, Arts. 19–45; "Bamberg." Arts. 27–55.

[6] *Ibid.*, 16: "So soll jn der richter mit peinlicher ernstlicher frage zu bekantnuss der warheyt halten, damit inn solchen unzweiffenlichen misthatten, die entlich urtheyl und straff mit dem wenigsten kosten, als gesein kan, gefürdet und volntzogen werde."

[7] "Item so der beclagt nach gnugsam beweysung noch nicht bekennen wölte sol der alssdann vor der verurtheilung mit peynlichen frage weiter angezogen werden, mit anzeygung das er der missetat uberwisen sey, ob man dadurch sein bekentnuss dester ee auch erlangen möcht, ob er aber nicht bekennen wölt, des er doch (als ob stet) gungsam bewisen were, so solt er nicht dester weniger der beweysten missetat nach verurteylt werden."

[8] "Carolina," Art. 78 *et seq.*; "Bamb." Art. 91 *et seq.*

the arrival of the accustomed hour, the criminal hearing may be announced, in the usual way, by ringing of bells, and the judge and the judgers should repair to the place of justice, where the court of justice is usually held, and the judge should tell the judgers to seat themselves, and he himself should sit, holding in his hand his staff of office or his naked sword, according to the ancient custom of each place, and remain gravely seated, until all is concluded." [1] There the judge and the judgers decide, finding according to the old formulas that everything is in order.[2] The accused is brought in, the accuser, if there be one, being present; spokesmen, "avant-parliers," [3] or "Fürsprecher," are assigned to the parties. There is always one of these for the complaint and one for the defense; even when the prosecution takes place officially an "avant-parlier" proceeds to deliver the formula of the complaint in the name of the sovereign.[4] The spokesman for the accused makes a short speech claiming his acquittal.[5] This bears a great resemblance to a real oral action. But it is a mere matter of form; the judges have decided upon their judgment before the day of the hearing, and the judgment is already written. "Before the final sitting the judge and the judgers shall cause to be read all that has been written (that is to say, the process) . . . and which has been brought to their notice. Then the judge and the judgers confer among themselves and decide what judgment they will render; if they are in doubt, they shall seek advice among the jurisconsults, as is provided by this ordinance, and they shall cause the judgment decreed to be put in writing . . . so that it may be opened at the final sitting." [6] In fact, at the desired moment, the judge unfolds the written judgment and reads it aloud.[7]

This whole procedure was extremely harsh; but we find traces of a less implacable spirit in these laws. We find there the maxim: "It is better to acquit a guilty person than to condemn an innocent one to death." [8] There is a certain consideration for the defense. Before the employment of torture the judge should take care to ask the accused if he is not able to urge some justificative fact, such as an alibi, showing that he is innocent; and it is

[1] "Carolina," Art. 82; "Bamb." Art. 95.
[2] *Ibid.*, 84–85; "Bamb." 97.
[3] *Ibid.*, Art. 88 *et seq.*; "Bamb." 101 *et seq.*
[4] *Ibid.*, Art. 89: "Bitt des fürsprechen der *von ampts wegen* oder sunst klagt." — "Bamb." Art. 103.
[5] *Ibid.*, Art. 90; "Bamb." 105.
[6] *Ibid.*, Art. 81; "Bamb." 94.
[7] *Ibid.*, Art. 94; "Bamb." 110.
[8] "Bamberg." Art. 13: "Ist besser den schuldigen ledig zulassen das den unschuldigen zum tode zunerdampnen."

observed that this warning is necessary "because many, by ignorance or terror, although they may be innocent, have not sufficient knowledge to allege pleas in justification." [1]

It was not the law, but science, which was specially destined to regularize the German criminal procedure. At first, however, the scientific movement was ineffectual; the authors drew all their knowledge from the Italian doctors, of whose works they presented anæmic copies. They did not think much of the Carolina, and judicial practice was then bound to be somewhat hazy and uncertain.[2] In 1620 the Prussian "Landrecht" borrowed its criminal procedure from the work of the Flemish Damhouder, of whom we shall speak later.[3] But in 1635 appeared the work of a great jurisconsult, which had an immense vogue, namely, the "Practica nova imperialis Saxonica rerum criminalium" of Carpzov. The author made use of the Roman law, the Canon law, the Saxon law, and the Carolina; and he succeeded in constructing a complete and logical system.

In Carpzov's eyes, the accusatory procedure is still the usual procedure.[4] But he assigns the greatest place to the inquisitorial procedure, "nullo accusatore existente." It is true that he inquires, at length, whether this form can be lawfully defended "num processus inquisitorius jure defendi queat";[5] but that is merely a scholastic doctrine, and not a serious obstacle. He wishes merely to demonstrate that the inquisitorial procedure is based upon texts of the Roman law; he concludes by recognizing that in his time it is the "remedium ordinarium." He only admits it, however, for grave crimes. And he concludes by recognizing a possible combination and mixture of both forms.[6]

He divides the "inquisitio" into two parts, the "inquisitio generalis," which is none other than our "information"; "Tantummodo præparatoria ad inveniendum delictum et investigandum delinquentem;" then the "specialis," which "solennis et ordinaria est ad puniendum et condemnandum."[7] The rules as to the admission of evidence in the information were very much the same as in other countries. The "inquisitio specialis" ended in the appearance of the accused, who was interrogated as to the "articuli inquisitionales," drawn up beforehand, an essential

[1] "Carolina," Art. 47: "Und solcher erinnerung ist darumb not, das mancher auss eynfalt oder schrecken, nit fürschlagen weist, ob er gleich unschuldig ist, wie er sich des entschuldigen und aussfüren soll."

[2] *Biener*, "Beiträge," pp. 160, 161; *cf. Stintzing, op. cit.*, p. 630 *et seq.*

[3] *Ibid.*, "Beiträge," pp. 164, 165.

[4] Quæstio 103, No. 17.

[5] *Ibid.* 103, Nos. 23–30.

[6] *Ibid.* 107, No. 37.

[7] *Ibid.* 107, No. 14.

document of the procedure. Then came the production of evidence; it was doubted, however, whether the witnesses should always be confronted with the accused.[1] The theory of proofs and torture intervened under the conditions already known.

But the defense was admitted by Carpzov with a liberality unknown in France: "Cum in processu inquisitorio nec interrogatoria inquisiti nec reprobatio admittatur, utique omnis facultas probandi reo adempta sit, remedium defensionis legitime deducendæ ac probandæ ipsi concedendum erit. Idque tanto minus inquisitio est denegandum quanto certius est defensionem esse juris naturalis, adeo ut ne bestiis quidem, nedum homini imo diabolo auferri debeat."[2] "It must," he says again, "be held as certain and indubitable that he has the right (to offer a defense) during the whole course of the inquisitorial procedure . . . whether he offer to prove his innocence before the proof of the offense and the deposition of the witnesses, or whether he offer to do so later, and even after the torture, he ought to be heard."[3] Although in the following numbers he attaches some restrictions to this liberal principle, we are, here, very far from the "justificative facts" of the French Ordinance of 1670.

Carpzov's doctrine as to the means of presenting the defense is likewise very liberal: "Moribus fori Saxonici hactenus triplex modus procedendi obtinuit. Aut enim 1° inquisitus causas et argumenta innocentiæ judici significat, eaque simul articulis inquisitionalibus includit, ac testes super iis examinari rogat; 2° aut peculiares articulos defensionales, quibus argumenta innocentiæ continentur, judici exhibet, testes que producit ac eos desuper examinari facit; 3° vel etiam absque productione testium argumenta defensionis suæ, quæ vel in jure forsan consistunt, vel jam in inquisitione probata fuerunt, pro informatione judicis in scriptis disputat, deductionem innocentiæ conficit, vulgo *ein Defension-Schrift*, eamque judici exhibet."[4]

Carpzov has no hesitation in admitting that the accused is entitled to the assistance of counsel, and he very ably meets the objection, drawn from the Roman law, that one cannot act by attorney in a criminal proceeding.[5] He is not, however, overfond of advo-

[1] Quæstio 114, Nos. 75, 76.
[2] *Ibid.* 115, No. 1.
[3] *Ibid.* 115, Nos. 21–23.
[4] *Ibid.* 115, No. 69.
[5] *Ibid.* 115, Nos. 88–90: "Quæritur num ex parte inquisiti ad deducendam et probandam ejusdem innocentiam advocatus intervenire queat? Quod adfirmare non dubito, et si enim procurator inquisiti non admittitur, ut qui nec dominus litis est nec in eum sententia capitalis ferri potest, aliter tamen res se habet in advocato qui litis dominus non fit sed reum in judicio præsentem defendit et consilio suo juvat."

cates, and he does not admit them all indiscriminately: "Non tamen indifferenter admittendi sunt advocati, sed tantummodo honesti, probi et docti viri, non litium criminalium confusores, nec rabulæ loquentes non eloquentes . . . quales advocati ipsius diaboli sunt mancipia quæ lites alunt ut sua farciant marsupia, et litigaturientes denudent . . . idque ut assequantur majusque pretium lucrentur in deductione innocentiæ farraginem allegatorum hinc inde colligunt et scripta sua in infinitum fere extendunt, quod sæpissime haud absque tædio et insigni molestia acta inquisitionalia legens expertus sum." [1] But what exasperates him more than anything else is the presumption of advocates who dare to lecture the judge: "Audent scilicet informare judicem allegationibus suis et demonstrare ex Corpore juris, Glossa aut interpretibus quid de lite criminali judicandum, id quod venditant pro magisterio, *es sey ein Meister-Stück*, quod tamen æque ridiculum et inconveniens est ac si ægrotus medico curam præscribere vellet." [2] But he has nothing but respect for good advocates: "Abstineant ergo probi advocati (quorum officium honestissimum et humano generi non minus proficuum est quam militia) a tali stultitia et malitia." [3]

Before the right of defense can be useful to him, it is essential that the accused should know the charges. Carpzov recognizes that, according to the common law, a copy of them is given to him, but according to the practice in Saxony, it is considered sufficient to communicate the "acta" to the advocate. "Denique quæritur: an inquisito innocentiam, ac defensionem suam probanti ac deducenti danda sit copia indiciorum aliorum que actorum inquisitionialium? quod de jure communi difficultatem et dubium non habet secundum Julium Clarum, l. V. Sentent. § ultim. quæst. 49, n° 2 . . . et quod danda sit reo copia indiciorum dicit esse communem opinionem Ripa . . . sed in foro Electoratûs Saxoniæ paulo aliter res se habet: facultas enim indicia, testium attestata alia que acta inquisitionalia in judicio inspiciendi inquisito ejusque advocato conceditur, ita ut liberum sit ipsis indicia alia que quæ sibi proficua fore putant, ex actis inquisitionalibus decerpere et consignare. . . . Copia vero actorum dari non solet." [4]

The institution of the public prosecutor is unknown in Germany; in certain districts, no doubt, we find fiscals, but they are merely the agents of the accusatory procedure, which "follows

[1] Quæstio 115, Nos. 93–95.
[2] *Ibid.* 115, No. 96.
[3] *Ibid.* 115, No. 97.
[4] *Ibid.* 115, Nos. 99, 101, 102.

the same path whether one is face to face with a private prosecutor or a fiscal. In the 'Landesordnung' of Bavaria of 1553, the institution of a public prosecutor for crimes is provided for. A criminal Ordinance for Treves of the year 1726 regulates with considerable preciseness the official prosecution by a procurator fiscal."[1] But there never was a national institution of such a nature.

In the *Netherlands* the same movement was taking place as in the countries we have already noticed. In that country of local boroughs the administration of the criminal law remained in the hands of the municipal officers, but there also the secret and written inquisitorial procedure, the theory of legal proofs, and torture were introduced. In the 1500s the transformation is complete. Undoubtedly, the Ordinances of the 5th and 9th July, 1570, prescribed by the duke of Alba, appeared iniquitous and "almost in themselves gave rise to a revolution."[2] Nevertheless, they tallied pretty well with the generally admitted practice, and although they were suspended by the peace of Ghent (art. 5), a certain number of their provisions continued, in fact, to be observed.[3] However,one of their compilers, Jodocus Damhouder, of Bruges, had published a "Praxis rerum criminalium," which the edition issued in 1601, after the author's death, styles "opus absolutissimum,"[4] and which we may consider a faithful mirror of the Flemish practice.

Damhouder still gives the accusation the leading place; but he gives a wide field to the "inquisitio," "quam vulgo informationem præcedentem appellamus."[5] He admits it in all grave cases; "ad hoc requiritur ut crimen sit magnum, inquisitione dignum; non enim inquirendum est nisi de majoribus criminibus, puta læsæ majestatis, homicidii, sodomiæ, adulterii, perjurii, incestûs, raptûs, furti et hujusmodi."[6] Under the name of "inquisitio," however, he comprehends but the "information," which must take place officially, or following on a denunciation, or at the instigation of the fiscal. Then come the other parts of the proceedings, — except the confirmation and the confrontation, which are wanting,[7] — that is to say, the interrogation, the examination,

[1] *Biener*, "Beiträge," pp. 142–144.
[2] See *Allard*, "Histoire de la procédure criminelle au XVIe siècle," § 236.
[3] *Allard*, "Histoire," p. 425.
[4] Chap. V, 1601 edition.
[5] Chap. VIII, No. 6.
[6] Chap. VIII, No. 19.
[7] Chap. VIII, No. 19: "In inquisitionibus per judicem aut fiscum aut quempiam ex ipsorum mandato peragendis, nec ante nec post litis contestationem vocanda fuerit pars ad videndam informationis deductionem vel ad audienda testium juramenta."

the "visite" of the action, and the judgment. The theory of legal proofs and torture play their accustomed parts. Damhouder is even one of those authors who have furnished the most ample details as to torture. He has, however, formulated a maxim as to its employment as a means of proof for which he must be held to account: "Nunquam maleficus traditur quæstioni cum pars formalis et adversa offert criminis manifestam probationem aut quum res percipi potest per probationem ordinariam."[1] On the other hand, he admits certain rights of the defense unknown in France. First is the aid of counsel. "In quovis crimine tam capitali quam alio concessum est reo per se et item per causidicos, advocatos et procuratores in judicio respondere et proponere quaslibet suas exceptiones dilatorias, declinatorias, et peremptorias, sive rectius elusorias, perinde atque in civilibus negotiis: verum in principali rerum cardine plane oportet reum ipsum respondere, proprio ore fateri aut diffiteri."[2] As to the copy of the documents, Damhouder admits that it must be given to the accused as a rule, especially in the case of a prosecution brought upon the complaint of a private individual: "judex et fiscus obligantur dare parti inquisitionis copiam priusquam partem ream cogere possint ad respondendum, potissimum si fuisset facta inquisitio ex auctoritate voto et mandato ad instantiam partis, teste Angelo summi judicii viro." But when the prosecution has been brought officially by the judge he declares that the practice is rather to the contrary: "Sin autem facta fuerit ex mero judicis officio absque alicujus requisitione, non debet reo de jure tradi informationis copia. In praxi autem seu Concilio Flandriæ Procurator generalis nunquam dat parti inquisitionis seu informationis præcedentis copiam; licet id fieri videamus in multis aliis Flandriæ curiis ubi obligantur accusato aut denunciato etiam dare testium nomina ac cognomina nec non totius inquisitionis seu informationis copiam, si quando id postulet."[3]

In the United Provinces in the 1600s the same principles govern. We have, as testimony to this, an illustrious criminalist, Antonius Mathæus, professor at Utrecht, who, in his book "De Criminibus," after having studied books XLVII and XLVIII of the Digest, comments on the statutes of his town. He mentions the complete disappearance of the accusatory system: "Accusa-

[1] Chap. XXXV, No. 1. [2] Chap. XXXII, Nos. 1, 2.

[3] Chap. VIII, Nos. 21–23. It is apparent, from our various citations, that Damhouder is acquainted with the institution of the public prosecutor and has seen it in operation in Flanders. It came from France. See *Biener*, "Beiträge," pp. 211, 212.

toris in jure municipali civitatis hujus mentio vix nulla; sermo omnis ad prætorem dirigitur; cur id fiat non est obscurum, fere enim desierunt accusare privati, solusque fisci procurator ac prætor eo munere funguntur. Accedit quod Gallorum et reliquorum Belgarum moribus privatis quidem licet deferre, nunciare crimina, actione civili damnum pecuniarium persequi, non tamen accusare." [1] He treats very clearly of the "information" and of the decree following thereon, then of the interrogation. He repudiates the oath exacted from the accused: "Cur enim deferatur jusjurandum pejeraturo? aut cur speremus eum qui, spreto Numine, cædibus, adulteriis, sacrilegio se contaminavit, idem Numen reveriturum injecta jurisjurandi religione?" [2] Lastly, he allows the intervention of a defending counsel: "post interrogationem et responsionem rei, quoniam non solum de facto sed et de jure quæri solet, advocatus denegari non debet." [3] But he declares that the "information" shall not be communicated to the accused; "vero informatio reo non editur."

[§ 4 *a*. **Addendum on German Criminal Procedure from the 1400s to the 1700s.**[4]

(1) *Influence of the Canon Law upon German Criminal Procedure.* The Canon law [5] exerted a great influence in the development of the criminal procedure obtaining in the German States, because of the idea, inherent therein, of punishment as a means of atonement and expiation of crime, in the public interest.[6] Although this idea appeared in the beginning, only in relation to the criminal law of the Church, yet it later found a universal acceptance, and is important as an explanation of the origin of the inquisitorial procedure. The development of the inquisitorial procedure was also stimulated by the "denuntiatio evangelica," [7] although the

[1] "De criminibus," 1715 edition (pp. 627, 628).

[2] *Ibid.*, p. 632.

[3] *Ibid.*, p. 633.

[4] [This Addendum = Chapters XIV and XVII of Professor MITTERMAIER'S "Progress of German Criminal Procedure." For this author and work, see the Editorial Preface.

It was thought best to offer this additional survey of the German development, even though it covers the same period; first, because the German point of view is here desirable, and next, because two or three additional topics are considered. — ED.]

[5] See *Rocco*, "Jus canonic. ad civil. jurisprud. perficiundam quid attulerit" (Panormi 1839).

[6] *Jarke*, "Handbuch des deutschen Strafrechts," I, p. 51. *Guizot*, "Cours de l'histoire moderne, histoire général de la civilizat." pp. 12–17. *Abegg*, "Lehrbuch des gemeinen deutschen Criminalprozesses," p. 24. *Otto Meier*, "de diversit. summor. pœnal. princip. in jud. rom. et apud" (Goetting. 1843).

[7] This was based upon a passage in the Bible, — Matthew, xviii, 15–17.

original denunciation in the Christian congregation of a wrong that had been committed, was made only in the name of the Church and subjected the wrong-doer to penance.[1] From the early right of the Church to keep watch over the morals of its congregation,[2] there arose a certain ecclesiastical jurisdiction over the laity, in that the Church on account of certain offenses withdrew from the offender its privileges. As the power of the Church increased,[3] the greater became the range of its criminal jurisdiction, and the more so, as the Church was sustained in its punishment by the temporal power.[4] This expansion, however, resulted in the temporal power in Germany (as everywhere else in Europe)[5] declaring itself opposed to the encroachments of the ecclesiastical jurisdiction.[6]

(2) *Special reasons for this influence.*

Of especial importance was the institution of the "Sendgerichte."[7] These courts grew out of the old system[8] of visitation by the bishops (upon whom there was frequently imposed[9] a more stringent duty of visitation in their capacity as "missi dominici"), and were held at certain times of the year by the bishop or his representative, usually the archdeacon, for the purpose of investigating the morals of the Church and punishing transgressions. The custom of examining in the Church[10] certain sworn

[1] See especially *Jan. a Costa*, Com. ad decretal, pp. 334–349. *Schilling*, "De origine jurisdict. eccles." p. 66. *Biener*, "Beiträge zur Geschichte des deutschen Strafrechts," p. 17.

[2] *Walter*, "Lehrbuch des Kirchenrechts," No. 183. *Jarke*, I, p. 56. *Rosshirt*, "Geschichte und System des deutschen Strafrechts" (Stuttgart 1838), I, pp. 128–138; p. 172. *Hildenbrand*, "Die purgatio canonic u. vulg." (München 1841), p. 36.

[3] In regard to the ecclesiastical jurisdiction in the Middle Ages, see *Beaumanoir*, "*Coutumes* de Beauvoisis," chap. XI, and also *Beugnot*, in the preface to his edition (Paris 1842, 2 vols.), p. lii. *Hélie*, "Traité de l'instruction criminelle" (Paris 1845), I, p. 350. *Negroni*, "Della giurisdizione ecclesiastica nelle cose crim." (Novarra 1843). *Richter*, "Lehrbuch des Kirchenrechts," No. 191.

[4] Constitut. Friederici II, de jurib. princip. eccles. 1220. "Schwabenspiegel," K, 100, 345. *Kopp*, "Nachrichten von den geistlichen und weltlichen Gerichten in Hessen," I, p. 152.

[5] As to France, see *Mignet*, "De la féodalité des institutions de St. Louis, et de la législat. de ce prince" (Paris 1822), p. 156. As to England, see *Millar*, "Histor. Entwurf der englischen Staatsverfassung," Part I, p. 227; Part II, p. 94.

[6] *Kopp*, I, pp. 150, 155–158.

[7] *Boehmer*, "Jus eccles. Prot." Lib. III, Tit. 39. *Kopp*, Part I, pp. 118–143. *Walter*, "Lehrbuch," pp. 194–199. *Biener*, "Beiträge," p. 28. *Richter*, "Lehrbuch des Kirchenrechts," No. 185.

[8] Capit. 742, No. 3. Capit. 769, No. 7. *Biener*, p. 30. *Eichhorn*, "Grunds. des Kirchenrechts," II, p. 73. *de Kock*, "Diss. de potestat, civil. episcop." pp. 31–62. *Unger*, "Die altdeutsche Gerichtverfassung," p. 392.

[9] *de Kock*, "Diss. Trajectin. in regno Francor. initiis." Trajecti 1838. p. 19.

[10] L. 13. X. "de judic." *Rosshirt*, "Geschichte," I, p. 181.

synodal witnesses, in regard to wrongs and crimes known to them (the number of which was constantly increased),[1] laid the foundation of an institution which could easily destroy the old accusatorial procedure. The statement of these informants was the equivalent of an indictment ("infamatio"), and led to a further proceeding against the accused.[2] So great was the effect of the mere accusation of one of these informants that the accused who was regarded as "infamatus," was obliged to vindicate himself.[3] These "Sendgerichte" continued to exist well into the Middle Ages, although much opposition to them arose in the cities.[4]

The Canon law exerted special influence because of the fact that in the spiritual courts, over which judges presided, juridical proceedings, (with frequent reference to the Roman authorities), conducted in an attempt to ascertain the truth by systematic methods, brought about the development of a written procedure.[5] The accused was allowed a representative, "Fürsprecher," learned in the law, and the widely spread system of appeals made a written procedure necessary. Because of its inquisitorial basis and the views relative to the taking of evidence, the procedure gradually became a secret one.[6]

The Canon law was influential also because of the fact that, with its manifest advantage of a purer theory of proof, it soon declared itself opposed to certain features of the Germanic procedure; it was also opposed to the institution of appealing to a judgment of God (pronounced by the priests), — an institution[7] which for a long time obtained in several countries[8] — as well as[9] to trial by battle.[10] Because of this attitude it brought about a change in the Germanic procedure.

[1] *Boehmer*, c. 1, pp. 34–37. *Kopp*, pp. 124, 136. *Biener*, p. 34.

[2] *Biener*, p. 34.

[3] *Hildenbrand*, p. 102.

[4] *Warnkoenig*, "Rechtsgeschichte von Flandern," I, p. 436. As to their duration into the Middle Ages, see *de Kock*, "diss." p. 45. In Frankfurt there were "Sendgerichte" until 1370. See *Thomas*, "der Oberhof zur Frankfurt," p. 205, also p. 206 in regard to their jurisdiction.

[5] *Rosshirt*, "Geschichte," p. 129. *Hélie*, "Traité," I, p. 387.

[6] *Hélie*, "Traité," I, p. 491.

[7] *E.g.*, this was the case in Germany. *Hildenbrand*, p. 117.

[8] These forms were even used in the "Sendgerichte." See *Hildenbrand*, p. 104, and p. 22, as to early views of the Church.

[9] C. 1. 3. X. "de purgat. vulg." *Gonzalez de Tellez*, "Ad decretal, ad Lib. V. Tit. 35," vol. V, p. 497. Judgment of God was in use in the spiritual courts at an earlier date. c. 20. C. II, qu. 5. *Biener*, p. 34. In regard to the opposition of the Church to appeal to the judgment of God, see *Hildenbrand*, p. 118. *Rocco, loc. cit.*, p. 46.

[10] There was also judicial trial by battle in the spiritual courts. *Gonzalez de Tellez*, vol. V, p. 496. But at an early date, there were prohibitions of its use. C. 22. qu. 5 C. 1. X. "de cleric. pugnant."

There were also incorporated in the Canon law, many legal institutions, purely Germanic in origin.[1] They were here first moulded into the form [2] in which they later appeared in our common law procedure. On the other hand it is a mistake[3] to ascribe to the courts for the investigation of heresy [4] the development of institutions later passing over into the German procedure. The procedure obtaining in these courts was different from that developed by the other ecclesiastical courts, and rested [5] upon special sources of law.[6] There is no doubt,[7] however, that this special procedure against heretics, before certain heresy courts, was to be found both in Switzerland [8] and in certain parts of Germany.[9]

(3) *The "Carolina."*

Even in the early 1800s the chief and ultimate source of the German common law was the "Carolina." This was due to the appeal of the States to the Reichstag in 1498.[10] Preparation was made for it by the appearance of the "Bambergensis." [11] It

[1] *Hommel,* "De jure canon. ex german. leg." (Lips. 1755).

[2] *E.g.,* acquittal upon oath (Reinigungeid). Later it will appear that this oath was especially developed in the Canon Law. *Hildenbrand,* p. 49.

[3] For the correct view, see *Biener,* "Beiträge," pp. 60, 151. In regard to the relation of the heresy courts to the inquisitorial procedure, see *Biener,* "Über die neueren Vorschläge zur Verbesserung des Strafverfahren," p. 122.

[4] For a knowledge of these heresy courts, the book by *N. Eymenicus,* director-inquisitor, is especially useful.

[5] In Spain there were special sources. *Biener,* p. 64.

[6] Contained in the decrees of the councils.

[7] For a knowledge of the formation and procedure of the ecclesiastical courts a book dealing with the English courts is especially useful, *viz. Oughton,* "ordo judicior. sive method. procedendi in negotiis in foris eccl. Britan." (London 1778). See the report in the "Zeitschrift fur ausländ. Gesetzgebung," VII, p. 477, in regard to the statements relative to the English spiritual courts (1832 and 1833). For a knowledge of the practice of the spiritual courts, the commentators of the Middle Ages are important. See *Tancredus* (1214) in *Bergmann,* "Pillii Tancredi Gratiæ" lib. de judic. ordin. (Goetting. 1842). *Savigny,* "Geschichte des römischen Rechts," V, p. 107. *Rofredus* (Savigny, V, p. 164). Pope Innocence IV (*Biener,* "Beiträge," p. 84). *Durandus,* "Speculum juris cum Joann. Andr. Baldi et alior. not." (Patav. 1479) (*Biener,* p. 87. Savigny, V, p. 501).

[8] Important reference, *e.g.* in regard to the heresy trials of 1439, 1481, before the ecclesiastical "inquisitor hæreticæ pravitatis" in the French portion of Switzerland, can be found in *Matile,* "histoire des institutions judiciaires et législatives de la principauté de Neuchâtel" (Neuchâtel 1838), pp. 230–243.

[9] Since the Reformation the civil courts are believed to have taken action against heretics. However, see *Trummer,* "Vorträge uber Tortur," I, p. 111.

[10] *Malblank,* "Geschichte der peinlichen Gerichtsordnung," p. 174 (Nurnb. 1783).

[11] In regard to the importance of the Radolphzeller and Tyrolean "Halsgerichtordnung," which abolished publicity, see Neues Archiv des Criminalrechts (Halle), IX, p. 46. *Mittermaier,* in Archiv des Crim. Neue Folge (1836), p. 319. *Waechter,* "Ad histor. const. crim." (Lips.

was compiled by Freiherr von Schwarzenberg, the author of the work last mentioned, and published in 1532.[1] It cannot be doubted that in the writing of the "Bambergensis,"[2] which formed the basis of the "Carolina," there were present in the mind of the author[3] certain law books[4] which existed in particular parts of the empire. One need not, however, therefore assume that Schwarzenberg used these laws as the foundation of his work. The particular merit of his work lay[5] in the assertion of fundamental principles; in a scientific interpretation of criminal law; and, as far as criminal procedure is concerned, in the arrangement of a system of procedure in harmony with the newly developed forms, and with a better theory of evidence, and calculated to better protect the innocent.[6] Schwarzenberg everywhere conformed to the common law of his time.[7] Yet he also drew heavily upon the opinions laid down by the learned jurists of the Middle Ages, relative to the application of Roman and Canon law,[8] with an effort[9] to give to the unlearned judges exact instructions; to rectify certain errors that had crept in; and to insert into the procedure, wherein torture was necessary (for the purpose of procuring a confession), certain conditions that would render it less dangerous to the innocent.[10] Both the accusatorial and inquisitorial forms of procedure were allowed. The former was pre-

1835). As to the importance of other early compilations and sources of law, contemporaneous with the Carolina, see *Birnbaum*, in Neues Archiv, XI, No. 14.

[1] *Rosshirt*, in "Neues Archiv," IX, No. 10.

[2] See important explanations in *Zöpfl*, "Das alte Bamberger Stadtrecht als Quelle der Carolina" (Heidelberg 1838), p. 167.

[3] As to the influence of the "Tyrolensis," see *v. Wendt*, in the Baier. Annalen, 1834, Nos. 137–153. *Zöpfl*, p. 159.

[4] The "Landgerichtsordnung" by Maximilian for Austria (1541) which was published by Prof. *Heyn*, in Vienna, in the Zeitschrift für österreich. Rechtswissenschaft, is especially valuable.

[5] *Rosshirt*, "Geschichte und System des deutschen Strafrechts," I, p. 238.

[6] *Tittmann*, "Geschichte der deutschen Strafgesetzg." (Leipzig 1832), p. 266.

[7] *Zöpfl*, p. 170. As to the relation of the "Carolina" to the epitomes thereof, see *Zöpfl*, "Die peinl. Gerichtsordnung und Projekte" (Heidelberg 1841).

[8] The opinion of *Gerstacker*, in Archiv, VII, pp. 367 and 462, and in the "progr. num origo const. crim. bambergens. a Torquemadæ instruction ib. repeti possit" (Lips. 1837), that he followed the Spanish inquisitions for heresy, is without foundation. *Biener*, "Beiträge zur Geschichte der Inquisitionsprocesses," p. 151. *Frey*, "observat." p. 53. The contents of notes 26–30, in Chapter XIV, *ante*, apply here. See also *Biener*, "Über die neuern Vorschläge der Verbesserung des Strafverfahrens," p. 123.

[9] *Rosshirt*, in "Archiv," IX? p. 616. *Rosshirt*, "Geschichte," I, p. 243. *Biener*, "Beiträge," p. 151.

[10] Art. 20, 48–61, C.C.C.

sumed to be the regular form,[1] but it was altered by the insertion of provisions to the advantage of the accused;[2] also by the employment of torture and by an increased activity of the judge. Likewise in the inquisitorial form of procedure[3] there was inserted an accusatorial element, in that a trial day[4] was set at its conclusion, on which only the proceedings theretofore taken place were read. This inadequate formality would seem to be a remnant of the old publicity.

The official complaint,[5] in the form of an accusation lodged by a public accuser, since it was in use in many countries, was given recognition. As to the inquisitorial procedure, it is apparently true that this was regarded as applicable only in the case of the gravest crimes, and even then only in case no accuser appeared.[6] The procedure was written.[7]

On the whole, the "Carolina" seems to have regarded the theory of proof,[8] as advanced by the practitioners of that time, as an important matter, and especially to have made an effort, in cases where the evidence, however strong, was only circumstantial, to prohibit punishment, and allow only the application of torture (to obtain a confession).

(4) *Influence of the "Carolina."*

It was impossible that the "Carolina" should immediately gain a general acceptance everywhere in Germany, or be everywhere accepted to the same extent.[9] It depended upon how much the

[1] Art. 11, 99, 181, C.C.C. *Leue*, "Der öffentl. mundliche Anklageprocess und der geheime schriftliche Untersuchungsprocess" (Aachen, 1840).

[2] Art. 47, C.C.C.

[3] Art. 6, 10, 211, 212, C.C.C. It is certain that the inquisitorial procedure in its later dangerous development was not anticipated in the C.C.C. *Maurer*, "Geschichte des Gerichtsverfahrens," p. 355.

[4] "Rechttag." Art. 81, 91, 92, C.C.C. compared with the "Bambergensis," Art. 94, 107, 123, shows that in the latter, this institution was not so definitely established as in the C.C.C. *Biener*, p. 156. As to the nature of the "Rechttag" of that time, see *Maurer*, p. 357. *Leue*, p. 65.

[5] Art. 88, 89, 188, 165, 201, C.C.C. *Biener*, p. 142. *Schweizer*, Vierteljahrschrift, 1842, 4 Hft., p. 550, contains valuable information relative to the continuance of the old forms and official accusations.

[6] A valuable description of an accusatorial procedure conducted in Brandenburg in regard to a murder is given in the Baierischen Annalen, 1835, Nos. 37–39. (Explanations by *Wendt.*) Therein is shown the wide range of the accusatorial procedure, and with what difficulty even at that time the inquisitorial procedure was admitted.

[7] Art. 73, 92, 181–203, C.C.C. The old procedural steps were otherwise very simple and short. See also *Leue*, p. 60.

[8] Art. 32, 69, C.C.C. That *Schwarzenberg* had in mind the "Reformation" of Worms (1495) is certain. *Mittermaier*, Archiv, IX, p. 57.

[9] It is interesting to notice the manner of the development of criminal procedure in accordance with the C.C.C., in countries other than Germany in which the C.C.C. was received, *e.g.* in that of Lüttich. Relative hereto,

German institutions were still adhered to, and especially upon the extent to which the "Carolina" was applied in conjunction with the Roman law.[1] In any district, the longer the folk courts remained, the longer the accusatorial form of procedure continued to maintain its existence.[2] The special ordinances of the 1500s, dealing with the regulation of the courts,[3] and also the formula books of that time,[4] reveal many traces of the old institutions.[5] The system of having a public accuser on the trial day[6] lodge a formal complaint upon which the trial would take place is found in several of the old court rules.[7] The development of criminal procedure was brought about through the usage of the courts and by the publicists who exercised an influence upon its growth and taught the relation of the passages of the Roman and Canon law to the provisions of the "Carolina." [8]

see *Sohet*, "Instituts de droit pour le pays de Liège," Liv. V, Tit. 35. For a presentation of the local criminal procedure, see *von Theilen*, "Forme et maniere de proceder en criminel." (Herve 1789). *Birnbaum*, in the Krit. Zeitschrift für Rechtswissenschaft und Gesetzgebung des Auslandes, I. Thl., p. 198. *Wynants*, "Rep curiæ brab. decis." In the 2d part is an excellent chapter; "de publicis judiciis," p. 257.

For the Netherlands, the "crimin. ordinantie" of Philip II (1570) is important. See also *von Voorda*, "De crim. ordantien etc." (Leyden 1792). For the history of criminal procedure in the Netherlands see *Boscher Kemper*, "Wetboek van Strafverordering" (Amsterdam 1838), vol. 1, pp. lxiv–cxxiii. The C.C.C. was accepted in Friesland. As to the Dutch criminal procedure, see also *van Linden*, "Regtsgeleerd practicaal," p. 387 *et seq.*

[1] As to the procedure in Kiel, shortly after the C.C.C., see *Falks*, Staatburgerl. Magazin, IV. Bd., p. 209. As to the brevity of the criminal proceedings of that time, see *Dreyer*, "Nebenstunden," p. 173. *Maurer*, p. 356. As to the length of time before the C.C.C. was accepted in many parts of Germany; *Birnbaum*, in Archiv, XI, p. 422. In Hamburg, even in the 1500s, there was a public penal accuser. It was not until the 1600s that the inquisitorial procedure came to prevail. *Trummer*, "Vorträge über Tortur" (Hamburg 1844).

[2] Examples in *Dittmer*, "Das Sassen und Holstenrecht" (Lubeck 1843).

[3] Such were the "Badisches Landrecht" of 1588, Thl. V; the "Pfalzische Landrecht" of 1582; and especially the "Henneberger Landesordn." of 1539, Book XII. "Reformat. der brandenburger Halsgerichtsordn." of 1582.

[4] *Tenglers*, "Laienspiegel," Fol. 132–144. *Sawr*, "Strafbuch," p. 447. *Brand*, "Klagspiegel," Fol. 103. *Alciat*, "Compend. processus civil." p. 285. In regard to the works of *Perneder*, *Rauchdorn*, see *Waechter*, in Archiv (Neue Folge 1836), p. 115. *Rosshirt*, "Geschichte," I, pp. 287, 230.

[5] A remarkable trial in the Freiburg "Malesizgericht" of 1555, in *Schreiber*, "Fortgesetzte Beiträge zur Geschichte von Freiburg," p. 35.

[6] As to its form in the interesting "Henneberger Landesordn." of 1539, Buch VII, Tit. 3. "Badisches Landrecht" of 1588, Buch V, Tit. VI.

[7] "Badisches Landrecht" of 1588, Buch V, Tit. VI, No. 2. Also for later traces, see *Maurer*, p. 357.

[8] Here belongs: *Carpzov*, "Pract rer. crimin." (1635); *Brunemann*, "Tract. de inquis." (1674); *Kayser*, "Praxis crim." (1678); *Ludovici*, "Einleitung zum peinl. Proc." (1707). See *Beiner*, "Beiträge," p. 165.

(5) *Later development of German procedure.*

Because of the victory of the newer political and social conditions and opinions, the old criminal procedure gradually but completely disappeared,[1] and the inquisitorial form of procedure supplanted the accusatorial.[2] Because of the custom of referring cases and actions to the universities for decision, and because of the peculiar attitude of the unlearned "Schöffen," who could no longer satisfy the requirements of scientific knowledge, and of their own accord withdrew from the courts, the old system of "Schöffen"[3] gradually disappeared, and the trial day ("Rechttag") was done away with in practice or by statute.[4] The loss of the desire for civic freedom,[5] the development of the active functions of the police, and the nature of the court organization, in which the civil and criminal jurisdiction was exercised by the same officials, brought about the result, that, in the German procedure, the disadvantage of the secret written inquisitorial procedure was made more and more evident.

The deterrent theory of crime, becoming prevalent, produced many harsh features in criminal procedure. Imprisonment of the accused was favored; acquittal and appeal were restricted; and the inquisitorial method was applied without restriction. On the other hand it came about in German procedure, through the effort of the judicial body, which seems to have been satisfied

Rosshirt, "Geschichte," I, p. 291. See especially *Waechter*, "Gemeines Recht," p. 92, as to *Carpzov*, p. 103.

[1] Traces of the continuance of the old forms are frequently found. See *Oesterlei*, "Handbuch über das Verfahren in Straffallen für das Königreich Hannover" (Göttingen 1820), III. Thl., p. 104, note, for the interesting procedure, as late as 1802, in the "Strafgericht Jork." And as to the continuance until 1756, in Baden, of the old criminal courts, degenerated into a mere comedy, see *v. Drais*, "Geschichte der Regierung von Baden unter Carl Friedrich," Bd. I, p. 60. See also a Protocol of 1726 in *Duttlingers*, Archiv für die Rechtspflege in Baden, I. Bd., p. 547. And for remnants of the old forms, *cf. Zentner*, "Das Geschwornengericht mit Oeffentlichkeit" (Freiberg 1830), pp. 147–176. For an interesting collection of statutes showing publicity, see Niederrheinischen Archiv, IV. Bd., pp. 200–236. A remarkable mingling of the old and the new (although not for protection of the innocent) can be found in the democratic "Urcantonen" of Switzerland. See *Siegwart Muller*, "Das Strafrecht der Kantone Uri, Schwyz" (St. Gallen 1833), p. 112. Examples of "Blutgerichten" in Switzerland in 1634, in *Schauberg*, Zeitschrift für ungedr. schweizerische Rechtsquellen, I, pp. 142, 147. See also *Reyscher*, in Zeitschrift für deutsches Recht, VI, p. 355.

[2] A Prussian statute of August 24, 1724, entirely abolished the accusatorial procedure.

[3] *Jarke* in Archiv, IX, p. 84. *Maurer*, p. 353.

[4] Interesting reasons in the "baier. Malefizordnung" of 1616, Tit. VI, Art. 4.

[5] *Mittermaier*, "Ueber die offentliche mundliche Strafrechtspflege" (Landhut 1819), p. 15.

only if it could obtain a confession of the accused, that the aim of the entire investigation was, through ingenious contrivances, to procure a confession. Therefore the procedure tended to become more slow.

While the German procedure sought to insure the safety of the accused by means of various reasonable restrictions upon the proceedings against him, through the withdrawal of the lay judges ("Schöffen"), and by means of theories of evidence given statutory expression, and also by means of a multiplication of legal remedies, yet the foundation was too faulty for these means to guarantee a procedure corresponding to the demands of the times and in accordance with the prevailing respect for freedom. The custom of referring cases to faculties, which rendered opinions, tended only to the development of the form and classification of procedure.

For the court regulations of the 1700s, the Hanoverian Criminal Instructions,[1] the Gothia Regulations of Procedure,[2] the Prussian Criminal Regulations,[3] and the Bavarian Statute Book [4] give a picture of the common law procedure of that time. The Saxon statutes [5] were directed rather towards the satisfying of special local requirements.]

§ 5. **England.**[6] — Everywhere upon the continent, in France and elsewhere, the inquisitorial procedure, secret and written, was

[1] "Hannoverische Criminal-instruction" of April 30th, 1736; printed in the "Churbraunschweig-luneb. Landesverordn." (Göttingen 1740), II. Thl., p. 796. See especially *Freudenheit*, in the supplement volume of the Archiv, 1838, p. 62, and see also p. 68 in regard to the "Criminal-instruction" published on December 6th, 1748.

[2] "Gothaische Processordnung" of 1776 in 3 vols. (often corresponding almost word for word with the Hanoverian).

[3] "Preussische Criminalordnung" of 1717. See relative thereto, *Beiner*, "Beiträge," p. 183. *Abegg*, "Geschichte der preuss. Strafgesetzgebung" (Neustadt 1841), p. 81.

[4] "Codex Maximil. bav. crim.," 1751. As to this, see *B. v. Kreitmaier*.

[5] "Generalverordnung wegen des Verfahrens in Untersuchungssachen," of October 27th, 1770. "Instruction, die Abstellung der Marter" of December 2d, 1770. "Generale wegen des Verfahrens in Untersuchungssachen" of April 30th, 1783. See also *Pfotenhauer*, "Handbuch der neuesten in Sachsen erschienenen Criminal-Gesetze" (Leipzig 1811). For the best treatment, see *Weiske*, "Handbuch der Strafgesetze des Königreichs Sachsen von 1572 bis auf die neueste Zeit" (Leipzig 1833). *Volkmann*, "Lehrbuch des im Königreich Sachsen geltenden Criminalrechts" (Leipzig 1831). *Weiske*, "Handbuch des Criminal-proc. mit Rücksicht auf sächsisches Recht" (Leipzig 1840).

[6] When the present book was written in 1880, for an award of a competition by the Academy of Moral and Political Science, and appeared in 1882, the history of the English jury was far from being as well defined as it is today. There had already been published, on the origin of the jury, the authoritative work of BRUNNER, "Die Entstehung der Schwurgerichte," which has retained its place of authority, and Bigelow's two books, the

now established, a product of the Roman and the Canon law, with their defects more or less accentuated according to the country. One European nation, however, had resisted and escaped the contagion, and was destined later to serve, to a large extent, as a model for the legislation of the French Revolution. This was England. By utilizing and developing those elements which had to the same extent existed upon the continent, but had there become sterile, it had constructed a criminal procedure of its own, which, though it was not exempt from defects, was oral and public, and offered material safeguards to the defense. This result it owed chiefly to two causes, the institution of the jury and the accusatory principle. It had, at the same time, reduced the preliminary examinations to the limits of strict necessity.

The jury is used by the English in both civil and criminal actions; and in criminal matters it is used twice in the course of each action, as the *grand jury*, or jury of accusation, and as the *petty jury*, or trial jury. Although it is only with these two juries that we are here concerned, it is necessary, first of all, to speak briefly of the jury in general, and of the civil jury in particular.

1. Brunner established the fact, confirmed by the later English works, that the jury in Normandy and afterwards in England, is, in its origin and early manifestation, merely an application of the Carlovingian "inquisitio," a method of proof employed when the king's interests were concerned, or those of persons to whom he conceded the right of recourse to this procedure. It was a proof by witnesses, but very different from that of the common law, where the witnesses had merely to affirm upon oath a formula settled by the judgment. In the "inquisitio," on the other hand, he who conducted it chose from among the inhabitants of the place where the deed was done a certain number of the most notable and credible, and, binding them on the faith of their oath to tell what they knew of the matter, received their report.

The practice of the "inquisitio" was preserved in French law, with applications varying according to the districts and according

"Placita Anglo-Normannica" and the "History of Procedure in England." But the writings of POLLOCK and MAITLAND,[1] of THAYER,[2] and of HOLDSWORTH,[3] which shed such a great light upon the development of this institution, had not yet appeared. Sir James Fitzjames Stephen's "History of the Criminal Law of England" itself was published in 1883.[4] I have therefore taken the opportunity in the present translated edition to rewrite completely my original accounts, in the light of these notable works.

[1] "The History of English Law before the time of Edward I," 2 vols., 1895.
[2] *Thayer*, "A Preliminary Treatise on Evidence at the Common Law" (Boston, 1898).
[3] *Holdsworth*, "A History of English Law," vol. 1 (1903). I shall principally cite the two last-mentioned works, those of Thayer and Holdsworth.
[4] *Sir J. F. Stephen*, "A History of Criminal Law in England," 3 vols., 1883.

to the times; it was especially preserved in Normandy, whence it passed into England at the time of the Norman Conquest. It was used most of all in administrative and fiscal matters, which is to be expected from its origin. The authors above mentioned state that a great portion of the data contained in the "Domesday Book" are the result of such "inquisitiones."[1]

The jurors were, therefore, originally witnesses, and they retained this leading characteristic for a long time. But they were always witnesses of a particular kind. Not only did they differ from the common law witnesses, but, from their origin, they were *chosen* from among the aggregate of the inhabitants,[2] and they were not always interrogated minutely, but often replied by a mere formula, which was like a judgment ready prepared.[3] Thayer says, very truly, that they were "selected persons," who gave, upon interrogation, "a sworn answer."[4] The same author remarks, moreover, that for more than a century after the Conquest we are without information as to the operation of the "inquisitio" in England. "In trying to follow its English history we remark at once that for more than a century there is little clear, authoritative information. We get our knowledge mainly from the scattered accounts of cases in the Domesday Book and in chronicles and histories. These have been collected by a competent and careful hand in the 'Placita Anglo-Normannica' of Dr. Bigelow. The noble series of extant English judicial records does not begin until 1194 (Trin. 5 Richard I). Our first law treatise, Glanvill, was written not before 1187. Our existing law reports begin not earlier than two centuries and a quarter after the Conquest, in 1292."[5]

From Glanvill's time, however, the jury really exists, not merely in civil, but also in criminal matters, and we have but to follow the development of the institution. It was, moreover, regulated in civil matters earlier in Normandy than in England, in the pro-

[1] *Thayer*, "Evidence," p. 50. — *Holdsworth*, *op. cit.*, vol. I, p. 145.

[2] See especially the document of the year 892, quoted by *Flach*, "Les origines de l'ancienne France," vol. III, p. 381, note 3: "Itaque ex his omnibus xiiii electis, in ecclesiam sancte Marie progressi itemque ab ipso viciscomite per ordinam interrogat et discussi absque ulla varietate testificantes jurati dixerant."

[3] *Brunner*, "Zeugen- und Inquisitionbeweis der Karolingischen Zeit," p. 157: "Nicht immer gehen die Aussagen der Geschworenen so sehr in's Detail. Häufig werden sie im derselben knappen Form abgegeben, wie die Zeugenaussage, welche bekanntlich mitunter That- und Rechtsfrage zugleich umfassen. Die Aussage beschränkt sich auch bei den Geschworenen nicht selten auf die einfache Formel *Res plus debet esse Petro quam Martino*, so dass die Nebenzeugungsmomente, welche den Einzelnen zu dieser Aussage veranlassen, latent bleiben. Die Aussage hat in solchen Fällen den Charakter eines Ausspruches."

[4] *Thayer*, "Evidence," p. 48.

[5] *Ibid.*, p. 50.

ceeding of "recognitiones,"[1] and we shall see presently that it was introduced at a later date and with greater difficulty in crimes than in civil actions. For the moment I merely wish to state in what sense its general and civil development took place.

The institution was slow in taking definite shape. Certain characteristics which appear essential to the English jury were not settled until very late. Thus the number of twelve jurors, which would appear to be one of the fundamental points in the organization of the trial jury, was not settled until a somewhat late date. Not only has the grand jury, the jury of accusation, remained at twenty-four jurors (twenty-three in reality, in order that the majority of twelve, entailing the arraignment, can come into play), but the early constitution of the civil and petty jury was rather fluctuating and complicated. It included, besides the knights and the "legales homines" of the county and the "hundred," men from the four "villæ" adjacent to the place where the events happened.[2] Various combinations, moreover, were formed, sometimes of multiple juries and separate juries for the same matter.[3] Then, for the petty jury, we see the figures, without being fixed and unchangeable, usually being settled at the number twelve, and oscillating around that number, — fourteen and sixteen, for instance,[4] and sometimes ten or eleven. About the end of the 1300s the necessity for a jury of twelve members was finally regarded as essential.[5] Although it was the old elements which conduced to that result, they took effect very slowly. The intrinsic merits recognized in the number twelve, and its multiples and submultiples,[6] also undoubtedly played a part in the matter.[7]

Another characteristic and important feature of the English jury is that its verdict must be unanimous. This was a safeguard which would appear to be fundamental. But this was not an original rule. It was perfectly natural, for it is in conformity

[1] *Thayer*, "Evidence," pp. 53–55, 59.

[2] *Ibid.*, pp. 53, 83. This appearance of the four "villæ" in the proceedings appears to tally with very old ideas. A chapter of the "Lex Salica" treats "de hominem inter duas villas occisam" (Merkel's edition, t. 73). The new jury charged with the trial of the members of a former jury, accused of malversation by an "attaint," usually consisted of twenty-four members (*Thayer*, p. 86).

[3] *Ibid.*, p. 93.

[4] *Ibid.*, notably pp. 53, 57, 61–63, 82, 84, 86.

[5] *Ibid.*, pp. 88, 89.

[6] *Ibid.*, p. 90. — *Cf.* "Bull of Boniface VIII," preceding "Liber Sextus": "Senarium (qui est numerus perfectus) librorum, illo adjuncto, comprehendens."

[7] Upon this question of the number of jurors fixed at twelve, see *Holdsworth*, *op. cit.*, vol. I, pp. 149, 155 *et seq.* — *Cf. Blackstone's* "Commentaries," Book IV, p. 302.

with the primitive tendencies of the popular mind. We often find it in the old elections. But it was not enjoined upon the English jury during the early ages of its existence; a majority was sufficient.[1] A passage quoted by Stephen from Britton is quite emphatic and suggestive in this respect. "And afterwards let the jurors be charged of what fact they are to speak the truth, and then go and confer together and be kept by a bailiff. . . . If they cannot all agree in one mind, let them be separated and examined[2] why they cannot agree; and if the greater part of them know the truth and the other part do not, judgment shall be according to the opinion of the greater part. And if they declare upon their oaths that they know nothing of the fact, let others be called who do know it."[3] It was only about the end of the 1800s that the rule of the necessity for unanimity was introduced.[4] It was, apparently, a consequence of the other rule which required twelve jurors to constitute a petty jury; it was thought that the declaration of twelve jurors was necessary to make a valid verdict and, the jury comprising it being henceforth solely and essentially twelve in number, that it was their unanimity which was necessary.[5]

The jurors being, originally, witnesses of a peculiar kind, and not judges, no means of proof were at first produced before them, neither witnesses, nor other proof. It was they themselves who, in a way, produced proof to the Court. Fortescue, who was chief justice of the King's Bench from 1442 to 1460, in his essay "De laudibus legum Angliæ," probably written before 1470, contrasted this system of proofs with that of the proof by witnesses (especially in civil cases) in use upon the continent. "Slender in resource must he be thought, and of less industry, who out of all men he knows cannot find two so void of conscience and truth as to be willing, for fear, favor, or advantage to go counter to the truth. . . .[6] Who then can live in property or person under law like this, giving such aid to any one who would harm him (c. 21). Under that system (c. 23) justice constantly fails from the death or failure

[1] *Thayer*, "Evidence," p. 82 *et seq.* — *Holdsworth*, vol. I, p. 157 *et seq.*

[2] The rôle of witnesses is apparent here as well as that of jurors; it recalls certain "inquisitiones" of the Carlovingian monarchy.

[3] *Britton*, *Nichol's* Edition, p. 31. — *Stephen*, *op. cit.*, I, p. 258.

[4] *Thayer*, "Evidence," pp. 88, 89.

[5] In the grand jury of twenty-three, a majority of twelve is still sufficient.

[6] In the 1400's and the early 1500s suborned and bribed witnesses were numerous in France. Rabelais is full of satire on this point. Reform was brought about in this respect in 1566, by the Ordinance of Moulins, which restricted testimonial proof in civil matters to unimportant actions.

of witnesses. In England, on the other hand (c. 25, 26) the witnesses must be twelve; they are chosen by a public official of high standing, acting under oath, from among persons of the neighborhood where the matter in question is supposed to exist or take place, men of property, indifferent between the parties, subject to challenge by both, acting under oath." [1] The method of the constitution of the jury also rendered possible the operation of such a system in early days. The jurors were not taken indifferently throughout the whole county. They must be men of the neighborhood "de vicineto." [2] The sheriff always chose a certain number of them in the same "hundred" where the affair took place, and these had frequently a decisive influence over the others.[3] It was according to their own knowledge of the facts that the jurors decided, and not according to proofs furnished them by a regular procedure; in 1499 their verdict was approved although it was rendered without any evidence having been produced before them previous to their separation.[4]

They had, however, certain means of getting information privately. They were allowed to make a visit and entry upon the places,[5] and they must sometimes have heard witnesses then. The parties were allowed to give information to the jurors before the trials. "Long afterwards it was regarded as the right of the parties to 'inform' the jury after they were empanelled and before the trial."[6] In 1361, in a real action, the officer charged with the custody of the jurors received a box containing a deed which he transmitted to the jurors.[7]

But the admission of the methods of proof, testified to before the jurors in open court, and placed at their disposal, was arrived at slowly and with difficulty. It began, it would seem, by the submission to the jurors, for their examination, of written and anthentic writings (charters and other documents).[8] This kind of proofs was even what appears to have first borne the name of "evidence." [9] Then the practice extended its scope; and the comparison of documents not authenticated was allowed.[10] But progress was attended with more difficulty in regard to witnesses. The story is admirably told by Thayer.[11] At first there were admitted, following a tendency common to many systems of old

[1] *Thayer*, "Evidence," p. 130 summarizing Fortescue.
[2] *Ibid.*, p. 90.
[3] *Ibid.*, pp. 90, 92.
[4] *Ibid.*, pp. 132, 133.
[5] *Ibid.*, p. 167.
[6] *Ibid.*, pp. 91, 92.
[7] *Ibid.*, p. 110.
[8] *Ibid.*, p. 104.
[9] *Ibid.*, p. 104.
[10] *Ibid.*, pp. 106, 107.
[11] *Ibid.*, pp. 105–133.

law, only documentary witnesses, in confirmation of the documents to which they had been witnesses.[1] Gradually, however, testimonial proof was more freely admitted. From the first half of the 1300s the witnesses are clearly distinguished from the jurors.[2] But during the whole of the 1400s, there are only voluntary witnesses, and these could only testify with the authority of the Court.[3] And they often incurred a heavy liability by the mere fact of giving their testimony. What appears to have played an important part in this development was the intervention of the counsel of the parties, who had a great influence from the 1300s. The explanation made by them of the pleas urged by their clients in the statements of counsel carried great weight, and in the 1400s were even regarded as evidence.[4] They announced and explained the testimony which it was in their power to bring, and the hearing of that was, in a measure, a supplement to the statement. It often happened that the witnesses announced by the counsel were not heard; but even in the 1400s they were not usually in Court.[5] It was in the 1500s that the general rule was at last introduced, according to which the witnesses testified in open court, before the jurors, and were examined by the Court or the jurors.[6]

But now that the proofs were produced before them, the jurors necessarily became judges — judges of the fact,[7] and ceased to be witnesses. That involved two things. Logically, the jurors must altogether cease to play the part of witnesses. Otherwise, confusion would arise; two kinds of witnesses appearing in the case, one set at the same time judging the testimony of the other.[8] But although the status of judges of the fact became more and more dominant as regards the jurors, the result was slow in taking place. In 1670, in Bushel's case, the Court of Common Pleas, in an opinion of Chief Justice Vaughan, still admitted very plainly that the jurors could rely upon the proofs of which they had a "private knowledge," and which were unknown to the Court. "The judges cannot know all the evidence which the jury goes upon; they have much other than what is given in court. They are from the vicinage, because the law supposes them to be

[1] *Thayer*, "Evidence," pp. 92 *et seq.*, 102, 113.
[2] *Ibid.*, p. 100.
[3] *Ibid.*, pp. 129, 130.
[4] *Ibid.*, pp. 112, 119.
[5] *Ibid.*, pp. 119, 121–123.
[6] *Ibid.*, pp. 102, 133. *Cf.* upon the whole history of witnesses, *Holdsworth, op. cit.*, I, 158 *et seq.*
[7] *Thayer*, "Evidence," p. 165 *et seq.* *Holdsworth, op. cit.*, I, p. 164 *et seq.*
[8] *Thayer*, "Evidence," p. 137.

able to decide the case though no evidence at all were given in court on either side. They may, from this private knowledge of which the judge knows nothing, have ground to discredit all that is given in evidence in court." [1] No doubt it had been endeavored, by the doctrine of "maintenance," [2] to repress the abuse of the influence which one juror might be able to exercise over the others in favor of one of the parties. But the principle remained intact; the jurors could use and rely upon their personal knowledge.

This principle, however, was destined to disappear; it was essential that the jury should be led to decide solely upon the proofs furnished in court. But that rule was introduced slowly and gradually. The court began by inviting those of the jurors who possessed a personal knowledge of the facts to produce it, as a witness would, in open court.[3] Finally it became a rule of law that the jurors could not rely upon their personal knowledge, but only upon the evidence produced in court: "It was necessary to accompany this practice by an endeavor to make the jury declare publicly their private knowledge about the cause. This effort prospered but slowly. The old function of the jury was too deeply ingrained to give way in any short time; the judges long contented themselves with advice, with laying it down as a moral duty that the jury should publicly declare what they knew. But while the jury's right to go upon their private knowledge was emphatically recognized in 1670, and continued to be allowed in the books well on into the next century, yet the enlarged practice of granting new trials, and the growth and development in the seventeenth and eighteenth centuries, was steadily transforming the old jury into the modern one; and at last it was possible for the judges to lay it down for law that a jury cannot give a verdict upon their private knowledge." [4]

The English law had, in this way, applied to the jury one of the fundamental rules of the Romano-Canonic system, as that governed upon the continent; it was, indeed, its point of departure that the judge must judge "secundum allegata et probata," and that he must take into consideration only those facts which he knew as a judge and not as an individual.

I have said that, to make the jury true judges of the fact, a second element was essential, and that also related to the system of legal proofs. It was admitted that the jury must decide according to the evidence, the testimony.[5] But that was open to two

[1] *Thayer*, "Evidence," pp. 167, 168.
[2] *Ibid.*, p. 126 *et seq.*
[3] *Holdsworth, Op. cit.*, I, 160.
[4] *Thayer*, "Evidence," p. 170.
[5] *Ibid.*, p. 162.

constructions. In the first place, it might be understood as applying the system of "moral proofs," that is to say, making the convincement of the jury the sole rule by which to weigh the value of the testimony and the evidence in general. It cannot be doubted that this was the rule first of all followed, and it was a necessary consequence of the rule allowing a juror to decide according to his private knowledge: "An independent original knowledge of the facts was attributed to the jury, and not a merely inferential and reasoned knowledge. So long as this theory was true and was really a controlling feature of trial by jury, witnesses must needs play a very subordinate part. They were not necessary in any case. When they appeared, the jury could disregard all they said; and should, if it were not accordant with what they knew. Gradually it was recognized that, while the jury might not be bound by the testimony, yet they had a right to believe it, and that they were the only ones to judge of its credibility." [1]

But the juridical minds of the English, at an early date, decided against this complete independence of the jury, as so understood. It was always admitted that the court, that is, the judges, must direct it and exercise a certain control over it. It was always the presiding judge who had the function of "charging" the jury, that is, reminding them of their duties and pointing out to them the questions which they had to solve. And in good time the theory of legal proofs took shape in civil matters, destined to lead to the modern law of evidence.[2] The proofs were objective, and the judge had to follow them; should the jury not be made to respect them? Must the court allow them to render verdicts contrary to the manifest proofs, "against law and evidence"? [3] It was thought not; but, on the contrary, that the jury should be punishable when it rendered an arbitrary verdict, and one contrary to the law: "It became the chief question whether they had such evidence before them as justified their verdict. If they had, they were not punishable." [4] But how were the jury to be compelled to act thus? "If they had not (sufficient evidence), why punish them for what, perhaps, they did not know?"[5] The old English law recognized a proceeding, the "attaint," by which the injured

[1] *Thayer*, "Evidence," pp. 137, 138. See also, upon the question of "moral proofs" and "legal proofs," *ibid.*, pp. 105, 109, 111, 114, 120, 133, 137, 139, 140, 162, 164.

[2] *Ibid.*, p. 179 *et seq.*; Ch. VI, p. 263 *et seq.*

[3] *Ibid.*, pp. 164, 167, 169, 181.

[4] *Ibid.*, p. 138.

[5] *Ibid.*, p. 138 (this is the remainder of passage cited in the preceding note).

party could have the jurors who had rendered an unjustifiable verdict sentenced to severe punishment and could also have the reversal of the judgment pronounced. This form of action, originally restricted to certain hypotheses, became generalized (except in criminal cases); the accused jurors were judged by a new jury, who could only consider the evidence produced on the first trial.[1] But this method was ineffective; the proceedings were complicated, and the jurors for the "attaint" were indisposed to serve against those of the first action. The "attaint," therefore, fell into desuetude.[2] Another system was then introduced; the guilty jurors were proceeded against penally, for the infliction of an arbitrary penalty or imprisonment. Numerous prosecutions took place, under these circumstances, before the Star Chamber, especially on account of acquittals in political actions.[3] After the abolition of the Star Chamber, the courts of common law were themselves in the habit of sentencing to imprisonment or fine jurors whom they considered guilty of having rendered groundless verdicts, contrary to the court's directions.[4] But the law changed. In 1670 it was finally settled in Bushel's Case that the jury could not thus be condemned under these conditions, as they were judges of the fact.[5]

The courts, however, bethought themselves of another proceeding, which had received prior applications, but which was enlarged, extended to new hypotheses, and which contained nothing penal. It was, to consider the verdict as void and to grant the party complainant a new trial. "The courts found a remedy by a simple extension of their very ancient jurisdiction of granting new trials in case of misconduct. If a jury should accept food from one of the parties while they were out, or should take from him a paper not delivered to them in court, and should afterwards find for him, the court would refuse judgment and grant a new 'venire.' Why not, then, if the jury should go plainly counter to law, or should give an irrational, absurd, or clearly false verdict, do the same thing?"[6] This practice developed in the second half of the 1600s and in the 1700s;[7] and English judges had thereby arrived at the point of imposing upon the jury a system of legal proofs. This is what makes the English jury so different from the French jury, in criminal cases (although

[1] *Thayer*, "Evidence," p. 143 *et seq.*—*Holdsworth*, *op. cit.*, I, p. 165 *et seq.*
[2] *Ibid.*, "Evidence," p. 149 *et seq.*
[3] *Ibid.*, pp. 162, 163.
[4] *Ibid.*, pp. 163, 164.
[5] *Ibid.*, pp. 165–168.
[6] *Ibid.*, p. 169; *cf.* p. 139.
[7] Upon the growth of new trials, see *Holdsworth*, *op. cit.*, I, p. 169 *et seq.*

a new trial is not granted as a general rule in England); the French jury following, and even exaggerating, the system of moral proofs. The English system of legal proofs — the "law of evidence" — is, moreover, very wide in a certain sense: all methods of evidence are always admitted, on principle; but, to constitute evidence, the data offered ought, in such and such a case, to present prescribed characteristics; for instance, witnesses who have only learned facts from hearsay are not competent. The judge tells the jury what constitutes evidence and what does not, and they must follow his instructions under pain of seeing the verdict (in civil actions) set aside by the granting of a new trial by a higher court. The instructions given by the judge to the jury are thus of vital importance, and under the existing law a new trial ought also to be given in case of misdirection by the judge.

2. The application of the jury to crimes presents certain special features. It began, it would seem, by the *jury of accusation,* or grand jury. It distinctly appears in the Clarendon Assize of 1164.[1] It is manifestly an application of the jury of denunciation, which we have seen in the Capitularies and the Church procedure. The jurors were obliged to denounce the culprits of whom they knew as to crimes specified by the authorities. But the denunciation thus made did not entail, as a necessary consequence, that the persons denounced should be tried by a jury. It would seem to be lawful that, according to the tradition of this system, they should exculpate themselves by the "ordeals" or by the oath-helpers, "co-jurantes"; but the Assize itself appears to discard the ordeals in favor of another solution, which it does not clearly indicate, except as to imprisonment, which may be of prolonged duration.

The *trial by jury* was, however, already there, and it is known to Glanvill, who describes it. He already calls it by its name of "inquest by the country"; he who submits himself to it is said to refer to the "patria" — to the country. But it makes its appearance with a very notable characteristic, and one which it will retain, partially at least, down to the 1800s. Trial by jury must be expressly *accepted* by the accused. He could not merely declare whether he acknowledged himself to be guilty (in which case sentence followed without further procedure), or whether he claimed to be innocent (pleaded guilty or not guilty),[2] but must

[1] *Thayer,* "Evidence," p. 57. — *Holdsworth,* I, 147.

[2] *Cf.* "Très-ancienne Coutume de Bretagne," *Planiol's* edition, c. 101, p. 144.

also expressly declare that he "put himself upon the country." This was even a rule which would be retained in the arraignment. He who remained silent and persisted in not making this declaration could not be tried, either as confessing or denying. To compel him to accept, a horrible torture was made use of, the "peine forte et dure," which, however, came into vogue gradually,[1] and which is well enough known to us, for it is described by Victor Hugo in his novel, "L'homme qui rit." It would have been a simple enough matter to regard this silence as equivalent to a confession. Bracton already suggested this solution in the 1200s; but it was only adopted by the English in 1772 in the majority of cases, and absolutely in 1827.[2]

What was the reason for this necessity for acceptance? Various reasons are given by the English authors. According to some, it arose from the fact that, proof by jury having succeeded the old methods of proof, which had never been abolished, the consent of the defendant was necessary, so that the proceedings should be regular; it was, in a way, a renunciation on his part, of his right to make use of the old methods. Others (and this is fundamentally the same idea in another guise) claim that it is merely an application of the "jurata," which was, in civil matters, an application of the jury, which latter intervened, aside from any lawful provision, from the consent of the parties to the cause.[3] But it would seem that another derivation is possible. The inquest by the country, in our ancient France, had to be accepted; now, the English trial jury bears the same name, and, in its origin, is certainly a descendant of that institution. We have even seen that, in Normandy, when the inquest by the country had replaced the ordeals in criminal matters, imprisonment "with little to eat and drink" was used to compel the accused to accept it.

The criminal jury was not yet much in use in Glanvill's time.[4] But it gained ground in the 1200s and especially in the 1300s.[5]

[1] *Thayer*, "Evidence," p. 69 *et seq.* This erelong consisted in a horrible proceeding. The prisoner was put in a dungeon, and stretched, naked, upon his back; an iron weight, as heavy as he could bear, was placed upon him, and, for sustenance, he was given, the first day, nothing but a piece of bread, the second day, three mouthfuls of stagnant water, found nearest to the prison, and so on, on alternate days, until he died or answered. Before pronouncing this sentence, a triple admonition, "trina admonitio," was made to him, recalling what we have found in our own proceedings against voluntary mutes. See *Blackstone*, IV, p. 327 *et seq.*

[2] *Holdsworth*, I, pp. 153, 154.

[3] *Thayer*, "Evidence," pp. 59 *et seq.*, 69 *et seq.* — *Holdsworth*, I, 151 *et seq.*

[4] *Thayer*, "Evidence," p. 64.

[5] *Ibid.*, p. 67; see the information as to the years 1307 and 1346 there given, and especially the notable bull of Clement V.

However, the old procedure by battle, the "appeal," always remained in existence; it was not to be abolished until in the 1800s. While that is true, it gradually lost public favor. At an early date the exception "de otio et atia" could be opposed to an appeal, allowing the accused to claim trial by jury.[1] But the event which most contributed to render the use of the jury usual was the suppression of the ordeals, decreed by the Lateran Council of 1219.[2]

But (laying aside the number of jurors) how was the petty jury, the trial jury, composed? It seems highly probable that, most frequently, the jurors were taken from among the members of the grand jury, to judge the affairs of the same "inquisitio." It therefore happened that it was, in part at least, the same persons who in the first place decided upon the arraignment, and then upon the guilt of the accused. But a reaction set in; it was acknowledged that the grand jurors and the trial jurors ought to be different persons, and from the beginning of the 1300s the accused could challenge whosoever had made a part of the grand jury for that reason alone.[3] The system of challenges, in effect, was established at an early date; it is a feature differentiating the jurors from witnesses and assimilating them to judges. The dignity of the jury, moreover, always continued to increase, and in the 1500s Thomas Smith calls them "the representatives of the people."[4]

The criminal jury, like the civil jury, first of all judged without "evidence," without witnesses testifying before them.[5] The jurors were deemed to have made each his own inquiry beforehand. Only the party complainant, the pursuer, was permitted to explain the case. A passage in Britton, quoted by Stephen, and which we have already used, furnishes important information in this respect. "We will also that any man, when he is indicted of a crime touching life and limb and perceives that the verdict of the inquest upon which he has put himself is likely to pass against him, desires to say that any one of the jurors is suborned to condemn him . . . the justices thereupon shall carefully ask the jurors whether they have reason to think that such slander is true. And often a strict examination is necessary, for in such a case inquiry may be made how the jurors are informed of the truth

[1] *Thayer*, "Evidence," p. 68.

[2] *Ibid.*, p. 69. — We have seen the same statement in the "Summa de legibus Normanniæ."

[3] *Ibid.*, "pp. 81, 82; *cf. Stephen*, "History of Criminal Law," vol. I, p. 253.

[4] *Thomae Smithii Angli*, "De republica Anglorum libri tres," Lugduni Batavorum, 1630, Book III, ch. 26, p. 237.

[5] *Stephen*, "History of Criminal Law of England," Vol. I, p. 255 *et seq.*

of their verdict; when they will say by one of their fellows, and he peradventure will say that he heard it told for truth at the tavern or elsewhere by some ribald or other persons unworthy of credit, or it may be that he or they by whom the jurors have been informed were intreated or suborned by the lords or by the enemies of the person indicted to get him condemned, and if the justices find this to be the fact, let such suborners be apprehended and punished by imprisonment and fine. And if the jurors be in doubt of the matter and not certain, the judgment ought always in such case to be for the defendant." [1]

The introduction of witnesses before the jury followed very closely the same development in criminal as in civil cases, except for particular rules, which will be mentioned a little later on. It was in particular because of acquittals rendered by the jury contrary to the evidence that the judges of the various courts pronounced punishment of fine against the jurors during the whole of the 1500s and the greater part of the 1600s.[2] Certain special rules, however, prevented their action from being as effectual as in civil matters. In the first place, the "attaint" was quite possible against the grand jury,[3] but not against the petty jury; which appears to have reference to the rule according to which the "attaint" was not possible when both parties had expressly accepted the jury.[4] Finally, according to a rule of law settled in the second half of the 1500s, a new trial was not granted in criminal cases for felonies (neither in case of acquittal nor in case of conviction), neither for nor against the king; it could be granted, but very rarely, for simple misdemeanors.[5] There was still another special jury in criminal affairs, which was not a trial jury, but a jury of accusation; it had a tremendous importance in the eyes of the men of the 1700s, and it is still in existence; this is the coroner's jury. The coroner ("coronator," — representative of the crown) was of very ancient origin. Stephen, following Stubbs, makes the office date from the year 1194;[6] but more recent researches attribute to it a greater antiquity. It probably goes back to the early days of the Norman monarchy, which in this had only to follow the customs of the Anglo-Saxon monarchy. The coroner was originally an officer charged with watching over the fiscal interests of royalty, and, for that purpose, he made adminis-

[1] *Stephen*, "History of Criminal Law," Vol. I, p. 259.
[2] *Thayer*, "Evidence," p. 62 *et seq.*
[3] *Ibid.*, p. 161.
[4] *Ibid.*, pp. 161, 162.
[5] *Ibid.*, pp. 163, 175–179. — *Holdsworth*, I, pp. 85, 86.
[6] *Stephen*, "History of Criminal Law," Vol. I, p. 217.

trative "inquisitiones" by "jurati," whom he convoked. Among his many duties he had the task of visiting the spot when a murder had been committed or a sudden and suspicious death had taken place. His duty was to inquire into the cause of the death, and, in case of crime, to search for the guilty parties. For this purpose, be convoked a jury of twelve members and four, five, or six persons from each of the adjacent "villæ." These four "villæ," in case of murder, the corpse being found, already played a part in Anglo-Saxon laws.[1] This coroner's inquest was kept up and regulated.[2] The coroner had power to compel the witnesses he had heard to come to testify judicially at the time of the trial. The verdict rendered by the coroner's jury, when it is affirmative against one or several certain persons, allows him alone, without other accusation, to prosecute them criminally: "The inquisition of the coroner always was and still is a formal accusation of any person found by it to have committed murder or manslaughter (or to have found and concealed a treasure),[3] and a person may be tried upon an inquisition without any further accusation."[4]

3. The English criminal procedure is essentially accusatory, and it is a system of *free accusation*, that is to say, the right to prosecute and accuse belongs indiscriminately to every citizen, "cuivis ex populo," whether he be or be not personally interested in the crime which he prosecutes. Stephen gives the following striking formulæ of this system: "In England and so far as I know, in England and some English colonies alone, the prosecution of offenses is left entirely to private persons or to public officers who act in their capacity of private persons and who have hardly any legal powers beyond those which belong to private persons. . . . The [modern] director of public prosecutions, when he has instituted a prosecution for the most serious offense and one in which the whole country has a deep interest, has no other powers than a private person would have in respect of the prosecution of a fraud which affected no one but himself. — It is perhaps more singular that the converse is true. Every private person has exactly the same right to institute any criminal prosecution as the Attorney-General or any one else. A private person may not only prosecute any one for high treason or a seditious conspiracy, but A may prosecute B for a libel upon C, for an assault upon D, or a fraud

[1] *Holdsworth*, I, pp. 148, 149.
[2] *Stephen*, "History of Criminal Law," Vol. I, pp. 217, 218, especially the details as to the "Statute de officio coronatoris" of 1276.
[3] This is one of the powers remaining to the coroner in fiscal matters.
[4] *Stephen*, "History of the Criminal Law," Vol. I, pp. 218, 219.

upon E, although A have no sort of interest in the matter, and C, D, and E may be altogether averse to the prosecution." [1]

This system, well known in ancient history, and which was in full vogue at Rome at the period of the "questiones perpetuæ," permits the admission of two distinct elements.

In the first place, the procedure is thoroughly accusatory in this respect, that there can be no criminal action *without an accuser*. In the 1500s this applied even in a formal manner. At that time, even when a person had been arraigned by the grand jury, even when he had confessed before the magistrate, he was released if no accuser presented himself before the trial jury and a formal appeal was drawn up petitioning for the accuser.

This is explained by Thomas Smith in very clear terms: "Ex quibus apparet delationem aut in judicium postulationem (*indictment*) nihil aliud esse quam duodecim virorum (the twelve jurors making the majority) prejudicium quod finem tamen principali negotio nullum affert, sed conjecturam aut opinionem verius, quinetiam de absentibus etiam inquiritur et de non citatis. Nam tametsi aliquis delatus fuerit, si nemo eum in judicio stantem reum peregent, nemo ibi aliquid objecerit, confertim absolvitur. . . . Æterum ubi incarceratus omnino non est delatus sed in carceren ex vehementi aliqua suspicione traditus, neque aliquis illum facti insimulat, dracone judiciario hoc verba clara voce recitante: '*AB vinctus ad sceptum Curiae adstat. Si quis illum criminis postulare voluerit, accusationem nunc instituat, nam vinctus liberationem expectat.*' Si nemo eum tunc accusavierit, in libertatem pristinam asseritur, postquam ergastulario stipendia sua persolverit. Qui sic liberantur voce preconis liberati dicuntur." [2]

At the present day, the grand jury always makes its presentment and finds the indictment upon an accusatory document, a "bill," which is presented to it by the prosecutor. There is always a prosecutor, although these are of very different kinds: "Some one is bound over to prosecute — sometimes the person who has been injured, sometimes a policeman, sometimes the magistrate's clerk. There is a considerable diversity of practice in different parts of the country, and in some towns one and the same person — a solicitor — is bound over to prosecute in every case." [3] To this rule is related the power which belongs to the courts occa-

[1] *Stephen*, "History of the Criminal Law," Vol. I, pp. 493, 495.
[2] "De republica Anglorum," Book III, ch. XXVI, pp. 228, 229.
[3] *Maitland*, "Justice and Police," p. 138.

sionally to compel certain persons to prosecute, or to take their recognizances in that respect.[1]

The second element of the system is the right, referred to above, of *every citizen* to institute any prosecution whatsoever. How did this system arise? It was not original. The grand jury, when it appeared, appears first of all as a jury of denunciation, whose members were obliged to name those whom they believed to be guilty of certain crimes. In the 1700s the grand jury had still the right of spontaneously arraigning those whom they deemed guilty, without any "bill" having been laid before them. This was a "presentment" in the strict sense of the word, and it is with this that Blackstone begins his explanation of the methods of prosecution: "A presentment, properly speaking, is the notice taken by a grand jury of any offense of their own knowledge or observation, without any bill of indictment laid before them at the suit of the King, as the presentment of a nuisance, a libel and the like; and upon which the officer of the Court must afterwards frame an indictment, before the party presented can be put to answer it."[2] It is evident from these last words that there was an endeavor being made as far as possible to restore the "presentment" to the common law.

How, then, is this accusatory system arrived at? Not by preconceived idea or by legislation, although the English authors readily present it as offering to society all safeguards.[3] This is what Stephen says in this respect: "I do not think that the existence of this state of the law can properly be regarded as the result of design. It seems rather to have been the effect of historical causes already referred to. One cause is no doubt to be found in the system of appeals or private accusations. They were in nearly every respect in the nature of civil actions, and were conducted like other private litigations. But another cause is to be found in the history of trial by jury. So far and so long as trial by jury retained its original character of a report made by a body of official witnesses of facts within their own knowledge, a criminal trial was a public inquiry, or rather a report upon a public inquiry, into the truth of an accusation of crime; but, when the jury assumed its present character, the preparation of a case for trial consisted no longer in inquiries made by the jurymen themselves, but in the collection of evidence to be submitted to them. No

[1] *Maitland*, "Justice and Police," p. 138.
[2] "Commentaries," IV, c. 23, 301.
[3] *Stephen*, "History of the Criminal Law," Vol. I, pp. 495, 496.

direct express provision was ever made for this purpose, unless the appointment of justices of the peace is to be regarded in that light. Justices did no doubt concern themselves with the detection and apprehension of offenders and the collection of evidence against them to a greater extent and down to a later period than is commonly known, and to that extent they may be regarded as having for some centuries discharged more or less efficiently and completely the duties which in other countries are imposed upon public prosecutors. By degrees, however, their position became that of preliminary judges, and the duties which they had originally discharged devolved upon the police, who have never been intrusted with any special powers for the purpose of discharging them. It was thus by a series of omissions on the part of the legislature to establish new officers for the administration of justice, as the old methods of procedure gradually changed their character, that English criminal trials gradually lost their original character of public inquiries and came to be conducted in almost precisely the same manner as private litigations. Perhaps the strongest illustration of the length to which this process has gone is to be found in the way in which business is conducted before a coroner. The coroner was the predecessor of the justice of the peace, and it was his duty on the one hand to receive appeals or private accusations and on the other to inquire into cases of homicide in the interest of the public. The inquiry was made originally by the reeve and the four men of a certain number of townships. It is now made by a jury, before which witnesses may be and are summoned, but if the inquiry appears likely to result in a criminal charge the inquest practically assumes the form of a litigation. The friends of the deceased and the suspected person are represented by advocates, and are entitled, or at all events permitted, to examine and cross-examine witnesses exactly as if the suspected person whom it is proposed to accuse was on his trial, and the coroner and jury occupy a position closely analogous to those of a judge and a jury, and very unlike the positions of persons holding an inquiry and pursuing their own independent investigations for the discovery of the truth." [1]

May a foreigner be permitted to add some comments? The old "appeals" were certainly private accusations, but they could only be instituted by the victim or his nearest relatives as in our old French law.[2] The principle of the "publica accusatio"

[1] *Stephen*, "History of the Criminal Law," Vol. I, pp. 496–498.
[2] *Blackstone*, "Commentaries," IV, c. 23, pp. 214, 216.

was, therefore, not introduced by these actions. But this principle nevertheless existed in the very old English law and manifested itself by way of "appeal" in case of high treason; any subject could accuse another on that ground. This right was, it is true, abolished as to its principal application in the reign of Edward III,[1] but it could easily be transformed into a right to accuse and to instigate an *indictment*, and thence to pass on to accusation for *felonies*. The *grand jury* could decide upon a *bill* presented to it by a private individual, as well as upon *its own knowledge* by way of presentment, and it is conceivable that this more convenient practice was introduced without difficulty.

Another cause should likewise have helped to facilitate the admission of the "publica accusatio." This is, that, by the doctrine of "pleas of the crown," the crime was not prosecuted in the name of the private individual, but of the king; crimes were always prosecuted and indictments issued in the name of the king.[2] As Blackstone says somewhere, the king could not but lend his name and his authority to private prosecutors.[3]

4. Thanks principally to the jury and the system of accusatory procedure, England had escaped the criminal procedure which had swept over the continent. It had, however, been threatened by this system, founded upon the Roman and the Canon law, and it had for a time experienced some of the defects which it entailed.

It was notably in the special courts which were recognized in the 1500s and the 1600s that this deviation took place. The High Court of Commission for Ecclesiastical Causes, from 1558 on, compelled accused persons to answer the interrogatories on oath.[4] This occasioned a prolonged struggle, and the practice was only in course of disappearance when Coke became Chief Justice of the Common Pleas.[5] But it was not forbidden by

[1] *Blackstone*, "Comm." IV, ch. 23, 314: "It was anciently permitted that any subject might appeal another subject of high treason, either in the courts of common law, or parliament, or (for treasons committed beyond the seas) in the court of the high constable and amiral . . . but that in the first was virtually abolished by the statutes 5 Edward III, *c.g*, and 25 Edw. III, c. 24, and in the second *expressly* by statute Henry IV, c. 14."

[2] *Pollock and Maitland*, "History of English Law," Book II, ch. IX, and Book II, pp. 491–496. — For the contemporaneous *indictments*, *Maitland*, "Justice and Police," p. 137.

[3] Another advantage was that the prosecutor bore the costs of the proceedings: *Stephen*, "History of the Criminal Law," Vol. I, p. 498.

[4] *John H. Wigmore*, "The Privilege against Self-crimination," chap. 78 § 2250 in "A Treatise on the System of Evidence in Trials at Common Law" (1905), Vol. IV, p. 3077.

[5] *Ibid., loc. cit.*, pp. 3079–3080.

law and generally until 1641: "In March, 1641, a bill was introduced to abolish the Court of Star Chamber as well as (then or shortly after) a bill to abolish the Court of High Commission for Ecclesiastical Causes. These were both passed July 2–5 of the same year; and in the latter statute was inserted a clause which forever forbade, for any ecclesiastical court, the administration *ex officio* of any oath requiring answer as to matters penal." [1] The celebrated Star Chamber had adopted the worst practices of the inquisitorial procedure. This was early recognized, and Blackstone says so frankly. But the fact is definitely established by researches made and published in our own days, based upon the proceedings followed before the Court. Not that modern historians attack the Star Chamber; they rather incline to rehabilitate it, doing justice to the services which it rendered.[2] But it is certain that it practised the interrogation of the accused, who was obliged to take the oath.[3] It also employed torture,[4] which was at the time practised in Scotland. It could not, it is true, inflict capital punishment; but it imposed imprisonment, enormous fines, and mutilation.[5] The Star Chamber was finally abolished in 1641 and its system of practice died with it.

In certain respects, however, analogous practices were followed before the courts of Common law with the jury. In many cases in the 1500s and the 1600s a preliminary procedure was carefully carried out before the justices of the peace and the trial begun by the reading to the jury of the official report which had been made of it: "Most notably it was required that every accused felon be examined by the justices of the peace, and his examination to be preserved for the judges at the trial; and, so far as appears, not a murmur was ever heard against this process till the middle of the 1700s; and no statutory measure was taken to caution the accused that his answer was not compellable, until well on in the 1800s. The everyday procedure in the trials of the 1500s and the 1600s, and almost the first step in the trial, was to read to the jury this compulsory examination of the accused." [6]

[1] *John H. Wigmore, loc. cit.*, p. 3082.
[2] *Holdsworth*, I, p. 284 *et seq.* *Thayer*, "Evidence," p. 162 *et seq.*
[3] *John H. Wigmore, loc. cit.*, p. 3080 *et seq.* *Holdsworth*, I, p. 280.
[4] *Holdsworth*, I, p. 280.
[5] *Ibid.*, I, p. 279.
[6] *John H. Wigmore, loc. cit.*, pp. 3084, 3085.—This, moreover, did not prevent the accused from pleading guilty, even if he had confessed during the preliminary examination. *Thomas Smith*, "De republica Anglorum," Book III, ch. XXVI, p. 232: "Si reum se esse pernegaverit . . . tametsi factum coram seirenarcha (justice of the peace) prius non inficiatur aut in flagranti crimine deprehendatur, scriba forensis ipsum interrogat quo modo decerni velit."

That is not all. In the course of the trial the accused was subjected by the judge to a formal examination, properly so called: "Furthermore, as the trial goes on, in all this period of 1500–1620, the accused is questioned freely and urged by the judges to answer."[1] He was not, it is true, compelled to answer under oath; he had not even the right to do so, for it was thought that the taking of the oath (which would in all probability be broken by him) would give a greater weight to his answers;[2] this is an idea which we may find among the English to-day.

In the 1700s the reading of the official report of the information and the interrogation of the accused vanished. But in two other respects the freedom of the defense was for a long time trammeled. The accused could not have witnesses heard in his defense, or have the assistance of a counsel. These restrictions were both justified in this way, that the accused could not be condemned unless clear and convincing proofs, "luce clariores," were brought against him, and that the judge attended to the interests of the accused better than an advocate could have done.

In the latter half of the 1600s, however, the practice of the courts was relaxed in severity. The accused in capital cases was allowed to produce witnesses in his defense, but they were heard without taking the oath. Thayer cites a whole line of precedents to this effect, running from 1640 to 1685.[3] The law at last intervened to allow witnesses for the defense to take the oath, first of all in cases of treason in 1685, and then in prosecutions for felony in 1707. The aid of counsel remained forbidden, as a rule, and Blackstone gives the standard reasons therefor.[4] It did not become a legal right until 1836. In the 1700s, however, it was often tolerated by the courts, but with material restrictions.[5]

5. Let us glance rapidly at the criminal action as it has developed according to these principles. As early as the 1500s Thomas Smith presented an interesting picture of it; he shows its equitable and reasonable character, without speaking, it must be understood, of the absence of witnesses for the defense and of counsel. But what chiefly concerns us is the procedure of the 1700s, be-

[1] *John H. Wigmore, loc. cit.*

[2] *Ibid.*, p. 3085. "He is not allowed to swear, for the reasons already noted, but he is pressed and bullied to answer." *Ibid.*, p. 3084, note 81: "the reason for this was merely, as before, that the oath was thought to give to the accused's statements a solemnity and a weight which would be too great an advantage."

[3] See the passages from *Coke*, cited by *Thayer*, "Evidence," p. 158, note. See upon the question the whole of Thayer's long note, beginning on page 157 (note 4) and ending on page 160.

[4] "Commentaries," IV, 355.

[5] *Thayer*, "Evidence," p. 161, note.

cause it served as a model for the Constituent Assembly. It is principally to Blackstone that we appeal for information.[1]

Each case necessarily passed before two juries, one of accusation and one of trial. It began with a kind of preliminary examination, very short and quite elementary. The prosecutor began by asking for a warrant or summons against the person he accused, and for that purpose he usually had to apply to the magistrate, who had become the chief officer of judicial police, the justice of the peace. The latter investigated the facts alleged by the prosecutor, from whom he required an affirmatory oath, and he issued, if there was cause, the warrant or order for arrest.[2] It was the duty of the officer charged with the execution of the warrant to bring the person arrested before the justice of the peace, who then made a kind of examination, "And to this end, by statute 2 and 3 Ph. and M. c. 10, he is to take in writing the examination of such prisoner and the information of those who bring him; which, Mr. Lambard observes, was the first warrant given for the examination of a felon in the English law. For, at the common law, 'nemo tenebatur prodere seipsum.' "[3]

This was the only examination to which the accused was subjected during the whole course of the proceedings; and English custom, in its solicitude, even provided, subsequently to the period we are writing about, that the justice of the peace must expressly warn the accused that he is not bound to answer, and that what he says can be afterwards used against him. — This first part of the proceedings might be secret.

The justice of the peace then comes to a decision. If there appears no serious charge, he releases the prisoner and discharges him from the prosecution; in the contrary case, he must detain him pending trial; that is the "commitment." But both custom and law provide that if the accused furnishes a sufficient surety, he must be released on bail. In the time of Blackstone, however, although liberation on bail was a matter of right for minor crimes, it was not permitted in the case of a capital crime.[4] Certain specified classes of suspected persons were

[1] See especially "Recherches sur les Cours et les procédures criminelles d'Angleterre, extraites des commentaires de Blackstone sur les lois Anglaises," preceded by an essay upon the provisions of these procedures and upon the abolition of capital punishment, Paris 1790.

[2] *Blackstone*, Book IV, p. 290: "It is fitting to examine upon oath the party requiring a warrant, as well to ascertain that there is a felony or other crime, without which no warrant should be granted."

[3] *Ibid.*, p. 296.

[4] *Ibid.*, Book IV, ch. XXII, No. 1: "Commitment being only for safe custody, where a bail will answer the same intention it ought to be taken,

declared not bailable. Individual liberty was protected by the laws, which punished the magistrate when he unjustly refused bail or fraudulently exacted an exorbitant amount, and by the statute of Habeas Corpus, which allowed proceedings for release from unlawful imprisonment to be brought before all the higher courts of England.

At this stage of the case, it becomes necessary, before proceeding further, to ask the grand jury to make the presentment. This grand jury is composed of freeholders, convoked by the sheriff to decide upon the indictments, at every session of assizes held by the high judges in each county. The grand jury is composed of at least twelve persons and twenty-three at most, and renders its decisions by a majority of twelve votes. Previous to this there had been drawn up an "indictment," one of the most important documents of the English procedure; the formal wording of which is a somewhat difficult matter. The indictments were presented by the crown officers in the name of the king, but at the request of private individuals.[1] Besides the information contained in the indictment, the jurors heard the witnesses, but only "for the prosecution"; they then finally decided whether the charges were sufficient and whether there was or was not cause for prosecution; in the former case, they wrote at the bottom of the indictment "billa vera," or, a true bill; in the latter, "ignoramus," or "not found."

The presentment being made, it was essential to proceed to the trial. There was no recourse to the ordeals, as in the olden days, but, instead, to the trial jury or petit jury. These trials were had at the assizes, which, at the time of which we write, were already of two kinds. The first, called sessions "of oyer and terminer and general jail delivery," were held twice a year in each county by the chief judges of the Court of Westminster.[2] They owe their name to the fact that the judges were required to terminate all the actions and empty the prisons of all the individuals held for trial. The other assizes, or quarter sessions, were held by the justices of the peace of the county assembled every three months, but they tried only the minor offenses. The jurors, "boni et legales homines de vicineto," were convoked

as in most of the inferior crimes; but in felonies and other offenses of a capital nature no bail can be a security equivalent to the actual custody of person."

[1] *Blackstone*, Book IV, p. 303.

[2] As to these circuits of the grand judges see *Max Budinger*, *op. cit.*, p. 153 *et seq.*, and *Bigelow*, *op. cit.*, ch. III.

by the sheriff to the number of forty-eight; and from among these the twelve judgers were chosen.

The indictment, already voted by the grand jury, merely served to put matters in such a form that the accused should and could be tried by the trial jury. It was still essential that he should have denied his guilt and that he should accept the trial by jurors.[1] For this purpose, the prisoner was brought into open court. This is the "arraignment": The indictment was first read to the accused "in the English language," and the judge then asked him if he was "guilty or not guilty." If he confessed, the intervention of the jury was needless; nothing remained but to award the punishment. We see here the weight of the confession as shown in the feudal procedure; it is the weight which it naturally retains in every procedure where no effort is made to obtain the confession. If the accused pleaded not guilty, it was furthermore necessary that he should accept, or, at least, that he should not refuse to submit to, the judgment by the country. If he absolutely refused to answer, or if, after having pleaded not guilty, he refused to put himself "on the country," the progress of the proceedings was impeded and the trial could not go on. This led to the application of the "peine forte et dure." In the 1700s that was still the state of the law, and it was not until George III's reign that, in all cases, voluntary silence was held as synonymous with a confession.[2]

It is conceivable that the accused usually accepted the judgment by the jury; and then the *trial* proceeded. [3] The names of the jurors were drawn by lot, and the accused had the right of challenge. He could always challenge for cause, but he could also make use of thirty-five peremptory challenges. The twelve jurors thus obtained were sworn and the trial began. Nothing is more simple than this trial, which does not allow of any interrogation of the accused. The indictment was read, and then the counsel for the party prosecuting, whether it was the king or a private individual who prosecuted, produced his evidence, and had his witnesses heard. The trial was essentially oral.[4]

It is a strange thing that, in this system, where the rights of

[1] By doing so he is said to "put himself on the country."

[2] See note 1, p. 333.

[3] He was entitled to an interval between the arraignment and the trial, but usually the latter followed immediately.

[4] "When the jury is sworn . . . the indictment is usually opened, and evidence marshalled, examined and enforced by the counsel of the crown or prosecution." *Blackstone*, Book IV, p. 355.

the accused are respected to the extent of not making him submit to an examination, two features nevertheless recall the procedure followed upon the continent. First, no counsel could be granted to the accused where a capital crime was concerned, English judges and jurists, like the Ordinance of 1670, justifying this rule by saying that "the judge shall be the counsel for the prisoner";[1] second, it was admitted, as a common practice "derived from the civil law and still observed to-day in the kingdom of France," says Blackstone, that the accused "*cannot exculpate himself by the testimony of any witnesses.*"[2] The practice of hearing the witnesses on behalf of the prisoner was, however, slowly introduced, but "not upon oath."[3] It was not until the reigns of William III and Anne that the latter restriction disappeared.

The trial at an end, it remained for the jurors to give their verdict. Having received the judge's instructions, they retired to deliberate and vote if the case presented any difficulty. Unanimity, in either direction, was essential to a valid decision. This is a strange rule, which, moreover, does not always appear to have been followed in England.[4] We know, besides, what methods of indirect constraint the English law allowed to be employed. The verdict having been found, the judge had nothing to do but conform the sentence to it; this was due to the distinction between the question of guilt and that of punishment, between the fact and the law.

The sentence thus passed was not, on general principles, susceptible of any recourse; the jury is not compatible with the system of appeals. Except where the decision was given by a jury without jurisdiction, a jury "non légal," as our law will subsequently express it, there was no recourse except by "writ of error." That was brought, against the decisions of the inferior courts, before the Court of King's Bench, and, against the decisions of that court before the House of Lords.[5] But it was only permitted in the case of an error in law, if, for instance, there had been an erroneous application of the punishment or the omission of an essential formality. Aside from these cases, the condemned person could only petition for pardon from the king.

Finally, the English law recognized a rather curious procedure

[1] *Blackstone*, Book IV, ch. XXVII; he adds, it is true, that this rule "seems to be not at all of a piece with the rest of the humane treatment of prisoners by the English Law."

[2] *Ibid.*, IV, 359. [3] *Ibid.*, Book IV, pp. 359, 360 and citations supra.

[4] See *Brunner, op. cit.*, pp. 363, 371; *cf. Blackstone*, Book III, ch. 23.

[5] *Blackstone*, Book IV, ch. 30.

by contumacy, resulting in the confiscation of the chattels and the outlawry of the accused, thus keeping up the traditions of the feudal period.

Such is, in its main features, and laying aside a great number of sometimes very interesting details (the benefit of clergy, for instance), the trend of that English procedure which, although possessing serious imperfections, presented the most rational form of criminal proceedings yet known to humanity, and which the philosophy of the 1700s even considered as perfect. It had, however, its weak points, especially the preliminary proceedings and examination; and, in its desire to imitate it even upon these points, we shall see the French legislation go astray in its early reforms, and waver long before finding its equilibrium.

6. English criminal procedure has remained, in the 1800s and the 1900s, substantially as it was in the 1700s. Several material changes have, however, been made in it, which it is important briefly to scan. I do not refer to the abolition of the "appeals," by "wager of battle" in 1833; that was a legislative declaration of their desuetude; I allude to more real innovations. There is, first of all, the adaptation of the accusatory system in such a way as to counteract its disadvantages. In 1869, the legislature, with reference to a whole series of offenses, subjected the private prosecution to the preliminary consent of certain judicial authorities or upon special conditions.[1] Before that date the action of the attorney-general could interpose to put an end to it.[2] For another thing, the creation of a Director of Public Prosecutions in 1879 added a new and important factor to the public action,[3] and we are aware that by very simple means a private prosecutor could always be found, when that was necessary or expedient.[4] Lastly, the law permits the courts to relieve the private prosecutor of the costs of the proceedings.[5]

But most notable of all is the part taken by the police department in the pursuit of offenders and the search for evidence. It is in reality, in almost all cases, the active agency in this respect. Without losing its individual character, it has become the necessary and invariable auxiliary to the judicature. It fulfils the task which, with us, devolves upon the collaboration of the State's attorney and the examining magistrate in the pre-

[1] *Maitland*, "Justice and Police," p. 138.
[2] *Stephen*, "History of Criminal Law," Vol. I, p. 96.
[3] *Ibid.*, "History of Criminal Law," Vol. I, p. 501.
[4] *Maitland*, "Justice and Police," p. 138.
[5] *Stephen*, "History of Criminal Law," Vol. I, pp. 498, 499.

liminary examination. The most authoritative English writers no doubt state that, save on certain points, the officers of the police have no privileges; that they exercise the same rights as a private individual. "The police," says Stephen, "in their different grades are no doubt officers appointed by law for the purpose of arresting criminals; but they possess for this purpose no powers which are not also possessed by private persons. They are, indeed, protected in arresting innocent persons upon a personal suspicion that they have committed felony, whether a felony has in fact been committed or not; whereas the protection of a private person in such a case extends only to cases in which a felony has been committed, and they are, and private persons are not, under a legal duty to arrest when the occasion arises; but in other respects they stand upon precisely the same footing as private persons. They require a warrant and may arrest without warrant in the same cases. When they have arrested they are under precisely the same obligations. A policeman has no other right as to asking questions or compelling the attendance of witnesses than a private person has; in a word, with some few exceptions, he may be described as a private person paid to perform as a matter of duty acts which, if so minded, he might have done voluntarily."[1] But this interpretation of the principles does not accord with the actual facts. It is a great deal for a police officer to have the right of arresting, without a warrant, a person whom he suspects of having committed a crime, and of being shielded from all liability in regard thereto, if he acts in good faith, although no crime has been committed. We may add that he has, to a great extent, the right of search. Although the rights of private individuals may be ample in such matters, they must hesitate to exercise them, for they will involve themselves in liability. It is, therefore, plain that a policeman occupies a peculiar and privileged position, and it is quite evident that the arrest of accused persons and the search for proofs and witnesses are matters for him. It is true that he cannot try to extract confessions from the person arrested; but the examination of the accused no longer figures in the English procedure. It is true that, in order to validate the arrest, he must bring the prisoner before the magistrate with the least possible delay; but that is only just, and this appearance before the magistrate has transformed the "preliminary examination" in England.

[1] *Stephen*, "History of Criminal Law," Vol. I, pp. 493, 494. — *Cf. Maitland*, "Justice and Police," p. 122.

We have seen how this preliminary examination was formerly made before the justice of the peace. Before him it can always be made. But in important towns it is made before the magistrates, — the "stipendiary magistrates," — attached to the Police Courts created in the 1800s in London and other cities.[1] It is before the magistrate, often an eminent man, who holds this court, that the person arrested must be brought, and the preliminary examination there made; and this proceeding has acquired a new and notable form in its new environment. This form is now a judicial one. The judge has no doubt the right to bar the public from this trial, but it is one of which he rarely avails himself. Usually everything takes place in open court. The prisoner is warned that he is not compelled to say anything, but that everything he does say can be used against him. The witnesses produced by the police, or by the private prosecutor, are heard, and the solicitor of the prosecutor examines them should he desire to do so. The accused is entitled to have his counsel, who cross-examines these witnesses, makes a statement, and produces witnesses for the defense if he wishes. This is really a judicial trial, and, as Maitland says, a "preliminary trial."[2] The evidence is reduced to writing, but the rule is that it cannot be read to the jurors at the "trial" proper.[3] On the conclusion of the trial the magistrate gives his decision. If he does not find the charge to be serious, he sets the prisoner at liberty. In the contrary event, he decides that he shall appear at the assizes, and continues the imprisonment, unless he releases him on bail.

But this preliminary examination, thorough as it is, does not dispense with the indictment by the grand jury, which must always intervene. But the composition of that body has changed. "In practice at the assizes the grand jury for counties is always composed of the county magistrates, whose names are called over by the officer of the court until twenty-three at most have appeared. The magistrates, however, have no special legal right or duty in the matter."[4] It is conceivable that, in these circumstances, the grand jury generally ratifies the decision of the magistrate in the preliminary examination. Maitland says, however, "Their inquiry is quite independent of that which has taken place before the magistrate. The grand jury system saves a certain number

[1] *Maitland*, "Justice and Police," p. 101 *et seq.; Stephen*, "History of Criminal Law," Vol. I, p. 232 *et seq.*
[2] *Ibid.*, "Justice and Police," p. 129; *cf.* p. 123.
[3] *Ibid.*, "Justice and Police," p. 132.
[4] *Stephen*, "History of Criminal Law," Vol. I, p. 254.

of innocent persons from the shame and annoyance of public trial, and seems necessary so long as proceedings before a magistrate are not made essential in all cases; but such proceedings are now so usual that for a grand jury to ignore a bill has become a rather rare event." [1]

The abolition of the examination of the accused during the trial often rendered the accused a mere passive participant in the proceedings, especially when he was represented by counsel.[2] This was peculiar, and fruitful of disadvantages. The courts, it is true, usually allowed him to make a "statement" when he desired to do so. But what he said, not being stated on oath, lacked authority, according to preconceived English ideas. The Criminal Evidence Act of 1898 made the accused a voluntary witness in his own behalf. He may, if he wishes, go into the witness box, take the oath, and testify. He is not obliged to do so, but he can no longer make a mere statement, as he could before the passing of that act.[3]

Lastly, the latest important reform has been brought about by the Act of 28th August, 1907, instituting a Court of Criminal Appeal and amending the law in so far as it concerns appeals in criminal matters.[4] The introduction of the appeal in criminal matters is a great reform. The older methods of recourse (writ of error and grant of a new trial) were lacking in efficacy in this respect. Proceeding to show this, Mr. Holdsworth, in 1908, thus begins his explanation upon this point: "It is a peculiarity of our system of criminal jurisdiction that there is practically no provision made for an appeal either from the finding of the jury on a question of fact, or from the ruling of the judge on a question of law." [5] The act of 1907 makes the appeal available on both questions. It is very important from a technical point of view of English law, but that is an investigation upon which we cannot enter. We may merely state that the English have not been restrained by any idea that, the jury being representative of the people in criminal matters, its verdict was incapable of reversal.

[1] *Maitland*, "Justice and Police," p. 139.
[2] *Dickens*, "The Old Curiosity Shop," ch. 63.
[3] *Esmein*, "Le 'Criminal Evidence Act' de 1898 et le serment des accusés en Angleterre," in the Revue politique et parlementaire of November, 1898.
[4] "Annuaire de législation étrangère," published by the Société de législation comparée, 1908, p. 14 *et seq.*
[5] "History of English Law," Vol. I, p. 84.

CHAPTER II

CRIMINAL PROCEDURE AND PUBLIC OPINION IN THE 1600s AND 1700s

§ 1. Reception of the Criminal Procedure in the 1600s. La Bruyère, Augustin Nicolas, Despeisses. — The public temper, in the 1600s, was by no means hostile to this inquisitorial and secret procedure which we have described. At that time it was looked upon as a necessary severity. It was accepted without question and instinctively, so to speak, like the absolute power of kings and religious intolerance. A great need of ready submission then filled all minds. This is well shown by the fact that it was possible to speak on the stage of the most odious feature of this procedure, torture, and that not in a satirical vein, but in the light of a jest. We know the scene in the "Plaideurs" and Dandin's proposal to Isabelle:

"D. Have you never seen the torture administered?
"I. No, and I do not believe I ever shall, all my life.
"D. Come with me, I want to satisfy your desire.
"I. Oh! sir, how could we look at the sufferings of the unfortunate people?
"D. That will be all right! it will serve to pass an hour or two!"[1]

Racine no doubt puts a sympathetic tone in a woman's mouth; but he does not mean to hold Dandin up as a monster and excite the horror of the audience. In the same way, Molière makes Harpagnon, whose cash-box has been stolen, say: "I am going to seek out the judge, and have the torture administered to all my household, servants, valets, son, and daughter, and myself into the bargain."[2] That made no one shudder, and yet Harpagnon's idea, so far as his valets were concerned, might have been

[1] "Les Plaideurs," Act III, sc. 4 (1668). [2] "L'Avare," Act IV, sc. 7.

a stern reality any day. The master's accusation constituted a presumption sufficient to cause a domestic servant to be put to the torture. Madame de Sévigné mentions torture very unconcernedly.[1] Among the littérateurs, La Bruyère is almost alone in protesting against torture. But his protest is a vehement one. It might be classed with his famous tirade upon the peasant. "Torture is a wonderful invention and may be counted upon to ruin an innocent person with a weak constitution and exonerate a guilty person born robust. The punishment of a guilty person forms a warning to scoundrels; the condemnation of an innocent person is the affair of all honest men. I might almost say in regard to myself, 'I will not be a thief or a murderer'; but to say, 'I shall not some day be punished as such,' would be to speak very boldly. — The situation of an innocent man in whom haste and the procedure have detected a crime is lamentable. Could even that of his judge be more so?"[2] — And elsewhere: "I admit that imprisonment and corporal punishment are necessary things, but justice, laws, and necessities aside, it is always a strange thing to me to see with what ferocity human beings treat their fellows."[3] Truly, Beccaria and Voltaire do not put the case better; but this eloquent voice is a solitary one!

About the end of the 1600s, however, eleven years after the great Ordinance, another voice is raised, loud and touching. It is that of a magistrate, Augustin Nicolas, president of the Parlement of Dijon. He is an intellectual descendant of Pierre Ayrault, and one of those magistrates who unite science with nobility of heart. It may be said that he has been discovered in recent years by MM. Laboulaye and Faustin Hélie.[4] He is worthy of a place with Lamoignon in this historic study. He is a link between Ayrault and the publicists of the 1700s, and it is a pleasure to show that in France, even in the worst times of criminal procedure, the torch of truth was never quite extinguished, and that there were courageous men to pass from one to the other the sacred flame.

Nicolas's work is not a large book.[5] He does not deal with

[1] "At last, all is over, and La Brinvilliers is in the air; after the execution, her poor little body was thrown into a large fire and her ashes scattered on the wind. . . . They threatened her with the torture, though she said it was unnecessary and that she would tell everything. . . . In spite of this confession, they administered the ordinary and extraordinary torture to her; but she confessed nothing more." Letter of 17th July, 1676, edited by Monmerqué, vol. IV, pp. 528, 529.

[2] "Les caractères," De quelques usages. [3] *Ibid.*, De l'homme.

[4] See *M. Laboulaye*, Revue des cours littéraires, vol. II, p. 770.

[5] It is entitled "*Si la torture est un moyen sûr à vérifier les crimes secrets; dissertation morale et juridique, par laquelle il est amplement traité des abus,*

criminal procedure as a whole. He has concentrated all his efforts on a single point, the most hateful of them all; he treats of torture, and especially of its employment in proceedings against witchcraft. Augustin Nicolas, however, is no rebel. That would be strange in a magistrate of the 1600s. He respects all authority and dedicates his book to the king himself. In his preface, following the fashion of the period, he compares the king to Hercules: "You, Sire, will achieve with less effort than he the same results on behalf of the helpless and the innocent if you deign to undertake the protection of the present work, and add your authority to the reasons which support its argument. Only to a king as mighty as you, Sire, belongs the task of correcting throughout his dominions the abuses which these later ages have imbibed from the most corrupt sources. It is for a French monarch to extirpate from his kingdom by means of his absolute power, and to invite, by such a noble example, the other Christian princes to correct in their dominions, so many wrongful methods of arriving at the ascertainment and chastisement of crimes. So many poor innocents who have perished during all these years by the horrible violence of torture, so many poor women as cruelly martyred as unjustly condemned for witchcraft upon confessions forcibly extorted by unbearable torments, stretch out their hands to the throne of the great Lord of the universe, who has intrusted to you the government of so many people! . . . Not for the first time has your majesty taken pains to safeguard his dominions from the sad results of the chicanery and brigandage of so many improper procedures. France, which to-day leads all the nations in the world in regard to science and culture, furnishes you with great geniuses in abundance to whom this humble effort of one of your subjects may be submitted." Nicolas is so impressed with the importance of the ideas which he is promulgating that he addresses himself to all the kings of Christendom. "Since I think that in this discourse I am rendering to the Christian republic the highest service possible, I am not afraid to address it to all Christian princes, nor to pray them most respectfully to cause it to be read and investigated seriously."[1] In the same way as to witchcraft, he appeals to the approaching Council of Prelates.[2]

qui se commettent partout en l'instruction des procès criminels, et particulièrement en la recherche du sortilège. A Amsterdam chez Abraham Wolfgang, près de la Bourse. 1682."

[1] p. 188.

[2] "I humbly beg the first council-general which shall lawfully meet to investigate my reasons regarding these matters; to their judgment I implicitly defer."

Not only does he respect established authorities, but even contemporary prejudices. Although his whole book shows his disbelief in sorcery, he declares that "it is a very certain mark of ignorance to deny the existence of sorcerers."[1] He feels that the formidable power of preconceived ideas is against him. He has for long hesitated in "the fear of putting before the public something which might seem contrary to everyday opinions."[2] He is aware that he will have against him "those who think to refute an argument by assailing its author with the scurrilous reproaches of being an advocate of sorcerers and the protector of impunity."[3] But he also feels that he has a duty to perform, and he says in an elevated strain: "It would be futile to wait until monarchs take the matter up of their own accord. So long as the learned and the wise dare not give utterance to their opinions on the subject, princes who rely upon their officers in regard thereto will never have any authoritative information about it."[4]

There are, in this book, two intellects, so to speak, which intertwine like two different threads in the woof of a piece of cloth. On one side are the arguments addressed to his contemporaries. These may appear to us to be long, tedious, puerile perhaps; but they were the kind of arguments of use for the men of that period, couched in language they understood. Thus Nicolas insists that torture is an institution of Roman paganism, and he frankly declares it to be an invention of the devil.[5] He strives very hard to show that there is no trace of it in the Mosaic law, nor in the mild law of Christ, and that the Canon law does not allow it.[6] In particular, he subjects to a careful examination, too long for our purpose, all the texts of the Roman laws regulating torture, and the passages from Cicero and Aristotle invoked in its behalf. It must, however, be observed that he gives proof of the possession of a sufficiently accurate historic sense. He is well aware that "the early Romans who made use of it dared only practise it upon their slaves"; and that this was the case "during the good ages of the Roman Republic."[7] He shows clearly that the "ac-

[1] p. 153; but compare p. 154: "It is a kind of madness to believe that sorcerers are responsible for all the mischiefs attributed to them." — p. 137: "Whatever German doctors say as to the number of sorcerers in their country, they are not so great sorcerers as they imagine."

[2] p. 7. [3] p. 52. [4] p. 189.

[5] Here is one passage among many, p. 33: "Whoever reflects upon the origin and the originators of torture can hardly help agreeing that it is an invention of the Devil, suggested to pagans and tyrants, for the oppression of an infinitude of honest people."

[6] p. 190. Compare p. 81 *et seq.* [7] p. 10.

cusations de majesté" of the Roman law were totally different from the crimes of high treason of the French law.[1]

But apart from all that, there are other reasons, which certainly appear to him to be the proper and true ones. And here, speaking above the heads of his contemporaries, he addresses himself to the intellects of posterity which will be able to understand him. When he claims the rights of reason and of good sense, we seem to be listening to a man of the end of the 1700s: "Although I have as much respect for the authority of human laws as anybody, I cannot submit to it when common sense is repugnant to it, as in this case, and when natural reason contradicts it."[2] — "We are relegated to natural equality and to the justice of common right, which demands that where the danger is greatest we take the most abundant care and precautions for the sureness of the trial."[3] Augustin Nicolas, in fact, is not, in many respects, a man of his time. He is an advocate of religious tolerance,[4] and he has that regard for accuracy of observation and familiar and picturesque detail which characterizes our present day modes of thought.[5] He puts his personality into the foreground and appeals to the individual conscience. "I consider my own case first of all, and I frankly confess that I am one of those who would prefer a speedy death to such intolerable sufferings (as torture), . . . and I have no doubt that every virtuous man who is neither a stoic nor an athlete would make the same confession in regard to himself."[6]

From this mode of thought we can surmise how Nicolas regarded torture. "No one," he says, "will deny that a single half hour under torture contains more of martyrdom than three punishments of gallows or scaffold. . . . Do sufficient reasons exist for dismembering a man alive and exposing ourselves to the chance of finding him innocent, and at the most setting him at liberty, however criminal he may be, if he has the good fortune to possess a charm or a constitution to endure these torments, or to top the injustice by adding a final punishment to an innocent person who confesses himself guilty under compulsion, to the first martyrdoms which we have already made him suffer? Does not this happen every day?"[7] He sets forth numerous examples of

[1] p. 66. [2] p. 15. [3] p. 26.

[4] "Our profession of Christianity has not been exempt from these shameful excesses, when an ill-advised zeal has caused us to take arms against our brothers rebellious to avenge upon them the interests of the Divinity and any supposed impairment of his worship and the faith we owe him" (p. 50).

[5] See as to witchcraft, p. 105. [6] p. 29. [7] p. 18.

innocent people having confessed under torture, and shows with a striking verisimilitude the judge growing more and more exasperated at the accused who will not confess.[1] The torments he refuses to describe. "Whoever wishes to learn the apparatus used in this butchery has only to read the Italian authors who deal with the subject. . . . The Spanish vigil (torture by prevention of sleep), which compels a man to keep himself suspended in the air for the space of seven hours, so that he may not lean upon a sharpened iron which would puncture him in the rear, causing intolerable pain; the Marsile or the Florence vigil, . . . our half red tripods on which are seated imbecile women accused of witchcraft, macerated in a horrible prison, loaded with chains and manacles, half rotting in the filth of a stinking and gloomy charnel-house, emaciated and half dead,—and a human body is required to endure tortures so diabolical!"[2]

The style, it is apparent, is touching and highly colored; but the language is usually moderate, the outcome of pity, not of anger; the insight of a wise man is perceptible.[3] Sometimes, irritated by the language of authors who speak of torture in the manner of past-masters of the art, he raises his tone to powerful irony. "Binsfeld eulogizes the invention of Marsile, who had found a gentle method of making all kinds of accused persons confess without breaking their arms or legs (by the prevention of sleep). . . . Is this not a pleasing method of finding out lies and killing innocent people? And must it not be a strange strength of prejudice which would describe this to us by the lips of a priest and a theologian as a small martyrdom or, as Marsile says, a ridiculous torment?[4] The deplorable thing about these people who bow unreservedly to authority without any regard to reason is that as learned a man as Jean Bodin allowed himself to become infatuated with the barbarous and inhuman severity of these martyrdoms, citing the torture of the Turks, which is to fix iron points like awls between the nails and flesh of all the sufferer's fingers and toes, and that method of torture of Italy which he calls the *Florentine vigil*, admirable kinds of torments to cause a sufferer to

[1] p. 29: "There are criminal judges so implacable in drawing the confession from every accused person, that they delight in inventing new torments, in which they add some atrocity to those existing in order to compel an accused to confess at all hazards."

[2] p. 36.

[3] Maxims scattered here and there bear witness to this breadth of mind. p. 134: "It is an invariable rule that the majority of controversies evince more passion than reason."—p. 70: "It is a common enough failing for men to measure God by their own standard."

[4] p. 30.

say whatever he is wished. . . . Does not Binsfeld know that the Italians are the promptest people in the world to make use of torments, because it is an invention of their country? He says that Marsile caused the hardiest to confess, but he does not say that we shall know a day too late for many judges how many martyrs he has made in the belief that he was dealing with criminals." [1]

What could be said in reply to all this? One objection was possible, and Nicolas foresaw it. It is, that, granted the system of legal proofs such as we have described, torture appeared to be its necessary complement, being the only means of avoiding scandalous impunities. This objection does not stop him; and, although he does not clearly formulate the theory of moral proofs, he allows it at least to be hinted, and in this way, returning to the truth, finds the true solution. "But, it may be said, if you discard the confession extorted by torture, you breed impunity for crime in a State, and as conviction is not always very easy, you will be compelled to let several presumed criminals go for lack of proofs and confessions. There are enough criminals to keep them (men of law) busy when justice limits them to lawful methods of conviction, without staking its success and the equity of its judgments upon confessions extorted by dint of intolerable torments, and God will be no less well served by sparing the blood of so many innocents as by spilling that of some culprits.[2] . . . It is said that it is enough for a judge to content himself with probable certainty, and rest his conscience upon what the laws and practice lay down for the regulation of his conduct. But if it is apparent to his conscience that the proof upon which he bases his judgment upon the life of a human being is uncertain, I do not see how, in such a serious matter, he can have enough assurance to be easy in his own mind in regard to the matter, nor how the public authority which he wields can afford enough justification before God or man." [3] He shows, above all, the inanity of these innumerable precautions by pointing out that, in secret crimes, even witnesses open to objection are, in time, admitted.[4]

Nicolas's book, be it understood, convinced no one. It must not be thought, however, that it went unnoticed. In the 1700s, we shall see Rousseau de La Combe quoting it with the highest eulogiums.

We may finally register, for the 1600s, two other less striking protests against the criminal procedure then followed. There is,

[1] p. 32. [2] p. 43. [3] p. 55. [4] p. 17.

first, a short note by the Abbé Fleury, tutor to the Duke of Burgundy. This is what he says in his "Avis à Louis, duc de Bourgogne, puis dauphin" (p. 146): "To reform our criminal procedure derived from the inquisition; it tends more to the discovery and punishment of the guilty than the vindication of the innocent."[1] The other criticism is directed against the use of torture. It is buried in the "Traité des crimes et de l'ordre judiciaire observé ès causes criminelles" by Despeisses.[2] "Credence must not always be given to what is said under torture . . . for an uncertain fact the accused is made to suffer a certain punishment. This invention of torture is rather a trial of patience than of truth; for he who is able to endure (the torments) conceals the truth, and likewise he who cannot endure them. Suffering will as readily force me to say what is not true as it will compel me to confess what is. If he who has not done that of which he is accused is patient enough to endure these torments, why will not he who has done it, when such a handsome reward as that of his life is held out to him? *Etiam innocentes coget mentiri dolor!* Whence it happens that he whom the judge has put to torture to prevent an innocent man dying, dies innocent and punished! for thousands have burdened their souls with false confessions. It is a terrible thing to destroy a human being for a misdeed as to which there remains a doubt. What power has he over the judges' ignorance of the fact? Does it not seem iniquitous that in order to avoid killing a man without cause, one should do worse than kill him, submit him to this inquiry, more painful than corporal punishment? There are those who are so hardened to the torments that they might never tell the truth under them; and there are others who would rather die confessing falsely what they had not done than suffer the torments."

But these reflections of some isolated minds were not addressed to the multitude. In 1750 the lawyer Barbier finds nothing more to say in regard to an innocent person put to the torture than this: "A poor publican of Charenton, after a long imprisonment, was condemned to the torture, ordinary and extraordinary, which he suffered for highway robbery, of which he was innocent, according to the confession of the real thief, who has been captured and broken on the wheel. This is evidence of the delicacy of the judge's function in criminal affairs!"[3]

[1] Quoted by *Poullain du Parc*, vol. XI, p. 5.
[2] Part I, Title X (Lyons edition, 1750, p. 1713).
[3] "Journal," IV, p. 446.

§ 2. **The Philosophic Movement of the 1700s.** — Gradually, however, the old ideas, the old conception of society, were destined to yield to the pressure of a new way of thinking. The philosophy of the 1700s made its appearance; and it admitted only two principles for the decision of all social problems, reason, and that sentiment of sympathy for the human race which they called *humanity* or *human nature*.[1] The battle-cry of the philosophers, according to one of their disciples, was reason, toleration, and humanity.[2]

What could be more unreasonable than a criminal procedure in which the prosecution counts for everything and the defense for nothing; where the judge, armed with a terrible power, at the same time feels himself chained down by a theory of proofs which dictates his decision to him and controls his personal conviction? What a strange idea of infallibility, contradictory in its terms! What could be more inhuman than those long imprisonments, those secret and ensnaring interrogations, and, finally, that torture crowning the work? "I hear Nature's voice crying out against me," says Montesquieu, proceeding to expound torture.[3]

"If these people are guilty," Servan says, "they are still deserving of pity; but if they are innocent, oh, the horror! oh, the pity of it! At that idea, humanity utters a terrible and sympathetic cry from the bottom of its heart!"[4] Beccaria declares that the fight must be carried on "with the weapons of reason"; he invokes the time "when gentleness and humanity achieve more than the power of princes."[5] Before these new authorities, the old criminal law could not long hold its ground.

That is not all. These active intellects, seeking universal reform, undertook a wide inquiry into the past and the present. They inquired into the former and the existing state of affairs abroad. And in these investigations the institutions of two nations especially attracted their attention: those of the Romans and those of the English. And they found that in Rome at the

[1] See *Taine*, "Les origines de la France contemporaine," vol. I, Book III, ch. III, pp. 266 *et seq.*; 276 *et seq.*; Book IV, p. 384 *et seq.*

[2] *Condorcet*, "Tableau historique des progrès de l'esprit humain, 9e époque." Condorcet defines the term humanity or human nature. "It is the feeling of a tender, active compassion for all the sufferings that afflict the human race, and of a horror of everything which, in our public institutions, acts of government, or private actions, adds new sufferings to those to which all flesh is heir."

[3] "Esprit des lois," Book XVI, ch. XVII.

[4] "Discours de Servan" (prefixed to *Serpillon's* "Code criminel," p.14). It concludes with these words: "He who does not love his fellow-men is a blind man who does not know nature. He who can hate them is a monster who outrages it."

[5] "Des délits et des peines," preface.

best period of its history and in England at that very moment, a criminal procedure totally different from that in France was to be seen, namely, publicity of trials, full liberty of defense, and judgment by jurors. No doubt, there was no lack of knowledge before that time as to what was the criminal procedure of the Romans. Old Ayrault had elucidated it in a scientific manner which makes his excellent book a classic, to which French and German criticism still go for information. It was, indeed, that example of the ancients which he incessantly invoked against the detestable methods of his age. But he had not been heeded. The historic idea of these facts none the less remained, as we find in Imbert.[1] Lamoignon said in the conferences upon the Ordinances: "If it is desired to compare our criminal procedure with that of the Romans and of other nations, it will be found that theirs is by no means so rigorous as that observed in France."[2] "At Rome," writes Muyart de Vouglans, "the prosecution was public, the accused had the opportunity of learning at the same time both who his accuser was, so that he could discredit him, and who the witnesses against him were, so that he was able to object to them, and, finally, of what crime he was accused, so that he could at once lodge his defenses, to which the accuser was obliged to reply immediately or within a brief delay granted to him; the accused could, moreover, have the aid of a lawyer."[3]

All this did not disturb our jurisconsults nor cause them to doubt the excellence of their practice. But the reformers eagerly picked up that weapon. Montesquieu constantly cites the Roman laws in criminal matters. Voltaire writes: "Among the Romans the witnesses were heard publicly, in the presence of the accused, who could reply to them, question them himself, or employ an advocate to do so. That procedure was noble and frank; it breathed Roman magnanimity."[4] In the Constituent Assembly the jury is spoken of "as among the Romans."[5] But it is especially towards England that they look, the country which had known how to maintain its political liberty and with that all the other liberties. Our philosophers often put their political theories in the mouth of an Englishman.[6] Their criminal procedure is among the most perfect of the institutions of the English people. Montesquieu

[1] "Pratique," Book III, chap. XIII, No. 3. [2] "Procès-verbal," p. 163.
[3] "Instit. crim." Part III, ch. II, p. 69.
[4] "Commentaire sur le Traité des délits et des peines," ch. XXII.
[5] *M. Mougin*, "The establishment of some jurors according to the method formerly in use among the Romans." Sitting of 27th October, 1790. Moniteur of the 29th.
[6] *Mably*, "Des droits et des devoirs du citoyen."

often cites it, even without naming it,[1] and Voltaire constantly refers to what passes on the other side of the Channel. "C. Which of all the nations appears to you to possess the best laws, and a system of justice most conducive to the general welfare and the happiness of the individual? — A. Our own country (England) unquestionably. That is proved by the fact that in all our arguments we always extol our own excellent Constitution, while in nearly all other countries they are sighing for a change. Our criminal laws are equitable and by no means harsh. We have abolished torture, against which nature cries out in vain in other countries. This shocking method of destroying a weak innocent person, and vindicating a robust criminal came to an end with our infamous Chancellor Jeffreys, who made use of the atrocious custom with a savage joy in James II's reign. We do not put a witness who has given his evidence too heedlessly to the necessity of lying by punishing him should he retract. We do not make the witnesses testify in secret; that would breed informers. The proceedings are public; secret trials are the invention of tyrants." [2] — "Fortunately, in England no trial is secret, because the chastisement of crimes is intended to be a public lesson to the people and not a private vengeance; the examinations are made with open doors and accounts of all the trials of interest are published in the newspapers." [3] — "In England, the slightest unjust imprisonment is indemnified by the official who ordered it." — "In England, that island famous for so many atrocious crimes, and so many good laws, the jury were themselves the advocates of the accused. Since the time of Edward VI they assisted their weakness, and suggested to them every way of defending themselves. But in the reign of Charles II, the assistance of two counsel was granted to every accused, because it was considered that the jury were only judges of the fact, and that the lawyers were better acquainted with the snares and evasions of the law. In France the Criminal Code seems framed purposely for the destruction of the people; in England it is their safeguard." [4]

Erelong de Lolme's imperfect but very lucid book was to draw attention to the procedure by jury as to all other English institutions; [5] the translation of Blackstone's Commentaries was to pass

[1] "Esprit des lois," Book VI, chs. II and III; Book XII, ch. II.
[2] "L'A. B. C., ou Dialogues entre A, B, et C" (fifteenth conversation).
[3] "Histoire d'Elisabeth Canning et de Calas," "Comment. des délits et des peines," ch. XXXII.
[4] "Prix de la justice et de l'humanité," Art. 23 (1777).
[5] "Constitution de l'Angleterre," by *M. de Lolme* (new edition, Geneva, vol. I, Book I, chs. XI and XII. On criminal justice.

from hand to hand;[1] and when the Revolution comes to give effect to the programme of the philosophers, it is England that is to furnish the Constituent Assembly with a model for criminal law.

These are the new principles and the new models which it is proposed to follow. The old criminal law and the old procedure are assailed from every side. In 1721, Montesquieu, in the "Lettres persanes," lays down his profound axioms on the nature and effectiveness of punishments.[2] Then, in Books VI and XII of the "Esprit des lois," he lays down the true principles of the criminal law and of criminal procedure. Afterwards comes Beccaria, Montesquieu's disciple (1766). Rousseau, preoccupied above all with moral and political problems, concerned himself little with the criminal law. He devotes a passing word to them in the "Contrat social." But upon the criminal law his principles are destined to have the greatest influence in the future. Voltaire was the greatest apostle and propagator of the wholesome and proper doctrine in these matters. He returns to it unceasingly in his numerous writings: "Mémoires pour les Calas;" "Histoire d'Elisabeth Canning;" "Relation de la mort du chevalier de La Barre;" "La méprise d'Arras;" "Procès criminel du sieur Montbailly et de sa femme;" "Commentaire sur le Traité des délits et des peines;" "Traité de la tolérance;" "Prix de la justice et de l'humanité." The list is a long one, and is still incomplete. These are but the loudest voices. Alongside of the masters speak their numerous disciples. We cannot mention their works in detail; but it appears to us to be useful to analyze the ideas of the three men who, among the philosophers, did the most for the reform of criminal law: Montesquieu, Beccaria, and Voltaire.

§ 3. **Montesquieu and Beccaria. The Criminal Law in Voltaire's Works.** — In regard to criminal procedure, as in regard to criminal law, Montesquieu keeps to general ideas: "Political liberty," he says, "consists in security, or, at least, in the idea that we enjoy security. This security is never more dangerously attacked than in public or private accusations. It is, therefore, on the good quality of criminal laws that the liberty of the subject chiefly depends. . . . The knowledge already acquired in some countries, or that may be hereafter acquired in others, concerning the safest rules to be observed in criminal judgments, is

[1] See also "Recherches sur les cours et les procédures criminelles d'Angleterre, extraites des Commentaires de Blakstone," 1790.
[2] "Lettres persanes," Letter 78.

more interesting to mankind than any other thing in the world. Liberty can be founded on the practice of this knowledge only; and supposing a State to have the best laws imaginable in this respect, a person tried under that government, and condemned to be hanged the next day, would have more liberty than a pasha in Turkey."[1] That is an excellent axiom. The criminal procedure does not only consider the evil-doers; it is the safeguard of the liberties of all; it is as Rossi said: "The English Jury and its Parliament are columns of the same edifice."

But under what conditions will the criminal laws be really protectors? Two things are necessary, certain forms and the possibility of liberty of defense. "In republics, it is plain that as many formalities at least are necessary as in monarchies. In both governments, they increase in proportion to the value which is set on the honor, future liberty, and life of the subject. In moderate governments, where the life of the meanest subject is deemed precious, no man is stripped of his honor or property until after a long inquiry; and no man is bereft of life till his very country has attacked him — an attack that is never made without leaving him all possible means of making his defense."[2] Add to this the necessity for fixed laws that leave nothing to the judge's discretion,[3] and we have Montesquieu's doctrine. As we have said, he has not dealt much with details; only two or three points have been selected by him. In regard to the prosecution, he admits the institution of the public prosecutor, a necessary survival of the ancient law, after a short disappearance: "We have at present an admirable law, namely, that by which the prince, who is established for the execution of the laws, appoints an officer in each court of judicature to prosecute all sorts of crimes in his name; hence the profession of informers is a thing unknown to us, for if this public avenger were suspected to abuse his office, he would soon be obliged to mention his author."[4] Montesquieu stigmatized torture;[5] but, strange to say, he gives his approbation, if not to the entire system of legal proofs, at least to the rule providing that two witnesses shall be necessary to justify a condemnation;[6] upon this point Voltaire was more far-seeing.

The "Treatise on Crimes and Penalties" of the Marquis of Beccaria was published at Milan in the Italian language,[7] but a trans-

[1] "Esprit des lois," Book XII, ch. II.
[2] *Ibid.*, Book VI, ch. II.
[3] *Ibid.*, Book VI, ch. III.
[4] *Ibid.*, Book VI, ch. VIII.
[5] *Ibid.*, Book VI, ch. XVII.
[6] *Ibid.*, Book XII, ch. III.
[7] As to the influence of the French philosophers on Beccaria, see *M. Paul Janet*, "Histoire de la philosophie morale et politique," vol. II, p. 412 *et seq.*

lation into French by Morellet appeared in February, 1766.[1] Its influence, which was immense, was even much greater in France than in Italy.

With Beccaria we enter into details. After several chapters devoted to the necessity for fixed punishments, he attacks the abuse of detention pending trial (ch. VI), secret accusations (ch. IX), the oath imposed on the accused (ch. XI), ensnaring questions (ch. X), and lastly, torture. He demands publicity of judgments and proceedings. "Let the judgments be public; let the proofs of the crime be public, and public opinion, which can be the only social restraint, will keep violence and passion in check" (ch. VII).

As to the system of proofs, he evidently has a leaning toward moral proofs. He prefers "the ignorance which judges by sentiment" — "all that is necessary to judge is mere good sense, and this guide is less misleading than the learning of a judge." He also says, however, "It is important, in a good system of laws, to determine in a precise manner the degree of confidence which should be placed in the witnesses and the nature of the proofs necessary to establish the offense" (ch. VII).

It is apparent that the reforms Beccaria demands are, in reality, not particularly daring. They do not go very far beyond those already demanded by President Lamoignon. But the fact that this was all claimed by right of reason makes the great commotion which the book caused comprehensible. Besides, the principles of criminal law, properly so called, held an important place in the book. "Beccaria," says Condorcet, "refuted in Italy the barbarous maxims of French jurisprudence." Morellet, the translator of the work, sent Beccaria the congratulations of all French philosophers. "I am especially enjoined to send you the thanks and compliments of M. Diderot, M. Helvetius, M. de Buffon. . . . I have submitted your book to M. Rousseau. . . . M. Hume, who has been staying with me for some time, commands me to tell you a thousand things on his part. . . . M. d'Alembert is going to write to you."[2]

Voltaire annotated the "Treatise on Crimes and Penalties"; but his works devoted to criminal law possess for us a much more living interest than Beccaria's book. In Voltaire, in fact, instead of elevated generalities and magnificent tirades, we shall find accu-

[1] Letter from *Morellet* to *Beccaria*, 1766: "It was M. Malesherbes, with whom I have the honor to be connected, who suggested to me the translation of your work into our language. My translation appeared eight days ago."

[2] Letter of *Morellet* to *Beccaria*, February, 1766.

rate, almost technical, criticism of the Ordinance of 1670. He brings to it the insight of his admirable good sense, in addition to his gift of accurate information, a very necessary quality.

"The Criminal Ordinance," he says, "seems on several points to have been directed only towards the destruction of those accused. It is the only uniform law in the whole kingdom. Should it not be as favorable to the innocent as it is terrible to the guilty? [1] This procedure is much more rigorous since 1670; it would have been much milder if the majority of the commissioners had been of the same mind as M. de Lamoignon." [2] We can follow all the phases of the procedure in Voltaire's criticism of it. He says nothing about the complaints and denunciations by which the proceedings begin; and, in fact, there was nothing in regard to them but wise provisions, which have survived.[3] Arrived at the information, he finds himself face to face with two abuses; secrecy and the monitories: "Although there are some cases in which a monitory is necessary, there are many others where it is very dangerous; it invites men from the dregs of the people to bring accusations against their superiors in rank of whom they are always jealous. . . . There is probably nothing more illegal in the tribunals of the Inquisition; and a great proof of the illegality of these monitories is that they do not proceed directly from the magistrates; it is the ecclesiastical power which issues them." [4]

He has much to say about the secrecy of the procedure: "All these secret procedures may, perhaps, be compared to a match, which burns imperceptibly, but sets fire to a bomb." — "Is it for justice to be secret? Secrecy belongs to crimes alone. It is the procedure of the Inquisition." [5] — "With us, all is conducted in secret. A single judge, only attended by his clerk, hears each witness separately. This custom, established by Francis I, was confirmed by the commissioners who were employed to digest the Ordinance of Louis XIV in 1670; which confirmation was entirely due to a mistake. They imagined, in reading the code

[1] "Commentaire du Traité des délits et des peines," ch. XXIII.

[2] *Ibid.*

[3] By a strange idea, he regrets the disappearance of the old accusation by *formal party:* "Happy are those nations that have been wise enough to ordain that all accusers should be confined in prison as well as the accused! Of all laws that is the most just." "Prix de la justice et de l'humanité," Art. XXII, § 3.

[4] "Relation de la mort du chevalier de La Barre." "There was no proof against my relatives," says Donat Calas in his "Mémoire," "and there could be none, so they had recourse to a monitory. . . . The crime was suspected, so they demanded the disclosure of proofs."

[5] "Prix de la justice," Art. XXII, § 5.

'de Testibus,' that the words, 'testes intrare judicis secretum' signified that the witnesses were examined in private; but 'secretum' means here the chambers of the judge. 'Intrare secretum,' if intended to signify private interrogation, would be false Latin. This part of our law, therefore, is founded on a solecism."[1] Here Voltaire yields to that propensity to anecdote that often leads him to seek in insignificant facts for the cause of great events; we no doubt find in Bornier, whom he quotes, that misunderstanding cited as the cause of "that custom, or rather that abuse of hearing the witnesses secretly,"[2] but we know how the secret procedure was introduced and kept up. However, everything was fish that came into the publicist's net. The confirmation did not appear less defective to Voltaire than the first deposition: "The deponents are usually from the dregs of the people, whom the judge, when he is shut up with them, can make say anything he likes. These witnesses are heard a second time, still in secret; this is what is called the confirmation."[3]

How is the accused to be able to confute these witnesses? By means of the confrontation; but "it would seem as if the law compelled the magistrate to conduct himself towards the accused rather as an enemy than as a judge. It is in the judge's option to order the confrontation or omit it ('if need be, confront,' the Ordinance says). Custom in this respect seems to be contrary to the law, which is ambiguous. There is always confrontation; but the judge does not always confront all the witnesses; he omits those who do not seem to him to be favorable enough for the prosecution. However, any such witness who has not testified against the accused in the information can testify in his favor at the confrontation; the witness may have forgotten certain circumstances favorable to the accused. The judge himself may not have at first recognized the importance of these circumstances and may not have recorded them."[4]

The confrontation, moreover, is illusory: "If, after the confirmation, they retract from their deposition, or vary in any material circumstance, they are punished as false witnesses. So that if a simple, honest fellow, recollecting that he has said too much, that he misunderstood the judge or the judge him, revoke his deposition from a principle of justice, he is punished as a reprobate. The natural consequence of this is, that men will confirm a false

[1] "Comment. sur le Traité des délits et des peines," ch. XXIII.
[2] *Bornier*, upon article 11, title VI of the Ordinance of 1670 (vol. II, p. 82).
[3] "Commentaire sur le Traité des délits et des peines," ch. XXIII.
[4] "Commentaire des délits et des peines," Art. XXIV.

testimony rather than expose themselves, for their honesty, to certain punishment." [1]

Furthermore, the accused is cut off from everybody, and without counsel: "To cast a man into a dungeon; to leave him there a prey to the horrors of imagination and despair; to examine him only when he is bereft of his memory by the anguish of pain, and his whole frame is disordered; is it not like enticing a traveller into a den of thieves to assassinate him? Nevertheless that is the custom of the Inquisition. That single word impresses the imagination with horror." [2] — "A man, being suspected of a crime, knowing that he is denied the benefit of counsel, flees the country; a step to which he is encouraged by every maxim of the law. . . . Do your laws, then, allow the privilege of counsel to an extortioner, or a fraudulent bankrupt, and refuse it to one who may possibly be a very honest and honorable man?" [3]

Finally comes the crowning cruelty, the crowning absurdity, torture: "Since there are yet Christian people — What do I say? Christian priests and Christian monks, who make use of tortures for their principal argument, we must begin by telling them that a Caligula, or a Nero, never dared to inflict such cruelties on a single Roman citizen. . . . We meet with nothing in the books which take the place of a code in France but these horrible words: preparatory torture; ordinary torture; extraordinary torture; torture under reservation of proofs; torture without reservation of proofs; torture in presence of two counsellors, torture in presence of a doctor, of a surgeon, torture to be administered to women and girls, if not with child. One would think that all the books had been written by the executioner." [4]

Later, quoting a passage from d'Aguesseau, in which the latter states that if the proof is not complete, torture or a further inquiry cannot be ordered, he cries: "What then is the power of precedent, illustrious chief of the magistracy? What! you have no evidence, and for two hours you punish an unfortunate man with a thousand deaths, in order to deal out to him a single one which will only last a moment. . . . Can it be possible that you are capable of ordering torture or a further inquiry! What a frightful and ridiculous alternative!" He was well acquainted with the judicial practice on this point: "Unfortunately we are not too well agreed as to what presumptions are strong

[1] "Comment. des délits et des peines," Art. XXIV.
[2] "Prix de la justice," Art. XXXIII.
[3] "Comment. des délits et des peines," ch. XXIII.
[4] "Prix de la justice," Art. XXIV.

enough to induce a judge to begin to dislocate the limbs of his fellow-man by torture. The Ordinance of 1670 has decided nothing regarding that shocking preliminary operation. A presumption is nothing more nor less than a conjecture. Torture should not be ordered in France until a 'corpus delicti' is established, at all events."[1]

Voltaire has attacked legal proofs more savagely than any one else, without, perhaps, taking into consideration, too carefully, their importance in the system as a whole: "God of justice! what examples of these mistaken murders appear every year in Europe, in almost all the courts that are governed by the Tribonian compilation, or by the ancient feudal custom! . . . The heart shudders, and the hand trembles, when we reflect how many horrors have issued from the bosom of the laws themselves. Then ought we to be contented to wish that all laws were abolished, and that there were no others but that of the conscience and the good sense of magistrates? — who would answer that this conscience and this good sense would not go astray?"[2] And elsewhere: "The Parlement of Toulouse has a very curious custom in its proofs by witnesses. Elsewhere half-proofs are admitted, which is a palpable absurdity, for we know that there are no half-truths. But at Toulouse they allow quarters and eighths of a proof. For instance, a hearsay may be considered as a quarter, and another hearsay, more vague than the former, as an eighth; so that eight hearsays, which, in fact, are no other than the echo of a groundless report, constitute a full proof. It was upon this principle that Calas was condemned to the wheel. The Roman laws required proofs 'luce meridiana clariores.'[3] . . . Who would not be terrified at such a procedure? Who could be sure of not falling a victim to it? Oh, judges, if you would not have the innocent accused take flight, facilitate the means of his defense!"

The rights of the defense — these words are in all mouths. What is necessary to insure the payment of proper respect to these sacred rights? Publicity, the assistance of an advocate, the abolition of torture, the doctrine of legal proofs; for the time being the claims of the publicists are limited to these points; on these they demand legislative reform. "If it should ever happen in France," says Voltaire, "that the laws of humanity soften some of our rigorous customs, without facilitating the commission of

[1] "La méprise d'Arras." [2] "Prix de la justice," Art. XXII, § 2.
[3] "Commentaire du Traité des délits et des peines," ch. XXII. In addition to the passages quoted, see another in which Voltaire summarizes his whole argument ("Comment." ch. XXIII).

crime, we may hope for reformation in these legal proceedings wherein our legislators seem to have been influenced by too much severity." [1]

But, beyond all that, the philosophers looked forward to something higher and more just, the trial by jury: "In England," says Montesquieu, "the jury give their verdict whether the fact brought under their cognizance be proved or not; if it be proved, the judge pronounces the punishment inflicted by the law, and for this he needs only to open his eyes." [2] Montesquieu does not merely praise the jury; he lays down the rule which should govern their action: "The people are not jurists; all these restrictions and methods of arbitration are above their reach; they must have only one object and one single fact set before them; and then they have only to see whether they ought to condemn, to acquit, or to suspend their judgment." [3] "That is a very wise law," says Beccaria, "and one invariably leading to satisfactory results, which provides for the trial of every one by his peers; for, when the fortune and the freedom of the subject are at stake, all sentiments conducive to inequality ought to be suppressed." [4] In Voltaire's "A. B. C.," one of the speakers, as we have seen, mentions England as the country possessing the best laws: "Every person accused," he says, "is tried by his peers; he is not accounted guilty unless they are agreed upon the fact. The law condemns him, not upon the arbitrary sentence of the judges, but for the crime as proved by the evidence." [5] — "Not only the freeman," Voltaire writes elsewhere, "but the stranger, finds equal security in their laws, since he is at liberty to choose six out of the twelve who are to judge him. The privilege is available to the whole universe." [6] Rousseau also extols the jury: "In England, when a man is accused of a crime, twelve jurors are shut up in a room to give their opinion, based upon the examination of the proceedings, as to whether such accused is guilty or not; and they are not allowed to leave that room, and get nothing to eat until they come to an agreement, so that their verdict is always unanimous, and decisive of the fate of the accused." [7]

§ 4. **Opinions of the Jurists of the 1700s.** — We have seen how the philosophers, in the name of reason and humanity, passed

[1] "Commentaire du livre des délits et des peines," ch. XXII.
[2] "Esprit des lois," Book VI, ch. III. [3] *Ibid.*, Book VI, ch. IV.
[4] "Des délits et des peines," ch. VII.
[5] "L'A. B. C." (fifteenth conversation).
[6] "Prix de la justice," Art. XXIII.
[7] "Correspondance," year 1761. Letter to M. d'Offreville, at Douai. — *Cf.* "Rousseau juge de Jean-Jacques," Dialogue I.

sentence upon the criminal procedure. What estimate did the jurisconsults, who commented upon it in their books and applied it in their courts, put upon it? Here the scene is changed and the spectacle is sometimes saddening. The governing principle of the jurists, so different from that we have been studying, consists of two things excellent in themselves, but apt to be fatal when carried to an extreme: the spirit of conservatism and respect for the law. It is not that they are, to all appearance, opposed to the prevailing spirit of the age. All of them, even the most inflexible, bow to the contemporary divinities, reason and humanity. "I pride myself on sensibility as much as any other," says Muyart de Vouglans in a curious tract in which he sets out to refute Beccaria's book.[1] "This solemn decree left the law to stand as it was in all its authority, and reason loses none of its rights," says Louis Séguier.[2] But this compliance comes to nothing. Some tax their ingenuity to prove that the criminal procedure is not opposed to the principles of philosophy;[3] others, and these are the most numerous, acknowledge the chief defects of the Ordinance, but they nevertheless bow before the law. This Ordinance of 1670, so solemnly discussed, already in force for a century, and whose rules go still farther back into the past, appears to them to be inviolable. Even the faultfinders do not dream of disobeying it. The spirit of authority stifles the spirit of reform within them. The Ordinance has spoken, they say, and they bow down. The remark has been made that "the jurisconsults are accustomed to live with the existing law; they contract a respect for it; and, not being excessively cultured, they delude themselves; they imagine that the alteration of existing things will involve a revolution. . . . The jurisconsults are useful, they are a conservative element; they cling to the laws of the past, but as to the future, it is never they who demand change, but people outside of the profession."[4]

Among the most ardent apologists for the Ordinance of 1670, Muyart de Vouglans figures in the first rank. His is probably the clearest intellect among the criminal law writers of the 1700s. He has expounded his opinion on the subject "ex professo" in his "Institutes au droit criminel;"[5] but it is especially in his polemic against Beccaria that he must be studied. Here we feel that he

[1] p. 4.

[2] Decree of the Parlement of Paris of 11th August, 1786, condemning Dupaty's Memorial to be suppressed and burned. "Réquisitoire," 1786, p. 175.

[3] "To do otherwise than assert that they could never be really inharmonious is to wrong reason and law." *Séguier*, p. 175.

[4] *M. Laboulaye*, Revue des Cours littéraires, 1865, p. 745.

[5] p. 69.

does not understand the situation; he thinks he has to deal with a madman,[1] or a criminal, with whom he takes very high ground,[2] and whom he picks out for castigation. "I leave," he says, "to those who are specially concerned with this branch of our public law, the task of using their censure and employing all their authority to arrest the contagion."[3] It is not the author's revolutionary spirit which surprises him most, nor his "disrespect even for the sacred maxims of government, morals, or religion."[4] It is to find a book on criminal law which is not, above all things, technical and devoted to positive law. "You, sir, no doubt expect, like myself, to find under the title of a 'Traité des délits et des peines,' an accurate and methodical study of the laws and principles relating to the subject, citations of authorities on the questions which may arise thereupon, and especially a precise enumeration of the different kinds of crimes and their punishments, as well as the proceedings necessary to arrive at their establishment and proof. You will, however, be astonished to see that nothing of the kind is to be found in this book."[5]

He has the most perfect faith in the law as it exists; a belief in it without the shadow of a doubt.[6] And he contrives to extract from Beccaria's book and hold up to public indignation[7] a list of propositions now regarded, for the most part, as truths of good sense and axioms of criminal law. His amazement at the principle of equality of punishments and the exclusion of the idea of divine vengeance in criminal prosecution is unbounded. "The author claims," he says, "that the status of the victim of the crime should no longer influence the infliction of the punishment, and the only reason he gives for this is that everybody is dependent chiefly on the social body to which he belongs. For the same reason he wishes that those of the highest rank be punished

[1] "This sham illuminee in whose eyes the Solons, the Lycurguses, the Papinians, the Cujas, in a word, the wisest philosophers of Greece, Italy, and France are but pure sophists, and the ages of Augustus and Louis XIV but ages of errors and darkness" ("Lettre contenant la réfutation de quelques principes hasardés dans le Traité des délits et des peines," Geneva 1767, p. 22).

[2] "Undoubtedly I do not have the highly strung organization of our modern criminalists; for I have not experienced the pleasing shudders they speak about. The feeling which has affected me most, after reading several pages of this book, has been that of surprise, to say the least of it." p. 4.

[3] p. 17. [4] p. 5. [5] p. 25.

[6] "It may be said for the honor of France that its jurisprudence has reached a stage of perfection which gives it a distinguished place among civilized nations; so much so that some of them have even taken it as a model for the reform of their criminal codes," p. 20. *Cf.* p. 50.

[7] pp. 6–17.

like the lowest of the people. The danger and absurdity of such a principle is self-evident. . . . Following out this system, the author goes so far as to claim that the seriousness of the crime in relation to its offense against God should not be taken into consideration."[1] Finally, without the slightest hesitation, he defends all the atrocities of the old system, and especially the oath of accused persons and torture. The fragment deserves to be quoted almost in its entirety. "The author cries out against the compulsory administration of the oath to the accused, and with so little reflection that he does not even cite the most specious reason which could be given against it, one which has led certain nations, Germany among others, to relinquish this practice; namely, that it is presumable that a person who has been capable of committing the crime is capable of committing perjury to conceal it. The reasons adduced by our author are, on the one hand, that it is unnatural for the culprit to accuse himself; and on the other, that experience proves that the oath has never made a guilty person tell the truth. But if it is necessary to abolish the oath because it is not natural for the culprit to accuse himself, the interrogation must be abolished for the same reason, notwithstanding that the author acknowledges that to be an essential step of the procedure. As to experience, it is indeed necessary that it should be as well established as the author claims, for this practice has been preserved with us and almost all other civilized nations, despite the reiterated efforts which have been made for its abolition.[2] If the author is to be believed, the abolition of torture is also necessary, as a proceeding at once cruel, unjust, useless, and dangerous. We may, at the outset, refute in a single word everything the author says on this subject by observing that he merely repeats what has been said by other authors, who have, like him, inveighed against this practice without having been able to prevent its perpetuation down to the present time. The non-success of these early attacks may even be the more plausibly opposed to him seeing that these authors all wrote before the Ordinance of 1670. That Ordinance, by the rigorous precautions it established, has, for the most part, remedied the disadvantages which aroused the zeal of these authors. We have, while treating of the procedure, indicated the nature of these precautions, and demonstrated that they are such that the person likely to experience this torture must be regarded as more than half convicted of the crime, so that the danger of confusing the innocent with the

[1] pp. 102–104, 106. [2] pp. 70–72; *cf.* "Institutes du droit criminel," p. 358.

guilty is not nearly so much to be feared as before the law was passed. It may also be confidently asserted that for a single example of an innocent person who has yielded to the violence of the torture for a century, a thousand others can be cited to prove that, without the aid of this proceeding, the majority of atrocious crimes, such as murder, fire-raising, and highway robbery, would have remained unpunished, and this impunity would have engendered disadvantages much more dangerous than those of torture, by making a multitude of people the innocent victims of these wily rascals. . . . Several other instances might be adduced where experience has equally proved the utility of torture, if that utility were not found to be otherwise sufficiently proved, both by the peculiar advantage the accused himself finds in its rendering him the judge of his own cause and putting it in his power to evade the capital punishment entailed by the crime of which he is accused, and by the impossibility hitherto experienced of substituting for this proceeding another means as effectual and subject to fewer disadvantages. A final argument in its favor is the antiquity and universality of the custom, which dates back to the early ages of the world, and has been adopted, as we know, by every nation, including the Romans themselves. Although the latter, in early times, usually employed it only against slaves, they did not fail to extend it afterwards to freemen. . . . Besides, the examples of one or two nations claimed to have discarded the custom form but exceptions the better to confirm the general rule. But finally, were it a question of deciding by precedent, such might be cited which would appear less suspicious and, at the same time, more to be respected in the author's eyes than those furnished him by his own country or generally by any of the States descending from the Empire. It is sufficient, to leave no ground for his objections upon this point, to meet them with the provisions of Articles 54 and 61 of the Ordinance of Charles V, commonly called the Carolina." [1]

After this astonishing outburst, Muyart de Vouglans calms down and bequeaths his ideas to posterity. "We cannot do better than conclude this analysis with those general reflections based upon unalterable principles, tried by constant experience, and against which any systems born of a spirit of contradiction and innovation are bound to fail." [2] It is almost incredible that this should have been written and published in 1767.

On the very eve of the Revolution, we find another apologist

[1] pp. 73–81. [2] p. 118.

for the Ordinance, less hysterical, but no less resolute. This is Attorney-General Louis Séguier, who, on 7, 8, and 10 August, 1786, delivered a long address before the Parlement of Paris, demanding the suppression of a memorial become famous under the name of the "Mémoire pour trois hommes condamnés à la roue." Dupaty was the author of this memorial, and it made criminal procedure the subject of a vigorous onslaught. Séguier's address was like the swan song of the old legislation. Séguier did not have to justify torture. At that period, as we shall state immediately, the most reprehensible torture, namely, the preliminary torture, had been suppressed, and the attorney-general was able to congratulate himself on that.[1] But in his opinion, "during successive generations our laws have attained that stage of perfection of which human legislation is susceptible."[2] He is indignant at the attack on the Ordinance. "This law, framed by the coöperation of the most profound, experienced, and cautious intellects, this law, based on such judicious reasoning and of such venerable authority, so inviolable in its execution, is unblushingly held out to a gracious monarch as an attempt to subvert natural law, as emanating from the courts of justice of Tiberius and the prisons of the Inquisition, as worthy of the heart of Claudius or Caligula. How astonished would be the illustrious shades of Lamoignon and d'Aguesseau, of Molé and Talon to hear it contended that this law is based upon a maxim invented in one of the dark ages of the human intellect! The age of Louis XIV, the rival of the age of Augustus, an age of darkness and barbarity! Has it been reserved for our administration to reply to such indecent charges?"[3] Séguier also does not hesitate to justify all the severities of the Ordinance, against which the public temper of the time protested. In his eyes "the jurisdiction of the provosts is of evident utility;"[4] the oath required of the accused is perfectly lawful.[5] He approves of the accused not being allowed to present his justificative facts until after the inspection ("visite") of the process or to prove them except by the judge's consent.[6] For him "secrecy is the immovable foundation of the law. It is enjoined in order to avoid the snares of bad faith, and to prevent conspiracies leading to subornation. It is enjoined because the attorney-general is the sole prosecutor, and in no case can he be suspected of prosecuting an accused from animosity or a desire for vengeance."[7] Lastly, he glories in the absence of counsel for the

[1] "Réquisitoire," p. 48. [2] *Ibid.*, p. 221. [3] pp. 245, 246.
[4] p. 26. [5] p. 162. [6] p. 171 *et seq.* [7] p. 246.

defense. "What would be the use of an advocate in important criminal proceedings? Experience teaches us that if a counsel is allowed, the proof of the crime is lost in the midst of the formalities prescribed for arriving at the judgment. Does not the accused know what he has done as certainly as the witness knows what he has seen or heard? In a criminal action there is most frequently only one principal fact, and to answer to such a simple fact a counsel is useless. Preparation shows more plainly the desire to distort the truth than the wish to do it homage."[1] This plausible ingenuity confuses the mind.

Séguier was, however, well aware that those laws which discarded counsel and ordered secrecy in the proceedings did not always rule in France.[2] But in his opinion the severities introduced are so many improvements realized. He knew that at Rome the procedure was formerly accusatory, public, and fully confrontative.[3] But he had little respect for the customs of "popular or semi-popular States."[4] This man, speaking on the eve of the Revolution, knew of Ayrault, one of whose opinions he reproduces verbatim without acknowledging its source;[5] yet he is insensible to the sentiments which stirred the heart of the old jurist. He was also acquainted with the English procedure, for which he has nothing but distrust. "The use of the double examination was not buried under the débris of the Roman Republic. It still exists to-day in the English courts of judicature. One of the laws of their national constitution is that all accused persons must be tried publicly and by their peers. This form is maintained there because of its analogy to the constitution of a state where the nation enjoys legislative power and controls the ministry by its representatives . . . in a word, shares the public authority. In ordinary crimes the judges hear the accuser; the accused presents his pleas in defense, the witnesses are heard, objected to, publicly confronted, and the accused is free, if he gives bail, throughout the whole examination. The jurors decide, but they decide only the question of fact; the law alone inflicts the punishment. . . . The British laws bear the impress of the genius and customs of the people who established them. The thoughtlessness and restlessness of some minds would like to see this form of procedure naturalized with us. Do the French Anglomaniacs fully understand this system of laws of which they declare themselves the admirers? Who among them would not be afraid to be left to the discretion of twelve judges known as jurors, who have no other

[1] p. 247. [2] p. 230 *et seq.* [3] pp. 217, 218. [4] p. 220. [5] p. 229.

way of giving their opinion than by the words, 'Guilty' or 'Not Guilty'? And these judges, chosen from each class of the people relatively to the accused's station or calling, remain shut up, unable to leave until they are of an unanimous opinion, — a kind of conclave in which he whom nature has endowed with the most robust constitution can compel his associates, by dire necessity, to come to his opinion upon innocence or guilt; with the result that a single juror can decide the fate of the guilty or of the innocent. Strange laws!"[1]

Séguier detests "those citizens, foreigners in their fatherland, who reserve their admiration for the States adjacent to France, or those reformers occupied solely in overturning our laws under the pretext of assimilating them to the Code of Nature."[2] He is sparing neither of exhortations nor ominous prophecies. "Such are the principles transmitted to us by our wise predecessors, and a virtuous indignation fills us at the sight of the contrary principles which to-day find supporters. It is the opinion of some enthusiasts that some people would substitute for public opinion.[3] Who will dare to deny the prudence of maintaining a Code of laws which has been in existence for several centuries, precisely because it does exist? The disadvantages of the laws in force we know; we can only learn by experience the disadvantages of the laws proposed to be substituted for them, especially when it is desired to proceed on a principle absolutely opposed to that of the old laws. An abrupt and unexpected change might shake the political constitution, and a new law has sometimes been the origin of a revolution."[4] The Revolution was, in fact, about to break out; but it was certainly not precipitated by the putting in operation of reforms.

Séguier's strange speech has taken us a little ahead in point of time. Let us return to the jurisconsults of somewhat earlier date. Poullain du Parc, in the beginning of the first of the two volumes which he devotes to criminal procedure, examines the question as a whole. "The forms of criminal procedure," he says, "are entirely different from those prescribed for civil procedure. Those who do not thoroughly examine the reasons for these forms cry out against the rigor of the law, which, in a matter touching the honor and the life of an accused, presumed innocent until he is convicted, holds out a constant snare to him and does not permit him to prove his innocence until after the examination ('instruction') has been completed. It is sufficient, to justify

[1] p. 218, 219. [2] p. 13. [3] p. 255. [1] p. 224.

the law against this reproach, to say that since the establishment of these forms it is exceedingly seldom that the innocent have suffered the punishment of the guilty, and that, in spite of the rigor of the law, several culprits prosecuted have escaped punishment for lack of sufficient proof. But further reflection, leading to a recognition of the spirit of the different provisions of the Ordinance of 1670, proves the excellence of the law. From the time the prosecution is instituted, the sole aim which should be adhered to is the discovery of the crime, of the perpetrator, and of his accomplices. The public safety requires that to be done promptly, and that would be impossible if a procedure, confrontative between accuser and accused, was admitted from the commencement, like that established in civil matters between plaintiff and defendant. But in ordaining that this examination be rigorous and prompt, the law has taken every precaution that the accused be kept secure from calumny." [1]

Our author then briefly describes the various documents of the procedure, and continues: "Such is the general spirit of the law. . . . I am also surprised to find the judicious Abbé Fleury make, in a few words, the most extravagant criticism of our criminal procedure. He expresses himself thus: 'To reform our criminal procedure derived from that of the Inquisition. It tends more to the discovery and punishment of the guilty than to the vindication of the innocent.' This is to attribute to the procedure an origin as false as it is odious. The Inquisition admits, as witnesses, all kinds of informers, whom it does not confront with the accused, — convicts, prostitutes, the nearest relatives, son against father, brother against brother, spouses against each other, are considered unimpeachable witnesses. The accused is compelled to guess at and confess his crime, real or suspected. The most secret thoughts are judged, and they do not stop at holding out continual snares to the accused in order to find him guilty; it would seem as if they avoided and endeavored to destroy every means of finding him innocent. These are the principal defects of that tribunal, erected at once in the face of the liberty of the people and the power of their rulers. It is surprising that any one should have thought of comparing this detestable procedure with that of France, where the tribunal of the Inquisition, after having made its early ravages, came to nothing of its own accord, as it were, by reason solely of its defective constitution and procedure." [2]

[1] "Principes de droit français suivant les maximes du Parlement de Bretagne," Rennes 1771, vol. XI, pp. 2, 3.

[2] Vol. XI, pp. 5, 6.

Poullain du Parc, like Séguier, resents the idea of the introduction of the English procedure into France. "Some authors, in their condemnation of our criminal procedure, laud that of England, where the whole of the examination, including the depositions of the witnesses, takes place in presence of the accused. I do not know whether that form has any disadvantages in a nation whose lowest subject considers himself independent of those of the highest rank; but in France, the subordination existing in the various stations of life would be sufficient to intimidate those witnesses who would have to testify in presence of an accused of superior rank. The genius and temper of the two nations are so dissimilar that it is impossible to draw just conclusions from a comparison of their respective procedures." [1]

He is not inimical to all reform, however, and he makes this suggestion. "The only excessive severity to be found in our criminal procedure is from the time of the confrontation. When that has revealed to the accused all the details of the charges, why should he not be entitled to claim the full communication of the criminal process, so that he may be put in a position to bring together everything that can help in his vindication and to prove the contradictions or the falseness of the depositions, the nullities in matters of form, the inadequacy of the examination, and the means neglected to be employed by the judges in thoroughly investigating the truth? However little of complexity there may be in the examination, it is impossible for the most observant accused to remember all the important points brought to his notice in the confrontation. So it may be said that the intention of the law is to devolve the defense of the accused upon the judges, since it puts the employment of all lawful pleas out of his power and permits counsel to be granted to him in a few matters only. Is this severity in accordance with the aim of all the laws, which is to use every possible means for the preservation of the honor and the lives of innocent people?" [2]

The other criminalists do not examine the question of legislation directly and as a whole. But, it must be admitted, they often point out the severity of the Ordinance, without, however, demanding any reforms. The following are some opinions on the principle points. First of all, Serpillon gives an account of the debate which took place in the conferences as to the oath imposed on the accused, and adds: "These observations . . . resulted for the first time in a precise law prescribing the necessity for the

[1] Vol. XI, p. 7. [2] Vol. XI, pp. 6, 7.

oath. . . . It is, however, notorious that there is actually almost as much perjury as there is oath on this occasion; but the accused cannot be punished for such false swearing." [1] Pothier remarks "that there is in the official report of the Ordinance an admirable speech against the use of the oath." [2] "Among the Romans," says Serpillon, "and even in France, an accused might be defended by an advocate even for the most serious crimes; but it was found to be more fitting to compel accused persons to defend themselves without the aid of any brief or prompting at hand." [3] Rousseau de La Combe recalls "that formerly the accused might plead through the agency of advocates and not by their own word of mouth, or interrogation; the charge might often be decided upon a pleading." [4] And Pothier: "In regard to capital crimes, the Ordinance forbids counsel to the accused, even after the confrontation. In this respect our system of practice is more severe than that of any other European country." [5]

The dominant note in these remarks is usually nothing more than a feeling of regret. Serpillon criticises the provision compelling the accused to lodge his objections to the witnesses before the reading of the deposition. "The Ordinance," he says, "is certainly strict as to the examination. . . . Ayrault, in his 'Pratique judiciaire,' also inveighs against the provision of the Ordinances in this respect, and in reality, even to-day, if an accused alleges strong objections to a witness and sets forth notorious facts, there are few judges who would not be influenced thereby, although the facts might not be proved in writing." [6] He speaks in similar terms about the article regulating the proof of justificative facts. "It may be said that this provision of the Ordinance is severe, since it requires an accused, often illiterate and imprisoned in the dungeons, sometimes for a year, to nominate his witnesses immediately. . . . The Ordinance does not even allow the judge to grant him a delay." [7]

The critics are somewhat more severe on the subject of torture. Pothier, as we know, protested in quite a personal way: "They avoided assigning to him criminal actions wherein it was foreseen that torture might be ordered, because he could not endure the sight of the sufferings; an inability which was occasioned a great deal more by the sensitiveness of his physical organization than by

[1] "Code criminel," p. 659.
[2] "Procédure criminelle" (Bugnet edition).
[3] "Code criminel," p. 662.
[4] *Ibid.*, p. 341.
[5] "Procédure criminelle" (Bugnet edition), p. 341.
[6] "Code criminel," p. 730.
[7] *Ibid.*, p. 1212.

moral sentiment."[1] Despite the explanation of his panegyrist, we ought to note with pious care this mark of feeling in the great jurisconsult. "The public," Serpillon writes, "has complained of torture for a long time. Protests were even made about it at the time of the conferences on this title. . . . Nothing more cruel or unjust than the preparatory torture can be found. The Romans administered it to their slaves, but that was because they looked upon them as domestic animals. They never condemned a citizen to it, and there is much stronger reason why Christians and Christian races ought to abstain from it. . . . These disadvantages have decided several sovereigns to abolish this torment. This was done about fifteen years ago in Prussia; the prince did not wish the innocent to suffer with the guilty. Torture is no longer in use in England, according to Despeisses, who has declaimed very loudly against its use in France. Several innocent people have died under the torture: that is a fact too notorious to need to be proved in detail."[2] And Rousseau de La Combe: "Accused persons hardly ever confess anything, so that usually the preparatory torture is ineffective. The accused suffer the torments of torture without confessing anything, and if they do speak, it is to deny everything. . . . We may take the liberty to represent to magistrates that to condemn an accused to the preliminary torture is a very delicate matter. . . . He is often crippled for life, although cleared of the charge by the final judgment. . . . An old criminalist makes the remark that torture is rather a trial of patience than of truth. . . . We have a considerable number of writers against torture, among others M. Nicolas, president of the Parlement of Besançon, in a special treatise in which he gathers all that could be said to show the uselessness of torture. . . . However that may be, it must be admitted that, at least, the preliminary and final torture are often wonderfully effective in regard to the discovery of accomplices."[3]

§ 5. **D'Aguesseau's Reforms.** — Whatever the opinion of the jurisconsults might be, they were no longer the speakers to be listened to. The real ruler of the age was the public temper; its progress may be traced step by step, for its history has been written.[4]

[1] "Éloge de Pothier." "Œuvres" (Bugnet edition), vol. II, p. 54.

[2] "Code criminel," p. 907. Also, speaking of the torture administered at the Autun presidial: "We find it so cruel," he says, "that we have, since these accidents, refrained from condemning any one to it preparatorily."

[3] "Mat. Crim." pp. 424–426.

[4] "L'esprit révolutionnaire avant la Révolution," by *M. Félix Rocquain*, 1878.

We are about to look on at its triumphs, from our particular point of view. For a long time confined within books, the spirit of reform is about to assert itself officially. It will gain admittance into the solemn hearings of the courts and into the literary societies, sometimes even into the legislature. No reform, in the direction we are about to point out, had been brought about under Louis XV. D'Aguesseau, however, entertained the idea of ameliorating the French laws, and bringing them together in a single body.[1] He went to work on almost the lines followed for the reform of justice under Louis XIV, calling for memorials, consulting the principal members of the Parlements,[2] and having all the questions revised by a higher commission, which did duty as his privy council. It consisted of Joly de Fleury, Machault d'Arnouville, two elder sons of the Chancellor, d'Argenson, Fortia, with, sometimes, the addition of Ormesson and Trudaine.[3] This work naturally included criminal procedure. The Ordinance of 1670 must be taken up again, but, it would appear, only to perfect it technically; at least that is presumable from an examination of some detached portions of the whole, which, ready before the rest, saw the light of day.

At one time, the Chancellor writes as follows to one of his friends: "The memorial upon forgery is to be immediately examined by the council, and, apparently, there will remain very little to do but give it the finishing touches. The next most pressing matter is the jurisdiction of judges, and marshalcies, and the title upon defaults and contumacies."[4] These various points were made, under Louis XV, the subject of Declarations or Ordinances. First comes the Declaration in the form of an Edict of June, 1730, concerning criminal proceedings. Its object is merely "to interpret, by additions, Articles 2, 3, 7 and 9 of title XVII of the Ordinance of 1670," regulating matters of detail alone.[5] In 1736 appeared the Declaration as to prévôtal and presidial crimes, of which we have already had occasion to speak. Here also the desire of the legislature is merely to regulate. The preamble recalls that "one of the principal objects of the Ordinance of 1670 was to fix definite limits between the ordinary judges and the provost marshals . . .

[1] See *Francis Monnier*, "Le Chancelier d'Aguesseau," 2d edition, 1863, p. 286.

[2] *Ibid.*, pp. 288, 290, 293. [3] *Ibid.*, p. 288. [4] *Ibid.*, p. 339.

[5] "These articles concerning defaults and contumacies met with very many difficulties in practice in respect to the places where the search for the accused ought to be made, and the summonses given." *Sallé*, "Esprit des Ordonnances, Édits et Déclarations de Louis XV" (vol. III, pp. 155, 156).

experience had taught that there remained several important points which every day gave birth to dispute between the ordinary courts and the judges of prévôtal cases." These are the difficulties it was desired to remedy.

Finally, the Ordinance upon forgery of 1737 is one of d'Aguesseau's chief titles to glory. It is really a law of almost perfect technical accuracy. The preamble would even seem to disclose the idea of amending the Ordinance of 1670 as a whole, but not of changing its general features. It states merely that "the diversity of opinions and the different constructions placed upon the diverse provisions have produced such a great variety in the practice of several courts, that proceedings which appear regular and sufficient to some, are considered by others null and defective." It is thought "that instead of being satisfied with curing the defects of procedure as they appear, it would be much more expedient to drain their source by a new Law, which would form at once a supplement and an interpretation of prior Ordinances. But, laboring as we do under the necessity of dividing up such an extensive work, we concluded that the revision of the Ordinance of 1670 upon criminal procedure should first of all engage all our attention. And we have deemed it proper to make a choice even in that Ordinance by commencing such a useful work by the titles on the acknowledgment of writings or signatures, and forgery, principal and incidental."

In Louis XVI's reign we verge on the era of true reform. Those reforms which were brought forth before the convocation of the States-General were, however, insufficient. We note for the time only one Declaration of 24th August, 1780, which, without entirely abolishing torture, does away with its most reprehensible application, the preparatory torture. "We were of opinion," the king said later, "that torture, always unjust when used to perfect the proof of offenses, might be necessary to obtain the disclosure of accomplices."[1]

§ 6. **Progress of the Spirit of Reform.** — The new spirit, however, made rapid progress. It won over the great mass of the citizens; it insinuated itself into the constituted societies of the State; Royalty itself received it very kindly. This is what a man holding court appointments wrote in 1775, in a book dedicated to the king, and of which the king accepted the dedication:[2]

[1] Preamble of the Edict of 1st May, 1788.

[2] "Les devoirs du prince réduits à un seul principe, ou Discours sur la justice," dedicated to the king, by Moreau. See Didot's "Nouvelle biographie générale," vol. XXXVI, p. 480. "Moreau was commissioned

"You will no doubt one day inquire if, in our criminal Ordinances, the oldest of which was for the repression of the fiercest barbarity, more was not thought of the conviction than of the defense of the guilty; if that formidable and profoundly secret examination, which takes the accused unawares, so to speak, is not as much fitted to cause consternation in the heart of an innocent person as to spread terror into the heart of the guilty; if there are any kinds of prosecutions in which it could be just to refuse the accused the aid of a counsel; if it is not more consistent with the spirit of humanity to leave him, from the beginning of the proceedings, the same liberty to prove his innocence as the accuser has all the time to prove the crime; if it is right to compel the accused to wait, before presenting his justificative facts, until the edifice of accumulated proofs against him has acquired all the perfection of which it is susceptible. . . . It would seem, in effect, Sire, that our criminal laws have looked upon the accused in the light of an already convicted culprit, and although it is to-day very difficult for the latter to escape the punishment which he deserves, it is also very easy for the honest man, or the person accused by public mistake, or arrested from private malice, to become the victim of the pain and vexation caused him by oppression. It has hardly ever happened in France that the arrested criminal has evaded condemnation; but it has happened more than once that innocence, unjustly prosecuted, has not been recognized until after the infliction of the punishment. The wisest and most just courts have sometimes had to tremble for a murderous mistake, into which they have been led by the very regularity of their procedure. The law has nothing with which to reproach them in such a case, but justice might probably blame the imperfection of their forms." [1]

The spirit of reform, despite the opposition of a section of the magistracy, is affirmed in the "Discours de rentrée" of the Courts. In 1766, Servan delivers that celebrated oration, in which he wages war against detention pending trial, the insidious interrogations, torture, and the doctrine of legal proofs. He throws doubt upon the lawfulness of capital punishment, and demands settled and accurate laws. It is hard to conceive of anything more daring

by the Court to draw up several works, among others the preamble of the Edicts of Chancellor Maupeou, and was rewarded for his zeal by the offices of the king's brother's first counsel, librarian of Queen Marie-Antoinette, and historiographer of France." The work quoted was originally written for use in the education of Louis XVI. See its preface, pp. 10, 11.

[1] *Op. cit.*, pp. 436–438.

from the lips of a magistrate. "Raise your eyes," he says to his colleagues, "and see over your heads the likeness of your God who was an innocent accused; you, who are a man, be human; you, who are a judge, be reasonable; you, who are a Christian, be charitable. Man, judge, or Christian, whoever you be, respect misfortune."[1] In conclusion he loudly demands the amendment of the Ordinance of 1670.

This was not an isolated case. Servan had imitators. In 1786, for instance, Attorney-General Hérault de Séchelles predicted the passage of new laws in the near future.[2] The literary societies, which exercised such a great influence at this period, eagerly assigned for competition questions of criminal legislation. "The learned societies and the academies, which swarmed in the 1700s, assisted in conserving this new spirit in the provinces, and the latter, following the example set by Paris, applied themselves to problems of criminal reform. It became a fashion. . . . In 1777 the 'Société Economique' of Berne offered a prize of twelve hundred francs to the author of the best memorial drawn up according to this programme: 'To compose and write out a complete and detailed plan of criminal legislation from this triple point of view: 1st, crimes and the proportionate punishments to be applied to them; 2d, the nature and weight of proofs and presumptions; 3d, the method of attaining them by means of the criminal procedure, so that mildness of examination and of punishment may be reconciled with the certainty of prompt and exemplary chastisement, and so that society shall find the greatest possible security for liberty and humanity.' When Voltaire saw this programme, of which he has been suspected of being the author, he was seized with enthusiasm, sent fifty louis more, and himself published a reply to these questions. His book is entitled 'Prix de la justice et de l'humanité.' . . . Competitors appeared from all quarters. The Society of Berne, after having adjourned the award of the prize, gave it, in 1782, to two Germans, Von Globig and Hulster. Their book was printed in German; it does not appear to have received any consideration in Germany.

"Among the competitors were two men destined to play, later, a great part in the Revolution, and who at that period contended

[1] See "Discours" prefaced to Serpillon's "Code criminel," p. 26.

[2] See "Réhabilitation de deux accusés et justification de trois autres," by *M. Godard*, advocate, Paris, 1787, p. 113. "We are permitted to announce discoveries which may make a nation happier, to predict the passage of new laws, told in a solemn address by a young and eloquent magistrate."

for the prize for justice and humanity. One was Brissot, the publicist of the Girondists, and the other a person less noted for his humanity, Marat. The latter had his work printed in 1781 and published at Paris in 1790. . . . That work is one of extraordinary mediocrity. . . . Not so with another work, written by Brissot, which was more successful. It is entitled "Théorie des lois criminelles,' a work which the Society of Berne did not allow to compete, because it had been published." [1]

In 1780, a French society, the Academy of Châlons-sur-Marne, decided a competition which it had set upon the following subject: "On the means of softening the rigor of the French criminal laws, without detriment to the public safety." [2] The Society, in publishing the addresses, declares that "it does not intend to ratify the views of the authors, but has given its approbation to their talents, their humanity and the useful ideas which it has thought to have discovered in their works. The very nature of the subjects suggested shows its desire to spread new lights upon philosophy and political economy. But at a time when zeal against the old prejudices too often degenerates into innovations still more dangerous, it thinks it proper to announce that it has made a rule to exclude from the competition any memorial not written with all due respect to Religion and Government."

At least twenty memorials were sent to the Academy. Two of these were awarded prizes, that of Brissot de Warville, and that of Bernardi, an advocate in the Parlement of Aix. They all put forward claims, tending more and more to constitute a common programme and which were to be registered in the Cahiers of 1789. They demand publicity of the proceedings,[3] the suppression of the oath by the accused,[4] and of torture,[5] complete liberty of defense,[6] and the system of moral proofs.[7] They, finally, demand the jury, as the restoration of an ancient national institution.[8] They call

[1] *M. Laboulaye,* Revue des Cours littéraires, vol. II, 1864–1865, pp. 782, 783.

[2] "Discours couronné par l'Académie de Châlons-sur-Marne en 1780," followed by the second best, and by extracts from several other memorials presented to the Academy. Châlons-sur-Marne 1780.

[3] *Brissot,* p. 94; *Bernardi,* pp. 176, 177.

[4] *Brissot,* p. 95; *Bernardi,* p. 162.

[5] *Brissot,* p. 103; *Bernardi,* pp. 164–166.

[6] *Brissot,* pp. 96–98; *Bernardi,* pp. 178–182.

[7] *Brissot,* p. 101 *et seq.*; *Bernardi,* p. 145 *et seq.*

[8] *Bernardi,* p. 202. "Let us remark that this usage that every man be judged by his peers was formerly followed in France; that it was the introduction of jurist judges and of the Roman law that led to its abolition; and that the reason for its existence still in England and some of the districts of the North is that they have known better than we how to preserve the wise and equitable principles of their ancestors."

for early reforms, in that bombastic and inflated diction characteristic of the 1700s: "People! Oh, ye who have so long groaned under the weight of your chains, — at last you begin to breathe; raise a serene brow; the age of tears is past; your misfortunes approach an end. . . . let the torch of reason burn a little longer and the universe will know no more gloom."[1] — "Happier reigns are dawning over Europe. Oh! friends and brothers, let this work prove to you my desire for the alleviation of your sufferings!"[2]

These demands, prayers, and appeals at last come to be addressed to the judges themselves. They do not make themselves heard in legal pleadings, for pleading there is none in criminal cases. But what cannot be said may be printed, and the "Mémoires justificatifs" for innocent people unjustly condemned continue to multiply in the years immediately preceding the Revolution. That method of appeal in the last resort, the import of which we have explained, is used. Royal orders are obtained allowing the stay of executions and the review of actions. The authors of these memorials, eagerly read by the public, are advocates, sometimes magistrates, who become the heroes of the hour.[3] Each of these pleadings, speaking for a people rather than for an accused, contains an appeal for necessary reforms. Let us briefly refer to some of these cases.

In 1785, there is the case of an unfortunate girl, Catherine Estinès, sentenced by the bench of Rivière to be burned alive for parricide. It is discovered, ere long, by the Parlement of Toulouse, that the process has been falsified. A complaint for forgery is lodged against the officers of Rivière and a justificative memorial for the accused is presented by M. Lacroix, advocate.[4] The author, in concluding, makes his client say: "Who knows whether, the report of my misfortunes reaching the throne, this example, added to so many others, may not hasten the reform of our criminal laws, so earnestly desired by all honest people! Oh! how I should then bless my past torments and my

[1] *Brissot*, p. 111.

[2] *Bernardi*, p. 218.

[3] The charges are freely communicated. It is often "tender-hearted" jailers who take to heart the facilitation of the defense. "They brought me the promised information," says M. Lecauchois, in his memorial for the girl Salmon; "a little over two hundred and fifty pages small-hand folio." — Lecardé, clerk of court, keeper of the prisons of Rouen, bears witness to the influence he exercised on the salvation of the girl Salmon: "The public will learn that the keeping of prisons is not incompatible with kindness and humanity. . . . I have collected a mass of inportant information for the clearing up of the action."

[4] "Mémoire pour Catherine Estinès," Toulouse, 1786.

present sufferings! A proper system of criminal laws is the best gift a sovereign could make to his people. France respectfully waits such a gift, worthy of her and of her king. . . . Our criminal Ordinance contains so many wise provisions; and it would cost so little to modify those less wise." [1]

In 1780, five individuals were sentenced by the Parlement of Dijon, for nocturnal burglary accompanied by threats, to various punishments: one was hanged, another died at the galleys; one of them had been subjected to the preliminary torture. They were innocent; the real culprits were subsequently discovered and condemned. Letters of review were then obtained and a justificative memorial drawn up by M. Godard, advocate at the Paris bar.[2] An opinion is annexed to the memorial, signed by MM. Target, Thétion, Sanson, Martineau, de La Croix, Blonde, Hardoin de la Reynerie, Fournel, Bonhome de Comeyras, Henry, Lacretelle, de Sèze, and Bonnet. "This great error," says the author of the memorial, "will make the cause of five unfortunate men a national cause, in which people of all classes will take part, since it will force them to turn their attention to their own case; and it will finally no doubt bring to a head that long looked for reform in our criminal laws. . . . He will be the descendant of Lamoignon. . . . He will inherit his virtues and his insight, as well as his fame, who, taking up after more than a hundred years the immortal thoughts of his predecessor, will cause the sovereign to give them the sanction due to them, and will obtain from the beneficent justice of the monarch a new code, the first object of which will be the happiness of this empire, and which will afterwards enlighten foreign nations, as the recent codes of two great European princes now enlighten ours." [3]

In 1786 there is another cause, that of a poor servant girl, Marie-Françoise-Victoire Salmon.[4] Condemned to be burned as a poisoner by the Parlement of Rouen, on 17th May, 1772, the keeper of the prison and certain clergymen interested themselves in her case; a reprieve was obtained, and the action was reviewed. This time she was condemned to an indefinite further inquiry and detention in prison; finally the validity of this new sentence was itself contested before the King's Council. M. Lécauchois, an ad-

[1] "Mémoire pour Catherine Estinès," p. 54.
[2] "Réhabilitation de la mémoire de deux accusés et justification de trois autres," Paris, 1787.
[3] pp. 112, 113.
[4] See "Mémoire justificatif," by *M. Lecauchois* (Paris, printed by Cailleaux, 1786).

vocate of Rouen, drew up two memorials for the girl Salmon and to the second is annexed an opinion by Fournel, an eminent Paris advocate.[1] This action stirred public opinion to a great degree. "Her protectors having aroused public sympathy, charitable contributions to a large extent found their way to the girl Salmon in her prison."[2] The memorial had an extensive sale. Finally, a decree of the Parlement of Paris, deciding her appeal, was issued on 23d May, 1786, discharging the accused from all the accusations and complaints brought against her; and all Paris joined in an ovation to the unfortunate woman and her defender.[3]

But the most celebrated cause was that which soon bore the name of the "Trois Roués." For nocturnal robbery, three unfortunate men, Bradier, Lardoise, and Simare, are, in 1785, condemned to the galleys for life by the bailiwick of Chaumont. The Parlement of Paris increases the punishment to that of the wheel. A reprieve is obtained, an appeal to quash lodged, and very soon a justificative memorial appears, followed by a short opinion.[4] The opinion was signed by Legrand de Laleu. The memorial was anonymous, but everybody knew the author to be Dupaty, magistrate, philosopher, and literary man, and president of the Parlement of Bordeaux. The memorial was immediately followed by another document entitled: "Pleas in law for Bradier, Simare, and Lardoise, condemned to the wheel."[5] These were notable and impassioned works, which went far beyond the material interests involved in the cause. The memorial in particular is an excellent piece of pleading, forcible and glowing, expressing in an ardent style the claims which erelong will prompt the law. Importunate and fiery appeals to royal justice and clemency succeed each other: "No, I will not be silent as to the defects and severities of our criminal Ordinance, now that France and humanity have Louis XVI to appeal to. . . .[6] Magistrates,

[1] "Consultation pour une jeune fille condamné à être brûlée vive," Paris, 1786.

[2] "Mémoire pour le sieur Lecardé," keeper of the prisons of Rouen, p. 28.

[3] Witness the recriminations of M. Lecardé, who desired his share in the glory: "From that day he (M. Lecauchois) has continually dragged her to play-houses of all kinds, the Théâtre François, the Comédie Italienne, Ambiguë-comique, Vaux-Hals, Ruggieri, Musée, Boulvard, etc. — swaggering beside her and showing himself off like a part of the play" (p. 25).

[4] "Three Men broken on the Wheel." "Mémoire justificatif pour trois hommes condamnés à la roue," 1786, Paris.

[5] Printed at Paris by Philippe-Denys Pierre, 1786.

[6] "Mémoire," p. 233.

there exists in your Ordinance a law, which grants, — I should rather say, which orders that every deaf and dumb accused shall have a counsel. . . . Extend, extend that humane law to the poor and indigent. It certainly concerns them. . . . the disability of misery is at least as deserving as natural disability. Nay, more so. The poor and indigent are themselves deaf and dumb, not merely by the irreparable loss of the organs of speech and hearing, but by the resourceless deprivation of the intellect which comprehends, and the reason which elucidates." [1]

"Ah! Sire, from the height of your throne, in the midst of that resounding chorus of Fame which spreads your wisdom and glory throughout the universe, deign for a moment to lend an ear to the blood of Calas, Montbailly, Langlade, Cahusac, Barreau, and their fellows, and the innocent blood of the three unfortunate men about to flow. All that innocent blood, in the midst of gallows and wheels, continues to cry out to you in piteous tones: Oh, prince, friend of mankind, do not leave your throne without deigning to listen to us! . . . Deign, deign from the height of your throne to cast a single glance upon all the bloody reefs of our criminal laws whereon we perished, whereon innocent people perish every day. . . . [2] Sire, do not believe those who may tell you that it is essential to maintain laws, rigorous, no doubt, but so old, — centuries old. Sire, reason and humanity are eternal; — do not believe those who tell you that systems of laws ought to be stable in empires, so that the empires themselves may retain their stability, as if the laws, designed to follow individuals, communities, and mankind in the circle within which they revolve, ought not to have their share in such revolutions and run a course, like mortal things; — do not believe those who tell you that it is dangerous to diminish the respect due to the laws by too open criticism, as if anything could dishonor them more than the mildew of barbarism which covers them, or the innocent blood with which they drip, — who, finally, tell you that the making of a new criminal code is a difficult work, which requires time and meditation to ripen, as if that were not an additional reason to go about the task without delay!" [3] . . . "Sire, the Code we crave from you has not still to be made. It is made, written, and engraved. God himself has engraved it in your heart, and nothing remains for you to do but to have it interpreted immediately by the chief of your magistracy, who ought not to find it difficult to

[1] "Mémoire," pp. 237, 238; *cf.* p. 57; *cf.* "Moyens de droit," pp. 43, 44.
[2] "Mémoire," p. 240.
[3] *Ibid.*, I, pp. 243–245.

understand and to give an example of it to your Empire, to the whole world!"[1] — "Hasten, oh, prince, friend of justice, truth, and humanity . . . for perhaps in some remote province of your Empire, your criminal laws, and especially the laws of your criminalists, are, even at this moment, sending to the scaffold men who, like Bradier, Lardoise, and Simare, are deprived of all counsel, who languish in prison like them, have for years been, like them, the sport of the injustice and the ignorance of the lower judges, and, like them, are innocent. You are the king. . . ."[2]

Dupaty's memorial had a prodigious effect. It was extensively sold, with the author's portrait and that of Legrand de Laleu. Louis Séguier himself bears witness to the great emotion it caused in the motions which he lodged for the suppression of this document, and which we have already analyzed. "This memorial, claimed to be justificative, has permeated the capital, all France, the whole of Europe. It was ostensibly written to sell for the benefit of the three condemned men, in order the further to engage public sympathy. . . . This venal distribution, hitherto unaccustomed, has produced the keenest ferment; the cause of the three criminals has become that of nearly every citizen. . . . At this time of ferment a general clamor is raised against the criminal Ordinance."[3] The attorney-general considers all this as a passing excitement. "It is reserved for our administration to vindicate a public accuser, to reassure minds prone to be led astray, to lay down the true principles, unknown to the majority of citizens of all ranks and stations, to justify the laws and to settle their true meaning, to reëstablish the authority of jurisprudence, by opposing the calmness of reflection to the transports of the imagination, the general welfare to the empty desire for notoriety, to enable this and every nation to realize that it is merely a mania for reform which guides the pen of this writer."[4]

What Séguier took for a passing storm was the all-powerful breath of the French Revolution.

[1] "Mémoire," I, p. 248.
[2] *Ibid.*, I, p. 249.
[3] *Ibid.*, I, pp. 3–5.
[4] *Ibid.*, I, p. 5.

Part III

HISTORY OF CRIMINAL PROCEDURE SINCE THE FRENCH REVOLUTION

TITLE I

THE LAWS OF THE FRENCH REVOLUTION

CHAPTER I

THE AMENDMENTS TO THE ORDINANCE OF 1670

§ 1. **The Edict of 1788.** — The growing pressure of public opinion was bound to lead to reforms in Louis XVI's reign, even before the convocation of the States-General. In this respect, however, as in other matters, the amendments made at that period were partial and wavering. They precede by very little the convocation of the States-General, and will disappear in the great renovation following 1789. In 1788 a step forward was made.

An edict was introduced in the famous Bed of Justice of 8th May, one of the last throes of the old monarchy. The necessity for a wholesale reform of the criminal procedure was recognized by the government. Homage was paid to the great Ordinance of 1670 in the preamble of the Edict, but the necessity of a revision was at the same time announced. "We shall not conceal that while retaining the greatest number of its provisions, we could advantageously change several of its principal articles and amend it without abolishing it. We have taken into consideration that in bringing order out of the chaos of criminal jurisprudence, the Commissaries were not able to provide for every contingency, that the official reports of their conferences bear witness that they were often at variance upon important points, and that their decision did not appear always to sanction the wisest opinions; that the advance of knowledge alone since the drawing up of that Ordinance should be sufficient to induce us to revise its provisions carefully, and to attune them to that public reason, to the level of which we would adjust our laws . . . from the example of the legislators of antiquity, whose wisdom limited the authority of their Code to a period of a hundred years, we have noticed that, this period having now expired, we ought to submit this Criminal Ordinance, which has undergone the judgment of a round century, to a general revision."[1] The keeper of the seals, in his speech at the bed of justice, was still more precise. "The necessity of a reform of the criminal Ordinance and of the criminal code is universally recognized. The whole nation demands this important work of legislation from the king, and His Majesty has resolved in the councils to accede to the wishes of his people."[2] But it was desired that this general reform should be the fruit of long planning. The method of inquiry proposed was notable. "To undertake this great work with the requisite order and wisdom, we propose to surround ourselves with all the intelligence we can gather around the throne on which divine Providence has placed us. All our subjects shall have the power to take part in the execution of the plan, by addressing to our keeper of the seals such observations and memorials as they deem fitting to enlighten us. We shall thus raise to the rank of laws the results of public opinion, after these shall have been subjected to the test of a mature and deep investigation."[3]

Pending this general reform, the Edict abrogated "several abuses which this appeared a moment to remedy."

1st, The use of the prisoner's seat was abolished. "We ordain that there shall be placed, in our courts and jurisdictions, behind the bar, a wooden seat or bench, sufficiently raised that the accused can be seen by all their judges; we leave it to the choice of the said accused whether to sit or remain standing; the presidents of our courts and the judges who preside at the trials in the jurisdictions shall warn them of their rights" (Art. 1).

2d, The rendering of judgments not evidentially based was forbidden. "Neither our judges nor our courts shall be entitled to pronounce sentence, *for the crimes resulting from the action;* it is our will that every decree or judgment shall set out and expressly name the crimes and offenses of which the accused shall have been convicted . . . we except decrees merely affirmative of the sentences of the judges in the first instance, in which the said crimes and offenses are expressly set out; provided that the courts shall cause to be transcribed in the introductory part of their decrees the said judgments of the judges of the first instance, all on pain of nullity"

[1] *Isambert*, "Anc. lois," t. XXVIII, p. 727.
[2] *Buchez* and *Roux*, "Histoire parlementaire," vol. I, p. 239.
[3] Preamble of the Edict. *Isambert*, t. XXVIII, p. 527.

(Art. 3). This was a very wise reform, and one long needed. "The very dignity of our judgment demands the express statement of the offenses," said the keeper of the seals. "What tribunal could be anxious for the prerogative of inflicting capital punishment without giving a reason for its decrees? — The king therefore thinks, gentlemen, that every solemn condemnation, which makes punishment follow the offense, should show the offense as well as the punishment." [1]

3d, The abolition of the preparatory torture was confirmed, and preliminary torture was abolished (Art. 8). "New reflections have convinced us of the deceptiveness and the inconveniences of this kind of proof, which never leads to the discovery of the truth with certainty, usually fruitlessly prolongs the punishment of the condemned, and may more frequently mislead our judges than enlighten them." A final interrogation by the judge commissioner was substituted for it. This was made on the very day of the execution, with confirmation and confrontation, if need be (Arts. 9–12). This was substituting a moral constraint for physical torture, the condemned person being obliged to take oath in this interrogation as in the others, according to the general rule, which was retained. It was "a milder, but no less effective, method to compel evil-doers to name their accomplices. We have thought that, the law having intrusted to the faith of the oath the greatest interests of society, since it makes the lives of human beings depend upon it, it might adopt it as a safeguard of the public safety, in the final declarations of the guilty persons. We have decided to try this method provisionally at least, reserving the right, although with regret, to reëstablish the preliminary torture if, after some years' experience, it is shown by the reports of our judges to be absolutely necessary." [2]

4th, A majority of two votes was no longer enough to sustain a capital punishment; three were necessary (Art. 4). Finally came two provisions, which appeared to the legislature to be the most important of all it decreed, and which are, in reality, very important.

5th, It was said: "No sentence involving natural death shall be executed until one month after being passed . . . except judgments rendered for the crimes of sedition and riot, in which the said judgments shall be executed on the day they are

[1] *Buchez* and *Roux*, "Histoire parlementaire," vol. I, p. 241.
[2] *Isambert*, t. XXVIII, p. 528.

pronounced." Why this delay, not allowed by the Ordinance? Was it to inflict upon the condemned the agonies of a horrible suspense? No. In spite of that disadvantage, which seems to have been taken into consideration, the intention was a noble one.[1] "The king wishes to insure to all condemned persons the time necessary to beg for his mercy and to make sure of his justice." It was a very humane measure, loudly demanded by Voltaire. "It is well known," said the keeper of the seals, "that in the most enlightened countries of Europe all capital sentences are subject to the approval of the sovereign." The better to insure this safeguard, the edict provided that the attorneys-general should transmit capital sentences to the keeper of the seals with the necessary information (Art. 5). These provisions, which were bound to be "equally valuable for preservation after the reform of the criminal laws," are not found in the laws of the intermediary period. That is comprehensible; the right of pardon then no longer existed, and the appeal to quash had henceforth a suspensive effect in criminal matters. Subsequently, although the right of pardon was reëstablished, the Code of Criminal Examination, copying the Code of Brumaire, year IV, ordained, in Article 375, the execution of capital sentences immediately they became final. The Ordinance of 1670 was to the same effect.[2] But that authority was not applied, and a circular of the keeper of the seals, of 27th September, 1830, even orders attorneys-general to lodge a memorial upon every capital condemnation. The keeper of the seals himself, after the matter has been considered by the directorship of pardons, addresses a report to the head of the State. "Pardon may be granted in the interests of justice and humanity." It is evident that it is really the provision of the Edict of 1688 which has been revived in our own times.

6th, Finally, it is notable that accused persons who were acquitted were awarded an honorable reparation. "I am able to state," says the keeper of the seals, "that His Majesty has been very much surprised to see that the laws of his kingdom have not yet made any provision in their favor, and that if there was no private prosecutor to the action who could be condemned in the costs of the printing and publishing of the judgments of acquittal, even that small indemnity was not granted to inno-

[1] Speech of the keeper of the seals. *Buchez* and *Roux*, "Histoire parlementaire," vol. I, p. 240.

[2] Title XXV, Art. 21.

cence."[1] Article 7 therefore provided as follows: "Our courts and judges shall order that every decree or judgment of acquittal rendered in the last resort, or which is not appealed, shall be printed and published at the expense of the private prosecutor, if there is one, and if not at the expense of our exchequer."[2]

Such was the Edict, which left the system of the Ordinance intact, but which was more liberal upon certain points than the subsequent laws proved to be. We know what opposition it raised in the Parlements. It is an interesting historic document; but it was not, in reality, a law which was ever applied. This was the last time royalty exercised, in criminal matters, the absolute and independent legislative power recognized in it by ancient France. On 5th July, 1788, the decree of the Council in regard to the convocation of the States-General was issued.[3] After that date it is the nation that speaks. Before observing how its representatives are going to interpret its wishes, it is expedient to find out how it expresses these in certain famous "Cahiers"[4] which the constituents then delivered to their representatives.[5]

§ 2. **The Cahiers of 1789.** — In regard to criminal legislation the Cahiers are a faithful mirror of the public mind. We shall once more here meet with the majority of the demands already voiced by the publicists, and again the path traced out by some of them will be faithfully followed by the Constituent Assembly. On important points the three Orders are almost always unanimous.

The publicity of the proceedings is the first thing demanded. "The publicity of the proceedings, formerly established in France, and in practice in all ages with nearly all enlightened nations, should be reëstablished, and henceforth the examination should take place with open doors and in full audience."[6] — "Above all, let the publicity of the procedure be reëstablished."[7] — "As to the reform of the Criminal Code, the Clergy's desire would be

[1] *Buchez* and *Roux*, "Histoire parlementaire," vol. I, p. 242.

[2] The number of copies allowed by the State varied from one hundred to two hundred, according to the importance of the jurisdictions.

[3] *Isambert*, t. XXVIII, p. 601.

[4] [The "Cahiers," or "Portfolios," were the written instructions given by the respective constituencies to their delegates or representatives elected for the assembly of the States-General. They contained a report of the united views and wishes of the constituencies as to matters likely to come up for legislative reform. — Trans.]

[5] We follow the "Résumé des Cahiers," by *Prudhomme;* 3 vols., 1789.

[6] "Cahier du Tiers," City of Paris, *Prudhomme*, III, p. 159. For the unanimity of the Cahiers of the Third Estate and of the Nobility in this direction, see *Prudhomme*, III, p. 588; II, p. 387.

[7] "Noblesse," City of Paris, II, p. 145.

. . . that the examination of criminal proceedings take place publicly, — the interrogation, deposition of witnesses, confirmation, and confrontation." [1]

The accused should be allowed the aid of counsel. On that point the Cahiers of the three orders are unanimous.[2] Certain of the Cahiers demand that the defending counsel be appointed gratuitously; this is the official advocate of the future.[3] Sometimes it is desired that the accused have the aid of counsel from the beginning of the proceedings. "Let counsel be assigned to the accused in all cases and from the beginning of the examination, and let him be authorized to have communication of the process whenever he shall find it necessary." [4] — "A judicial defender should be assigned to him from the beginning of the criminal action." [5] Others wish that the defending counsel intervene only after the interrogation of the accused. "Let a counsel be assigned to the accused after the first interrogation." [6] — "Let the accused have counsel for the confrontation and the subsequent proceedings." [7]

The oath imposed upon the accused ought to be abolished.[8] "Let the oaths or rather the perjuries required from the accused be suppressed." [9] — "The oath exacted from the accused being clearly contrary to the natural sentiment of self-preservation common to all, is but a violence done to human nature, unavailing for the discovery of the truth, and only qualified to impair the horror of perjury." [10] The Clergy are no less urgent than the Third Estate. "The suppression of the oath required of the accused should be demanded; it compels him to perjure himself." [11] — "Let the reform of the criminal code also be taken up, the means of defense assured to the accused, and the use of the oath, which nearly always makes the accused perjurers, be abolished." [12]

The defense should be put upon an equal footing with the prose-

[1] "Clergé," Mantes and Meulan.
[2] Unanimity of the Cahiers of all the bailiwicks: "Clergé," *Prudhomme*, I, p. 335; "Noblesse," II, 377; "Tiers," III, p. 548.
[3] Vannes, "Cahier du Tiers," III, 161.
[4] La Rochelle, "Cahier du Tiers," III, 161.
[5] City of Paris, "Cahier du Clergé," I, 159.
[6] Lyons, "Cahier du Tiers," III, 163.
[7] *Ibid.*, "Cahier de la Noblesse," II, 146.
[8] Prudhomme points out the unanimity in this direction of the Cahiers of the Third (III, 348), and the Cahiers of the Clergy of ninety-one bailiwicks (I, 335).
[9] Vannes, "Cahier du Tiers," III, 161.
[10] City of Paris, "Cahier du Tiers," III, 162.
[11] Douay, "Cahier du Clergé," I, 162.
[12] Auxerre, "Cahier du Clergé," I, 162.

cution in the sense that the accused could, from the start, allege and prove facts in support of his acquittal; and the justificative facts be no longer driven into the most remote corner of the proceedings. This was expressly stated in numerous Cahiers. "We would ask for the accused the power of alleging and establishing their justification by right, or by inquests immediately after their first interrogation."[1] — "Let a counsel be appointed for the accused, free, after the first interrogation, and every document of the proceedings be communicated to such counsel, who shall have free communication with the accused persons at all times, and shall plead in their favor and upon free paper their justificative pleas at every stage of the case."[2] — "Let the accused be entitled, with the constant aid of his counsel, to bring all justificative proofs from the beginning to the end of the procedure, and all judges be forbidden to refuse to allow them aid to do justice."[3]

It was necessary to restrict the great powers of the examining judge, who, alone, as we know, pronounced the ruling to the "extraordinary" action and issued the decrees, who confronted and confirmed alone, thus bringing together the written documents on which the action was decided. "A judge who hears the witnesses in the first instance, and takes their depositions, is often a judge of little education and sometimes prejudiced. The accused is already practically condemned to death, without any hope of escape, since the appellate court judges only upon the procedure, and upon the depositions taken by the trial judge."[4] We thus find many Cahiers demanding the presence of two or three judges, or even the intervention of the whole bench before proceeding with the informations and interrogations or issuing decrees.[5] "Let it be no longer permissible for the judge to proceed with the interrogations and other steps of the examination except with the assistance of two other judges; let it be forbidden to issue warrants of arrest or personal citation except with the advice of two judges."[6] — "Let the informations take place, not before a single judge, but before two judges, and the interrogations before the entire body whose duty it is to judge."[7] — "Let the informa-

[1] Saintes, "Cahier du Tiers," III, p. 159.
[2] Vannes, "Cahier du Tiers," III, p. 162.
[3] Dourdan, "Cahier de la Noblesse," II, p. 146.
[4] Blois, "Cahier de la Noblesse."
[5] According to *Prudhomme* (II, 399), the Cahiers of the Nobility are unanimous in demanding that a judge should never be entitled by himself to issue a warrant of arrest.
[6] La Rochelle, "Cahier du Tiers," III, p. 160.
[7] Toul, "Cahier du Tiers," III, p. 160.

tion and the first interrogation take place in the presence of three judges." [1] — "Let no decree be issued in criminal matters except by all the assembled judges of the jurisdiction." [2]

Other reforms are demanded which had already been effected by the ephemeral Edict of 1788. The decrees, including even those of the supreme courts, ought to be evidentially based in a precise fashion.[3] Torture was to be abolished forever, and the use of the prisoner's seat suppressed.[4] The abolition of exceptional courts was desired. "Let the jurisdiction of the provosts be abolished, so that every person accused may have the benefit of two steps of jurisdiction." [5] The extraordinary commissions in criminal matters are doomed.

Individual liberty was to be effectively protected. The interrogation of the captive ought to take place within twenty-four hours.[6] Liberation on bail should be granted whenever serious crime is not involved. "Let provisional release on bail always be granted after the first interrogation, except in those cases where the prisoner is held for an offense involving corporal punishment." [7]

The practitioners (who often drew up the Cahiers of the Third Estate) did not forget the provision of the Ordinance which punished as a false witness the witness who retracted at the confrontation. "Freedom is also asked for the witnesses to retract at the confrontation without the risk of incurring the punishment for forgery so long, at least, as the retraction is not fraudulent." [8]

The Clergy alone, strange to say, demand the suppression of the monitories, "except in the more serious cases." [9] But again, the Third Estate demands that the ecclesiastical courts have no longer a place in criminal procedure. "We would ask for the abolition of the joint examination by officials and criminal lieutenants, as a dangerous custom, calculated to double the costs, and increase the opportunities for quashing. The conferring on the ordinary

[1] Lyons, "Cahier du Tiers," III, p. 162.

[2] Nivernois, "Cahier du Tiers," III, p. 163.

[3] Unanimity in this direction in the Cahiers of the three orders: Clergy, I, 351; *cf.* p. 153; Nobility, II, p. 399; *cf.* p. 147; Third Estate, III, p. 573; *cf.* p. 172.

[4] Unanimity of the Cahiers: Clergy, I, 161; Nobility, II, 149; Third Estate, III, 165.

[5] Alençon, "Cahier de la Noblesse," II, p. 154; in this direction, the Nobility of forty-three bailiwicks, II, p. 400.

[6] I, 122; 352.

[7] Alençon, Labour; "Cahiers de la Noblesse," II, p. 145; in this direction, the Nobility of fifty-nine bailiwicks, II, 391.

[8] III, 159, and in this direction, the Third in thirty-two bailiwicks, III, p. 594.

[9] I, pp. 154 and 168.

royal judges of the cognizance of these privileged cases of which the clergy could be accused would follow, without prejudice to separate prosecutions which the promoters could bring for the maintenance of ecclesiastical discipline." [1] The citizens of 1789 were here claiming exactly the same measure as Louis XIV's commissioners had proposed in 1670. The publicists had been preaching all these reforms for fifty years. The desire was now to put them into effect without delay. But the Cahiers show that the public temper had gone beyond them. It was to England that they went for models for the organization of criminal justice, as they did for the foundation of political liberty.[2] It was, first of all, necessary to suppress the crying abuses of the old system, and then to introduce with us the oral procedure, by juries.

The Third Estate of fifty-eight bailiwicks demanded the discrimination of judges of the fact from judges of the law.[3] "In criminal matters the *determination* of the fact should always be kept separate from the *judgment* of the law. The institution of jurors for the *determination* of the fact appearing more favorable to personal safety and public liberty, the States-General should find out by what means this institution could be adapted to our jurisprudence." [4] Others we find pointing to the "twelve sworn peers pronouncing solely and exclusively upon the facts, and whose unanimity is essential to entail condemnation." [5] These are the characteristic features of the English jury.[6] Other Cahiers, it is true, refer to old French customary laws erroneously construed. "Let no criminal action be examined against any citizen unless the judge be assisted in every step of the proceeding by one or more citizens of the same rank as the accused, and let all citizens enjoy the same rights and privileges as the clergy, conformably to the old French usage." [7]

Lastly, the Cahiers demand the suppression of that reserved

[1] III, p. 122, in this direction, the unanimity of the Cahiers of the Third, III, p. 560.

[2] "Let there be formed at the beginning of the next session of the States-General a council composed of the most enlightened persons to deal with such an important subject as the reform of the Criminal Code. This council ought not to consist of magistrates and jurisconsults alone. The most enlightened virtue is not altogether proof against the wiles of prejudice. Citizens of all the estates, of all the orders, and *especially those who have had the opportunity to study the criminal jurisprudence of England* must be admitted into it." — Blois, "Cahier de la Noblesse," II, 142.

[3] III, 574.

[4] City of Paris, "Cahier du Tiers," III, 163.

[5] II, 144.

[6] Ninety-one Cahiers of the Nobility demand that "the unanimity of the sworn peers should be necessary to bring about a conviction subjecting an accused to capital punishment." II, 387.

[7] Vermandois, "Cahier de la Noblesse," II, 144.

justice, and that exercise of absolute power, which had been causing so much trouble in the administration of justice. The "lettres de cachet" are to be abolished.[1] They have been stigmatized by the man who is to be the first great mouthpiece of the Revolution. As for the letters of pardon, they can no longer intervene until after the judgment. "He should not be entitled to a grant of letters of pardon except after the final judgment and in the last resort."[2] — "It should be in the king's power to commute all punishments pronounced to a less severe punishment, and to pardon at his pleasure by letters emanating from His Majesty in due form, except in the case of the crimes of treason, peculation, and extortion; but in no case should he be entitled to prevent the pronouncing of the judgments."[3] The above, in their broad outlines, are the reforms that the Constituent Assembly is about to put into operation.

§ 3. **First Reforms effected by the Constituent Assembly; the Decree of 8–9 October, 1789.** — The Constituent Assembly passed two Laws on the subject of criminal procedure, both of the greatest importance; that of 8–9 October, 1789, and that of 16–29 September, 1791. It may appear strange, at first sight, that these Laws should have been passed in such rapid succession, and that the Assembly should so soon have thought it necessary to retouch its work. But the explanation is simple. The first of these two Laws carries out the reform of the graver abuses which would not wait; but as its preamble shows, it merely establishes a provisional state of things.[4] The second effects that adaptation of the procedure by jurors, and, in a more general way, of the English procedure, which has been ranked among the definitive institutions of France.

The Decree of 1789 by no means destroys the order of procedure in use down to that date. The Ordinance of 1670 still remains in full force. "The Ordinance of 1670 and the edicts and rulings concerning criminal matters shall continue to be observed so far as consistent with the present Decree, and except as otherwise formally ordained" (Art. 28). We still find the same written

[1] Unanimity in the Cahiers: Clergy, I, 352; Third, III, 576 and 58; for the Nobility, II, 56 *et seq.*

[2] Meaux, "Cahier du Tiers," III, 174; in this direction the Third of eighty-eight bailiwicks, III, 570.

[3] Tourraine, "Cahier de la Noblesse," II, 152.

[4] "Although the execution of the whole of this reform requires leisureliness and the maturity of the deepest reflection, it is, nevertheless, possible to enable the nation to enjoy the benefit of various provisions, which, without subverting the order of procedure at present followed, would reassure the innocent and facilitate the vindication of those accused."

and complex procedure. The information, the decrees, the interrogation, the ruling to the "extraordinary" action, the confirmation and the confrontation, the report of the action, the final interrogation, — all these find their places in the new text (and, at the same time, there are no jurisdictional changes). But certain novel elements are added to the old work. These consist of defense allowed and assured, and a wide publicity. In these respects the act grants safeguards which will subsequently disappear. The knowledge of this enables us better to understand how, at the time of the drawing up of the Code of Criminal Examination, certain minds wished to return purely and simply to this, the first reform effected by the Revolution.

The safeguards assured to the accused by the Decree of 1789 consist principally of the publicity of the procedure and the aid of counsel. It was not, however, the intention of the legislature to let in the full light of day from the first steps of the arrest and the examination. So long as proofs were still being sought for, which it might be easy to conceal, it would be highly inexpedient to put all the interested parties upon the alert. The complaint and the denunciation are made secretly: "the information preceding the decree will continue to take place secretly" (Art. 6). But another safeguard is originated, to form a substitute for the publicity which would be dangerous at that early moment. The judge is given colleagues, "adjoints," citizens appointed by the municipalities or communities of residents. Their presence takes the place, as far as possible, of the control by public opinion; and, at the same time, all danger is avoided, for "they take oath to the commune (administered by the municipal officers or the syndics) . . . faithfully to discharge their duties, and above all to maintain inviolable secrecy regarding the contents of the complaint and other documents of the procedure" (Art. 2).[1] In being present they, in a measure, personify the public, and they also take the place of counsel. That this is their rôle is well shown by the fact that, when publicity is established and counsel admitted, they retire and disappear. When the accused appears,

[1] These notables should be twenty-five years old at least, and chosen "from among the citizens of good principles and acknowledged probity." In the cases of urgency and capture in the act, they might be replaced by "two of the principal residents who are not to be heard as witnesses in the case, and who will immediately take oath before the examining judge" (Art. 8). Under another hypothesis (necessity for traveling to points too far from the chief place of the jurisdiction) they might be replaced by "members of the municipality of the place, chosen by the examining judge" (Art. 5).

"all the steps of the examination shall take place confrontatively with him, publicly, with the doors of the chamber of examination open; from that moment, the aid of the 'adjoints' shall cease" (Art. 11). Such is the general idea prompting the act. Let us briefly examine it in detail.

The provisional scope of the law is shown from the very beginning of the proceedings, when the judge is made to take cognizance by the private prosecutor or by the public prosecutor. If they begin by a *complaint*, "it can only be presented to the judge in the presence of two witnesses, produced by the complainant. . . . The fact of their presence and their names will be stated in the order which is issued upon the complaint, which they will sign, along with the judge, on pain of nullity" (Art. 3). In the case of an official prosecution, the "adjoints" are present, and the law requires that the king's procurator shall then state if he has an informer, and who he is, so that such informer "may be known to the judge and the 'adjoints' at the information, before it is begun" (Art. 4). "Two 'adjoints' should also be present at the drawing up of the official report (which is drawn up upon the spot) to establish the 'corpus delicti.'" "They are entitled to make any remarks they wish, which will be noted, and they will sign the official report on pain of nullity" (Art. 5). Two "adjoints" are present at the information and hear the witnesses (Art. 6). They are "bound, on soul and conscience, to make to the judge such observations as well for the prosecution as for the defense as they shall find necessary for the explanation of the testimony of the witnesses or the clearing up of the facts testified to" (Art. 7).

The information ending there, it remains to issue the writ. On that point, the law fully satisfies the demands of public opinion, recorded in the Cahiers. "Warrants of arrest cannot be issued against residents, except in the case of a crime entailing corporal punishment," and "warrants of personal citation or of arrest cannot be granted except by three judges at least or by one judge and two graduates" (Art. 9).[1]

If the accused obeys the warrant or is arrested, the procedure immediately becomes public, and he will have the aid of a counsel from the first interrogation. If he is not able to have one of his own, the judge will appoint one for him officially, on pain of nullity (Arts. 10 and 12). When the accused appears before the judge, the latter begins by "causing to be read to him the com-

[1] "The judges could, nevertheless, order immediate arrest in the case of capture in the act or of resisting the law."

plaint, the statement of the name of the denunciator, if there is one, the official report and reports and the information," then "he shall ask him if he has chosen or intends to choose a counsel, or if he wishes one to be appointed for him officially; in the latter case, the judge shall appoint the counsel *and the interrogation shall not be commenced until the following day*" (Art. 13). Have we not here a law which respects the rights of the defense, even to the point of exaggeration? The English law, which to-day orders the justice of the peace or police magistrate to warn the prisoner brought before him that he is not bound to reply, "that he ought not to obey from any fear, or yield from any hope," is, in truth, less liberal.[1]

It must be understood that in this interrogation, to prepare for which the accused has almost a day and a night, no oath is required from him. There is, however, one case in which the prisoner must still take oath, namely, "when he wishes to object to the competency of the witnesses."[2] But in that case it is a kind of "juramentum calumniæ."

Immediately after the interrogation, "a copy of all the documents of the process, signed by the clerk of court, shall be delivered to the accused, free of charge, upon free paper, if he asks for it."[3] His counsel is at all times entitled "to see the minutes" (Art. 14). The proceedings being from that time public, the continuation of or additions to the information, if any, took place publicly and in presence of the accused (Art. 15) who could question the witness after his deposition; but "the confessions, variations, or retractions of the witness at that early stage did not constitute him a false witness" (Art. 16).

The information at an end, ruling to the "extraordinary" action might take place, as before. But it was said: "Criminal actions cannot be ruled to the extraordinary except by three judges at least" (Art. 17). The confirmation of the witnesses and the confrontation immediately followed. All this took place publicly. The accused was present from the time of the confirmation, and his counsel was also entitled to be present, but "without being entitled to speak on behalf of the accused or suggest to him what he ought to say or reply, unless in the case of any new examina-

[1] *Stephen*, "Commentaries on the Laws of England," vol. IV, p. 347 (1873 edition).

[2] Art. 12. "The accused's oath shall not be required for this or any other interrogation, and he shall not take it during the whole course of the examination, unless he wishes to object to the competency of the witnesses."

[3] Art. 14. This provision repeats the prior law, but in criminal cases only, and the time for the delivery of the copy is deferred.

tion ('visite') or report whatsoever, when he could make remarks, which had to be noted in the official report" (Art. 18).

The freedom of the defense was assured. "The objections to the competency of the witnesses may be lodged and proved at any stage of the action, after as well as before cognizance of the charges, and the accused shall be allowed to prove them, provided they are found by the judges to be relevant and admissible" (Art. 17). The accused could also, as the Cahiers demanded, "plead his defenses and justificative facts or facts in extenuation, at any stage of the case, including even the fact of insanity, although it had not been set forth in his interrogation or other documents of the proceedings. The witnesses the accused may wish to produce, without being bound to name them at once, shall be heard publicly, and may be heard at the same time as those of the accuser, upon the continuations of or additions to the information" (Art. 19). These witnesses for the defense no longer had to be cited by the public prosecutor. The accused had the option "either of summoning them on his request, or of pointing them out to the public prosecutor, so that he might subpœna them." But he ought to act "within three days from the decree allowing the proof" (Art. 20).

The procedure, besides, retained, as we have said, its characteristic of being a written procedure. The various steps which we have described were carried through before the examining judges and were then recorded in the documents which swelled the record of the action. So that when the time came to appear before the court to obtain judgment, the formality of the *report* was still necessary. "The report of the action shall be made by one of the judges, the public prosecutor's motions lodged immediately thereafter, with the reasons assigned therefor ('motivées'), the final interrogation made, and judgment pronounced, all in public court" (Art. 21). Except for the introduction of publicity, it would seem that nothing in the last act of the judicial drama was changed. Even "the accused shall not appear at this hearing except during his interrogation, after which, if he be a prisoner, he shall be again removed" (Art. 21).

Another important modification had, however, been introduced. The accused, even when absent, could be represented by his counsel, who could speak, and lodge pleas in defense. "The counsel shall be entitled to be present during the whole sitting and speak for the defense after the report has been concluded, the motions lodged, and the final interrogation taken." Criminal lawyers were once more about to make the court-rooms resound, whose echoes they have not disturbed for a good many years.

The judges were then required to retire to the council chamber for deliberation; after which they immediately resumed "their public session for the pronouncement of the judgment" (Art. 21). Reasons must be assigned for every condemnation to *afflictive* or degrading punishment whether in the first instance or in the last resort (Art. 22). No condemnation to an *afflictive* or degrading punishment could be pronounced except by two-thirds of the votes cast, and final sentences of capital punishment could be passed only by four-fifths of the votes (Art. 25). The usages of torture and of the prisoner's seat were abolished forever (Art. 24).

Such are the new features under which the old procedure was presented in the Decree of 1789. That law, for which its authors did not look for more than an ephemeral existence, was, nevertheless, harmoniously put together. The fact was that it had been in readiness for a long time; and the reforms it introduced, often demanded, had been, so to speak, digested by public opinion. It proved to be more liberal in regard to the first part of the criminal action, that is, the information, the interrogation, and the warrant, than were the subsequent laws. The latter established a safeguard, which, in contemporary opinion, formed a substitute for all the rest, that double barrier protecting English liberties, as Blackstone says, the grand jury and the petit jury.

One point worthy of remark is that the Decree of 1789 is silent on the subject of the doctrine of legal proofs. Was that an intentional omission? Was it considered unnecessary to abrogate by a law that system, which had not been imposed by any law, but was merely the creation of jurisprudence?

In addition to that Decree and the Decree of 22–25 April, 1790, explaining and completing it, the Constituent Assembly prescribed several other temporary provisions before constructing its final work upon criminal procedure. By a Decree of 12–19 October, 1790, it provisionally commissioned the district tribunals to try criminal causes. It had previously suspended the procedures and the trials of the "prévôtal" courts.

In the month of September, 1791, there was promulgated a Law organizing criminal procedure on totally new foundations. The Ordinance of 1670 is from that time abrogated; that is the hour of its death. It had existed as a law in force for a hundred and twenty years; and although henceforth its text appears only as a matter of history, its influence, totally obliterated for a time, will later make itself forcibly felt.

CHAPTER II

THE CODES OF THE INTERMEDIARY PERIOD

§ 1. **The Procedure by Jury. Law of 16th and 29th September, 1791. System Originated Thereby.**—The Cahiers of 1789 demanded trial by jurors in criminal matters; they recommended the study of English institutions. For at least fifty years the eyes of France had been turned towards England, that country where every person accused is tried by twelve of his fellow-citizens. These wishes were about to be given effect to by the Constituent Assembly. England was to be the model for imitation; and in order to make the imitation complete some of the finest creations due to French genius were to be sacrificed. The institution of the public prosecutor, that admirable feature so well elucidated by Montesquieu, was to disappear temporarily from our judicial organization. The English laws were incessantly cropping up in the debates. "It is easy to see," says M. Bergasse on 17th August, 1789, "that no methods are talked about here except those furnished by the system of jurisprudence adopted in England and free America for the prosecution and punishment of offenses. This system, in fact, formerly in use in our own country, is the only humane system of practice; we cannot do better than adopt it without delay, ameliorating it, however, in certain details."[1] Later on, in the debate on the Law of 1791, Thouret made this statement: "We have had the benefit of conferences with several of the first jurists of England, who have passed some time in this capital."[2]

The importation into France of the English criminal procedure was, however, an arduous task. The two systems of legislations

[1] *Buchez* and *Roux*, "Hist. parlement," vol. II, p. 257.
[2] Sitting of 28th December, 1790; Moniteur of the 29th.

were in direct opposition upon most points, even now when publicity had found its way into French procedure, and the accused had, with us, the aid of a defending counsel, a privilege which the English law still hesitated to grant them. In France, the prosecution was wholly, so to speak, in the hands of the public prosecutor; the private parties could merely proceed for damages. In England, while all crimes (felonies) were presented to the grand jury by pleas of the crown, only the private prosecutor came to the front in the procedure, which was, of necessity, accusatory; the attorney-general only rarely constituted himself prosecutor. In England, the examination prior to the trial did not amount to much; intrusted almost entirely to justices of the peace, it formed but an insignificant element in the final action. In France, down to that date, the examination of the action by the examining judge had absorbed the greatest part of the procedure; it was the groundwork and the keystone of the whole edifice. Again, in England the procedure was entirely oral, and the law did not even permit the reading of written depositions to the trial jury. In France, writing played a preponderant part, even after the reforms brought about in 1789; the actions were judged chiefly upon the written documents. This is enough to show the absolute contrariety between the two systems, although we have taken notice only of the most salient points. Was it possible to introduce the English system with us, as a whole; could it exist in the midst of usages and traditions so different from those which had presided at its birth and followed its slow development? For another thing, in the event of the retention of the old French institutions, how were the grand jury and the trial jury, voted by acclamation in the sitting of 30th March, 1790, and which ought to figure in the number of essential safeguards guaranteed by the Constitution, to be amalgamated with them?

There was, as a matter of fact, little hesitation in the minds of the compilers of the new plan. They sacrificed the traditional institutions to the principles of the English procedure. — "Your committee have felt from the outset that this new institution (that of the jury) cannot be in any respect in accord with our Ordinances and our present form of examination. It has appeared to us to be necessary to recast everything so as to form a complete and harmonious system."[1] The principles of the English law were,

[1] M. Duport on behalf of the committees on Legislation and Criminal Jurisprudence. Sitting of 26th December, 1790; Moniteur of 27th. —

in fact, peculiarly in harmony with the spirit of the Revolution. The dominant power of the justice of the peace at the commencement of the action, the wide initiative left to citizens in the prosecution of offenses, should, in the eyes of the members of the Constituent Assembly, be sufficient to hold in check the institution of public prosecutor. It was clear that no servile imitation of the English system was possible; that must be changed in many particulars before acclimatizing it with us. This was done by the bill which was destined to become, almost without modification, the Law of 16th September, 1791.

The party representative of tradition did not yield without a struggle. A long and bitter debate arose, not upon the details of the plan, but upon two or three of its fundamental principles. A number of members of the Assembly desired to retain the ancient procedure, shorn of its defects and its harshness, with or without the jury. They protested against any daring innovations, attributable to foreign importation. This Ordinance party, if it is allowable so to describe it, was, for the time, completely vanquished. The majority of their demands were, moreover, inspired by a mistaken desire for conservatism. It was partly in the right, however; some of the institutions which it then wished to save from destruction had not long to wait for reappearance and restoration. Later still even, this party will be found on the point of taking complete revenge at the time of the drawing up of the Code of Criminal Examination.

On 26th December, 1790, M. Duport, on behalf of the committees on Legislation and Criminal Justice, introduced in the Assembly the draft bill upon the procedure by jurors. Its principal features must be sketched at this point; these are, summary examination before the officer of judicial police, at the canton; — district trial before the grand jury; — final trial and judgment before the criminal court of the department: such were the three phases through which the proceedings ran.

The justice of the peace was primarily the magistrate of detective police ("sureté") "par excellence."[1] He caused the appearance before him of those accused of crimes or misdemeanors by means of a *warrant for production* of the accused ("mandat d'amener") analogous to the warrant of the justice of the peace, executory, if need be, by the public authorities.[2] He

M. Bergasse had already said on 17th August, 1789: "The culprit should not be brought before any judges other than the justice of the peace" (*Buchez* and *Roux*, *op. cit.*, vol. II, p. 294).

[1] Tit. I, Art. 1.

[2] Tit. I, Arts. 2–4.

proceeded with the first steps of the information;[1] that is to say, the hearing of witnesses and drawing up of official reports. If, after interrogating the accused, he thought there was no ground for criminal prosecution, he liberated him; if not, he caused his imprisonment by virtue of a *warrant of arrest.*[2]

The justice of the peace acted either officially, or on the suggestion of private individuals. He acted officially in the case of capture in the act,[3] or, again, when a death was brought to his notice, the cause of which was unknown or suspicious, in which case it was his duty to visit the spot.[4] — Private individuals put him in action by means of the complaint or the civic denunciation. The complaint was the act of the injured party.[5] In that particular the terminology of the ancient law was preserved; but the share of the private individual was much more important than formerly. The justice of the peace was obliged to take the depositions of the witnesses produced by the complainant,[6] and to draw up, if need be, official reports upon his requisition. He was certainly not obliged in this case to issue the warrant of arrest, nor even that of production; he could, no doubt, refuse to summon the accused, or liberate him if he had summoned him. But the party complainant could demand from him "a document showing refusal";[7] and the former then had the right to submit the matter directly to the grand jury. The denunciation by a person not interested, being a civic duty, bore the name of "dénonciation civique." If the denouncer "signs and affirms his denunciation," it was the duty of the justice of the peace to proceed as in the case of a complaint, and the denouncer had the same recourse as the complainant.[8] If the denouncer refused to sign and affirm the denunciation, the justice of the peace was not bound to do anything, but he was entitled to prosecute officially if he thought proper. — The officers of the gendarmery exercised the functions of judicial police concurrently with the justice of the peace, except in cities where there were several justices of the peace.[9]

The cause went from the canton to the district. The grand jury sat there, the jail was there, and a permanent magistrate was there, called *director of the jury,* chosen by rotation every six months from among the judges of the district court. He took

[1] Tit. V, Art. 8; Tits. III and IV; Tit. IV, Art. 3.
[2] Tit. VIII, Arts. 5–7.
[3] Tit. IV.
[4] He was also required to secure the presence "of two active citizens," Tit. III, Arts. 2 and 3. This is a reminder of the "adjoints" of the Decree of 1789; and also of the procedure followed before the English coroner.
[5] Tit. V, Art. 1.
[6] Tit. V, Art. 6.
[7] Tit. V, Art. 20.
[8] Tit. VI, Art. 3.
[9] Tit. I.

the control of the case. He received the documents of the proceedings made out by the justice of the peace, inspected them, and even interrogated the prisoner in jail.[1] If he was of opinion that there was no occasion for prosecution, he submitted the matter, within twenty-four hours, to the district court, which pronounced upon that question after having heard the king's commissary. If he thought there was ground for prosecution, or if, contrary to his opinion, the court so determined, it became the duty of *the director* to draw up the "acte d'accusation" for presentation to the jury, as in the case of the *indictment* of the English procedure.[2] He could, in the meantime, go on with the examination.[3] If the eventual punishment was merely degrading, and sufficient bail was offered, he could grant the prisoner provisional liberty.[4]

If there was a civic denouncer or a complainant in the action, these rules underwent material modification. Provided this party presented himself within two days, the director of the jury no longer retained his full freedom of action. If he thought there were grounds for prosecution, he must act in concert with the party in drawing up the indictment; in case of disagreement, each drew up his own indictment, and the jury subsequently made their choice between the two. If the director of the jury thought, on the contrary, that there was no ground for prosecution, he could not, as formerly, have the question decided by the district court; but the party could, nevertheless, draw up his indictment alone.[5] Moreover, if the justice of the peace had refused to act, the complainant and the person who had affirmed his denunciation

[1] See "Instruction du 21 Octobre, 1791" upon the execution of the decree settling the procedure by jurors. "As the formality of the hearing of the accused within twenty-four hours is obligatory, and it is important to know if it has been complied with, the director of the jury should draw up an official report of it, which should contain the statements and answers of the accused. It is unnecessary to observe the old forms of interrogations, or to take the oath of the accused, that he will tell the truth; mere good sense shows the uselessness and inquity of such an oath, which places the accused between perjury and punishment. . . . The director of the jury should not allow himself to put any captious questions; he ought to hear the accused's free statement."

[2] Part II, Tit. I.

[3] Part II, Tit. I, Art. 16. "The witnesses who have not made their statement before the police officer shall make it before the director of the jury. These statements shall be received in writing before the witnesses are examined orally by the grand jury." Here also care is taken to insure that this examination is of quite another character from that formerly made. — Instructions as to the jury of 21st October: "If there are new witnesses who have not yet been heard, the director of the jury shall receive their depositions secretly, and they shall be transcribed by the clerk of court, not in the form observed under the Old Régime for the inquiries, but as mere statements designed to serve as information only."

[4] Part II, Tit. I, Arts. 30, 31.

[5] Part II, Tit. I, Art. 12.

could, respectively, on the "refusal stated" of the justice of the peace, "present their charges to the grand jury directly."[1] But all the indictments had to be submitted to the king's commissary, who put his "visa" on them; "the law authorises"; or his "veto"; "the law forbids"; but, in the latter case, the dispute was decided by the district court.[2]

The jury of accusation, consisting of eight jurors,[3] was presided over and instructed in its duties by the director of the jury; the documents of the proceeding were sent to him "with the exception of the written statements of the witnesses." — "First of all, the documents were read, then the witnesses produced were heard orally, as well as the party complainant or the party denouncing, if present."[4] All this took place with closed doors. Then the jurors, left alone by the director of the jury, and having for foreman "the oldest," deliberated and decided by a majority. The foreman then wrote at the foot of the indictment "there are grounds," or "there are no grounds," formulas synonymous with the English "found" or "not found." If the jury allowed the prosecution, the director of the jury issued "immediately an order of arrest against the accused, by virtue of which, if he has not been already arrested, he will be seized wherever he may be found and brought before the criminal court;"[5] or, again, in a proper case, liberation on bail was granted by the criminal tribunal, if it had not been already done.[6]

The matter then passed to the criminal tribunal established

[1] Part II, Tit. I, Art. 12.

[2] Part II, Tit. I, Art. 13. The investigation of the king's procurator is merely for the purpose of ascertaining whether the offense, in the event of its being proved, deserves corporal or degrading punishment. See Instructions as to the jury, of 21st October: "This opposition by the king's commissioner stops the presentation of the indictment to the jury if, besides, the director of the jury was of the same opinion as the king's commissioner; for in that case the party would be the sole judge of the nature of the offense; but the law allows the question to be then determined by the court, to whom the party, the king's commissioner, or the director of the jury may refer it. . . . It decides whether the offense is or is not of a nature deserving of corporal or degrading punishment;" in case of a negative decision, "the indictment is void, and the same judgment pronounces the release of the prisoner."

[3] Upon the method of constituting the jury of accusation, see Part II, Tit. X. "Every three months the syndic procurator of each district draws up a list of thirty citizens from among all the citizens in the district possessing the qualifications of electors. . . . Eight days before the day of the Assembly, the director of the jury causes the names of thirty citizens registered upon the list to be put into a vase, and in the centre of the courtroom, in presence of the public and of the king's commissioner, he causes the names of eight citizens to be drawn." — Instructions as to the jury.

[4] Part II, Tit. I, Art. 20.

[5] Part II, Tit. I, Art. 29.

[6] In case of a negative answer by the jury of accusation, the accused should be set at liberty, if he had been arrested.

in each department, composed of three judges and a president, whose duty it was to determine the punishment, while the jury decided upon the question of fact. Attached to this tribunal were also a public accuser and a king's commissary. The former, an elective functionary,[1] was charged with "the prosecution of offenses on indictments approved by the first jury."[2] He produced the witnesses for the prosecution,[3] explained the case and spoke for the prosecution.[4] He was, in reality, a public prosecutor; the complainant, moreover, had also the right to have his witnesses heard in support of the prosecution. — The king's commissary was a magistrate charged with seeing to the execution of the law and securing its application.[5] It was he who, in the case of an affirmative verdict, asked for the application of the punishment.[6]

The president of the criminal court interrogated the accused within twenty-four hours of his arrival at the court-house,[7] in presence of the public accuser, and notes of this interrogation were taken. He could, besides, continue the examination in a general way, hear new evidence produced by the public accuser, the private party, and even by the accused.[8] But it was understood that these written depositions were only to be used as information; they were neither read nor submitted to the jury.[9]

English tradition was not followed in regard to the constitution of the trial jury. A somewhat unsatisfactory system was contrived. Every citizen entitled to vote must be enrolled in a register kept for the purpose by the secretary-clerk of each district (Part II, Title XI, Art. 2). These entries, sent to the attorney-general-syndic of the department, constituted a general jury list, from which the said magistrate every three months chose two hundred names, which, after the choice had been approved by the director of the department, composed the session lists (Art. 6). On the 1st of every month, the president of the criminal court caused the list of the trial juries for the session which was to open

[1] Part II, Tit. II, Art. 5.
[2] Part II, Tit. IV, Art. 1.
[3] Part II, Tit. VI, Art. 12; Tit. VII, Art. 3.
[4] Part II, Tit. VII, Arts. 3, 18.
[5] Part II, Tit. V, Art. 1: "He must acquaint himself with the documents and proceedings and be present at the investigation and the judgment." — Art. 2: "The king's commissioner is always entitled to lodge with the judges all the requisitions he may deem proper, of which he shall be given an official certificate."
[6] Part II, Tit. VIII, Art. 5.
[7] Part II, Tit. VI, Art. 10.
[8] Part II, Tit. VI, Art. 12.
[9] Part II, Tit. VI, Arts. 11, 12; "These new depositions, as well as the old, will all be laid before the president, to serve as information only."

on the 15th to be made up. For this purpose, in presence of the king's commissary and of two municipal officers who took an oath of secrecy, he presented the list of two hundred jurors to the public prosecutor, who was entitled to exclude twenty without assigning cause. The remaining names were put into a box, and twelve trial jurors were drawn by lot. But the accused's right of challenge had to be taken into account. For this the list of twelve names was exhibited to him, and within twenty-four hours, he could challenge those composing it, which were replaced by lot (Art. 10). In this way he was entitled to make use of twenty peremptory challenges. This privilege exhausted, he could still challenge indefinitely, but only on assigning the reasons for his challenges, of the validity of which the criminal court were the judges. This fantastical system of successive and "out of presence" challenges was undoubtedly one of the mistakes which hampered the working of the jury at the outset.

The accused was at last brought before the criminal tribunal, composed of the magistrates we have mentioned and twelve jurors. There an oral and public, and very simple, procedure took its course. It is described in Titles VI, VII, and VIII of the second part of the Law of 1791, which fixed in a definite manner the rules for actions before the jury. These rules have been expanded and stated precisely by the "Code of Offenses and Punishments," and simplified by the "Code of Criminal Examination," but their broad features remain as they were traced in 1791. We shall not dwell upon the details, which will be found in the modern treatises upon criminal procedure; but it must be noted that the oral character of the procedure was most carefully and insistently specified. "The examination of the witnesses shall always be made orally and without writing out their depositions." [1] The only documents the jurors received were the indictment and the official reports, if there were any.[2] At the same time, the legislature expressly declared its intention to repudiate the system of legal proofs and to refer the matter to the personal conviction of the jurors alone. This was shown by the phraseology of the

[1] Part II, Tit. VII, Art. 3. *Cf.* Tit. V, Art. 16: "The witnesses can nevertheless be heard at the trial, although they have not been summoned or received to *depone preliminarily in writing.*" — "During the investigation, the jury and the judges may take note of what appears important to them, provided the discussion is not thereby interrupted" (Tit. VII, Art. 16).

[2] Instructions as to the jury. "They ought to examine the documents in the action, among which need not be included the written statements of the witnesses, which ought not to be submitted to the jury, but only the indictment, the official reports, and other such documents."

oath administered to them. "You swear . . . to give your decision according to the charges and the pleas in defense, and following your conscience and your personal conviction, with the impartiality and firmness proper in a free man."[1] Elsewhere it was said: "The accused shall be entitled to bring witnesses to attest that he is a man of honor and probity and of irreproachable conduct; the jurors shall give reasonable consideration to this testimony."[2]

English tradition was discarded in one important particular. In England, the judge, whose influence upon the jurors is very great, re-states at the conclusion of the argument the issues which must be solved. The French legislature certainly ordained such a statement;[3] but it did more; it provided from the outset, that the issues should be put to the jurors in writing, so that they had only to reply by "yes" or "no." This idea was a fertile one; a most ingenious mechanism was bound to result from it. After prolonged efforts to perfect the working of this tool, as delicate as it is certain, a happy precision was arrived at, which still grows more precise every day. The first principles were laid down in 1790. Montesquieu's idea, in particular, namely, to present to the jurors but one fact, a single fact at a time, was followed in practice. It was not obligatory, moreover, to follow the indictment alone in the stating of the issues. That might be imperfectly drawn or "have changed by the accused's defense and the proofs furnished by him." — "The impossibility of limiting the jurors strictly to the contents of the indictment without revolting injustice must be acknowledged. The law therefore ordains that, when they have found the commission of the offense and that the accused was guilty of its commission, they shall return a third equitable finding as to the particular circumstances of the fact, either to determine if the offense was committed wilfully or involuntarily, or with or without intent to injure, or pronounce in extenuation of the particular character of the offense."[4] But how are all these degrees to be treated? "Must they put to themselves in every case as many questions as

[1] Part II, Tit. VII, Art. 24.

[2] Part II, Tit. VII, Art. 14.

[3] Wise advice was given in this respect from the beginning. Instruction as to jurors: "The president of the court makes a statement of the case, reducing it to its simplest points. He specifies the principal proofs produced for or against the accused. This statement is intended to enlighten the jury, to concentrate its attention, and to guide its judgment, but it ought not to restrain its freedom. The jury owe to the judge respect and deference . . . but they do not owe him the sacrifice of their opinion, for which they are accountable only to their own consciences."

[4] Instruction as to the jury.

there are admissible degrees between wilful murder and lawful homicide? That would result in a useless and absurd complexity in the stating of the questions. . . . It will therefore be for the judge who superintends the procedure and who presides over and directs the course of the action, carefully to group the various issues relative to intent, to which the nature of the deed and of the charges could give rise, to be pointed out to the jury and its deliberation directed to these points. After having taken the opinion of the court upon the manner of putting the questions, he will put them in presence of the public, the accused, counsel, and jurors, to the last of whom he will submit them in writing, arranged in proper order for deliberation." [1]

The English traditional rule requiring the jury's decision to be unanimous was not adhered to. "But the opinion of three jurors ought always to be sufficient, in the accused's favor, either to decide that the fact is not certain, or to decide in his favor the questions put by the president relative to intent." [2] The theatrical spirit of the time was well shown in the way in which the jurors gave their opinions. One of the judges appointed by the president, the king's commissary, and the foreman of the jury met in the council chamber. There, each juror in succession, beginning with the foreman, "in the absence of each other," had to give his verdict, "putting his hand upon his heart." Each, then, as a check, deposited in a white or black box a ball of the same color, for each verdict. The boxes were opened in presence of the assembled jurors, the votes were counted, and the foreman of the jury announced the verdict in open court.[3] The judges then decided upon the terms of the punishment, beginning with the youngest and ending with the president.[4]

There was no appeal from the jurors' decision. That appears to be a universal characteristic of the jury in criminal matters. "The jurors' decision can never be subject to appeal. If, however, the court is unanimously of opinion that the jurors are mistaken, it will order three jurors to be added to the first twelve to give a verdict by four-fifths of the votes." [5] An appeal to the Court of Cassation was alone possible, either on behalf of the condemned, or on behalf of the king's commissary in the name of the law. It had to be lodged within three days; and in case of acquittal the commissary must act within twenty-four hours. The only grounds

[1] Instruction as to the jury. Law, Part II, Tit. VII, Arts. 20 and 21.
[2] Part II, Tit. VII, Art. 28.
[3] Arts. 23, 29, 30, 32, 33.
[4] Tit. VII, Art. 9.
[5] Part II, Tit. VIII, Art. 27.

for appeal were the omission of the forms prescribed on pain of nullity or the erroneous application of the law. In the case of quashing, a new trial began before a different criminal tribunal, unless there was merely error in the application of the law, in which case the first jury's verdict stood.[1]

We see that practically nothing of the ancient institutions remains. One main fact is that the institution of the public prosecutor suffered total destruction. Not only were the duties formerly fulfilled by the king's procurator uselessly shared between the king's commissary and the public accuser,[2] but the prosecution of crimes did not in reality belong to the latter at all. Undoubtedly, the law gave him "supervision over all the police officers of the department, whom he could admonish in case of negligence on their part, or even bring before the criminal tribunal for discipline;"[3] but he did not intervene personally until the prosecution had been already decreed — he only appeared in the same way as an advocate chosen after the commencement of the action. The accuser could prosecute only when an officer of judicial police was guilty of breach of office;[4] in any other case, on receipt of a denunciation he had to transmit it to the justice of the peace.[5] However, M. Duport, the reporter of the bill, congratulated himself on this result. "It is now by the decision of his fellow-citizens that he (the prisoner) is prosecuted. Society is about to intrust to a public officer the duty of exercising its rights and of prosecuting in its name. This officer, who will be the public accuser, ought not to be any of those who have already acted . . . such a man will be more considered, more formidable than the law itself . . . he will have the superintendence of all the police officers; but he will not be entitled in any way to supplant them in the exercise of their duties."[6]

[1] Part II, Tit. VIII, Art. 14 *et seq.*

[2] It was, besides, the application of a general system based upon an erroneous idea: "In England, the king is the sole executive power. The execution of the laws, once they are made in Parliament, belongs to him alone, and for that purpose he appoints executive officers, judges, administrators, fiscal officers. . . . In France, the king is merely the supreme head of the executive power: he does not appoint the executive officers for the interior, he merely makes use of their services; it is the country which chooses them for him, which puts them into the king's hands, to be employed by him. . . . The fundamental maxim of our government is that the executive arm of the monarch can never reach individuals except by the necessary medium of agents elected by the people. Now, this principle would be violated if the king's commissioners could accuse citizens." Duport, sitting of 26th December, 1790; Moniteur of the 27th.

[3] Part II, Tit. IV, Art. 5.

[4] Part II, Tit. IV, Art. 7.

[5] Part II, Tit. IV, Art. 2.

[6] Sitting of 26th December, 1790; Moniteur of 27th. It is certain that,

The right of prosecution was partially conferred on mere private individuals. The action of complainants and civic denunciators was incomparably more efficacious than that of the old civil action. Either could constrain the justice of the peace, if not to issue warrants, at least to begin an examination by taking depositions. They could, afterwards, of their own authority, cause the grand jury to take action. In all cases they took part in the drawing up of the indictment. Again, the power of the justice of the peace to proceed officially, not only in case of capture in the act or suspicious death, but even upon a mere unconfirmed denunciation, united in his person two qualifications which should have been kept separate: those of prosecutor and of examining magistrate.

The preparatory examination, which formerly took in nearly the whole of the action, was reduced to a mere trifle. It consisted merely of summary examination by the police officer, possible hearing of witnesses by the director of the jury, and interrogation of the accused by the president of the criminal tribunal. This fragmentary inquiry, at different hands, could neither be quite real nor quite complete. Finally, its characteristic of orality was absolute. The depositions were certainly taken in writing before the various examining magistrates, but their purpose was to serve merely for information; they were submitted neither to the grand jury nor to the trial jury; for that very reason, the public accuser, as well as the president of the criminal tribunal, had cognizance of them; but they were communicated neither to the accused nor to the counsel chosen by him, or officially appointed for him by the president at the time of the interrogation. The jury judged only according to what was said before them, and nothing of what was then said was written down.

§ 2. **Discussion of the Bill by the Constituent Assembly. Struggle between the Old and New Principles.** — This radical revolution in criminal procedure was not consummated, as we have said, without strenuous opposition. The foregoing analysis of the Law shows, of itself, how complete was the defeat of its opponents. It is no less interesting to recall the principal incidents of the discussion. This will show that, although the majority of those who opposed these innovations were magistrates imbued with the principles of the old law, they sometimes had supporters whom we are surprised to find fighting on their side.

having an elective character, the public accuser, master of the prosecution, would have been a formidable power; this was a mischievous circle.

Among those who opposed the bill were, first of all, the warm upholders of tradition, who did not hesitate to present as ideal the old procedure, ameliorated, and the Ordinance of 1670, corrected and amended. "M. Duport," said M. Mougin, "has seen everything from a philosopher's, and almost nothing from a magistrate's, point of view. First of all, I appeal to all who are acquainted with the principles of criminal law if the Ordinance of 1670, regulating the formalities of accusations and complaints, does not exhibit, after some few amendments, a perspective and a clearness in its principles, calculated to reassure society as to the protection of innocence and the detection of crime? And you have put into force the very amendments which that Ordinance required to attain perfection. The friends of humanity have witnessed with emotion the attainment of what was entreated by reason and justice. A counsel is granted, a thing the civil law has no right to refuse, because it is conceded by natural law. You have ordained that tutelary publicity, which can only be detrimental to ignorance and bad faith. You have proscribed that shameful prisoner's seat, the use of which ignominy dared to dispute with the pity which created it. The ferocious institution of torture also is no more, that impious remnant of the barbarous ages. Add to all these reforms, demanded by nature and humanity, the establishment of several jurors, following the method in use with the Romans, and you have done all that is possible for justice and humanity."[1] M. Rey spoke to the same effect at the sitting of 28th December, 1790; and the Abbé Maury reminded his hearers that the Ordinance of 1670 had governed France for upwards of a century and that it was proper that ineradicable traces of it should remain. But such proposals were nipped in the bud. The majority of the Assembly, in common with the majority of the country, ardently desired the jury, that institution which had grown with the growth of English liberty. The men of that time felt vaguely that here was an institution which formed a true distinguishing mark of free countries.

Upon certain matters of detail the opponents of the bill were sometimes better inspired. At the sitting of 28th December, M. Prugnon referred to the disappearance of the public prosecutor, and the great void thereby left. "Is there to be a public party charged with lodging complaints and prosecuting crimes?

[1] Sitting of 27th December, 1790; Moniteur of the 29th. This is what the speaker understood by the jury of ancient Rome: "The jury were not chosen for every individual crime. Ten or twelve citizens were appointed every year who performed the duties until the following year."

It seems to me of the highest importance in all the systems, that you should consider the utility of this officer, suppressed by your committee, who played such an essential part in the old criminal procedure; for it surely will not be claimed that his place is filled by the public accuser who is proposed to you and who will be charged with almost useless functions. You must be the judges whether it is necessary to call upon all the people, as your committee proposes to do, to publicly denounce their fellow-citizens." [1]

The choice of police officers was also criticised, from various quarters. These were, as we know, the justices of the peace and the officers of gendarmery. M. Prugnon attacks the former. He is indignant "at seeing the right to arrest a citizen without preliminary formality intrusted to a man on whom it was not thought desirable to confer the trial of matters above fifty livres." He remarks that the English justices of the peace, taken as a model, are quite different types of personages from those of France. "The English justices of the peace do not resemble ours; not only do they receive no salaries, not only is their jurisdiction more extensive, not only are they chosen from among the most enlightened citizens, but they must have an income of £100." [2] — The same speaker also deals with the officers of gendarmery. It is wished "to combine in the same hands, namely, in those of an officer of the marshalcy, the two most horrible despotisms, judicial despotism and military despotism." M. Mougin asks "if any one believes it to be prudent to entrust to a marshalcy trooper or a justice of the peace the terrible right to issue a warrant of arrest, or, what is the same thing, a warrant of production." [3] Robespierre, finally, makes a protest to the same effect: "I am at a loss to know in what respect the Old Régime was more defective than this. It is almost enough to make us regret even the 'prévôtal' jurisdiction, less odious in many respects, and which had all the appearance of a political monster, precisely because it put in the same hands a civil magistracy and the military power." [4] In spite of all, that part of the bill devoted to the police of safety was retained. The question of ascertaining to whom these functions should be intrusted had been reserved to begin with. These Articles were subsequently adopted in their original form.

But the keenest strife centred upon two points of vital impor-

[1] Moniteur of 29th December, 1790.
[2] Sitting of 28th December, 1790.
[3] Moniteur of 29th December, 1790. [4] *Ibid.*

tance. Here the adversaries of the bill appeared at first to have the upper hand. By a combination excellent in appearance, they wished to add the benefit of new principles to the old practices. Depositions in writing would continue to be taken, and these documents would be submitted to the jurors, who, however, would hear the witnesses testify orally; precise documents would thus come to the aid of their personal memories, sometimes evanescent. This procedure permitted an easy review of criminal actions; and the Abbé Maury exclaimed, in the course of the debate, referring to a very celebrated case: "If we had not had the written procedure, Calas could not have been rehabilitated." [1] M. Rey stated the undeniable fact, that the written procedure renders the task of the counsel for the defense easier, and their aid more efficacious.[2] The law was to determine what proofs must be brought together to warrant a condemnation; but the judges should never, whatever the charges might be, condemn an accused contrary to their personal conviction.

These ideas and proposals were brilliantly debated on opposite sides of the Assembly. "Your committee," said M. Mougin, "abjures written proofs; everything is done orally; the judgment alone will be written, the proof will not be written . . . that is to say, an accused will be judged on speculation and upon a mere rough estimate. And if the juror and the judges are mistaken, the accused will be without hope, as without recourse." [3] — "To intrust the depositions to memory alone, is like writing upon water . . . the committee wishes to transport us back to the ages before the invention of writing . . . it must be that since the 'Hôpital' all our legislators have been raving." — "If legal proofs are no longer necessary to establish the guilt of an accused, everything must become conjectural, and the life and honor of the citizens are brought before a court of conjectures . . . the proof will lie in the individual perception of each juror." M. Prugnon thus expresses himself at the sitting of 3d January, 1791.[4] Next day M. Rey, M. Goupil, and Robespierre, whom we find among the opponents of the bill, speak to the same effect. "The law," says Robespierre, "has laid down certain rules for the investigation into, and the admission of, proofs, rules without the observance of which the judges would not be entitled to condemn, whatever their personal conviction may be . . . it is necessary to establish

[1] Sitting of 17th January, 1791; Moniteur of the 19th.
[2] Sitting of 28th December, 1790; Moniteur of the 29th.
[3] Sitting of 27th December, 1790; Moniteur of 29th.
[4] Moniteur of 4th January.

undeniably that these have been followed, and the method of doing so is by writing . . . the confidence due to legal proofs must be united with that warranting the judge's personal conviction." He makes the following motion: "1st, The depositions shall be reduced to writing; 2d, The accused cannot be declared convicted in the absence of legal proofs; 3d, The accused cannot be condemned on legal proofs, if they are contrary to the knowledge and the personal conviction of the judges." [1]

The man who spoke most authoritatively in this direction was Thouret. At the sitting of 5th January, without, however, saying anything about the doctrine of legal proofs, he proceeded to maintain the advantages of the written procedure combined with the oral testimony of the witnesses. This he did with great moderation, sometimes quoting striking anecdotes, and, on concluding, he proposed an amendment in the following terms: "The Assembly ordains that the criminal examination and procedure shall be conducted publicly, in the presence of judges and jurors, that it shall be written and immediately put before the jurors to receive their reasonable consideration." This speech made a great impression upon the Assembly, which voted for its printing, and the debate was even adjourned for several days to allow the representatives to reflect upon these difficult questions.

How were the supporters of the bill able to repulse these attacks? How did they come to refuse to accept the written procedure and the system of legal proofs, as it was presented to them, that is, hitherto apparently harmless and only beneficial? Such conduct might appear inexplicable; however, it must be acknowledged, although these men had the logic of reasoning against them, they had in their favor the logic of facts. They sometimes found it difficult to make their ideas understood, but they felt very plainly an incompatibility between the old method of trial and the new, that the two systems could not be mingled, and that to import into the trial by jurors the complexities of writing and the learned theory of legal proofs, would be to impair an admirable institution, under color of ameliorating it; this was a graft the young tree could not bear. This was maintained by Duport, Chabroud,[2] Baumetz,[3] and Pétion.[4] "The institution of the jury," said Duport, "is a primitive one, which still bears the impress of its rude origin, and breathes lustily of nature and instinct. We do not speak of it

[1] Sitting of 4th January, 1791; Moniteur of the 5th.
[2] Sitting of 3d January; Moniteur of the 4th.
[3] Sitting of 4th January; Moniteur of the 5th.
[4] Sitting of 17th January; Moniteur of the 19th.

enthusiastically, or love it passionately, but a strong and healthy heart is necessary to appreciate all its beauty, or perhaps, even, to employ it at all. . . . The pleasing element in the establishment of the jury is that, with it, everything is decided by force of honesty and good faith, a simplicity much preferable to that useless, melancholy mass of subtleties and forms, called, down to this day, justice." [1] Later on, in a more precise discussion, he demonstrated how the written procedure could not be combined with the oral procedure. The collection of all the testimony in writing would indefinitely prolong the actions; the tired jurors would lose interest in an action the course of which they could no longer follow; when they returned to the chamber of their deliberations, instead of taking away with them a sufficiently clear impression to dictate their judgment, they would get lost in the inspection of a voluminous procedure, a task beyond their capacity. "Some have thought that it would be very advantageous to combine the written proof and the oral proof, and thus to have the benefit of both systems; but that is impossible. . . . Arrived in their chamber, the jury would read the depositions, weigh them and compare them, like the judges of the Tournelle, and the result would be, as I have said, bad judges instead of good jurors." [2]

The same speakers maintained that there was an equal incompatibility between the institution of the jury and the system of legal proofs, even construed in favor of the accused. Here the matter was not so clear. It was no doubt clear that the minute and complex theory elaborated by traditional practice, which had never found a place in the law, was too delicate a tool to put into the hands of jurors; but it was a different matter with regard to certain very simple rules, such as that which required two eye-witnesses for a condemnation. That rule was, in certain cases, observed in England in the procedure by jury; and to-day, still, the theory of proofs plays a great part before the English jury.[3] There was, however, every reason to reject the system "in toto." In England, in effect, the rules of evidence in criminal cases are really only a series of rather elastic maxims established by judicial practice, and the observance of which is imposed upon the jurors by the president of the assizes, by virtue of his high authority. To settle by a law the evidence necessary for condemnation would have been to pass a delusive measure. The jury, not being re-

[1] Sitting of the 26th December; Moniteur of the 27th.
[2] Sitting of 4th January; Moniteur of the 5th.
[3] *Blackstone*, Book IV, chap. 27; see *Mittermaier*, "Traité de la procédure criminelle en Angleterre," *Chauffard's* translation, § 20.

quired to assign a ground for its decisions, would always have been able to evade it; and it would, above all, have had the effect of furnishing the jurors with a convenient pretext for unjustifiable acquittals.

When, on 17th January, 1791, the Assembly resumed the debate, a change had already taken place in the members' opinions. A vehement speech by Maury, defending the written procedure, was no doubt still listened to. Attacking Anglomania, he asserted that the reason the English procedure was oral was, that in the 1200s, when the jury was instituted, no one was able to write. But Tronchet, representing the spirit of compromise, proposed a middle course, a system less pronounced than that of Thouret. "The procedure shall be oral, but the accuser and the accused may require an epitomized official report of the actions." Arrived at this point the cause of Duport and his supporters might be said to be won; Tronchet's motion had really no bearing on the question, and was therefore rejected, and the bill was definitely adopted in the form in which it had been presented.

Such was the work of the Constituent Assembly in regard to criminal procedure. To pass judgment upon it, it must, we believe, be divided into two parts. In regard to the proceedings before the trial jury, definite rules were laid down. The Assembly had endowed France forever with this magnificent institution, which has since spread throughout Europe with the representative régime. It is one of the great benefits for which we must be eternally grateful to it. But in respect to the arrest and preliminary examination, always necessary in these serious matters, the Assembly had disorganized the old institutions due to French genius, and had substituted for them an imperfect and inadequate mechanism, which could never work in a satisfactory manner. It had mixed up the public action and the civil action, overturning that equitable distinction, elaborated in the protracted evolution of the ancient law. After long hesitation, the institution of the public prosecutor was again taken up. The Assembly had left this difficult problem unsolved; how was the preliminary examination, necessarily written, to be welded with the necessarily oral procedure by jurors?

The Law of 1791 being as we have described it, it would seem as if nothing at all remained of the old procedure. We may, however, find some traces of it left by the Ordinance of 1670. The reception of complaints by a police officer (Tit. V, Arts. 2–5) is, in respect to its details, copied almost verbatim from Title III of the Ordinance. For Title IX, on Contumacy, a part of the provisions of the Ordinance had been borrowed, particularly the proceedings ending in the verdict of contumacy and the resolvable character of the sentence.[1] But there again the jury made its appearance, although the procedure was not oral in the true sense of the word: "the depositions of the witnesses taken in writing shall be read to the jurors, who shall be drawn by lot." — The provisions on forgery are an echo of those of the Ordinance of d'Aguesseau. Finally, in its Title XIII, the Decree repeated certain precepts of the Ordinance of 1670.[2] These are but slight vestiges, but we note them here. Although there are only broken links here, we shall find, later, important fragments of the chain.

The Law of 29th September is not the only one devoted to criminal procedure passed by the Constituent Assembly; it had previously organized the municipal and correctional police in the Law of 19–22 July, 1791, adopted almost without discussion on the report of Desmeuniers.[3] Here, concurrently with the initiative of the citizens, the Law organized the action of a kind of public prosecutor. "Art. 44. The prosecution of these offenses shall be made by the procurator of the commune or his deputies if any such there be, or by lawyers empowered to that effect by the municipality." Nobody, however, appears to have had the right of direct citation before the correctional tribunal; the pursuers must make their denunciation to the justice of the peace, who, having summoned the prisoner before him by a warrant of production, remanded him, if there was cause, before the tribunal (Arts. 45 and 57). The examination took place in public court (Art. 58); a summarized official report of the action was drawn up by the clerk of court; and appeal to the district court was permissible.[4] In municipal police matters, the prosecution took place on the petition of the procurator of the commune or of private individuals, and the court took action by virtue of a direct summons issued in the name of these persons (Art. 35).

§ 3. **The Code of Offenses and Punishments of 3d Brumaire, year IV.** — The Law of 1791 was not destined to last much longer than that of 1789, for which it had been substituted; it had to yield place to the Code of Offenses and Punishments of 3d Bru-

[1] Contrary to the provisions of the Ordinance, the law for the first time treats alike, in the proceedings for contumacy, the escaped prisoner and the fugitive who has never been arrested (Art. 14).

[2] See Tit. XIII of the Law of 1791, Arts. 4, 5; and Tit. XIII, Ord. 1670, Arts. 6, 25.

[3] Moniteur of 6, 7, 8, 9, 13, 14, and 21 July, 1791.

[4] Law of 16th August, 1790, Tit. XI, Arts. 2 and 6.

maire, year IV. It was not invariably respected during the time of its rule. This is not the place to speak of the revolutionary tribunals and procedures, which proceeded to erect, alongside of the common law, a frightful exceptional system of law; still, it is unquestionable that numerous illegalities crept into the ordinary procedure.[1] But the forms introduced by the Law of 1791 were, none the less, looked upon at that period as a completed institution, and it was not for its destruction, but for its perfection, that the Convention took up the work of the Constituent Assembly.

The special purpose, in compiling the new Code, was to have a work at once synthetic and detailed, as distinguished from the prior laws. It was to embrace the procedure in regard to misdemeanors and contraventions as well as crimes. The Convention, on 3d Floréal, year II, commissioned Cambacérès and Merlin to prepare a general work upon the legislation as a whole. Merlin devoted himself in particular to criminal legislation, and at the end of eighteen months, he presented to the Convention the Code of Offenses and Punishments, unfinished, but comprising 646 Articles, the first 598 and the 646th of which were devoted to criminal procedure. The Assembly, on the eve of breaking up, passed it on trust and without debate. Here preliminary labors were lacking. As documents they are limited to this short report by Merlin: "By a Decree of 23d Fructidor, you commanded your commission of eleven to present to you a draft 'Code of police of safety and correctional police' adapted to the Constitution, and in consonance with the judicial organization. In devoting itself to the carrying out of this Decree, your commission of eleven thought that, the better to fulfil your wishes, it ought to extend the scope of its labors, and propose to you a general recasting of all the laws passed since the beginning of the Revolution, to regulate and direct the prosecution and punishment of offenses of all kinds. You already perceive the innumerable advantages which ought to result from such a work. The maintenance of the republican Constitution, accepted by the French nation, is your desire as well as your duty. The most important steps to attain that end are the repression of anarchy, the establishment of the reign of law, the guarantee in a thoroughly efficient

[1] See the Law of 22d Vendémiaire, year IV, forbidding any police officer to bring before the director of the jury any citizen for an act not provided for and specified in the criminal laws, and declaring null all indictments drawn up on account of such acts. *Cf. Taine*, "Les origines de la France contemporaine." The Revolution. Vol. II, pp. 184, 251, 255, and 329.

way of the safety of person and property; they are, in other words, to give to the police and the courts of judicature all possible power of action and elasticity, and this you can only accomplish by simplifying and classifying in a clear and methodical order the innumerable regulations proper for the guidance of magistrates in the search for and the repression of offenses. There is no worse state than that of a government whose magistrates do not know, or are liable to know only imperfectly, what their duties are; but, that is the position in which our public functionaries charged with the repression of offenses find themselves, owing to the multitude and confusion of our criminal laws. That obstacle, however, you can very easily remove. All that is required is to give the nation a sufficient Code of Offenses and Punishments, and it is the draft of such a Code which we now offer for your inspection. Begun eighteen months ago, in pursuance of the Decree which ordered the classification and recasting of the laws promulgated by three representative assemblies, this draft has required much research, long study, laborious work, and it is not yet as complete as its title would seem to indicate."[1]

The Code of Brumaire, year IV, was really the work of Merlin, a prodigious task for one man. And it exhibits a character in strict conformity with its origin. It would be difficult to find a composition with parts forming a more harmonious whole. We feel that the backing and filling of parliamentary commissions has had no share in this, and that the brain of a capable jurisconsult is responsible for this comprehensive law. No law could be more punctilious and minute; it increases the safeguards of the defense, and traces step by step the path which ought to be followed; but at the same time it unconscionably multiplies the protecting formalities, so that the magistrate can make no progress in the midst of nullities, ready to bar his way. No law has ever regulated more logically the questions for the jury, and that part of the Code of Brumaire is no less ingenious than the delicate and learned composition of the Roman Formulæ; but the jurors, still more than the magistrate we have mentioned, are bound to find themselves at a loss before this over-learned apparatus, before these really complicated simplifications.[2] We know that this theoretical

[1] Sitting of 30th Vendémiaire (Journal des Débats, No. 1124, pp. 458–459).

[2] See Arts. 373–379. This is, as we know, the system of specific issues carried to extremes. In reality, the Code of Brumaire made little innovation on this point. As elsewhere, the precepts included by the constituents in their Instruction as to the jury of 21st October, 1791, were incor-

masterpiece was found to be exceedingly defective in practice; this admirable machinery had been conceived without taking the inevitable friction into account. But it is not from that point of view we would study the Code of Brumaire; we must, above all, find out if it absolutely continues the tendency of the Law of 1791, discarding to the same extent the rules of the old French law. There was no change in the broad features; but important alterations were made in the details. Some of the excessive principles affirmed in the Law of 1791 were somewhat palliated, and, upon certain points, a partial return to ancient tradition was noticeable.

We find one distinction in the introductory articles of the Code of Brumaire, a fundamental axiom of the ancient law, abolished by the Law of 1791, the distinction of the public action from the civil action. — "Art. 5: The object of the public action is to punish injuries to social order. It is essentially a function of the people. It is exercised in their name by functionaries appointed for that purpose. — Art. 6: The object of the civil action is reparation for the damage caused by the offense. It belongs to those who have suffered the damage. — Art. 8: The civil action may be prosecuted at the same time and before the same judges as the public action, or separately." These are, almost verbatim, Articles 1 and 3 of our Code of Criminal Examination, but the same thing was said under the rule of the Ordinance, and in the "Idée de la justice criminelle," for example, with which Jousse prefaces his Commentary, we find the distinction expressed in identical terms.[1] From that time, as a matter of fact, the popular accusation, instituted by the Law of 1791, disappeared. The rights of private individuals in the prosecution are, no doubt, still very important. The civic denunciation remains in the Code of Brumaire with all its effectiveness (Arts. 87–93). The denunciators and the complainants no doubt still participate in the drawing up of the indictment (Arts. 224–227).[2] But we know that now the private party acted merely for the purpose of obtaining damages (Art. 430); this leading principle was clearly laid down, that the action for penal satisfaction belongs only to the people and

porated in that law. We pass over the details, which are to be found in all the treatises upon criminal procedure.

[1] Page xxiii: "In our practice two classes of persons concur in the punishment of crimes: First, the private prosecutor, who claims reparation for the trespass committed against him, and his damages; Second, the public prosecutor, who prosecutes the punishment of the crime and the sentence to the punishment it merits."

[2] It appears, however, as we shall state later on, that the private prosecutor can no longer directly put the jury of accusation in action; he must address himself to the director of the jury.

the functionaries chosen by them, a principle which, still obscure in application, is subsequently to bear fruit; it contains the germs of the reconstitution of the public prosecutor.

The Code of Brumaire retains the officers of judicial police instituted in 1791, the justices of the peace and the officers of gendarmery; but it adds to the list the police commissaries and the wardens of fields and forests. For the first time, the directors of the jury, who, down to that time, were merely examining magistrates in the second degree, could, in certain cases, prosecute crimes and take cognizance directly (Arts. 21, 140, and 142). The law established a certain hierarchy among the police commissaries and the wardens (Arts. 2, 5–47). They still confused in their hands the prosecution and the examination; they acted "either upon an official denunciation, or upon a civic denunciation, or a complaint, or officially." The denunciator who signed his civic denunciation and affirmed that it was not dictated by any personal interest, thereby compelled even the police officer to issue a warrant of production (Art. 90), but he could not directly put the grand jury in action. As for the complaint, it obliged the justice of the peace to hear the witnesses produced, but that was all. This magistrate could refuse to proceed further. In case of refusal, the complainant could no longer, as formerly, move the grand jury to action. He could only appeal to the director of the jury (Arts. 98 and 147). This provision, again, recalled a principle of ancient law, namely, that the judge is not bound by the complaint.

The chief officer of judicial police was always the justice of the peace. He performed the most important part of the preliminary examination; for the results at which he arrived were subsequently obligatory on the director of the jury.[1] The Law of 1791 was exceedingly brief regarding this examination; the Code of Offenses and Punishments, on the contrary, goes very fully into details. Articles 102 to 131, devoted to this subject, are grouped under the headings of "official reports," of "hearing of witnesses," and of "documents of conviction." Many of them were subsequently to pass, with slight alterations, into the Code of Criminal Examination. The rules as to the official reports and the hearing of witnesses were a strangely perfected imitation of Titles IV, V, and VI

[1] Art. 242: "The director of the jury has no right to investigate whether, in a proceeding brought by an officer of the judicial police, relative to an offense entailing, by its nature, corporal or degrading punishment, the circumstances or the proofs are or are not serious enough to determine upon a prosecution; and he cannot, on that pretext, refuse to draw up the indictment."

of the Ordinance of 1670. The testimony of the witnesses was, as formerly, reduced to writing on a separate cahier. The witnesses were heard separately and apart, but the new law ordained that, if the accused was already under arrest, the deposition should be taken in his presence (Art. 115); and if he was not arrested until afterwards, the justice of the peace, before interrogating him, should grant him a perusal of the depositions taken, without giving him a copy (Art. 116). These precautions already indicate that writing is in future to play a more important rôle in the procedure than in the past.

The warrants were the subject of Articles 36 to 80. The Law of 1791 recognized but two, that to bring the accused before the court (" d'amener "), and the writ of attachment; it did not, in repressive matters, allow of citation pure and simple, analogous to the summonses of the civil procedure, showing itself, in that respect, more severe than the Ordinance, which, along with the decree of arrest, placed not only the personal citation, but the decree of summons to be heard. The Code of Brumaire introduced a new warrant, in the nature of a simple citation, that of *appearance;* but its use was very restricted. The warrant for production or to cause to appear (" d'amener ") was always the first to be issued; but when the accused had obeyed this warrant, if the offense was punishable " by a fine above the equivalent of three days' work " the justice of the peace "ordered the accused to appear on a specified day before the director of the grand jury."

The case passed, as formerly, from the justice of the peace to the director of the jury; that magistrate, chosen by rotation every three months from among the judges of the district court (Arts. 171, 211), at the same time held the position of president of the police correctional court. He carried the examination that had been commenced to its completion. He interrogated the accused within twenty-four hours of his arrival at the departmental prison, and caused a note of his replies to be made. He could also hear new witnesses, but on this occasion the hearing did not take place in the presence of the accused. The law provided that the director of the jury " should take their statements *secretly* and have them written down by the clerk of court " (Art. 225). That done, after having stated that the procedure was in order, he issued an order (" de renvoi ") to remand the accused either to the court of correctional police, or before the grand jury (Arts. 219, 220). All these ordinances must, on pain of nullity, be preceded by the conclusions of the commissary of the executive power, and within three days an abstract of them must be delivered to the public accuser. As we already know, the director of the jury could not issue an order of "not found" based upon the insufficiency of the charges, when the process had been transmitted to him by an officer of the judicial police.[1] For the moment no recourse against these orders was possible.

The director of the jury must also decide upon requests for provisional liberty. According to the principles laid down by the Law of 1791, the Code of Brumaire decided that setting at liberty was a matter of right whenever the eventual punishment was merely degrading or correctional, subject always to the bond of a solvent bondsman, who must deposit 3000 livres (Art. 222). If a crime involving afflictive punishment was concerned, provisional liberty was never allowed. It was either a matter of right or it was not. The powers of the director of the jury were then completed and detailed by the Code of Offenses and Punishments. The examining judge, who, later on, was to be distinguished from the director of the jury, was already designated. Some features of the new plan are borrowed from the old law; the hearing of witnesses secretly, for example, and the conclusions of the commissary of the government, prior to the orders.

After the order "de renvoi," sending the accused before the grand jury, the director of the jury drew up the indictment, the private party participating under the same conditions as before (Arts. 226–230); and he immediately communicated it to the commissary of the executive power, who put his "visa" on it (Art. 230). The procedure before the grand jury, as set out in the Code, was not altered. The director of the jury explained to the jurors their duties, and read to them a long instruction, the text of which has passed into the Code of Criminal Examination. Then the commissary of the executive power read the documents of the procedure, with the exception of the depositions and the interrogations; the witnesses and the party complainant were heard.

If the jury decided that there were grounds for prosecution, the director issued an order of arrest against the accused (unless he had been admitted to bail[2]), by virtue of which he was conducted

[1] No doubt he could decide that there was no ground of prosecution, when he was invoked by the party complainant, in appealing from the refusal to act opposed by the justice of the peace (Art. 98), or when, by exception, he had been able spontaneously to begin the prosecution.

[2] In this case, the director issued an order enjoining the accused to present himself before the criminal court at all the steps of the proceedings, and to remain in the place where the court sits. (Art. 257.) The arraignment did not terminate the provisional freedom.

to the court-house. There he was notified of the order of arrest and the indictment (Art. 259). From that time the action was carried on before the criminal court. There was little change in the composition of the criminal court. "It is composed of a president, a public accuser, four judges taken from the civil court, the commissary of the executive power, attached to the same tribunal, a deputy specially appointed for him by the executive directory for service in the criminal court, and a clerk of court" (Art. 226). The public accuser did not intervene, as in the past, until after the arraignment (Art. 278); although he had the superintendence of the various officers of the judicial police, he did not have the direct prosecution (Art. 283). However, he could, henceforth, receive denunciations and complaints, not only from the various authorities, but also from private citizens (Art. 281): "he transmits them to the officers of judicial police and sees that they are followed." Was this a survival of the system in which the king's procurator was specially charged to receive the denunciations? The commissary of the executive power still retained his other function of public prosecutor; he made the requisitions by virtue of the law (Art. 293).

The president of the criminal court interrogated the accused within twenty-four hours after his arrival at the court-house, and the official report of the interrogation had to be "added to the documents" (Art. 315). The public accuser, the private party, and the accused were entitled to a hearing of new witnesses before him. It was only then, contrary to the Law of 1791, that the regularity of the proceedings was solemnly verified. The commissary wrote upon the indictment the words, "the law authorizes" or "the law forbids," and it was the president's duty to assemble the court within twenty-four hours "to decide in court upon the legality or illegality either of the warrant of arrest, or the examination" (Art. 326). If a nullity was discovered, the court ordered matters to be taken up anew at the point of the earliest null document.

The Code of Brumaire dealt minutely and at length with the proceedings before the trial jury. It was the development of institutions unknown to the old law, and it gradually became precise and regularized, without borrowing anything from a legal system which had never had a jury. What place did the Code make for the written procedure in this final stage of the action? The Law of 1791 had pushed to an extreme the fear of seeing writing insinuate itself into the procedure by jurors. While maintaining firmly the principle of *orality*, the new law was less exclusive. Not only had the preparatory and written examination increased in importance; but a place was made in the trial for the production of these writings. Until then these documents had only been communicated to the public accuser, who alone gathered information from them; henceforth, they are communicated to the accused, who, by their means, with the aid of his counsel, can bring together the elements of his defense; a plan of defense was as possible as a plan of attack. The texts are precise. Article 319 says, speaking of the depositions taken by the president of the criminal court: "They shall be communicated to the public accuser and to the accused on pain of nullity of all subsequent proceedings." And Article 320 adds: "The accused, after his interrogation, receives in the same way, and under the same sanction, a copy of the other documents of the procedure. This copy is delivered to him gratis by the clerk of court." Some of the depositions were already known to the accused; those taken by the justice of the peace had been read to him; but he was ignorant of the contexts of those collected secretly by the director of the jury. This written procedure was, to a certain extent, to figure in the trial. Articles 365 and 366 state in effect: "Article 365; No written deposition of witnesses not present in court can be read to the jurors." "Article 366; As to written statements which the witnesses present have made, and written notes of the interrogations to which the accused has been subjected before the police officer, the director of the jury, and the president of the criminal court, nothing but what is necessary to bring to the notice, either of the witnesses or of the accused, the variations, contradictions, and differences which may be found between what they say before the jurors and what they said previously, can be read in the course of the trials." Finally, in pursuance of Article 382, the president puts before the jurors "all the documents of the action, with the exception of written statements of the witnesses and written interrogations of the accused." Such was the combination by which Merlin had thought to utilize the preliminary examination in the oral procedure. It was a wise compromise, and it has turned out that these rules have been almost definitive; these provisions, somewhat modified, have passed into the Code of Criminal Examination.

The doctrine of moral proofs was maintained with more firmness than ever. A long instruction, designed chiefly to bring them to the notice of the jurors, was required to be read to them by the president and posted conspicuously in the jury room. The method of composing the trial jury, the system of challenges (Arts. 502–512), the majority by which the verdict should be rendered, and the mode in which the jurors gave their opinion, and finally the appeal to quash, remained very nearly as they were in the Law of 1791.

In the procedure for contumacy, the Code of Offenses and Punishments, like the Law of 1791, to a certain extent reflected the provisions of the old law. Although there were jurors, the witnesses were not heard; their written depositions were read (Art. 471). The appearance of the condemned within the prescriptive period of twenty years *ipso facto* extinguished the judgment, and the proceedings went on in common form, subject at that time to the admission of an exception to the principle prohibiting the reading to the jury of the depositions of absent witnesses. "Article 477. The written depositions of witnesses who have died during his (the contumax's) absence shall be read to the jurors, who will give them reasonable consideration, always bearing in mind that the written proofs do not alone control their decisions, but are to be used only informatively."

The court of correctional police was composed, according to the Code of Brumaire, "of the director of the jury, who presided, and two justices of the peace." It took office either by virtue of the order of "renvoi" of the director of the jury after preliminary examination, or of the direct citation of the injured party, who thus acquired a new right. This citation must invariably be previously indorsed ("visé") by the director of the jury, who had to assure himself that he had before him a correctional offense (Arts. 180–182). Appeal, always possible, was taken to the criminal court (Art. 198). The right of appeal belonged to the condemned, the civil party, the commissary of the executive power, and the public accuser of the department. The majority of these rules, as well as those settling the procedure either in the first instance, or on appeal, have passed into the Code of Criminal Examination. The municipal police court was composed of the justice of the peace and two assessors (Art. 151); the prosecution took place either at the request of the commissary of the executive power attached to the municipal commission, or at that of the injured party. The examination always took place in open court; there was no appeal.

The Code of Offenses and Punishments had really made few alterations in the rules laid down by the Law of 1791. An unquestionable tendency, however, existed in it to make the preliminary examination, secret and written, the important prelude to the proceedings before the jury. Very soon a further step was destined to be taken. France, wounded and weary, lost her interest in the liberty for which she had suffered. By a violent reaction, she returned to the principle of authority. She then turned her eyes towards the institutions of the ancient monarchy; and little was lacking to put the Ordinance of 1670, almost as it had been amended by the legislators of 1789, into its old place among our laws.

CHAPTER III

THE LAWS OF THE YEAR IX

§ 1. **Law of 7th Pluviôse, Year IX. The Magistrates of Detective Police. Public Prosecutor Reconstituted. Changes in Examination.** — Criminal procedure, as organized by the Code of Brumaire, year IV, was destined very soon to undergo radical changes. In practice it had shown itself ineffectual for repression. This was partly due to the enfeeblement of the prosecution and the preliminary examination, but it was due principally to the environment in which the institution of the jury did its work at the outset. Perverted by political passions, powerless to cope with the brigandage which spread over a whole section of France, its destruction in the terrible crisis which shook the country at that time was assured. To the desire for progress succeeded an overwhelming need of rest, and the difficulties of the present well-nigh gave the victory to the past.

An early amendment of the rules of criminal procedure was brought about by the Constitution of the 22d Frimaire, year VIII. It combined the duties of the public accuser and those of the commissary of the executive power attached to the criminal court; and the functionary to disappear was he who took his title by election.[1] The old office of public prosecutor appeared in its entirety at the hearings in the criminal courts; but it was of more importance still to reconstitute it fundamentally, and hand over to it the prosecution; and that was the work of the Law of 7th Pluviôse of the year IX.

This Law did more. It at the same time reorganized the preliminary examination, following a type which bore a strong re-

[1] Const. of 22d Frimaire, Art. 63. The Law of 27th Ventôse, Art. 35, allowed of the appointment of a deputy to this commissioner, in those towns where the government thought it beneficial.

semblance to the old procedure, and materially altered the proceedings before the grand jury. "The dominant idea of the bill," said Thiessé, chairman for the bill in the Tribunate, "is the idea of a public prosecuting party and an examining judge, with a distinct distribution of their duties." [1] It created in each arrondissement deputy governmental commissaries, true state's attorneys, appointed by the First Consul and revocable at will (Art. 24); they were deputies of the commissary, in the same sense that the king's attorneys had formerly been deputies of the attorney-general.

They were charged not only with the search for, but with the prosecution of, all correctional police offenses and all crimes (Art. 1). It was, henceforth, their duty to receive denunciations and even complaints (Art. 3). The justices of the peace and officers of the county police still retained the right to receive them also, but these officials were placed under deputies' orders, and so became mere assistants of the public prosecutor (Art. 4); a rôle they have retained ever since.

The power of arrest was the subject of new rules. The justices of the peace and officers of the county police could have the accused seized in three cases: capture in the act, accusation by public rumor (Art. 4), and in the case of an offense entailing afflictive punishment, provided there were sufficient presumptions.[2] But the agency ordering the arrest was bound to have the accused brought before the deputy with the least possible delay. The deputy then issued a warrant of commitment ("de dépôt") against the accused and had him imprisoned in the departmental prison (Art. 9). He had also received the complaints and official reports, collected or drawn up by his assistants, the police officers.

This was a new creation, which certainly gave the public prosecutor a power he never had before. The barrier said to have been erected between the examination and the prosecution was lowered for him. All the documents found their way into his hands and he ordered the detention pending trial. But, as a counterbal-

[1] Sitting of the Tribunate of 27th Ventôse, year IX ("Archives parlementaires de 1800 à 1860," vol. II, Part I, p. 94); *cf.* "Exposé des motifs": "The present bill constitutes a true public prosecutor, who, raised above all local influences and considerations, can display all the zeal and activity demanded by his duties. . . . The division we have made into what concerns the judgment and what concerns the prosecution extends to all parts of the criminal procedure, and presents a regular and complete double system of hierarchy."

[2] In the first two cases, the mayors, "adjoints," and commissioners of police have the same right.

ance to this power, the law limited its duration. Within twenty-four hours after the issue of the warrant of commitment, it was his duty to advise the director of the jury, who was bound to "take cognizance of the matter and to proceed therein with the least possible delay" (Art. 8). From that time the examination proceeded nearly in accordance with the principles of the ancient practice. The public prosecutor and the examining magistrate acted in concert, the former charging, the latter deciding and examining (Arts. 12 and 13). The witnesses were, as formerly, produced by the public prosecutor and the civil party.[1] A most important fact was the reappearance of the secret procedure. The witnesses must be heard "separately and out of the presence of the accused." This was overturning the rules in force since 1789. The rules as to the interrogation were changed at the same time. The judge did not, at the outset, give the accused any information as to the charges brought against him. Something still remained, however, of the liberal spirit of the prior laws. After the interrogation, the director of the jury was obliged to grant to the accused a perusal of the depositions, and the latter could insist upon being interrogated anew (Art. 10).

On the conclusion of the examination, it was communicated by the director of the jury to the deputy, who must, within three days, lodge his motions in writing;[2] then the examining magistrate issued an order reminiscent of the old ruling to the "extraordinary" action. "According to the various cases, and considering the nature and weight of the proofs," he set the accused at liberty (no grounds), or remanded him to the police court, or the police correctional court, or the grand jury (Art. 15). In case of an order of remand, he granted provisional liberty, if that was proper under the old rules, or regularized the detention pending trial by means of the writ of attachment.

The decision of the examining magistrate was subject to revision, however, at the instance of the public prosecutor. Whenever the order was not in conformity with the requisitions of the deputy, the matter was necessarily taken before the district court, which decided it after hearing the deputy and the director of the jury (Art. 16). The deputy could thereupon, if he thought proper, send the documents to the commissary attached to the criminal court, who put that court into action in the third instance (Arts.

[1] Art. 9: "The witnesses pointed out by the deputy and by the party complainant shall be summoned by citation of the director of the jury." Cf. "Ordonnance de 1670," Tit. V, Art. 1.

[2] *Cf.* "Ordonnance de 1670," Tit. XVI, Art. 17 *et seq.*

17, 18).[1] In the last place, the commissary could appeal to the Court of Cassation against the decision of the criminal court. No right of appeal on the part of the accused was anywhere mentioned.

The new Law, a complete Code of preliminary examination, radically altered the procedure before the grand jury, substituting the written procedure for the oral procedure. "The indictment," said Article 20, "is drawn up by the deputy commissary attached to the criminal court; the director of the jury causes it, as well as all the documents relative to it, to be read to the jury in his presence." — "The party complainant," adds Article 21, "shall not be heard before the grand jury, and the witnesses shall no longer be summoned before it; their depositions shall be submitted to it with the interrogations and all the documents in support of the indictment."

It is apparent that the Law of 7th Pluviôse marked a very distinct return to the past. It restored all the secret, preliminary examination dropped by the Laws of 1791 and of the year IV. The reforms it brought about related to the following points: 1st, the creation of a public prosecutor and an examining judge; 2d, the introduction of the warrant of commitment; 3d, the hearing of witnesses out of the presence of the accused; 4th, the substitution of written proofs for oral proceedings before the grand jury. It is interesting to see how each of these features was praised in the debate before the Tribunate.

The creation of a public prosecutor met with general approval. Costé,[2] Boutteville,[3] Goupil-Prefeln,[4] Challan,[5] Caillemer,[6] Chabot de l'Allier,[7] and Gillet,[8] successively upheld its legality and its necessity. The system preferred by the men of 1791 was not, however, abandoned without a contest. It found a warm supporter in Ganilh. He recalled the memorable debate of 1790: he invoked the shades of the famous orators taking part in it, whose fame had grown since that time, and several of whom had added the glory of martyrdom to their reputation for wisdom. Then, reviving the memories of the Terror, he pointed out the dangers of a public prosecution intrusted to the governing power.[9]

[1] He could appeal "not only on the ground of jurisdictional questions or the erroneous application of the law to the nature of the offense, but also on the ground of flaws in the examination or the procedure" (Art. 18).

[2] 1 Pluviôse, "Arch. parl.," *loc. cit.*, p. 119.

[3] 2 Pluviôse, "Arch. parl.," p. 141.

[4] 3 Pluviôse, "Arch. parl.," p. 145.

[5] 1 Pluviôse, "Arch. parl.," p. 123.

[6] 2 Pluviôse, "Arch. parl.," p. 139.

[7] 3 Pluviôse, "Arch. parl.," p. 149.

[8] 3 Pluviôse, *ibid.*

[9] Sitting of 2 Pluviôse, "Arch. parl.," pp. 133, 134.

But answers to this were not lacking. The best reason given was the necessity for strengthening the prosecution. "France has had the fatal experience of inseparable disorders, first, the absence of all government, and then a social organization too feeble to escape extinction or to avoid usurpation." [1] Chabot, in refutation of the subtle theories borrowed from the Constituent Assembly, remarked that the organization then established had totally disappeared. "Is not the government, as it is constituted in France, in itself the sole executive power? That being so, the execution of the laws belongs to the government alone, and to it belongs the duty of finding out and causing the prosecution of violations of these laws." [2] Finally, Gillet points out with much plausibility the dangers of the popular accusation which it was desired to introduce into our law. "We fear, in future, to confide the prosecution of offenses and its instigation to three hundred functionaries, yet we are not alarmed at the thought that this power of instigation at present exists in the hands of three millions of people." It is notable that two speakers attributed the reconstitution of the public prosecutor to Montesquieu's influence. The authority of the author of the "Spirit of the Laws," weakened during the troubled times, was greater than ever.[3]

The warrant of commitment met with the most vigorous opposition. It was a new creation, something hitherto unknown. Several speakers had nothing for it but distrust, and truly it should be acknowledged that their fears were well founded, if we think of the good luck experienced by this youngest born of the warrants of criminal procedure. An exact definition by the law of the forms of this new warrant at least was demanded.[4] Gillet, it is true, very ably defended the bill: "The warrant of commitment," he says, "is a new term in the Criminal Code, but the thing itself is no novelty. The preliminary examination, between the time of the seizure of the accused and that of the issuance of the writ

[1] *Goupil-Prefeln*, 3 Pluviôse, "Arch. parl.," p. 145.

[2] Sitting of 3 Pluviôse, p. 146; *cf. Goupil-Prefeln*, p. 145: "I ask of what use would the power of bringing the accusation before the trial jury be to the government if the research and the prosecution before the judges charged with the examination devolved upon functionaries independent of it."

[3] *Caillemer;* sitting of 2 Pluviôse (p. 138). *Gillet;* sitting of 3 Pluviôse. It is curious to notice that *Chabot* claims for the judges the right of taking action directly, as formerly: "I have made a second general observation upon the bill as a whole to the effect that the bill does not leave to the judiciary authorities the right of research and prosecution of offenses in cases where the government officers neglect or refuse to make researches or prosecutions" (p. 148).

[4] *Costé*, 1 Pluviôse, p. 120; *Chabot*, 3 Pluviôse, p. 148.

of attachment, is not always so simple and easy that it can be carried through immediately and in a breath. . . . Well, during all this interval, it would be worse than imprudent to leave the accused at liberty . . . the same police officer, therefore, exercises three totally distinct powers upon the person of the accused: 1st, he issues the warrant to bring the accused before the Court; 2d, he orders the accused to be provisionally detained during the course of the examination in a place pointed out by him, and that is what may be called the warrant of commitment; 3d, he issues the writ of attachment. These officers being scattered throughout a multiplicity of communes possessing no departmental prisons, are often under the necessity of lodging the accused in a guard-house, an inn, often in the old seigniorial prison, and sometimes even in the village belfry. . . . According to Article 7, the accused could no longer be lodged anywhere except in a departmental prison, and, looked at in this light, the warrant of commitment put in the power of the public prosecutor is, to say no more, already much less irregular and alarming than those orders for provisional detention emanating from justices of the peace."[1] So that the warrant of commitment, in the opinion of the legislators, was but a means of regularizing a practice, till then illegal, but unavoidable. It was, in all cases, an essentially provisional and temporary expedient, and it is not difficult to understand why the law, in putting it in the hands of the public prosecutor, did not require that, like the writ of attachment, it should state the cause of the arrest.[2]

The secrecy introduced into the preliminary examination was strenuously contested. It was felt that this was a serious measure, and, we are in fact, still under the threat of the decision then made. Ganilh was its most energetic opponent. He showed, very correctly, that not only the rules of the Codes of 1791 and of the year IV, but also those of the Law of 1789, were, in this respect, abandoned. "It is proposed to you to-day, not only to have the depositions written, but to have them taken secretly, even when the accused is under arrest and could be present. It is proposed to you to reëstablish a part of the secret procedure, that odious procedure, the suppression of which was demanded by the Cahiers of all the bailiwicks, and which, before the institution of the jury, necessitated the adjunction of two notables in

[1] Sitting of 3 Pluviôse, pp. 156, 157.

[2] According to *Challan* (sitting of 1st Pluviôse, p. 124), this formality ought, however, to be observed.

every information. It is proposed to you to make this occult and treacherous procedure the foundation of the grand jury's decision, and to infect our criminal procedure, one of the greatest blessings of the Revolution, with one of the greatest defects of the criminal procedure under the Monarchy! Such an impure mixture cannot be made; an insuperable obstacle interposes itself. There can be no alliance between the oppressive forms of the Monarchy and the protective forms of the Republic. They are naturally repugnant to each other, and cannot concur in bringing about the same end." [1] Remarkable words these. It was clearly to the system of the Ordinance that a return was here made. One important point of difference existed, the communication of the charges to the accused after his interrogations; but that difference was destined to disappear in the course of a few years. It is perfectly certain that an effort was made to attain a composite system, which would borrow from the Ordinance the preliminary examination, and from the laws of the intermediary period the procedure before the jurisdictions of judgment. This mixture was possible, whatever Ganilh might say, as experience has thoroughly proved.

Chairman Thiessé vindicated the new provision as follows: "The existing method is no doubt more liberal, but does it lead more certainly to the manifestation of the truth? Such is not the opinion of your commission. The situation of the witness in the presence of the accused is, at first, painful: and calmness and confidence are necessary to him to testify to what he knows, which should be done confidentially to the magistrate; the moment of the trial proper will come later. The witnesses and the accused will then enter into all necessary explanations, either for the conviction of the crime, or for the manifestation of innocence. Till that time the statements, like the interrogations, can be collected by the magistrate. Innocence can lose nothing thereby, and truth may be the gainer. The same remarks ought to apply to article 10, which requires the accused to answer before being aware of the charges, and the examining magistrate, in his turn, not only to make him acquainted with them after the interrogation, but also to receive all the answers which he wishes to make afterwards to the charges. The first interrogation should thus establish the truth, the second correct errors arising from surprise." [2] Gillet presented analogous observations. "It most frequently happens

[1] Sitting of 2 Pluviôse, p. 137.
[2] Sitting of 24 Ventôse, p. 94.

that the accused is not present when the witnesses testify before the police officer, for the good reason that the information ought to precede the warrant of production, and that when the witnesses arrive the accused has not yet appeared. If, however, the accused does happen to be present, and if, from that early moment, when the production of the charges is begun, he has his eyes and ears upon the witnesses who are developing them, the truth thereby is apt to be greatly distorted. The witness is intimidated, and explains himself with less confidence and frankness. . . . Untruthful replies are easily adjusted in proportion to the necessity of each charge as it crops up. . . . The (new) path is clear since, in following it, the accused has always and necessarily cognizance of the charges before the warrant of arrest, and every facility is allowed him to refute them."[1] After 1789, the point of view changed; the interests of the prosecution were given precedence over the rights of the defense.

Of all the changes introduced by the new law, the most strenuously contested was that substituting the written procedure for the oral procedure before the grand jury. That may, at first sight, appear surprising, for it appears to us to-day to be the least serious. Since that time, we have expunged the grand jury from our laws, and nobody asks for its reëstablishment. Even in England, the country of its origin, it is retained more from force of tradition than from public approbation. But this opposition is explicable, if we consider that this was a first blow struck at the system of proofs established in 1791. "Without the oral testimony of witnesses," said Chabot, "and with written documents, there is, in reality, no grand jury. We may dare to assert that written proofs may be sufficient for the jurors, but that is evidently to recommence the fight between legal proofs and moral proofs. It is to raise the question whether the procedure by jurors is preferable to the Ordinance of 1670, whether, in short, the sublime institution of the jury ought to be preserved or destroyed." And the same speaker invoked his personal experience as a magistrate. "As a commissary under a director of the jury, I have been present for three years at assemblies of grand juries, and I can testify that I have often entered without having been able to form a definite opinion upon the merits of the case, and if it had been necessary for me, upon the mere perusal of the documents, to fulfil the duties of a juror, I would have experienced grievous doubts. . . . I rarely failed to leave these assemblies better informed on

[1] Sitting of 3 Pluviôse, p. 158.

the main points of the case than I was before."[1] — "Visit," said another speaker, "all the nations possessing trial by jury, that is, all free countries (for liberty and that sacred institution invariably go hand in hand), ask the English, the Americans, go as far back as the time when the Romans still had jurors, and ask them all what they think of a written deposition."[2]

One consideration, however, was of great weight in favor of the bill, namely, that the accused was not present before the grand jury. To suppress the oral testimony was to put the parties on a more equal footing. This was brought forward by Challan,[3] Caillemer,[4] and Gillet, who added other observations of considerable practical value. "It is inadvisable that the testimony against him (the accused) should appear alive, as has been said, with all the sensations that render them expressive, while that in his favor only appears expressed in writing. . . . An eternal and incurable human malady urges the average man to wish to extend his power beyond its just limits; so that it often happens that, in spite of every care of the magistrate who instructs the jurors, the latter are tempted by the ignorance of their inner consciousness to substitute themselves in place of the trial jurors, and that they, in effect, deliberate with the same reasoning, and on the same grounds, as if they had to pronounce the judgment. The method proposed leaves them one illusion less to cause them to make mistakes. . . . The function of witnesses in criminal matters has become, in the present state of things, a very onerous burden, since it requires at least three sessions and as many as five if the indictment is annulled . . . we ought to congratulate ourselves on having, by suppressing the institution, at the same time relieved the public treasury and the citizens."[5]

In the Legislative Body the same considerations were debated by the speakers of the government and of the Tribunate. The Law was there adopted by 226 white balls against 48 black. We have dwelt at some length on this Law of the 7th Pluviôse; but, we believe, not to an improper excess. It is, in fact, very important, inasmuch as it forms the natural and necessary transition between the Codes of the intermediary period and the Code of Criminal Examination. It marks the point of time when the ordinary current of ideas changes its course. Along with it reenters into our legislation some of the principles registered in the

[1] Sitting of 3 Pluviôse, p. 152.
[2] *Boutteville;* sitting of 2 Pluviôse, p. 145.
[3] 1 Pluviôse, p. 125.
[4] 2 Pluviôse, p. 140.
[5] Sitting of 3 Pluviôse, p. 159.

Ordinance of 1670 and rejected by the Revolution. This element, thus introduced anew, was to coalesce with the rules on oral and public proceedings forever sanctioned before the trial jurisdictions; and that was to constitute the modern law.

The year IX witnessed the appearance of another Law, which, considering that it contained but transitory measures, was of no less importance. It responded to the need for security which at that time took precedence of all other needs, and it was, in great part, borrowed from the traditions of the old law. In concluding the debate on the Law of 7th Pluviôse before the Tribunate, Thiessé made a distinct allusion to this other bill; he declared that "it is in consequence of having neglected to give all the necessary expedition to the search for and the prosecution of crimes, that we often have recourse to extraordinary institutions, always exceedingly dangerous."

§ 2. **The Jury Put to Trial: Political Passion; Brigandage.** — Political passion, whose terrible current at this time seized upon everything, had swept away the jury in its flood. This was proved in the clearest way in the debate, in the year IX, on the bill as to special tribunals. "The jury," said Jean Debry, "belonged to the dominant faction, from which its judgments religiously took their color. It was not a case of facts, but of the opinions of persons who spoke from a misguided conscience. It would probably have taken a long time to give it that character of impartiality which alone inspires respect and reassures innocence." [1] — "Till now," said Chazal, "all and sundry have been taken as jurors; the function has been permeated by revolutionary passion. Till now the judgment by jury has been neither the judgment of God, nor that of the people, nor has it been the 'palladium' of liberty. It has usually been nothing but the judgment of a collection of ignoramuses, and during all the time of factions we have been witnesses of the scandalous iniquity of the shameless acquittal by the factionists of their accomplices, though men of the most nefarious character, and the remorseless destruction of their enemies." [2] — "The temporary juries of the year II were no less fertile in assassination than the permanent jury of the revolutionary tribunal. The Septembrist jury, which acquitted its accomplices, was lawfully constituted. The juries of the reaction, under whose protection the republicans were for long slaughtered with impunity, were lawfully constituted. The juries of the departments of the

[1] Sitting of 5 Pluviôse, p. 190.
[2] Sitting of 6 Pluviôse, p. 204. *Cf.* 13 Pluviôse, p. 277.

West and the South, which acquit all guilty persons, even when taken in the act, are also lawfully constituted. . . . Immediately the prosecution and the defense assume a political character and address themselves to the passions, the jury becomes terrible to innocence, and the safeguard of robbers."[1] This woful influence of political passion upon the jury was proved anew in the State's Council of the Empire, at the time of the debate on the Code of Criminal Examination;[2] but it would not have been sufficient, in itself, to create a permanent state of insecurity.[3] The jury would very soon have recovered its proper position if it had not had to struggle against a scourge which, from its very nature, it was powerless to battle with: we refer to brigandage.

The original germs of this existed, and attained considerable development, under the old monarchy. Recent works have shown how miscreants, poachers, smugglers, and vagrants were in open strife against social order;[4] and, in regard to certain districts at least, official documents of later date show that the mischief was by no means of recent growth. Read what one of the commissioners, sent in the year IX by the First Consul to make a general inquiry into the state of the South, says about that district: "It would be unjust to ascribe to the Revolution all the crimes committed in these unfortunate districts during the past ten years. It can only be asserted that it found elements most propitious to all kinds of disorders, and that the various interregna of governments and the absence or weakness of public authority have allowed evils at other times scarcer and more circumscribed to assume a more general and widespread character."[5] He spoke with extraordinary accuracy. The destruction of the old organization, the uncertainties and the weakness of the new authorities, anarchy, fierce passions, all furnished an environment wonderfully suitable for the development of these fatal germs. Erelong civil war and foreign war did their share in furnishing new and terrible

[1] *Bérenger*, 14 Pluviôse, p. 301.

[2] Sitting of 30 January, 1808 (*Locré*, vol. XXIV, pp. 578–580). Sitting of 8 Brumaire, year VII (*Locré*, vol. XXIV, p. 439. See also vol. XXV, p. 580).

[3] "With us, since the Revolution, the jury has not quite come up to the expectations conceived of it except in regard to the repression of ordinary offenses, such as murder, theft, arson, etc.; whenever these crimes present themselves the jury become inexorable." *Delpierre*, in the Tribunate, 7 Pluviôse, p. 216.

[4] *Taine*, "Les origines de la France contemporaine," I. "The Old Régime," p. 498 *et seq.*

[5] "Rapport de Français de Nantes, chargé de l'inspection de la 8e division militaire." — *F. Rocquain*, "L'état de la France au 18 brumaire," p. 4.

recruits to the great army of brigandage. Where could deserters find a better refuge? And among those who took up arms in the name of a political principle, how many were also tempted by the hope of pillage, and, the civil war once at an end, continued to carry on the campaign on their own account? "The origin of this brigandage (in the Maritime Alps) is due," it was said, "to the disbanding of several military bands called companies of Barbets. The increase of brigandage since the union is attributable to two causes: an increase in the number of travellers, and especially of Frenchmen going into Italy, and to the molestations suffered by the inhabitants, either to their persons or their property, at the hands of troops." [1] In Brittany, "besides the Chouan party, there are brigands hardly distinguishable from them; in both of these bands are to be found Austrian deserters from their regiments." [2] — "Some leaders of the old Vendean rebels have put themselves at the head of worthless characters of these departments, such as deserters, and artisans out of work, and plunder the carriages upon the roads and in the forests. . . . These are a remnant of the civil wars and internal broils; the dregs of the Revolution." [3] In the middle districts, the causes of brigandage are, according to Lacuée, "the defective organization of houses of correction, deserters, conscripts, the lack of police upon the highroads and throughout the country, vagrancy, mendicity, and the facility of carrying arms." [4] Thiers speaks of "that breed of bandits formed from the débris of the armies and disbanded soldiery of the civil wars," — "the Chouans and the Vendeans, unemployed since the termination of the civil war, and who had contracted tastes which the peace could not satisfy, ravaged the highroads of Brittany, Normandy, and the outskirts of Paris; refractory conscripts, and a number of soldiers from the army of Liguria, whom misery had driven to desert, committed the same acts of brigandage upon the roads of the Centre and the South." [5] The great companies were threatening to re-form. Finally, dire want went a long way to foster these disorders. "The distress in these departments" (one of the "missi" of the year IX is

[1] "Rapport de Français de Nantes." — *Félix Rocquain*, "L'état de la France," p. 14.

[2] "Rapport de Maille-Marboise," of 13 Nivôse, year IX, upon the state of the thirteenth military division. *F. Rocquain, op. cit.*, p. 121.

[3] "Rapport de Fourcroy," of 13 Nivôse, year IX, upon the 12th military division. — *F. Rocquain, op. cit.*, p. 146.

[4] "Rapport sur la première division militaire." — *F. Rocquain, op. cit.*, p. 253.

[5] "Histoire du Consulat et de l'Empire," vol. II, p. 161.

speaking of Brittany) "is frightful; the seamen are without employment or wages, the artisans and sailmakers have stopped work, for lack of openings, or because the excessive price of bread and the scarcity of buckwheat ('blé noir') no longer permits the employment of day-laborers. These causes, which have lasted a long time, have afforded the bandit leaders a certain means of maintaining the strength of their bands." [1]

This scourge, always on the increase, called for exceptional measures; such emergencies, involving a struggle for life, are beyond the scope of the ordinary laws. First of all, the Law of 26th Floréal, year V, inflicted capital punishment for the thefts struck at by Articles 2 and 3 (Second part, Tit. II, § 2) of the Criminal Code of 1791, when accompanied by one of the following circumstances: "1st, If the culprits have gained admittance to the house by force of arms; 2d, If they have used their arms in the house upon those they found there; 3d, If the violence used against those found in the house has left such traces as wounds, burns, or bruises." This law had been called forth by the odious practices of the "chauffeurs," [2] as the executive Directory had explained in urging this measure on 11th Frimaire of the year V: "Thieves, distinguished by the name of 'chauffeurs,' are scattered throughout several departments and harass town and country. They are not isolated malefactors . . . they are brigands mustered in bands, organized under leadership, marching according to instructions, forming, in short, in the very heart of our social system, a kind of confederated army, aiming at its elemental destruction." [3] Rousseau introduced the bill in the Council of the Elders, and he had great difficulty in vindicating this severity of an evident necessity. Muraire even secured an adjournment of the vote; but the bill was passed on 26th Floréal. It was, however, a totally inadequate measure. Montesquieu's axiom that preventive effect is produced, not by the severity, but by the certainty, of the punishment was to be verified once more.

Consider what magistrates the law appointed for the prosecution and trial of these bandits! Justices of the peace and jurors; timid functionaries and timorous citizens. The jury was no match for brigandage; that is a truth which Italy has recognized in our own days. Let us quote some interesting testimony extracted from the reports and debates of the year IX. "The jus-

[1] "Rapport de Barbé-Marbois." — *Rocquain, op. cit.*, p. 122.

[2] [So called from their practice of applying fire to the soles of their victims' feet to compel them to reveal their hidden treasures. — Trans.]

[3] "Journal des Débats," No. 566.

tices of the peace of the South are execrable, and complaints are made in all four departments about the grand juries and trial juries, destestable on account of their ignorance." [1] — "Can you conceal from yourselves that the subjection to the ordinary procedure of the brigands who incessantly attack public conveyances, and murder soldiers and citizens, practically means the insurance of their impunity, either because of the defects which still encumber the institution of the jury, or of the effect of the terror inspired by these wandering hordes?" [2] — "You would call upon the juries, the ordinary courts? Well, tribunes, visit these courts in several departments of the Republic. Here you will see, on the one hand, audacious crime-laden bandits, still dyed with the blood of their victims, insulting the judges, threatening the witnesses, defying the jury, and braving the scaffold. There you will find witnesses, stupefied, silent, motionless; further on, jurors more concerned about the means of their safe return home than with the hearing of insignificant actions, placed between the alternatives of acquitting the culprits or delivering themselves over to the vengeance of their accomplices. Let us pass into another department. Here the jury is composed entirely of citizens shut up within the walls of the town. It is impossible to assemble them in any other section of the department. Jurors and witnesses alike much prefer to allow themselves to be sentenced to pecuniary penalties, to exposing themselves, upon the highways, to penalties much more serious, those imposed by crime, not upon their purses only, but also upon their lives. These are not the only results of the existing state of affairs. The gendarmery have resigned in brigades, because, after having fought against the brigands, risking their lives in these actions, shed their blood, and fulfilled the expectations of their country, incapable juries have acquitted brigands captured with arms in their hands." [3] On the 18th Frimaire of the year IX, the minister of general police writes to the First Consul: "Although the thefts from stage-coaches have not yet ceased, and the pillage of the public funds continues, the fault cannot be imputed to the police department. The departmental prisons are all filled with brigands, and hardly a single crime committed has not been followed by the death or arrest of some of its perpetra-

[1] *F. Rocquain, op. cit.*, p. 25. "Rapport de Français de Nantes."

[2] *Trouvé*, at the Tribunate, 7 Pluviôse, year IX, "Arch. parlement," vol. II, Part I, p. 130.

[3] *Roujoux*, at the Tribunate, 14 Pluviôse, "Arch. parlement," p. 300; *cf. Carret*, 13 Pluviôse, p. 277; *Garat*, 13 Pluviôse, p. 296; *Delpierre*, p. 216.

tors. Although these disorders have not yet come to an end, it can be confidently asserted that many courts and jurors do not do their duty. Scoundrels taken with arms in their hands have been acquitted and set free by the tribunals." [1]

The necessity for exceptional courts was incontestable, but successive measures, usually inadequate, were the means adopted. A Law of 30th Prairial of the year III had conferred the trial of the Chouans, Barbets, *and others*, upon the military courts. Another Law of the 1st Vendémiaire of the year IV provided that "the rebels, known as Chouans, or by any other name, and all those described in Article 3 of the Law of 30th Prairial, shall be tried by the military councils established by the Law of the second complemental day;" [2] that is to say, by the courts-martial. These rather vague provisions dealt especially with rebels. They were affirmed by the Code of Offenses and Punishments.[3]

In the year VI something more was done: it was desired to make a complete organization of the exceptional courts, settling clearly their jurisdiction and the procedure to be followed before them. The new Law specified the crimes constituting brigandage and entailing capital punishment (Arts. 1 to 6); it then provided that if these deeds, subject as a rule to the ordinary courts, had been committed by an assemblage of more than two persons, the prisoners, accomplices, aiders, and abettors should be court-martialed. The warrant to bring the accused before the court could then be issued by the director of the jury, the justice of the peace, the police commissary, the municipal agent or "adjoint" in communes of under 5000 inhabitants, or by officers of the county police, with the full concurrence of all these functionaries (Art. 9).[4] The better to determine the jurisdiction, there was a regulation analogous to that formerly practised in the "prévôtal" jurisdictions, made by a civil magistrate, the director of the jury (Art. 11; *cf*. Arts. 12 to 16); this magistrate in all cases proceeded with the preliminary examination.[5]

The bill was presented by Rœmers to the Council of the Five Hundred, where several of its provisions were attacked. "The

[1] Speech by *Honoré Duveyrier*, speaker for the Tribunate in the Legislative Assembly, 17 Pluviôse, year IX, "Arch. parlement," p. 308.

[2] See the Report of *Dubois-Dubay*, "Journal des Débats," Vendémiaire, year IV, No. 1093, p. 5.

[3] Art. 598.

[4] See also Art. 10.

[5] The measure was, moreover, temporary. "Art. 22. It will remain in execution for a year only, dating from its promulgation by its insertion in the 'Bulletin des lois'; after that time it will be 'ipso facto' abrogated, failing its renewal by the Legislative Body."

name of military commission alone was a source of terror," says one of the speakers. "You are afraid to intrust the civil jurisdiction to the military, and to recall an abhorrent system, all resemblance to which must be avoided."[1] The Law was, however, passed by the Council of the Five Hundred on the 19th Ventôse of the year VI, and approved by the Ancients on the 29th Nivôse. It was renewed in Brumaire of the year VII, but not in the year VIII. The military commissions, who tried the brigands, did not, on that account, disappear. They survived by virtue of the Law of the 30th Prairial of the year III.[2]

But even this jurisdiction could only produce proper effects with the help of physical force; it was really necessary to make war upon the brigands. Expeditions performed by mobile columns were necessary. Meanwhile, things had come to such a pass that it was necessary to arm the conductors of public conveyances and have them escorted by soldiers. There was a lack of troops. "These brigands had chosen for their diffusion through the country the moment when the absence abroad of nearly all the military had deprived the interior of the forces necessary for public safety."[3] In the year VIII the evil was at its height, as an official document clearly shows: "Whole communes have been victims of their (the brigands') devastations and cruelty. . . . All these departments beg for prompt aid, in the shape of men, arms, and ammunition. These have been often promised, but the supply has, so far, been insufficient."[4]

It was the desire of the First Consul to be that destroyer of brigands whom France had for a long time called for, whom it then invoked, and who would afterwards be celebrated in mythological allusions.[5] Numerous columns traversed the infested districts, and in their train military commissioners tried the prisoners; "the First Consul instituted military commissions in the train of the mobile columns which pursued brigandage. . . .

[1] "Journal des Débats," Floréal, year VI, No. 240, p. 154.

[2] *Savoye-Rollin* at the Tribunate, 13 Pluviôse, year IX ("Arch. parlement.," p. 284).

[3] *Thiers*, "Le Consulat et l'Empire," vol. III, p. 287.

[4] "Résumé des comptes rendus au Ministère de l'Intérieur par les commissaires du Directoire exécutif près les administrations centrales des départements," published by *Rocquain*, *op. cit.*, p. 377.

[5] "The peoples of Greece raised altars to the heroes who delivered them from bandits" (Debate in the Council of the Ancients in the year VI). —"Nothing less will do than the mighty hand of the modern Hercules, who comes to our assistance, for the extermination of the brigands and the prevention of the ruin of the social edifice" ("Exposé des motifs du livre II, Tit. II," of the Code of Criminal Examination, *Locré*, vol. XXVIII, p. 52).

These military commissions had already produced salutary effects in Pluviôse of the year IX. The judges in military uniform, who composed them, were not afraid of the accused; they reassured the witnesses testifying, who were often the soldiers themselves who had arrested the brigands with arms in their hands." [1]

But it must be acknowledged that this work of repression had been somewhat irregular if singularly expeditious. Français de Nantes states in his report, already quoted: "The result of the military commissions from the Decree of 29th Frimaire (which instituted them in the Var and the Bouches-du-Rhône) to the 30th Germinal following, that is, for a period of four months, has been twenty-three brigands shot and taken bearing arms; a hundred and sixty shot after examination and judgment; fifty-eight set free; seven remitted before the ordinary judges; one sent to the Toulon bagnio; fifty remitted as strongly suspected before the general in command of the division, who asks for authority to transport them for life. Two female receivers of stolen goods and accomplices of brigands have been condemned to death." [2] Farther on he deprecates "the way in which armed force has been employed against the brigands. The columns of scouts never appeared in a commune without accomplishing some pillage. Their leaders seem to have had no other end but to get money. . . . Some individuals, arrested as Barbets, have been shot without trial, either from personal hatred, or because they did not give up the amount demanded. . . . Most of these facts are well known throughout the department." [3] In Brittany, Barbé-Marbois also demands that a check be put "upon the excessive readiness of the gendarmes to fire upon the fugitives they are pursuing, and still more upon the executions of those they have overtaken and arrested, even if they were notoriously guilty. There are instances of such executions, but it must be said that they are rare. Not a single one must be allowed, and the institution of exceptional courts does away with the pretext for them." [4]

§ 3. **The Law of 18th Pluvôise, Year IX. Special Tribunals. Revival of the "Prévôtal" Courts.** — The government was about to demand, in effect, the establishment of exceptional courts. They were generally demanded by the prefects; [5] and if an exceptional jurisdiction was necessary for the brigands, it must at least be regular. The proposal would therefore seem to have been made

[1] *Thiers*, "Le Consulat et l'Empire," vol. III, p. 339.
[2] *Rocquain, op. cit.*, p. 69.
[3] *Ibid.*, p. 15; *cf.* pp. 5, 6.
[4] *Ibid.*, p. 126.
[5] *Ibid.*, pp. 5, 19.

under very favorable conditions. The condition of France, in the matter of amelioration, was far from being satisfactory. The various characteristics by which we have attempted to portray the plague of brigandage are taken, for the most part, from the reports of the State's Councillors sent on missions of inquiry in the year IX, or from the debates in the Tribunate of the same year.[1]

The bill relative to the establishment of a *special criminal tribunal* was presented to the Tribunate, with an able explanation of reasons drawn up by Portalis, 17th Nivôse in the year IX.[2] According to the provisions of this bill, the government had the right to establish, in the departments where it should be deemed necessary, special criminal courts (Art. 1). These tribunals were composed of the president and two judges of the criminal court, three military men not under the grade of captain, and two citizens having the qualifications required for judges. All five of these were appointed by the First Consul (Art. 2). It looked like a revival of the provost marshals and their assessors. The jurisdiction of these special courts still more strongly recalled that of the old "prévôtal" courts. We find in the law of the year IX all the deeds struck at by the Declaration of 5th February, 1731. In the first place the *cases prévôtal on account of the status of the accused,* that is, crimes committed by vagrants, and those without means of subsistence, or not rehabilitated (Arts. 6 and 7); vagrancy properly so-called and the escape of prisoners (Art. 7); — then the *cases prévôtal from the nature of the crime;* thefts on the highways or with violence, or the use of means or circumstances aggravating the offense (Art. 8), thefts in the country and in habitations, and country buildings ('bâtiments'), accompanied by breaking in . . . or when the crime was consummated with bearing of arms or by an assembling of two persons at least (Art. 9); false money (Art. 11); seditious assemblages, the parties having been surprised in the act of such assemblages (Art. 12); murders contrived by armed assemblages, the crime of enticing away, and machinations practised outside the army and by civilians, to corrupt soldiers, requisitionnaires, or conscripts (Art. 11). To this list, taken almost verbatim from the Declaration, were added certain deeds the severe repression of which was demanded by the new state of affairs: fire-raising and threats, excesses, and assaults committed

[1] See also: *Rocquain, op. cit.,* pp. 5, 69, 70, 146, 147, 170, 252, 253, 262, 263; and the debate on the Law of Pluviôse ("Arch. parlement.," *loc. cit.,* pp. 308, 309; 105, 106; 222; 299).

[2] "Arch. parlement," II, Part I, p. 70.

on the recipients of national property, because of such acquisition (Art. 11); finally, the special courts had also a concurrent jurisdiction with the ordinary courts, of premeditated murder (Art. 10).[1]

These crimes and offenses were officially prosecuted by the government commissary, without any party complainant (Arts. 3 and 15). All officers of gendarmery and police officers were entitled to issue the warrant "d'amener" (Art. 17). The details as to the official reports to be drawn up, the inventories, the interrogation, and the hearing of witnesses in the preliminary examination, were borrowed from the Ordinance and the Declaration.

The special court having taken office on sight of the complaint, the additional documents, interrogations and answers, and informations, and the government commissary having been heard, the court must first of all determine its jurisdiction, and that without appeal (Art. 24). This was a survival of the past. The provosts had their jurisdiction determined by the presidials, and the latter determined their own jurisdiction when they took cognizance of "prévôtal" causes.[2] This determination, intimated to the accused within twenty-four hours, must be, within the same period, intimated to the minister of justice for submission to the Court of Cassation, which was obliged to take cognizance and decide, to the suspension of all other matters (Arts. 25, 26). This appeal, which, however, did not stay either the examination or the judgment, but merely the execution (Art. 27), was borrowed from the Law of the 29th Nivôse of the year VI. Finally, the sternest feature of the "prévôtal" courts, namely, the fact that their decisions on the merits were not subject to any appeal, also characterized the special court; neither appeal nor review to quash were allowed (Art. 29).

But the Law of the year IX differed materially from the provisions of the Ordinance from other points of view. In conformity with the principle of the new law, it insured public hearing,

[1] If, the examination having been begun by reason of one of these misdeeds, the accused was incriminated by reason of ordinary offenses, "the special court," it was said, "shall examine and judge, whatever may be the nature of these misdeeds" (Art. 13). The natural meaning of this clause was that the special court would become incidentally cognizant; that was what the old laws decided (Ord. of 1670, Tit. II, Art. 23; "Déclaration de 1731," Art. 18). The reporter *Thiessé* gives it another construction: "That is to say, that the special court will not be ousted from the examination and the judgment of the crimes conferred on it by the law because of any misdeed foreign to its jurisdiction" ("Arch. parl.," *loc. cit.*, p. 112); but see *Benjamin Constant's* reply (p. 321).

[2] Ord. 1670, Tit. II, Art. 15; Tit. I, Art. 17. See *Chazal*, at the Tribunate ("Arch. parl.," *loc. cit.*, p. 208).

the benefits of oral trial and moral proofs, and the aid of counsel; there was an indictment, drawn up by the government commissary, perusal of which was allowed.(Art. 28). Finally, the concluding article provided "that the special court should be revoked, ipso facto, two years after the peace (Art. 31)." [1]

It would seem that the bill should have been passed without difficulty in this troubled period. The Laws of the year III and the year VI had raised but few objections, and the bill offered safeguards rather than new severities. Nevertheless, it raised a storm of opposition. In the Tribunate it gave occasion for long debates, which lasted from the 17th Nivôse to the 16th Pluviôse. More than twenty speakers were heard, and among the adversaries of the proposal we find Benjamin Constant, Daunou, Isnard, Chazal, and Chénier.

Whence came this opposition? The Constitution of the year VIII, like those which had preceded it, guaranteed (Art. 62), for all deeds coming under the head of crimes, judgment by jury. But it was replied that another article of the Constitution, article 92, decided that in case of armed rebellion or troubles threatening the internal safety of the State, the law could, in determined times and places, suspend the rule of the Constitution. Well, it was said, here we do not go so far; the authority of the Constitution is only partially suspended. Moreover, the same constitutional difficulty existed to a still more serious extent then, and it was not raised; the real motive for the opposition must be sought for elsewhere.[2]

[1] The following is a comparative list, showing to what extent the bill was copied from the provisions of the old laws dealing with the "prévôtal" courts:

Law of Pluviôse		Declaration of 1731
Art. { 6. 7.	—	Art. { 1. 2.
Art. { 8. 9. 10.	—	Art. { 2. 5.
Art. 3, end	—	Art. 2.

Law of Pulviôse		Ordinance of 1670, Tit. II
Art. 14.	—	Art. 23.
Art. 21.	—	Art. 9.
Art. 22.	—	Art. 10.
Art. 23.	—	Art. 12.
Art. 24.	—	Art. 25.

[2] "Neither the establishment of these (military) commissions, nor the details of their powers, nor the law of 29th Nivôse, introduced by myself, have excited among the representatives of the two councils or among the citizens, the uneasiness which might be expected to-day." *Jean Debry* in the Tribunate, 5 Pluviôse, "Arch. parl.," *loc. cit.*, p. 190.

It was felt that this was not merely a temporary measure, but a system tending to become permanent. It was desired to establish two jurisdictions, one of common law, the other of exception; for some the jury, for others the special courts. Duveyrier, the chairman, did not conceal this. "Do you wish to safeguard the feeble and valuable remnants of the jury? Strip it, from now on, of the usage which weakens and denatures it every day. Let its purpose be to distinguish the vast difference between those offenses which threaten social order in troubled times and those rare errors which disturb it in a more peaceful time. Let it be, so to speak, the prerogative of those people who occasionally transgress, but who do not live for and by crime; who wound, but who do not wage war on the established régime. Let an act tried by the jury be such that if it does not carry with it a presumption of innocence, at least does not bear the character of a fault which has not been unworthy of that beneficent institution. Let it, in short, exist for those to whom it belongs, imperfect, but always susceptible of improvement by wisdom and experience." [1]

This duality was put forward merely as a make-shift: the truth was that the provisional state of matters was bound to change into a definite state. The government did not acknowledge the fact at that time, but it declared it openly later in the "Exposé des motifs" of Title VI, Book II, of the Code of Criminal Examination, which maintained the special courts as a permanent institution. M. Réal there said: "It was speedily recognized that the law ought to be permanent and of universal application. The same experience which had decided upon the necessity for its existence had also decided upon the necessity for its permanence and its universality; and the celebrated Ordinances, truly national and popular, of Orléans, Moulins, and Blois have ordained this special institution for all times and for all places. The commissaries who drew up the Ordinance of 1670 had the good sense to place the exception alongside of the ordinary rule. . . . Twelve years of abuses have depraved public opinion to such an extent that at the very moment when we return to principles, a well-informed and powerful, but moderate and prudent, government, which desired the guidance of nothing but prudence and conviction, was compelled to compromise with that public opinion, and the Law of

[1] Sitting of 29 Nivôse, "Arch. parl.," *loc. cit.*, p. 107. *Delpierre*, 7 Pluviôse, p. 219: "It must, in good faith, be acknowledged that the establishment of special criminal courts comes very near to being the suspension of the procedure by jury."

18th Pluviôse of the year IX received, not in its universality, since the government could apply it to all the departments, but in its duration, a limitation, since it must cease to exist two years after the peace. But although it was wise for an ameliorating government not to seek for the permanence of the institution until after proof by provisional trial, the government ought to be accused of want of foresight and cruelty if to-day . . . it foreshadows, in presenting but an ephemeral institution, a period of misfortunes and desolation, where the public safety will be once more delivered over to the mercy of all the brigands." [1] The foresighted minds of the year IX were not deceived on this point. The system was destined to pass into the Code of Criminal Examination. The special courts were afterwards, in 1815, to be replaced by "prévôtal courts," a temporary institution, it is true,[2] but to which article 54 of the Charter of 1830 was to render the return forever impossible.

What was thus revived was one of the most odious institutions of the Old Régime. M. Réal's report subsequently stated this very plainly, and he put together all the links of the chain. This was not acknowledged in the year IX, but the matter was too evident to escape all eyes. "Were the proposed law," said Benjamin Constant, "not infinitely more vague and the powers given by it to the special courts much more extensive than what were called under the Old Régime 'prévôtal' judgments, I would not have broken silence." [3] Desrenaudes evokes "the idea of these frightful commissions against which are raised, what do I say? have been raised for a century, the voices of all the men honored by humanity, and the question is immediately asked if the splendid conceptions of Montesquieu, Beccaria, Rousseau, Dupaty, Servans, and so many others are to be destroyed in a day, or relegated to the restricted sphere of some obscure crimes and some mean offenses." [4] — "The speaker for the government," says Garat, "will find these principles in the Ordinance of 1670; but it is not these precedents we ought to follow or that should be proposed to us." [5] Chazal contributed the most complete elucidation. "The government," he began by saying, "asks you to establish exceptional courts, which it has conceived upon the model of the old 'prévôtal' courts organized by the Ordinance of 1670." [6] Then, taking separately, on one side the various

[1] *Locré*, vol. XXVIII, pp. 54, 55. [2] Law of 20th December, 1815.
[3] In the Tribunate, 5 Pluviôse, "Arch. parl.," *loc. cit.*, p. 187.
[4] 6 Pluviôse, "Arch. parl.," *loc. cit.*, p. 193.
[5] 13 Pluviôse, "Arch. parl.," p. 294.
[6] 6 Pluviôse, "Arch. parl.," p. 204 *et seq.*

provisions of the bill and on the other those of the Ordinance and of the Declaration of 1731, he showed their identity; he made it clear that in some respects the severities of the old law had been increased; he regretted not to find in the bill the power in the accused to be heard at the time of the jurisdictional judgment, the judgment ruling to the "extraordinary" action, and the old formal confrontation.

This was all so clear, that, in future, the speakers in support of the bill could not misunderstand its parentage, and they were obliged, to obviate the comparison, to insist upon the ephemeral nature of the new law. "It is impossible to institute comparisons between an essentially temporary institution in our political system and a class of courts inherent in the monarchy and coördinated to the general aspects of its criminal legislation."[1] Portalis, addressing the Corps Legislatif on behalf of the Tribunate, said: "The provosts of the Old Régime, like the special tribunal, are the outcome of disorder and brigandage. They were not instituted by Louis XIV; their origin is of earlier date; they were sanctioned by the deliberations of the States-General. But the provosts were permanent; the special tribunal is but temporary."[2] Several even attempted a mild rehabilitation of the "prévôtal" jurisdictions. "Whatever the 'prévôtal' jurisdictions had of value, so far as compatible with the present régime, has been taken and the Law of 29th Nivôse blended therewith, and thereby ameliorated. A fatal dart was thought to have been launched against the bill by saying that it is framed on one of the most despotic establishments of Louis XIV. The 'prévôtal' jurisdictions were not originated by Louis XIV; they go back to much earlier times, when, as at present, France, devastated by audacious hordes, had need of a justice armed to war against them. The 'prévôtal' jurisdictions were not essentially bad; they merely had the defects inherent in our old criminal procedure, which are not to be found in the bill. The procedure here is not secret; the accused pleads his defense publicly. The trials are open as in the ordinary tribunals. The jurisdiction, which the provosts settled by calling on the graduates within easiest reach, is controlled in a much more reassuring manner."[3]

The Law was voted, but it passed the Tribunate by the majority of forty-nine votes against forty-one only; in the Legislative Body

[1] *Laussat*, sitting of 12 Pluviôse, "Arch. parl.," *loc. cit.*, p. 258: *cf. Trouvé*, p. 231; *Carret*, p. 279.

[2] 1 Pluviôse, p. 332. [3] 17 Pluviôse, "Arch. parl.," *loc. cit.*, p. 316.

the bill obtained one hundred and ninety-two votes against eighty-eight. It was a part of the Ordinance of 1670 which entered into our laws; and that is why we have dwelt at some length on this curious page of our parliamentary history. Many speakers declared that in voting for the establishment of special courts, their intention was to save the institution of the jury, which would have been destroyed forever by prolonged proof of its powerlessness. It is useful to record these testimonies, which we shall utilize a little later. Here are some of them. First of all, Duveyrier, the chairman for the bill in the Tribunate, says: "The institution of the jury, a benefit and safeguard of liberty among all free nations, is with us, of all the gifts of the Revolution, that which a miracle alone can save in the midst of revolutionary storms. But we all admit that, originally imperfect and inaccurate, it was also discredited in the popular opinion by the barbarous use to which the most atrocious tyranny condemned it; hampered since then by a complexity of abstract forms and metaphysical combinations, it drags along to-day, marking at each step its inadequacy against the excessive evils of the times and scarcely allowing the good which it might some day accomplish to be apparent. — Do you wish to accelerate and consummate its destruction? Would you render it forever incapable of its natural functions? then leave it to struggle against obstacles which it cannot overcome; . . . crush it under the daily proofs of its nullity and powerlessness, until it is no more in the eyes even of its most zealous partisans than a fine philosophical conception, impossible to carry into practice, and at all events inapplicable to our age and our social condition. If, on the contrary, it is your desire to protect its deficient but precious remnants, strip it from now on of the practice which continues to impair and distort it."[1] — Trouvé: "It is of course distressing to discard, even for the shortest period, the benefit of one of the most sublime institutions, to throw a veil, so to speak, over this 'palladium' of civil liberty. But suppose this veil is the means of its ultimate preservation; suppose this momentary suspension is indispensable to the safety of the State!"[2] — Caillemer: "The improvement of the institution of the jury! As if this improvement did not require radical, and consequently, gradual changes; as if, besides, this improvement could produce the effect looked for from it before the extinction of all revolutionary passion, and the complete

[1] 29 Nivôse, "Arch. parl.," *loc. cit.*, p. 107.
[2] 7 Pluviôse, p. 230.

reëstablishment of morality."[1] — Roujoux: "A decade of tranquillity may not suffice to bring back our minds to the feeling of the sublimity of the institution of the jury. The memory of its present ineffectiveness will not be easily obliterated. Save, then, tribunes, save this institution from the outrage of circumstances, if you would preserve the benefit of it."[2] — Bérenger: "The juries of the departments of the West and the South acquit all culprits even when captured in the act . . . this institution is not rendered tutelary by its forms, but by the jurors' impartiality, existing, in case of ordinary crimes, even in time of revolution, and rendering them capable of judging one accused of theft or murder, when these offenses are isolated. But immediately the prosecution or the defense assumes a political character, and addresses itself to the passions, the jury becomes terrible to innocence, and is the safeguard of brigands. Reserve it for times and places favorable to it, and do not force it to undergo a comparison which will render it detestable. Let us calm public opinion, which so many prolonged evils and so many unpunished crimes stir up against it; let us save this liberal institution from the wreck of the Revolution by adopting the bill."[3]

All agreed in declaring that the jury had not given the results looked for, and it was acknowledged by its most ardent supporters that it was necessary to bring about radical changes in its organization. "In my opinion," said Daunou, "(the jury) is not so much a prerogative as an incidental form, merely an essential part of our judicial system, a part whose organization is no doubt still very defective, but which it will be better worth while to ameliorate than to suspend. The Constitution, which is confined to sanctioning its existence, cannot prevent its improvement, and this work, at least set in motion by the trials and observations of ten years, will be more worthy of the enlightened men who now draw up our laws, more worthy of their talents and the wisdom of the principles they profess, than these long and wretched decrees of exception and circumstances which they propose to us."[4]

[1] 8 Pluviôse, "Arch. parl.," *loc. cit.*, p. 243.
[2] 14 Pluviôse, "Arch. parl.," p. 300.
[3] 16 Pluviôse, "Arch. parl.," pp. 301, 302; *cf. Delpierre*, 7 Pluviôse, p. 216.
[4] 7 Pluviôse, "Arch. parl.," *loc. cit.*, p. 224; *cf. Chazal*, p. 204; *Garat*, p. 296.

TITLE II

THE FRENCH CODE OF CRIMINAL EXAMINATION, 1808

CHAPTER I

THE DRAFT OF THE CRIMINAL CODE

§ 1. **The Draft of the Code. The Jury and the Ordinance of 1670.** — The substitution of the Empire for the Consulate brought no change in the institutions which we have described. Certain appellations were replaced by others, that was all; the criminal courts took the name of "Courts of Criminal Justice"; the government commissioners attached to the courts of appeal were called "attorneys-general," the commissioners attached to the other courts, "imperial attorneys." The public prosecutor resumed his ancient titles.[1] There was one single new creation — that of the Imperial High Court, instituted by the Senatus-Consultum of 28th Floréal in the year XII (Arts. 101–133). But from that time on a recasting of the criminal laws was in preparation. It was a matter of necessity and was bound to figure among the new codes at that time promised to France. The Criminal Code had not been retouched since 1791, and its practice had disclosed numerous imperfections. On the other hand, the criminal procedure had been radically changed by the Laws of the year IX; the Code of Offenses and Punishments needed complete remodeling. Finally, and above all, the rules as to the composition of the jury must be remodeled and improved.[2]

[1] The deputies created by the Law of 7th Pluviôse, year IX, are, however, still called *magistrates of police* in the draft of the Criminal Code.

[2] This composition had, moreover, varied very much during the Revolution. The general jury list, instituted by the Law of 1791, including all

The preliminary labor had been commenced in the year IX; a Decree of the consuls of 7th Germinal of that year appointed a commission, composed of MM. Vieillard, Target, Oudart, Treilhard, and Blondel, whose duty it was to draft the Criminal Code and to meet at the house of the Grand Judge Minister of Justice, the work to be ready in Messidor of the same year.

This commission, indeed, drew up a vast plan comprising at once the criminal law and criminal procedure, and containing 1169 Articles. In the second part, devoted to criminal procedure, and which alone interests us, the commissioners had, subject to very numerous modifications in detail, preserved the existing institutions and the forms then in force. They were very far from thinking of suppressing the trial by jury: "The Law of 16th September, 1791, which introduced the trial by jury among us, would be one of the finest productions of the 1700s, if the legislature had not been drawn in an opposite direction as much by revolutionary violence, as by the force of old habits. The trial by jury placed in the hands of the most useful and enlightened part of the citizens could never be either oppressive or anarchic." So M. Oudart expressed himself in the remarks preceding the second part of the draft.[1]

The creation of magistrates called "prætors" was proposed, who should hold assizes successively in several departments.[2] They were to compose the criminal court, assisted merely by another magistrate or "propraetor," "causing the same justice to rule everywhere and subjecting the passions to the government of the same laws." This was a return to the imitation of English institutions; the "prætor" was none other than the English chief justice, and it was desired to give to the sessions of the jury something of the solemnity of the English assizes. The "propraetors" assumed the functions formerly exercised by the directors of the jury. "Under the rule of the existing law, the director of the jury exercises criminal functions for three or six months, and quits them precisely when he is somewhat more in a condition to properly exercise them; thereupon the order of the

the electors, had suffered the counterblow of all the changes made upon the electoral laws; it had been successively altered by the Laws of 2d Nivôse, year II, and of 6th Germinal, year VIII, and by the Senatus-Consultum of the 16th Thermidor, year X.

[1] "Projet de Code criminel," p. xxxiv.

[2] A Law of 9th Ventôse, year VIII, had formerly regulated this point: "Since this law, the First Consul selects from the Courts of Appeal as many judges as there are departments, and sends them to preside for one year over the criminal courts." "Observations" of *M. Oudart*, p. xxxviii.

list calls upon that one of the judges who is found to be the least fitted. In our draft the 'proprætor' is appointed for life like any other judge, and as were the criminal lieutenants and assessors."[1]

Important changes were introduced as to the method of choosing the jurors: "Since the month of Nivôse in the year II," said M. Oudart, "the list of special petty jurors ought to be thirty, and the list of ordinary jurors ought to contain as many citizens as there are thousands of inhabitants. . . . According to this division a panel of 665 jurors was made at Paris every three months, which made in the course of the year twenty-seven hundred to twenty-eight hundred ordinary and special jurors. Since the law provides that such a great number of citizens should be called upon at once, many more bad selections are made than good ones and the government cannot hold anybody to account for an act essentially vicious. The care of drawing up these lists is also almost everywhere left to clerks, who, without more ado, copy the pages of the registers of the population. Professional thieves, dead men, men who have long left the district, men afflicted with incurable diseases, and men who cannot either read or write have been registered on these lists." It was therefore endeavored to obtain a better choice, above all requiring jurors subject to a certain census qualification. The challenges must henceforward be made upon a quadruple list and *in court*. "We can," said M. Oudart, "finally restore to the parties the invaluable right to challenge in court, a formality religiously observed in England."[2] There was an attempt to simplify the system of questions put to the jury, but in this respect Articles 869 and 870 admitted discussions among the jurors themselves and conferences of the jurors with the judges, which presented serious inconveniences. Finally, the rule of unanimity was suggested for the decisions of the trial jury, as in England. This system, illogical in itself, and difficult of acceptance by the French spirit, had never been admitted with us for acquittal; for condemnation the Laws of 1791 and of the year IV had required ten votes out of twelve; the Laws of 19th Fructidor of the year V, and of 18th Frimaire in the year VI, in principle, required unanimity, but at the end of twenty-four hours spent in vain efforts to obtain it a division of votes went to the benefit of the accused, and a mere majority was sufficient for a condemnation. The draft (Art. 864) exacted unanimity of votes to acquit as well as to condemn, and it fixed no limit of time for the deliber-

[1] "Observations," *Locré*, vol. XXV, p. 17. [2] *Locré*, vol. XXV, p. 25.

ations.[1] We shall very soon have to bring up again several important features of this primary draft. We have analyzed these few provisions to show that the commissioners had borrowed the principles of the reforms which they suggested rather from England than from the old French legislation.

A current, however, very powerful and always growing stronger, existed, setting in towards the past. The nation was then tired of political liberties, and the governing bodies, the magistrates above all, turned their eyes with regret towards the criminal procedure of the Ordinance. The jury appeared to them to be a barbarous and dangerous institution. They could not understand why the evanescent oral testimony should be preferred to the permanent written record, ignorance to knowledge, irresolution to experience and to the professional sentiment of duty. Was it not necessary to judge the tree by its fruits, and to return to the old procedure, not certainly such as had been settled by the Ordinance of 1670, secret and merciless, but such as the first reforms of 1789 had purified? Many gave utterance to this idea and it wanted little to give them the victory. It was they who spoke loudest in the great inquiry which had opened upon the draft of the Criminal Code.

§ 2. **"Observations" of the Supreme Court and the Courts of Appeal.** — An extensive inquiry was, indeed, ordered for the purpose of collecting the observations of the magistracy upon the work of the commissioners. The Court of Cassation and the Grand Judge, the Appeal Court and the Criminal Courts in turn gave their opinions. The Supreme Court and the Grand Judge were required to express their opinions in a solemn fashion. By virtue of a resolution of the 5th Ventôse in the year X,[2] the Court of Cassation must every year in Fructidor send a deputation of twelve of its members to acquaint the consuls, the State's Council, and the ministers present of the defects which the experience of the year had made apparent, and the changes and improvements proper to be wrought upon the laws. In the same sitting the Minister of Justice was required to give an account of the observations which he had made upon the same subject. Now, on the third complemental day of the year XI, in obedience to the aforesaid resolution, the First Minister, M. Muraire,[3] expressed himself

[1] See *M. Oudart* (*Locré*, vol. XXV, pp. 41, 42).
[2] *Sirey*, "Lois annotées," I, p. 572.
[3] Along with M. Muraire, the deputation included MM. Maleville, Cochard, Lassaussade, Bailly, Zangiacomi, Cassaigne, Brillat-Savarin, Baris, Schwendt, Minier, Lachèse, and M. Merlin, government commissary.

in regard to the jury in terms condemnatory of the institution. "The sad result of the impunity of the greatest crimes, offending public morality and terrifying society, has almost led to the doubt whether the institution of the jury, so fine theoretically, has not to-day been more harmful than useful in its effects. And very soon, this first doubt, leading to a second, may make it necessary to-day to investigate by the light of experience what was done by the Constituent Assembly, but in a speculative manner; perhaps it may be to examine if in a country where there is neither class distinction, nor feudality, nor privilege, the institution of the jury offers very real benefits; if the institution adapts itself perfectly to the national character; if it can properly be allied with that too usual sentiment of generosity and indulgence in some, of timidity and carelessness in others, which will always induce to commiseration the man who is not fortified in the habit of trying and who sees before him merely the man whom he is going to strike, society being but in his eyes an abstract and invisible thing." [1]

The Grand Judge on his side said: "Afraid of the result of these trials, and considering, according to accurate report, that the complexity of the subject, the subtlety of the discussion, and ignorance and weariness, invariably embarrassed and often overwhelmed the trial jury, composed of men strangers to that description of duty, many fine minds and a number of enlightened magistrates have thought that it would probably be preferable to keep merely the grand jury, taking pains to fix the necessary method of arriving at the best choice of jurors. In this system we confer upon the courts the examination of the proceedings as well as the judgment in regard to the individuals who have been declared indictable, we maintain the publicity of the examination and also the communication of the documents to the accused as well as his counsel, and we leave them both all necessary latitude to plead the facts and justificative pleas. The inequality of class distinctions having been abolished, there is no longer reason to fear either the prejudices or the oppression of one caste or one order. The judges are, like the jurors, the true peers of the accused, and they have, what the jurors have not, study, knowledge, and experience of affairs." [2] He did not, however, dare to propose the abolition of the jury. "Despite the sad experience which we have had, the supporters of the procedure by jury are very far from thinking, as many others believe, that this institution cannot be acclimatized

[1] "Projet de Code criminel," p. 192; *Locré*, vol. I, p. 207.
[2] "Projet de Code criminel," p. 212.

in France; they maintain, whatever may be said, that this institution is quite compatible with the genius and character of the nation, that if down to the present time it has encountered obstacles, these must be attributed principally to the numerous dissensions to which the Revolution has given birth, and that these dissensions being necessarily bound very soon to disappear by the effect of time its progress and success will not be further hindered except by slight obstacles which it will not be difficult to overcome. Now! do not refuse an additional trial, and let a third experiment decide between them and their adversaries." [1]

The observations of the Courts of Appeal are very interesting.[2] Twelve courts: Aix, Amiens, Bourges, Colmar, Douai, Metz, Nancy, Nîmes, Orléans, Pau, Riom, and Turin give their decision against the procedure by jury; five merely demand its maintenance: Agen, Angers, Caen, Rennes, and Toulouse; five do not give any opinion upon this grave question; the courts of Bordeaux, Brussels, and Trèves furnish upon the plan merely observations of detail; Ajaccio and Montpellier present a vague commendation.[3] The Courts of Appeal hostile to the institution of the jury, bolder than the Supreme Court and the Grand Judge, expressly demand its suppression; some, however, express their opinion with caution: "In the uncertainty of the opinions, the Grand Judge proposes a third trial of the institution of the jury. The expedient is no doubt good, but the court sees in it great inconveniences, that of prolonging the abuses of the jury and retarding the final reformation of the criminal procedure." [4] Metz demands, for the moment, but the abolition of the grand jury: "The grand jurors still more than the trial jurors are exposed to entreaties and seduction, because they are more approachable by the parties." [5] Orléans desires the suppression of the trial jury, but an institution dare not be absolutely renounced "the defect of which is not generally enough demonstrated and above all not generally enough recognized." [6] But the majority are altogether in the affirmative: "Everybody uniting intelligence with experience has declared against the jury. What good will a new trial be? Nothing brings the authorities into disrespect more than useless and dangerous

[1] The grand judge says "third experiment," because the jury had already been established twice, by the Law of 1791 and by the Code of Brumaire, year IV.

[2] "Observations des cours d'appel sur le projet de Code criminel," Paris, year XIII, 2 volumes. Imprimerie impériale.

[3] Ajaccio, "Observ.," p. 1; Montpellier, p. 2.

[4] Amiens, "Observ.," p. 2.

[5] Metz, "Observ.," p. 21.

[6] Orléans, p. 16; *cf.* Aix, p. 2; Colmar, p. 4.

experiments." [1] — "An almost universal cry is raised against the institution of the jury, and the majority of the court shares public opinion in this respect." [2] — "The defects of the institution of the jury being generally felt and universally recognized, the best form of procedure in criminal matters will be to confer that power upon the regular courts." [3] — "The institution of the jury is not suitable to France; it will be dangerous to make a new trial of it." [4] — "Experience has proved that the procedure by jury offers too favorable opportunities to crime." [5] — "What originally was such a fine and seductive speculation in practice offers nothing but the worst results." [6] — "It appears to us that the moment has not arrived to try the new experiment proposed, and that it will be necessary to reserve it for that happy period when our descendants see in the different French Revolutions nothing more than historic facts." [7] However, the objections which these courts advance regarding the jury were those which we have seen brought forward in the discussion of 1791, and those which will always be brought forward whenever the quarrel recommences: the ignorance and inexperience of the jurors, their fears, their hesitations, their passions; the repugnance of citizens to become jurors and the difficulty of making up the lists; the superior merits of the written procedure, incompatible with the jury, and of which the advantages are brought forward even for the defense; all this was brought forward. One of the characteristics of the jury naturally repugnant to the magistrates was also urged, namely, the establishment of traditions and a settled practice with a constantly renewed and changing body.[8]

It was the example of the English which had formerly popularized the institution of the jury in France; it was the English procedure which served as a model for the compilers of the Law of 1791, and the authors of the new bill had also borrowed from it in their principal reforms. The courts whose words we shall quote set themselves to point out that there was in all this merely a troublesome mania of imitation; and this demonstration might at that time be heartily indorsed. England had become the implacable enemy of France, and much blood had flowed since 1789. "We do not envy the English their tastes, their habits, their enthusiasm for their laws; we oppose to these declamations the experience and

[1] Bourges, p. 3. [2] Douai, p. 22. [3] Nancy, p. 6. [4] Nîmes, p. 9.
[5] Pau, p. 16. [6] Riom, p. 11. [7] Turin, p. 3.
[8] Bourges, p. 4: "The greatest defect of juries is that they are always composed of new people. What is this strange system of discarding in this respect the light of experience?"

the opinion of one of the greatest magistrates of our time,[1] to whom we could add an infinitude of others."[2] — "There is a jury in England, there must be one in France; grand jury in England, there must be the same in France. But is this people wiser, better governed, or happier than we? If these institutions do not exist here, it is by reason of their antiquity."[3] — "Let the English people feed themselves upon illusions under a government which oppresses them; the French people desire free institutions and such as reach their mark; it has been proved by too long a chain of experiences that none of the English institutions, which it is wished to transport into France, prosper here, not even that of justice of the peace."[4] — "The judgment by jurors has been transplanted from England into France, but it is clearly shown that the French character is not suited to this institution and that our ways are not consistent with it. . . . Let us then allow the English to live in their own way and let us live in ours."[5] — "The changing picture of the crimes of that nation, which uses assassination and the plague to repulse an enemy which it has provoked into breaking a solemn treaty hardly signed, ought not to induce us to adopt its system in criminal procedure. The jury has not rendered that people better; and if we recall what travellers have told us, there is no European country where theft, especially upon the highways, is more frequent and better organized than in that island."[6]

If a wrong road was taken in following the example of the English, the national tradition must be taken up again; it was necessary to return to the point where it was abandoned. It is towards the Ordinance of 1670, almost as it had been reformed in 1789, that the Courts of Appeals turn their eyes. "We do not hesitate to think that the Ordinance of 1670, modified by the Decrees of 1789, offers more guarantees and more real grounds of safety. . . . With the aid of counsel to the accused and the publicity of trials, the Ordinance of 1670, amended, would probably be, we do not hesitate to repeat, what would come nearest to perfection."[7] — "The criminal courts have been too much decried, notwithstanding that they have done less damage during the one hundred and twenty years following the Ordinance of 1670 than the jury within the short space of time which has followed its establishment."[8] — "The principal objections made to the procedure established by the Ordinance of 1670, are the want of publicity and the lack of

[1] *Séguier*, in his address of 1786 analyzed above. [2] Aix, pp. 10, 11.
[3] Bourges, p. 5. [4] Douai, p. 25. [5] Nancy, p. 5.
[6] Nîmes, p. 7. [7] Aix, pp. 2 and 12. [8] Bourges, p. 3.

ability experienced by the accused in making his defense heard. The experience of several years has shown how easy it was to do away with these inconveniences, however grave they may be supposed to be. The Constituent Assembly had called for the reform of these abuses; it might be added that it had prescribed the power to grant to the accused peremptory challenges of one or two judges. . . . Why seek among our neighbors an evanescent perfection which always escapes at the moment when it appears to be within reach, while it is so easy to give a valuable improvement to our laws, already the best of all those which have so far been in existence?"[1] — "Undoubtedly it cannot be denied that the Ordinance of 1670, the fruit of the reflections of the most famous jurisconsults of the age of Louis XIV, has not attained in many ways perfection in criminal legislation, and that, although it can be reproached with some defects, it is inherent in all the works of man in some point to pay a tribute to humanity."[2] — "The procedure established by the Ordinance of 1670 was justly censured for two principal reasons: the first was that the examination was secret; the second, that the accused was without counsel. Instead of changing this defective order, the system of the Revolution adopted an institution foreign to our usages."[3]

Finally, the court of Nancy sketched out the broad features of this French procedure. The courts of the arrondissement, with five judges at least, took cognizance in the first instance of all the offenses entailing afflictive and degrading punishment; the magistrates of police remained as the Law of Pluviôse had established them. A commissioner attached to each general court performed the functions formerly attributed to the criminal lieutenant; he heard the accused and the witnesses and caused the answers to be recorded, but with the assistance of a substitute of the same court; then came the requisitions of the public prosecutor and the investigation of the procedure by the entire bench to decide if there was cause for indictment. "The witnesses who should have been heard in writing would be confirmed and confronted by one and the same operation in the council chamber by the judge performing the function of the criminal lieutenant, in the presence of the substitute who had assisted him in the information and of the accused, who obtained the assistance of a counsel and of the magistrate of police. . . . The public would not be admitted at this step of examination of the procedure. At the hearing, the witnesses would be exempted from appearing

[1] Metz, p. 17. [2] Orléans, p. 16. [3] Pau, p. 107.

on account of the confrontation previously made. . . . The magistrate of safety would perform here the functions of public prosecutor; a reporter would be appointed for the purpose of reading all the documents, the accused would be represented by his official counsel, before whom all the documents of the procedure would previously have been laid. The report and the judgment would be public; appeal would be a matter of right." [1] This was the resurrection of the written procedure. Some of the courts, however, which condemned the jury, demanded the maintenance of the oral and public procedure: "Let the procedure of the investigation and of the judgment remain public and oral; let a president supervise the trial, and let the judges secretly deliberate as a trial jury, the president being excluded. . . . Let the judges publicly give their opinions *as a jury*, without being subject to any other proof than their personal convictions, and let them afterwards join with their president in deliberating *as a court* upon the punishment to be inflicted upon the guilty party." [2]

What of the courts who were favorable to the maintenance of procedure by jurors? They recalled the enthusiasm of the early days and the real benefits of the institution; they showed that the temporary lack of success was due merely to circumstances and defects of organization: "Do not infect the general legislation with what can be useful only under certain circumstances and for certain men. . . . And has that end not been obtained by creating special courts? Those are sufficient for the extraordinary cases of which we speak. Let them be allowed to remain so long as the social interest shall demand them, and pray to Heaven that this violent remedy be very soon needless and leave in all its purity the ordinary institutions upon which our happiness and that of posterity rest." [3] — "This ameliorative institution, independently of the abuses for which it has been blamed, the outcome of times of trouble and political strife, can nevertheless be suited to our existing ways, and strike deep roots in proportion as minds keep calm and congratulate themselves on being well governed." [4] — "The institution of the jury, for a long time awaited by humanity, had signalized the first works of our modern legislature, at the time when there existed in France but one single desire, that for good institutions and good laws. This new system of criminal jurisprudence was also universally approved and its benefits were generally felt. But very soon this excellent harmony, which

[1] Nancy, pp. 10 and 11.
[2] Colmar, p. 5.
[3] Agen, p. 4.
[4] Angers, p. 7.

looked at things from the true point of view, was disturbed; party spirit took possession of all minds; there was no hesitation in finding bad what had formerly appeared to be good; not only that, but an attempt was made to abuse it, and every means was employed to run down this institution. The true cause of the discredit of the procedure by juries is to be found in party spirit, in a system followed for the destruction of the best institutions produced by the Revolution."[1] It required a certain courage in the magistrates to use such pointed language at such a time.

§ 3. **"Observations" of the Criminal Courts.** — The observations furnished by seventy-five Criminal Courts were also published by order of the government,[2] and we believe they may be classified in the following way. A fairly large number, twenty-three, present merely remarks on matters of detail, and do not explicitly give an opinion in favor of the jury, maintained in the draft code, nor do they give an opinion against it;[3] twenty-six pronounce against the institution of the jury,[4] some rather feebly it is true; twenty-six demand its maintenance.[5]

Here also a large number of speakers demand the return to the written procedure without the co-operation of a jury; the reasons invoked were those which we have found in the observations of the Courts of Appeal, sometimes presented with a great deal of exaggeration. It is above all on the national character that they fasten: "Experience is undoubtedly the surest of all guides, but when the nations to be governed by it have arrived at maturity, it is their own and not the experience of foreign nations which must be chiefly consulted; and personal experience tells us that the Ordinance of 1670 offered to good order a surer safeguard and

[1] Caen, p. 2; *cf.* Toulouse, p. 3.

[2] "Observations des tribunaux criminels sur le projet de Code criminel," 6 vols. Imprim. impériale, year XII.

[3] Criminal courts of the following departments: Aisne, Basses-Alpes, Hautes-Alpes, Alpes-Maritimes, Aube, Charente-Inférieure, Corrèze, Gers, Gironde, Léman, Jemmapes, Indre-et-Loire, Loire-Inférieure, Meuse, Montblanc, Morbihan, Oise, Pas-de-Calais, Pô-et-Doire, Rhin-et-Moselle, Sarthe, Yonne.

[4] Ain, Allier, Ardèche, Ariège, Aude, Aveyron, Bouches-du-Rhône, Dyle, Doubs, Dordogne, Haute-Garonne, Forêts, Eure-et-Loir, Hérault, Isère, Lot, Meurthe, Lys, Lozère, Orne, Basses-Pyrénées, Var, Vaucluse, Haute-Vienne.

[5] Cantal, Excaut, Gard, Indre, Indre-et-Loire (only the attorney-general), Haute-Loire, Loire, Marne, Manche, Maine-et-Loire, Lot-et-Garonne, Moselle, Nièvre, Puy-de-Dôme, Hautes-Pyrénées, Pyrénées-Orientales, Bas-Rhin, Haut-Rhin, Roer, Saône-et-Loire, Sarre, Seine-et-Oise, Stura-et-Tanaro, Vosges.

more real grounds of safety than the institution of juries and prætorships." [1] — "What a difference there is between our manners, our customs, and our national character and those of the English nation! Without entering upon the subject in detail and at length . . . it is sufficient to instance the comparison of Shakespeare's plays and those of other English tragedians with those of Corneille, Racine, and Voltaire. . . . In a word, the sad experience which we have had with the institution of the jury, notwithstanding the various changes to which it has been subjected, proves that it is irreconcilable with the national customs and character, with those feelings of toleration and natural pity in the Frenchman which incline his heart to commiseration." [2] — "The Englishman at the theatre only cares for apparitions, madmen, dreadful criminals, murders long drawn out; he runs to animal fights, and probably regrets those of the gladiators; who knows if he does not seek the functions of a juror for the sake of the pleasure of watching a criminal struggling with his conscience, with the death that awaits him? The Frenchman, on the contrary, is delicate in all his tastes; he eagerly flees from any sight which could disagreeably awaken his sensitiveness; could he have any pleasure in wielding the bleeding sword of justice?" [3] — "The French Empire is in the centre of Europe, and Europe has only courts without juries. The Revolution merely expanded and strengthened the national character, it did not alter it. The French will never cease to be what they have always been, gallant, bellicose, witty, and frivolous. The reason that the institution of the jury is analogous to the English constitution is probably because they have based the former upon their constitution alone. It is the essential counterbalance of the royal prerogative, of class distinctions, privileges, and of the feudality which it has been their desire to retain. For the same reason the jury, which would have been necessary before the abolition of the three orders and feudality, has probably become useless here since all citizens have become equal before the law." [4] — "We unite in the general desire for its abolition, and we say to the genius who has saved France, and to all the generous and enlightened citizens whom he has consulted, that there was a time when civil liberty should have allowed the existence among us of the institution of the jury, but that we have now arrived at the time when the interests of

[1] Ariège, vol. I, p. 1.
[2] Aveyron, vol. I, pp. 15, 16.
[3] Doubs, vol. II, pp. 7, 8.
[4] Bouches-du-Rhône, vol. I, p. 75; *cf.* Dordogne, vol. II, p. 25; Eure-et-Loir, vol. II, pp. 9, 10; Haute-Garonne, vol. II, p. 41.

that same liberty demand its destruction."[1] — "We think that the institution of the jury is the most undesirable gift which England has made to us, and that it has against it not only the result of an unfortunate experience but also the principles of sound philosophy."[2]

The courts which demand the maintenance of the jury usually speak less firmly; most frequently they seize upon the idea expressed by the Grand Judge, that it is necessary to make a new trial of it.[3] Some, however, speak boldly: "The trial by jurors, notwithstanding all the blemishes which tarnish it and all the imperfections which disfigure it, has always appeared to us to be the finest and the most liberal of the institutions which the French people have derived from their political regeneration."[4] — "The institution of the jury has still detractors. These usually judge institutions only from the abuses which might result from them in some particular, and not by the aggregation of good achieved by them. If we go through the judicial records since the institution of the jury we shall not find a single instance of an innocent person having been condemned. It is true that guilty persons have often escaped, but is it not much better that a hundred culprits should succeed in evading the sword of the law than to see one innocent person succumb to it? On the other hand, go through the annals of the old penal legislation; what a large number of innocent persons have perished upon the rack in the name of the law! How much larger still the number of culprits who have not been punished! This parallel is sufficient to render homage to the wisdom of the institution of the jury, and to carry conviction of the necessity for its preservation. The criminal court of Maine-et-Loire combines the two special courts of 18th Pluviôse, year IX, and 25th Floréal, year X. It has been, and it still is, easy for it to estimate which of the two methods is preferable, either the institution of the jury or the courts judging alone the fact and the law. It does not hesitate to adopt the draft of the Code and to maintain the institution of the jury."[5] — "Is it imagined that a people must be almost entirely composed of philosophers and legists, and do we look for an assembly of jurors equal in wisdom to the Areopagus? No people will ever be mature-minded enough

[1] Nord, vol. V, pp. 6, 7. [2] Vaucluse, vol. VI, p. 9.

[3] Phrases like the following are often found: "We agree with the magistrates, as respected as they are enlightened, who have already given their opinion in favor of the preservation of the jury" (Sarre, vol. VI, p. 6).

[4] Loire, vol. III, p. 2. [5] Maine-et-Loire, vol. IV, pp. 22, 23.

to suit those who are so exacting. Everywhere we find a few philosophers, many of the rabble. Between these two extremes the mass of the population is composed of simple honest men of good sense. . . . We are not as good as the ancients, it is said; we are not even as good as the English; I know nothing of that. . . . That does not decide the question. The function of a juror is to determine whether an accused is guilty of the deed imputed to him. Well, what qualities are requisite to solve that problem? There must be attention to the evidence, sufficient intelligence to grasp it, and enough integrity to state in good faith the impressions received from it. To say that the French are not worthy of enjoying the institution of the jury is to say that they are not capable of attention, or that they have not a certain degree of intelligence and integrity." [1] — "We cannot conclude without manifesting our very pronounced desire for trial by jury. We are thoroughly persuaded that it is the palladium of civil liberty. . . . We are not less thoroughly alive to the necessity of preserving to the innocent accused the surest of safeguards. The whole evil comes not from the institution itself, but from the defective organization of the jury." [2] — "Let the jury be abolished and the duty imposed anew and forever on some jurisconsults, whom I shall even suppose to be chosen from among the most upright and clear-sighted, of pronouncing upon the honor and the life of accused persons, and very soon they will regard as faulty that expression of the inner consciousness, which we call conviction, whose voice is so clear and powerful. They would have recourse (this we are forced to believe, because a great many lawyers, and many judges, think so even now), to the old rules of law in regard to evidence. . . . And without desiring it they would be led into error much oftener than juries could be, and in a manner much more regrettable." [3]

It must be noted that in no particular were the opinions always absolute. Some in insisting on the maintenance of the trial jury demanded the suppression of the grand jury; others, on the contrary, wished merely to preserve the latter. "Experience has shown that the grand jury is the most important part of the institution of the jury. It is the door of the criminal sanctuary; and if it is always obstructed, as it has been down to to-day, it must be closed altogether and an institution which offers more disadvantages than advantages discarded." [4] — "It has been shown that private citizens called upon to perform these sacred duties

[1] Manche, vol. IV, pp. 56, 57. [2] Pyrénées-Orientales, vol. IV, p. 13.
[3] Sambre-et-Meuse, vol. VI, pp. 18, 19. [4] Aisne, vol. I, p. 8.

are never thoroughly imbued with the object of this institution. It is impossible to make them understand that they are not judges of the offense itself, but that other jurors are charged with that duty." [1] — "I think that the institution of the grand jury is useless and that it even has bad effects. Without wishing to be accused of desiring to innovate in attacking an established institution, I dare to say that our constituent legislators in proposing to create among us a new system of criminal procedure have not been sufficiently on their guard against the spirit of imitation, which has caused the introduction into their plan of proceedings well adapted to the English system, but which are out of place in theirs." [2] — "The grand jury will not be the subject of our observation. The institution in this particular is wanting in its chief element. The jurors no longer judge upon oral depositions; they become in a way judges of the written action." [3] — The following are opinions to the contrary: "The members of the criminal court of the department of Lot are of opinion that with the help of a better choice, which is proposed to be made, of the jurors, only the grand jury ought to be preserved, and that the rest of the examination and the judgment should be confided to the courts." [4] — "We do not consider that the grand jury presents nearly so much danger to society as the trial jury. Experience has proved that the jurors more willingly determine to prosecute than to condemn. . . . The adoption of this expedient would be to take the happy medium between the opinion of those who would preserve the institution of the jury and that of those who think it ought to be entirely rejected." [5] — "The Grand Judge in his report, where he discusses the organization of the jury, also seems to wish for its abolition. That fact appears more strikingly on pages 214 and 215, relative to the opinion which would preserve merely the grand jury, a brilliant idea, which, wisely carried through, would probably be the best way out of the difficulty of all the systems proposed." [6] It may be asked if those who wished to keep the grand jury only really believed that that institution could exist for any length of time deprived of its natural support. It was, we think, important to set down the principal data of the inquiry; it is curious to note the prophecies then put forth on one side and the other, now that time has given the solution.[7]

[1] Loir-et-Cher, vol. III, p. 24.
[2] Manche, vol. IV, p. 13.
[3] Eure-et-Loir, vol. II, p. 8.
[4] Lot, vol. IV, p. 12.
[5] Orne, vol. V, pp. 8, 9.
[6] Basses-Pyrénées, vol. V, p. 15.
[7] We may say that the majority of the criminal tribunals were favorable to the retention of the jury. We may even regard as being won over

§ 4. **The Jury and the Publicists.** — Besides the official inquiry there was another open, to which all were summoned; it was spontaneously made in books and pamphlets. The great question of the jury preoccupied all minds; the academies, as formerly, offered prizes in regard to the question of criminal legislation.[1] The pamphlets for and against the jury multiplied.[2] There was, with much less lustre and buoyancy, something recalling very remotely the movement of ideas preceding the reforms of the Revolution. We had arrived at the moment of lost illusions; the spirit of scepticism replaced the generosity of the early days; both camps no longer invoked the voice of nature, but the lessons of experience. Let us say something of MM. Bourguignon and Gach, whose works then attracted attention. In the year X the Institute had offered for competition the question, "What are the means of perfecting the institution of the jury in France?" This was clearly to indicate that the maintenance of procedure by jury was not in doubt, and M. Bourguignon so states at the beginning of his memorial, which won the prize. "The importance of the subject bears witness to the great wisdom of the learned men who have proposed it and the general and liberal intentions of the government, which manifests the most constant desire to ameliorate that institution." [3]

This memorial is an ardent pleading in favor of the jury. He begins with a rapid comparison of the jury as it exists in France with that of the Athenians, the Romans, and the English. "The lessons of experience are worth much more than abstract theories." [4] Then, studying the principles which ought to determine the formation of the lists of jurors, the author demands that only citizens be admitted who have a certain amount of property,

to that opinion the tribunals who do not give an opinion, acting on advice which appears to come from the Grand Judge and the Court of Cassation.

[1] "Mémoire qui a remporté le prix en l'an X sur cette question proposée par l'Institut national: Quels sont les moyens de perfectionner en France l'institution du jury," by *Bourguignon* (Paris, year X). — "Moyens de perfectionner le jury," by *F. Canard*, crowned work (Moulins 1802).

[2] See *Bourguignon*, "Deuxième et troisième mémoire sur le jury." — "De l'excellence de l'institution du jury et du système des lois pénales adoptées par l'Assemblée constituante," by *Porcher* (Orléans 1804). — "Des vices de l'institution du jury en France," by *M. Gach* (Paris 1804). — "Résultat de l'expérience contre le jury français," by M. . . . (Paris 1808). — *Cf.* "Développement des lois criminelles par la comparaison de plusieurs législations anciennes et modernes," by *Scipion Bexon* (Paris year X).

[3] "Deuxième et troisième mémoire sur le jury," p. 2. The author adds in a note: "A commission composed of magistrates of the highest merit is, by order of the government, exclusively employed in the preparation of a bill upon this important subject."

[4] "Deuxième et troisième mémoire sur le jury," p. 7.

and that they be *chosen* and not drawn by lot. Further, he says, "Experience has proved that it is more disadvantageous to confide the formation of that list to administrators than dangerous to confer it upon magistrates . . . the administrative and judicial authorities might, however, be made to concur in the choice of jurors."[1] He demands that the method of challenge be altered,[2] and that a simple majority of votes should suffice for condemnation. "It is true," he says, "that according to our old criminal laws the severest sentence only prevailed when it obtained a majority of two votes. This strange provision was no doubt adopted to serve as a corrective or palliative of the barbarous forms with which that Code was infected; but it is not from that source that the means for perfecting the jury ought to be drawn."[3] He presents very wise observations upon the drawing up of the questions to be put to the jury, some of which might even be very useful to-day.[4] All these ideas, and many others contained in the work, were perfectly judicious and capable of offering the legislator an interesting subject for reflection.

M. Gach's work seems to have produced a rather striking impression upon the minds of his contemporaries; it was fairly frequently quoted in the discussions of the State's Council. It was a violent attack upon the institution of the jury, "that eldest born of the French Revolution, the illustrious conquest of the eighteenth century over the wisdom of the preceding centuries;"[5] but this pamphlet really contained nothing new, merely repeating all the grievances we have so often heard raised, and that we shall hear so often raised again; the frivolity of the national character, the ignorance of jurors. "Considered in itself," said M. Gach, "this institution is one of the finest conceptions of the human mind; but as experience has taught us to mistrust the most brilliant theories in matters of civil and political legislation, I undertake to prove that the institution of the jury is merely a beautiful philosophical dream, impossible of realization among us. French soil, in other respects so fertile in celebrated and estimable men of

[1] "Deuxième et troisième mémoire sur le jury," p. 34.
[2] *Ibid.*, p. 42. [3] *Ibid.*, p. 90.
[4] pp. 50–96: "The first method consists in publishing legislative information as to the Penal Code, which shall include the exact and detailed definition of every offense, in inserting in every indictment the legal definition of the offense, and in charging the magistrate, whose duty it is to sum up the evidence, to explain to the jury how the characteristic features of the offense may be applied to the fact. . . . And I cannot help observing on this occasion that this want of legal definition of offenses is an important defect in our Penal Code" (p. 79).
[5] *Gach*, "Des vices du jury en France."

all descriptions of talents and merits, will never produce good jurors; the obstacle is in the character, manners, vices, and even the virtues of the nation. What advantages do you claim to draw from the example of ancient and modern nations? Is there any resemblance between the tribunals of Rome or Athens and the French jury? What have the Greeks and Romans in common with us, their manners with our manners, the time when they lived with that in which we live? The example of the English people cannot be of great weight; no nation in Europe except ours has yet imitated them on this point; and it is not reasonable to think that the English alone are better advised in this particular than the other nations of Europe." Elsewhere he says: "The mass of jurors being composed of citizens of all classes, functionaries excepted, such jurors cannot usually but lack in intelligence. It may be averred that the most intelligent nation in Europe, as well as the most polished and good-tempered, is probably one of the worst-informed. . . . There is no country where the mass of citizens stagnates in more profound ignorance of everything relating to the laws and public administration; lacking the wish to learn and too uneducated even to feel the value and necessity of education, the Frenchman in general does not read, does not observe, does not reflect." This thesis was, moreover, relieved by accurate observations upon the operation of the jury as then organized.

Bourguignon, however, resumed his pen and published two more memorials upon the jury. In the second of these[1] his object is to reply to the attacks against trial juries which in general had their birth among the magistracy. "I have heard jurisconsults and magistrates of the greatest merit cast doubt upon the superiority of this procedure . . . the want of success, they say, which it has obtained in France since it has been observed there, proves to a nicety that, good as it is, it cannot be adapted to our manners."[2] In his second memorial he sets out to refute M. Gach's work, the endless objections in which, he says, have been brought together and explained with very much force by a very talented writer.[3] In these two works the courageous and generous magistrate does not bring to bear any new elements to

[1] "Deuxième mémoire sur l'institution du jury," read in the general sitting of the Academy of Legislation of the first Nivôse, year XIII.

[2] "Deuxième mémoire," p. 3.

[3] "Troisième mémoire sur le jury," by *M. Bourguignon*, one of the magistrates of the "parquet" of the imperial high court, judge in the court of criminal justice of Paris (Paris 1808), p. 52.

the debate, but he takes up ardently and lucidly the well-grounded reasons for the maintenance of the jury. He furnishes, however, some rather valuable statistics. In the second memorial he compares the results obtained at Paris by means of the jury on one side and the special court on the other in the years X and XI. Seven hundred and eighty-eight accused had appeared before the jury, of whom five hundred and nineteen had been condemned and two hundred and nine acquitted. Before the special court one hundred and ninety-three accused had been brought; one hundred and twenty-seven had been condemned and sixty-six acquitted.[1] In the third memorial he completes this information. "During the years IX and X there were acquitted only one-fourth of the accused persons tried by jury, although the very same court acquitted more than a third of those that it has tried specially and without jurors. The comparative abstract of the decrees rendered by the same court during the years XI, XII, XIII, XIV and onwards have given me almost the same results."[2]

But it was thoroughly felt from that time that the solution of this great problem depended upon the man in whose hands France, weary and wounded, had placed her destinies. Bourguignon, in his second memorial, addressed him without naming him, when, in a rather specific enumeration, he cites the celebrated men who have been the partisans of the jury and those who have been its adversaries. Among the first he counts Solon, Pericles, Aristotle, Demosthenes, Lysias, the sons of Cornelius, Servilius Cœpio, Plautius, Silvanus, Marius, Sylla, Cicero, Pompey, Cæsar; in England Alfred the Great, John I, Henry III, Edward I; among the latter the thirty tyrants, and in England Henry IV, Henry VII, Henry VIII, James I, Charles II.[3] He concludes by invoking Augustus, a transparent allusion wanting neither in courage nor dignity: "Augustus employed this all-powerfulness to pacify the universe and procure for the Romans peace and safety; but unfortunately he transmitted it entirely to his successors, who abused it in the most shameful fashion. Posterity will have no right to address these reproaches to him: Cæsar, thou hast invested thyself with absolute power, destroyed our institutions, overturned the constitution of our ancestors; What hast thou substituted for these foundations of Roman greatness? The *lex regia*, that is to say, absolute and arbitrary despotism. . . . Cæsar, thy improvidence has rendered it the author of all the acts of tyranny

[1] "Deuxième mémoire," pp. 70, 71.
[2] "Troisième mémoire," p. 92.
[3] "Deuxième mémoire," pp. 59, 60.

by which they (thy successors) have sullied the annals of the Empire."[1] In concluding the preface to his third memorial he puts up a prayer to his all-powerful master. "The polemical discussion now taking place in regard to the jury will soon be finished. . . . Persuaded that the advantages resulting from this improved institution will not escape the vast genius which presides over the destinies of the Empire, I would consider this final pamphlet absolutely useless if it did not serve to destroy the prejudices sown among the different classes of society against a procedure too little known."[2]

[1] "Deuxième mémoire," p. 60.
[2] "Troisième mémoire," preface, p. 2.

CHAPTER II

THE QUESTION OF THE JURY BEFORE THE STATE'S COUNCIL

§ 1. **First Discussion of the Draft of the Criminal Code before the State's Council. Interruption of the Work.** — The draft of the Criminal Code had been sent, with the results of the inquiry, to the section of the State's Council on Legislation, then presided over by M. Bigot-Préameneu, and composed of MM. Berlier, Galli, Réal, Siméon, and Treilhard.[1] The debate in the State's Council in regard to the Code, which, as formerly in regard to the Ordinance of 1670, was necessarily to be the principal phase of the preliminary work, did not begin till the 2d Prairial, in the year XII (22d May, 1804). The official report of that first sitting is very brief: "His Majesty, who presides over the sitting, authorizes the section on Legislation to present within fifteen days the fundamental questions on the draft of the Criminal Code."[2] On 9th Prairial Napoleon renews this invitation; he declares moreover, and this is very important, that the decision come to upon this point shall not be final, "the Council remaining at liberty to revise their first resolutions."[3] It was also decided that the commissioners who had prepared the draft should be present at the sittings of the State's Council, but not at those of the section on Legislation, where they would have formed the majority. From that time everything is in readiness; the work is about to commence and was to be prosecuted until the 29th Frimaire, year XIII. Then a long interval ensues, and it is only on 23d January, 1808, that the discussion is resumed, this time to end in the presentation and the passing by the Legislative Body of the Code of Criminal Examination.

[1] *Locré*, vol. I, p. 205. The observations of the Courts of Appeal were brought together only in the course of the year XII; they are in general dated in the months of Germinal, Floréal, Messidor, and Thermidor of that year.

[2] *Ibid.*, vol. XXIV, p. 8.

[3] *Ibid.*, vol. XXIV, p. 9.

One question for a long time delayed the State's Council; namely, the one we have always met since 1789 whenever criminal legislation has been discussed: Shall the procedure by jury be preserved, or a return made to the traditions of the old French procedure? The judicial police, the prosecution, and the preliminary examination also made some difficulty, but upon this point the Law of Pluviôse had cleared the way. As to the procedure before the trial jurisdictions, the broad features, as we have said, had been definitely fixed by the Laws of the Intermediary Period.

Of the list of questions dealing with general principles, drawn up by order of the Emperor and presented in the sitting of 16th Prairial, year XII, the first eight deal with the jury.[1] Immediately discussion arises upon this point. Although the jury has numerous opponents, it also counts supporters, and M. Regnaud de Saint-Jean d'Angély even proposes a kind of duel between them by the creation of two rival commissions.[2] MM. Siméon, Dupuy, Portalis, and Bigot-Préameneu were heard in their turn, — to cite but the chief speakers, — demanding the return to the old forms of procedure, modified and rendered less severe. We already know their arguments; they are those which we have found in the observations of the Courts of Appeal and of the Criminal Courts: "At the commencement of the Revolution useful reforms were made in criminal procedure, by introducing into the information 'adjoints,' who supervised the examining judge, by rendering the confrontation public, by giving counsel to the accused, and by giving him communication of all the documents. The wish for the best, which has done us so much harm in the Revolution, subsequently led to the proposal of the jury."[3] — "In the publicity of the procedure and the trials lie the true safeguards of individual liberty. With that publicity one would be better and more justly tried by men whose office it is to do so,

[1] The following is the complete list:

"I. Shall the institution of the jury be preserved?

"II. Shall there be a grand jury and a trial jury?

"III. How shall the jurors be appointed; from what class shall they be appointed; by whom are they to be appointed?

"IV. How is the challenge to be exercised?

"V. Shall the examination be purely oral, or partly oral and partly written?

"VI. Shall several questions be put to the jury, or only one:—'Is the accused guilty or not guilty?'

"VII. Shall the verdict of the jury be unanimous or shall a certain number of votes determine the issue?

"VIII. Shall there be magistrates entitled to hold assizes in certain district criminal courts?" *Locré*, vol. XXIV, pp. 11, 12.

[2] *Locré*, vol. XXIV, p. 22.

[3] *M. Siméon, Locré*, vol. XXIV, pp. 3, 14.

and who have made a study and profession of it, than by all and sundry."[1] — "The results of the jury may be judged from what takes place among the English; there is no country with a worse police and less individual safety."[2] — "Portalis thinks that the jury ought to be suppressed. . . . The best jurisconsults (English) are not favorably impressed with the jury. In England the jury is the cause of very many disorders."[3] — "The only point in the new institutions which has obtained the general assent, is the publicity of the examination. . . . Neither the accused nor society finds a sufficient safeguard in the jury."[4]

These are very categorical and rather strange assertions; other speakers arrive at the same conclusion, but by a less direct road. "The institution of the jury has more disadvantages than advantages, but it would probably not be proper to suppress it suddenly now that we have become accustomed to it."[5] Without absolutely repudiating the jury, the archchancellor defends the written procedure: "It is exceedingly extravagant to expend enormous sums for a procedure of which no trace remains . . . it is no less surprising that the law attaches so little effect to the examination made by the magistrate of police and by the director of the grand jury, that it cannot be used even to enlighten the jury. See, besides, how the written procedure could be established. The examination made by the magistrate of police would constitute a charge against the accused, save for the proof offered by the evidence. The evidence would not be written, but the confessions of the accused and the variations of the witnesses would be contained in the official report signed by them."[6] Cambacérès, too, is a supporter of the Ordinance of 1670: "We ought not to be afraid of taking some of the provisions of the Ordinance of 1670. . . . The deprivation of counsel and defenders and the interrogation upon the prisoner's bench certainly ought not to be reëstablished, but that does not apply to the confirmation in which a witness can correct himself, or to the confrontation where the accused is allowed to object to the competency of the witnesses and to dispute their depositions. With some alterations, the articles of the Ordinance of 1670 upon this subject could be usefully employed in our new legislation."[7]

Everybody, however, protests against the doctrine of legal

[1] *M. Siméon, Locré*, vol. XXIV, p. 21.
[2] *M. Dupuy, Locré*, vol. XXIV, p. 29.
[3] *Locré*, vol. XXIV, pp. 34–36.
[4] *M. Bigot-Préameneu, Locré*, vol. XXIV, p. 40.
[5] *M. Boulay, Locré*, vol. XXXIV, p. 22.
[6] *Locré*, vol. XXXIV, p. 27.
[7] *Ibid.*, vol. XXXIV, p. 28.

proofs. The magistrates who would replace the jury should form their conviction "not upon the proofs called legal, but with the same means, the same elements as the jury and according to the evidence."[1] Portalis even tries to show that heretofore the doctrine of legal proofs existed only in a sense favorable to the accused: "It would be a mistake to suppose that this doctrine would *compel* the judge to condemn when two witnesses agreed upon the same fact; it is limited to preventing the judge from condemning when there are not at least two such witnesses."[2]

There were in the Council, however, men who did not abandon the principles of that Revolution, which had in some cases drawn them from obscurity and from the lowest ranks of the people to carry them to honor and power. The jury found capable and eloquent defenders: MM. Berlier, Treilhard, Defermon, Cretet, Bérenger, Frochot, and, lastly, the high constable M. Regnaud de Saint-Jean d'Angély declared themselves in favor of its maintenance. They invoked the equitable and protective character of the procedure by jury; they showed above all that it had not, so far, been in operation in France under normal conditions: "Probably, had we been living under the rule of the Law of 1789, prudence, the enemy of innovations and trials, would have counselled us to remain as we were; but the step has been taken, and the same prudence forbids us to renounce an improvement so dearly acquired."[3] — "Why do the English still so jealously guard it (the jury system)? There is reason to believe that it is because nothing is more terrible than to give to a few the perpetual right of life and death over all the others."[4] — "To-day, when the legislature can follow the counsels of wisdom and reëstablish the jury in all its purity, the nation will probably see with surprise such a liberal institution obliterated from the Code of its laws, under a leader whom it knows to be strongly attached to liberal sentiments."[5] — "The nation is attached to the institution of the jury for the reason that, although it has been the means of several scandalous acquittals, it has at least the advantage of never putting the accused at the mercy of individual passion."[6] — "So long as the institution of the jury has not been vitiated, it has had none but advantageous results."[7] — The high constable declares that "he

[1] *M. Siméon, Locré,* vol. XXXIV, p. 19.
[2] *Locré,* vol. XXXIV, p. 53. [3] *M. Berlier, Locré,* vol. XXIV, p. 25.
[4] *M. Cretet, Locré,* vol. XXIV, p. 30.
[5] *M. Treilhard, Locré,* vol. XXIV, p. 33.
[6] *M. Frochot, Locré,* vol. XXIV, p. 44.
[7] *M. Defermon, Locré,* vol. XXIV, p. 37.

has always heard the jury spoken of as one of the principal advantages which the French have derived from the Revolution, and as one of the most certain safeguards of liberty." [1] — M. Regnaud de Saint-Jean d'Angély asserts that "the gravest inconveniences would follow its suppression. . . . From 1789 to 1791 attempts were made to bring to the form of procedure, introduced by the Ordinance of 1670, the only modifications of which it was susceptible. That trial had not been a happy one. Then the jury was established, and obtained general approval." [2]

The defenders of the jury especially triumphed when they pointed out that it alone was compatible with that doctrine of moral proofs that everybody would respect: "No law enjoins upon criminal judges the subordination of their moral conviction to legal proofs, although the legal proofs *might* often prevail." [3] — "It would be arming professional judges with too formidable a power to call upon them to decide upon the fact, and to allow them to allege no other grounds for their judgment than their private opinion, their conscience. The judgment of the fact could not be intrusted to them without reëstablishing the doctrine of legal proofs; but since that system is acknowledged to be pernicious the result is that it is not necessary to constitute permanent jurors, and it *is* necessary to return to the jury." [4] — "Might it not happen that each court would create its own principles and constitute a body of doctrine upon the choice of circumstances which ought to entail acquittal or condemnation?" [5]

The supporters of the jury, moreover, accepted, either as a transitory measure or as a permanent institution, the special tribunals for the more dangerous criminals: "If allowance can be made for special circumstances by temporary restrictions, why destroy the principle and deprive our descendants of the benefit of the institution?" [6] — "The right to be tried by jury is a civic right: hence it cannot be claimed by vagrants and vagabonds. There is no objection to the establishment for them of a 'prévôtal' court of justice, provided it be better organized and less rapid in its movement than the old. The crime of forgery should also be remitted to these courts." [7]

In this important discussion, however, which really should

[1] *M. Defermon, Locré,* vol. XXIV, p. 44.
[2] *Ibid.,* vol. XXIV, p. 38.
[3] *M. Berlier, Locré,* vol. XXIV, p. 25.
[4] *M. Bérenger, Locré,* vol. XXIV, p. 43.
[5] *M. Cretet, Locré,* vol. XXIV, p. 31.
[6] *M. Berlier, Locré,* vol. XXIV, p. 24.
[7] *M. Regnaud, Locré,* vol. XXIV, p. 39.

have been decisive, although it was recommenced later on, all eyes were turned towards the chief who presided over it. Napoleon had intervened several times; he appeared greatly struck with the system expounded by M. Siméon: "His Majesty says that no reply has been made to what M. Siméon has advocated, that the judges, not being compelled to decide according to the legal proofs, are no more than jurors, but have this advantage over the ordinary jurors, that they are better trained and better chosen; that it would be from such citizens that jurors would have to be taken, although they were not invested with the character of judges."[1] But the discussion took a turn more and more favorable to the maintenance of the jury. "M. Berlier says that the more the debate progresses, the more satisfied he is of the sufficiency of the institution of the jury, and that it merely needs some improvements."[2] Then the Emperor found it expedient to close the debates; but he took care to observe: "that he does not regard the Council as bound by the resolution which has been taken, and that if, in organizing the system, unforeseen obstacles should be encountered, the Council are at liberty to revert to their original opinion."[3] He took the opportunity, however, of giving his opinion: "On both sides very strong reasons have been adduced for and against the institution of the jury, but it cannot be denied that a tyrannical government would have a greater advantage with the jury than with judges, who are less under its control, and who would always oppose it more vigorously. Had the most terrible tribunals juries? Had they been composed of magistrates, the customs and the forms would have been a rampart against unjust and arbitrary condemnations. The severity which the continued exercise of these functions could impart is little to be feared, since the procedure is public, and there are defenders and debates. His Majesty, however, has no objection to the jury if it is possible to insure its proper composition. . . . It will also be necessary to organize exceptional courts to take jurisdiction of offenses committed by non-residents or by those united in bands."[4] From that time (for the moment at least) the question was decided: "The Council adopts the principle of the preservation of the institution of the jury."[5] Immediately afterwards the second question: "Shall there be a grand jury and a trial jury?"

[1] *Locré*, vol. XXIV, p. 33.
[2] *Ibid.*, vol. XXIV, p. 45.
[3] *Ibid.*, vol. XXIV, p. 46.
[4] *Ibid.*, vol. XXIV, p. 47.
[5] *Ibid.*, vol. XXIV, p. 48.

was answered in the affirmative, after very brief remarks by MM. Treilhard and Bigot-Préameneu.[1]

The choice of jurors was the next thing to occupy the State's Council's attention; this point, however interesting it may be, we may pass over; but incidentally one of the debates brings up the old ideas. Napoleon asks if in the opinion of the Council lawyers should be allowed as counsel;[2] and opinions unfavorable to the liberty of the defense made themselves apparent. "M. Miot says that in England the accused have not as a matter of right the power to choose defenders. In all cases advocates are not admitted to this duty because it is feared that they would obscure the facts. Counsel sit near the accused and help them with their advice, but they plead only when they have obtained permission to do so."[3] M. Regnaud de Saint-Jean d'Angély went farther: "In the civil courts the agency of lawyers is always necessary because there the disputed points present questions of law, which could not be discussed except by men versed in the knowledge of the law; but it is different in criminal courts, where the only point is the discovery of the truth of a fact. There, the accused himself can, by the explanations he gives, clear himself from the charges brought against him; it is, therefore, not necessary for him to have a defender. There are, it is true, men whom ignorance or timidity prevent from explaining themselves, and it would be necessary to make an exception in their case. The president of the court would decide whether or not it was proper to admit this exception and to grant a defender." This was, in fact, what was formerly said in justification of the Ordinance.

This proposition, however, which Lamoignon had formerly vainly opposed, gave rise to protests: "M. Bérenger says that it would never be possible to find an organization and forms perfect enough to give to the judge the certainty that he never condemned an innocent person. Sometimes appearances are against the accused, and because his confusion and fear prevent him from explaining them away, he appears to be guilty. It is therefore always necessary that he should have the aid of a defender. This aid, moreover, cannot be refused without recalling a too notorious law with which our criminal procedure ought not to have any relation. M. Treilhard says that the accused to whom

[1] *Locré,* vol. XXIV, p. 48.

[2] A few moments before he had said: "It is important to admit as defending counsel for the accused men unacquainted with the customs of the bar." *Locré,* vol. XXIV, p. 52.

[3] *Locré,* vol. XXIV, p. 52.

a defender is refused would be convinced that there was a desire for his destruction. The rule which M. Miot declares exists in England is part of the law, but in fact an accused is never refused permission to have a counsel." [1] It was not difficult to show that the provision which would exclude counsel would be illusory and that, moreover, their aid was legitimate and often necessary.[2] "It would be preferable to give a discretionary power to the president, to authorize him to silence any advocate who does not keep within the limits of a legitimate defense, and even to bar such an advocate from the court when circumstances demand it." [3]

In the same sitting, the Council decided upon the question of the written procedure. In this respect the reformatory tendencies seemed to triumph. Cambacérès expounded the proposal of which we have spoken before: "As matters exist at present, the examination is wholly oral; for what has been written only serves as information for the direction of the trial. . . . The first information will continue to be made by the magistrate of police. . . . This procedure will be transmitted to the director of the jury, who will make the confirmation of witnesses. . . . All these proceedings will be sent to the Court of Criminal Justice along with the accused, who will be allowed to have a counsel visit him in his prison. The trials will be opened by the reading of the proceedings conducted by the magistrate of police and the director of the jury. Witnesses will be summoned; the accused, aided by counsel seated near him, will be entitled to urge objections to their competency and to disprove their depositions. The official report will not contain the evidence in detail, but the attorney-general and the accused will have the right to have the results thereof stated. The whole will be submitted to the jury." — "His Majesty adopts the idea of submitting a copy of the information to the jury. He nevertheless thinks that that made by the police ought not to be communicated to them; for the police examines chiefly with a view to discover all the culprits and all the circumstances of the crime; for this reason it ought to work in secret. The examining judge, on the contrary, has no other purpose than to arrive at the

[1] *Locré*, vol. XXIV, pp. 53, 54.

[2] "M. Siméon says that the regulation which would exclude advocates would be evaded; they would compose the pleas for the defense. [This reminds one of the "logogriphs" of Athens.] We should, moreover, see gathering about the criminal courts, as formerly before the consuls, men who are not graduates, who would exercise the office of defending counsel and would very soon acquire the art of circumventing justice as well as the lawyers" (p. 52).

[3] *M. Bérenger, Locré*, vol. XXIV, p. 54.

truth of the facts." — "The proposals of his Royal Highness, the Archchancellor, are adopted with the modification that the examination made by the police is not to be communicated."[1] This was a very important decision; it was making that mixture of the written procedure and the procedure by jury, which the wisdom of the Constituent Assembly had repudiated. This would probably have resulted in the destruction of the very institution, the maintenance of which had been decided upon; but happily this idea, as we know, was not carried into effect.

The debate continued throughout the sittings of 23d and 30th Prairial. Other questions of principle were decided, the most of which concerned criminal law, properly so called. The institution of "Prætors," against which the majority of the Courts of Appeal and the Criminal Courts had given their opinion, was vigorously opposed; it was decided that the Courts of Criminal Justice should be stationary.[2] The discussion passed to the articles presented by the section on Legislation (this was the first part concerning the criminal procedure to be taken up), which occupied the sittings of 17th, 21st, 24th, and 28th Fructidor in the year XII; and 3d, 10th, 14th, 17th, 21st, and 24th Vendémiaire in the year XIII.[3]

Everything appeared to be going smoothly, when all at once the jury was put in question anew. In the sitting of 1st Brumaire, in the year XIII, presided over by Napoleon, M. Bigot-Préameneu reported a deliberation which had taken place in the section on Legislation "upon the union of the criminal courts and the civil courts." The idea of the Revolution had been, on the contrary, completely to sever the two courts of justice, and to have criminal courts distinct from the civil courts. But the new proposal appeared to simplify and increase the dignity of the magistracy. The union of courts had already been recognized in regard to the correctional police by the Law of 27th Ventôse in the year IV; the judgments were henceforth rendered in that matter by the courts of the first instance; it was destined very soon to be the same in regard to the ordinary police courts, save for one slight exception which has disappeared in our days.

The following was the proposed procedure in criminal matters.[4] The accused would be brought by the examining magistrate before the court of the first instance (which would fulfil the func-

[1] *Locré*, vol. XXIV, pp. 56, 57.
[2] *Ibid.*, vol. XXIV, p. 99.
[3] *Ibid.*, vol. XXIV, pp. 108–419.
[4] A bill was introduced in regard to this in the sitting of 8th Brumaire, year XIII (*Locré*, vol. XXIV, p. 428 *et seq.*).

tions of the grand jury), composed of six judges, with the addition of the examining judge. The Courts of Criminal Justice were united to the Courts of Appeal and bore the name of Imperial Courts. In these courts one section was constituted, — renewed every year like the "Tournelle" of the old parlements; before it were brought not only the appeals of the correctional police, but also the criminal actions in regard to which arraignments had been decided upon. In the bill the jury was preserved, Article 19: "The judgments in criminal matters will be rendered upon the verdict of a jury."

A considerable revolution was thereby wrought in the working of the jury. Up to that time, the union of the juries in each department had always been a principle, and it had become customary. The provision requiring the carrying to the chief seat of the court of all the criminal matters of the jurisdiction had the effect of rendering jury service, already obtained with great difficulty, impossible. It also meant the substitution, in the near future, of the written procedure for the oral procedure, the transportation of the witnesses to the chief seat of the court becoming too difficult and too costly. It was an indirect method, making the new practice re-establish, by its own workings, the old procedure. All this was foreseen from the very first; it was acknowledged by the opponents, as well as the supporters of the jury. "It is true," says M. Boulay, "that the union of the criminal and civil courts means the ultimate destruction of the jury. It is certain that when the public sees on one side enlightened magistrates and on the other ignorant and inexperienced jurors, the parallel will not be advantageous to the latter; it seems, then, that it would be proper, if we decide upon the union, to decide frankly at the same time upon the suppression of the jury."[1] M. Treilhard, with a new warmth, takes up the defense of the threatened institution. "The jury," he says, "is getting along much better than in the past; it will get along still better in the future. . . . How, without enormous expenses and delay in the actions, can the accused, the witnesses, and the jurors of seven or eight departments be transported to the chief places of the Courts of Appeal? . . . Would you dispense with the hearing of the absent witnesses? That would mean the destruction of the accused." Finally, he addresses to the Emperor a personal argument, containing at once a flattery and an irony, but really also containing the truth: "The institution of the jury," he tells him, "will succeed if people are

[1] *Locré*, vol. XXIV, p. 416.

thoroughly persuaded that it meets with Your Majesty's views." [1] Napoleon wished to mitigate the effect produced by the bill and to conceal its consequences: "It is not," he interjected, "a question of the institution of the jury," [2] and later he added: "That if it was wished to return to the question of the maintenance of the jury, it should be approached frankly, but that question had been decided, and His Majesty shared the opinion of those who thought the jury ought to be maintained. This method of procedure appeared to be the best; and besides, it was enough to insure His Majesty's adoption that it had not been unanimously rejected." [3] Erelong, in a long speech, he endeavored to refute M. Treilhard's objections. But the truth was not long in reappearing. The Archchancellor made this statement: "It may be objected that this system is incompatible with the procedure by jury; His Royal Highness is not in favor of that institution and he thinks that public opinion is not favorable to it." [4]

In the following sitting, the question was directly broached. The suppression of the grand jury was proposed. M. Treilhard showed that the motion was unconstitutional, the constitution of the year VIII guaranteeing the double jury. Deception was tried; it was said that the grand jury was not really suppressed, that it was proposed merely to "convert the judges into jurors." [5] But Napoleon himself declared that "the constitution declares too imperatively that the accusation shall be admitted by jurors to allow of this power being conferred upon judges without a senatus-consultum." [6] This question was not of very great fundamental importance. MM. Treilhard and Berlier brought the debate back to the leading point, that is to say, the trial jury, the early destruction of which was assured by the bill; for "to maintain an institution on paper means nothing when the germ of its destruction is planted there." [7] They demanded urgently that the question should be definitely settled, and they easily won their

[1] *Locré*, vol. XXIV, pp. 420–422.

[2] *Ibid.*, vol. XXIV, p. 420.

[3] *Ibid.*, vol. XXIV, pp. 422, 423.

[4] *Ibid.*, vol. XXIV, p. 439. Napoleon also expressed the idea that he desired large judicial bodies, "because it is necessary that, if the public prosecutor neglects his duties, the criminal court should be able to send for him and order him to prosecute." M. Treilhard replied that "all this time the office of the person who prosecutes has been distinguished from that of the person who judges, because it would be contrary to law to make the same individual a judge and a party." — "His Majesty says that it does not enter into his ideas to allow the courts of judicature to directly prosecute crime, but that he wishes that the courts may be able to order the prosecution thereof" (pp. 418, 419).

[5] *M. Siméon, Locré*, vol. XXIV, p. 437.

[6] *Locré*, vol. XXIV, p. 439.

[7] *Ibid.*, vol. XXIV, p. 443.

point. "His Majesty allows the renewed discussion of the question of whether the jury shall be retained." The discussion was short. MM. Fourcroy and Montalivet spoke in favor of the jury, and the "Council adhered to the resolution which it had taken in the sitting of the 16th Prairial for the preservation of the jury." The strategy had been baffled almost without a struggle. But the battle was not yet finally won: the organization of the criminal courts was still threatened.

Then M. Berlier had a fertile idea. Adopting the principle of the union of the two Courts of Judicature, he found the means of reconciling this with the normal working of the jury: "Let us commence by uniting all the judges of both jurisdictions, so that they will form but one body, from which will be taken successively judges who will proceed to hold, in criminal matters, periodical assizes in the chief place of each department, and who, on their return to the Court of Appeal, will there decide upon the civil disputes of their fellow-citizens."[1] This was, it is evident, the system which was destined to triumph, and which experience has sanctioned, — a system much preferable, it must be said, to that of the Constituent Assembly, because the president of the assizes is required to be a magistrate elevated in rank and chosen with care. M. Treilhard also openly came to his aid. This proposal, however, was contested by the Archchancellor; he declared "that if the jury is admitted, it is to please some noble minds, but he is persuaded that it will rather be by forming great bodies than by this institution that the establishment of a rigorous and imposing juridical system will be attained."[2] Finally, the Council decides the principle, "that civil and criminal justice will be rendered by the same court; that these courts shall be stationary, notwithstanding which, in cases of necessity, the criminal section could go and hold its assizes away from the place where the court sits."[3] A merely illusory concession was made to M. Berlier's idea; but the germ deposited was to grow till it penetrated everywhere.

In the sitting of 15th Brumaire, year XIII, the supporters of the jury gained a new advantage, which, however, could not be lasting: "the Council adopts the principle that the verdict that there is or is not ground for indictment shall continue to be given by jurors."[4]

The discussion of the bill upon the union of the two Courts of

[1] *Locré*, vol. XXIV, p. 445.
[2] *Ibid.*, vol. XXIV, p. 447.
[3] *Ibid.*, vol. XXIV, p. 452.
[4] *Ibid.*, vol. XXIV, p. 454.

Judicature was continued in the sittings of 22d and 29th Brumaire, and 20th Frimaire in the year XIII. Three new drafts were proposed and discussed. Suddenly an interruption occurred. Proceedings were taken "to report to His Majesty observations presented by the magistrates who have been summoned to the coronation." The chief justice declares that, consulted upon the union of the two systems of justice, "the president and attorneys-general of the criminal courts have not attacked the system in itself, but there appears to be a general fear that it cannot be reconciled with the summoning of jurors and witnesses. However, the magistrates are sure that the examination by juries has for some time taken a better direction. The increase in crimes is very much less."[1] The Archchancellor "has found more magistrates than he thought of the opinion that the examination by juries ought to be preserved, but with modifications. This opinion is shared even by those who were the loudest in their complaints on account of the direction the jury had taken in several particular circumstances; they agree that matters are improved and that there are fewer abuses. In regard to the union, the system appears to them to be good, but one difficult of execution, so far as regards the jury." — "Opinion is unanimous," says M. Treilhard, "upon the impossibility of preserving the jury if criminal and civil justice are united."[2] M. Berlier asserts that "according to several magistrates with whom he has had occasion to speak, the abolition of the jury will be the necessary and early consequence of the plan of union resolved upon in the recent sittings. But that does not constitute the only risk which this bill incurs; it also endangers the oral examination and the public trial. Now, although opinion is divided upon the institution of the jury, everybody at least agrees in thinking that the abolition of the oral examination of the trial will be a public calamity; that, however will not be long in happening if the bill goes through. . . . As n one dares to propose that it shall be sufficient to submit simpl copies of the depositions, as was practised under the Old Régime the existing courts must be maintained as the only kind of organiza tion to which the beneficent institution of the publicity of trial can be adapted."[3] — "M. Defermon says that the general opin ion is that the union would destroy the jury, in the course of tim

[1] *Locré*, vol. XXIV, p. 509; he adds later "that before having heard th observations of the magistrates he was persuaded that the institution the jury could be reconciled with the two systems of justice; now thought it impossible" (p. 516).

[2] *Ibid.*, vol. XXIV, p. 510.

[3] *Ibid.*, vol. XXIV, p. 510.

at least; but what is of especial importance is to ascertain if this institution can be abandoned without abandoning at the same time the public trials, which are the accused's safeguard."[1]

The Emperor then demanded if the tribunals had "expressed a *positive* opinion upon the institution of the jury."[2] The replies were very clear: "The majority," says the chief justice, "decide against any institution with which the jury cannot be reconciled;"[3] and the Archchancellor "has found the opinion of the magistrates more favorable to the jury than he thought." Public opinion was clearly expressed; so Napoleon, unveiling his true thoughts, declared that "the opinion upon the institution of the jury appears to be so doubtful that its suppression would not excite any regrets."[4] The Council, however, "resolves that criminal and civil justice shall continue to be administered by different tribunals."

From that time everything seemed to be at an end upon that point; there remained nothing but to discuss the articles of the draft of the Penal Code. This discussion was effectually resumed, and in the three sittings of 22d, 27th, and 29th Frimaire, in the year XIII, a new draft of the first ninety articles was examined. Then the work was suddenly stopped, and was not taken up again until after the lapse of three years, in 1808. How is this to be explained?[5] Was it not that the Emperor had determined on the suppression of the jury, but had decided that as the moment was not favorable, he must wait, thinking that probably several years would suffice to efface the sympathies which this institution still retained? The work, therefore, remained uncompleted and the thread suspended. "Pendent opera interrupta minæque!"

§ 2. **Resumption of the Work. Suppression of the Grand Jury. Retention of the Petty Jury.** — When the work was resumed in 1808, the great debate was again taken up. The first sitting (23d January, 1808) is opened by the report of M. Treilhard: "He reports regarding the trend of the discussion which took place in the year XII, and adds that the matter was reduced to the presentation of various questions, the solution of which ought to fix the foundations of the bill; that several have been decided, and that others remain undecided." He had these questions read, the first being: "Shall the institution of the jury be preserved?"

[1] *Locré*, vol. XXIV, p. 512.
[2] *Ibid.*, vol. XXIV, p. 516.
[3] *Ibid.*, vol. XXIV, p. 517.
[4] *Ibid.*, vol. XXIV, p. 519.
[5] Napoleon had previously stated that it was necessary to make haste; "there is no advantage in delaying the drawing up of the Criminal Code; next year would find them in the same state as at present. Time alone would not bring about unanimity of opinion, nor would it remove doubts or furnish ideas." *Locré*, vol. XXIV, p. 440.

The great problem still presented itself, mingled with that of the union of the two courts of justice, to which Napoleon steadfastly clung. In this first sitting the attack and the defense of the threatened institution took place under very much the same circumstances as in the years XII and XIII. Three times the Emperor asked how the jury had worked during the three years. The chief justice replied rather vaguely "that in general, the jurors fulfilled their functions rather feebly, and that they encouraged crime by the resulting impunity." [1] But M. Treilhard, while acknowledging that he could not speak to the point upon the existing condition of the jury, declared "that, after all, the number of offenses has diminished. The special tribunals, it is true, have contributed very much to stop the disorder; however, many crimes are still tried by juries." [2] M. Bérenger "remarks two facts: one is notorious, that offenses are diminishing in number; the other, which nobody disputes, is that there is not a single example of an unjust condemnation." [3] Cambacérès asserted anew that the jury "is not in accordance with the character of the nation," [4] and M. Jaubert "that the greater part of the French nation repudiates the institution of the jury." But Napoleon always intervened personally with great energy; there was a sort of argument between him and M. Treilhard: "M. Treilhard said that the bill had the disadvantage of destroying, in fact at least, the publicity of the trials, which is the greatest safeguard, and the want of which an examination in writing cannot supply; nothing was more disastrous than the secret procedure. — His Majesty said that there was no question of reëstablishing the secret procedure. — M. Treilhard replied that that was what would inevitably happen by force of circumstances. — His Majesty asked if the union of the two systems of judicature did not present any advantage. — M. Treilhard replied that it would form great bodies, but that he does not see in that the means of gaining more respect for the magistracy. — His Majesty said that there would result from it the ease of converting civil actions into criminal actions, whenever that was proper to be done. — M. Treilhard protested that this conversion was very rare.[5] — His Majesty said that it would be very extraordinary if, for the slightest civil interest, a citizen should have the option of being tried successively by two courts, and that when his honor and his life were concerned he should be allowed

[1] *Locré*, vol. XXIV, p. 579.
[2] *Ibid.*, vol. XXIV, p. 581.
[3] *Ibid.*, vol. XXIV, p. 591.
[4] *Ibid.*, vol. XXIV, p. 591.
[5] *Ibid.*, vol. XXIV, p. 587.

but one stage of jurisdiction. — M. Treilhard said that there were also two stages in criminal prosecutions, since the accused was examined by the grand jury and by the trial jury. — His Majesty said that did not constitute two stages." [1] Finally the Council, once more, "decides that the jury be preserved, but that the cognizance of certain offenses shall be reserved for special tribunals."

It might be thought that the question was irrevocably settled, that it would not appear again. That, however, was not the case; it was taken up in the following sitting, on 2d February, 1808. The first speaker was M. Jaubert, one of the most decided opponents of the jury, and his first words clear up the situation: "It is not denied that the opinion appears to be formed in the Council, that the maintenance of the jury is decided upon, and that there remains as a counterbalance to these deciding votes nothing but His Majesty's genius and authority." [2] M. Jaubert's forcible address, in which he maintains "that the old institutions had specific advantages over this modern institution," concludes with a demand "for the suppression of the jury, for the formation of a great body to exercise at once both forms of justice; for the organization of a procedure which shall preserve publicity of actions and the use of counsel in defense." [3]

Thereafter the discussion started again. The Minister of Religion disputed the possibility of separating law from fact; he asserted that in England the jury was regarded "as a regrettable institution"; [4] and that "although Europe has made great progress in civilization for several centuries, no nation has adopted the trial by jury." M. Berlier proceeded once more to defend the noble cause which he had hitherto so energetically supported: "The institution of the jury is thoroughly tested; it has in its present shape rendered great services to society, and it will render still greater services in its future form." [5] The Emperor himself appeared this time to have come to a decision: "His Majesty says that he prefers the old legislation to a system where the same judges would always decide as jurors; habit would render them callous, and the accused would no longer have the same safeguards as formerly. It is necessary that the functions of the juror be performed but rarely by the same person." The Council "adopts the trial by jurors anew."

[1] *Locré*, vol. XXIV, p. 588.
[2] *Ibid.*, vol. XXIV, p. 603.
[3] *Ibid.*, vol. XXIV, p. 607.
[4] *Ibid.*, vol. XXIV, p. 613.
[5] *Ibid.*, vol. XXIV, p. 618.

This decision was taken for the fourth time. The matter will not come up again. The institution, however, did not emerge entirely unscathed from the attacks made on it; the grand jury was abolished. M. Jaubert declared "that with the grand jury society has no longer a safeguard;" and Napoleon, in a very able statement, showed that this jury was singularly inappropriate for the task it ought to fulfil. "The Council decides that the grand jury shall be suppressed."[1]

There remained the important question of the organization of the criminal courts and the union of the two systems of justice. A plan had been submitted by Napoleon at the sitting of 23d January.[2] At that of 2d February he submitted a new one.[3] The section on Legislation set to work upon these proposals, and, in the sitting of 6th February, Treilhard presented another draft;[4] he stated that the section had blended the two plans, chiefly following the second: "Besides, it presents but the foundations for the opinions of His Majesty and his Council." A discussion then arose, resulting in the section on Legislation preparing seven new articles, which were discussed in the sitting of 16th February.[5] A fifth, sixth, and seventh draft were successively submitted. Finally, after all these waverings, it was decided, as M. Berlier had already proposed, that the criminal courts should be united with the civil courts, but that the juries of each department should meet at the chief place of each department. The two principles were reconciled by substituting for the permanent criminal court assizes presided over by members of the Court of Appeals, sitting along with assessors, chosen from among the members of the court, or from among those of the courts of the first instance. The solution of the problem had been found.

There was also some hesitation as to the arraignment: "The Council," said M. Treilhard, "originally placed the prosecution with the courts of the first instance; afterwards it was delegated to the Imperial Courts. In order to do away with this system, which the section believed to be dangerous, it attempted to put the matter in the hands of the imperial procurator and the examining magistrate."[6] If these two magistrates were agreed, the accused must be brought before the assizes; if they were of different opinions, the matter was referred to the court. This was something abnormal; and a new draft, that of 7th February, 1808,

[1] *Locré*, vol. XXIV, p. 622.
[2] *Ibid.*, vol. XXIV, p. 582.
[3] *Ibid.*, vol. XXIV, p. 591 *et seq.*
[4] *Ibid.*, vol. XXIV, p. 601.
[5] *Ibid.*, vol. XXIV, p. 624 *et seq.*
[6] *Ibid.*, vol. XXIV, p. 656.

here again furnished the solution to the problem. It created the Council Chamber, composed of three judges, including the examining magistrate whose duty it was to pass upon the conclusions of the public prosecutor in all matters in which the examination was complete. A single vote, if a crime were concerned, was sufficient to necessitate the submission of the documents to the court, the criminal section of which finally decided upon the arraignment, subject to appeal to the Court of Cassation. Then only was the indictment drawn up by the attorney-general.

The decision lay with the Council Chamber; this was the old ruling to the "extraordinary" action, with this difference, demanded by the Cahiers of 1789, that three judges took part in it instead of one alone: "Formerly," says M. Regnaud, "the decree finding a true bill was rendered by a single criminal judge; one can recall the applause excited by the resolution of the Constituent Assembly, appointing assessors to this judge, who up to that time acted alone. It was because the Council had counted upon the maintenance of that order of things that it had voted for the suppression of the grand jury."[1] The branch of the Court of Appeal which sat as the court of last resort was synonymous with the grand jury, whose functions were conferred upon certain magistrates. The new system had thus united and welded together the principles of the old jurisprudence and the rules of the recent laws. It was first thought that a "senatus-consultum" was necessary to sanction these radical changes in the organization of the procedure by jury, and a bill for the purpose was even presented in the sitting of 5th March, 1808.[2] But M. Treilhard, who, down to that time, had seen in every attack upon the jury an attack upon the constitution, maintained the contrary opinion, now that the trial jury was conclusively saved. "The constitutions," he says, "ordain that there shall be a grand jury, but they do not forbid that its duties be intrusted to a tribunal;"[3] and they passed on to other matters.

[1] *Locré*, vol. XXIV, p. 666.
[2] *Ibid.*, vol. XXIV, p. 667 *et seq.*
[3] *Ibid.*, vol. XXIV, p. 692.

CHAPTER III

THE ORDINANCE OF 1670 AND THE REVOLUTIONARY LAWS IN THE CODE OF CRIMINAL EXAMINATION

§ 1. **Separation of the Powers of the Public Prosecutor and the Examining Magistrate.** — In the great strife which lasted so long between the procedure by jury and the Ordinance of 1670, the former gained a decisive victory. Posterity ought to give recognition to the men who, in the State's Council of the Empire, were able to resist the undisguised will of the Emperor, and to whose courageous efforts was due the retention of the jury in our laws. But the system of the old procedure, finally discarded upon this point, left deep traces in other parts of the law where it sometimes has the upper hand; the preliminary examination was, in particular, marked by its harsh imprint.

When the Articles of the draft of the Criminal Code were discussed before the State's Council for the first time in Fructidor, year XII, and in Vendémiaire, year XIII,[1] they presented a rather curious system in regard to the preliminary examination. The bill retained a magistrate of police and an examining magistrate in each district; but their functions were very different from those finally resolved upon. The magistrates of police did not only act, they also examined; and in that respect an improvement was made upon the Law of the year IX.[2] They received denunciations and complaints (Articles 39 to 42; 44 to 52); it was they who, in the ordinary case, heard the witnesses; and Articles 64 to 79, placed under the heading of hearing of witnesses, which later passed

[1] *Locré*, vol. XXIV, pp. 408, 409.

[2] "Projet primitif," Art. 480: "The magistrates of police, considered as officers of judicial police, are charged, 1st, with receiving denunciations and complaints . . .; 2d, with establishing the traces of the offenses by official reports; 3d, with gathering the facts leading to presumptions and the proofs existing against those accused; 4th, with bringing them before the propraetors."

almost integrally into the Code of Criminal Examination, were copied from the Ordinance of 1670; in the discussion this was specially alluded to.[1] It was the magistrate of police who made house searches and seizures (Articles 80 to 86: "Concerning written proofs and documents of conviction"). It was also he who issued warrants to bring the accused before the court, summonses to appear and warrants of commitment, and who interrogated the accused (Articles 87 to 92). It must be noted that the warrant of commitment was defined as the order according to which "the accused was provisionally maintained in a state of arrest,"[2] and that the magistrate of police must "send within twenty-four hours either from the warrant of detention, or of appearance, or of any other final step of his proceeding, all the documents to the clerk of the correctional court, after having numbered them and advised the examining magistrate of what he had done." The examining magistrate did not appear until this moment (Articles 103 to 106);[3] he completed and even, if need be, recommenced the proceedings, communicating them immediately to the magistrate of police. It was his duty to interrogate the accused anew; in conformity with the Law of the year IX, the latter was then made acquainted with the charges,[4] and then the examining judge, if there was occasion, issued the writ of attachment. Lastly he issued the orders of "renvoi" or of "non-lieu" (no ground for prosecution), but should it happen that he did not adopt the requisitions of the public prosecutor, the questions of fact as well as of law were submitted to the Court of Criminal Justice in the Council Chamber; the decision taken could, within twenty-four hours, be attacked by the attorney-general before the Court of Cassation.

The first time that the Articles came up for discussion they passed

[1] Art. 72 provided that minors under fifteen years of age could be heard on making an affirmation and without taking the oath. The Arch-chancellor asks, "that in order to leave no doubt as to the use which the court could make of the affirmations spoken of in this article, these words should be added, which are found in the ordinances: 'except as may be considered reasonable.' M. Target says that these expressions of the Ordinance have been considered too vague." *Locré*, vol. XXIV, pp. 167, 168.

[2] Art. 80.

[3] Art. 103: "He is charged with completing the examination begun by the magistrate of police, or even with making it anew in whole or in part, when he deems that proper."

[4] "The examining magistrate shall interrogate the accused before the latter has had cognizance of the charges. He shall cause them to be read to the accused after his interrogation, and if he requests it, he shall be immediately interrogated anew." This communication by mere reading recalls, to some extent, the proceedings under the Ordinance.

without objection; but when they came up again in the sittings of 22d, 27th, and 29th Frimaire in the year XIII, there were several protests. In the new draft it was proposed to give to the imperial procurators, and in their absence, to their deputies, the functions of the officer of police (a point which was not discussed at that time); these functions, however, remained as we have described them. The Archchancellor observed "that functions have been transferred to the public prosecutor which formerly belonged exclusively to the judge. This is a return, it is true, to the existing system where the magistrate of police takes the double function of public prosecutor and examiner; but the old system had the advantage of putting two officials in action, in such a way that the inaction of a single official was not sufficient to stay the course of justice." M. Defermon said that "the old system also gave more safeguards to the accused; the public prosecutor claimed, the judge pronounced; so that the authority was not concentrated in the same hands. It was impossible to see without consternation the same official receiving the complaint or the denunciation, hearing the witnesses, and disposing of the liberty of the accused."[1] But to this were objected the necessity of a rapid procedure and the provisional character of the measures taken by the magistrate of police. The question, besides, was lost in the consideration of another greater one put by Napoleon: What should be the relations between the magistrates of police and the chief public prosecutors ("préfets")?

In 1808, when the discussion was resumed, the battle raged; it lasted throughout the sittings of 4th, 7th, and 11th June, 1808.[2] Once again the partisans of the old forms found themselves face to face with those who adhered to the proceedings followed in the laws of the intermediary period, but in this instance they had reason on their side, and they won their case. The Minister of Religion and the Archchancellor were very energetic: "From the nature of the institution the public prosecutor is a party; from his title it belongs to him to prosecute, but for that very reason it would be contrary to justice to allow him to conduct the examination proceedings."[3] — "The imperial procurator would be a little tyrant who would make the city tremble. . . . All the citizens would shudder if they saw in the same official the power of accusing them and that of bringing together proofs that might justify

[1] *Locré*, vol. XXIV, p. 552.
[2] *Ibid.*, vol. XXV, p. 123 *et seq.*
[3] *Ibid.*, vol. XXV, p. 124.

his accusation."[1] And M. Jaubert adds that "care is taken that the plan closes for a considerable time the access of justice to the unfortunate prisoner. The imperial procurator draws up the official report and he draws it up alone. . . . He hears the witnesses, he even takes custody of persons, and as long as they are in his keeping it is impossible to seek the aid of any authority. To whom is it proposed to intrust such a formidable power? To a dismissable officer and one under the orders of the procurator general . . . in this respect this ancient legislation, so loudly inveighed against, endangers the safety of the French people."[2]

Tradition, as we see, spoke against the draft: "On reading the draft of the Code, it is evident that many of its provisions are taken from the Ordinance of 1670. Among others is that concerning the ruling to the 'extraordinary' action. It is also necessary to bear in mind that, in the system of that Ordinance, the two functions were separate, and that the danger of combining them was always foreseen."[3] "Formerly the attorney-general had the most extensive power in regard to prosecution; the courts could not prevent him from using this power. . . . But the Ordinances consistently kept the attorney-general in the position of a prosecuting party. That position it is important to preserve."[4]

MM. Treilhard, Merlin, and Regnaud de Saint-Jean d'Angély, however, supported the draft: it was necessary, they said, that the attorney, in order to conduct the prosecution, should be acquainted with the facts; this was, besides, the system inaugurated by the Law of Pluviôse. They maintained that the old principles could no longer be applied; they stated that when the public prosecutor had made the first authentications it was his duty within twenty-four hours to put the matter before the examining judge. But their most specious argument was that speed was necessary, and that to compel the attorney to petition the judge would entail a dangerous delay. The Archchancellor, while making just allowance for what they said, made this objection: he admitted that in the case of capture in the act, if a crime were concerned, the imperial procurator should be authorized to take any urgent steps of examination: "In the case of capture in the act, it matters little by whom the fact is established. There is no disadvantage, for instance, in the imperial procurator establishing that a dead

[1] *Locré*, vol. XXV, pp. 129–131. [2] *Ibid.*, vol. XXV, p. 136.
[3] *Cambacérès, Locré*, vol. XXV, p. 130.
[4] *Ibid., Locré*, vol. XXV, p. 146.

body has been found, but it would be very dangerous to grant him that power except in the case of capture in the act. . . . Who would not shudder to see a single official, invested with such inquisitorial power, invade his home?"[1] This was satisfactory, and it must be acknowledged "that the distinction between captures in the act and other cases appears to have a very reasonable foundation for differentiating the powers discussed; by admitting it the public safeguard experiences no appreciable abatement."[2] M. Berlier also asked if it would not be possible "upon the claim of the master or head of a house to allow the same form of arrest or examination as in the case of capture in the act."

Thus the division of the functions between the judge and the attorney, and the distinction between the pursuit and the examination, were accepted with these modifications. This is how it happens that capture in the act has taken an important place in the Code of Criminal Examination, which it does not usually occupy except in primitive systems of law. For the same reason it happens that the Law specifies, besides capture in the act properly so called, a certain number of cases of a similar nature. In the sittings of 18th and 21st June, 1808, a new draft of Chapters IV and V was presented. The hearing of witnesses, the investigation of written proofs, and the issue of warrants were intrusted to the examining judge. Some traces of the original draft, however, have remained. The section treating "of the attorneys' method of proceeding in the exercise of their duties" contains the rules as to the making of the official reports of the examination, and that in regard to capture in the act. — Conformably to the logic and the traditions of the old law, the *complaints*, which put the court in action, ought to be as a rule addressed to the examining judge (Article 63), the denunciations being addressed to the attorney (Article 31); but the complaints could also be addressed to the attorney, who then transmitted them with his requisitions to the examining judge (Article 64).

The traditional principles of the old law, as to the division of functions between the two officials, thus triumphed. That could not be other than a matter for congratulation. But, at the same time, these principles were destined to reappear upon other points and to give to the preliminary examination those rigorous forms and illiberal rules, which it has for the most part preserved to the present time.

[1] *Locré*, vol. XXV, pp. 147, 148.
[2] *M. Berlier*, *Locré*, vol. XXV, pp. 130, 131.

§ 2. **The Documents and Forms of the Preliminary Examination.** — The preliminary examination, necessary in the case of a crime, and optional in the case of a misdemeanor, was to be a secret and written procedure. It did not include confrontation, and detention pending trial was the general rule, admitting very few exceptions. The preliminary examination of the Code of Criminal Examination is the procedure of the Ordinance of 1670, down to the ruling to the "extraordinary" action. First of all, the hearing of the witnesses takes place secretly. The accused cannot be assisted in the matter even should he be under detention when it takes place; each witness testifies separately in the presence of only the judge and his clerk. Articles 71 to 86, which deal exhaustively with the matter, reproduce title VI of the Ordinance almost verbatim. One rather important difference, however, should be pointed out. The Ordinance (Title VI, Article 1) declares that "the witnesses are brought by our attorneys or those of the seigneurs, as also by the civil parties." This absolutely prevented the judge from hearing the witnesses the accused wished to produce; the Code of Criminal Examination provides that "the examining judge shall cause to be summoned before him those persons who shall be pointed out by the denunciation, by the complaint, *or otherwise.*" The addition of these last words allows the judge to hear witnesses nominated by the accused, but it is purely a discretionary power in him; the accused could not cause his witnesses to be summoned directly and compel the judge to hear them.

These Articles were, however, adopted almost without discussion;[1] and upon that point the observations of the commission of the Legislative Body were insignificant.[2] The Law of Pluviôse had prepared all minds for the acceptance of these principles. The Committee's Report by M. Treilhard, is very laconic: "You will find, gentlemen, in the chapter on examining magistrates, very detailed rules upon complaints, upon the mode of constituting the private prosecutor, upon the way in which the witnesses ought to be heard, upon the oath which they ought to take, upon their obligation to appear when they are cited, upon the methods of coercion when they fail to appear, and upon the going of the judge to hear them when they are not able to be present. I merely allude to these provisions, which cannot be susceptible of any difficulty, and which, besides, are by no means new."[3]

[1] Sittings of 21st June, 1808, *Locré*, vol. XXV, p. 168 *et seq.;* 26th August, *ibid.*, p. 192 *et seq.;* 4th October, *ibid.*, p. 214.

[2] *Locré*, vol. XXV, p. 215 *et seq.*

[3] *Ibid.*, vol. XXV, p. 243.

In regard to searches and seizures, some safeguards are inserted in the law. They must take place in the presence of the accused if he has been arrested (Articles 39 and 89), and the latter was entitled to furnish explanations, identify the objects seized, and initial the seals. These provisions were borrowed not from the Ordinance, but from the Code of Offenses and Punishments (Articles 125 to 131). As to medical, legal, or other expert reports, no confrontation is open to the accused; Article 46, so important on this point, settles but the oath to be taken by the experts. The defense cannot contest the choice of an expert made by a judge; nor, with more reason, have a counter expert proceed officially. In this respect, it must be said, the Code of Offenses and Punishments was even less liberal than the Ordinance (Code of Brumaire, year IV, Article 103; Ordinance of 1670, Title V).

There remain probably the most weighty points of the preliminary examination: the appearance of the accused and his interrogation, the detention pending trial, and the possibility of provisional release. Here the old law reappears, although the majority of the terms employed are borrowed from the Laws of the Intermediary Period.

The four warrants, created successively by the Laws of 1791, the year IV, and the year IX, are all preserved, and usually retain their original character. The warrant of appearance and writ of attachment cannot be issued except by the examining judge; the same applies generally to the warrant to produce the accused (" d'amener "); however, in case of capture in the act, it can be issued by the attorney (Article 40). As a general rule the proceedings opened with a warrant to produce the accused; only in a case where the accused was domiciled and where a mere misdemeanor was concerned, could the judge content himself with first issuing a warrant of appearance (Article 91). This new function of the warrant of appearance was introduced at the request of the commission of the Legislative Body: "Experience," it was said, "has proved that there might be great inconveniences in causing a resident person to be arrested and exposed by being openly led away by the police, such person being accused of having committed in a moment of passion what, if proved, would entail but fifteen days' or a month's imprisonment. . . . These reflections lead us to regard it as advantageous to leave to the discretion of the examining judge whether to issue against the persons accused of police offenses mere warrants of appearance. We might recall the wisdom of the article of Title

X of the Ordinance of 1670, where it is said: 'According to the nature of the crimes, the evidence, and the persons, it shall be ordered that the party be summoned to be heard, cited to appear, or arrested.'"[1] The warrant of arrest established the detention pending trial; it required the preliminary conclusions of the public prosecutor, and stated the fact, the object of the prosecution, and the law characterizing the act as a crime or as a misdemeanor (Article 96). The warrant of commitment was retained, but with its provisional character; it was issued by the imperial procurator when, a warrant to produce the accused having been issued, the accused was found, more than two days from its date, outside of the district of the officer who had issued such warrant and more than fifty kilometres from the domicile of that officer (Article 100).[2] The warrant of commitment had, in the Code of 1808, only two other cases of application, relating to exceptional hypotheses.[3]

The Code of Criminal Examination does not deal with the interrogations except to fix the time within which the first interrogation must take place (Article 93); but the observance of that delay is the only safeguard which it insures to the accused in the matter. The interrogation is to take place in secret, as the rule has always been; the accused, alone in presence of the judge, knows nothing of what has been done against him up to that time except what the judge sees fit to communicate to him. All the safeguards granted to the defense since 1789 had gradually disappeared. In 1789 the complaint and all the documents which had been brought together by the judge were read to the accused before he was interrogated; he had from that time a counsel with whom he could confer before answering. The Law of 1791 provided that if the accused had been arrested he should be present at the hearing of the witnesses (Title V, Article 15). The Code of

[1] *Locré*, vol. XXV, pp. 228, 229. M. Dhaubersart's report also signalizes the warrant of appearance as a revival of the decree of summons to be heard. *Ibid.*, p. 255.

[2] The Code of Brumaire, year IV, decides (Art. 74) that in such a case the accused could "have himself kept in sight or put in a state of provisional arrest."

[3] 1st, Art. 193. It deals with a prosecution brought for forgery in the correctional police court, the act being of a nature to entail an afflictive or degrading punishment. "The tribunal can immediately issue the warrant of commitment or writ of attachment, and transfer the accused before the examining magistrate having jurisdiction." 2d, in case of appeal from a judgment of the correctional police (Article 214): "If the judgment is annulled because the offense is of a kind meriting an afflictive or degrading punishment the court or the tribunal will issue, in a proper case, the warrant of commitment, or even the writ of attachment."

Offenses and Punishments contained the same provision (Article 115), and it also decided that, if the witnesses had been heard before the appearance of the accused, or before his arrest, their statements must first of all be read over to him, without giving him a copy thereof (Article 116). The Law of the year IX was less liberal; it provided that the accused should be heard and interrogated without having had communication of the charges, but he must afterwards be made acquainted with them and could reply to them. Even this resource exists no more under the rule of the new Code. During the whole course of the examination, the accused might remain in complete ignorance of the proceedings; he does not receive a notification of any step, for the Code of 1808 opens to him no right of opposition to the decision of the judge except in the single case when he disputes the jurisdiction of the examining judge, and the latter has not admitted his declinatory plea (Article 539). No doubt the judge can orally communicate the charges to persons accused, confront the latter among themselves or with the witnesses, but that is a mere discretionary power in the judge. This is a return to the rules of the Ordinance of 1670. Except for the want of some formalities in the writings, a criminal lieutenant of the Old Régime would find matters such as he practised them.

Release on bail was one of the conquests won by the Revolution. The old law did not recognize it, so to speak, for it did not admit it in matters ruled to the "extraordinary action." The Code of Brumaire, year IV, had established a very simple system, excluding all arbitrariness. It recognized only two situations: either provisional liberty was a right for the prisoner, or it could not be granted. The first case occurred when the eventual punishment was correctional or merely degrading; the second when it was corporal (Article 222). The draft of the Criminal Code reproduced this distinction, attaching to it, however, other consequences; it declared release impossible when corporal punishment might follow, but in the judge's discretion if the punishment was only degrading or correctional; this was a radical change from the previous legislation. It would seem as if the memory of the laws in force had been lost, for M. Treilhard declares that "the section had followed the system of the Constituent Assembly." [1] The draft was found to be even too tolerant; MM. Cambacérès, Jaubert, and Regnaud de Saint-Jean d'Angély, as well as the chief justice, asked that the discretionary release be restricted to the

[1] *Locré*, vol. XXV, p. 184.

case of a correctional police action;[1] they gained their point. M. Berlier attempted to have an absolute right recognized in the defense in this respect, observing that "since release on bail applies only to police correctional offenses, the judges can have no good reason to refuse that benefit to accused persons who have complied with the law." — The Archchancellor said that "police misdemeanors might entail imprisonment, and it would be impossible to release indefinitely without bail those who are accused; it was sufficient to leave that power to the judge."[2]

The Code of Criminal Examination did not therefore regard provisional release as a right of those accused of minor offenses; it was absolutely prohibited in the case of a crime (Article 113), and also in correctional matters, when the accused was a vagrant or had been convicted (Article 115). Bail of at least five hundred francs was invariably required. The council chamber decided upon the requests for release on bail, and its decisions could be attacked by the imperial procurator and the private prosecutor, but not by those accused of minor offenses (Article 135).

All the provisions which we have analyzed except that on provisional liberty passed the State's Council almost without debate. The longest time was spent in the consideration of Article 10, conferring on the prefect certain powers of judicial police. This was supported by Napoleon personally.[3]

Supposing the examination concluded, the judge now submitted its results to the Council Chamber, so that the latter might decide how to deal with the matter. In a criminal case, this control was nominal rather than real, for a single voice, that of the examining judge, was sufficient to have the documents transmitted to the attorney-general and to have the arraignment branch put in action.[4] The proceedings before the arraignment branch were secret, like the first information or inquiry: "the judges see neither the accused, nor the private prosecutor, nor the witnesses for either side. Immediately after the reading of the documents, the attorney-general retires, leaving his statement, written and signed. — The greatest secrecy ought to preside over the deliberations of the Imperial Court in all criminal matters submitted to it."[5] Since

[1] The institution was even radically attacked: "M. Regnaud says that the Constituent Assembly has only established the system of provisional liberty in imitation of the English, who release on bail, even when the most severe punishments are concerned. But it is a question for ascertainment whether this theory conforms to our customs." *Locré*, vol. XXV, p. 186.

[2] *Locré*, vol. XXV, p. 191.

[3] *Ibid.*, vol. XXV, p. 205 *et seq.*

[4] "Exposé des motifs," by *Treilhard*, vol. XXV, pp. 246, 247.

[5] "Exposé des motifs," by *M. Faure*, vol. XXV, p. 566.

the Law of 7th Pluviôse, year IX, the same applied to proceedings before the grand jury. The new Law merely generally transferred to the arraignment branch the powers of the jury; and a part of the Articles regulating its functions were copied into the Code of Brumaire, year IV; sometimes, even, the adaptation was hasty and the amalgamation badly made.[1] On one point, however, the new jurisdiction acquired a power which the old lacked. The grand jury had no power "to investigate if the deed specified in the indictment merits corporal or degrading punishment" (Code of Brumaire, Article 241). The Chamber of Accusation, on the contrary, examines into the classification of the deed (Inst. Crim. Article 231); that is logical, as the judges take cognizance of the question of law, which the jury is forbidden to do.

If the Chamber of Accusation remits the case to the Court of Assizes, it falls to the attorney-general to draw up the indictment, which formerly preceded the arraignment, of which it formed the basis.[2] In the "Exposé des motifs" by M. Faure, in the report of M. Riboud,[3] this change is made a matter for congratulation; but in reality the indictment merely reproduces, with some additional details, the decree of "renvoi"; undoubtedly it, as well as the latter, ought to be read to the jury, but that is a mere formality. It is in practice a rapid reading, to which the jury pays little attention; they are about to hear the witnesses and the accused, and to see the drama unfold itself before their own eyes.

§ 3. **The Proceedings before the Trial Jurisdiction. Moral Proofs.** — When, after the proceedings before the tribunals of examination, we consider the trial before the tribunals of judgment, the contrast is complete. We pass from obscurity into the full light of day. There the procedure was secret, written, and always favorable to the prosecution, not leaving to the defense even the right of confrontation; here everything is publicity, oral trial, free defense, and full discussion. In the one case, there are the traditions of the Ordinance of 1670; in the other, the principles announced by the Constituent Assembly and put in operation in the Laws of the Intermediary Period.[4] Whatever may be

[1] For instance, Art. 225: "The judges shall deliberate among themselves without dispersing and without communicating with anybody." This was the last paragraph of Art. 238 of the Code of Brumaire; but although very appropriate for the jury, it was hardly applicable to magistrates, as was observed in the State's Council. *Locré*, vol. XXV, pp. 431, 432.

[2] *Locré*, vol. XXIV, p. 507.

[3] *Ibid.*, vol. XXIV, p. 589.

[4] This truth was recently recognized in an official document: "The compilers of the Code of 1808 adopted a system of conciliation: they

the tribunal before which appearance is made, the examination is public, otherwise void (Articles 153, 190, and 309); the rights of the defense are the same in every respect as those of the prosecution; it can produce its witnesses, and these are even the last heard, just as the defending counsel and the accused are the last to address the court. The accused may always have the assistance of a defending counsel; the law officially assigns one to all those accused.

But between these two extreme and opposed situations, is there not an intermediary stage, within which the defense may begin to become organized and make itself acquainted with the written proceedings, in which, so far, all the proofs have been concentrated, and from which the prosecution, to which it has been constantly available, draws its weapons? In criminal matters, where a preliminary examination has perforce taken place, the legislature established this intermediary phase, this period of transition. When the decree of "renvoi" has been rendered and the indictment drawn up, these documents were at once disclosed to the accused (Article 242), who, within twenty-four hours, must be removed to the court-house. Twenty-four hours after his arrival there, the accused must be interrogated by the president of the Court of Assizes or by the magistrate who takes his place (Article 294). By this means he has the opportunity to have his complaints heard by a magistrate of high rank. This is not all; the president ought to warn him that he has the right to contest the validity of the decree of "renvoi" before the Court of Cassation, ask him if he has chosen a counsel for his defense, and, if need be, assign him one officially (Article 294). This is one of the noblest provisions of French law; the reformers of the Revolution devised it in the nobility of the national character; it was not a borrowing made from England, where this liberal law was unknown.

From that time counsel could freely communicate with the accused, examine all the documents of the process (Article 302),

endeavored to satisfy both interests involved and to combine the different elements offered by the various periods of our history. From the feudal period (?) they borrowed publicity of hearing, the jury, oral proofs, and the right of appeal; from the monarchical régime they took the institution of the public prosecutor, permanence of judges, and the use of proceedings recorded in writing. They flattered themselves they had done enough for the accused in assuring him impartial judges, the aid of a defending counsel, and publicity of trial, at the moment when, the examination being concluded, he was about to establish his innocence, if it had been unrecognized." "Projet de loi tendant à réformer le Code d'instruction criminelle," presented in the name of *M. Jules Grévy*, president of the French Republic. Journal Officiel of 14th January, 1880, p. 302, col. 2 and 3.

and have a copy thereof taken (Article 305). A copy of the official reports and the written statements of the witnesses is even gratuitously delivered to the accused. This provision was contained in the Code of Offenses and Punishments (Article 320); according to it a copy of all the documents of the process was delivered, although the formula employed by the Code of Criminal Examination excludes from the gratuitous copy the interrogations of the accused. But these equitable provisions are made to apply only to criminal matters; the law does not deal with the case where the preliminary examination was made in view of a correctional offense. In the latter case there is no advocate officially appointed, no communication of documents. The communication to the advocate did often take place in practice, but it is merely a gratuitous concession on the part of the office of the public prosecutor. In important correctional police actions this is a regrettable omission. It is conceivable that the texts regulating the proceedings before the trial jurisdictions when the police court, the correctional police court, or the Court of Assizes is concerned were borrowed from the Code of Offenses and Punishments. A glance over both Codes is sufficient to assure us of this fact.

The operation of the jury was slightly altered; experience had proved the necessity for such an alteration. The composition of the jury lists was materially changed. Article 382 indicated the categories of persons from whom the jury must be chosen. These were first of all the members of the electoral colleges, as composed by the "senatus-consultum" of 16th Thermidor, year X (Articles 14, 15, 18, and 19), that is to say, electors of the second degree,[1] and the three hundred who were added; then came four "alinéas," which effected for the jury what will be called later the adjunction of capacities. Finally, Article 387 permitted persons who did not belong to any of these classes to petition for "the honor of being admitted to jury duty"; the prefect could include them in the lists if he had obtained "favorable information" regarding them, and if the Minister of the Interior gave his authority. The prefects drew up the session lists "composed of sixty citizens." Article 387: "The prefects shall form upon their own responsibility a list of jurors, whenever they shall be required to

[1] They were appointed by the assembly of the canton "composed of all the citizens resident in the canton, who were included in the communal list of the district." There were two hundred at the most and one hundred and twenty at least for the electoral college of the district; three hundred at most and two hundred at least for the electoral college of the department. They were appointed for life.

do so by the presidents of the Courts of Assizes. This requisition shall be made at least fifteen days before the opening of the session."

It is evident that the choice of jurors, so poorly made during the Revolutionary period, was restricted within narrow limits. They had even gone to the opposite extreme from the looseness of the old laws. The composition of the jury was entirely in the hands of the prefects, since they chose the session lists at their pleasure and at a date very near to the opening of the sessions of the assizes. Drawing by lot played no part except in the composition of the trial jury. The challenge in court was regulated; there could be no more challenges for cause assigned (Article 399).[1]

The system of questions put to the jury was simplified. Here they went even too far, and from one extreme they fell into the other. A single question, the simple formula of which stamped at once the material and moral element of the offense, comprised the whole contents of the indictment; that is to say, it stated not only the principal fact, but also any aggravating circumstances by which it might be accompanied (Article 338). This was eventually to oblige the jurors to make distinctions, and to enter into an analysis (Article 365), which the previous laws had wisely wished to spare them. The solution of this problem had not yet been found.

Upon another point they were better inspired. Article 387 declared "that the decision of the jury should be reached for or against the accused by a majority, otherwise to be void. In case of a tie, the opinion favorable to the accused should prevail." Rejecting the English principle of unanimity, and the hesitations of the Intermediary Period, the Code of Criminal Examination adopted this very logical and reasonable law of the mere majority, which, however, was destined to be again rejected, to be finally returned to in our own times. But the legislature of 1808 had not dared to announce this principle in an absolute manner; it had accompanied it with a restriction which was in reality illusory. Originating an extravagant and complicated system, it provided that, if the decision had been given against the accused by a mere majority of votes, the jury should give its verdict to that effect

[1] It was thought necessary to prescribe strenuous means to compel the citizens appointed to serve on the jury. Not only were fines imposed, as at present, against defaulters, but furthermore, Art. 392 declared that those who neglected, without just cause, to comply with the requisitions addressed to them for jury service were ineligible for judicial and administrative positions.

(Article 341), and then the court itself, composed of five members, was called upon to deliberate upon the question of guilt. This is how the court's vote was combined with the vote of the jury: Article 351 "If the opinion of the majority of the jurors is adopted by the majority of the judges, in such a way that in adding together the number of votes that number exceeds that of the majority of jurors and the minority of the judges, the opinion favorable to the accused will prevail."

How did the Code decide two important points, upon which the old practice and the law of the Revolution radically differ: the written or the oral trial, and the theory of proofs? First of all, the oral character of the trial is maintained; but the Code of Criminal Examination is less distrustful of writing than were the prior laws. In the procedure before the jury, the Code of Brumaire had pointed out very emphatically the use which could be made of the information, and no trace of the trial was recorded in writing. Article 365: "No written deposition of witnesses not present at the hearing can be read to the jury." — Article 366: "As to written statements made by the witnesses present and written notes of the interrogations to which the accused has been subjected before the police officer, the director of the jury, and the president of the criminal court, nothing can be read in the course of the trial except what is necessary to bring to the notice, either of the witness or the accused, the variations, contradictions, and differences which may be found between what they say before the jury and what they have previously said." — Article 382: "He (the president) also submits to the jury all the documents in the action, with the exception of the written declarations of the witness and the written interrogations of the accused." From these three articles the first has disappeared, and this fact is important; for, although the compilers of the Code had no idea of derogating upon this point from the prior law,[1] we shall see what judicial practice has deduced from this omission. As to the other two provisions, they were maintained, but in a form which somewhat enlarged the function of the written

[1] This results from an article of the title on "Contumaces"; Art. 477, providing for the confrontative trial which takes place when a contumacy is purged, is in these terms: "In the case provided for by the preceding article, if, for whatever cause, witnesses cannot be produced at the trial, their written depositions and the written replies of others accused of the same offense shall be read at the hearing; the same shall apply to all other documents, which shall be deemed by the president to be of a nature likely to shed light upon the offense and the guilty parties." If that had been possible according to the common law, it would not have been included in the article.

documents. Article 318: "The president shall cause a note to be taken by the clerk of court of the additions, changes, or variations which may exist between a witness's deposition and his previous statements. The attorney-general and the accused may require the president to have notes taken of these changes, additions, and variations."[1] Article 341: "The president puts the written issues before the jury in the presence of the foreman of the jury; he adds thereto the indictment, the official reports establishing the offenses, and the documents of the action other than the written depositions of the witnesses." Henceforth the documents submitted contain the interrogations of the accused persons.

Upon one point the written procedure was plainly improved. In case of contumacy the Code of Brumaire provided that the jury should intervene, as in the procedure of confrontation (Articles 462 to 482). The Code of Criminal Examination decided, on the contrary, that the jury should not intervene; the court itself decided upon the merits after having established the regularity of the procedure (Article 470). This was logical, in effect, and the reform was useful, as is very well shown in the "Exposé des motifs" by M. Berlier: "Since everything is reduced to the reading of documents, to the investigation of a written procedure, and to a cold analysis of circumstances more or less thoroughly established in the action, it would be overthrowing all ideas not to leave to the judges the duty of deciding upon the matter. To reëstablish them in this right is, moreover, to disentangle the examination of the contumacy from elements which uselessly complicate it without advantage to the contumax."[2] In such an action, there is no defense, no oral trial; it is a matter for the magistrates rather than for a jury. The rules of the procedure in contumacy, which the previous laws had in great measure borrowed from the old French law, were, moreover, retained in the Code of Criminal Examination.

In correctional police, there could be no question of forbidding the judges to consult the information when one had been made; and this necessarily would influence their decision, although the oral and public trial should always be the chief basis of that decision. Before the courts of correctional police, as in ordinary

[1] *Cf.* Art. 372: "The clerk of court shall draw up an official report of the sitting for the purpose of establishing the fact that the prescribed formalities have been observed. No mention shall be made in the official report of the replies of the accused or the contents of the depositions, always without prejudice to the application of Art. 318."

[2] *Locré*, vol. XXVII, p. 159; *cf.* Report of *M. Cholet*, *ibid.*, p. 72.

police matters, the Code of Criminal Examination, following that of Brumaire, provides that, if not the entire trial, at least its principal points should be set down in writing.[1] In regard to police courts, Article 155 (which Article 189 makes applicable to courts of correctional police) declares "that the witnesses shall take oath at the hearing to tell the whole truth and nothing but the truth, and the clerk of court shall take note of their names, surnames, ages, professions, and residences, and of their *principal statements*." It was desired by this means to render less costly the procedure on appeal; this is a germ which is destined to future development.

The legislature had maintained the system of moral proofs, one of the reforms for which the 1700 s had fought most keenly, and which constituted a decided and final conquest. Before the jury this doctrine retained its absolute sway: whatever might be the proof furnished, the jury could always acquit, and in the same way an affirmative verdict could be rendered, whatever might be the weakness of the evidence. Like the Code of Brumaire, the Code of Criminal Examination puts before the eyes of the jury a long warning in which they are reminded of this doctrine. Article 342: "The law does not ask the jury to account for the means by which they are convinced. It does not prescribe to them rules on which they must particularly base the fulness and sufficiency of proof. It enjoins them to interrogate themselves in silence and meditation, and to seek in the sincerity of their conscience for the impression made upon their reason by the proofs brought against the accused and his pleas in defense. The law does not say to them: 'You will hold as true such a fact attested by such and such a number of witnesses;' no more does it say to them: 'You shall not regard as sufficiently established any proofs which shall not be constituted by such an official report, by such a document, by such presumptions;' it only asks them this one question, comprising the whole measure of their duties: 'Are you thoroughly convinced?'"

Before the other tribunals the same principle still prevailed; but it allowed of several qualifications. Sometimes, though very rarely, the judge could not decide according to the proof; the law chose several specially for him. This was the case in the offense of adultery (Article 338, C. P.). In the same way certain contraventions, fugitive and ascertainable with difficulty, could not

[1] Code of Brumaire, Art. 155: "Their names (the witnesses'), ages, and callings are inserted in the judgment; — the clerk of court takes a summary note of their principal statements, as well as of the principal pleas in defense of the accused."

be proved except by a regular official report; this is, at least, the way in which judicial practice interprets the Laws of 17th Brumaire, year VI, in matters of gold and silver, and of 9th Floréal, year VII, in regard to the customs, and the Decree of 1st Germinal, year XII, upon the customs (Article 34). Conversely, in certain cases, the decision, whatever might be the judge's opinion, will be entailed by the production of a certain proof; this is true of official reports, as to the material facts which they state (Article 154, Inst. Crim.): some constitute evidence even in support of an allegation of forgery, and so far as the allegation of forgery has not been successfully brought they are binding on the judge; the others are good until met by contradictory proof, but this proof must be offered and produced in order to deprive them of their authority.

The Code of Criminal Examination introduced few alterations into the system of methods of appeal. The appeal was retained and always admitted in correctional matters; for mere police cases it was open to a sufficient degree. The appeal to the Court of Cassation, with the exception of alterations in detail, was regulated as in the Codes of the Intermediary Period.

§ 4. **The Special Courts.** — But this was merely the common law procedure. There was also an exceptional procedure in criminal cases. This took place before the "Special Courts" (Articles 583 to 599, Inst. Crim.). These courts were the offspring, but with a different title, of the special tribunals organized by the Laws of 18th Pluviôse, year IX, and of 22d Floréal, year X. They were composed of five magistrates sitting in the Court of Assizes, and three military men having the rank of captains at least (Article 556). They had jurisdiction of all crimes committed by vagrants or vagabonds or by those condemned to corporal or degrading punishments, as well as the crimes of armed rebellion, armed smuggling, false money, and murder brought about by mobs and assemblages (Articles 553 and 554). The whole of the preliminary examination was the same as for a case brought before the jury, and it was submitted to the Chamber of Accusation, which, in a proper case, ordered the transfer of the proceedings to the special court (Articles 566 and 567). This decree of transfer, determining the jurisdiction, was officially submitted to the criminal branch of the Court of Cassation (Articles 568 and 570). Before the Special Court, the trial was oral and public, and the defense free, as before the Court of Assizes (Articles 573 and 579). The judgment was rendered by a majority, a divided court benefiting the accused alone (Article 582). It was the decision of the court of last resort, and could not be attacked on appeal (Article 597).

These Articles, compared with the Law of 18th Pluviôse, presented material ameliorations; the cases withdrawn from the jury were less numerous, and they were made subject to appeal in the debate in the State's Council.[1] In reality there was an aggravation in the sense that the system became definite; it was no longer an expedient for emergencies, but a regular and durable institution. The same spirit that prompted this change had, under the old law, created and developed the prévôtal jurisdictions, and on this point the Ordinance of 1670 triumphed. It was recognized openly; we have already cited very explicit passages from M. Réal's Committee Report. The secret procedure of the Old Régime was alone repudiated. "Formerly there was the examination, already very severe, of the Ordinance of 1670, intrusted to the provost and his assessor. Thus the judge extraordinary, that is, the military judge, alone took possession of the accused from the first, and did not leave him during the examination; the assessor was the reporter of the action. . . . Add to this procedure, thoroughly 'extraordinary,' the severity of forms, the two kinds of torture, the perpetual secrecy which it borrowed from the 'ordinary' procedure of 1670. . . . In the Law which we present to you the ordinary judge examines in the ordinary form against the crime of those accused persons who may belong to the jurisdiction of the special court, because this first secret and rapid examination is sufficient in both cases. . . . It must be added that the judgment of jurisdiction is no longer pronounced by an inferior court, as by the system of 1670, nor by the director of the jury, as was allowed by a later Law, nor by the Special Court itself, as was provided by the Law of Pluviôse, year IX, but by the Imperial Court, composed of the most experienced and the most enlightened magistrates."[2] It was also declared that the examination was "in every respect superior to the prévôtal jurisdictions of the Old Régime"; but it was the old tradition which was adopted. In this respect, M. Réal's very able Report is most interesting. It contains a brief history of the prévôtal courts. It commences by recalling that that institution "was recognized and claimed by the States-General" of the 1500s and that "the Ordinance of 1670 merely collected and assimilated the old provisions scattered throughout the ordinances." He

[1] Sitting of 9th August, 1808, *Locré*, vol. XXVII, p. 19.
[2] *Locré*, vol. XXVII, pp. 68, 70.

afterwards recalls that these courts were not affected by the early reforms of 1789, and that the provost marshal continued to exist down to the first month of 1790. "But on 6th March, in an evening sitting, on the occasion of a complaint brought to the bar of the Assembly by the municipality of Paris against a provost of the Marshalcy of the Limousin, a member of the Assembly, by an incidental motion, demanded that the prévôtal jurisdiction should from that time be suppressed. It is true that this suppression was postponed, but at this time it was provisionally decreed that all the proceedings begun by the provost should be suspended. This strange provisional decree decided the question on its merits, and was equivalent in its results to the final suppression of the prévôtal jurisdictions, of which nothing more was heard. . . . Strange thing! It seemed that the vagrants were less to be feared than the provosts; it appears that the prévôtal jurisdictions were among those privileges destroyed in the memorable night of 4th August, 1789, and that the whole nation must consequently renounce the *honorable privilege,* which separated it from evildoers."[1] It is no less curious to see how the speaker explains that no place was made for the exceptional courts in the Codes of the Intermediary Period: "At the time when the new Criminal Code was elaborated, the ideas of that severe and simple style, which the great talents had introduced into the fine arts, had spread among all minds; at the same time the principles of equality advanced rapidly towards exaggeration. The legislators could not entirely withdraw themselves from the influence of that double impulse, and in the construction of the criminal system they frequently sacrified solidity to regularity. In the repair of that old edifice, the column supporting the central part of it, — this special jurisdiction of which neither the strength nor the importance was divined, — was suppressed because it was probably somewhat contrary to the symmetry of the details and the unity of the plan."[2] It really seems as if David and his school were the cause of Merlin's not having admitted the prévôtal courts into the Code of Offenses and Punishments!

M. Réal, it is true, presented more serious arguments. He recalled the inconsiderate ardor, the desire for change, the distrust of established authority which characterized the Revolutionary period, contrasting therewith the invariable tradition which deprived convicts of the benefit of the common law. "It was precisely at the moment when a Code more appropriate to the man-

[1] *Locré,* vol. XXVIII, pp. 48, 49.

[2] *Ibid.,* vol. XXVIII, p. 49.

ners, to the needs, to the opinions of the nation and the age, and consequently milder and more humane, was about to replace the Code of 1670, that it was necessary to preserve the exceptional jurisdiction, such as it was, to keep down the brigands. How was it that it did not occur to these legislators that what was merely useful under the régime of 1670 became absolutely necessary, indispensable, under the milder and more humane régime which was about to replace it?"[1] The speaker finally recalled the brigandage which had devastated France, and the Law of the year IX, with its happy effects: "It was very soon recognized that the Law ought to be permanent and universal. . . . The laws of circumstance, the provisional laws, were no longer suited to the nation; still less did they suit that genius, which gives birth but to secular plans, to the hero who founds empires and dynasties, who, after having long revolved his vast conceptions, engraves them upon bronze, and gives them the determined character which the founders of Rome alone have down to this day imprinted on their laws, as upon their imperishable structures."[2] The report of M. Louvet, much more colorless, was but a repetition of some of these considerations; the speaker was probably not completely convinced of what he laid down as veritable truths, for he declares that it was "necessary to leave to time the care of altering or even abolishing this institution, if the ameliorations which might be made in the state of manners of the nation should one day make such a necessity felt."[3]

There was no opposition to the bill in the State's Council; it is even interesting to state with what unconcern certain speakers noticed the extravagant consequences of some provisions.[4] In the debate on the first draft of the Criminal Code in the year XII some scruples were still manifested, but these, it must be said, were quickly set at rest. Let us note these words of M. Treilhard, in the sitting of 30th Prairial, year XII: "M. Treilhard says that

[1] *Locré*, vol. XXVIII, p. 51.

[2] *Ibid.*, vol. XXVIII, pp. 55, 56.

[3] *Ibid.*, vol. XXVIII, p. 78.

[4] Art. 372 of the bill is discussed: the article is to the effect that the judgment of the court shall be formed by the majority on pain of nullity. "Count Muraire says that the nullity will be illusory, since the judgment is not subject to review. And it is therefore sufficient to state the rule that the judgment shall be formed by the majority.—Count Berlier says that, as M. Muraire has observed, the law does not allow of review, and therefore it should not speak of nullities for which no redress could be obtained. Therefore the last words of the article should be omitted; but if the rule of the majority of votes were not followed in the decree (a hypothesis almost imaginary!) such a serious error, if it were thoroughly established, would undoubtedly be ground for an action of damages against the judges."

the section is devoting itself to the organization of exceptional courts; this institution in itself has appeared dangerous to him because some circumstances can always be found which might be abused in rendering any of the citizens justiciable by the exceptional courts. This abuse would only be evaded by giving jurisdiction to these courts, not on account of the nature of the crime, but on account of the status of the person. Second offenders, for example, could be remitted to them. Besides, this institution already exists in the special courts which try the crimes which it is not proposed to submit to the exceptional courts. — The special courts must remain for two years after the peace. The section has thus thought that if between the present and that time the jury should fulfil the hopes conceived of it, these courts might be dispensed with; that if, on the contrary, the new trial which is going to be given to the jury should not be satisfactory, they could be prorogued."[1] But this did not suit Napoleon: "His Majesty says that the majority of those who have voted for the maintenance of the jury have been swayed merely by the certainty that the exceptional courts would continue to exist. . . . His Majesty is of opinion that attempts against the gendarmery should be judged by these courts, also second offenses and crimes committed by banded malefactors."[2] Cambacérès supported these observations by rather curious reasoning: "It must not be thought that the establishment of exceptional courts must *weaken the jury;* but the thing is to send before these courts only the men who have not the right to claim trial by jury. To be tried by jury is, in effect, to be tried by one's peers; so that if this privilege is to be given to vagrants and brigands we must have them tried by other vagrants or brigands."[3] From that time the matter was decided; the question came up again several times before the Council, but no further objections were raised.[4] If these various deliberations are considered together in their successive gradations from the great debate which preceded the vote on the Law of 18th Pluviôse, year IX, we shall see what changes were made in their minds. A few more observations upon two important points, and

[1] *Locré*, vol. XXIV, p. 106. [2] *Ibid.*, vol. XXIV, pp. 106, 107.

[3] *Ibid.*, vol. XXIV, p. 107. M. Treilhard having asked if before drawing up a bill for this purpose it would not be necessary to wait for "the arrival of the observations which had been asked for from the tribunals, . . . His Majesty says that the section can, in the meantime, go on with this work, and that the observations of the tribunals would be considered at the time of the discussion."

[4] See particularly the sittings of 23d January, 1808 (*Locré*, vol. XXIV, p. 591), and of 6th February (*ibid.*, p. 613).

we shall have finished with the draft of the Code of Criminal Examination.

§ 5. **Res judicata. Reserved Justice. Rehabilitation and Revision.** — We recall the slight respect that the old judicial practice had for "res judicata." When the judgment was favorable to the accused absolution was very rarely pronounced, and when evidence was lacking the "further inquiry" was the rule. This is one of the points against which the public conscience protested most vehemently, and the liberating and final effect of the acquittal by the jury was inserted in the Constitution of 1791. The Code of Brumaire, year IV, twice made application of it: in dealing with the grand jury, and in dealing with the petty jury. Two perfectly contrary systems were thus brought face to face.

Was there to be a turning back and the resumption of the tradition of the old law? For an instant this might have been feared. In the sitting of the State's Council of 30th Prairial, year XII, the Archchancellor of the Empire spoke as follows: "At the present time the head of a criminal court is not armed with sufficient means to hold in check the accused, the defending counsel, and the public. He has not even the right to imprison on the spot those who disturb the hearing. Is it desired that he should act with proper firmness? that he should be invested with discretionary power; that the court should be able to dismiss the juror faithless to his trust, that he should not be restricted to pronouncing acquittal, pure and simple, of the accused for whom the verdict of the jury is favorable, but that he should be able to place him in the bonds of a 'further inquiry,' and under police supervision?"[1] Previously he had said in the sitting of 9th Prairial: "There is still an alteration no less important, that the acquittal of an accused should not always be a complete triumph for him, but that the judges should find in the law the power to put him under a 'further inquiry,' and to place him under police supervision."[2] But this opinion found no favor, and in the course of the debate it was not mentioned again; the articles of the Code of Criminal Examination, which reproduced the two texts of the Code of Brumaire, year IV, of which we have spoken above, passed without discussion whenever they came under the eyes of the Council. The liberative effect of the acquittal was even further strengthened. Henceforth the appeal to the Court of Cassation could not be lodged except in the interests of the law

[1] *Locré*, vol. XXIV, p. 98. [2] *Ibid.*, vol. XXIV, p. 28.

against an acquittal pronounced in the Court of Assizes, and against the procedure which had preceded it. The Court of Assizes also has, in one case, the power to render ineffective the decision of the jury, but that is when, the verdict being affirmative, the court thinks the good faith of the jury has been deceived or misled, and that the condemnation would be unjust.

We have not forgotten the important part played in the old criminal procedure by the letters of justice and pardon. These letters disappeared even before royalty did. They were certain applications of reserved justice; and from 1789 it was agreed that all justice emanates not from the king but from the nation. For some of these letters, those which tended to hinder the courts of justice, stopping prosecutions or imposing on the judges a mandatory acquittal, the suppression was destined to be final. Although the head of the State, when the form of government was the Monarchy or the Empire, since that time enjoyed the right to grant amnesties, this was in no respect a return to the old letters, which were quite individual. As to the letters of remission and pardon which formerly served to find not guilty homicides committed in lawful self-defense, they constituted a bizarre system for which there was no longer a *raison d'être*.[1] But there were others which answered real needs: letters of reprieve, of rehabilitation, and of revision. During the Intermediary Period endeavors were sometimes made to satisfy these needs by means of new institutions; sometimes it was considered that they were not legitimate or deserving of the interference of the legislature.

In regard to the right of reprieve, the Constituent Assembly had deemed it incompatible with the new principles.[2] It was considered to be a kind of attack upon the decisions of the courts of judicature, and Montesquieu had already declared that this right was only admissible in the purely monarchical state. On the other hand the sentences rendered upon the verdict of a jury appeared to present such safety that all tampering with them was useless. However, the reprieve answers a need which is the same under all governments and in all countries: to ameliorate too severe sentences, to correct judicial error, to compensate the efforts of the condemned towards well-doing. So the right of reprieve appeared under the consulate; the organic "Senatus-Consultum" of the 16th Messidor of the year X granted it to the

[1] See the "Exposé des motifs" of Title VII, Book II of the Code of Criminal Examination (*Locré*, vol. XXVIII, p. 164).

[2] See the Penal Code of 1791, Part I, Title VII, Art. 13.

First Consul.[1] Under the Empire the right to grant letters of reprieve, an absolute right in the hands of the Emperor, could be explained by a return to ancient principles; according to the "Senatus-Consultum" of the 28th Floréal, year XII, justice was rendered in the name of the Emperor.

The rehabilitation had not been, like the reprieve, expunged from our laws during the Revolution. It had even become a right for those offenders who, after having suffered their punishment, returned to proper paths; but, conformably to the new ideas, it could not emanate from the executive power. The spirit of the time is recognized both in the choice of the authority charged with taking into account the improvement of the offender, and in the spectacular forms by which the rehabilitation was surrounded.[2] The authority which decides it is the general council of the commune (Articles 3 to 5).[3] If the vote, which takes place after a delay of a month, is favorable, "two municipal officers wearing their scarves of office . . . shall conduct the offender before the criminal court of the department in the territory in which he is presently domiciled . . . they shall appear with him in the court-room in the presence of the judges and the public. After having caused the judgment pronounced against the condemned to be read, they shall say in a loud voice: 'such an one has expiated his crime by suffering his punishment; meantime his conduct is irreproachable; we demand in the name of his country that the stigma of his crime be effaced'" (Article 6). The president of the court then intervened, but only to register the decision and to pronounce a formula (Article 7). "The president of the court without deliberation shall pronounce these words: 'upon the attestation and the demand of your country, the law and the court efface the stigma of your crime.'"

The rehabilitation was little practised under this form, which put in a vivid light the crime of which it was desired to obliterate the traces. The institution was very unpopular at the time when the draft of the Criminal Code was under discussion.[4] The ques-

[1] Art. 86: "The First Consul has the right of pardon. He exercises this right after having heard in a privy council the grand-judge, two ministers, two senators, three State's councillors, and two judges of the Court of Cassation."

[2] See the Penal Code of 1791 (Part I, Title VII).

[3] It is necessary that ten years elapse after the expiation of the punishment, and that the person liberated shall have resided for two consecutive years in the same commune (Arts. 1 and 2).

[4] Sitting of 30th Prairial, year XII, "M. Regnaud says that under the old laws rehabilitation was put in force by letters from the king; that the Constituent Assembly has adopted a different method, but that circum-

tion of ascertaining if it should be maintained was one of the points which is singled out from the beginning as one which ought to be first of all decided. The prevailing opinion was that the institution should not be expunged from our laws, but there was an inclination to return purely and simply to the letters of rehabilitation of the Old Régime. "The Archchancellor observes that the Constituent Assembly resolved upon the rehabilitation under circumstances much less favorable than those in which we find it: at that time the letters of reprieve were suppressed and the sovereign could not interfere to grant the rehabilitation or to modify it. It was granted to all the condemned, and the local administrations pronounced it indiscriminately and without investigation. Meanwhile, a different mode might be adopted, one which would make the rehabilitation a useful institution. It must not be intrusted either to the general councils or to local administrations, but granted only by letters from the prince, which should be issued with a knowledge of the cause and with suitable modifications."[1] This idea, however, which was a pure and simple return to the traditions of the Old Régime, was not followed. A mixed system was adopted, bearing the imprint of the systems which had successively been in force. The condemned, if he was not a second offender, at the end of the time of probation fixed by the law, had to present his claim to the Court of Appeal with the certificates of the municipal councils of the communes where he had successively lived. The Court could deny the claim or, on the contrary, allow it. Even if it admitted it that was not all; the rehabilitation only resulted from the "letters" of the chief of the executive power, who was entitled to refuse it. "The rehabilitation," says the Archchancellor, "ought only to be put in operation by decree of the court, rendered with a knowledge of the cause, upon the demand of the condemned, supported by the certificate of the municipality, and upon the motion of the public prosecutor. The court ought to have the right to suspend it, and the decree should not become executory except by virtue of letters from the prince."[2] This composite system did not pass without being contested in favor of the old system. M. Regnaud declares "that he would prefer that the letters from the prince should be obtained first of all and that they should afterwards be ratified."[3] But M. Ber-

stances have not permitted its employment. This method had also the disadvantage of sending back indiscriminately into society those who had suffered their punishments" (*Locré*, vol. XXIV, p. 104).

[1] *Locré*, vol. XXIV, p. 105.
[2] *Ibid.*, vol. XXVIII, p. 123.
[3] *Ibid.*, vol. XXVIII, p. 124.

lier replies that "the act of the sovereign would thus be placed at the mercy of the courts, and this old and dangerous prerogative of the parlements should certainly not be resuscitated." In reality, the new combination contained more than an inversion of the order of the operations formerly followed. M. Réal brought this out in his "Exposé des motifs": "Since," he says, "it is no longer a question of the right of reprieve and of its application pure and simple, since it concerns the recognition of an acquired right, the courts cannot remain in ignorance of the examination preceding the judgment; it is thus necessary, in this mixed matter, to admit the concurrence of the courts in allowing recourse to the prince." [1]

The aim of revision has always been to correct judicial error. The Constituent Assembly did not allow it, thinking that it was enough to grant to the accused free defense and judgment by the country; in this there was a reaction against the practices of the Old Régime, where the letters of revision were frequent. The Convention, however, introduced the revision, but in one single case, that of two irreconcilable convictions, and it made it a method of recourse before the Supreme Court. The Code of Criminal Examination admits it, with the same characteristic, and makes it available in three cases in favor of those condemned to criminal punishment. Upon this point the system of the Ordinance does not reappear.

Concerning "lettres de cachet," as a matter of right at least, there could be no question. However, in the debate in the State's Council allusion was made to them. The draft of the Criminal Code contained a strange institution. This was a "family jury" it was to judge the simple misdemeanors or contraventions committed "by a son of the family not married or not establishe[d] in business, or by a married woman not separated from her hus-band" when there were no stranger accomplices, and when stran-gers could not raise any claim for civil damages. The decision o[f] this jury, which decided upon the guilt and upon the punishmen[t] under the presidency of the justice of the peace, only became ex-ecutory on confirmation by the president of the Court of Appea[l] who could reduce the punishment. This plan, which answere[d] the sentimental ideas of the 1700s very well, was at first favorabl[y] received. Some criminal courts even extolled it in their observa-tions.[2] But when it was discussed in 1808, the practical spir[it]

[1] *Locré*, vol. XXVIII, p. 165.

[2] Tribunal of Loir-et-Cher, p. 36 ("Observations," vol. III); Tribun[al] of Hérault, p. 66 (*ibid.*).

had gained the upper hand, and the proposal was rejected in the State's Council. However, a serious discussion of the matter still took place, for it was recalled that the "lettres de cachet" had formerly often filled a function analogous to that which it was wished to attribute to this family jury. "Count Regnaud de Saint-Jean d'Angély fears that this institution would introduce arbitrariness. He acknowledges that formerly, when the 'lettres de cachet' were in vogue, there was still more arbitrariness; but the 'lettres de cachet' were not much issued."[1] In the sitting of 23d August, 1808, M. Treilhard also supported the family jury: "He says that he does not claim that this institution is necessary, but that he is persuaded that it would be beneficial, were it but to prevent a return to the 'lettres de cachet'; powerful and influential men would not fail to invoke the authority of the sovereign, if the law does not give them means of repressing internal disorders in their families."[2] But the institution was not capable of surviving; it was not allowed to see the light of day, and the "lettres de cachet" have not reappeared.

[1] *Locré*, vol. XXVIII, p. 107.

[2] *Ibid.*, vol. XXVIII, p. 142.

CHAPTER IV

CRIMINAL PROCEDURE IN FRANCE SINCE THE CODE OF 1808

§ 1. **Legislation and Judicial Decisions.**—Our task would seem to be at an end. We began our study at the period where the first traces of the inquisitorial and secret procedure show themselves in our laws. Then, following the course of the times, we have seen this procedure expand, become imperative and grow precise in detail, and finally become settled within the inflexible limits of the great Ordinance. In the second half of the 1700s a new spirit brings up for examination the Criminal Procedure, in common with all the institutions of the old French social system; and erelong a great breath of liberty passes over France. The Laws of the Revolution, copied from the English laws, establish among us the jury, the oral and public procedure, and the free defense of the accused. But some of the wisest institutions of the ancient law were needlessly sacrificed; in the midst of the terrible circumstances which form its environment, the new procedure shows itself inefficacious; little is wanting but a strong wave of reaction to secure the revival of the Ordinance of 1670. The institution of the jury, however, has been saved after much discussion and strife, and we have witnessed the slow elaboration of the Code of Criminal Examination, a composite work and one of compromise, which borrows from the Laws of the Revolution almost all its rules regarding trials and judgments, and from the Ordinance of 1670 almost all those of the preliminary examination. It would seem that our explanation should be at an end, for the Code of Criminal Examination is still in force at the present time. A last chapter remains for us to write, however. The Code of Criminal Examination is to-day already an old law; it is more than one hundred years old, and since its promulgation it has undergone numerous alterations, some of them very material, although relating to matters of detail. The strife has continued between the two tendencies, between which the legislators of 1808 wished to establish a durable compromise and a definite equilibrium. Although there could be no question of new conquests for the procedure of the past, although the ground yielded by it was definitely lost, the spirit of free defense was bound to insinuate itself at those points where it had not been able to penetrate in 1808. The discussion has, in fact, continued ever since, in press and in parliament, in books and in speeches. This time, contrary to what took place in the 1700s, the attack has frequently been made by the criminalists; their voices have been loudest in favor of humanity and wise liberty. It is sufficient to mention the celebrated and honored names of Faustin Hélie and d'Ortolan.

It must be said, however, that, with the exception of certain reforms closely connected with the recollection of celebrated trials, such as the rehabilitation in favor of the dead, these demands have not aroused public opinion to the point of passion. The governments which have proposed and adopted ameliorations and reforms have yielded to scientific deduction rather than to the exigencies of public opinion. It is easy, we believe, to explain this tranquillity of mind, which is by no means indifference. We have the trial by jury for the graver infractions; for all of them the procedure is public and oral and the defense entirely free. It is, therefore, certain that in law and in fact innocence can easily triumph before the trial jurisdiction at the end of the contest. Whatever may be the severity of the examination, it cannot abolish the sentiment of safety given by the final proceedings. We shall not describe the movement of minds as it appears in the parliamentary debates, in the press and in books; it is the very environment in which we live; let us point out briefly what has been done by legislation, from 1808 to the present time. We shall also note the tendencies and the results of judicial practice where they have been inspired rather by a general view than by the minute interpretation of authorities; judicial practice is everywhere and always one of the most puissant factors among those contributing to the development of a nation's laws.

§ 2. **Changes in Procedure before Trial.** — The Code of Criminal Examination, as we have seen, is composed of two quite distinct parts: the rules concerning the judgment, and those regulating the examination. The former ought to be more stable than the latter; they have derived little from the institutions of the past. One borrowing, however, has been made from the most unfortunate inspiration of the Old Régime. The special courts, descendants of the old prévôtal jurisdictions, formed a dark stain upon the Code of Criminal Examination. They did not disappear along with the Empire. The constitutional charter of 14th June, 1814, maintained them as a normal institution. Article 62: "No one can be deprived of his natural judges." Article 63: "Commissions and extraordinary courts cannot be created. Under this denomination prévôtal jurisdictions are not included, should their reëstablishment be deemed necessary." A Law of 20th December, 1815, effectively organized prévôtal courts, composed of a president and four judges, chosen from among the members of the district court, and of a provost, taken from among the military or naval officers, having the rank of colonel and being thirty years old (Articles 2, 3, and 4). They took cognizance of all the crimes jurisdiction of which was conferred by the Code on the special courts, but in addition thereto, their jurisdiction comprehended a great number of political offenses (Articles 8 to 14), and this new jurisdiction was the real *raison d'être* of the institution.[1] The judgments rendered by these prévôtal courts were not susceptible of any review; the question of jurisdiction was submitted to the chamber of arraignments, which decided finally without the possibility of an appeal to the Court of Cassation (Articles 45 and 39). By the same means the special courts of the Code of Criminal Examination ceased to exist, and the new prévôtal courts were not destined to have a long life. Article 55 and last of the Law of 1815 provided "that the present law shall cease to have effect if it has not been renewed in the course of the said session." Well, it was not renewed; at the very opening of the session, on 5th November, 1817, Louis XVIII announced that he did not consider the preservation of the prévôtal court any longer necessary. The charter of 1830 prohibited their reëstablishment forever. Article 53: "No one can be deprived of his natural judges." Article 54: "Extraordinary commissions or exceptional courts cannot be created under any title or denomination whatever." On this point, again, the Ordinance of 1670 finally became a thing of the past; henceforward the prévôtal jurisdictions belong but to history. The common law jurisdictions remained: courts of assizes, tribunal of correctional police, and police court.

For the procedure before the Court of Assizes perfection was not attained in 1808 any more than in 1791 and the year IV. The

[1] *Sirey*, "Lois annotées," I, p. 931.

alterations made later could not but be, it is true, merely improvements in detail, but several very important points were retouched. The rules as to putting questions to the jury were altered: without returning to the complex simplifications of the Code of Offenses and Punishments, it was decided that the only question which, according to the Code of Criminal Examination, could clear the indictment, should be resolved into its necessary elements.[1] In this respect the practice of the presidents of the Courts of Assizes preceded the law and inspired the lawmaker.

Another reform assured the independence of the jurors in their voting. We have already told how, according to the Law of 1791 and the Code of Brumaire, the jurors gave their opinions aloud, one by one. The Code of Criminal Examination did not preserve these somewhat spectacular forms, but it maintained the principle of the oral verdict; it did not even isolate the jurors from each other as had been previously done. When they had retired into the jury room, and the discussion was at an end, the foreman of the jury questioned them one after another and took down their replies (Article 345). This method was bound frequently to put a restraint upon timid dispositions and even falsify the voting. It was changed by the Law of 9th September, 1835, establishing the vote by secret ballot. "It is asked," said the Keeper of the Seals, in the Committee Report, "why, when everything is done among us by ballot, it is not allowed to the courts of assizes to express one's private conviction, — the proceeding used in elections at all stages, and in the making of the laws." This new method of ballot was affirmed and detailed in the Law of 13th May, 1836.

In 1832 the jury acquires a new power, that of taking into consideration extenuating circumstances in favor of accused persons (Article 341). This reform, of prime importance, concerns criminal law more than it does criminal procedure. However, we ought to remark that it was a partial lowering of that barrier which it was desired to raise between the fact, left to the jury, and the question of punishment, reserved for the magistrates. In granting extenuating circumstances the jury are often swayed by the severity of the punishment: this is a tendency which could not be prevented; moreover, the Keeper of the Seals, in presenting the Committee Report, recognized to a certain extent the lawfulness of such verdicts. "Undoubtedly," he said, "the opinion of the jury will be found to be sometimes affected by the considera-

[1] Law of 9th September, 1835 (New Art. 345 of the Code of Criminal Examination); Law of 13th May, 1836.

tion of the severity of the punishment; but the influence of that consideration cannot be totally avoided. It is better to allow the jury some latitude than to expose ourselves to having the accused freed entirely without punishment, and to allow the dangerous doctrine of omnipotence to be sanctioned." [1] Force of circumstances baffled the preconceived ideas at first included in the law.

On two points numerous changes took place, the legislature wavering between contrary tendencies. These two points were the composition of the jury, and the majority by which it must render its verdict of condemnation. Every time, so to speak, that the government undergoes a notable change, a new law is made to alter the composition of the jury. Thus there came in succession the Law of 2d May, 1827, the Decree of 7th August, 1848, the Law of 4th June, 1853, the Decree of 14th October, 1870,[2] and the Law of 21st November, 1872. These frequent alterations, the result of current politics and changes, should not surprise us. Roman history presents the same spectacle at the time of the "quæstiones perpetuæ": the senators and the "equites" dispute the right to sit on the criminal jury; the changes brought about in the choice of jurors are a triumph for one of the parties; and the laws succeed each other at short intervals, all tinged with a political character.[3] We shall not enter into details at this point. Let us only say that since the Law of 1827 there is one more stage in the operations which ought to result in the petty jury. This law in effect created an *annual jury list,* from which the session lists are no longer chosen, but drawn by lot, fifteen days before the opening of the assizes. This was a happy creation, which has always existed since that time, and which even, in the more recent laws, has caused the general list, henceforth useless, to be set aside. What has varied, and will undoubtedly vary again, is the choice of authorities charged with drawing up this list every year.

The legislature of 1808 had adopted for the decisions of the jury the principle of a mere majority, but it had not openly proclaimed it, and had constituted an illogical and complicated system which could not last. The Law of 4th March, 1831, abolished this anomaly. It provided no longer "that the judges of the law should take part in the declaration of the fact"; but it provided

[1] *Sirey,* "Lois annotées," II, p. 126.

[2] It repealed the Law of 1853, and again put in force the Decree of 1848.

[3] See *Geib,* "Geschichte des römischen Criminalprocesses," p. 195 *et seq.* *Zumpt,* "Das Criminalrecht der römischen Republik"; Zweiter Band: "Die Schwurgerichte."

that the decision of the jury should not convict the accused except by a majority of more than seven votes. This was a partial return to the principles of the Laws of 1791 and the year IV; and it was granting accused persons a dangerous favor. Very soon, therefore, a reaction set in, and the Law of 9th March, 1835, reëstablished the rule of the mere majority: "It is asked," said the Keeper of the Seals, "why, in a government by majorities, it was to the minority that the right of deciding upon the life and the possessions of the citizens was left."[1] In 1848 a new oscillation of the pendulum took place in a contrary direction; there were even two laws passed upon this point in the same year. A first Decree of 6th March, 1848, destined to repeal the famous Laws of September, 1835, decided, in Article 4: "A conviction shall require a majority of nine votes; the decision of the jury shall, to be valid, bear these words: 'Yes, the accused is guilty, by a majority of more than eight votes.'" The preamble declares "that the conviction by the jury by a mere majority is a provision which has the disapproval at once of philosophy and humanity, and which is in direct opposition to all the principles laid down by our various National Assemblies." But on 18th October another Decree, passed by the Constituent Assembly upon the report of M. Crémieux, reduced the majority necessary for conviction to eight votes. Finally, the Law of 10th June, 1853, again amending Article 347 of the Code of Criminal Examination, reëstablished the principle of the mere majority, allowing the court, in Article 352, to "transfer to subsequent assizes a case where it was convinced of the commission by the jury of a judicial error."[2] It is not likely that such a wise rule, one that holds the balance equal between the accused and the society accusing him will be abandoned in the future; it has now been long sanctioned by experience, and it may be said to have passed into our customs.

[1] The Law of 1835, however, imported a restriction, very slight, it is true. Amending Art. 352, Inst. Crim., which, in the case of an affirmative verdict, allowed the judges, if they were unanimously of opinion that the jury were mistaken upon the merits, to adjourn the case to another session. It adds: "When the accused shall have been declared guilty by a mere majority only (which the jury must declare) it will be sufficient that the majority of the judges are of opinion that the judgment should be suspended and the case adjourned to the following session, in order that this modification be ordered by the court."

[2] The "Exposé des motifs" said: "This seeming innovation is not one in reality. For the sixty years that the jury has been in existence in our country it has not operated with specific majorities for verdicts of guilty except during fourteen years; it has operated during forty-six years with a mere majority." *Sirey*, "Lois annotées," 1853, p. 67.

To finish with the legislative amendments, which the organization of the jury has undergone, let us say that a recent Law of 19th June, 1881,[1] has suppressed the summing up made by the president of the Court of Assizes after the close of the parties' cases. This is a reform in favor of which a strong current of public opinion had set in for a long time. This summing up, which ought to present a faithful picture of the case, did not always represent fairly the prosecution and the defense. From an unconscious *esprit de corps,* from that professional sentiment which formerly rendered the judges of the Tournelle unfavorable to the defense, the president, however strong might be his desire to prove himself impartial, too often became the auxiliary of the attorney-general. The summing up was sometimes an amplification of the requisition of the public prosecutor. The prosecution and the defense were probably not on an equal footing when, at the moment when those waverings which precede difficult decisions were taking place in the minds of the jurors, the president threw the weight of his high authority into the scale. Conversely, moreover, it may be said that the jurors, now accustomed to their duties, had their minds made up at the close of the trial, and that they listened impatiently to a summing up, which prolonged their session, and delayed the decisive moment when the verdict was to be decided on and announced.

If it is now asked how in judicial practice the rules of procedure before the assize courts have been applied, we find first of all that it has maintained with the greatest rigor the necessary formalities in the procedure by jury: the forms are here one of the principal safeguards. The Supreme Court, enlarging in a spirit of justice the scope of nullities, declares to be error the omission of any formality which is really material to the defense, even when the law shall not have prescribed it on pain of nullity. But on the other hand, judicial practice has introduced to a rather large extent the use of written depositions before the Assize Courts. We have seen with what care the Legislature of 1791 and the year IV withdrew from the eyes of the jury the written depositions taken in the preliminary examination; not only was it forbidden to submit these documents to them, but also, with some exceptions, to have them read to them. The Code of 1808, while it was less precise and less strict, had not rejected this tradition, as we have shown

[1] New Article 346, Inst. Crim.: "The president, after the close of the trial, cannot, on pain of nullity, sum up the pleadings of the prosecution and the defense." In Belgium this summing up was abolished by Decree of 4th July, 1831.

above. Judicial practice, on the contrary, decided that the president, by virtue of his discretionary power, could always let the jury have a perusal of the written depositions. This law of the courts, established at an early date,[1] has been kept up in a consistent fashion. Originally the wording of the decisions seemed to restrict it to the case where the witness could not be cited or appear by reason of "force majeure," but the same principle was in course of time applied to the case where the witness might have, but had not been, cited; whether the witness was present or absent, the president could cause his deposition to be read.[2] This is a practice well established to-day, and one which raises no protest; it gives the defense the same assistance as the prosecution. Besides, although formerly the employment of written documents had been so carefully prohibited before the jury, it was in the fear that by this means the doctrine of legal proofs would be reformed of its own accord. It is easy to see that this fear was groundless. The system of moral proofs is enjoined by public opinion still more than by law.

In the procedure before the courts of correctional police, written proof gained much more ground, and that by virtue even of an express law. The organization of the appellate jurisdiction in correctional matters was in 1808 illogical and extravagant; it could only be justified by the difficulty of communication at that period. Some appeals only (those of the department where the court sat) were brought before the Court of Appeal; the others were brought before the court of the chief seat of the department; several to the court of the chief seat of an adjacent department. There was neither harmony nor true hierarchy, and historically as well as logically a wisely constructed hierarchy appears to be one of the natural conditions of the appeal. The Law of 13th June, 1856, abolished these anomalies. According to the new Article 201 of the Code of Criminal Examination, the appeal should always be brought before the court. But, in spite of the great development of the means of communication, this led to making rather difficult and very costly the appearance of the witnesses before the Court of Appeal. In the old state of things they usually appeared only in the trial court, and the judges of

[1] See *Cass.*, 10th January, 1817; *Cass.*, 9th April, 1818 (*Sirey*, "Collect. nouv.," vol. I, p. 463).

[2] The law, however, retains the rule according to which the dominant characteristic is that the proceedings are oral; so that when a witness appears and testifies before the jury, the reading of his written deposition cannot be made to precede his oral deposition. *Cass.*, 12th September, 1867 (*Sirey*, 68, I, 319).

appeal decided according to the notes of hearing, taken by the clerk of court in conformity with Articles 156 and 189 of the Code of Criminal Examination. In 1856 this fact was stated to the Legislative Body by the reporter of the Law, M. Nogent Saint-Laurent: "The witnesses are always heard in the trial court; before the magistrates charged with the appeal their hearing is always exceptional in practice."[1] Henceforward this practice could no longer be affirmed. What was to be done? Accept the necessity and the fact and, since the judges would most often judge upon the notes of hearing, see that they were complete and faithful. This was rather difficult to manage, the task being troublesome to the clerks of court. "How could they have sufficient and complete notes? Nothing but stenography could keep up with the testimony. Any other method dragged hopelessly behind. Go into the court-room and observe the clerk of court; he is attentive; absorbed; he glances from the deponing witness to the paper upon his desk. The testimony has hardly reached his ear before he is writing as fast as he can. . . . The trial goes on, however, without anybody concerning himself with the clerk. Nobody comes to his assistance. He has a great deal to do. . . . When the hearing is at an end his summary notes are riddled with blanks, gaps, and contractions. The summary notes should at all events present all the salient sides of the oral depositions, but they rarely do so. Under the bill, however, oral depositions, formerly so rare before the court, will become rarer still. The consequence of this is evident; the notes of the evidence will acquire a greater importance; consequently they must be improved."[2] To achieve that this is what was done. Article 189, as amended, contains the following provisions: "The clerk of court will take notes of the statements of the witnesses and the replies of the accused. The clerk's notes will be ratified by the president within three days after the rendering of the judgment." It was, therefore, no longer the *principal* statement (Article 155), but all the statements of the witnesses, and, furthermore, those of the accused, that the clerk must take notes of, and the president's certificate guaranteed the faithfulness of these notes. An amendment was presented by M. Picard, asking that the notes should be communicated to the defense, which should be entitled to examine them, and, if need be, make a protest, but this was not considered by the State's Council.

[1] *Sirey*, "Lois annotées," 1856, p. 58.
[2] Report of *M. Nogent Saint-Laurent; Sirey*, "Lois annotées," 1856, p. 59

A prior Law, that of 30th January, 1851, upon judicial assistance, had rendered the defense before the court of correctional police easier for the accused. According to Article 29, "the presidents of the correctional court shall appoint an official defender to accused persons prosecuted at the request of the public prosecutor, or detained pending trial, when they demand it, and when their poverty shall be established either by the documents referred to in Article 10, or any other documents." This same Law, in the following Article, rendered it also possible for indigent accused persons to have witnesses cited for the defense, although they are not able to defray the expenses of the citation. Up to that time the indigent accused had but one resource, to ask the public prosecutor of his good will to cause the witnesses pointed out by him to be cited (Article 321).[1] Two methods of recourse in criminal and correctional matters were enlarged or rendered easier. The Law of 29th June, 1868, amending Article 443 and the following Articles of the Code of Criminal Examination, provided that the appeal for revision, in the three cases where the Code admits it, could be lodged after the decease of the condemned in order to rehabilitate his memory; it makes this method of recourse available to those condemned to correctional punishments when the punishment is "imprisonment or total or partial deprivation of civil, civic, and family rights." Quite recently a Law of 28th and 30th June, 1877, amending Articles 420 and 421 of the Code of Criminal Examination, dispenses with the "mise en état" of the person condemned to a punishment depriving him of his liberty, who lodges an appeal to the Court of Cassation, when the duration of the punishment does not exceed six months; it also dispenses, in the same case, with the payment of the fine by any one "condemned to a correctional or police punishment entailing deprivation of liberty." This necessity, always imposed[2] by the "mise en état," was a tradition of the old law.

[1] "The presidents of the courts of assizes and the presidents of the correctional tribunals can, even before the day fixed for the hearing, order the citation of the witnesses who shall be indicated to them by the indigent accused, where the testimony of these witnesses shall be deemed useful for the discovery of the truth. All productions and authentication of documents can likewise be ordered officially."

[2] At least whenever the punishment carried deprivation of liberty for any length of time (old Article 421). — Along with these liberal Laws one may be cited which appears harsh; namely, that of 9th September, 1835, which allows of the expulsion from the hearing of accused persons who, "by means of outcries or any other means likely to cause disturbance shall obstruct the course of justice," and which, however, declares that they will be tried confrontatively in the same way as those who refuse to appear. This, at first sight, recalls the proceedings of the ancient law against *vol-*

We have seen above that the Code of 1808 had preserved in the clearest fashion the principle of *res judicata*, and the liberatory effect of the acquittal pronounced by the Court of Assizes. It is expedient to point out how the courts in general construed Article 360 of the Code of Criminal Examination. Under the rule of the Code of Brumaire, it was provided that the effect of the acquittal was to wipe out at once all the penal qualifications of which the fact was susceptible, even those which had transformed it into a simple misdemeanor, by the elimination or the modification of some of its elements. It is true that, on the other hand, the Code of Offenses and Punishments ordered the president to put to the jury the questions resulting from the trial which might modify the gravity of the charge.[1] Under the rule of the Code of Criminal Examination was this tradition to be followed, or was it, on the contrary, to be provided that, after acquittal in the Court of Assizes, the accused might be prosecuted before the court of correctional police for the same act, differently named and transformed into a misdemeanor? The question was not long in arising before the Supreme Court. On 27th August, 1812, the Court of Toulouse rendered a decree sustaining the prior rulings, "considering that the new Code of Criminal Examination has not in this respect made any change upon the maxim 'non bis in idem'; it had but substituted a chamber of accusation for the grand jury, and nothing prevents the president of the assizes from putting questions arising in the course of the trial."[2] But this doctrine was warmly contested by Merlin, in the sitting of the Criminal Chamber of 29th October, 1812, and in conformity with his motion the contrary theory was adopted by the Resolution of 29th October, 1812: "be it understood that according to Articles 374 and 379 of the Code of Offenses and Punishments, the questions which were submitted to the trial jury must necessarily relate not only to the fact which was the subject of the indictment, but also to all the circumstances which, according to the trial or the accused's defense, could modify the gravity of the deed, even though they changed its character; that in this way under the rule of this law, the acquittal pronounced in favor of an accused must absolutely free him from all prosecution, on account of the

untary mutes, but this comparison is hardly appropriate. The Law of 1835 applies only to accused persons who are in a state of open and violent rebellion against the court, when it takes numerous precautions to compel them to follow the course of the proceedings.

[1] See *Cass.*, 5th February, 1808; *Sirey*, "Collect. nouv.," II, p. 484.

[2] *Merlin*, "Répertoire, additions. Nobis in idem, No. V bis."

act charged, and also on account of all its modifications, and all the features of criminality of which it might be susceptible; but that the Code of Criminal Examination, by establishing other rules, has necessarily restricted this principle."[1] This Resolution settled the judicial law on this point, which has not varied since. This solution is probably regrettable, and with difficulty reconcilable with the broad and absolute terms of Article 360; but it must be acknowledged that it rests upon a very strong juridical reasoning;[2] and if it should ever be abolished by a law,[3] such a law must logically at the same time impose upon the president the obligation of putting to the jury the *subsidiary questions* resulting from the trial.

§ 3. **Changes in the Preliminary Examination.** — The preliminary examination was the part of the Code of Criminal Examination most open to criticism; and important reforms had been already carried out in regard thereto, and others, more important still, are in preparation. But before approaching the recital of these reforms and the investigation of these plans, let us see whether judicial law had in any way modified the system established by the legislature of 1808. The Courts had been able to do only one single thing: to open to the accused a recourse before the Chamber of Accusation against the orders of the Council Chamber, or against those of the examining judge, where the law had not granted it to him expressly, but had not absolutely refused it. In effect, it did something of the same kind in favor of the public prosecutor. The Code had not allowed to the public prosecutor and the civil party an appeal from the order of the Council Chamber except in a single case, namely, when this order set the accused at liberty.[4] But the Courts did not hesitate to enlarge this provision and to give to the public prosecutor the right of appeal in every case;[5] they relied upon the principle that in criminal matters appeal is a matter of right. "Is it necessary," said

[1] *Merlin*, "Répertoire," *loc. cit.*

[2] "If the president of the Court of Assizes," said *Merlin*, "ought not to have interrogated the jury upon this point, it is very clear that the accused cannot be deemed to have been put to trial upon this point before the jury."

[3] A bill for this purpose was submitted to the Chamber of Deputies.

[4] Old Article 135: "When the release of the accused shall be ordered conformably to Articles 128, 129, and 131 above, the imperial attorney or the private prosecutor shall be entitled to oppose his release."

[5] See *Cass.*, 25th October, 1811 (*Sirey*, "Collect. nouv.," III, I, p. 414); *Cass.*, 20th June, 1812 ("Collect. nouv.," IV, I, p. 128); *Cass.*, 19th March, 1813 ("Collect. nouv.," IV, I, p. 308); *Cass.*, 29th October, 1813 ("Collect. nouv.," IV, I, p. 308); *Cass.*, 29th October, 1813 ("Collect. nouv.," IV, I, p. 454).

Merlin in his motion, "that this order be expressly ranked by the Code of Criminal Examination in the class of those which are susceptible of appeal? Certainly not. It is sufficient that it be not excepted from it, and why? Because this power to attack all the acts of the Council Chamber of the court of the first instance is a matter of common law." He had formerly said: "It is not an appeal, properly so called. It is a method introduced for the same purpose as the appeal."[1] But if this were so, must not the same right of appeal be given to the accused? "It may be said for the affirmative," declared Merlin in another matter where this question presented itself, "that there is no Article of the Code of Criminal Examination allowing the accused to protest to the judge against an order of this nature; no more is there any which forbids him, which interdicts him from this method, although it is open to his adversaries, which destroys all equality between him and his adversaries . . . that, besides, the recourse to the superior judge against the orders of the first judges is a matter of common right, and it is upon this principle that you have relied in the Resolution passed by you on 29th October last, determining, notwithstanding the silence of Article 135, that the orders which are sent to the correctional police in the case provided for by Article 130 are subject to appeal." However, the eminent jurisconsult finds a reason for refusing to the accused the right of lodging appeal: "The common law," he continues, "is that the preliminary judgments are not subject to appeal. It is, therefore, conforming to the common law to refuse to the accused the power of protesting against the order sending him to the correctional police."[2] Probably, as a matter of good logic, it would have been possible by the same reasoning to deny the appeal of the public prosecutor; but, however that may be, Merlin's argument triumphed, and the Supreme Court decided that "the method of appeal is not open to the accused against the order transferring him to the correctional court, that this right belongs only to the public prosecutor and the civil party."[3] For a stronger reason it was determined that the orders of the examining judge were not, except for a juris-

[1] *Merlin*, "Répert. addit." Appeal from an Ordinance of the Council Chamber, No. 11.

[2] *Ibid.*, "Répert. addit." Appeal from an Ordinance of the Council Chamber, No. IX.

[3] *Cass.*, 20th December, 1813 (*Sirey*, "Collect. nouv.," IV, I, p. 497); — *Cass.*, 7th November, 1816 (*Sirey*, "Collect. nouv.," V, I, p. 244); — Grenoble, 29th March, 1834 (*Sirey*, 34, 2, 441); — Lyons, 31st January, 1834 (*Sirey*, 34, 2, 381).

dictional cause, capable of attack by appeal on the part of the accused.[1]

The revision of our Criminal Codes in 1832, so fertile upon other points, produced nothing new in regard to these matters. But under the Second Empire we find a series of very important reforms, although all bearing upon isolated points. The Law of 17th July, 1856, suppressed one of the institutions which appeared to the compilers of the Code of Criminal Examination to be the most happy, that of the Council Chamber. It transferred its powers to the examining judge alone; he in future had the duty of rendering the final decree which closes the examination, and decides what the result of it will be (Article 127 *et seq.*). In the eyes of the legislators of 1808 this had appeared a very important matter; it had recalled to them the ruling to the "extraordinary" action pronounced by a single judge, an abuse against which the Cahiers of 1789 had vigorously protested. But practice had shown that the examining judge had a preponderating influence in the Council Chamber. In law, if a crime was concerned, and, in fact, in all cases, it was easy for him to obtain an order of transference. He alone knew the proceedings thoroughly, and could present them under colors favorable to his opinion. By giving him the right to decide alone, the proceedings, the progress of which became more rapid, were simplified; the responsibility of the decision was held by everybody to lie upon him who usually gave it out. If we consider what was said in 1856 in justification of the new Law, it must be acknowledged that these observations were just. It must be noted, on the other hand, that the nations which have borrowed our Code of Criminal Examination, Belgium and Italy, for example, have retained the Council Chamber; and by giving it new powers they have made it one of the most useful parts of the general mechanism. We shall also see that it is proposed to reconstitute it in France upon that model. The Law of 17th July, 1856, still regulated this question of opposition to the orders of examination, which we have already seen decided by judicial law; and it adopted the majority of the solutions admitted by the Supreme Court. The new Article, 135, declares, in effect, that "the imperial attorney can, in all cases, lodge appeal to the orders of the examining judge. The civil party can lodge appeal to the orders issued in the cases provided for in Articles 114, 128, 129, 131, and 539 of the present Code, and to every order injurious to his civil interests." As for the accused, something

[1] Paris, 17th April, 1833 (*Sirey*, 33, 2, 289).

more was done in his interest than judicial law had done. He could lodge appeal, not only "in the case of Article 539," that is to say, when he objected to the jurisdiction of the judge, and when the latter was declared competent (which had never been contested), but also "to the orders issued by virtue of Article 114." Article 114 applies to the order of the judge deciding upon the demand for liberation on bail. But, at the same time, Article 135, by its very clear phraseology, as well as by reason of the explanations furnished before the Legislative Assembly, effectually prevented all judicial rulings aiming at the enlargement of the accused's right of opposition.

The question of detention pending trial and liberation on bail, which we have met in Articles 135 and 114, was the primary consideration of the legislators of the Second Empire in the matter of preliminary examinations. In 1855 they approached it for the first time. According to the old Article 94, the examining judge, after the interrogation, issued a writ of attachment when the act entailed corporal or degrading punishment or correctional imprisonment; but by the same authority he was bound thereby and no authority was given him subsequently to withdraw this writ spontaneously. The Law of 4th April, 1855, amending Article 94, provided that after the interrogation the judge could not issue anything but a warrant of commitment and that "in the course of the examination he could, upon the motion of the imperial attorney, and whatever might be the nature of the charge, withdraw every warrant of commitment, on condition that the accused should be represented at all the stages of the proceedings, and should be bound for the execution of the judgment immediately upon his being required." This was preserving to the warrant of commitment the character of a temporary measure, which had always distinguished it; and though here the temporary measure could very easily become absolute, this extension presented more advantages than disadvantages; it even allowed the rule forbidding liberation on bail, whenever a crime was concerned, to be disregarded. But this gave rise to a somewhat serious abuse. Subsequently a Law of 14th July, 1865, amending anew Article 94, allowed the judge to cancel the writ of attachment, like the warrant of commitment, but it none the less allowed him the option of issuing either a warrant of commitment or a writ of attachment after the interrogation; by this means it authorized the practice, well established to-day, which regards both warrants as identical in their functions as well as in their effects, although the warrant of commitment is far from affording the accused the same safeguards as the writ of attachment.[1]

The Law of 14th July, 1865, completely altered the matter of the arrest, of detention pending trial, and liberation on bail. Conceived in a truly liberal spirit, it allows the judge, whatever might be the seriousness of the charge, to issue in the first place against the accused merely a simple summons to appear; according to the old Article 91, the warrant to bring the accused before the Court (" mandat d'amener ") was essential when a crime was concerned. Then, withdrawing all the barriers and prohibitions formerly existing, it provides (Article 113, New) that " in every case, the examining judge can, upon the request of the accused and upon the motion of the imperial attorney, order the accused to be provisionally liberated, on condition of his engagement to be represented at all the stages of the proceedings and to execute the judgment immediately upon his being required." This was the first time since 1789 that provisional liberty was allowed in criminal matters. Furthermore, the judge could always exempt the accused from furnishing bail (Article 114). This provision was, it is true, of less importance than might be thought: a Resolution of 23d and 24th March, 1848, had suppressed the *minimum* of bail to be furnished. These articles gave the judge great powers of liberation; they gave him great powers, but they did not compel him to use them.

The Law of 1865, however, has gone farther, by providing that in certain cases provisional liberation shall be a matter of right, without being as broad in that respect as the Law of 1791 and the Code of Offenses and Punishments. Article 113 (New): " In correctional matters liberation shall be a matter of right, five days after the interrogation, in favor of a domiciled person, when the maximum punishment pronounced by the law shall be less than two years' imprisonment. The foregoing provision shall not apply either to prisoners already condemned for crime or to those already condemned to an imprisonment of more than one year." As a last favor, in this case the judge cannot exact bail from the accused. Article 114: " Provisional liberation may, *in all cases where it is not a matter of right*, be subordinated to the obligation to furnish bail." [2] We know that the accused could submit to the Chamber

[1] See Arts. 61 and 96, Inst. Crim.

[2] Articles 113 to 126, drawn up anew by the Law of 14th July, 1865, contain important details upon provisional release and bail which we must omit. Let us only say that it is not merely during the preliminary examination that provisional liberty can be claimed. Art. 116: "Provisional release can be claimed at every stage of the case." The prevailing practice,

of Arraignments the order by which the examining judge decides upon his request (Articles 135, 115, 113; *cf.* Article 119).

The Law of 14th July, 1865, has dealt with detention pending trial from another point of view; it has restricted, or, rather, regulated, the power of the examining judge to pronounce the "mise au secret," or prohibition of communication with the accused. A certain number of serious occurrences have drawn the attention of the public to the abuse of this practice. Article 613, drawn up anew in 1865, provides that "when the examining judge shall think proper to prescribe in regard to an accused a prohibition of communication, he can only do it by an order which shall be entered upon the prison register. This prohibition shall not extend beyond ten days; it can always be renewed. It shall be reported to the attorney-general."[1]

The Law of 14th July, 1865, whatever might be its importance in other respects, had only touched upon one point of the preliminary examination as organized by the Code. Another Law, a little earlier in date, that of 20th May to 1st June, 1863, had suppressed this examination for a whole class of infractions. These were "flagrants délits correctionnels," correctional offenses where capture in the act had occurred. This Law, in some of its provisions, also touched upon the question of detention pending trial. Down to that time detention pending trial and the preliminary examination were two things indissolubly united, only the examining judge being able to issue the warrant of commitment or writ of attachment.[2] This sometimes presented great inconveniences. When an individual was taken in the act, committing an infraction punished merely by correctional punishment (a very frequent thing, especially in large towns), and brought by the officers who had arrested him before the imperial attorney, the latter had but two courses to take, both of them somewhat unsatisfactory. If he did not wish to leave the accused at liberty and have him directly summoned before the court of correctional police (Articles 182, 184, Inst. Crim.), which would have been absurd, — in order to have him regularly incarcerated he would have had to require the examining judge to issue the warrant of commitment or writ of attachment; but this opened up an

however, by a somewhat strict construction of Art. 126, decides that liberty cannot be claimed before the Court of Assizes.

[1] Since 1875, the prohibition of communication can have no further object than to prevent communication with the outside, those detained pending trial having to be subjected to the rule of individual separation.

[2] It must be understood that we leave aside the quite exceptional hypothesis of Art. 100 (Inst. Crim.).

examination, which necessitated a certain number of steps and entailed inevitable delay. This examination, which the law did not impose in other matters, was entirely useless for such a simple case. The proofs were all collected; the witnesses were known, and usually they were the officers who had effected the arrest. Therefore Article 1 of the new Law, for the purpose of evading these difficulties, gives the imperial attorney, in such circumstances, the right to issue the warrant of commitment: "Every accused captured in the act, for a fact punishable by correctional punishment, is immediately brought before the imperial attorney, who interrogates him. . . . In this case the imperial attorney can put the accused under warrant of commitment." This warrant is, moreover, in this instance, of an essentially provisional character.

The Law of 1863, indeed, was not contented with suppressing the preliminary examination for capture in the act; it has materially accelerated and simplified the judgment. If, on the very day of the arrest, there is a hearing of the correctional police court, the imperial attorney can immediately bring the accused there (Article 1). The witnesses are then "orally summoned by any officer of judicial police, or officer of the public force. They are bound to appear under the penalties provided by Article 157 of the Code of Criminal Examination (Article 3)." The simple proceeding is thus settled without delay and almost without formality. This procedure was imitated by the Legislature of 1863 from that practised before the police courts in London, which had achieved such great success. If on the same day as the arrest there is no hearing of the correctional court, the imperial attorney is bound to have the accused summoned for next day's hearing. The court, if need be, is specially convoked (Article 2). Again, the accused could reject, or rather delay, this expeditious procedure. Article 4: "If the accused should demand it, the court grants him a delay of at least three days for the preparation of his defense." The Law of 1863 has been productive of excellent effects, although in practice its provisions are not altogether observed except in large towns, which result, however, was foreseen by the reporter before the Legislative Body. In the inferior courts, one hearing a week is devoted to matters of correctional police, and the court is not specially called together on the day following the arrest, as provided for in Article 2; the individual captured in the act may therefore remain for almost an entire week under the warrant of commitment issued by the State's attorney.

§ 4. **Plans for Reform.** — The movement and the progress of criminal legislation under the Third Republic have been more active and more extensive than they were under the previous régimes, since the years 1808 and 1810. They have not resulted, it is true, in new codifications, although a revision of the Penal Code and a partial revision of the Code of Criminal Examination have been projected. But numerous useful amendatory Laws have been elaborated. They are so important that the harmony of the texts of the Code of Criminal Examination and the Penal Code where they have been but partially inserted is thereby greatly disturbed, and the man who studied French criminal law thirty years ago and who has not kept in touch with the new legislation possesses no more than an old law very different from the present living reality.

Very many of these new laws deal only with the penal law properly so called; the principal of these are the Law of 26th March, 1891, upon the extenuation and the aggravation of punishments; the Laws of 14th April, 1885, 27th May, 1885, and 20th March, 1891, upon the banishment of the convict; the Law of 14th August, 1885, upon the conditional liberation of the convict; the Laws of 16th August, 1887, and 10th March, 1898, upon judicial rehabilitation; and the Laws of 5th August, 1899, and 11th July, 1900, upon legal rehabilitation, which operates by process of law upon the expiration of the delay fixed by the law, if no new conviction supervenes in the interval. These last-mentioned Laws of 5th August, 1899, and 11th July, 1900, regulate also the important institution of the judicial record (" casier"). Several of these laws at the same time deal with the criminal procedure in this respect that they have augmented the powers of the judges in such matters. Such are the Laws of 1885 and of 1898 upon judicial rehabilitation; the Law of 26th March, 1891 (with which the name of my eminent colleague, M. Bérenger, is connected), in so far as it allows the judges to suspend the execution of the sentence of imprisonment and fine in favor of certain kinds of offenders; it furnishes also a first example of legal rehabilitation, the sentence lapsing, if a new conviction, with imprisonment or to a heavier punishment does not intervene within five years after. The laws upon banishment have also given to the courts powers which they did not formerly possess. Such was the direct object of the Law of 28th October, 1888, which allows the court, on recognizing extenuating circumstances in correctional matters, which wishes consequently to substitute a fine for the imprisonment imposed by the law, then to inflict a fine of 1000 to 3000 francs.

But besides these criminal laws, which only incidentally touch upon the criminal procedure, there are also some among these new laws directly dealing with it and aiming at its reform. They relate to three heads. Some aim at the reform of the preliminary examination, the chief object of this study; a second group deal with the jury and the procedure before the jury; a last have reformed the procedure of revision. I shall examine them briefly in that order. I would observe before beginning that I lay aside what is peculiar to the procedure in matters of press offenses, regulated by the Law of 29th July, 1881, the principles of which I have explained elsewhere.[1]

§ 5. **Recent Legislation.** — The defects of the system of *preliminary examination* adopted by the Code of 1808 had often been pointed out and were well known. When the Republic was finally established and the government belonged to the Republicans, its reform imposed itself as a most essential task. A bill was, therefore, introduced for the reform of the Code of Criminal Examination, and it appeared in the Journal Officiel of 14th January, 1880. "The government could not remain indifferent in the presence of such a true statement of affairs. Already, in 1870, an extra-parliamentary commission had been charged to investigate the reforms to be introduced into the work of 1808. The melancholy events which almost immediately supervened did not allow of the accomplishment of its mission. But in the month of October, 1878, upon the initiative of the Honorable M. Dufaure, Keeper of the Seals, a commission, composed of jurisconsults and eminent criminalists, to whom were added several members of parliament, met under the presidency of the minister of justice for the purpose of studying and introducing into our laws the ameliorations demanded by theory and experience. Thanks to the activity displayed by its members, this commission was able, within the space of several months, to prepare a first bill containing the subjects in the first book of the Code of Criminal Examination."[2] This bill was presented to the Senate, in the sitting of the 27th of November, 1879, and proved to be of a very weighty character. It remodeled the whole of the first book of the Code and comprised a great number of articles (Articles 8 to 221), introducing a methodi-

[1] *Esmein*, "Eléments de droit constitutionel," 5th edition, p. 1050 *et seq.*
[2] Bill for the reformation of the Code of Criminal Examination. Exposé des motifs. Journal officiel of 14th January, 1880, p. 301, col. 3; 302, col. 1.

cal order where none had existed; but what we have to notice is the radical changes which it made upon the preliminary examination. The Committee Report shows on every page the result of a new spirit which permeates the law, entailing a thorough change of system.

First of all the origin of this preliminary examination, as regulated in 1808, is pointed out: "The system of the Code of Criminal Examination is no other than that of the Ordinance of 1670 with less harsh forms;"[1] and it must give place to new conceptions. There was, however, no thought of suppressing the preliminary examination, in order to establish a purely accusatory system modeled on the English procedure. The institution of the public prosecutor was highly extolled, and the dangers presented by the individual accusation, usable by any citizen, were forcibly pointed out.[2] Not only was the preliminary examination retained, but it must continue to be secret: "Our temperament is no less repugnant to the régime of publicity; not to speak of the difficulties which might result therefrom in regard to the detection of guilty persons, and notably of accomplices remaining at liberty, informed by the progress of the examination of the moment when flight or the destruction of the 'corpus delicti' would become necessary. Is it credible that it would be easy to collect positive statements from witnesses, exposed to the captious questions which have rendered celebrated the ability of the English advocates in their cross-examination? In France, it is hard to get a witness, even at the trial, to tell his story frankly, as he told it to the magistrate in secret. Is it credible that the inhabitants of our country districts, so timid when the accusation of a neighbor, whose rancor they fear, is concerned, would dare to speak in all sincerity before the accused, and before his relatives and friends, when they would be in addition exposed to the more or less malevolent criticism of an advocate? Let us add that with our temperament, the examination, if thus carried out publicly, would most frequently have the effect of forming opinions in a sense favorable to the accused or the contrary, and dictating in advance the judgment of the court or of the jury."[3]

But what they desired and thought to be capable of realization was to render the procedure confrontative in this first stage of the action, and to place the defense upon a broad basis: "While discarding the English system as impracticable, it is allowable to ask if it is not possible to extract from it and retain one of its im-

[1] Journal officiel of 14th January, 1880, p. 302, col. 3.
[2] *Ibid.*, p. 303, col. 1.
[3] *Ibid.*, p. 303, col. 1.

portant elements, that of confrontation, between the prosecution and the defense?"[1]

The expedients which the new bill brought together in furtherance of this result appear to us to group themselves logically around the three following points: First, the accused could have a defender beside him, and would receive communication of all the documents of the proceedings. Second, the defense would not have a merely passive part; it would be entitled to invoke on the part of the judge or set into direct operation the measures which should appear to it to be important for the discovery of the truth. Third, a series of methods of appeal is available to the defense against the principal decisions of the examining magistrates.

I. "It becomes necessary to place beside the prisoner, often ignorant and illiterate, from the first step of the information, the aid of a defender, who is not allowed in the existing system until the eve of the public trial."[2] (See Article 127 of the bill.[3]) As a general rule the counsel must be present at the interrogations. "Article 119. Except in case of urgency, if the prisoner is provided with counsel, the judge cannot interrogate him except in presence of the latter, or except he be duly summoned." The first interrogation of the prisoner was also a very limited one: "the examining magistrate establishes the identity of the prisoner, makes him cognizant of the facts charged against him, and receives his statements, after having warned him that he is at liberty to refuse to reply to the questions put to him."[4] — "The examining magistrate advises the prisoner that he has the right to choose a counsel, and in default of such choice, the judge, on his request, appoints one for him." This provision recalls, as will no doubt have been already noticed, the provisions of the Law of 1789. It is true that the following Article added: "The examining magistrate may, nevertheless, proceed with an immediate interrogation and confrontations, if urgency appears, from the condition of a witness in danger of death, or the existence of evidence on the point of destruction."[5]

From the time that the prisoner declared either to the judge or to his clerk, or to the chief warden of the prison (Article 127), that he had chosen counsel for the defense, "except in urgent cases, every time that the prisoner has to be interrogated or confronted,

[1] Journal officiel of 14th January, 1880, p. 303, col. 1.
[2] *Ibid.*, p. 303, col. 2. [3] Journal officiel of 15th January, 1880, p. 333.
[4] Art. 85. This is almost identical with the English law. [5] Art. 86.

the examining magistrate must summon the counsel at the same time, twenty-four hours beforehand, by prepaid letter or by any other form of notice which shall be decided upon by a regulation of public administration."[1] — "Counsel may go into the judge's office of examination with the accused, whether imprisoned or liberated, every time the latter is summoned there. He is forbidden to speak without having obtained the permission of the examining magistrate. If the judge refuses permission, the fact is mentioned in the minutes."[2] — "The State's attorney and the civil party's counsel both have the right to be present at the interrogation."[3] — "The public prosecutor should be present at the examination, with the same authority, and under the same circumstances, as the defending counsel. The examining magistrate decides between them."[4]

Free communication between the prisoner and his counsel was regulated in the following way: "Article 130. If the accused is kept prisoner, he may, immediately after his first appearance, communicate freely with his counsel." — "Article 131. The judge may, nevertheless, if he thinks it necessary, forbid communication of the accused with his counsel. . . . The prohibition cannot extend beyond the tenth day counting from the first appearance. When the necessities of the information demand it, the Council Chamber can always, upon the report of the examining magistrate, prolong the prohibition during a second period not extending beyond the twentieth day counting from the first appearance." The advocate henceforth was to appear at every moment of the proceedings. It was for him that the defense was to have cognizance of the more important documents.

The witnesses were heard secretly, as above stated. It was not even provided that the accused or his counsel be present at this hearing. The judge alone could admit them or the representative of the public prosecutor; but this was a power of which the examining magistrates probably did not make much use; the bill also provided for inspection of the written deposition by the accused or his counsel. "Article 64. The witnesses may be heard either in presence of the public prosecutor, of the civil authority, of the accused, and their counsel, or without their presence. In the latter case, the judge ought, as soon as possible, and at the latest before the end of the examination, allow to the accused or his counsel inspection of the depositions taken in their absence." Furthermore, according to Article 133, during the

[1] Art. 128. [2] Art. 129. [3] Art. 119. [4] "Exposé des motifs."

course of the examination, "counsel for the accused may examine (the process) if the examining magistrate is of the opinion that such production is compatible with the necessities of the examination.[1] — In every case, he must immediately be given, if he demands it, notice of every appealable order of the judge." Finally, in case of a view, the counsel is apprised and may be present at the investigation. Article 47: "In every case where it appears to be necessary, the examining magistrate visits the spot, after having apprised the state's attorney and defendant's counsel for the purpose of drawing up the official reports to establish the 'corpus delicti' and the condition of the place, and receiving the statements of the witnesses."

II. The defense, as we have said, did not play a merely passive part, and it sometimes took the initiative. In this respect, the bill contains a general provision. Article 37: "The public prosecutor, the civil party, *and the accused,* may require the examining magistrate to take all steps which they believe to be necessary to discover the truth."

This text, for the first time, gave the accused in a clear fashion the right to have witnesses heard on his behalf. Several Articles contained the application of this principle. Articles 124, and those immediately following, dealing with the confrontation, provide as follows. Article 124: "The accused may require that a confrontation be allowed between him and the witnesses heard by the examining magistrate in his absence. The judge may, according to the case, order or refuse the confrontation." — Article 125: "If the requested confrontation is refused, no use can be made of the deposition taken, unless the accused requires it by an express declaration. This prohibition does not apply if the witness is dead." — Article 126: "In every case, before the close of the examination, the accused, if he requires it, may be confronted with his co-defendants." These were very curious provisions; they took up old provisions of the Ordinance of 1670. The old formal confrontation was dropped at the time of the introduction of the oral and public trial before the trial court. It was proposed to return to the forgotten rules; the witness who was not confronted, could, as formerly, be called by the accused, but could not give testimony against him. This is a sure sign that, as we have said, the written procedure was regaining ground: since the written depositions were often used before the trial courts, it

[1] The public prosecutor can *request* for him production of the proceedings at all stages of the information. Art. 132.

was desired to surround them anew with safeguards which formerly allowed them to constitute proof.

In one particular matter, the defense had the right to insist. This concerned expert witnesses. The examining magistrate selected the expert from a list "drawn up every year for the following year by the courts of appeal on the opinion of the Faculties, learned bodies, tribunals, and chambers of commerce."[1] — But, according to Article 49, "the public prosecutor, the civil party, and the accused could select an expert from the said list, having the right to be present at all the operations, and to address all requisitions to the experts appointed by the examining magistrates, such expert being bound to record his remarks either at the foot of the official report, or following the report." Article 51: "The examining magistrate decides, subject to appeal to the Council Chamber upon all the incidental matters arising in the course of the expert examination." And "the experts' reports must be held at the disposal of the parties for forty-eight hours after they are lodged."[2] That is not all: "If the expert examination has been finished before the 'mise en cause'[3] or the arrest of the accused, the latter has the right, after the communication of the report, to choose from the annual list an expert to examine the work of the appointed expert, and lodge his observations."

III. The examining magistrate retains, according to the bill, very large powers; if he could grant very much to the defense, he could also refuse it very much. It was essential to give no finality to his decisions or place above him a tribunal to which the accused could appeal. This the bill did, and for this purpose it revived the Council Chamber. Article 136: "The Council Chamber of examination is composed of three judges and the clerk of court. *The judge who has examined the case is never entitled to take part in their deliberation.*" Its function was not, as formerly, to decide upon the result of the examination, when that was concluded; the examining magistrate retained the right of issuing the order of closure. It was charged with passing upon the principal decisions come to by the judge in the course of the information, when they were contested by the parties. "From the time when there are contentious decisions to be taken, he cannot remain judge in

[1] Art. 54: "The Council Chamber can always," the article adds, "when the circumstances require it, authorize the appointment of experts whose names do not appear upon the annual list."

[2] Art. 52.

[3] The act of bringing a third party into the cause. [TRANS. note.]

the last resort of the questions raised before him; it is therefore necessary to place about him a superior jurisdiction charged with deciding finally the path to follow in all cases where disagreement arises, and to decide upon certain questions which would entail too heavy a responsibility upon the examining magistrate. It is for this purpose that the bill reëstablishes a Council Chamber, suppressed by the Law of 1856 as a useless part of the machinery, which will find in the existing organization a different and necessary rôle." [1] Article 137 pointed out by whom, and in what cases, the Council Chamber could be put in motion; [2] but what chiefly concerns us is the methods of recourse available to the accused. Article 37 opened the appeal to him to a very great extent, by allowing him to take the initiative. This article, as we have said, gave to the accused, as well as to the other parties in the cause, the right "to require the examining magistrate to take all steps which he should think necessary for the discovery of the truth"; and "upon his refusal he has the right to go to the Council Chamber in the case provided for by the law." Various Articles applied this principle: when the accused demanded to be confronted with witnesses, the order refusing the confrontation bore the reason assigned; it was susceptible of appeal before the Council Chamber.[3] "The examining magistrate decides, *subject to appeal to the Council Chamber,* upon all the incidental matters arising in the course of the expert examination." [4] It was, as we know, the Council Chamber which decided upon the prohibition of communication with the defending counsel, when that extended beyond ten days (Article 133); and the prohibition of communication with other persons, which the judge could only pronounce for ten days, could also be attacked before the Council Chamber (Article 104). Finally, "where the examining magistrate has not granted liberation on bail, it can be granted upon request addressed to the Council Chamber" (Article 107). As a rule, the orders of the Council Chamber could not be attacked. Article 142: "No judgment of the Council Chamber is appealable except as regards

[1] "Exposé des motifs." Journal officiel of 14th January, 1880, p. 303, col. 3.

[2] Art. 137: "The Council Chamber is invoked in the course of the information in those cases provided for by the law, either by the examining magistrate (Arts. 99, 104, 131), or by the public prosecutor (54, 107), or by the private prosecutor or the accused (104, 107, 124, 153). It may be vested in office by anybody in the case provided for by Article 44 (relating to claims lodged in case of its vesting in office by the persons who claim rights in the matter) and by witnesses sentenced to pay a fine in the case provided for by Article 56."

[3] Art. 124.

[4] Art. 51.

the request for provisional liberation; appeal to the Court of Cassation cannot be lodged against any of its judgments."

Concerning the orders by which the judge closed the instruction, however, appeal was open to the accused in a certain number of cases before the chamber of arraignments; Article 152. The accused could lodge an appeal from the orders specified in the old Article 539, and in the following cases: 1. For want of jurisdiction; 2. If the act was not provided for and punishable by the law; 3. If the "action publique"[1] was extinguished; 4. On account of a nullity in the examination.

The bill also contained important provisions as to detention pending trial. As to provisional liberation it, in general, retained the rules established in 1865;[2] but it materially altered the system of *warrants*. It replaced the warrant for appearance by a summons to appear (Articles 73 to 75); as to the three others which it retained, it provided them with a safeguard which up to that time only the writ of attachment presented: "Article 77. Every warrant contains the statement of the act and the reference to the Law declaring that act to be a crime or a misdemeanor." The warrant of commitment resumed its true character, and the features which distinguished it well justified the epithet of *provisional* given to it: "Article 93. The provisional warrant of commitment is the order by virtue of which the examining magistrate may, after his first appearance, have the accused detained in prison for five days." — "Article 94. The warrant of commitment cannot be renewed." — "Article 95. Twenty-four hours before the expiration of the warrant of commitment the chief warden is bound to advise the signing magistrate of the day when the prisoner must be set at liberty. The accused shall be set at liberty at the beginning of the sixth day."

The bill also took care to limit the duration of the writ of attachment which might succeed the warrant of commitment. It was here undoubtedly still possible, on the expiration of the five days, to prolong the detention pending trial; but for this a decision of the Council Chamber was necessary: "Article 96. The writ of attachment is the order by virtue of which the examining magistrate could have the accused detained in prison *for thirty days.*" — It could not be issued against the accused who was present

[1] "Action publique": a prosecution entered by the public prosecutor against a person who has committed a wrong giving rise to a civil action for damages ("action civile") in favor of the injured party. (TRANS.)

[2] Article 107 expressly permits the Court of Assizes to grant provisional liberty.

except on the expiration of the warrant of commitment. — The writ of attachment could also be ordered against an accused who had fled. — "Article 99. If the judge is of the opinion that the period of thirty days provided for by Article 96 should be prolonged, he invokes the Council Chamber, which may, upon his report, order the warrant to be kept in force for a new period of thirty days. — This decision is renewable in the same way."

The bill of 1880 did not come to anything, although it has been several times amended and discussed by the Senate. Even the partial revision of a Code is, indeed, an arduous work, and a good deal of time is required for its accomplishment. But it may be said that it has been the basis, or at least the point of departure, of a reform much less complete, but very important, which has been effected in our preliminary examination by the Law of 8th December, 1897, the object of which is to amend certain rules of the preliminary examination in cases of crimes and misdemeanors. It is due in great measure to Senator Constans, former Fellow of the Faculty of Law. The eminent Senator was inspired by a thoroughly practical idea. Seeing that it would be impossible for a long time to consummate the complete reform of Book I of the Code of Criminal Examination which was proposed in 1879, he desired at least, without changing the principles and general rules of the system, to introduce into it material safeguards for individual liberty, — the liberty of the defense as far as that can exist without complete publicity.

This Law first of all insures to everybody taken into provisional custody for a crime or misdemeanor an appearance within a period of twenty-four hours at most before the examining magistrate, and in case of disobedience the law inflicts punishment upon the head wardens of prisons and the officers of the public ministry. A counsel is assigned to the prisoner, with whom he can always freely communicate, and the interrogation bearing upon the merits of the case cannot begin until the counsel has been chosen or appointed. The day before each interrogation the papers in the case are communicated to the counsel and he is immediately made acquainted by the clerk of court with every order rendered by the judge. The interrogations and confrontations take place in the presence of the counsel; the latter, it is true (Article IX), "cannot address the court until he has been authorised by the magistrates to do so," but "in case of refusal the fact is mentioned in the minutes." Another Law has suppressed the summing up of the evidence made by the president of the assizes to the jury, which was often nothing but a new address by the prosecution.

But liberal legislation did not stop there. On the second of March, 1909, the Senate voted at the second reading a bill dealing with *the safeguards of individual liberty.*[1] This was the result of a number of proposals. One was made to the Senate by M. Monis, former Keeper of the Seals. M. Clémenceau had introduced another before entering the ministry, and after becoming Minister of the Interior he introduced a bill. The text passed by the Senate first of all repealed Article X of the Code of Criminal Examination, mentioned above, and relates, besides, to the following subjects: First, its object is, without disarming the court, to extend with us the application of the provisional liberation of prisoners, which has been, since the Revolution, acclimatized in France with difficulty.[2] At the same time, the purpose of one of its provisions is to insure the exact observance of the forms prescribed by the law for the warrants putting a person in provisional custody or detention pending trial: "The non-observance shall always be punished by a fine of fifty francs at least against the clerk of court, and, if need be, injunction against the examining magistrate and the state's attorney, and even an action for damages ('prise à partie') on his failure." Second, the personal searches and domiciliary searches, either at the residence of the prisoner or at the residences of third parties, are for the first time strictly regulated. "The principle," said chairman Monis, "is the absolute inviolability of the home; the search may be a judicial necessity, but it can only be justified after an examination has been already begun. The frequent abuses which have been made of the domiciliary search tend to cause this judicial ceremony to be practised upon mere suspicion; they present themselves at a residence, make a thorough search, and carry away all the papers which they can find there, because, perhaps, by this police ceremony some incrimination may be discovered."[3] The text voted consequently reads: "The domiciliary search and the personal search are acts of examination; recourse cannot be had thereto, unless, the

[1] Journal officiel of 3d March, Senate, p. 153 *et seq.*

[2] *M. Ribot*, at the time of the first reading in the sitting of 9th February, 1905 (Journal officiel of the 10th, Senate, p. 90): "The number of provisional liberations in proportion to the number of detentions pending trial is too small. In England it is 22 per cent. With us it is 3 per cent in the whole of the departments other than that of the Seine, and it is 18 per cent in Paris. . . . It ought to be compared with the number of arrests, which is much too large. Paris alone has 28,000 detentions pending trial compared with 88,000 for the whole of France."

[3] Journal officiel of 19th February, 1909, Senate, p. 89.

examination having been begun, the individual in the residence which it is wished to enter is thought to be the perpetrator of the incriminating act, or an accomplice or is at least presumed to have in his house objects relative to the offense. In the absence of these conditions the examining magistrate who makes a domiciliary search commits an arbitrary act entailing an action for damages." It is also said: "Except in the case of capture in the act, the examining magistrate himself makes the searches, except in regard to what is said relative to commissions of inquiry." — Finally, the "prise à partie," or action of damages against the magistrates for the abuse of their powers, in cases where the law allows it, is rendered more available to private parties: "No magistrate can be sued for damages for abuse of his powers without the prior authority of the first president (of the Court of Appeal), who shall decide, after having taken the opinion of the attorney-general. — In case of refusal, which shall be based on evidence, the party complainant shall be entitled to invoke the Chamber of Requests of the Court of Cassation. He will be allowed the aid of an advocate and exempted from the deposit of a fine. The Chamber of Requests shall decide in ordinary form and in open court, after having heard the statements of counsel for the party complainant and the motion of the public prosecutor."

But in the Chamber of Deputies the bill did not pass. In March, 1911, the Monis Cabinet inserted this item in its proposals: "We request the Chamber to enact the bill repealing Article X of the Code of Criminal Instruction and instituting safeguards of personal liberty." But the Chamber was too engrossed with other measures to take action on this. Article X remains in force yet. In 1906, however, a ministerial circular of August 4, addressed to all prefects, declares that Article X is "a dangerous anachronism," and enjoins upon them "to make use of it cautiously and exceptionally, and only after prior application to the ministry."

In the discussion at the first reading, there was a question of also introducing into the preliminary examination a safeguard which would be worth all the rest, namely, publicity, — public hearing. M. Ribot was the first to speak of it, recalling that to-day, with the work of newspaper reporters and the indiscretions of the press, the secrecy of the chambers of the examining magistrate would be open to everybody: "If we are at the point where, by confidences drawn from I know not whom, perhaps from witnesses, perhaps from advocates, through depositions, we have arrived at constructing, besides the truth which is built up in the judge's chamber, another truth for the use of the purchasers of newspapers, I ask if it will not be wiser, as well as more courageous, to examine the problem as it stands, if it will not be necessary to take a step farther than in 1897, and come to confrontation throughout the whole examination. If you accept the principle of confrontation, save for allowing the judge to hear a witness separately in certain cases, — which, moreover, will be exceptional, — and if at the same time you accept publicity, which is the truest safeguard of all. . . ." — the chairman: "That is the solution." — M. Ribot: "Yes, that will be the solution; it is, I am convinced, the solution of the immediate future. It is not in the bill, but I have been of that opinion for a long time." [1]

This is, in effect, the English system, which is characterized by two salient features. On one side, all the preliminary researches, those which put us upon the track and most frequently lead to the arrest of the presumed perpetrator of the crime, are made, not by a magistrate, but by the police, and the ability of the English detectives is well known. The policeman, — the constable, — to-day possesses very extensive powers to effect arrest. But that accomplished, the prisoner is brought before the judge with the least possible delay; the judge in open court hears the policeman and the witnesses he produces, and so proceeds publicly with the examination, deciding at each appearance if the prisoner shall be set at liberty or remanded. We may see in the London police courts with what sureness and what safeguards this examination is made.[2]

In this debate of 9th February, 1909, Keeper of the Seals Briand showed himself favorable to the English system; but he added with the prudence imposed upon him by his office: "I ought to say that the application of this system in France will, because of the general conditions of our judicial organization, inevitably present certain difficulties in its execution, and it is because I have not found the means of solving these difficulties that I dare not, so far, make a solemn promise to the Senate; but the question, I repeat, is one to be studied." It is not merely our judicial organization which causes difficulty, but also the temperament, the manners, the habits of the French people; it was on that account that the bill of 1879 rejected publicity. I am, however,

[1] Journal officiel of 10th February, 1909, Senate, p. 91.
[2] See an excellent résumé of this system in *Maitland*, "Justice and Police."

of M. Ribot's opinion, that publicity is the solution of the future.

The Law of 8th December, 1897, remedied a very palpable defect in the organization of the correctional tribunals. Article 257 of the Code of Criminal Examination is to the following effect: "The members of the Imperial Court who have voted upon the arraignment cannot take part in the same case, nor preside at the assizes, nor assist the president upon pain of nullity. This also applies to the examining magistrate." This was just, for these magistrates, having already known of the matter, as far as the examination was concerned, necessarily have formed an opinion upon it, and it is reasonable to suppose that the public proceedings will not alter it. But, on the contrary, no text forbids the examining magistrate from sitting as a judge of the correctional tribunal in the trial of cases which he has examined, and in which he has ordered the transfer of the prisoner to the tribunal of correctional police. In fact, the examining magistrate almost always sits there, owing to the organization of our courts of the first instance and the small number of members composing them. And not only has he his opinion formed, but, knowing the case thoroughly, he almost always exercises a decisive influence upon the other members of the court. Article 1 of the Law of 8th December, 1897, renders this practice illegal: "The examining magistrate cannot take part in the judgment of the actions which he has examined."

The operation of the criminal jury and the procedure followed before it have, as a rule, remained the same. Certain characteristic modifications, however, have been made upon this procedure. The constitution of the jury is regulated by the Law of 21 to 24 December, 1872, still in force, — one of those excellent laws which we owe to the National Assembly (1871 to 1876). Generally speaking, all electors are qualified to be jurors, which gives a considerable range in a country of universal suffrage. Certain exclusions, however, there are, and these are amply justified. "No one," says Article I, "can fill the office of juryman on pain of nullity of the verdicts of guilty in which he shall concur, if he is not thirty years old, if he does not enjoy civic, civil, and family rights, or if he is in a state of incapacity or incompatibility established by the two following articles." Article IV adds "Domestic servants or hired servants (and) those who cannot read and write in French." The first of these rules comes from the Revolution; it was a traditional electoral incapacity in the laws of that period;

our modern law does not retain it in electoral matters, but it makes use of it in the selection of jurors; the second rule fixes the minimum qualification which can be required of them from an educational point of view.

The Law of 1872 has not established in each department a general and permanent jury list; it establishes an annual list of which it fixes the *maximum* and the *minimum*, and which is formed by a double operation. In each canton a list, containing twice the quota of jurors which each canton is required to furnish, is drawn up by a commission composed of the justice of the peace and his deputies and of the mayors of all the communes of the canton. The list of each district is then made up by a commission presided over by the president of the court of first instance, and composed of all the justices of the peace and general judges of the district; it reduces the number of jurors appearing upon the lists of the various cantons to the figure fixed for the district. It could also formerly add to it new names in a proportion of one-third. It also draws up a list of substitute jurors resident in the place where the court of assizes sits. The lists of each district so drawn up are final, and the annual list is obtained simply by the addition of all the lists of the district. From this district panel the panel of each session is obtained by means of a drawing by lot, at which the president of the civil court of the chief seat of the department presides in open court. From that session list, the drawing by lot, combined with the challenges, furnishes the petty jury.

The Code of Criminal Examination ordains that the president shall, on the termination of the trial, sum up the case to the jury. Article 336: "The president shall sum up the case. He will draw the jurors' attention to the principal proofs for or against the accused." This was, as we know, an adoption of the English practice, where the summing up of the magistrate is of such great importance. We also know that the English law has means of correcting the errors which the judge may commit in this matter: it grants a new trial on account of a misdirection of the jury by the judge. But with us, as an effect of inquisitorial procedure, which makes itself felt even in the trials of the court of assizes, the summing up of the president was looked upon as a final address for the prosecution pronounced by the magistrate who had the highest authority in the court, and to whom nobody could reply. It must be added that too often the summing up of the president justified these accusations. A Law of 19th June, 1881, has therefore abolished the president's summing up. The new article, 336, now reads: "The president after the close of the trial cannot, on pain of nullity, sum up the pleas of the prosecution and the defense." That is a measure calculated to surprise Anglo-Saxons. They could not understand a jury without a magistrate to direct them as to the rules according to which their verdict must be rendered. It is true that their theory of proofs (evidence law) renders this impossible. But their most enlightened and liberal minds admit that the judge may use his authority to make the jury feel the weight and the import of the evidence produced against the accused.[1]

A more recent law ranks in the same order of ideas. The jurors, in general, once they go into their chamber of deliberation, cannot leave it without having settled upon their verdict, nor communicate with any one. Article 343 reads: "Entry cannot be permitted during their deliberation for any cause whatever, except by the president and in writing." But judicial practice has come to the conclusion from these last words that the president himself can go into the jury room when he is sent for by the jury. They may wish to have explanations upon some point, or, as the French doctrine and practice admit that the jury may consider the effect of their verdict as regards the punishment and that the counsel for the defense can even point out to them the possible consequences of their verdict in that respect, probably they may desire to question the president on that point, and even obtain from him certain assurances. There were certain dangers in this secret conventicle in this respect. The Law of 10th December, 1908, has amended Article 343 as follows: "He (the president) shall not enter unless he is summoned by the foreman of the jury and accompanied by the counsel for the accused, the public prosecutor, and the clerk of court." This is still an interview outside of the court-room; but both adverse parties, the defense and the prosecution, are represented in it and there remains an official report of what has been said.

One of the features of our procedure before the court of assizes still frequently criticised is the interrogation of the accused by the

[1] "The letters of Charles Dickens," *Tauchnitz* edition, vol. III, p. 51 (to the Chief-Baron): "I really have not been able to repress my admiration of the vigorous dignity and sense and spirit with which one of the best of judges set right one of the dullest of juries in a recent case." — p. 57 (to M. de Cergat): "It is difficult to conceive any other line of defense than that the circumstances proved, taken separately, are slight. But a sound judge will immediately charge the jury that the strength of the circumstances is in their being put together and will thread them together in a fatal rope."

president. This is not a matter, it must be understood, of a summary interrogation for the purpose of establishing his identity, which is inevitable and harmless. I refer to the prolonged interrogation contrived to extort confessions or produce contradictions in the statements of the accused. It is with us a matter of invariable tradition. It is not prescribed by the Code of Criminal Examination; but the persistent influence of the inquisitorial procedure has kept up these learned interrogations of the judges in the same way as the spirit of the accusatory procedure has developed in the English courts the dexterity of English counsel in the art of examination and cross-examination. Several authors have wished to argue from this that Article 310 and the following Articles of the Code of Criminal Examination form a Chapter IV, bearing the heading: "De *l'examen* du jugement et de l'exécution," but, "examen" and "*interrogatoire de l'accusé*" are by no means synonymous.

Sometimes it is a regular duel between the president and the accused, which lasts during several sessions, and the conditions of which are certainly not equal. The Steinheil affair, which has interested the whole world, has sharply drawn attention to this point. Ministerial circulars have recommended to the presidents of the assizes moderation and prudence. An amendatory law has been prepared and should not fail to bear results.

In France, as in other countries, the oath of the jurors has raised difficulties; but that is somewhat outside the domain of criminal procedure.[1]

The jury seems thus to possess the favor and the full confidence of the legislators. There is being formed against it, chiefly in the press, a movement of public opinion, which I believe to be superficial, but which none the less exists.[2] It is provoked above all by numerous acquittals, manifestly contrary to the law and to legal truth. These take place, not merely in press prosecutions, those for political offenses and those which, although common law offenses, relate to strikes; there are also acquittals, legally unjustified, of crimes called crimes of the passions, and even crimes which do not present any particular or extraordinary feature. The French jury, very unlike the English jury in this respect, is particularly independent, impressionable, and jealous of its absolute authority. This results from several causes which have

[1] *Esmein*, "Éléments du droit constitutionel," 5th edition, pp. 1075, 1076.

[2] See the literature upon this point in *Garraud*, "Précis de droit criminel," 10th edition, 1909, p. 789, note 2.

already been, for the most part, pointed out. First of all, the high magistrates who preside over it have never been able, owing to the persistent memory of the inquisitorial procedure, to acquire a real authority over the jury and to assume direction of it efficaciously. On the other hand, and above all, there is the system of moral proofs, which rules the jury in the most complete fashion, and the jurors, with the naïve logic of the French mind, have a growing conviction that not only is the fact of their being convinced their only rule in deciding upon the guilt, but even that they have but to follow their personal sentiments, their own impressions as to the general questions of guilt and criminality in each particular case. This is especially true as to the consequences of the verdict upon the application of the punishment. We have seen above the topical facts in this respect and the phenomenon is so plainly evident that M. Briand, Keeper of the Seals, prepared a bill legalizing this irresistible tendency: he allowed the jury, under certain conditions, to deliberate and vote with the judges composing the court of assizes, upon the application of the punishment. Another consideration is that scientific and literary men, unfamiliar with political science, find unreasonable and unscientific this system where men without special or even general education or professional knowledge decide upon the guilt of citizens.

I believe, however, in the value of the jury in criminal matters. I believe in its persistence and in its beneficial future, in spite of defects, several of which, at least, can be remedied. The jury, in effect, is one of these institutions, the happy product of history in a particularly favorable environment, which is found to answer the crying needs of civilized humanity. Born among the English, adopted by the French Revolution, it is being propagated gradually along with modern civilization, like the constitutional government and the civil State. A great civilized nation cannot renounce it without losing its rank. It is, it may be said, one of those conquests which, once achieved, are final; the jury can no more be abolished than universal suffrage, whatever opinion may be held elsewhere about both these institutions. We have seen how the jury, before it had been twenty years in existence, victoriously resisted the opposition of Napoleon's terrible will; it has now existed among us for one hundred and twenty years; it is indestructible. The jury in criminal matters, in fact, satisfies two deep-seated needs and acts as a corrective of "that right to punish, so terrible among men," as Montesquieu said. It insures to the accused, upon the question of guilt, judges absolutely independent of political power. These twelve citizens, stepping for the moment from the ranks of the nation, and charged with this onerous duty, may be ignorant, undisciplined, full of prejudices; but they are not dependent upon any authority, and the citizen does not feel really safeguarded unless he has perfectly independent judges when his liberty or his life is in the balance.

In the second place, the necessary intervention of the jury in criminal proceedings has by its very defects been the means of rendering these proceedings *humane*. I mean by that that it renders the application of the criminal law, of the *right to punish*, conformable to the average conscience of society, to the popular conscience, in the broad sense of the word. When a jury refuses to recognize the guilt of an individual who is legally guilty, or when it grants extenuating circumstances to an accused who does not deserve it, considering too severe the punishment which a merely affirmative verdict would entail, it puts penal justice in agreement with impartial social feeling, and renders it comprehensible and acceptable to other citizens of the same mental caliber as itself. This is the necessary condition of the acceptance of repression without resistance by our modern society. Chance no doubt also takes part in this popular administration of justice; that is unfortunate, but inevitable. And such a system certainly also risks the weakening of repression: but before the danger can be really great the twelve citizens who judge must have a very strong feeling of it and they will conform their decision thereto. It is above all necessary that the public prosecutor, charged with the pursuit of crime, should act energetically and speak clearly; that he should not hesitate to bring a necessary and exemplary prosecution from fear of a possible acquittal, and that he explain to the jury firmly and dispassionately the necessity for repression: the chances are then all in favor of the twelve jurymen understanding and following him.

I have said that the English jury is very different from ours. It also has its detractors, however, especially in regard to the great part it plays in civil cases, but the English do not think of renouncing it: "The defects of the jury system are obvious. They are twelve ordinary men — a group just large enough to destroy even the appearance of individual responsibility. They give no reasons for their verdict. The verdict itself is not subject to any appeal,[1]

[1] This was written in 1903. Since that time the appeal in criminal cases has been made available against the verdicts and the sentences;

and it is apt, in times of political excitement, to reflect the popular prejudice of the day. Experience shows that they are capable of being intimidated. It is said that they are always biassed when a pretty woman or a railway company happen to be litigants. Though a good special jury is admitted to be a very competent tribunal, the common jury may be composed of persons who have neither the desire nor the capacity to weigh the evidence, or to arrive at a conclusion upon the facts in issue. In spite of these obvious defects, distinguished judges who have spent many years working with juries, have combined to praise the jury system. Fortescue, Coke, Hale, Blackstone, and Stephen are witnesses whose evidence should be conclusive. We may add to these names that of Judge Chalmers, whose experience in the new county courts leads him to the same conclusion."[1] The author of this passage brings to the aid of his opinion simple and convincing reasons. "The litigant gets a body of persons who bring to bear upon the facts of his case *average common sense*."[2] And he recalls the following profound remark of Hale in regard to the jury in criminal cases: "It were the most unhappy case," says Hale, "that could be to the judge, if he at his peril must take upon him the guilt or innocence of the prisoner."[3]

Different methods have been proposed to introduce, with us, the jury in correctional matters also. Logically that would appear to be only just; the reasons for it are the same as in criminal cases. But this appears to be impossible. Jury duty, already very heavy, would become intolerable for the citizen.

The Code of Criminal Examination made available the review of convictions for errors in law, but only to a very limited extent. It admitted it only for crimes, and only in cases specified and strictly resolved upon by Article 443: "(1) When, after a conviction for homicide, documents shall be lodged, calculated to exhibit sufficient presumptions of the existence of the claimed victim of the homicide; (2) when, after a conviction for a crime or misdemeanor, a new decree or judgment shall have convicted, for the same deed, another accused, and the two convictions cannot be reconciled, their contradiction shall be the proof of the innocence of one or the other of the persons convicted; (3) when one of the witnesses heard shall have been, subsequently

Act of 28th August, 1907, instituting a Code of Criminal Appeal and amending the law relative to appeals in criminal matters, "Annuaire de la Société de législation comparée," 1908, p. 14 *et seq.*

[1] *Holdsworth*, "A History of English Law," vol. I, pp. 166, 167.

[2] *Ibid.*, vol. I, p. 167.

[3] *Ibid.*, vol. I, p. 169.

to the conviction, prosecuted and convicted of false testimony against the accused."

But this power of revision has been successively and considerably enlarged. That has been done chiefly under the pressure of public opinion. It is a natural tendency of the French heart to be tender toward the innocent condemned. We have seen the first manifestations of this in the reign of Louis XVI, and the same phenomenon is repeated in our time with an added force. The first increase of the power of review was introduced in the last years of the Second Empire, in 1867. It was not at that time a matter of introducing the revision anew, but of allowing it after the death of the condemned. The case struck at was that of Lesurques, convicted and executed under the Directory for having attacked and murdered the Courier of Lyons; for the same offense a later conviction of another person appeared to be irreconcilable with the first. The family of Lesurques, a very respectable one, presented ceaseless petitions to the government and the houses of parliament. Public opinion became more and more interested in this question; the conviction of Lesurques was commonly considered as an undoubted example of judicial error, and a popular drama, "The Courier of Lyons," where the facts were presented, has attracted several generations of spectators. The Law of 29th June, 1868, promulgated 9th July, amending Article 443 *et seq.* of the Code of Criminal Examination, allows of review after the death of the condemned. It has also enlarged the law from another point of view. Without creating new cases for review, it has allowed it to be invoked by those convicted in cases of simple *misdemeanor*, as well as in cases of *crime;* it also makes the procedure more precise and improves the draft of the Article. The private interests, however, in view of which the amendment was effected, derived no satisfaction therefrom. The Lesurques case was appealed in 1868, but the result was the dismissal of the appeal by the Court of Cassation on 17th December, 1868 (Dalloz, 1869 s, 41). The Supreme Court ruled that the two convictions of separate persons for this crime were not irreconcilable.[1] The decisive step was taken in 1895. There were still almost certain judicial errors, which did not, however, come within the scope of the review, as it was then settled. The Bourras and Vaux cases gave a new impetus to public opinion. Numerous proposals, emanating from parliamentary initiative, were introduced in the houses of parliament, and the movement

[1] *Garraud,* "Précis de droit criminel," 10th edition, p. 947, note 2.

resulted in the Law of 8th June, 1895.[1] This time, among the numerous reforms which it introduced, the Law contained one provision of prime importance: it introduced a new cause for appeal, very liberally conceived. The new Article 443 allows a fourth cause for appeal: "(4) When, after a conviction, a new fact has happened or has come to light, or when documents unknown at the time of the trial are filed, tending to establish the innocence of the person convicted."[2] In this new case, moreover, there is a safeguard against too great a facility for review. While, under the other hypotheses, the right of filing the claim belongs not only to the Minister of Justice, but also to the person convicted and, after his death, to those of his successors designated by the law, in the fourth case it belongs only to the Minister of Justice, who does or does not file the appeal, after the opinions and deliberations prescribed by the new Article 444. The Law of 1895 (New Article 445) also authorizes the Court of Cassation, "in case of admissibility, if the case is not in shape, to proceed directly or by commission of inquiry, with all inquiries upon the merits, confrontation, examination as to identity, interrogations, and means proper to put the truth in evidence."

The Law of 1895 has increased the number of cases where the Court of Cassation itself decides upon the merits of the case and directly reviews it. The aim of the legislature at the outset was certainly that, the claim for review being declared admissible by the Court of Cassation, the latter should simply annul the judgment of conviction and should transfer the case to a court of the same grade as that which had pronounced the sentence, there to be proceeded with by a new trial. Only on the hypothesis where, after a conviction for homicide, the continued existence of the person believed to have been killed was established, did the law consider these new trials to be unnecessary, and did not prescribe a new trial. The impossibility of a new trial sometimes even rendered review inadmissible, as in the case of the death of the convicted person. The Law of 1895, while preserving the principle of a new trial, allows the Court of Cassation, in the fourth case, when only a single condemned person is concerned, to retain the case and decide upon the merits, if no punishable crime or offense exists after its judgment.

The Dreyfus case, which stirred France so grievously and so

[1] "Annuaire de législation française," published by the Society of Comparative Law, 19th year, 1896, p. 105 *et seq.*
[2] "Annuaire de législation française," above cited, p. 112.

long, twice brought the procedure of review under criticism. It did not, however, definitely result in any new legislative reform in this matter. It was really the means of having one imposed, however. The Code of Criminal Examination and the subsequent Laws of 1868 and 1895 gave the criminal branch of the Court of Cassation jurisdiction of claims for review. When that branch was vested with the first review in the Dreyfus case, the Law of 1st March, 1899, called the Law of Divestiture ("dessaisissement") intervened, which transferred the jurisdiction to the Court of Cassation (all branches together). Though this law was framed in general terms and applied to the future, it also applied to the case in hand, and it was for that that it had been passed. It was truly a law that fitted circumstances. For, although in the Dreyfus case, that passion in favor of innocent condemned persons, of which we have spoken above, had a powerful influence, political interests and passions operated in a contrary direction. Since that time, moreover, the Law of 5th March, 1909, has repealed that of 1st March, 1899, and given back to the criminal branch its natural jurisdiction. The second review of the Dreyfus case simply led the Court of Cassation, conformably to the motion of Attorney-General Baudouin, to construe the Law of 8th June, 1895, in the most liberal and widest sense.[1]

The Law of June, 1895, also effected another liberal and important reform. This was the reparation granted by it to the victim of judicial errors. This is of two kinds. The first consists of a kind of honorable reparation, consisting of a wide publicity given to the review obtained (New Article 446, end): "The decree or judgment of review, resulting in the innocence of the condemned person, shall be advertised in the town where the conviction was pronounced, in that of the seat of the jurisdiction of review, in the commune of the place where the crime or misdemeanor was committed, in that of the residence of the person claiming review, and of the last residence of the victim of the judicial error, if he is dead. It shall be officially inserted in the Journal Officiel, and its publication shall, besides, be ordered in five newspapers chosen by the claimant, if he shall request it. The expense of the above provided publication shall be borne by the Treasury." The other satisfaction is of a pecuniary nature; it consists of damages granted to the victim of the judicial error, or to his representatives. The principle of such a reparation in the case of an improvident and

[1] "Cassation, chambres réunies," 1st June, 1906. *Sirey*, 1907, I, 49; Journal des Parquets, 1906.

unfounded prosecution, resulting in an acquittal, existed in the ancient French law, but at the expense of the judge or of the procurator fiscal, or king's attorney, according to the cases. It was introduced along with the official prosecution, and the "Très ancien Coutume de Bretagne" makes precise and rigorous applications of it.[1] Where the prosecution was brought upon a denunciation, the responsibility fell upon the informer, even when he was not made a civil party:[2] the judge was not released by revealing the informer. These principles were retained in our ancient law with respect to the public prosecutor. The Constituent Assembly retained the rule in regard to the justice of the peace when he prosecuted officially without complaint or civic denunciation.[3]

Our law has not retained these principles, however, and, with the exception of the "prise à partie," the magistrate is not liable. The damages granted by the Law of 1895 to the victim of a judicial error are due to him, not from the public prosecutor, but from the State. It is the resumption of the principle contained in the Declaration of 1787. The Law of 1895 provides (New Article 446): "The decree or judgment of review, resulting in the innocence of a condemned person, may, upon his demand, allow him damages, because of the injury occasioned him by the conviction.—If the victim of the judicial error is dead, the right of claiming damages shall belong, under the same conditions, to his wife and his ascendants and descendants. It shall not belong to relatives further removed than such as can prove a material injury resulting to them from the conviction. — The claim shall be admissible at every stage of the proceedings for review. — The damages allowed shall be borne by the State, subject to its recourse against the civil party, the informer, or the false witness by whose fault the conviction has been pronounced. They shall be paid as expenses of criminal justice." This was a check, and a thoroughly justified one, on the general principle of the non-liability of the State by reason of acts of public authorities done in its name.

[1] When there is torture or "joux" (*Planiol* edition, c. 101, p. 145 *et seq*).

[2] "Très ancien Coutume de Bretagne" (*Planiol* edition, c. 103, p. 146).

[3] Decree of 6–29 September, 1791, upon the criminal police and police of safety. Title VI, Art. 8: "If the informer refuses to sign and affirm his information, the police officer shall not be bound to consider it; he can, nevertheless, take cognizance of the facts of his own accord, hear witnesses, issue a warrant to bring the accused before the court, and, in a proper case, a writ of attachment, provided that he will be personally liable if it is proved that he acted maliciously and from desire to injure."

TITLE III[1]

CRIMINAL PROCEDURE SINCE 1800 IN OTHER COUNTRIES

§ 1. **Importance of Comparative Law. Two Principal Groups of Laws: (1) Combination of the Inquisitorial and Accusatory Systems. (2) The Accusatory System as derived from English Law.** — It is no longer possible to conceive of the isolated study of any system of laws, without connecting it with its sources, following its evolution, and comparing it with the systems of other nations. Each of those European nations styled by the Romans barbarians had, about the beginning of the Middle Ages, its own particular customs in matters of criminal law, but the procedures of all of them possessed many features in common. The accusatory system, everywhere in force, itself tended to uniformity. Repressive laws are, we know, inevitably dependent upon political organization. It follows that the prevalence of the feudal system throughout Europe resulted in the judicial systems assuming a similar aspect almost everywhere. Then, when absolute monarchy began to take the place of feudality, it relied, for the impairment of the latter, upon the laws of the Roman Emperors; and the influence of Roman law, which had never altogether died out in certain European countries, even at the height of the reign of the barbarian laws, helped materially in the reconciliation of the various systems of law. But the dif-

[1] [Title III = Sec. IX of Professor Garraud's "French Criminal Procedure." For this author and work, see the Editorial Preface. — ED.]

ferent countries did not advance at the same pace along the path of the transformations which their procedures were destined to undergo. All, however, with the exception of England, had discarded the accusatory system and had substituted for it the inquisitorial system. The French Revolution, by its system of laws, exercised an influence in regard to the repressive organization and procedure which marks an era in the legislative history of European nations. The French Code of Criminal Examination of 1808, which constituted a kind of compromise between the two systems of procedure, served as a type and a model for a great number of nations. Its influence, more lasting than the conquest, still remains.

In considering the differences of detail which we shall set out in their proper places, he who seeks to segregate the principles governing the laws of procedure of the nations of Continental Europe discovers the fundamental unity which characterizes them. Everywhere there is the institution of the public prosecutor, the division of the procedure into two stages, that of the preliminary examination which borrows its rules from the inquisitorial system, and that of the trial ("jugement"), which takes up all the safeguards of the accusatory system. The jury has gradually conquered the systems of law of foreign nations, and countries like Spain and Austria, which have tried to suppress it, are forced to reëstablish it, owing to the imperious demands of the popular conscience, which sees in the jury the true safeguard of liberty. In contrast with this imposing group, which has found, in the French Code of 1808, the model and framework of its institutions, are ranked the Anglo-Saxon systems, which form an autonomous group, obeying proportionately the same inspiration and animated by the same spirit. They have been and still are the preservers of the accusatory system in Europe and America. In England there is no public prosecutor. The prosecution is left to private initiative. The equality of the struggle between the prosecution and the defense is safeguarded by a series of institutions which, thanks to the intelligence of the race, act without endangering too much the social welfare. In the Anglo-Saxon system the jury is the guarantee of the trial as well as of the accusation.

We shall point out briefly, on one hand, the legislative sources of criminal procedure in the most important countries, and on the other, the rules of that procedure, and attempt to distinguish their general and typical features, — what may be called the "dominants."

§ 2. **Legislation in Various Foreign Countries: Germany, Austria, Belgium, Principality of Monaco, Grand Duchy of Luxemburg, Spain, Italy, Switzerland, the Netherlands, Great Britain, Russia, Grand Duchy of Finland, the Balkans, Scandinavia, Turkey, Egypt, North America, South America.** — With the exception of England, where ideas of codification have, nevertheless, made some progress, all the European countries have now codified their criminal law.[1]

I. *Germany.*[2]

(*a*) *Demands for reform.* — Through the application of scientific investigation to criminal procedure,[3] and because of the gradually growing conviction of the injustice of torture,[4] the shortcomings of the German criminal procedure, inherent in the law itself, and rendered the worse by the practice, gradually became more apparent. Through the statutory prohibition of torture in many countries,[5] criminal procedure lost one of its chief fundamental elements. It became evident that many of the provisions of judicial inquiry depended for their force upon torture, and that many of the views of the German theory of proof could no longer exist. The legislation of the German States could no longer remain indifferent to the constantly increasing demands for reform.[6]

It was, however, insisted that the foundation of the secret

[1] We shall not arrange the countries in groups, for example, 1st, Anglo-American group; 2d, Romance group, north and south; 3d, German group; 4th, group of other countries. That would be to acknowledge that there is an ethnical relationship between systems of law, which is not the case. We are therefore compelled to proceed by numeration. Upon this point see *Franz von Liszt*, "Le droit criminel des peuples européens" (Berlin and Paris 1894), Introduction, pp. xv and xvi.

[2] [Paragraphs *a*, *b*, *c*, and *d*, of this account of German legislation are interpolated from Chapters XVIII and XIX of Professor *Mittermaier's* "Progress of German Criminal Procedure." For this author and work, see the Editorial Preface. — ED.]

[3] In all the French and Italian works in regard to the scientific treatment of criminal law, one of the chief subjects of discussion is the necessity of the revision of criminal law because of the abolition of torture, of publicity, and of the accusatorial procedure. As to the direction in which one must regard criminal law as having been improved since the middle of the 1700 s, see the interesting treatment by *Brabant* and the exchange of letters of the Austrian cabinet, as to the plans of Emperor Joseph for improvement. *Cf. Vischers*, in the "Revue belge" (Liège 1834), Heft 11, p. 297, and Heft 12, p. 379.

[4] *Gockinga*, "De doctrinæ juris. crim. incrementis inde a seculo duodevigesimo media jam parte elapso" (Groningen 1826).

[5] *Feuerbach*, "Themis oder Beiträge zur Gesetzgebung," No. V.

[6] The legislation of Tuscany of the 30th of November, 1786, relative to criminal law, is important as an expression of the views at that time obtaining for the improvement of criminal law. See *Carmignani*, in the "Zeitschrift für ausl. Gesetzgebung und Rechtswissenschaft," II Thl., No. 20.

inquisitorial procedure be retained, also the effort to procure a confession, and the German criminal procedure founded upon a statutory theory of proof. Torture was to be abolished, and the institutions therewith connected. The principles of evidence of the "Carolina" were to be extended and the abuses that had crept in were to be rectified.

(*b*) *Earlier legislation.* — These demands led to the Austrian code of 1803 [1] relative to crimes and punishments,[2] and the Prussian criminal rules [3] of 1805 [4] prepared through the introduction of

[1] In regard to the history of the Austrian law, see *Mittermaier*, "Handbuch," I, p. 116. *Graff*, "Vers. einer Gesch. der Criminalgesetzgebung in Steyermark." (Gratz 1817). *Jenull*, "Das österreich. Criminalrecht nach seinen Grunden und Geist." (Gratz 1803–1813), I Bnd., p. 74. *Maucher*, "Syst. Handbuch des oesterr. Strafgesetzes." (Wien 1844), I, p. 12.

[2] Under the title, — "Gesetzbuch über Verbrechen," published on September 3d, 1803. Here belong the commentaries of *Jenull*, "das oesterreich. Criminalrechts" (see *ante*), IV vol. (vol. I in new edition, 1820). *Hannamann*, "Das rechtl. Verfahren der Criminalgerichte über Verbrechen, nach dem Gesetzbuche in Beispielen dargestellt," 3d Thle. (Vienna 1806). *Luzac*, "Versuch einer Anwendung der Gesetze über Verbrechen." (Vienna 1806). *v. Wagersbach*, "Handbuch für Criminalrichter und Bezirksobrigkeiten" (Gratz 1812), 3 vols. Examples of statutes and discussion in *Zeillers*, "Jahrlichen Beiträge zur Gesetzkunde und Rechtspflege," 1800–1811, IV vol. *Pratobevera*, "Materialien für Gesetzkunde und Rechtspflege in Oesterreich." VIII vol. (Vienna 1816–1824). *Wagner*, "Zeitschrift für österr. Rechtsgelehr. und Gesetzkunde" (Vienna 1825–1831, and since 1833, continued by *Dollinger* and *Kudler*, yearly, 12 vols., later continued by *Stubenrauch*). *v. Wildner*, Zeitschrift, "Der Jurist." (Vienna, since 1839, yearly, 4 vols.). A collection of all the laws enacted for the Austrian Code, and instructions, in *Waser*, "Das Strafgesetz über Verbrechen sammt den dazu gehörigen Verordnungen" (Vienna 1839), and in fuller detail in *Mauscher*, "Syst. Handbuch" (Vienna 1844).

[3] "Criminalordnung," published on December 11th, 1805. Supplements thereto in *Hofmann*, "Repertor. der in Crim. Untersuchungssachen nähern Bestimmungen" (Zulichau 1817). *Berger*, "Rep. des preuss. Criminalrechts." (Zeiz 1819). *v. Strombeck*, in *v. Kamptz*, "Jahrbuch," XIII Hft., p. 35. *Paalzow*, "Comment. über die Criminalordnung" (Berlin 1817), 2 vols. Comments and illustrations in *Kleins*, "Annalen der Gesetzkunde und Rechtsgelehrsamheit" (Berlin since 1788), 26 vols. *v. Kamptz*, "Jahrbücher für die preuss. Gesetzgebung und Rechtswissenschaft" (since 1813), 127 vols to date. *Hitzig*, "Zeitschrift für die Criminalrechtspflege in den preuss. Staaten" (Berlin 1825), to date 48 vols. with supplements. See also *Abegg*, "Grundriss zu Vorlesungen über den gemeinen und preuss. Strafprocess." (Königsberg 1825). *Abegg*, "Lehrbuch des gemeinen deutschen Criminalproc." (1833), p. 36. *Richter*, "Handbuch des Strafverfahrens in den preuss. Staaten" (Königsberg 1830), 4 vols. *Temme*, "Comment. über Paragraphen der preuss. Criminalordnung" (Berlin 1838). *Alker*, "Handbuch des preuss. Criminalprocessverfahren" (Berlin 1842). For the later ordinances passed relative to the "Criminalordnung," see, preferably, *Mannkopf*, "Preuss. Criminalordnung in einer zusammenstellung mit der ergänzenden Verordnungen" (Berlin 1839). A later Prussian statute which is important is the one of August 5th, 1844, relative to the brief examination in court of summary jurisdiction. In regard to the progress of the Prussian legislation, see also *Temme*, in *v. Jagemanns*, "Zeitschrift," new edition, p. 307.

[4] As to its composition, see *Mathis*, "Jurist. Monatsschrift," IV, p. 232.

systematic court rules.[1] This latter, because of its failure to make a distinction between preliminary investigations and investigations in chief, because of its admission of extraordinary punishments and punishments for contempt, and also because of its numerous restrictions upon acquittal, could not satisfy the legitimate requirements.[2] The Bavarian Criminal Regulations,[3] because of the completeness of their provisions, because of the favoring of acquittal and means of defense, and especially because of the promotion of that which, for the improvement of the German inquisitorial procedure and for the correction of abuses, was proposed for legislation by scientific knowledge, seemed best to correspond to the demands of the time.

(*c*) *Defects of the earlier legislation.* — But while all these codes were so serviceable for their time, they contained only half measures.[4] They lacked a proper foundation, and since they contained the old court system with its inherent defects, they could not render the accused secure against arbitrary action. They retained the disadvantages of the inquisitorial procedure; they placed undue restriction upon acquittal; and through the admission of punishments for contempt they contained dangerous elements. Moreover, they did not assure to the judges the means of procuring the complete material requisite for a just verdict,[5] and because of the attempt at a theory of legal proof, they often

[1] As to the earlier history of Prussian law, see *Mittermaier*, "Handbuch," I, p. 120. The general outline of September 16th, 1804, in *Kleins*, "Annalen der Gesetzkunde," XXIII, p. 213. As to the influence of certain commentators on the Prussian procedure, see *Biener*, "Beiträge zur Geschichte des Inquisitionsprocesses," pp. 164, 182. See especially, *Abegg*, "Geschichte des preuss. Strafrechts," in *Hitzig's* "Zeitschrift," 1st Supplementband (1835).

[2] See criticisms in *Kleins*, "Annalen," Bd. 24, No. 2; and "Glossen zum preuss. Criminalrechts" (Breslau 1818). *Temme*, "Commentar über die wichtigeren Paragraphen des preuss. Criminalordnung" (Berlin 1838).

[3] Earlier history, see *Mittermaier*, "Handbuch," I, p. 109. The "Criminalordnung" formed the 2d part of the Criminal Code of 1813. The supplements ("Novellen") were collected in the "Sammlung der wichtigsten k. Rescripte in Beziehung auf das Strafgesetzbuch von 1813"; and *Doppelmair*, "Sammlung der Erläuterungen und Rescripte" (1824), and also the single supplements ("Novellen"), given by *v. Wendt*, "Grundzüge des deutschen und besonders baier. Criminalprocesses" (Erlangen 1826). See also *v. Gonner* and *Schmidtlein*, "Jahrbücher der Gesetzgebung und Rechtsk. in Baiern." (Erlangen 1818–1820), 3 vols. *Zurhein*, "Zeitschrift für Theorie und Praxis des baier. Rechts" (München 1835), 2 vols. *Seuffert*, "Blätter für Rechtsanwend. in Baiern." (Auspach, from 1836.)

[4] *Mittermaier*, in "Archiv des Criminalrechts" (Halle), XI, Nos. 7, 12, 15, 20.

[5] *Mittermaier*, in "Archiv" (Neue Folge, Halle 1837), p. 6. *Cf. Rosshirt*, "Zwei criminalist. Abhändl." pp. 3–88. As to the faults of the German procedure, see *Mittermaier*, in "Archiv" (1842), pp. 71–93, 103.

caused the release of the guilty.[1] The legislators hoped, through a mass of general rules, to be able to guide the course of procedure,[2] but in an unfortunate manner, they often went beyond what was requisite and hindered the necessary free exercise of discretion.[3] Moreover, they made so many exceptions to the rules that finally the rules were without significance.[4]

Political changes, the increasing opinion that the former German procedure did not satisfy reasonable requirements, the greater respect for civil freedom, and the realization of the necessity for securing it against attacks in the criminal procedure, gave rise in the ensuing period to scientific investigation, and much deliberation, *e.g.* in the legislative assemblies, in regard to a regular revision of German procedure.

The gradually increasing knowledge of French procedure, obtaining as law in many parts of Germany, and the occasional questions arising as to the retention of the French procedure, caused disputes,[5] stimulated interest, and made foreign legislation better known. In this way there increased in number scientific works relative to the improvement of criminal procedure, often occasioned by a discussion of codification. These also aimed at

[1] For a concession of the faults in the German procedure, see *Biener*, "Uber die neueren Vorschläge zur Verbesserung des Criminalverfahrens in Deutschland" (Berlin 1844). Also *Puchta*, "Der Inquisitionsprocess mit Ruchsicht auf zeitgemässe Reform" (Erlangen 1844). In consequence of this, *Martin* defended the German procedure in *Richter's* "Krit. Jahrbuch" (1843), p. 110.

[2] Notice the statements of *Feuerbach*, in his work, "Betrachtungen über Oeffentlichkeit und Mündlichkeit" (Giessen 1824), I Thl., p. 415, and in the description of crimes, II, p. 191, note.

[3] *E.g.*, in regard to the testing of evidence. *Gmelin*, "Uber die peinliche Rechtspflege in Kleinstaaten" (Tübingen 1831), p. 126.

[4] *E.g.*, in regard to arrest and the searching of premises.

[5] Here belongs *v. Sandt* and *zum Bach*, "Niederrheinisches Archiv für Gesetzgebung und Rechtswissenschaft" (Köln 1817–1820), 4 vols. Also the articles appearing in *v. Kamptz*, "Jahrbücher," especially Heft XXIII, pp. 91–202. *Hadamar*, "Die Vorzüge der öffentlich-mündlichen Rechtspflege" (Mainz 1815). "Grunde für und wider die mündliche Rechtspflege" (Mainz 1816). *Schramm*, "Freimuthige Bemerkungen über öffentl. mündl. Verfahren" (Elberfeld 1817). *Tritterman*, "Nachtheile des öffentlichen Verfahrens" (Düsseldorf 1817). *Mosqua*, "Prüfung der neuern Gründe fur öffentliches Verfahren" (Berlin 1818). See also *Mittermaier*, "Die öffentlich-mündliche Strafrechtspflege und die Geschwornenheit in Vergleichung mit dem deutschen Strafverfahren" (Landhut 1819). Especially valuable are the conclusions of the "Immediatcommission" (in Köln), "Uber das öffentl. mündl. Verfahren in Untersuchungssachen, über das öffentl. Ministerium, über das Geschwornengericht" (Berlin 1818). And in regard hereto, see also *Gravell*, "Prüfung der Gutachten der Immediatcommission" (Leipzig 1819), 2 vols. *Rebmann*, "Andeutung einiger Forderungen an eine gute Strafrechtspflege" (Wiesbaden 1819). "Bemerk über Einf. der Oeffentlichkeit des ger. Verf. und der Geschwornengerichte in Baiern." (München 1819). *v. Feuerbach*, "Ueber Oeffentlichkeit und Mündlichkeit" (Giessen 1821–1825), 2 vols.

a comparative study of the legislation of foreign countries, and of those of its principles differing from the common German procedure.[1] There was, however, the disadvantage that the legislators could not get away from their favorite deterrent theory and their desire to obtain a confession.[2]

(*d*) *Legislation of the early 1800s.* — In most of the German States, other than those whose criminal codes have already been referred to above, the legislation dealing with criminal procedure was in the form either of new codifications, or of new revisions of old codes, or else through special statutes dealing with particular subjects. The basis of most of their laws was the common German procedure, often changed, but not always improved, by a few statutory enactments.

In several countries, single far-reaching statutes were passed relative to individual points of criminal procedure, while for the most part the common German procedure was retained. Such was the case in: Baden,[3] the Kingdom of Saxony,[4] Braun-

[1] *Abegg*, "Beiträge zur Strafprocessgesetzgebung" (Neustadt 1841). *Leue*, "Der mündliche öffentliche Anklageprocess und der geheime schriftliche Untersuchungsprocess" (Aachen 1840). *Hepp*, "Anklageschaft Oeffentlichkeit und Mündlichkeit des Strafverfahrens" (Tübingen 1842). *Leman*, "Über Oeffentlichkeit und Mündlichkeit des Strafverfahrens" (Berlin 1842). *Molitor* in *v. Jagemanns* and *Nollners*, "Zeitschrift für Strafverfahren," III. Bd., No. 1. *Folir*, "Über Mündlichkeit und Oeffentlichkeit des Gerichtsverfahrens" (Carlsruhe 1843); and *Geib*, in his reference to *Folir* in *Richter's* Krit. Jahrbüchern (1844, Feb., p. 20). *Biener*, "Über die neueren Vorschläge zur Verbesserung des Criminalverf." (Berlin 1844). Here also belong the legal writings of *Schirach*, in regard to the improvement of criminal procedure in Schleswig-Holstein: "Über die von holsteinischen Standen beanträgte Reform des Strafverfahrens" (Kiel 1843). The articles by *Falk*, *Hermann*, *Graba*, in the new Kieler Blätter, 1843, III Bd., p. 75; VI, p. 209; VII, p. 258. *Brinkmann*, "Über Schwurgerichte in Strafsachen" (Kiel 1843). *Esmarch*, "Über Reform des Gerichtverfahrens in Schleswig" (1844). *Cartheuser*, in the "Jurist. Zeitschrift des schlesw. Advokatenvereins," I Annual, 2. Hft., p. 269. As to the improvement of procedure, see especially *Puchta*, "Der Inquisitionsprocess mit Rucksicht auf eine zeitgemässe Reform" (Erlangen 1844). *Rintel*, "Von der Jury" (Münster 1844). *Hopfner*, "Über den Anklageprocess und den Geschwornengericht" (Hamburg 1844). *Mittermaier*, in "Archiv," 1842, Nos. 2, 8, 15.

[2] *Hepp*, "Darstellung der deutschen Strafrechtssysteme," 2d Abthl., pp. 383–392.

[3] Strafedict of 1803, with the supplements and examples of 1812, edited by *Rhenaus* (Mannheim 1823). See also *Donsbach*, "Verfassung und Processverfahren der Untergerichte" (Karlsruhe 1822). *v. Hohnhorst*, "Jahrbücher des badischen Oberhofgerichts zu Mannheim" (1823–1831, 6 vols.). *Duttinger*, *Ketternaser* and *v. Weiler*, "Archiv für die Gesetzgeb. und Rechtspflege in Baden" (Freiburg 1830, 4 vols.). Among the later statutes dealing with criminal law, the statute of November 25th, in regard to the abolition of punishments for contempt, and the statute of August 3d, 1837, in regard to retrial in criminal cases, are important.

[4] See *ante*, Chapter XVII, and especially the statute of March 30th, 1838. Changes of special features in the procedure in criminal cases —

schweig,[1] Holstein and Schleswig,[2] Hanover,[3] Mecklenburg,[4] Anhalt-Dessau,[5] Weimar,[6] Altenburg,[7] Schwarzburg,[8] the Grand Duchy of Hesse,[9] and Oldenburg.[10]

In other German States there was a secret written procedure, in-

see also in regard to the Saxon criminal procedure, the excellent article in the "Zeitschrift Criminalist. Jahrbücher für das Königr. Sachsen," by *Watzdorf* and *Siebdrat* (Zwickau 1837–1841, and "Neue Jahrbücher" since 1842). A new draft was laid before the High Court in 1843. It occasioned many written articles. There was not an agreement as to fundamental principles and so the draft was withdrawn by the government. See *Mittermaier*, in regard to this proposed revision in the "Archiv des Criminalrechts" (Halle 1842), p. 424.

[1] Verordnung of January 15th, 1814; of February 3d, 1814; of March 20th, 1823; and the statutes of 1832 and the statute of February 23d, 1837. *Scholz*, "Abriss der Gerichtsverfassung und des Verfahrens in Strafsachen in Braunschweig" (Altenburg 1841).

[2] *Esmarch*, "Prakt. Darstellung der Strafverfahrens in Schleswig," 1840, with the supplements of 1843.

[3] *Puffendorf*, "Introd. in proc. crim." (Luneburg 1732). *Oesterlei*, "Handbuch über das Verf. in Straffallen für das Königreich Hannover" (as vol. III of the "bürgerl. und peinl. hannov. Proc.") (Göttingen 1820). Statute relative to the abolition of torture, of March 15th, 1823. In June, 1829, a revision of the criminal procedure was proposed ("Archiv des Criminalrechts," X, No. 1). *Gans*, "Entwurf der Criminalprocessordn. für Hannover" (Göttingen 1836). In regard to the acts of the Commission, see "Archiv," Neue Folge, 1837, p. 20. Statute of September 8th, 1840, in regard to the judicial procedure in criminal cases. Statute of November 19, 1840, in regard to offenses subject to the jurisdiction of a police magistrate. *v. Bothmer*, "Erörterung und Abhändlung aus dem Gebiete des hannov. Criminalrechts und Criminalprocesses" (Hannover 1843).

[4] Criminalgerichtsordnung of January 31st, 1817; see "Neues Archiv," I Bd., No. 28. In regard to the Mecklenburg criminal procedure, see *Richter*, "Handbuch des Meklenb. Criminalproc." (Gustrow 1830). Also much in *Kammerer*, "Das Rechtsmittel der Revision in Criminalproc." (Rostock 1833). The statute of January 12th, 1838, in regard to the regulations dealing with the jurisdiction of the "Criminalcollegium," is important. Also the statute of January 13th, 1838, in regard to "Niedergerichte"; the statute of January 15th, 1838, in regard to the order of speeches in criminal investigations; and the statute of January 12th, 1841, in regard to evidence.

[5] Explanations, changes, and supplements to certain titles of the Anhalt Landesordnung, of July 10th, 1822 (pp. 141, 150 deal with criminal procedure).

[6] Weimar Criminalgerichtsordn. of October 5th, 1810. Weimar Verordnung of May 7th, 1819, in regard to the abolition of torture, the admissibility of punishments for contempt, and circumstantial evidence. Statutes of April 7th and 9th, 1839.

[7] Altenburg. Statute in regard to circumstantial evidence of April 15th, 1837, and the statute of January 27th, 1837, in regard to successive appeal.

[8] Statute of February 2d, 1837, in regard to legal remedies.

[9] *Ruhl*, in *Bopp*, "Materialien," I, p. 33. *Bopp*, "Nachträge zur hessen-darmstädt. Civilprocessordn. und peinl. Gerichtsordnung" (Darmstadt 1838). The statutes passed at the introduction of the new Criminal Code of September 17th, 1841, have an influence upon procedure.

[10] There was later introduced a Bavarian Criminal Code, with many improvements. See "Archiv," IV, p. 471. Important additions by way of explanation of October 11th, 1821. An edition of the Code containing all additions prior to 1836 appeared in 1837.

quisitorial in nature, joined with a certain publicity and an oral method of pleading, so that at the end of the procedure there was, as it were, a public conclusion. This was the case especially in the systems of many of the Swiss Cantons, *e.g.*, Zurich,[1] Lucern,[2] Bern,[3] Thurgau,[4] Glarus,[5] and Freiburg.[6] In this category also belonged the Criminal Regulations [7] of Würtemburg,[8] which contained a limited oral conclusion in the case of graver crimes,[9] and certain other institutions of the accusatorial procedure.[10] The Prussian Revision had in view a similar public conclusion.[11]

Other legislation chose as its foundation the French procedure, yet with a limitation upon the passing of judgment by jurors, and with the effort to conduct the preliminary investigation thoroughly, and to widen the range of the discretion of the presiding judge. Here belong the codifications of the Netherlands,[12] and of the

[1] Statute of June 10th, 1831.

[2] Lucern. Strafprocessordn. of June 17th, 1836.

[3] Statutes of March 7th, and December 15th, 1834 ("Archiv," Neue Folge, 1837, p. 194).

[4] Statute of June 19th, 1834, and of November 19th, 1837, in regard to the administration of justice.

[5] Strafprocessordn. for the Canton Glarus, 1837.

[6] Statute of May 27th, 1839.

[7] As to the statutes preceding the new regulations for criminal procedure, see Ordinance of November 18th, 1811; IV Organisationsedict of December 31st, 1818, Nos. 193–226, and the edict of July 17th, in regard to criminal forms and institutions. See also *Hofacker*, "Systematische Uebersicht des gemeinen und würtemburg. Strafprocesses" (Tübingen 1820). Also *Hofacker*, "Jahrbücher der Gesetzgebung und Rechtspflege in Würtemburg" (Stuttgart 1824–1830). A revision of the criminal statutes was proposed in the Assembly ("Stande") in 1830. See criticism of the administration of justice, in *Gmelin*, "über die peinliäche Rechtspflege in Kleinstaaten mit bes. Beziehung auf Würtemburg" (Tübingen 1831). See also many articles in regard to the Würtemburg criminal procedure in *Sarwey*, "Monatsschrift für die Justizpflege in Würtemburg" (Ludwigsburg, 1837 to 1844, yearly, 4 vols.).

[8] Of June 22d, 1843. *Holzinger*, "Commentar über die Strafprocessordnung für Würtemburg" (Ellwangen 1844). Also *Knapp*, "Die Strafprocessordnung von Würtemburg mit Anmerk." (Stuttgart 1843.)

[9] That this is insufficient, see *Mittermaier*, in "Archiv," 1842, pp. 88, 278 (as to the proceedings in the assembly, p. 270). *Folir*, "Über Mündlichkeit und Oeffentlichkeit der Gerichtsverfahrens" (Carlsruhe 1843), p. 27.

[10] *Hepp*, "Darstellung des deutschen Strafrechtssysteme," II Abth., p. 384.

[11] *Mittermaier*, in "Archiv," 1842, p. 293. *Folir*, p. 28. *Temme*, in the Zeitschrift of *Jagemann* (New edition), I, p. 311.

[12] The last code went into effect in 1836. "Wetboek van Strafverordering." Relative thereto, see *Asser*, in the "Zeitschrift für ausländ. Gesetzgebung," X Bd., Nos. 11, 20. Valuable remarks in regard to the revision of 1828 in *Rappard*, "het Ontwerp van een Wetboek van Strafverordering" (Zutphen, 4 vols.). See also *den Tex* and *van Hall*, "Anmerkingen over het Ontwerp" (Amsterdam 1829, 4 vols.). As to the revisions prior to 1828, see *Mittermaier*, in the "Zeitschrift," Bd. I, No.

Canton[1] of Vaud, the Criminal Regulations for Baden,[2] and the code of Hungary.[3]

(*e*) *Legislation under the Empire.* — Since the proclamation of the Empire, the task of the legislative unity of Germany has been the constant subject of political thought. The year 1877 constitutes, in this respect, an important date in the history of the country. It was marked by the promulgation of four leading laws, the Code of Judicial Organization, the Code of Criminal Procedure, the Code of Civil Procedure, and the Bankruptcy Code. We propose to deal here only with the first two of those.

(I) The Judicial organization law[4] substitutes, throughout the German Empire, one and the same system of civil and criminal tribunals in place of the different local jurisdictions. Justice is administered by "amt" tribunals, district courts, superior district courts, and the tribunal of the Empire. The principle of the unity of civil and criminal justice governs this organization, with two qualifications. In the lower stage of the hierarchy, the "amt," which corresponds very nearly to the French canton, there are two tribunals, one civil, the "amt" court, "Amtsgericht"; the other correctional, the tribunal of lay assessors, "Schoeffengericht." The "amt" judge sits in both: in the former, alone; in the latter, assisted by laymen. In the higher stage, assizes are periodically held at the district tribunals to try criminal cases which are not within the cognizance of the correctional chambers or of the supreme tribunal of the Empire. The organization of the German assize courts is identical with that of the French assize courts. They are composed, on the one side, of a president and of two judges, and on the other side of twelve jurors.

20; II, No. 6. There is a valuable treatment of this statute in *Voorduin*' "Geschiednis en beginselen der nederlandsche Wetboeken" (Utrecht 1839), 2 vols. *Bosch-Kemper*, "Wetboek van Strafordering" (Amsterdam, vol. I–III, 1840). *Lipmann*, "Wetboek van Strafordering" (Amsterdam 1842).

[1] "Code de procédure pénale du Canton de Vaud," Lausanne, 1836. (See "Archiv," Neue Folge, 1837, p. 171.)

[2] The earlier revision was in 1835. See "Archiv," 1842, p. 80. The date of the code is March 6th, 1845.

[3] "Entwurf einer Strafgesetzgeb. für das Königr. Ungarn," 2 Thl. (Leipzig 1843).

[4] Code of 27th January, 1877. *Dubarle*, "Code d'organisation judiciaire allemande," Introduction and translation (Paris, 2 vols., 8vo, 1885). This Code forms part of the collection of the principal foreign Codes published under the supervision of the committee on foreign legislations of the Ministry of Justice. See also "Annuaire de législation étrangère," 7, p. 77. *Laband*, "Le droit public de l'Empire allemand," translated by *Gaudillion* (6 vols., 8vo, 1900–1904, Paris), may be consulted generally on the judicial organization.

(II) The German Code of Criminal Procedure is directly derived from the French Code of Criminal Examination.[1] The variations between them important enough to be noticed here are not sufficient to make a distinct type so far as the procedure is concerned. Prior to this unifying legislation, the systems of law of the German States might have been grouped as follows: Certain states, notably the two Mecklenburgs and the two Lippes, followed the German common law, from which they had borrowed a procedure fundamentally inquisitorial. Two states, Lübeck and the Duchy of Saxe-Altenburg, had adopted the accusatory system, but without jury or assessors. Finally, in the great majority of the states, the laws of procedure retained, at least in the trial, the accusatory system, by causing either jurors or assessors to take part in the trial.[2] It is in this last group that the legislators of 1877 sought their type and from it have taken their model, sanctioning that evolution of the criminal procedure which in Germany, as in the majority of the States of the European continent, had followed the three successive phases;—the accusatory phase, the inquisitorial phase, and the mixed phase. In the last system, which sums up the existing traits of the German procedure, the arraignment, which is the starting-point of the action, is, as a rule, the work of special functionaries. The examination reproduces the forms of the inquisitorial procedure. But after the trial jurisdiction is reached, everything takes place in the broad daylight of courtroom and confrontation. The proofs are not formal, but moral, and the judge has only his conscience to guide him in his estimate of the facts and the culpability.

A law modifying the Code of Judicial Organization and the Code of Criminal Procedure of date 27th May, 1898,[3] has intervened to put the judicial organization in agreement with the new German Civil Code on one hand and on the other to

[1] *Fernand Daguin*, "Code de procédure allemand" (1st February, 1877), translated, with notes (Paris 1884). The introduction is particularly notable.

[2] On the history of German procedure: *Daguin*, "Introduction," p. vii *et seq.; Feuerbach*, "Lehrbuch des gemeinen in Deutschland gültigen peinlichen Rechts," edited by *Mittermaier* (14th ed., 8vo, Giessen, 1847); *Ch. Lévita*, "Précis de l'histoire du droit pénal allemand depuis la Caroline jusqu'à nos jours," translated and annotated by *Bourneville de Marsangy* (Extract from the "Revue crit. de législation," 34 pages, 8vo, Paris, Cotillon, 1862). For the very ancient law, *J. J. Thonissen*, "L'organisation judiciaire, le droit pénal et la procédure pénale de la loi salique" (2d ed. 8vo., Paris, Chevalier-Maresq, 1882). See also, for the bibliography of German criminal law, "Le droit criminel des États européens," Germany, appendix, p. 363.

[3] Review, analysis, and translation in "Ann. de législation étrangère," 1899, 38, pp. 142–150.

remedy several disadvantages of procedure pointed out by experience.[1]

II. *Austria-Hungary, etc.* — The Austria-Hungarian Empire is composed of an amalgamation of States, nationalities, and legal systems.

(*a*) The Austrian Code of Criminal Procedure bears the date 23d May, 1873.[2] It is the fourth which has been promulgated in Austria since the beginning of the 1800s. This country has, in fact, been governed by the Codes of 1803, 1850 and 1853; it is now governed by that of 1873. The Criminal Code of 1803 was both a Penal Code and a Code of Procedure.[3] As regards the procedure it merely reproduced and developed the rules of the pure inquisitorial system. The Code of 1850 was modeled on the French Code; it introduced the oral and public procedure, the accusatory principle, and the institution of the jury. But it was swept away by the storm of reaction which raged in 1851. The Act of 31st December, 1851, declared that a Code of Criminal Procedure should be made for the whole Empire. That was the Code of the 29th July, 1853, which remained in force until January 1st, 1874. That Code suppressed the jury, allowed publicity to subsist only in a relative degree, admitted of no defense until after the close of the examination, and retained a system of legal proofs.

The liberal movement and the constitutional reforms which followed 1860 and 1861 attracted attention to the defects of the criminal procedure. Numerous plans were successively studied. In 1872, Minister of Justice Glaser, who had, in his capacity of chairman for several of the commissions on reform, contributed more than any one else to the preliminary labors, submitted the draft

[1] Consult, for the systematic explanation of German criminal law, "Encyclopaedie der Rechtswissenschaft" of *Franz von Holtzendorff* (6th ed.), II. The criminal law is divided into three articles. To *M. Wachenfeld* is committed the general penal law, *M. Beling* explains the general criminal procedure, and *M. Weiffenbach* has specially treated of military penal law and criminal procedure. *Ernst Henrich Rosenfeld*, "Der Reichs-Strafprozess" (Berlin, Gutentag, 1903) may also be consulted.

[2] This Code bears the title "Oesterreichische Saf process-Ordnung vom 23 mai 1873." It has been translated by *MM. Edu. Bertrand* and *Ch. Lyon-Caen* under the inaccurate title of "Code d'instruction criminelle annoté" ("Collection des Codes étrangères," imprimerie national, 1875). See the introduction, which treats of the three following matters, Austrian criminal procedure subsequent to the Codes of 1803, 1850, and 1853, the history of the compilation of the Code of 23d May, 1873, and a general sketch of the new Code.

[3] It has been translated into French in the collection of civil and criminal laws of modern nations, published under the supervision of *M. Victor Foucher* (vol. 1 of the collection).

which became the Code of 1873. Conforming to Germanic traditions, this law is called Regulations ("Ordnung") of Criminal Procedure,[1] but it is neither more nor less than a Code. In the procedural legislation of the European continent, this Code may be signalized as the expression of a progress remarkable both on account of the prior state of Austrian legislation, and of the variety of races, traditions, and customs of the nations who have entered into the formation of Austria. Its fundamental principles had been already fixed by the Constitution of 21st December, 1867, that is, the oral nature and publicity of the trial proper, the accusatory trial and the jury for the more serious offenses, political offenses, and those of the press. For these last, the jury began to act under the law of 9th March, 1869.

The Austrian Code of 1873 has received the unanimous approbation of criminalists. It is inspired, no doubt, by the French Code of Criminal Examination, of which it reproduces the type; but how much modified and improved! The scientific mind of Glaser is forcibly imprinted upon a law of procedure adapted to the necessities of practical life. The influence of this Code of 1873 upon the contemporary orientalization of criminal procedure is also a fact which must be taken into account. Since the French Code of 1808, no legislation peculiar to one nation has been more widely quoted and imitated elsewhere.

(*b*) The history of criminal procedure in Hungary is the history of the strife of a century between the inquisitorial and accusatory systems. The Code of Criminal Procedure of 22d December, 1896, which now governs this country, has made uniform a system of laws formerly very diversified, and has introduced the jury, not only for press offenses, but for the more serious misdemeanors. It institutes the accusatory procedure, with the public prosecutor.[2]

(*c*) Bosnia and Herzegovina are governed by the Code of 30th January, 1891, which came into force 1st January, 1892.[3]

(*d*) Croatia-Slavonia has a Code of its own; the Regulation of 17th May, 1875, modeled upon the Austrian Code of 1873. The jury, however, has not been instituted in this province.

III. *Belgium.* — Belgium has retained the French Codes, notably the Code of Criminal Examination of 1808. But its

[1] And not of criminal examination ("d'instruction criminelle") as the translation of *MM. Bertrand* and *Ch. Lyon-Cæn* has it.

[2] Upon this Code, review by *Meyer* in "Ann. de législation étrangère," 1897, pp. 397–409.

[3] See the review of *Meyer*, Bull. soc. lég. comp. 1891–1892, vol. 21, p. 398.

Constitution of 1831 directed their "revision with the least possible delay" (Art. 139). This great work has been only partially accomplished. Only, on the one hand, the preliminary title of a new Code of Criminal Procedure, a title adopted in preference to that of Code of Criminal Examination, has been promulgated, 17th April, 1878,[1] and on the other hand, title IX of book III, replacing Articles 443, 444, 446, and 447 of the Code of Criminal Examination, that is to say, modifying the rules of appeal.[2]

The history of criminal procedure in Belgium embraces three periods, which correspond with the periods of its contemporaneous history.[3] From 1795 to 1814 Belgium was French soil. It then passed successively under the régime of the Code of Offenses and Punishments of the 3d Brumaire, of the year IV, and of the Code of Criminal Examination of 1808. After the events of 1814, Belgium, as a part of the new Kingdom of the Netherlands, lived, like the rest of that country, under the rule of the Napoleonic legislation. But the Code of 1808 was almost immediately amended in two important particulars; the jury was abolished and "the publicity of the trial in criminal and correctional matters prior to the pleadings" was suppressed (Resolution of 6th November, 1814). After 1830 Belgium, henceforth forming an autonomous kingdom, took up again the French system of laws, which, however, has been modified and amended by a series of provisions which were the subject of a special investigation appropriate to each of the institutions to which these provisions respectively relate.

IV. *The Principality of Monaco.* — The Code of Criminal Examination of the Principality of Monaco, which bears date 31st December, 1873,[4] is, as might be supposed, mainly copied

[1] "Annuaire de législation étrangère," 1879, text, review, and notes by *Georges Louis*, pp. 443–457. All the parliamentary documents relating to the introductory title of the new Code have been reproduced "in extenso" and coördinated by *Nypels* under the title of "Commentaire du Code de procédure pénale" (Brussels 1878).

[2] This law, which bears date 18th June, 1894, is contained in the "Annuaire de législation étrangère" (1895, vol. 24, pp. 504–514. Review and notes by *A. le Poittevin*). On the plan of reform of the Belgian Code generally, *S. Mayer*, "Das Strafprozessrecht Belgiens," in "Archiv für Strafrecht" (1886); *Vacca*, "Le reforme del codice di procedura penale nel Belgie," in "Rivista penale," 30, p. 109 *et seq.*

[3] Bibliography: *Haus*, "Principes généraux de droit pénal belge," vol. 2, book IV; *Thonessen*, "Travaux préparatoires du Code de procédure pénale," "Reports made to the Chamber of Representatives"; *Lindotte*, "Le Code de procédure pénale appliqué et annoté"; "Revue critique de droit criminel" (Criminal procedure); *Ferdinand Thiry*, "Cours de droit criminel" (2d ed., 1895), Second part, "Procédure pénale"; "Pandectes belges," *passim; Nypels*, "Législation criminelle de la Belgique," 3 vols., 8vo.

[4] Official edition, Nice, Cauvia & Co., 1874.

from the French Code of 1808. It, nevertheless, differs from that in various respects, and notably in regard to the order of the matters dealt with. The chief characteristic of this procedure is the exclusion of the trial jury from criminal proceedings.[1]

V. *Grand Duchy of Luxemburg.* — The criminal legislation of the Grand Duchy of Luxemburg does not possess the merit of originality. The Luxemburg Criminal Code, promulgated 18th June, 1879, reproduces the Belgium Penal Code of 1867. The procedure of the Grand Duchy is still regulated by the French Code of Criminal Examination of 1808, in which, however, important changes have been made.[2]

VI. *Spain.* — The Spanish Code of Criminal Procedure is dated 14th September, 1882.[3] The chief reform effected by this Code is the substitution of the oral trial for the written procedure. The Spanish people had been "educated for centuries in the written procedure, secret and inquisitorial"; they have renounced that system to adopt the accusatory system, "carrying it, so to speak, even into the preliminary examination, since the legislature grants to the prisoner the guarantees which the ancient laws refused him, and which the secrecy of the examination has maintained solely within the limits necessary to prevent the facts leading to presumptions of the offense from disappearing." [4]

The jury, suppressed in 1875, was reëstablished by the Act of 20th April, 1888,[5] which gave it jurisdiction to sit in cases of the more serious misdemeanors.

The origin of the Spanish public prosecutor appears to be of very old date; but the present organization of the office is traceable to the laws of 1812. Its members, who are also called "representantes del ministerio fiscal" have the same powers as in France in the repressive procedure. They institute the public action

[1] Articles 76, 355, 358, and 444 of the Code of Criminal Examination have been modified by a sovereign ordinance of 16th August, 1888, and Article 467 by an ordinance of 22d May, 1891. Besides this, a plan for the general revision of the Code was in preparation. See on this plan, *De Rolland*, "Projet de Code de procédure pénale" (3 vols., 8vo, 1899–1903). It is about to be sanctioned. See "Code de procédure pénale de la principauté de Monaco" (8vo, 1905).

[2] See *Jacques Delahaye*, "Bull. de l'Union intern. de droit pénal," 1903, p. 63.

[3] Translated in the collection of foreign codes by *Gabriel Verdier* and *Joseph Depeiges* (Paris, Imprimerie national, 1898). See also *Thouralt*, "Notice sur le Code de procédure criminelle du 14 Septembre, 1882" ("Annuaire," t. XII, p. 693). On the history, *Du Boys*, "Histoire du droit criminel de l'Espagne" (1 vol., 8vo, 1870).

[4] Report of the Minister of Pardons and Justice.

[5] This law has been translated in an appendix to the translation of the Codes by *Verdier* and *Depeiges*.

in all cases except in those which, by law, cannot be prosecuted except at the request of the injured party.

VII. *Italy.* — The organic repressive law is at present represented, in united Italy, by two chief authorities: 1st, the fundamental statute of the kingdom and the laws of constitutional and political order; 2d, the Code of Criminal Procedure and the laws on the judicial organization.

(*a*) The royal statute contains several declarations and constitutional provisions relating to individual liberty (Art. 26); the inviolability of the home (Art. 27); the exclusion of exceptional tribunals (Art. 71); the publicity of hearings (Art. 72); the immunity of senators (Art. 37); the political guarantee of deputies (Art. 15); the institution of a High Court of Justice (Art. 36). Other laws of a constitutional or political nature relate to certain points of judicial organization or of procedure, such as the Act of 13th May, 1871, upon the prerogatives of the sovereign pontiff, the edict or law relating to the press of 26th March, 1848, etc.

(*b*) The Italian Code of Criminal Procedure is dated 1865.[1] It must be supplemented, either by the law upon the judicial organization of 6th December, 1865, which is itself followed by a regulation of 14th December, 1865, and by other laws, too numerous to be mentioned here, relating to the magistracy and its functions. Among these, however, must be noted that of 6th December, 1888,[2] which confers on the Court of Cassation of Rome the exclusive jurisdiction of all the penal matters of the kingdom and suppresses the criminal branches of the six other Courts of Cassation. The judicial organization greatly resembles the French organization. The prætors, magistrates analogous to the French justices of the peace, form the lowest step in the judicial hierarchy. Assize courts, constituted like the French Courts of Assizes, administer justice in criminal matters.[3] The office of public prosecutor is organized on analogous lines.

(*c*) Plans for the reform of the Italian Code of Criminal Procedure are as numerous as they are varied. There can be no

[1] *Marcy,* "Code de procédure pénale du royaume d'Italie" (2 vols., 8vo, 1881, Paris). The two principal commentaries on this Code are *Borsari* and *Casorati,* "Codice di procedura penale commentato" (5 vols., Milan 1885); *Saluto,* "Commenti al Codice di procedura penale" (8 vols., 8vo, 3d ed., Turin 1884).

[2] "Annuaire de législation étrangère," vol. 17, p. 512.

[3] Law of 8th June, 1874 ("Annuaire de législation étrangère," vol. 4, p. 357), and the law of 16th December, 1886, amending it (Annuaire, vol. 16, p. 395).

discussion here of those which are due to parliamentary initiative. But, among the plans presented in the name of the government, I shall cite, in chronological order, the plan of Falco of 19th April, 1866, that of Filippo of 1868, that of Villa of 9th March, 1880, and of Taiani of 25th November, 1885, etc. Finally, by the Decree of 1st October, 1898, Keeper of the Seals Aprile instituted a commission charged to study and propose amendments of which the Code of Criminal Procedure may be capable, in the direction of a more efficacious protection of individual liberty and a greater celerity in the penal action.[1] The proceedings of this commission have been published.[2] The commission finished its labors in June, 1904. Without modifying the essential bases of criminal procedure, it provides a series of reforms in matters of detail which bear upon all the stages of the criminal action.[3]

[(*d*) This Draft Code was finally enacted on June 20, 1912, and now represents, in many respects, the most advanced views in Continental criminal procedure.[4]]

VIII. *Switzerland.* — The Codes of Criminal Procedure of the Swiss Cantons may be divided into three ethnical groups: 1st, the cantons of German Switzerland; 2d, the cantons of French Switzerland; and 3d, the Italian canton of Tessin.

(*a*) The cantons of German Switzerland, Argovie, Saint-Gall, Basle, Basle-Campagne, Lucerne, Schaffhausen, Zurich, Thurgau, Grisons, Soleure, Appenzell, Unterwalden, Berne, Glarus, Schwyz, and Zug, all have Codes of Criminal Procedure whose provisions differ in their details, but which reproduce, in broad outlines, the mixed system of procedure. It will suffice to cite one of the most original of the laws of procedure, that of the canton of Appenzell of 25th April, 1880.[5]

(*b*) The laws of western Switzerland have almost all undergone the influence of the French Codes. The peoples of the French-

[1] See *Lucchini*, "Giustizia per tuti," "Revista penale" ("Justice for All," "Penal Review"), vol. 54, p. 489.

[2] "Lavori preparatori del Codice di procedura penale pel regno d' Italia" ("Preliminary Proceedings for a Code of Criminal Procedure in the kingdom of Italy"), 3 vols., 4to, Rome. The first two volumes contain the minutes of the commission. The third contains reports upon the principal problems of criminal procedure. The Italian government with courteous generosity has placed these volumes at the service of foreign criminalists.

[3] See the résumé of the discussions of the commission in the "Scuola positiva" (1904), p. 441.

[4] [See V. Manzini, "Trattato di Procedura Penale secondo il nuovo Codice di Procedura Penale Italiano" (1913, Boica, Turin). — ED.]

[5] It is analyzed in the "Annuaire de législation étrangère," vol. 10 (1881), p. 447.

speaking part of Switzerland have lived too long under the rule of these codes to be able to reject completely and radically the traditions and modes of thought which they have borrowed from France. In the canton of Geneva, for example, the Code of 1808 remained in force until 1884. The existing Code is dated 25th October, 1884, and was promulgated 4th January, 1885.[1] The Code of Criminal Procedure of the canton of Friburg is dated 24th May, 1873, and was put in force 1st January, 1874. The Code of Criminal Procedure of the canton of Valais, of 24th November, 1848, entered into force 1st July, 1849. The last-mentioned Code might, however, have been dated a hundred years earlier, offering, as it does, the curious example of a procedure of the 1700 s. It retains the system of legal proofs; it still speaks of half-proof, and the uniform depositions of two unimpeachable witnesses are necessary to establish a fact. There is certainly an oral trial, since the parties plead before the tribunal, but the tribunal does not hear the witnesses, and judges solely from the documents of the proceedings. In the canton of Vaud, the Code of Criminal Procedure of 1st February, 1850, went into force 1st July, 1850. The Code of Criminal Procedure of Neuchâtel, one of the most recent and progressive, is dated 25th September, 1893, and came into force 12th March, 1894.[2] These various Codes differ so widely and fundamentally from each other that it would be very difficult to make a useful comparison between them.[3]

(c) In the canton of Tessin[4] the constitutional Decree of 8th November, 1894, contains the foundations of a new organization in criminal matters. According to the Act of Judicial Organization of 4th May, 1895, promulgated in pursuance of that Decree, justices of the peace have jurisdiction of offenses punishable by a maximum of one hundred francs fine or seven days' imprisonment; the district assizes of offenses punishable by more than one hundred francs fine or seven days' imprisonment or detention; the cantonal assizes of offenses coming under the head of crimes. An important innovation is that the assize courts are composed of magistrates and jurors, sitting together and having jurisdiction of the fact, the

[1] See *Lefort*, "Annuaire de législation étrangère," vol. 14 (1885), p. 571.

[2] The earlier Code was dated 7th April, 1875 ("Annuaire de législation étrangère," vol. 5, p. 762 *et seq.*).

[3] This work has been done and well done by *A. Gautier*, only so far as relates to the procedure of the examination ("instruction"). See "La réforme de l'instruction préparatoire" ("Revue pénale suisse," 1904, pp. 253–273). As to the trial procedure, we shall often have to cite the Geneva Code, which has established the correctional jury.

[4] See "Annuaire de législation étrangère" (1896, vol. 25, p. 560).

law, and the punishment. This Act, in 36 articles, was followed, on the same date, by a Code of Criminal Procedure containing 344 articles.

IX. *The Netherlands.* — Holland possesses a Code of Criminal Procedure which is characterized, like the rest of the laws of that country, by its conciseness and brevity (49 Articles). It is divided into twenty-two titles in which the subjects are arrayed in an order very similar to that of the text of the French Code. The absence of the jury is a matter for remark, as is a system of legal proofs in a sense favorable to the defense. An Act of 15th January, 1886, introduced into this Code certain modifications to put it in accord with the Penal Code of 1881, but the general principles remain unchanged.[1] Private persons cannot, as a rule, take part in the bringing of the criminal action except by way of denunciation (Art. 11). The two actions, criminal and civil, are quite distinct. This Code has absolutely forbidden the civil action before the criminal jurisdiction. It has retained it before the correctional and police jurisdictions only when, the sum demanded being below a certain amount, it would be prejudicial to the parties to oblige them to bring a second action (Arts. 231 and 233).

X. *Great Britain.* — We must take separately the procedure in England, Scotland, and Ireland.

(*a*) In England the criminal procedure has not been codified. This also applies to Scotland and Ireland. Even the attempts due to Sir James Stephen, which were made in 1878 and 1879, to obtain from the English Parliament the adoption of a plan of codification, have been limited to the penal law. In the three countries the procedure is based partly on the common law and partly on the statute law. The common law is the customary law contained in the decisions of the tribunals, or the law which is created anew by the judges by the analogous application of the provisions in force.[2] Statute law is simply legislative law.

[1] See *Van Swinderen,* "Esquisse du droit pénal actuel dans les Pays-Bas et à l'étranger," 5 vols., 4to, 1891–1903. The last two volumes are supplements. The Code of the Netherlands has been translated by *Tripels.* The Code of Criminal Procedure has been amended, as stated in the text, by an Act of 15th January, 1886 ("Annuaire de législation étrangère," 1886, p. 111).

[2] See as the source of our information on the English judicial organization and procedure, *de Franqueville,* "Les institutions politiques, judiciaires et administratives de l'Angleterre" (2d ed., 1864, 1 vol., 8vo); "Le système judiciaire de la Grande-Bretagne" by the same author (2 vols., 8vo, 1893); *Glasson,* "Histoire du droit et des institutions politiques, civiles et administratives de l'Angleterre" (6 vols., 8vo, 1881–1883); *Mittermaier,* "Traité de la procédure criminelle en Angleterre, en Ecosse et dans l'Amerique du Nord," translated into French by *Chauffard* (1 vol.,

The characteristics of English procedure are: 1st, the system of the free individual accusation; 2d, the absence of a preliminary examination by a judge; 3d, the institution of a double jury, the grand jury and the petty jury; 4th, the institution of functionaries, police judges, in certain towns, who have the right to try summarily slight offenses and to remit serious cases to a higher jurisdiction; 5th, the necessity of unanimity of opinion of the trial jury to determine culpability; 6th, the assistance of a counsel to the defense at every stage of the procedure; 7th, arrest facilitated by custom, but incarceration rendered difficult and exceptional; 8th, the interrogation and examination of the witnesses by the counsel of both parties, accuser and accused, by way of cross-examination.

In England, as in France, offenses are divided into three classes (treasons, felonies, and misdemeanors). But this classification is not coördinate with the judicial organization. The jury is the common law judge. The only division which has a jurisdictional interest is that of causes into *summary* and *indictable.* The former are within the jurisdiction of the inferior or summary jurisdictions, — justices of the peace, courts of petty session, and police courts. The latter are begun in these inferior jurisdictions, but remitted to the superior jurisdictions and submitted to the verdict of the jury.[1]

(*b*) The Scotch criminal procedure [2] is halfway between two great historical currents, — the Continental system and the English system. In certain parts it is strictly inquisitorial,[3] in others it is clearly accusatory. For example, the penal action is intrusted to special functionaries, at whose head is the Lord Advocate, a member of Parliament; but alongside of the official accusation, the

8vo, 1868); *A. Prins*, "Etude comparative sur la procédure pénale à Londres et en Belgique" (Brussels 1879); *du Boys*, "Histoire du droit criminel de l'Angleterre," volume 3 of the history of criminal law of modern nations (Paris 1860); *Halton*, "Etude sur la procédure criminelle en Angleterre et en France" (doctorate thesis, Paris 1898); *Seymour Harris*, "Principii di diritto e procedura penale inglese," translated by Bertola (Verona 1898) [and now the report of *Edwin R. Keedy* and *John D. Lawson* on "Criminal Procedure in England," American Journal of Criminal Law and Criminology, 1910, vol. I, p. 607.— ED.].

[1] *Glasson, op. cit.*, vol. 6, p. 569.

[2] *J. Dove Wilson*, professor in the University of Aberdeen, "De la procédure criminelle en Ecosse," "Bull. de l'Un. int. de droit pénal," vol. 11, 1903, pp. 71 to 82. See generally, *J. H. A. Macdonald*, "A practical treatise on the criminal laws of Scotland" (2d ed., 1877), pp. 246–550 [and now *Edwin R. Keedy*, "Criminal Procedure in Scotland," American Journal of Criminal Law and Criminology, 1913, vol. III, p. 728. — ED.].

[3] It is generally thought that the preliminary procedure is modeled upon the French system of the 1500s, to which, however, the Scottish system originally bore a greater resemblance than it does now.

subsidiary accusation by the injured party is allowed.[1] In order that the Lord Advocate may be absolutely independent, he is responsible only to Parliament for his acts. His action, therefore, can have no effect when public opinion is against him.

(*c*) The Irish procedure is partly borrowed from the mixed system, and is without any peculiar feature worthy of note.[2]

(*d*) In the English colonies, the local laws and customs are respected.

A Code of Criminal Procedure for the East Indies was promulgated 22d March, 1898. It takes the place of the successive Codes of 1861, 1871, and 1882.[3]

XI. *Russia.* — The great social reforms which, in Russia, marked the beginning of the reign of the Emperor Alexander II, such as the enfranchisement of the serfs in 1863, and the reconstitution, on the same date, of the provincial administration, "Zemstvo," were the prelude to the judicial laws of 1864.[4] On 20th November, 1864, the laws of criminal procedure which still prevail in Russia came into force. The new judicial organization rests on the principles of the separation of the administrative and judicial powers, and the irremovability of the magistracy, and upon the participation of the people in the administration of justice by the institution of the jury and the election of justices of the peace. The written and secret procedure is replaced by the oral and public procedure, the theory of legal proofs by that of moral proofs. The number of steps of appeal, which entailed indefinite delays, is limited, and instead of the official appeal from judgments it is left to the parties interested to attack them. Finally, the institution of a tribunal of Cassation, put into the care of the directing Senate, insures everywhere the correct application of the law. This code of criminal procedure takes the French system as its basis, but it adapts that system to Russian ways and traditions. It is a national work, and not a mere copy of foreign codes.[5]

[1] The private action has, however, fallen into desuetude. See *Mittermaier*, *op. cit.*, pp. 214, 215; *Glasson*, "Histoire du droit et des institutions politiques, civiles et judiciaires de l'Angleterre," t. 7, p. 732.

[2] The same phenomenon as in Scotland, the abandonment of the private action.

[3] See review and analysis in "Annuaire de législation étrangère," 1899, vol. 28, pp. 968–976.

[4] *Kapnitz*, "Code d'organisation judiciaire de l'Empire de Russie," edition of 1883–1890, translated and annotated, 8vo, 1893.

[5] Among the works written in Russia on criminal procedure, the most important are those of *Foinitski*, "Cours de procédure pénale" (1885) *Tollberg*, "Cours de procédure pénale" (1890); *Ishebyshev-Dmitriev*, "La procédure pénale russe" (1875); *Sloutshevski*, "Cours de procédure

Following the political and social events which marked the end of the reign of Alexander II, and the horrible crime of 1st March, 1881, a reaction against this liberal system made its way. This is especially shown by the Act of 1889, which suppresses the election of justices of the peace and again blends the judicial and administrative powers, subordinating the former to the latter. Nevertheless, the judicial laws and those of procedure of the 20th November, 1864, have exercised the happiest influence on Russian juridical life. At the same time that the reform of the penal Code is in process of completion, an analogous reform of the judicial laws is in course of execution.[1] The labors of the commission ended in 1899. They have been published, and the plan has now been submitted to the Council of the Empire. Its principal innovation consists in the principle of a confrontative procedure from the beginning of the examination.[2]

The Grand Duchy of Finland, which is united to Russia, has a special and autonomous system of laws. Its substantive law has the same origin as the Swedish substantive law, and the history of the law of the two countries took the same course down to the time when the political separation of Finland and Sweden allowed each of these laws to develop in its ethnical direction. The present Penal Code of Finland is dated 19th December, 1889. It went into force on 1st January, 1891.[3] The criminal procedure is not codified. It has been the subject of numerous and successive laws, notably those of 27th April, 1868, 24th February and 3d March, 1873, etc., which also deal with civil procedure.[4]

XII. *The Balkan Countries.* — We group under this head Bulgaria, Servia, and Roumania.

(*a*) In Bulgaria, since the time of the Russian occupation, the

pénale" (1890–1892). None of these works, which are in Russian, has been translated into French.

[1] See *Margoline,* "Aperçu critique du nouveau Code pénale russe" (Paris, 1905), with *Garraud's* preface.

[2] These reforms were inspired by the former minister of justice, Mourawiëw, who sought to give all questions concerning the administration of criminal justice a very liberal and forceful direction.. See *Kapnitz,* "Documents relatifs à la revision des Codes d'organisation judiciaire et de procédure civile et criminelle enterprise par ordre de S. M. l'empereur Alexander III, du 7 Avril, 1894."

[3] The Penal Code of Finland has been translated into French by *Ludovic Beauchet,* professor in the Faculty of Law of Nancy (Paris 1890). See the very interesting appreciations of this system, by *Henri Joly,* "A travers l'Europe" (Paris, Lecoffre, 1898), In Finland, pp. 6–44. On the legislation of Finland, a review by *K. Montgomery* ("Annuaire de législation étrangère," vol. 9, 1880, pp. 727–756).

[4] On the judicial organization, "Répertoire général alph. de droit français," Finland, t. 22, p. 256.

different procedures have been the subject of provisional regulation inspired chiefly by the Russian Codes. These regulations have since been replaced by new laws. The law relative to criminal procedure alone remained in force. It has been replaced by the Code of 1897,[1] divided into five books, 1st, concerning jurisdiction; 2d, concerning the preliminary examination; 3d, concerning the procedure before the departmental tribunals (the procedure before justices of the peace is regulated by a special law of 3d June, 1880[2]); 4th, concerning the methods of appealing against judgments; 5th, concerning the execution of sentences. The laws of 17th January, 1900, 26th January, 1901, and 20th January, 1902, have amended and completed this Code of Criminal Procedure.[3]

(*b*) The Servian Code of Criminal Procedure is dated 16th June, 1865. It is a faithful copy of the Austrian Code of 1853, which served as its model. The provisional judicial regulations, elaborated at the time of the creation of the principality, have been replaced by new laws, and the Code of 1865 was greatly modified in 1880.

(*c*) The Roumanian Code of Criminal Procedure, inspired by French legislation, was promulgated in 1864. The judicial organization and the procedure of this country present a very close analogy to the French judicial organization and procedure.

XIII. *Scandinavia.* — This group includes Denmark, Sweden, and Norway.

(*a*) The Danish criminal procedure is governed by various laws, the most important of which go back to 1845.[4] The public prosecutor has the initiative in prosecutions. But the Danish Penal Code of 1866 provides that, for certain offenses the prosecution may be exercised by the injured party and in the forms of civil procedure, in cases of slander and minor offenses of violence, for example (§§ 116, 200, 212, 215 to 222, 226, 233). For others the criminal action is subordinated to the complaint of the party injured, for example, in cases of adultery, outrages against morals, petty larceny, etc. (§§ 159, 174, 235, 236, 254, 278).

[1] Review and analysis in "Annuaire de législation étrangère" (1898, vol. 27, pp. 809–817).

[2] A law of 1896 has modified the criminal procedure before justices of the peace ("Annuaire de législation étrangère," 1896, p. 778).

[3] The analysis will be found in the "Bulletin de l'Union internationale de droit pénal," vol. 12, p. 108.

[4] *C. Goos*, "Der danske Straffesproces" (Danish criminal procedure) (Copenhagen, 1880). *C. Goos* must also be credited with the most important work on criminal law which has appeared in Denmark.

There is no jury. The criminal and police tribunal of the lowest grade, regulated, at Copenhagen, by two laws of 28th February, 1845, and 24th May, 1879, is composed of eleven members, a president and ten judges, irremovable, and appointed by the king.[1] Every case must be tried by five magistrates. The tribunal takes cognizance of all penal matters and tries without assessors or jury, whatever may be the gravity of the offense. But every sentence imposing a punishment exceeding a fine of twenty crowns can be carried, by appeal, to the Supreme Court.

(*b*) Sweden is still governed by the Codes of 1734 (civil, penal, and commercial) amended by a series of statutes which have adapted it to existing institutions and conditions.[2]

(*c*) The Norwegian Code of Criminal Procedure of 1st July, 1887, came into force 1st January, 1890. Its chief innovation consists in the introduction of the jury, formerly unknown in Norway, and the adaptation of the procedure to the new institution.[3]

XIV. *Turkey and Egypt.* — The Turkish Code of Criminal Procedure bears date 25th June, 1879. It contains 487 Articles.

Egypt is governed by the Code of 3d November, 1883, amended in 1899.[4] There is little difference between these systems and the French type which served as their model.

The Soudanese Code of Criminal Procedure bears date 2d October, 1899.[5]

XV. *North America.* — The United States of North America are organized as a federal republic. They have two kinds of systems of law, just as they have two kinds of tribunals: the federal laws and the special laws of each State. The Constitution contains the following provision: "The powers not delegated

[1] *P. Dareste,* "Annuaire de législation étrangère," vol. 9, p. 660; *Beauchet,* "Etude sur l'organisation judiciaire dano-norvégienne," "Bull. soc. legisl. comp.," 1884, vol. 13, p. 128.

[2] See *Grasserie,* "Les Codes suédois de 1734," followed by the laws subsequently promulgated down to the present day, translated and annotated (1 vol., 8vo., 1895).

[3] *P. Dareste,* "Annuaire de législation étrangère," vol. 17, p. 711. This Code has been translated into Italian by *Brusa,* "Codice di procedura penale norvegese" (Traduzione, note e ragionamento, Turin 1900). I refer to that work, which is preceded by a remarkable introduction on the history of criminal procedure in Norway and the chief features of the new Code.

[4] Review by *Vidal-Bey,* "Annuaire de législation étrangère," 1884, p. 782. Amendments in 1899, "Annuaire de législation étrangère," 1900, vol. 29, p. 534. The Turkish Code of Criminal Procedure is translated into German in the collection of foreign Codes in the supplement to the "Bulletin de l'Union internationale de droit pénal," Berlin 1905.

[5] Review and analysis in "Annuaire de législation étrangère," 1900, vol. 29, pp. 572–675.

to the United States by the [Federal] Constitution nor prohibited by it to the States are reserved for the latter respectively." In consequence of this provision, the Federal tribunals, the Supreme Court of the United States, and the Circuit and District Courts, have an exclusive criminal jurisdiction over certain offenses, such as high treason against the United States, offenses committed within a Federal territory, etc., and a concurrent jurisdiction with the court of the State where the criminal act was committed over certain offenses, such as counterfeiting and uttering.

The law of the United States is derived from the English system of law, from which it has borrowed its common law and its ancient statutes, so that it was for a long time exclusively composed, as in England, of customary provisions perfected and modified by special statutes. For several years past a movement in the direction of codification has set in in the majority of the States, and now many of them possess either Codes relating to a special branch of law or Codes comprising several matters in juxtaposition. In this way the criminal procedure has been notably codified in the State of New York.[1] Its Code of 1881, which reproduces sufficiently closely the average of the American institutions, may be taken as a type of the system of criminal procedure in that country. In this respect, the laws of the United States show the following variations from those of England: 1st, There is a public prosecutor charged with the prosecution of crimes and misdemeanors in all the States of the Union and in Federal jurisdictions.[2] Before the inferior courts (those not of record) alone is his action optional. 2d, The composition of the grand and the petit jury differs in the two countries, being more democratic in the United States. In the majority of the States the names of the jurors are drawn by lot from a list drawn up by a commission of functionaries and magistrates. In England it is still the sheriff who is charged with choosing the jury of session from a list of persons uniting certain con-

[1] "Code de procédure criminelle de l'Etat de New-York," translated by *André Fournier* (Larosse, 1893).

[2] It is only in this respect that French influence makes itself felt in the criminal legislation of the United States. The insecurity and impunity which, in a new country, and one constituted of different ethnical elements, would have been the consequence of the English system of prosecution, which leaves repression to private initiative, have led the American people, since the end of the 1700s, to intrust to a special functionary the care of prosecuting and of insuring repression. But the attributes relative to the judicial police and to the execution of the judicial decisions have remained foreign to the province of the American public prosecutor. *Fournier* (*op. cit.* p. 9) observes that the imitation was made by taking as a model the office of public prosecutor as it was constituted in the courts of the French Old Régime.

ditions of income, domicile, and capacity, made up by the parish churchwardens and the administrators of the poor law. 3d, The procedure is less formal in the United States than in England. Technical errors in the procedure are immaterial unless they impair the material rights of the defense. A solemn affirmation may be substituted for the oath.

But, apart from these differences, and if we consider the criminal procedure of the United States as a whole, it is the accusatory English system of which this procedure reproduces the type: First, In the preliminary examination, public and confrontative, the accused has the right to the aid of a counsel and need not submit to interrogation; Second, Detention pending trial, reduced to the minimum of severity and duration, cannot be aggravated by the prohibition of communication; Third, The arraignment is directed by a special jury; Fourth, Every person prosecuted in a penal matter has the right, unless he waives it, of trial by jury; Fifth, Witnesses are examined by each party, and the impartiality of the judge is assured by his neutral rôle during the furnishing of the proof; and Sixth, Numerous safeguards are given to the accused, — by the unanimity required to find a verdict of guilty, by prohibiting the character of the accused to be used as evidence against him, by the delay which must take place between the verdict and the sentence, and by the delays in and the nature of the methods of appeal.

XVI. *Latin America.* — The States of Latin America present, in their laws of criminal procedure, numerous varieties, but the points of comparison between them are connected with what these laws derive from the Spanish legal system.

A Penal Code and a Code of Criminal Procedure were promulgated in Venezuela, 14th May, 1897, and came into force 20th February, 1898.[1] The legislative power of the different States and that of the federal district are authorized to adopt the institution of the jury, which is to perform its functions conformably to rules established by the Code of Criminal Procedure.

The Code of Criminal Procedure of Mexico was promulgated on 6th July, 1894.[2] This Code has not modified the procedure; in that part of it relative to the organization and action of the jury it reproduces the law of 24th January, 1891 (Ley de Jurados).

In Bolivia, the existing Code is dated 6th August, 1888. It is

[1] Review and analysis in "Annuaire de législation étrangère," 1898, vol. 27, pp. 963–966.

[2] "Annuaire de législation étrangère," 1895, vol. 24, pp. 946, 947.

really but a revision of the Code of 8th February, 1858. This system reproduces the general outlines of the Spanish system, from which it has borrowed its principal rules.[1]

The Code of Criminal Procedure of the Argentine Republic, adopted 4th October, 1888, came into force 1st January, 1889.[2]

The Code of Ecuador is dated 9th September, 1890.[3]

§ 3. **Chief Features of Prosecution, Examination, and Trial under the Principal European Systems.** — The three chief problems raised by criminal procedure concern the organization and the working either of the *accusation*, the *examination*, or the *trial*. How have these problems been solved by European legal systems?

I. Conformably to the old Germanic saying, "No accuser, no judge,"[4] criminal tribunals are to-day called upon to try only offenses which are submitted to them. In France, "action for the enforcement of punishments belongs only to those functionaries to whom it is committed by law," that is to say, to the public prosecutor (Code Instr. Cr., Art. 1). But the authority of the public prosecutor is limited by the right recognized in the injured parties to go either before the tribunals or the examining magistrate.

This is the system which is almost everywhere recognized among European systems of law. The institution of the public prosecutor, the origin of which is essentially French, has penetrated everywhere. It exists, with inevitable organic differences, in the majority of the nations. Three systems may, however, be taken as typical studies, with respect to the rôle which they reserve for the private parties.

In the German Code, the accusation is, on principle, intrusted to the public prosecutor. But the injured party has no right of action, even in regard to his civil interests, before the criminal courts. He must seek reparation before the civil tribunals for the detriment occasioned to him. There are, however, two principles which tend to limit and show the reason for this peculiar characteristic of the Germanic procedure. The German Code contains a great number of infringements as to which the law leaves the initiative to the injured party or to his legal representatives, according to the opportunity for prosecution, the public

[1] See the succinct analysis made by *H. Prudhomme*, in "Bulletin de l'Union internationale de droit pénal," vol. 12, pp. 148–152.

[2] See *Daireaux et Theurault*, "Annuaire de législation étrangère," 1888, p. 1042.

[3] *Henri Prudhomme*, "Ann. de légis., etc.," 1890, p. 973.

[4] "Wo kein Kläger ist, ist kein Richter."

prosecutor having no right to act except in so far as his intervention has been requested by the victim. The injured party can also join his action with the criminal action when the law gives him the right to demand a composition (Basse). This composition or compensation is a pecuniary reparation of a special nature differing from both damages and fine; from damages, inasmuch as it is not commensurate with the injury, and can only be demanded from the guilty party in connection with the punishment and within the limits of a maximum fixed by the law; from fine, inasmuch as it does not belong to the Treasury, but to the injured party, and cannot, in case of non-payment, be converted into imprisonment.

In Austria, although the public prosecutor is the principal representative of the prosecution, he is not the exclusive representative. Two principles limit his power. The prosecution may be maintained by the injured person in a great number of cases (Art. 16 *et seq.*). Further, the Code of 1873 admits of the private subsidiary prosecution, that is to say, in case of the abandonment of the criminal action by the public prosecutor, the right in the injured party to take it up in place of the public prosecutor and move for the application of the punishment (Art. 48). Finally, the public prosecutor or the private accuser is master of his action in the double sense that he can directly avail himself of the trial court without reference to a magistrate of examination at all (Art. 207), and that, after having done so, he can abandon his accusation and divest the judge. These are the characteristic features of the Austrian procedure in respect of the participation of private individuals in the criminal accusation.

In Spain, the public prosecutors, or fiscals, "representantes del ministerio fiscale," have other powers than those in France in regard to the bringing of the criminal action. But, on one hand, the Spanish Code allows the private accusation for certain misdemeanors, such as calumny, insult, and certain offenses against morals, and directs the public prosecutor to join with the injured party. On the other hand, apart from these exceptions, the action aiming at the repression of punishable acts is free to all; any citizen in the enjoyment of the plenitude of civil rights may bring it. Society does not remain supine in the face of the habitual inertia of mere interested parties. Its representative, the public prosecutor, or fiscal, is free to institute prosecutions whenever it appears to him to be proper to do so. The Spanish practitioners whom we have been able to consult declare that it is, in fact, always the fiscal who prosecutes.

The institution of the public prosecutor was historically lacking in England. "When an offense has been committed, no official can assume the right to take into his hands the interests of menaced society. But every private person, injured or not, has the right to prosecute. Nobody can be restrained from constituting himself accuser, save with rare exceptions, and, on their side, the magistrates cannot prosecute unless a formal accusation has been drawn up."[1] Until very recent times the attempts to constitute a public prosecutor in England have failed, and the attorney-general and his assistant, the solicitor-general, had no function in criminal justice.

[[2]The director of public prosecutions is an official appointed by the government, whose duty it is, under the superintendence of the attorney-general, to institute or carry on criminal proceeding in cases which appear to him to be of importance or advise persons concerned in such proceedings; and to appear for the Crown in criminal appeals.

The office of director of public prosecutions was created by the "Prosecution of Offenses Act," October, 1879, which defines his duties and powers as follows: "It shall be the duty of the director of public prosecutions, under the superintendence of the attorney-general, to institute, undertake or carry on such criminal proceedings (whether in the Court for Crown Cases Reserved, before sessions of oyer and terminer or of the Peace, before magistrates, or otherwise), and to give such advice and assistance to chief officers of police, clerks to justices, and other persons, whether officers or not, concerned in any criminal proceeding respecting the conduct of that proceeding, as may be for the time being prescribed by regulations under this act or may be directed in a special case by the attorney-general."

In certain cases it is the settled duty of the director of public prosecutions to institute and carry on the prosecution: (1) Murder.—By the regulations of January 25, 1886, made under the Prosecution of Offenses Acts, 1879 and 1884, it is the duty of the director of public prosecutions to prosecute in cases of murder. (2) Bankruptcy Offenses. — By 46 & 47 Vict., c. 52, s. 166, "Where the court orders the prosecution of any one for an offense under the Debtors Act, 1869, or Acts amending it, or for any offense arising out of or connected with any bankruptcy

[1] *Glasson, op. cit.*, t. 6, p. 724.

[2] [From the report of *Edwin R. Keedy* and *John D. Lawson*, published in the American Journal of Criminal Law and Criminology, 1910, Vol. I, p. 607. — ED.]

proceedings, it shall be the duty of the director of public prosecutions to institute and carry on the prosecution." (3) Corrupt and Illegal Practices. — By 46 & 47 Vict., c. 51, s. 45, it is the duty of the director of public prosecutions to institute any prosecution for any corrupt or illegal practice in reference to any election.

The consent of the director of public prosecutions is required in prosecutions for incest, and for being an habitual criminal; and the Criminal Appeal Act requires him to appear for the Crown on appeals to the Court of Criminal Appeal.]

The types of the public prosecutor which exist in Scotland and Ireland offer certain analogies to the French organization. Scotland has for a long time possessed an official prosecution so strongly constituted that the private accusation is a thing of the past.[1] Ireland has an attorney-general, assisted by crown solicitors, whose functions are permanent.

The majority of the United States of America have a public prosecution represented by an attorney-general and official district attorneys, who remain members of the bar.

II. The majority of the European States find a place in their systems of laws for the preliminary examination.

This procedure has its origin in the idea that it is necessary to submit to the trial tribunals only those accusations sound in fact and in law, and to guarantee the individual liberty of the accused by raising a barrier against prosecution. Introduced by the French Code of 1808, this procedure has made remarkable progress in penal legislation. It has passed into the majority of the Codes of Continental Europe, and for more than half a century has been considered a triumph of juridical wisdom. For several years a very strong scientific current appears to have set against it. On the one hand, the objection is raised to the obligatory and absolute principle of control of the accusation by the judicial power, and the practical impossibility for the magistrates to make a conscientious study of the record. On the other hand, it is maintained

[1] On this organization see *J. Dove Wilson*, "Bulletin de l'Union internationale de droit pénal," t. 11, pp. 71–73: "The prosecution of crimes in Scotland belongs to the public prosecutor and is made at the State's expense. When the public prosecutor takes up the matter, the complainant has no right to bring a complaint in a criminal court. If the public prosecutor should refuse to interfere, the complainant has the right to prosecute. It is very seldom, however, that a complainant exercises this right, and, in the course of a long experience, I have never seen it exercised successfully."

that the prosecution is impeded and that the responsibilities are scattered, without any tangible benefit to the accused.[1]

In France, the examination is obligatory in criminal matters, and optional in correctional matters; it has no place in police offenses. This distinction between the small and the great degrees of criminality is generally accepted, with differences of detail in its application. In Germany, for example, matters within the jurisdiction of the lay assessors' courts are not subject to any preliminary examination. The procedure of preliminary examination is, on the other hand, obligatory when prosecutions before the Assize Court or the tribunal of the empire are concerned. In the matter of infringements amenable to the district courts, an information can be filed when the public prosecutor makes a request for it or when the accused demands a judicial inquiry in the interest of the defense. The court may also, contrary to the rule in France, order the filing of an information (Art. 200). In Austria, the preliminary examination is not obligatory unless a crime of which the Assize Court should take cognizance is concerned (Art. 91).

The majority of the Codes distinguish and endeavor to separate the preliminary inquiry conducted by the police, from the examination, properly so called, confided to the court. In all the countries of the European continent, the latter function is in the hands of a judge, a member of the court of first instance. The examining judge is invested with the most extensive powers to hear the witnesses, to interrogate the accused, to make inspections on the spot, to order domiciliary searches and seizures, to proceed with the arrest of the accused and to put him in the hands of the law. But by what appropriate institutions is the exercise of these formidable powers, which it is essential to give to the examining judge and to the public prosecutor at this stage of the procedure, to be limited and controlled? It might be thought at the outset, by the safeguard offered by the publicity of the examination. None of the Continental Codes sanctions this. The Aus-

[1] The development of these criticisms may be studied in the following works: *Romagnosi*, "Progetto del codice di procedura penale pel cessato regno d'Italia," 4th ed., 1838; "Ultime aggiunte e riforme al progetto," p. 251. — *Glaser*, "Ueber besetzung in Anklagestand" in "Kleine Schriften über Strafrecht und Strafprozess," 2d ed., 1883, XVII, pp. 437–520. — *Bar*, "Recht und Beweis in Geschwornengericht," p. 152. — *Carrara*, "Opuscoli," t. 6, p. 440. — *Casorati*, "Il processo penale e le riforme," 1881, VII; "Il giudizio di accusa e le riforme," 1881, VII. — *Cesarini*, Rivista penale, 1879, p. 300. — *Manducca e Vacca*, "La procedura penale e la sua evoluzione scientifica," 1888, p. 23. — *Alimena*, Rivista penale, vol. 37, 1893, p. 125.

trian Code mentions only the publicity of the trial proper (Art. 228). The secrecy of the examination has been preserved in Germany. The Codes of Friburg and of Valais declare, in categorical terms, that the records of the examination shall not be public. In Geneva, the draft of the Code of Criminal Examination, presented in 1884, introduced complete publicity into the procedure of examination. But this proposal was rejected. In Neuchâtel, the Code of 1893 left to the examining judge the option between publicity and the closed door, giving him the choice, in every case, of the method most favorable for the discovery of the truth.

The most effectual method of protecting the accused from the abuses of this examination is to grant him the aid of a counsel capable of enlightening him as to his rights, of putting him on his guard against the snares which may be laid for him, and of suggesting to him the course to take and the pleas to urge. The French Law of 8th December, 1897, effected, from this point of view, a long-demanded reform; it effected it by measures which place the French system of law in the vanguard of progressive legislation. But we must note that in Austria, since 1873, the accused has been authorized, even during the examination, to choose a counsel "either to take care of the preservation of his rights at each stage of the proceedings which directly concerns the establishment of the fact and which cannot be taken up later, or to pursue his appeal already lodged by him" (Art. 45). The counsel cannot, it is true, take part in the interrogation of the accused, nor in the hearing of the witnesses, but the law expressly gives him the right to the inspection of documents (Art. 45).

The German Code authorizes the accused to have the assistance of a counsel from the filing of the information (Art. 137); it even allows the judge to appoint one of his own accord when the accused has neglected to choose one himself (Art. 142). At the same time, this counsel has only a very barren rôle. He can take part neither in the interrogation of the accused (Art. 190) nor in the hearing of the witnesses (Art. 191). His rights consist in the power to assist, either alone or with the accused, in some subsequent steps of the proceedings. The complete record cannot be shown to him unless the judge deems that its production is without inconvenience in regard to the purpose intended to be reached (Art. 147). In Switzerland, the Codes are divided. Those of Friburg and Valais refuse a counsel to the accused as long as the examination lasts. The codes of Vaud, Neuchâtel, and

Geneva allow a defense more or less completely during the examination. In Russia, the preliminary examination, in its chief features, reproduces the French procedure, as that existed before the Law of 9th December, 1897. The examining judge must make the inquiry, whether he has been apprized by the police, or by a complaint of the victim, or by a requisition of the public prosecutor. The procedure of this examination is secret. Assistance in the defense is not allowed. The plan of reform of the Russian statute of Criminal Examination of 1864 as regards confrontation is allied with the system of the Austrian Code of 1873 and not with that of the French Law of 1897.

A last counterbalance to excessive powers of the examining judge consists in the establishment of tribunals of examination distinct from and independent of the judge, and charged either with supervising the acts of examination or with weighing the results of it. Three chief systems exist and find expression in present-day systems of law. The first is independence and autonomy of the examining judge, both in the course of the examination and at its close. That is the system of examination, of the indictment by the same judge who has conducted it. The second is independence of the judge in the course of the examination, but reviews of the indictment by a special tribunal. That is the system followed in all the Swiss Codes of the French-speaking cantons. The third is control of the judge both in the course of the examination and the completion of the proceedings by an independent tribunal. That is the system of the German and Austrian Codes.

But this last system, under the scientific influence of Glaser, contains, in this respect, a measure which appears to reconcile happily the different interests which conflict in the examination. It discards the proceeding, obligatory among almost all the Continental nations, of sanctioning the indictment bench court. This function is assigned, as the rule, to the public prosecutor; the approval of the indictment by a department of the Court of Appeal does not exist, except in case of objection by the accused to the indictment of the public prosecutor. A consequence of this new feature is the disappearance of the defects of the French type often pointed out. The court is reinstated in its natural judicial rôle, which consists in being arbiter in a dispute between the accuser and the accused. This new system has been adopted by the Hungarian Code of Procedure of 1896, and by the Tessin Code of 1865.

The English procedure is entirely different from that of the Continent. In England there is no examining judge, and no secrecy. The police before the courts are in the same position as any party complainant; they are put upon the same footing as private individuals. Every individual arrested must be taken before the magistrate, who, as an impartial arbiter between the prosecution and the defense, inquires into nothing by himself. In order to understand the method of conducting the action, it is necessary to distinguish summary from indictable causes. The former are remitted directly, without other examination than that made by the complainant, to courts of petty session, or in certain towns, to police courts, and tried at one sitting, without preliminary examination. The latter, the indictable causes, so called because they cannot be tried except on information (indictment), are taken indifferently before the courts of petty session or the police courts, which play the part of magistrate of examination. These courts hear the witnesses, interrogate the accused, and collect the facts. All this is done publicly, after hearing of parties. The records of the proceedings are written out by the clerks of the courts, signed by the witnesses, and sent, with the indictment, to the Court of Assizes.[1]

There is not at the present day any examining magistrate in Scotland.[2] The mechanism for criminal prosecutions consists of the public prosecutor and the criminal courts. There are in the Scottish counties several functionaries known as "procurators fiscal," who are really king's procurators. The public prosecutors attached to the various courts are almost invariably solicitors; some of them are advocates. With the exception of the chief, the Lord Advocate, and his staff, who must resign their offices with every political change, the king's procurators are irremovable and hold office "ad vitam aut culpam." To the public prosecutor belongs the duty of collecting the evidence, and the practice is invariably to make this examination as much for the defense as

[1] Upon all these points, see *Glasson, op. cit.*, t. 6, p. 754; *Mittermaier, op. cit.*, pp. 81–109; *Guérin*, "Etude sur la procédure criminelle en Angleterre et en Écosse," 1890. The interesting particulars furnished on the subject of the English procedure of examination by *Sir Howard Vincent* (at one time chief of criminal police in London and author of "The Police Code," now in its twelfth edition) to the Congress of the International Union of St. Petersburg (Bull. de l'Un., 1903, pp. 176–182 and 204) may be referred to. [And see the report of *Edwin R. Keedy* and *John D. Lawson*, above cited 589.—ED.]

[2] [On this see the report of *Edwin R. Keedy*, above cited. There is at least a private official examination corresponding to the French system in principle.—ED.]

for the prosecution. The Lord Advocate decides, upon the papers which are transmitted to him by the public prosecutor, upon the propriety of prosecution, and determines at the same time, according to the maximum punishment which he considers should be inflicted, whether the case should be taken before the Supreme Court, or before the sheriff or a jury, or whether it should be tried summarily. There is no appeal possible against the decision of the Lord Advocate in any case, either for or against the prosecution. The only recourse admitted is political, before Parliament.

III. The trend of the trial procedure, in the various European countries, is shown rather by common characteristics than by essential differences. Evolution occurs everywhere in the following directions. First, The separation, into several groups, of courts and procedures, corresponding to the different groups of offenses; but equality of all persons accused before the penal law and procedure. Second, The introduction and development of the jury summoned to sit beside or with the professional magistrates. The jury exists in nearly every country of Europe and America. There may be mentioned, as exceptions, the Netherlands, where even felonies are tried by provincial courts composed of magistrates who have not taken part in the examination, and the Scandinavian countries, which are opposed to the institution of the jury.[1] Third, Publicity, confrontation, oral testimony. In every country, in Germany, England, Austria, Belgium, Portugal, etc., the trials are public or else are void. The rule universally followed is that the witnesses shall testify orally. Finally, The trial is confrontative; the accuser and the accused must be placed on an equal footing; the aid of a defending counsel is universally provided for.

IV. In minor cases, and notably in cases of trivial misdemeanors or contraventions, the general tendency is to simplify the procedure in order to make repression more expeditious and less costly.[2] The different methods of simplification adopted by existing legislation are divided into the three following systems: First, Summary procedure by immediate appearance; Second,

[1] In Denmark, except in Copenhagen, it is only when the pronouncement of the capital sentence is involved that the judge must be assisted by four jurors having a deliberative voice. *Beauchet*, "Bull. de la Soc. de législ. comp.," vol. 13, p. 133. In Norway the Code of Penal Procedure of 1st July, 1887, introduced the jury for the first time. In Sweden the jury exists for press offenses only.

[2] See, on this point, *Tcheglovitov*, "La procédure en matière de contraventions" ("Bull. de l'Un. inter. de droit pénal," vol. 10, 1902, p. 352–365).

The release of the criminal action by the voluntary payment of the fine with which the delinquent is threatened; Third, Penal orders without judicial procedure.

(1) The first system relies upon a procedure which is distinguished from the ordinary procedure only by its rapidity; the accused appears without citation, on mere notice, or even by being immediately brought to the bar of the tribunal. The French law knows and practises two institutions which have this character and this aim of simplification; — the procedure of capture in the act and the appearance before the police tribunal on mere notice.

The two other methods dispense with all prosecution before the tribunals, in default of any objection in case the accused fails to file exception to the decision.

(2) Voluntary payment of the fine is not recognized in French law, except in the matter of fiscal torts, indirect taxes, customs duties, etc., in which the legal fine may be modified by the department interested, which has the right to compromise before judgment. The Penal Code of the Netherlands contains a provision, Article 74, sanctioning the abandonment of the criminal action on payment by the accused of the maximum fine which he would have incurred on account of the incriminating act. All judicial procedure becomes practically useless in this case, since the guilty party submits to the full rigor of the law. But this system would not be practicable were it not permissible for the public prosecutor or the judge to compromise, before every judgment, by making the prisoner who confesses his guilt pay a sum regulated according to the circumstances of the case.

(3) On this conception depends also an institution which has no analogy in the French legislation, that of penal orders ("Mandatsverfahren"), by which the judge convicts the accused without hearing him and without prior proceedings. This summary method has been borrowed by the Austrian Code of 1873 from the old Codes of several German States. By the terms of § 460 of the Code of 1873, when an information has been filed against an accused who is at liberty charging an offense punishable by imprisonment for a month at most, or merely by a fine, the judge may, if he finds that there is no cause for an imprisonment of more than three days or for a penalty exceeding fifteen florins, pronounce, by a penal order ("Strafverfügung"), the penalty incurred, on the petition of the public prosecutor, without prior proceedings. A right of objection to the order of the judge is reserved to the

convicted person if he on his part prefers that the forms and guarantees of the ordinary procedure be observed. This system has been generalized in Germany, by the Code of the Empire of 1877, § 447 of which reads as follows: "In matters which are within the cognizance of the aldermanic courts, the judge of the 'amt' may, without preliminary trial, and when the public prosecutor shall request it in writing, pronounce a judgment by a written penal order. No other punishment may be inflicted by penal order than the maximum fine of one hundred and fifty marks, the deprivation of liberty for not more than six weeks, and, in a proper case, confiscation." The right of objection to the penal order is regulated by §§ 449 to 452.

The system of penal orders is in operation in several cantons of Switzerland, among others, in those of Soleure (Code of Criminal Procedure of 1866, Art. 388) and of Glarus (Code of Criminal Procedure of 1899, Arts. 171 to 186). It has been adopted by the Hungarian Code of 1896 (Arts. 532 to 535), and by the Norwegian Code of 1887 (Arts. 287 to 290). In Norway penal orders are issued by the public prosecutor. There is a question of the introduction of the system of penal orders into Italy, Russia, and Denmark. This procedure, the chief advantage of which is to allow the accused to avoid public trial, is much esteemed in the countries in which it is in practice. Provided the privilege of recourse to the ordinary procedure is reserved to the convicted person, this system would not appear to be out of harmony with the fundamental principles of criminal procedure.

APPENDICES

APPENDIX A[1]

THE SCIENTIFIC LITERATURE OF CRIMINAL PROCEDURE

§ 1. **Two Eras in the Literary History of the Science of Criminal Procedure, before and after the Code of Criminal Examination of 1808.** — Two extensive eras in the history of the scientific literature of criminal procedure are easily distinguishable. The first ends and the second begins with the promulgation of the French Code of Criminal Examination. Its appearance in France and the spread of its influence throughout Europe mark a decisive date.

Criminal law has really been scientifically studied only since the beginning of the 1700s. Before that time the right of society to punish appeared to be so evident that the search for the grounds of the right and the reasonable regulation of its exercise were not thought of. The sources utilized for criminal law as well as for criminal procedure prior to the French Revolution were customary law, Roman law, Canon law, and the royal Ordinances. All these sources became blended in the teaching of the criminalists, and the result of their fusion, constituting scientific criminal law, made possible and paved the way for the work of codification.

§ 2. **The Writers of the First period, prior to the Code. Glossators, Practitioners, and Forerunners.** — The writers of the first period may be classed chronologically in three categories: the *Glossators*, the *Practitioners*, and the *Forerunners*.

I. The first Glossators, who studied criminal law as a branch of civil law, contented themselves with applying to the portions of Justinian relative to criminal matters, — Books 47 and 48 of the

[1] [Appendix A = § X of Professor GARRAUD's "French Criminal Procedure." For this author and work, see the Editorial Preface. — ED.]

Pandects and Book 9 of his Code, — the methods of interpretation which have earned for them the name of Glossators. After a short gloss or commentary on the text, more or less correctly comprehended, they coördinated it with the edicts of the kings, the local customary laws, and the rules of judicial practice. These fragmentary studies produced some results, the credit for which is traceable to the Roman laws. Their labors produced some fortunate mistakes, by which the progress of juridical science profited.

It is sufficient to mention, among the Glossators, PLACENTINUS,[1] AZO,[2] ROFREDUS,[3] and ACCURSIUS.[4] Rofredus is probably the one among the Romanists whose influence was the most decisive on the evolution of criminal procedure. In his "Libelli de jure pontifico" he shows that the method of inquisitorial procedure was derived from the Roman law and that Innocent III had but regulated its form. These doctrinary assertions helped, at a time when the revived Roman law aroused a widespread enthusiasm, to bring about the adoption of the inquisitorial procedure by the secular courts. Among the canonists of the 1100s who treated of criminal law, it is enough to mention TANCREDUS,[5] and WILHELMUS DURANDUS,[6] whose "Speculum juris," written about 1271, was a recognized authority among the ecclesiastical and secular tribunals. It is from this work, his chief title to the extraordinary reputation which he enjoyed at that period, that Wilhelmus Durandus acquired his surname of "Speculator."

II. In the latter half of the 1200s the study of criminal law begins to assume its due importance. Criminal law becomes a branch distinct from civil law; then a generation of jurists arise who collect, under the titles of "Praxis," "Practica," "Libellus," and "Summa," the customary laws and write manuals of practice in which the criminal law and the procedure are seldom separated. The oldest collection exclusively devoted to

[1] Placentinus came from Italy to be professor at Montpellier, where he died in 1492.

[2] Azo, who died not later than about 1230, taught at Bologna, and afterwards at Montpellier.

[3] Rofredus died in 1242.

[4] Accursius, professor at Bologna, died in that town in 1260. He is the author of the Glossa ordinaria of all the law of Justinian.

[5] Tancredus of Bologna wrote several works at the beginning of the 1200s. Chief of these is a work on canonical procedure which was translated, after the 1200s, into French and German, the "Ordo judiciarius."

[6] Died at Rome in 1296.

this branch of criminal practice is the "Libellus de maleficiis" of ALBERTUS DE GANDINO.[1]

It was in Italy, which remained the classic land of criminal law, that this particular literature had its birth and development. Very soon its influence spread throughout Spain, France, Germany, and the Netherlands. Down to the latter half of the 1500s the manuals of ALBERTUS DE GANDINO, of JACOBUS DE BELVISIO,[2] of ANGELUS ARETINUS,[3] and of HIPPOLYTUS DE MARSILIIS [4] were authoritative before the tribunals of all these countries.

PHILIPPE DE BEAUMANOIR,[5] of whom Loysel said, "He it was who broke the ice and opened the way," represents the secular science in the 1200s. First of all the jurists, he draws an outline of the whole of the civil and customary law. Beaumanoir gives few explanations of the criminal procedure, because, at the period when he wrote, this procedure did not differ essentially from the civil procedure. The same tribunals and the same judges pronounced in all litigations, and as the penal law was not well settled, they had an almost arbitrary power, not only to vary the punishment, but also to adapt the forms of the procedure to circumstances. The only customs regulated with any certainty were the two confrontative procedures, — the judicial combat and the inquisition, — the first of which represented the old ways and was on the decline, while the other expressed the new ideas and ways. At that period of transition, the work of Beaumanoir is valuable in making us acquainted with the institutions of the time.

The works of the criminalists of the end of the 1500s felt the beneficial influence of the Renaissance. The art of explaining ideas and coördinating them in their natural order was almost unknown until that time. The authors presented their thoughts as these offered themselves to their minds, without method or logical sequence. Starting with the end of the 1500s, it is no longer mere collections of usages and manuals of legal practice

[1] This treatise, printed for the first time at Venice, in 1491, was afterwards added to the "Tractatus maleficiorum" of Aretinus. It appears to have been written about 1262.

[2] This jurisconsult, born 1270, died 1355, is the author of a "Practica judiciaria in materiis criminalibus," printed at Lyons in 1515.

[3] Author of "De Maleficiis tractatus," printed at Lyons in 1551. Neither the date of his birth nor that of his death is exactly known. He lived in the first half of the 1400s.

[4] Author of the "Practica causarum criminalium," born 1450, died 1529.

[5] "Les Coutumes du Beauvoisis," by *Philippe de Beaumanoir*, French jurisconsult of the 1200s (new edition published by Count Beugnot, 2 vols. 8°, Paris, Renouard, 1842). *Beugnot's* preface (cxxxi pages) is still of interest.

which see the light of day, but scientific treatises, that is to say, systematic essays on the sources. Among the Italian jurisconsults, who were the true founders of scientific criminal law, must be mentioned especially two names: that of JULIUS CLARUS,[1] who was the most noted criminalist of his age, and that of FARINACIUS,[2] whose scientific reputation has probably been exaggerated, but whose influence upon the direction of the procedure was only too real and too decisive.

The first treatise on criminal law published outside of Italy was written by a Belgian practitioner, JODOCUS DAMHOUDER. His "Praxis rerum criminalium," [3] the most important part of which is devoted to procedure, served as a guide for a long time to the practice of the tribunals in the Netherlands and in Germany.

But in the 1600s, the authority of a German, BENEDICT CARPZOV, supersedes and effaces that of Damhouder, Farinacius, and even of Julius Clarus. His "Practica nova imperialis Saxonica rerum criminalium in partes tres divisa," first published at Würtemberg, in 1635, served as a guide to German practice and legislation for more than a century.

Treatises on criminal law were published from that time during the 1700s in constant succession for the methodical exposition of the procedure; but their authors did not cease to write them with an eye to legal practice. They confined themselves to explaining the laws, customs, and usages which governed the punishment and the forms of procedure, and to synthesizing the law derived from these sources, without thinking of examining, in a rational way, the problems which brought the institutions into force, or criticising the abuses of the inquisitorial procedure.

The criminalists most in vogue in the 1700s and whose works may still be consulted with profit are: JOUSSE [4] and MUYART DE

[1] Born in 1525 at Alexandria, Italy; died in 1573. We owe to him the "Sententiarum receptarum," in 5 books, of which the fifth book, the most important and the largest, is devoted to criminal law. This work has often been reprinted.

[2] The "Opera Omnia" of this jurisconsult have often been reprinted. He was born in 1554 and died in 1613. Farinacius has a heavy, solid intellect. The seven folio volumes in Latin which comprise his works are rather difficult to read.

[3] This work was printed for the first time at Bruges in 1551, but of this edition no trace remains. Damhouder himself translated it into French under the title "Pratiques judiciaires ès causes criminelles" (Anvers 1574, 12mo).

[4] *Jousse*, collaborator with and friend of Pothier, his colleague at the presidial of Orléans, author of the "Traité de la justice criminelle de France," 4 vols., 4to, 1671. This work is not very original, but it is very complete, methodical, and clear. A perusal of the preface well affords an idea of the mentality of a criminalist of the time of the Revolution.

VOUGLANS[1] in France; RENAZZI and CREMANI, in Italy; and SAMUEL FREDERIC BUCHMER in Germany.[2] These, magistrates or professors, were men of peace living in the midst of a stirring age; preoccupied only with the established legal system, they knew nothing of the great advance of ideas which was taking place around them; they had no presentiment of the revolution which was in preparation. But their works were necessary; they were the systematization of the law in force, and paved the way for the codification which would have been almost impossible without this preliminary labor.

III. The inquisitorial criminal procedure had already been criticised in the 1500s and the 1600s. Some forerunners had proposed its abolition. First must be mentioned PIERRE AYRAULT,[3] who attacks with a sagacious vigor the secrecy of the procedure,[4] and who speaks of having read the description of publicity in criminal actions, made more than one hundred and twenty years before, that is to say, about 1492, by his maternal grand uncle, Jean Belin, Lieutenant-General of Anjou, and who cites in testimony of the publicity the last traces of it which were exercised in France "at the doors of the churches, castles, markets, and public places where the seats of the judges still remain." AUGUSTIN NICOLAS,[5] the Jesuit THÉODORE SPÉE,[6] in the 1600s, protest very courageously and openly against torture.

But, in the latter half of the 1700s, the reformers submit the ancient procedure to critical observation and attempt to extract an ideal of liberty and to lay down a minimum of claim on the part of the prosecution.

[1] *Muyart de Vouglans*, counsellor to the Grand Council at Paris. He took part in the Parlement Maupéon. His two principal works are "Lois criminelles de la France dans leur ordre naturel" and the "Instituts au droit criminel." The law in force appeared to him to be the last word of human reason. He died upon the scaffold.

[2] I do not speak of *Pothier*, who has published, among his little treatises, in which he has with admirable clearness simplified and popularized French law, a "Traité de la procédure criminelle" (reprinted in the Works of Pothier by *Beugnot*, in Vol. X, pp. 387–511). Pothier did not criticise the criminal procedure of his age. We know, however, that when he sat on the Orléans presidial bench in criminal affairs it was the custom to avoid putting before him proceedings in which the question might arise.

[3] Born 1536, died 21 July, 1601.

[4] In "L'ordre, formalité and instruction judiciaire, dont les Grecs et les Romains ont usé ès accusations publiques." The Lyons edition of *Jean Caffin*, 1642, is the best.

[5] *Augustin Nicolas* published a brochure entitled "Si la torture est un moyen sûr à vérifier les crimes secrets." He was president of the Dijon Parlement.

[6] *Spée* published an important work, "Cautio criminalis contra sagas liber," Rhurtel 1631, Cologne 1632. Compare *A. du Boys*, "Histoire du droit criminel de France, depuis le XVIe siècle jusqu'au XIXe," 1874, vol. 2, p. 147 *et seq.*

France and Italy take the lead in the movement. France has VOLTAIRE, SERVAN, and BRISSOT DE WARVILLE; Italy has FILANGIERI, RISI, and chiefly CESARE BECCARIA. In that "fiery pamphlet,"[1] the "Traité des délits et des peines," published in 1764, a notable date in the history of penal law, Beccaria attacks that monstrosity, torture, demands the abolition of secrecy in the examination, and proposes that the accused have a counsel. This programme was so daring that it brought upon its promulgator persecution in Italy.

§ 3. **Writers of the Second Period, subsequent to the Code. Italian, French, and German Writers.** — The later criminalists of the 1700s, by their striving, in their works, after some kind of system, might be ranked among the authors of the second literary period. But it is really only since the promulgation in France and the spread through Europe of the influence of the Code of Criminal Examination of 1808 that a new method of studying and explaining criminal doctrines begins. This corresponds with the new legislative method of codification.

In France the first commentator on the Code of Criminal Examination was CARNOT, Councillor in the Court of Cassation. His treatise, "De l'instruction criminelle," which appeared in 1812,[2] contains an independent interpretation, based on reason alone, of the new Code. Following him, a magistrate, J. M. LEGAVEREND, published a "Traité de la législation criminelle en France,"[3] which is something more than a mere commentary on the authorities. It is a systematic and constructive study of criminal procedure according to the new legislation.

But the greatest work, which in this class of teachings remains to this day a model, the value of which has in no way been surpassed, is the "Traité de l'instruction criminelle" of FAUSTIN HÉLIE. The first volume of this work was published in 1845; the ninth was completed only in 1860. The second edition, in eight volumes, appeared in 1866. No other work has had, during the 1800s, such an influence as this upon the judicial practice of the tribunals and upon the scientific direction of the procedure. Its authority has extended beyond French frontiers, and wherever

[1] *Lerminier* writes very correctly in his "Introduction à l'histoire générale du droit": "Beccaria made, in the 'Traité des délits et des peines' (Naples 1764), not a scientific book, but a fiery pamphlet which pleased the righteous effervescence of opinion. It was a petition which Europe used to present to its sovereigns."

[2] Published by *Nève*, Court of Cassation, 2 vols., small 4to.

[3] This work has reached three editions. The last appeared in 1830 (2 vols., 4to), revised and corrected by *Duvergier*.

the type of procedure systematized by the Code of Criminal Examination of 1808 has penetrated, the work of Faustin Hélie has been acknowledged as its best commentary. The interests of the defense and the guarantees of individual liberty have had no more authoritative and strenuous an interpreter than Faustin Hélie. In a biographical notice, written for the sixth edition of the "Théorie du Code pénal," M. Faustin-Adolphe Hélie declares that his father "attached no importance to any authority." He thought "that democracy ought to develop itself freely and unrestrainedly, without the counterbalance of authority." This bent of mind is detected at the bottom of Faustin Hélie's chief doctrines, and these give to his treatise a liberal and individual character which has not been without influence upon the best impulses of French criminal procedure.

In the first half of the 1800 s, Italy is chiefly represented by two criminalists, CARMIGNANI and NICOLINI; the first more of a philosopher, with his work, where law and procedure are treated together, "Teorica delle leggi della sicurezza sociale":[1] the other, more of a historian and practitioner, with his "Procedura penale nel regno dello due Sicilie." Less illustrious, but not without merit, are CONTOLI, with his "Considerazioni sul processo e giudizio criminale," ADEMOLLO, with "Il giudizio criminale in Toscana," ARMELLINI, with his "Corso di procedura penale." Then the Italian science undergoes an eclipse, and for years presents nothing but some treatises in the form of exegetic commentaries, some studies, and some critical works on legislative reform. The formation of Italian unity begins to give a new impetus to the scientific spirit. FRANCISCO CARRARA, with his "Programma del corso di diritto penale" (Sect. III, Del giudizio criminale),[2] TOLOMEI, with his treatise of "Diritto e procedura penale," PIETRO NOCITO, with the "Prolegomeni alla filosofia del diritto giudiziario penale e civile," CANONICO, with the "Del giudizio penale," ENRICO PESSINA, with the "Sommario di lezioni sul procedimento penale italiano," ZUPPETTA, with the "Sommario delle lezioni di ordinamento giudiziario penale e di codice di procedura penale," PESCATORE, with his "Sposizione compendiosa di procedura civile e criminale," etc., bring to Italian literature interesting contributions. These criminalists belong to the school which sees in the procedure the best guarantee of liberty and which does not consider that the

[1] Pisa, 1831, 4 vols., 8°. *Carmignani*, born 1768, died 1847. He was professor of criminal law at the University of Pisa.

[2] *Carrara* was Carmignani's successor at the University of Pisa.

interests of social defense need suffer by safeguarding the rights of the individual. The Code of Criminal Procedure of 1865 gave birth to a multitude of treatises, in the form of commentaries, among which the most complete and the most reputed are those of SALUTO and BORSANI E CASORATI. We may mention finally, as an interesting attempt to adapt criminal procedure to the new times, the "Principii fondamentali di diritto giudiziario penale"[1] of PUGLIA.

German culture, in the field of procedure, was exercised upon the "Carolina," which governed a great part of Europe down to the beginning of the 1800s. But the German authors cultivated much more assiduously the laws and the special Codes which were promulgated, in the countries of German race, after that period. We may mention, among the criminalists whose works were of note at the beginning of the 1800 s, STUBEL,[2] HENKE, ABEGG,[3] FEUERBACH, BAUER,[4] and, later, BIENER, KOSTLIN, MÖHL, PLANCK, ZACHARIAE, JAGEMANN, MITTERMAIER, and FRÜHWALD.

When the two great States of Germanic race, Austria, in 1873, and Germany, in 1877, codified and unified their criminal procedure, this important event of their juridical life made a point of departure for a period of strenuous scientific life. In Austria must be mentioned, among the notable works, those of ULLMANN, MAYER, BAR, MITTELBACHER, RULF, RIEL, VARGHA, GLASER, etc. The last-mentioned criminalist, who was the inspirer of the Austrian Code of 1873, was commissioned by the élite of German jurisconsults, at whose head was the criminalist, BINDING, to collaborate with DOCHOW, SCHWARZE, GEYER, and MEYER on the first edition of the Encyclopedia of Holtzendorff, and to expound in that work the German Code of Criminal Procedure of 1877. Other names should be added to this list. The commentaries and text books of LÖWE, JOHN, DOCHOW, GEYER, VON LISZT, and BENNECKE have become classics in Germany.

[1] Milan 1899.

[2] "Das criminalverfahren in dem deutschen Gerichten bis im Sachsen" (Leipzig 1811).

[3] "Lehrbuch des gem. Criminal-Prozesses" (Königsberg 1833).

[4] "Anleitung z. Criminalpraxis" (Göttingen 1837).

APPENDIX B[1]

HISTORY OF THE CONTINENTAL SYSTEM OF EVIDENCE

§ 1. **Three Points of View from which Evidence must be considered.** — Evidence must be considered from three points of view: —

First, As to its sources (elements of evidence).

Second, As to the method of its research and manifestation (methods of proof).

Third, As to its demonstrative value (probative force).

§ 2. **Historic Evolution of the System of Evidence. Four Phases.** — Historically, the evolution of the system of evidence corresponds very closely with that of the system of punishments. This evolution may be followed through the four phases through which evidence appears to have passed, the *ethnical* phase, the *religious* phase, the *legal* phase, and the *scientific* phase.[2]

[1] [Appendix B = § XLVI of Professor GARRAUD's "French Criminal Procedure." For this author and work, see the Editorial Preface. — ED.]

[2] *Ferri* especially has pointed out, in the evolution of the probatory system, the four distinct and characteristic stages almost parallel with the successive stages of the penal system: "Sociologie criminelle," trans. by *Terrier*, 1905, No. 76, p. 515. See to the same effect, *Tarde*, "Penal Philosophy" (trans. *Howell*, Modern Criminal Science Series, Little, Brown & Co. 1912), p. 429, and especially p. 484. "In fact," says Tarde, "there exists a bond, during each phrase of legal evolution, between the nature of the proof which 'gives their tone' to the others and the character with which the penalty has a tendency to clothe itself. I have distinguished four species of proofs which have been, or are beginning to be, in vogue: ordeals, torture, the jury, scientific expert testimony. Now to the first of these corresponds a penalty which is *expiatory:* so much so that the offering of a victim to the gods sometimes dispensed with a capital execution.

The *ethnical* phase, — during which, in the primitive groups, then in the city itself, a familial criminal law exists side by side with an interfamilial criminal law. Within the family the right to punish is founded at one and the same time upon the lawfulness of paternal correction, upon the utility of intimidation, and upon the necessity of social defense. From one family to another and from one group to another the relations of primitive hostility are felt. There is no culpability for acts of fraud or violence. Only the individual and his family are exposed to the law of retaliation.[1] In this period evidence is abandoned to "the empiricism of personal impressions."[2] Capture in the act is the type of the procedure; and capture in the act dispenses with the necessity for any proof. The thing is then to establish it or its equivalent.

The *religious* phase, — during which the sentences are pronounced in the name of the gods. It is to the gods that their execution is abandoned in the most serious cases, so much so that the divinity — "the judgment of God" — is invoked to point out the perpetrator of a wrong, as it is invoked to punish the delinquent. The judgment of God, or *ordeal,* considered the judgment "par excellent," is a universal institution.[3] In a certain stage of social and religious development, the belief exists that the best way to end a litigation or determine a question of guilt is to expose at least one of the parties in the cause, sometimes even both,

To the second, that is to torture, corresponds a penalty which is essentially one of intimidation and which is *exemplary:* the wheel, quartering, burning at the stake, tortures which are more horrible than ever. To the third, that is to proof by means of the popular conscience, by the jury, corresponds a penalty which is mild and pretendedly *correctional.* Finally, what is the penalty which is going to correspond to the fourth, to proof by dogmatized science, that is, to expert testimony? Is it not a penalty, before every thing *sanitary . . .?"*

[1] See particularly as to what relates to the old Greek customs, *Gustave Glotz,* "Études sociales et juridiques sur l'antiquité grecque" (Hachette 1906), pp. 3–9.

[2] *Ferri, op. et loc. cit.*

[3] See *Glotz, op. cit.,* "L'Ordalie," p. 69–97. "From France to Polynesia, from the Scandinavian regions to the confines of Africa, there is probably no country in the world where, to prosecute one's right or prove one's innocence, one may not submit himself to a mortal test. It may be an ordeal, by boiling water or by cold water, by fire or by poison. . . . The idea which is manifested in this formidable and hallowed procedure is plainly manifest in a preliminary rite: At the supreme moment, those who call on heaven to intercede, especially he whose body is going to be put to the test, offer a prayer, a direct and formal appeal to divine providence. Among those societies where the priesthood is the prerogative of a caste, it is the man of God who comes forward to make the solemn invocation. Among those having no priesthood caste, it is the culprit who makes use of an analogous formula." See *Kovalevsky,* "Coutume contemporaine et loi ancienne," pp. 397, 398.

to some very serious danger and thus to compel the divinity to play the part of justice. "Ordeals," according to Tarde,[1] "are to a certain extent the divine-legal expert testimony of the past."[2]

The *legal* phase, — where the law itself determines in advance the different methods of proof, as well as the degree of proof necessary or sufficient to warrant a punishment. It is in this period that the confession of the culprit is held to be the "*queen of proofs*," and that, to obtain it, that method of interrogation is employed — torture — which has appeared so natural and necessary that it was called "the question."

The *sentimental* phase, — in which, going to the other extreme, the conscience of judge and juror is relieved of all responsibility as to the proof, by referring him to his own personal opinion, that is, to the approval of his conscience.[3]

The *scientific* phase, — in which the proof "par excellence" is to be furnished by *expert inquiry* and will aim at the methodical search for and weighing of the experimental data of nature to establish the doing of the wrongful acts and of the diverse individual and social factors which have produced its existence. The expert will become the successor of the juror, and the scientific management of the evidence will consist in extending, regulating, perfecting, and directing the judicial qualifications of the expert.

It is the third phase that present-day legal systems have reached, with a tendency, becoming more and more marked in legal practice, to utilize scientific means to arrive at the speedy and certain detection of criminals and to diminish the terrible number of crimes unpunished and criminals undetected.[4]

[1] "Penal Philosophy," p. 430.

[2] *Tarde* adds: "They correspond to the mythological phase of the human mind, just as our actually existing expert testimony has begun to correspond to its scientific phase, which is just beginning to come into existence."

[3] *Tarde* (*op. cit.*, p. 431) sees in this system the consequence of "another superstition, the optimistic faith in the infallibility of individual reason, of common sense, of natural instinct." He calls moral proof, "proof by jury," "an assumed revelation of the truth by a non-enlightened and unreasoning conscience." "Proof by jury ought to have been conceived of," he adds, "during the century in which the verdict of common sense served as a foundation not only for the Scottish philosophy, but for every philosophy, and in France suggested the dogma of the sovereignty of the people."

[4] One of those scientific processes, and that which has rendered the greatest of services in the discovery, either of the identity of prisoners, or of their antecedents, is the system of criminal anthropometry. The first idea of this process is due to *Quetelet*, director of the Observatoire and perpetual secretary of the Belgian Royal Academy, who, in 1871, published the work entitled "Anthropométrie ou mesure des différentes facultés de l'homme." This idea was applied and utilized by *M. Alphonse Bertillon*,

§ 3. **The Two Principal Systems. Legal Proofs and Moral Proofs.** — The two chief systems of evidence, the system of legal proofs, which is a thing of the past, and that of moral proofs, which is now in force, have successively appeared in modern Europe. They are in contrast to each other as two contrary types.

The first consists not merely in defining the means of searching for and establishing the guilt, which is indispensable in every law of procedure, but in holding it as demonstrated by the conjunction of certain circumstances, the union of which necessarily entails the persuasion of the judge, and in the absence of which he should declare himself not convinced. The second consists in proving a fact by all the methods proper to establish its existence, and in leaving the judge entirely free to declare that he is convinced or not convinced.

No legal rule can measure beforehand the value of each proof. The independent impression made on the conscience of the judge by the oral examination and cross-examination, in a word, the fact that he is thoroughly convinced, is the only criterion which the law should recognize when it has confidence in the judges whom it appoints.[1] But it is necessary to lay down legal rules to govern either the process of the search for proofs in the preliminary examination, or that of the furnishing of evidence in the final examination. It is to the study of this double rule that the theory of evidence in criminal matters leads, generally speaking, at least at the present time. Thus the penal tribunal is free to form its conviction, to believe or not to believe in the evidence produced, but it is subject to fixed rules in the method to employ in seeking, admitting, and furnishing the evidence. These are the two systems which we are about to elucidate.

§ 4. **Origin of the System of Legal Proofs.** — The system which consists in proving a judicial fact, like a fact of any other kind,

and the process of identification which he invented and which has had such a great success to-day bears the name of its author, — Bertillonage. This process was inaugurated at the Dépôt of Paris in 1882. On the use of scientific methods to prove the offense: *Tarde*, "Penal Philosophy."

[1] *Ferri* has applied an epithet to this system which would lead to the belief that the legislature had acted from "sentiment" in regulating it. Unless by substituting for it a system of scientific proofs, that is to say, substituting the *expert* for the *juror*, it is difficult to see what system could replace it. "Certainty," says *Faustin Hélie*, "cannot be commanded or regulated by any law; it is, like thought, essentially free and independent of all external power." The question of the jury, however, is quite distinct from that of the laws of evidence, as *Tarde* has shown in his "Penal Philosophy," p. 440 *et seq.* The eminent criminalist quoted above, who is an admirer of the jury, is also a firm supporter of this system of proof. See "Instr. cr." vol. 4, Nos. 1771–1774.

by seeking, without premeditated plan and without hindrance. for everything which can establish it, is the most natural system, for it resembles the course we instinctively follow to discover the truth.[1] The Roman procedure, so formal in so many respects, adapted itself, in all that concerned the proof, to this natural principle, and down to the last days of the Empire the rules which, elsewhere, demanded the persuasion of the judge were almost unknown.[2]

But this system of proof appeared incompatible with the intellect of professional judges. The development of the opposite system coincided, in fact, everywhere, with the appearance and progress of the institution of professional and permanent judges.[3] We see it take rise in the later days of the Empire, when the abolition of the old "ordo judiciorum" had given over to the magistrate the entire judicial power. It reappeared and developed, throughout modern Europe, from the time when the jurists replaced the "hommes jugeurs."[4] The Criminal Ordinance of 1670 contained no exposition of the minute and complicated rules of the system of legal proofs: the theory of the system had been built up by jurists and it had ended by being made equal to law. In the 1500s and 1600s, the system was completely established, and it existed as long as the inquisitorial procedure lasted. It is necessary to point out its broad features, taking for a guide the authors who wrote on our ancient criminal law in the course of the 1700s.[5]

[1] See *Bentham*, "Judicial Evidence," Book I, ch. 3.

[2] A mandate of Adrian quoted in lib. XXII, 5, 3, § 2, Dig. is often cited on this point: "Quæ argumenta et ad quem modum probandæ quique rei sufficiant, nullo satis certo modo definire potest. Sicut non semper, ita sæpe sine publicis monumentis cujusque rei veritas deprehenditur. Alias numerus testium, alias dignitas et auctoritas, alias veluti consentiens fama confirmat rei, de qua quæritur, fidem. Hoc ergo solum tibi rescribere possum summatim, non utique ad unam probationis speciem cognitionem statim alligari debere; sed ex sententia animi tui te æstimare oportere, quid aut credas aut parum probatum tibi opinaris." The doctrine of legal proofs, however, finds a germ in the writings of the jurisconsults. See *Faustin Hélie, op. cit.*, p. 403. The report made by *Count Portalis* to the Academy of Moral and Political Science upon two memoirs treating of evidence in criminal proceedings may be also consulted ("Rev. de légis. et de jurispr." 1840).

[3] See on this point *Bonnier, op. cit.*, 131.

[4] It should be noted, however, that, in the institution of "cojuratores" and the custom of judicial proofs are found the first germs of legal evidence. See *Faustin Hélie*, "Instr. cr." vol. 4, 1764.

[5] Especially *Muyart de Vouglans*, who devoted to the theory of legal evidence the sixth part of his "Instituts au droit criminel," pp. 303–354. Comp. *Jousse, op. cit.*, vol. 1, pp. 654–837. But there will be found, in the writings of the legists of the 1600s and the 1700s, besides the exposition of legal rules, conceptions of a philosophy and a psychology of the noblest and truest kind in regard to confessions, evidence, and presumptions. This is a part of the true judicial psychology.

§ 5. **Four Methods of Proof. Proof of the Corpus Delicti; Proof of Culpability.** — The four methods of proof which we still distinguish to-day — the *confession,* or oral proof, *proof by witnesses,* or testimonial proof, *documentary evidence,* or instrumental proof, and *presumptions,* or conjectural proof, were then classed and graded according to their importance. The objective was a *complete proof,* which alone warranted the pronouncement of capital punishment, for this is the type of action which is always taken; capital crimes constituting, according to our ancient authors, the very foundation of penal law.[1] For less serious charges, the exigencies of the system were, in effect, relaxed. The criminalists of the time finally analyzed and dissected the logical process which consists of showing, in order to bring about the conviction of the accused, two things, the commission of the crime, and the *guilt* of its perpetrator.

I. To establish the first point meant seeking and establishing the "corpus delicti."[2]

In this respect two kinds of offenses were distinguished. The first were those which left material traces, "delicta facti permanentis," such as a homicide or a fire. In this case the first duty of the judge was to find out these traces. He did this, either himself, by drawing up official reports or "minutes" of the case, or by means of reports by physicians, surgeons, and other experts.[3] The Ordinance of 1670 had carefully regulated this matter,[4] and, astonishing as it may appear, judicial practice recognized the accused's right to demand a counter-expert.[5] As a rule, no other proof, outside of the reports or "constats" by the judge or by ex-

[1] Most crimes were punished or might be punished with capital punishment. "As there is no law," said *Poullain du Parc, op. cit.,* t. 11, pp. 112, 113, "which can authorize the punishment of the innocent, there must be a complete proof, whatever the crime may be, to warrant capital punishment, and that proof can only be made according to the forms lawfully laid down." And elsewhere, p. 116: "In charges which are not capital it is evident that such strong evidence is not necessary. . . . But when there are only strong indications their strength can warrant only pecuniary punishments, if the judge does not have recourse to the suspension 'quousque,' that is, to the further inquiry." Compare *Jousse, op. cit.,* vol. 1, Nos. 43[illegible] and 433, p. 833.

[2] See *Muyart de Vouglans,* "Inst." p. 508.

[3] The inspection of the "corpus delicti" by skilled men is a very ol[d] custom. See *passim Edmond Locard,* "La médecin judiciaire en Franc[e] au XVIIe siècle" (Lyons 1902).

[4] Tit. IV and V. Title IV, entitled "Des procès-verbaux des juges; title V, "Des rapports des médecins et chirurgiens."

[5] The accused "may request permission to have a second examinatio[n] made at his expense by other surgeons, which is readily granted provide[d] the request be presented within a few days of the first." *Muyart* [de] *Vouglans,* "Inst." p. 226.

perts was admitted to prove the "corpus delicti," except in exceptional cases where it was impossible to proceed in this way.[1] And the confession of the accused constituted no proof against him unless the "corpus delicti" had been first established by other means.[2]

The offenses of the second kind were those which left no lasting traces, "delicta facti transeuntis," slanders, for example. In this case, the proof of the "corpus delicti" could not be separated from the proof of guilt. It was not, therefore, produced separately and as a preliminary.

II. The evidence, in its employment for the demonstration of guilt, was classed, according to its degree of strength, as "complete proofs," "proximate indications," and "remote indications." The judge was required to limit himself to specifying the admissions, the testimony, the presumptions, and the indications or facts leading to presumptions, that is to say, the elements of proof which were found in the cause; each of these elements had, according to the circumstances, a legal value; and this valuation must be given effect by the judge, whatever his personal opinion might be.

§ 6. **Testimonial Proof.** — The *proof by witnesses* was considered the best proof in criminal cases; but, in order to be *complete,* it must fulfil certain conditions, difficult of realization: 1st. Two competent witnesses must first of all be found testifying to the same fact.[3] An isolated testimony was certainly not held to be valueless, but it was not allowed to be ground for a capital sentence.[4] 2d. It was also necessary that the two witnesses should be eye-witnesses. Hearsay witnesses ("testes ex auditu alieno"), those who testified "to having heard the threats of the accused and the cries of one dying" ("testes ex auditu proprio"), those called "testes ex parte accusati," who affirmed having re-

[1] See *Muyart de Vouglans,* "Inst." pp. 308, 309, and *Poullain du Parc, op. cit.,* t. 11, p. 81.

[2] See *Jousse, op. cit.,* v. 1, No. 20, p. 661. (This is still the system of the New York Penal Code, § 395 (translated by *Fournier,* note pp. 218–219).

[3] This is a traditional rule, "Testis unus, testis nullus," or as *Loysel* said, "The voice of one is the voice of none." *Paul Viollet,* in his "Histoire du droit civil français" (Paris 1893), p. 30, has shown that this rule, which "has dominated the whole matter of testimonies and inquiries during the whole of the Middle Ages and down to modern times," is undoubtedly derived from scripture. It is formulated in St. John and St. Matthew (St. John viii, 17); "And we may affirm," adds *Viollet,* "that this rule of two witnesses, invariable in the Middle Ages, and retained in the 1800s in several legal systems of the United States of America, is of Hebraic origin."

[4] *Jousse, op. cit.,* v. 1, pp. 663, 695.

ceived from the accused the confession of his crime, could not, whatever might be their number, constitute a complete proof. 3d. The witnesses must be *affirmative.* If they expressed themselves in language of doubt, such as "If I am not mistaken —" "If I remember rightly —" "It might have been so," they were called *vacillating,* and their statements had not even the value of an indication. 4th. It was necessary that the depositions be identical in the three interrogatories undergone by the witnesses at the beginning of the information, at the confirmation ("récolement"), and at the confrontation. 5th. Finally, the witnesses must be neither *impeachable* nor *impeached.* In this respect, the ancient procedure, while seeking to do away with the usage of the right of impeachment, had multiplied and even exaggerated the grounds for it.

Two perfect testimonies, when they coincided, inevitably led to conviction, for they necessarily entailed the convincing of the judge.[1]

§ 7. **Written Proof.** — After the testimonial proof came the *written proof,* obviously rarer than the first. The jurists, after some hesitation, had come to recognize that this method of proof must be employed in certain crimes which could hardly be established except by writing, "because they consisted principally in the thought, such as heresy, 'confidence,' plotting against the prince, usury, subornation of witnesses"; and for others, such as forgery, testimonial proof and instrumental proof might concur. But in every case in which writing was admitted, before it could make a *complete proof,* it was necessary: 1st, that it should be precise as to the fact of the crime; 2d, that it should be authentic, or, if the writing was signed, that it should be acknowledged by the accused. One verification of handwriting could never furnish a complete proof. The conjectural art of handwriting experts was with reason distrusted.[2]

§ 8. **Presumptions.** — Complete proof could still be furnished by *presumptions,* considered incontrovertible, provided, it must be borne in mind, that the facts upon which they were based should be themselves regularly established.[3] In that case, indications,

[1] *Jousse, op. cit.,* v. 1, p. 673. The evidence "which is looked upon as most certain is that which results from the testimony of two or more persons who have seen the crime committed."

[2] As to the conjectural nature of the art of handwriting experts, our old authors are unanimous. See *Muyart de Vouglans, op. cit.,* p. 330; *Rousseau de Lacombe,* "Matières criminelles," p. 371. *Cf. Poullain du Parc,* t. 11, p. 191 *et seq.; Jousse, op. cit.,* v. 1, p. 743.

[3] Here is an example given us by *Muyart de Vouglans* (*op. cit.,* p. 346): "When a murder has been committed, two unimpeachable witnesses tes-

leading to presumptions, were given the force of absolute conviction. It was generally admitted that the *confession* did not constitute a complete proof: "Nemo auditur perire volens." It was essential that there should be, in addition to the confession, proximate indications or the testimony of a qualified witness.[1]

§ 9. **Proximate Indications.** — *Proximate indications*, called, by some jurists, *half-proofs*, could not, by themselves, cause the capital condemnation of the accused. But they formed, in conjunction with the *voluntary* or *involuntary* ("*forcé*") confession, a complete proof. The chief effect of proximate indications, in serious charges, was thus to allow of the administration of the torture, so that the theory according to which a capital sentence could only be based upon a complete proof, apparently so favorable to the accused, resulted in making torture almost inevitable; torture, as it has been said, "became the indispensable complement of this system of evidence."[2]

The facts constituting proximate indications were always left by the Ordinances to the discretion of the judge. Certain rules have, however, been evolved by judicial practice. Thus, among the half-proofs there figured originally testimonial proof or incomplete writing, the testimony of a single eye-witness, a writing authenticated by expert evidence, or the extra-judicial confession of the accused, when, having been denied by him, it was sworn to "by two qualified witnesses." Then, presumptions, based upon the indications, might be either general or peculiar to certain crimes.

§ 10. **Remote Indications.** — All the proximate indications allowed the application of torture. However, for a considerable number of crimes, it was necessary to add to these at least one *remote indication*. Here a third class of indications, comprehended under the name of "adminicules," came into play. Muyart de Vouglans, as the forerunner of modern anthropologists, gives, as

tify to having seen the accused, with the naked and bloody sword in his hand, leave the place where, some time after, the body of the deceased was found wounded by a sword stroke." Although this indication is very close, very telling, it is not conclusive, because it would be possible to prove suicide, for instance.

[1] In Chap. III, Part II, *ante*, may be read the discussions between our old authors upon this question of the weight of the judicial confession. See also on this point, *Bonnier, op. cit.*, No. 365. *Jousse, op. cit.*, v. 1, No. 660, asserts, however, that the evidence is complete when it is based upon "the pure and simple confession of the accused."

[2] Certain jurists maintained that the indications might be added together. But this combination was usually rejected. "The half-proof," said *Poullain du Parc* (*op. cit.*, t. 11, p. 116), "is no more conclusive than a half-truth, and for the same reason that two uncertainties cannot make a certainty, two half-proofs cannot make a full proof."

an example of signs ("signes") of guilt of this kind, "the bad expression ('physiognomie') of the prisoner." It is evident that little was required to constitute a remote indication.

§ 11. **Legal Proofs in Ancient French Criminal Law. Necessity for Confession. Interrogations. Torture.** — To sum up, the theoretic characteristic of the system of legal proofs in the ancient French law was, that there could be no capital sentence without a complete proof, and that evidence had this character only under certain exceptional conditions very difficult of realization. This tyranny of the proof compelled the judges to procure by any and every means, "per fas et nefas," a confession from the guilty person. To attain this end, custom originated two proceedings, the secret *interrogation* ("interrogatoire"), in which the accused, without counsel, must swear to divulge the truth, and by means of which the so-called *voluntary confession* was obtained; and torture, by which the *involuntary confession* ("confession forcée") was obtained. Thus, the system of legal proofs, originally introduced in the interest of the accused, and as a necessary counterbalance to the absence of guarantees resulting either from the tribunal being composed of professional jurists, or from the inquisitorial and secret procedure, led fatally to the use of torture. And it is unquestionable that the maintenance of this great injustice down to the time of the Revolution was due to the fact that the convincing of the judge could hardly ever be obtained without the confession of the culprit.[1]

The true cause for the employment of torture, which spread, by a strange contagion, from the beginning of the 1100s, throughout all Europe, and the original home of which was that corner of Italy where the school of Bologna resuscitated the Roman law, was everywhere that, "on one hand, ordeals and oath-helpers ('cojureurs') were no longer believed in, and on the other hand, a conviction would not be pronounced on indications alone, whatever their strength might be." What was necessary for the judges of that time was the confession at any cost, or proof of the impossibility of getting the confession.[2]

[1] See *Despeisses*, "Œuvres," t. 2, p. 213, No. 10; *Aug. Nicolas*, Master of Requests in the Parlement of Bourgogne, "Si la théorie de la torture est un moyen de vérifier les faits," Amsterdam, 1682.

[2] See the interesting observations of *Tarde*, "Penal Philosophy," pp. 432–437, on torture, its origin, history, and causes. *Jousse, op. cit.*, t. 1, pp. 689–694, lays down the theory "of the confession of the accused by the 'question' or torture." His first words judge the proceeding from the point of view of the confession: "It may be taken as a general rule that torture is a dangerous expedient by which to compel a witness to divulge the truth. Several examples are to be found in history of persons who under

Nevertheless, if the prisoner resisted this shocking method of extorting his confession, if nothing could be got from him, it must not be thought that the justice of the time was done with him. The action was suspended, or an "extraordinary" punishment was dealt out to him.

§ 12. **Origin of the System of Convincing Proofs.** — The institution of the jury and the abolition of torture necessarily entailed the destruction of the system of legal proofs.[1] However, by a combination, excellent in appearance, certain legislators of the Constituent Assembly wished to join to the advantages of the ancient usages the benefit of new principles. They proposed to put upon the law the burden of determining what proofs it should be necessary to produce in order to warrant a sentence, but they did not wish ever to compel the judges, whatever the charges might be, to condemn an accused without being thoroughly convinced. This was an ingenious system, which claimed to unite "the confidence due to legal proofs with that which is deserved by the judge's being thoroughly convinced."[2] But how delusive, with the institution of the jury, would have been a system restricting by legal limitations the evidence necessary to convict! One of two results must follow. Either the jury, not being compelled to assign a reason for their decision, would always be able to avoid that obligation; or, if they thought it their duty to respect the obligation, they would be able to find in it a convenient pretext for unjustifiable acquittals. The legislature also formally declared that it rejected the system of legal proofs and insisted only on the jury's being thoroughly convinced.[3] This was shown in the lan-

the influence of pain have confessed to crimes which they did not commit." Consequently "the confession made by an accused during torture did not make a sufficient proof among the Romans any more than among ourselves, when there was no other proof." But "the confession made by an accused under torture which is afterwards ratified by him when he is free and out of pain makes a complete proof against him." *Jousse* afterwards discusses the case where the confession extracted by torture is retracted and the case where torture is inflicted as the sequel of void proceedings: "If the proceedings are invalid, the confession made by the accused under torture does not make it valid."

[1] The philosophers of the 1700s had attacked legal proofs. *Beccaria* ("Des délits et des peines," chs. VII and VIII) shows that certainty could not be comprehended within the rule of a scientific proof. *Filangieri* ("Science de la législation," book 3, ch. XV) asserts that certainty can have its place only in the conscience of the judge.

[2] This is the formula which Robespierre used in the sitting of 4th January, 1891 (Moniteur of the 5th). It has perhaps not been sufficiently noted that the idea of this combination was criticised by the Italian criminalist *Ellero*, in his brochure upon the "Critica criminale," printed in his "Trattati criminali."

[3] The Constituent Assembly was confronted with the question by the report which *Duport* made at the sitting of 26th December, 1790, on be-

guage of the oath which was administered to them: "You swear . . . to decide according to the charges and the pleas in defense, and following your conscience and your personal conviction, with the impartiality and the firmness becoming a free man."[1] Elsewhere, it was said, in the Law of 16th September, 1791,[2] "The accused may bring witnesses to testify that he is a man of honor and probity, and of irreproachable conduct; the jury shall give this testimony reasonable consideration." And the Instructions of 29th September, 1791, state precisely the principle of the moral proof in these terms: "It is particularly upon the examination and the trial which have taken place in their presence that the jury must base their personal conviction, for it is their personal conviction which is here concerned; it is that which the law asks them to declare, and it is that to which society and the accused appeal." In the Code of the 3d Brumaire, year IV (Art. 372), the theory of moral proofs was maintained with more firmness still; a long instruction especially intended to remind the jury of it was required to be read to them by the president and posted up in the jury room. This instruction has passed, with the same characteristic, into the Code of Criminal Examination of 1808, where it forms the provision of Article 342: "The law does not require the jury to state the reasons for their convictions; it prescribes no rules on which they should make the weight and sufficiency of a proof particularly depend; it orders them to question themselves in silence and meditation, and in the sincerity of their conscience, to look for the impression which the evidence brought against the accused and his pleas in defense have made upon their reason. The law does not say, 'You will regard as true every thing testified to by such and such a number of witnesses,' nor does it say to them, 'You will not hold as sufficiently established all proof which may not be formed of such documents, of so many witnesses, or of so many indications'; it asks them only this one question, which embraces the whole measure of their duties, 'Are you thoroughly convinced?' "

half of the committees on constitution and criminal jurisprudence. The bill proposed to abolish all written proof before the jury, and to give no other foundation for its verdict than its sense of being thoroughly convinced, based on the oral trial. *Faustin Hélie* ("Instr. cr." v. 4, No. 1768, pp. 336–340) has reported the chief passages of the discussion which took place on this subject. The committee's bill was adopted in the sitting of 18th January, 1791.

[1] Law of 16th September, 1791, 2d part, Tit. 7, Art. 24.

[2] Second part, Tit. 7, Art. 14.

§ 13. **Convincing Proof really "Jury Proof."**—The proof by convincement thus came into existence along with the jury and seems to be inseparable from it.[1] But the formula, impregnated with revolutionary lyric, which has become Article 342 of the Code of Criminal Examination, has given birth to many errors as to the

[1] Nobody has shown this better than *Tarde*, in a passage which I may be permitted to transcribe ("Penal Philosophy," *Howell's* translation, "Modern Criminal Science Series," pp. 437–439): "The jury does not in any way come from the German forests; it came into existence in 1215, as has been demonstrated by Du Boys and other authors, owing to the embarrassment experienced by the itinerant justices of England in doing without the ordeals which the Lateran council had just prohibited. Whereas upon the Continent the idea of torture suggested itself as being the proper thing, the English, with infinitely more sagacity no doubt, devised the expedient of assembling twelve of the neighbors of the accused when he did not admit his guilt, and regarding 'their belief relative to the existence and the perpetrator of the crime' as being the equivalent of the judgment of God. This was the more natural, as for a long time past the embryo of the jury, under the name of 'proof by the country,' existed in the English system of bringing an accusation; and this form of proof was placed in the same category as that of 'proof by battle.' The accused had the right of choosing between these two.

"In this manner the fact that the ordeals and the jury were the equivalent of each other is attested. We must recollect that at this period men were prone to believe that the Holy Ghost was present at every reunion of Christians carried out with any solemnity; a jury might seem to be a species of council inspired from on high. Even the jury was destined to furnish the illusion of certainty. A presumption of oracular infallibility was attached by religious belief, as later on by philosophical and humanitarian belief, to decisions, *the grounds of which were not stated.* Furthermore, from its origin, as we see, the verdict has only been, as it is still in our day, a supreme act of opinion, a 'constat' of fact and not a judgment properly speaking. . . .

"The English juries were to so great an extent looked upon as mere witnesses, in early times, that until after the time of Edward III in the 1300s, absolutely no testimony could be brought before them, and even in our own time, in England, when the accused confesses, the jury is incompetent because then the proof is complete. It is because the jury is a species of inspired witness that it has never been asked to state the grounds of its verdict, and that the idea is even repelled, just as much as the idea of a decree without any grounds would be repelled. . . .

"At the beginning of the French Revolution, France found herself in an embarrassing position similar to that of the 'justitiarii itinerantes' of 1213; torture having been done away with, it became necessary to find a substitute for it. . . .

"It was knowingly, furthermore, that the English jury was imported into France."

The "Cahiers" of 1789 had demanded judgment by a jury in criminal matters; they recommended that a study should be made of English institutions. During the discussion before the Constituent Assembly of the system of proof before the jury, Thouret clearly expressed these ideas. "Written evidence is incompatible with the establishment of the jury. — The necessity for this subsequent transcription, the moral idea which makes the jury *the means nearest to infallibility,* and which leads through the medium of debates between the witnesses and the accused to *such a degree of persuasion that it is impossible for human reason to go farther* . . . the conviction of the juror is the law which it is the juror's duty to follow. Moral conviction overcomes everything when it is felt. It can neither be commanded, nor inspired. It is the true touchstone of moral veracity."

rights and duties of the jury. What appears to stand out prominently is the feeling that there is here an arbitrary power, to solve the most formidable question which can be propounded to mortal men. The jury appears to be placed above the law and authorized to judge on an *impression*. It is to this formula even more than to the system of the moral proof that the false doctrine of the *omnipotence* of the jury must be traced.

§ 14. **Disappearance of the System of Legal Proofs.** — The system of legal proofs, which prevailed in modern Europe down to the end of the 1700s, has almost everywhere disappeared, and whatever vestiges of it remain are gradually vanishing. It is hardly necessary to mention, as a matter of archæological curiosity, the provisions of the Code of Criminal Procedure of the canton of Valais of 29th November, 1848, which are still devoted to and minutely regulate the legal proof. This "fossil legislation" is a sole exception! But, in the Anglo-Saxon laws, where the accusatory system remains in force, and where the method of proof is the same in civil and criminal matters, two characteristic traits of the old system of evidence should be noticed. The first, already noted, is the rule which compels the accused to undertake a plan of defense from the very beginning of his appearance, and to plead guilty or not guilty. And when he confesses or pleads guilty he must prove all the pleas which he urges against the indictment. For, in this respect, the confrontative procedure places the parties upon the same plane, and by putting in a defense the accused becomes complainant in the action; "*reus excipiendo fit actor.*"

INDEX

C.

D.

Q.

R.